The L/L Research Channeling Archives

Transcripts of the Meditation Sessions

Volume 18
April 2, 2006 to May 27, 2008

Don Elkins

Jim McCarty

Carla L. Rueckert

Copyright © 2009 L/L Research

All rights reserved. No part of this book may be reproduced or used in any form or by any means—graphic, electronic or mechanical, including photocopying or information storage and retrieval systems—without written permission from the copyright holder.

ISBN: 978-0-945007-92-0

Published by L/L Research
Box 5195
Louisville, Kentucky 40255-0195

E-mail: contact@llresearch.org
www.llresearch.org

About the cover photo: *This photograph of Jim McCarty and Carla L. Rueckert was taken during an L/L Research channeling session on August 4, 2009, in the living room of their Louisville, Kentucky home. Jim always holds hands with Carla when she channels, following the Ra group's advice on how she can avoid any possibility of astral travel.*

Dedication

These archive volumes are dedicated to Hal and Jo Price, who faithfully and lovingly hosted this group's weekly meditation meetings from 1962 to 1975,

to Walt Rogers, whose work with the research group Man, Consciousness and Understanding of Detroit offered the information needed to begin this ongoing channeling experiment,

and to the Confederation of Angels and Planets in the Service of the Infinite Creator, for sharing their love and wisdom with us so generously through the years.

Table of Contents

Introduction 6
Year 2006 8
    April 2, 2006 9
    April 14, 2006 16
    April 16, 2006 21
    April 18, 2006 28
    May 7, 2006 33
    May 28, 2006 41
    July 7, 2006 48
    August 25, 2006 54
    September 3, 2006 59
    September 17, 2006 66
    September 26, 2006 73
    October 1, 2006 77
    October 8, 2006 82
    November 12, 2006 88
    November 16, 2006 94
    November 19, 2006 101
    December 10, 2006 105
    December 17, 2006 111
Year 2007 117
    January 7, 2007 118
    January 21, 2007 125
    February 4, 2007 131
    February 11, 2007 137
    February 18, 2007 145
    March 18, 2007 150
    March 25, 2007 154
    April 8, 2007 161
    April 14, 2007 167
    April 22, 2007 173
    May 6, 2007 178
    May 19, 2007 183
    May 20, 2007 189
    July 31, 2007 195
    August 7, 2007 202
    August 12, 2007 207
    September 2, 2007 214
    September 7, 2007 223

September 8, 2007	230
September 22, 2007	236
October 6, 2007	242
October 13, 2007	248
October 27, 2007	254
November 10, 2007	259
November 24, 2007	265
December 15, 2007	272
December 29, 2007	277
Year 2008	**284**
January 7, 2008	285
January 12, 2008	293
January 19, 2008	299
February 10, 2008	305
February 10, 2008	312
February 10, 2008	319
March 15, 2008	327
March 22, 2008	333
March 29, 2008	339
April 12, 2008	345
April 26, 2008	353
May 4, 2008	359
May 4, 2008	364
May 10, 2008	371
May 13, 2008	377
May 24, 2008	384
May 27, 2008	390

Introduction

Welcome to this volume of the *L/L Research Channeling Archives*. This series of publications represents the collection of channeling sessions recorded by L/L Research during the period from the early seventies to the present day. The sessions are also available on the L/L Research website, www.llresearch.org.

Starting in the mid-1950s, Don Elkins, a professor of physics and engineering at Speed Scientific School, had begun researching the paranormal in general and UFOs in particular. Elkins was a pilot as well as a professor and he flew his small plane to meet with many of the UFO contactees of the period.

Hal Price had been a part of a UFO-contactee channeling circle in Detroit called "The Detroit Group." When Price was transferred from Detroit's Ford plant to its Louisville truck plant, mutual friends discovered that Price also was a UFO researcher and put the two men together. Hal introduced Elkins to material called *The Brown Notebook* which contained instructions on how to create a group and receive UFO contactee information. In January of 1962 they decided to put the instructions to use and began holding silent meditation meetings on Sunday nights just across the Ohio River in the southern Indiana home of Hal and his wife, Jo. This was the beginning of what was called the "Louisville Group."

I was an original member of that group, along with a dozen of Elkins' physics students. However, I did not learn to channel until 1974. Before that date, almost none of our weekly channeling sessions were recorded or transcribed. After I began improving as a channel, Elkins decided for the first time to record all the sessions and transcribe them.

During the first eighteen months or so of my studying channeling and producing material, we tended to reuse the tapes as soon as the transcriptions were finished. Since those were typewriter days, we had no record of the work that could be reopened and used again, as we do now with computers. And I used up the original and the carbon copy of my transcriptions putting together a manuscript, *Voices of the Gods*, which has not yet been published. It remains as almost the only record of Don Elkins' and my channeling of that period.

We learned from this experience to retain the original tapes of all of our sessions, and during the remainder of the seventies and through the eighties, our "Louisville Group" was prolific. The "Louisville Group" became "L/L Research" after Elkins and I published a book in 1976, *Secrets of the UFO*, using that publishing name. At first we met almost every night. In later years, we met gradually less often, and the number of sessions recorded by our group in a year accordingly went down. Eventually, the group began taking three months off from channeling during the summer. And after 2000, we began having channeling meditations only twice a month. The volume of sessions dropped to its present output of eighteen or so each year.

These sessions feature channeling from sources which call themselves members of the Confederation of Planets in the Service of the Infinite Creator. At first we enjoyed hearing from many different voices: Hatonn, Laitos, Oxal, L/Leema and Yadda being just a few of them. As I improved my tuning techniques, and became the sole senior channel in L/L Research, the number of contacts dwindled. When I began asking for "the highest and best contact which I can receive of Jesus the Christ's vibration of unconditional love in a conscious and stable manner," the entity offering its thoughts through our group was almost always Q'uo. This remains true as our group continues to channel on an ongoing basis.

The channelings are always about love and unity, enunciating "The Law of One" in one aspect or another. Seekers who are working with spiritual principles often find the material a good resource. We hope that you will as well. As time has gone on the questions have shifted somewhat, but in general the content of the channeling is metaphysical and focused on helping seekers find the love in the moment and the Creator in the love.

At first, I transcribed our channeling sessions. I got busier, as our little group became more widely known, and got hopelessly behind on transcribing. Two early transcribers who took that job off my hands were Kim

Howard and Judy Dunn, both of whom masterfully transcribed literally hundreds of sessions through the eighties and early nineties.

Then Ian Jaffray volunteered to create a web site for these transcriptions, and single-handedly unified the many different formats that the transcripts were in at that time and made them available online. This additional exposure prompted more volunteers to join the ranks of our transcribers, and now there are a dozen or so who help with this. Our thanks go out to all of these kind volunteers, early and late, who have made it possible for our webguy to make these archives available.

Around the turn of the millennium, I decided to commit to editing each session after it had been transcribed. So the later transcripts have fewer errata than the earlier ones, which are quite imperfect in places. One day, perhaps, those earlier sessions will be revisited and corrections will be made to the transcripts. It would be a large task, since there are well over 1500 channeling sessions as of this date, and counting. We apologize for the imperfections in those transcripts, and trust that you can ascertain the sense of them regardless of a mistake here and there.

Blessings, dear reader! Enjoy these "humble thoughts" from the Confederation of Planets. May they prove good companions to your spiritual seeking. ♣

For all of us at L/L Research,

Carla L. Rueckert

Louisville, Kentucky

July 16, 2009

Year 2006

April 2, 2006 to December 17, 2006

L/L Research

L/L Research is a subsidiary of Rock Creek Research & Development Laboratories, Inc.

P.O. Box 5195
Louisville, KY 40255-0195

www.llresearch.org

Rock Creek is a non-profit corporation dedicated to discovering and sharing information which may aid in the spiritual evolution of humankind.

ABOUT THE CONTENTS OF THIS TRANSCRIPT: This telepathic channeling has been taken from transcriptions of the weekly study and meditation meetings of the Rock Creek Research & Development Laboratories and L/L Research. It is offered in the hope that it may be useful to you. As the Confederation entities always make a point of saying, please use your discrimination and judgment in assessing this material. If something rings true to you, fine. If something does not resonate, please leave it behind, for neither we nor those of the Confederation would wish to be a stumbling block for any.

© 2009 L/L Research

Sunday Meditation
April 2, 2006

Jim: The first question is from A. It reads, "I am soon to be a high school teacher. I had some classroom experience about a year ago and found the emotional environment nearly overwhelming. Many students want to test the boundaries on an authority figure, which is normal behavior for teenagers. However, so many students doing it all at once is difficult. How can I best maintain my strength over a sustained period?"

(Carla channeling)

We are of the principle known to you as Q'uo. Greetings in the love and in the light of the one infinite Creator, in Whose service we come to you this day. It is a great privilege and pleasure to be called to your circle of seeking and we thank you for this honor. It truly gladdens our hearts, because serving by sharing our thoughts is our chosen means of service to the one infinite Creator at this time. Consequently, you offer us the opportunity that we treasure the most: that opportunity to serve the Creator by serving those sub-Creators that, like we, are moving in that divine circle from one heartbeat of the infinite Creator to the next.

As always, we would ask that each of you be responsible for discriminating between those thoughts of ours that seem resonant and useful to you and those thoughts which do not. Please do not be concerned with any thought that does not seem to be something that you knew already but had forgotten for a moment. Things that resonate like that are apt and appropriate for your work. If they do not resonate, they may be wonderfully helpful to someone else but they are not part of your process and we would not wish you to be led off your path by our stray thoughts. We thank you for this consideration.

We thank the one known as A for the query about how to create the most pleasant atmosphere for both teacher and students in a classroom. As you already know, my brother, the mechanics of discipline are simple. We do not believe you are truly asking concerning discipline but rather how to deal with your dislike of disharmony. However, we would say that it is appropriate for a teacher to be an authority figure of a kind. That is, you and the students together have a precious gift to share. That gift is time.

When a group of students does not have boundaries and limits set on their behavior by a helpful teacher, the gift of time tends to be squandered in such a classroom because there is not enough energy left over from the ongoing and somewhat off-the-topic discussions of students that are not engaged in learning.

Therefore it is helpful to the students as well as to yourself to make a few simple rules and then to be very careful to act precisely the same way each time a rule is broken. The usual means of discipline is asking the student to spend time—again, that gift of time—paying his dues for the infractions of the rules. This is usually done by means of detentions or extra study halls. This is a perfectly good solution to misbehavior as perceived by the teacher.

As long as the rules are simple, understandable and maintained carefully with no favoritism or injustice of that kind going on, the tendency in such a classroom will be that that group of students becomes aware fairly quickly of the necessary ways to act in order to avoid punishment.

There is, however, another aspect to discipline. That is that aspect which involves the teacher or authority figure opening his heart and becoming vulnerable. For you, as a teacher, my brother, are also a student. You and the students in the classroom, together and equally, are students of the life experience itself. It is well to remember that what you are doing with them is a partnership and a group activity.

Consequently, see what you can do to open your heart to your students and explain to them at least once how you feel about being in the position that you are. Explain to them that you are going to need their help. If you are going to create an environment and then fill that environment with learning and laughter, shared experiences and deep comradeship as you hope to do, then you shall need their help, for you cannot create this atmosphere by yourself.

Indeed, this instrument at one time in her life was a librarian and she had to keep all of the study halls of that particular institution in which she taught. Therefore, she had students in her library at all times. And naturally, she was involved in disciplining them in order that the rest of the students could enjoy a quiet study hall and get their homework done.

Her technique for maintaining quiet was to go directly to the leader of whatever group was misbehaving and ask for that person's help. She would explain that she had the need to keep order in the library and there was a bit of conversation going on that was making it difficult for some of the other students to concentrate. She would then ask for that particular person's help in reminding others at her table if such a conversation began again.

Naturally, faced between two fires—one, helping the teacher who was asking pleasantly and courteously for her help, and [the other] being assigned detention, which would take away the fun of Friday afternoon—the trouble-maker would immediately agree to help, and, reluctantly or not, she would from that time forward be able to help the teacher maintain order at her table. This was all done without threats, raised voices or any accusation of wrongdoing.

Being vulnerable and asking for help are a very good ideas. It brings out the best in people if you are honest with them and explain what it is that you need and why you need it.

However, your question is more deeply and spiritually, or metaphysically speaking, more centrally a question about attitude.

It is well, when approaching the teaching of young souls, to remember beyond anything else that you and they are one. You are in this adventure together. It is easy for a teacher to assume that he will teach and that the children will learn. In actuality, it is always a teach/learning, learn/teaching situation.

In fact, you will find, my brother, that you learn more than they do. It is amazing what young souls have to offer. They do not have life experience but they have active and inquiring minds and they have, in many cases, hearts that have not yet been bludgeoned, as of yet, by the various cultural offerings of your society in ways that numb and deaden emotion. The thinking of the heart is emotion based.

Therefore it is well to remember that you are dealing with young plants who will turn to the sun of emotion. Therefore, see what you can, my brother, to be the sunshine in their lives. Think of what they would like to know—not only what the curriculum would like you to teach them. Become their advocate. Put yourself in their shoes. See things, as best you can, from their point of view.

Therefore, that seeping down into the deeper parts of your thinking as you move towards the day's work with the children will prepare you to deal with them as who they truly are: sons and daughters of the infinite Creator, as are you.

Even in cases of difficulty, we encourage you to maintain a remembrance of unity that underlies the relationship betwixt yourself and any and all of those who are in your classroom. A kind word in a bad situation is often a turning point for a tender mind or heart and you will have the power to offer either kind words or unkind words.

We also encourage the relaxation into what you are doing. You chose this type of livelihood because you hoped that you would be able to offer the gifts of your affection, your understanding, and your knowledge to those minds who are eager to learn. Do not be dismayed that they do not know yet that they are eager to learn. You may need to create for students that motivation that they now lack by making the things about which you are teaching pertinent, interesting, challenging and relevant to an ordinary, everyday life.

All of these positive ways of making the classroom time more fun, more challenging and more interesting will balance the fact that you must indeed serve as the authority figure that a teacher is.

As we said, to sum up, the key to discipline in the classroom is attitude. Walk softly, speak softly, be fair and the job will soon be done for that class, for that school term. It shall always, as you said, my brother, need to be done again when you have a new group. And sometimes there are entities in the classroom whose enjoyment is to disturb a classroom's pleasant aura of calm. Therefore, some discussions may be protracted.

However, in the end you will find your students grateful to you for creating a good atmosphere and increasingly responsive to a teacher who really, truly wishes to share the knowledge, the affection, and the comradeship that he has to offer.

Is there a follow-up to this question? We are those of Q'uo.

Jim: No, I don't believe so. Our next question is from B who lives in Michigan. For the last couple of years she's been suffering almost continuous psychic attacks and she has to pray continuously through the day for relief.

Her question is, "As Jesus instructs us in *A Course in Miracles*, 'All your problems have already been solved.' Can you please take me to the future, to the point in time when this problem that I'm now experiencing with negative entities and interference has already been resolved and I have been experiencing the desired state of peace and freedom from these causes and patterns of a negative interference for at least one year. Please ask my higher self exactly what I did to get to the desired outcome. Tell me the steps that my higher self suggested to the solution from the future, from the infinite wisdom of my higher mind, that I may better serve God and others."

We are those of Q'uo, and are aware of your query, my sister. We cannot tell you what your higher self would say to you concerning this or any other issue. We are not your higher self and your higher self indeed is within you.

We find in this instrument's mind that she has had other people ask her questions similar to yours, my sister, and she has always suggested to them the following technique if they are unable to break through to their own guidance system in the normal way, which is simply to pray and then to listen and to write down, as you would in a journal the ideas that come to you. Her suggestion has always been this: to find a hypnotherapist and to ask the hypnotherapist, after inducing the hypnotic state with you, to take you back before birth so that you are free of the veil of forgetting and are able to speak with your higher self.

You would then have the hypnotherapist ask you to contact your higher self. In the hypnotic trance state, this is a do-able thing and this instrument has seen it done, not once but many times.

The hypnotherapist then would ask the question that you wish to ask of your higher self and you would repeat that which the higher self says to you. It would be taped, for you would not necessarily be very able to remember exactly what was said if it were not taped. Therefore, be sure that such a session is recorded. In this way, you will use your free will to do your learning in your way.

We find that no question was asked concerning the spiritual principles involved in this kind of sustained psychic greeting so we will keep our comments minimal and simply say that it is well to think of such attacks as gifts. Think about the writings in the New Testament that are called the Beatitudes. "Blessed are they who mourn." That does not sound like a blessing. Each of the Beatitudes is similarly dour and sorrowful in its apparent nature, and yet each is a blessing. Why are they called "blessings" by the one known as Jesus the Christ? This is meat for you to ponder.

We are with you. Your guidance system is with you. Consciousness itself is with you and is you. The psychic greeting that you are experiencing is also part of you. It seems to come from elsewhere. Yet the creation of this experience within your life is as much of a gift and is as much a part of your learning as any other portion of your incarnation and its experiences.

Consequently, it is not something which it is appropriate to attempt to escape. Rather, we would suggest an attitude of quiet confidence, even though the surface of your emotions is roiled by the suffering which you have undergone. Dig deep within yourself for the underlying peace and power of your nature. This visitation has its purpose.

May we ask if there is another query at this time?

Jim: What are the metaphysical qualities of water?

We are those of Q'uo and are aware of your query, my brother. The metaphysical qualities of water begin with its place in creation. It is one of the classical four elements that this instrument learned in reading about white ritual magic of the West in the books by the one known as William.[1]

Water is that aspect or element of the creation which contains the sacred energies of the Archangel Gabriel. Water holds gifts and powers that move from the simplest physical observations to the most abstruse and occult applications of spiritual principles. But the central gift of water is its acceptance of the impressions of consciousness. Water can be magnetized to hold pure emotion. Consequently, water is a very magical element, a crystal that can be solid, liquid or gaseous, and yet is a crystal in terms of the way that it can hold ideas, thoughts and emotions.

This instrument was telling the one known as B earlier about a vision that she had several months ago, when she read an article by a scientist who had done experiments with water crystals.[2] He asked entities to project as pure an emotion as possible to these crystals and then he photographed the results. Interestingly enough, the crystals, when magnetized by thoughts of thanksgiving, joy and love, developed beautiful, flower-like patterns of crystallization. When ugly and angry thoughts were projected to these ice crystals, the ice crystals became malformed.

The intimacy of thought and water is very appropriate to consider as you look at your physical body. Your thoughts are impressing every cell of your body. You are a very watery being. A large percentage of your body is water. You are, therefore, a creature of the tides of your inner emotions. Be aware of how easy it is to magnetize water with an idea or a thought or, most importantly, an emotion. Tend your everyday self to thoughts of thankfulness, thanksgiving, praise, appreciation and joy. Remember how powerful you really are and impress your own body with the fire of your love. Let that love do its healing and organizing work within your physical body.

Is there a follow-up to this query? We are those of the Q'uo.

Jim: Our next question is, "Can you tell us what you know of the Creator, including any specifics regarding the masculine and feminine aspects?"

We are those of Q'uo, and are aware of your query. We do not know a great deal about the one infinite Creator, for the Creator is shrouded in mystery. We know that the Creator is not a being and does not have organs or eyes or a physical vehicle of any kind. We know that the Creator's very nature is love. We know that the creation which the Creator cobbled together out of this Thought of love and free will is a creation of love. We learn about the Creator by observing ourselves and other beings, all of whom carry the energy of the one infinite Creator within them.

Is there a follow-up to this query? We are those of Q'uo.

Jim: We have another query: "Can you discuss the numerological significance of repeating or recurring numbers?"

We are those of Q'uo, and are aware of the query. Numbers are interesting entities. There is a character and a personality to each of your digits, zero through nine. And indeed, larger numbers as well have energies to them in some cases either because of something inherent to that number or because it reflects the doubling or the tripling of another number that has significance.

For the most part, if you wish to use numbers as they are often used in systems like the *I Ching*[3], it is best to stay with the single digit numbers.

---

[1] William E. Butler.

[2] Read more on the web site, www.masaru-emoto.net/english/entop.html.

[3] Learn more by checking this site, http://en.wikipedia.org/wiki/I_Ching.

We are not saying that you can create a meaning to numbers but rather that numbers, in and of themselves, have a character that you may come to know. In terms of repeating numbers, it is interesting to know what number is being repeated. Sometimes, there is no meaning to the repetition except as a wake-up call. If it is 11:11 when you have just thought a certain thought, if you look up and see that number, it is as though the creation were saying to you, "What did you just think? That was an interesting thought. Pay attention to that thought."

In other cases, the number does have significance. Eleven, for instance, is a master number, so-called by this instrument and by the numerology books that she has read in the past. Therefore, if you are seeing 11:11 frequently, you are actually seeing a master number repeated, indicating that transformation is at hand. If you see 12:12 repeated, the energy of that number is an energy of completion. You may look further for yourself at the various numbers, one through nine and zero as well, to investigate this line of thinking further.

However, the most likely meaning of repeated numbers for entities who notice these things is that synchronicity from spirit that simply says, "Pay attention to your thoughts."

Is there a follow-up to that query? We are those of Q'uo.

Jim: I don't believe so. We have one more question here: "From your point of view, Q'uo, if you were to write a short pamphlet concerning the Earth for all those civilizations that have been transplanted here and are visiting here, something containing the basic information and spiritual insight on how to best make use of this Earth opportunity, what would you say?"

We are those of Q'uo, and are aware of your query, my brother. My brother, were we to write such a booklet, we would attempt to find as many ways as we could to describe the environment of Earth in such a way that entities could see into the way to work it.

We would develop an operating manual that would let people know that they were creatures of love; that their consciousness was love, but that they were carefully blocked from a direct apprehension of their nature so that they could use the school of third-density life in order to find that nature once again, by choice and by faith.

We would talk about the dimensions of that choice and why such a choice was necessary. We would talk about faith; not faith in something but the faculty of faith. For it is faith that tells you that all is well when the apparent picture is that all is not well. And it is by faith alone that the spiritual seeker begins his journey and moves his footsteps upon that path once it has begun.

We would talk about Earth as a spiritual distillery. This is a concept that we were speaking about in a channeling session done recently. It is helpful to understand, when one is an Earth being, what the situation is, what the rules of the game are, for there are rules to the game. There is a very simple dynamic that entities may observe.

All things have their opposite. The choice is a choice between the two largest dynamics that govern and help to create your experience. Those are the dynamics between the light and the dark, love and fear, helpfulness and greediness, service to others and service to self.

Those are two distinct paths. We would encourage people to choose the path that they wish to take and then to take it as purely and as honestly as possible, today and tomorrow and the next day, for the rest of a life.

Your school is a simple one. The subject itself is extremely difficult to comprehend. That is why you have a lifetime to work on it.

Is there a follow-up to that query? We are those of the Q'uo.

Jim: I don't think so, but I think T might have a question.

T: Yes, I recently had a feeling. It was just a state of mind that came over me as I was meditating. It just seemed like what I was meditating on became very clear and very easy to hold in my mind. This lasted for six to eight hours, maybe. And then the next day it was basically back to the same. It didn't come as easily. And while I'm still trying to do this, I would like to know if there is anything special that I can do when something like this does happen, how to nail it down maybe, and be able to come back to it. A linchpin that you can hang your hat on and come back to later and help to create that again.

We are those of Q'uo, and are aware of your query, my brother. We find in this instrument's mind memories of similar, special times, times in which she has been transported from the mundane world to a place of light where the perfection of the divine plan was quite clear.

It is a wonderful gift to have enhanced awareness and immediate apprehension of truth, or gnosis, as this instrument calls such experiences. We believe that your experience was of this type of gnosis or knowing that has nothing to do with facts but has everything to do with focused and centered emotion. The knowledge of the heart is of this nature.

(Side one of tape ends.)

(Carla channeling)

We must share with you the fact that we do not know a way reliably to help you nail down such a state of mind. Such enhancements are gifts. They let you know that things are possible that are outside the box, shall we say, of ordinary intellectual mentation.

They let you know that there is a greater truth, a higher reality, that overarches and interpenetrates that experience of everyday. It is immanent, nearer to us than our very physical vehicles. This awareness is so close to everyone at all times that it is surprising that such times of enhanced awareness do not occur more often.

However, we can encourage you, my brother, to appreciate those times when they come, and know them for the truth that they hold.

In terms of how to encourage such experience to happen more frequently, we encourage the basic concept of spirit. When you move into the silence, be aware that you are a crystal. Like a radio station, you may be tuned to different frequencies. We are not suggesting that you manipulate yourself, saying, "I want to be of this setting or that setting." We are suggesting that when you enter the silence, you enter it aware of its sacred nature and aware of yourself as a being worthy to rest in that sacred place.

Those things that brought you to that moment wherein a door opened for you and you were able to slip into a different frame of mind were a combination of your passion, *(inaudible)*[4] the rhythms of your body, your mind, and your spirit, and all of those elements within your universe that are cyclic.

Sometimes you are much more physically ready to experience *(inaudible)* depend upon the planets and the moon. To a certain extent they depend upon the health of your body. It may depend on many things. However, it is certainly always helpful for you to enter that silence aware of that sacred place that is the nature of silence. All of the universe lies within the stoppage of the busy mind.

May we ask, my brother, if there is a follow-up to that query?

T: No, that's fine. Thank you very much.

We are those of Q'uo, and this instrument has energy for another query, if there is one.

R: I have one question, Q'uo. Can you tell us how this circle of seeking looks to you, as opposed to the other times where we have just people in this location?[5] Do you see a double circle? Or is it brighter? We have people who are listening but not physically with us in this room.

We are those of Q'uo, and are aware of your query, my brother. We give this instrument the image of a lei. It is term used for a necklace of beautiful flowers. When this instrument was in Hawaii, she was given several of these flower necklaces. When you have a circle of seeking that is local, that is all in one place, it has a different energy to it than when there are entities from many different places that are coming together from all over the world.

It is not that it is brighter, but that it is a larger circle.

It is, however, of the same nature as a local circle in that the beauty lies in the relationships of all of those within the circle with each other and with the Creator. It forms a kind of kaleidoscope of color and texture and even sound, from our point of view.

---

[4] Throughout the latter portion of this session a large thunderstorm rolled through Louisville. Both of our tapes were compromised. After hours of careful work, comparing the two tapes, B was able to recover about 95% of the session's text. However, some words were too garbled to recover, as the lightning strikes seemed to cause the tape to entirely fail to record at times.

[5] This session was being broadcast into a "chat room" environment where a total of 23 people, from many places around the world, logged on and listened in.

When you have entities who are tuning in from varied locations, there is, in those entities, a good bit of passion and emotional focus because of the difficulty of dealing with the technological aspects of getting the connection made. So even though the entities are far away in terms of their being a part of the circle, there is not a double circle. It is simply a larger circle.

We ask you to pause for a moment and appreciate yourselves. Appreciate your beauty. Sense into your relationships with those entities you cannot see but whom you know are like birds of a feather that flock together in ways that you *(inaudible)*. We can see the *(inaudible)* affection, inspiration and love. We can see the health and wellness of this group and we can see its power to create a shift in consciousness. Each *(inaudible)*.

We would ask at this time if there is a final query? We are those of Q'uo.

R: Not from me, Q'uo, but for those who are listening or cannot speak to you, I know you can hear them, I thank you for your kind words.

B: No more questions [from the internet listeners].

We are those of Q'uo, and we thank you, my brother, on behalf of those people that are not physically present. We thank you for bringing those messages of thanks to us. Indeed, we are the ones who offer thankfulness and gratitude from the depths of our many hearts to you. It has been a true pleasure to share with this circle of seeking.

We leave you, as we greeted you. For all that there is, is love and its child, light. The unmanifested and the manifested worlds are created *(inaudible)*. In those two elements of Godhead, we leave you. We are known to you as the principle of Q'uo.

B: Thanks from the internet people.

Adonai. Adonai.

L/L Research

L/L Research is a subsidiary of Rock Creek Research & Development Laboratories, Inc.

P.O. Box 5195
Louisville, KY 40255-0195

www.llresearch.org

Rock Creek is a non-profit corporation dedicated to discovering and sharing information which may aid in the spiritual evolution of humankind.

ABOUT THE CONTENTS OF THIS TRANSCRIPT: This telepathic channeling has been taken from transcriptions of the weekly study and meditation meetings of the Rock Creek Research & Development Laboratories and L/L Research. It is offered in the hope that it may be useful to you. As the Confederation entities always make a point of saying, please use your discrimination and judgment in assessing this material. If something rings true to you, fine. If something does not resonate, please leave it behind, for neither we nor those of the Confederation would wish to be a stumbling block for any.

© 2009 L/L RESEARCH

SPECIAL MEDITATION
APRIL 14, 2006

Question from J: Could you offer a word to those whose energetic profile matches service-to-self entities, who have strongly developed lower and upper chakras and a muted heart chakra, and who are working to effect their positive polarization now on this planet.

For example: they have the advantage of possessing a great deal of personal gravity, will, intuitive force and perceptivity. Also, they have significant insight into the machinations of dark force operations now haunting this planet.

On the other hand, ingress into the heart of such is a tricky business because it demands the balancing of polarized emotions of immense charge. It's not so easy to accept one's complicity in perpetrating the horrors of creation.

The first question: can you recommend avenues of restitution and service?

(Carla channeling)

We are those known to you as the principle of Q'uo. Greetings in the love and in the light of the one infinite Creator, in Whose service we come to you this evening. It is a privilege to be called to your circle of seeking. We thank each of you for reserving these moments of your incarnation for seeking the truth and for calling us to your circle.

As always, we would ask of each that care be taken to discriminate in listening to our thoughts. If something seems resonant to you, by all means, use it. However, if our thoughts do not seem resonant to you, please lay them aside. Your cooperation in guarding the gates of your perception is much appreciated for it will allow us to speak freely and not be concerned with abridging your free will or your sacred spiritual process.

We would gladly speak a word to those whose profile matches the service-to-self energy pattern of well developed red, orange and yellow-ray energy centers, and well developed blue and indigo energy centers, but poorly developed green ray.

We would suggest that such entities experiencing this pattern of energy expenditure may profitably consider that they may well have chosen to incarnate in third density upon the Earth at this time in order to effect a more harmonious and full balancing of the energies which you may call love, light, power and peace. We offer these words to indicate the dimensions of love and wisdom, or the lessons of fourth density and fifth density, that are studied in sixth density in order to unify and solidify the point of awareness that contains all of the consciousness that is granted to all aspects of the creative principle.

Those who have experienced a far more comprehensive course of study in wisdom than in compassion move into third density not only to be of service to the planet and to its people but also to tackle a kind of strenuous metaphysical boot camp, if you will, in which your preincarnative desire is that you shall effect, within the athanor of incarnation, a more equitable and just integration of the energies of love and the energies of light or wisdom.

We wish to indicate that this is not, for an entity overbalanced into wisdom, a *beau geste* that is particularly easy to grasp or effectuate.

The chief stumbling block to one overbalanced in wisdom is a basic attitude with which this instrument is familiar that she calls pride. When she sees this element of character within herself, she confesses her pride.

However, we would perhaps use the term arrogance rather than pride. In pride, there is a conscious element: one is proud of something. There is a quantitative aspect to this concept of emotive structure. We do not wish to indicate that there is any conscious aspect to the structure involved in those who are wise at the expense of love. Therefore, we suggest the term arrogance, for arrogance is an unconscious attribute carried by those who are aware of the efficacy of their thinking processes.

We would say to those whose profile matches this distortion that it is time to become willing to be grounded in humility.

We would offer one figure before taking further queries. This instrument attended one of its Holy Week services yesterday evening. This particular service was devoted to focusing upon an evening meal held in an upper room tended by thirteen men, including Jesus the Christ.

During this meal the one known as Jesus offered two mandates as suggestions for loving each other. His first suggestion is memorialized in what this instrument calls the Holy Eucharist. The teacher known as Jesus took bread, the common, ordinary bread that was the substance of the night's meal. He blessed it. He broke it. And he shared it with all who were at the table.

And he said, "When you break bread, do it in remembrance of me."

And he took the wine, which was their common drink, blessed it and poured it out, sharing it completely with those present.

Again, the one known as Jesus said, "When you drink, do this in remembrance of me."

A second mandate, as a teacher that evening, as recorded in your holy work known as the *Bible*, was to ask those present to remove their sandals so that he could wash their feet. The one known as Peter at first refused, for he felt that it was far too humble a task for a teacher to offer to his students.

But the one known as Jesus said, "Unless I wash you, you shall not be clean." And so Peter immediately said, "Then, Lord, wash all of me." The one known as Jesus said, "You are clean and yet it does not hurt to wash the dust of the day off your feet."

Having washed the disciples' feet, he said to them, "If I am your teacher and I wash your feet, then perhaps you may see your way clear to washing each others' feet."

The one known as Jesus seldom spoke directly. However, you may see his intention was to indicate not only the value of service to others but also the value of absolute humility.

We ask all of those who find themselves wise and who know themselves clever, has it helped you to love? Has it opened your heart? We have often spoke through this instrument of the most difficult journey an entity such as those you have described will ever make. That journey is the fourteen or so inches from your head to your heart.

May we ask for the next query, my brother?

J: Can you make suggestions which make easier the polarization of these ones in particular?

We are those of Q'uo, and are aware of your query, my brother. We have perhaps made a modest beginning at suggesting the general strategy for working towards the full integration of wisdom and love. We have talked before about the heart chakra. It is a much misunderstood energy center encompassing two distinct aspects.

It is impossible to make a direct assault upon the closed heart. The heart itself is protected within what this instrument would describe as an outer courtyard. The overarching dome of light that signals the presence of consciousness is gently enswathed in the basilica of the inner heart.

Outside of that *sanctum sanctorum* is that place where entities come, in all their dirt, to see if they are ready to enter their own heart. The difficulty that entities find when attempting to enter their heart is that they must needs integrate all of their personality shell into that entity which stands at the door and seeks entrance. All entities carry the full 360 degrees of personality. The entire spectrum of light and dark lives and thrives within each spirit sent forth by the one infinite Creator before the world was.

For those who carry that arrogance of wisdom, there is subtle work to be done in emptying the pockets of self. It is lonely and unforgiving work to break yourself open to the point where you can see and acknowledge all of the factors that go into what on the surface is a simple and seamless attitude of confidence and self-knowledge. Nevertheless, this is the task ahead of one who wishes to open his heart.

It is a difficult thing to grasp because there is no cleverness involved in opening the heart. There is only the acknowledgment of the falsehood of any claim that one may wish to make to true wisdom. For wisdom uninformed by love is not stable or balanced, in terms of that lesson which entities such as yourself incarnated in order to balance.

The wiser an entity is, the more narrow his ability to see beyond his own intelligence. The ability to use higher chakras further confuses the issue, because from the viewpoint of manifestation, there seems to be such a likelihood that such powerful knowledge will be useful to the self, to the Creator, and to the planet.

In orienting you and those like you to the actual situation, we would ask each to move back in perspective until there is a broadness that takes in all of the third-density pattern. A pattern involves a choice of how to be and how to serve. In third density, the path to graduation involves a simple choice followed by a series of congruent choices which progressively tune the spirit under such discipline to the point where that spirit is able to surrender to love.

The difficulty is in releasing all of the intelligence and knowledge that is so proudly carried and so skillfully used in the outer manifestations of life on planet Earth.

In order to dig down into the treasure of self, you must break the container that holds all of that pride or arrogance of accomplishment. When you have released this structure, you will find that you are as vulnerable as a tiny kitten, such as the one that is snuggled up against this instrument's ankle at this moment. Only when you have become as a tiny child, free of the burden of your wisdom, can you at last break the bunker of self-consciousness.

My brother, how deeply and how truly you seek to do that! And yet how clever are the many, many thoughts and strategies that will gladly entrain your intelligence and distract your will. These forces within you do not wish for you to open your heart. They like having full pockets. They do not want you to empty your pockets of these things which, to the surface personality, seem to suggest selfhood. Yet there is a powerful voice within you that says that this is not true consciousness. And you hunger for that.

What is the "I" of a person and of a soul? When consciousness itself is the "I" of you, then shall your heart be free to open and blossom and radiate infinitely. And from that perspective alone shall you at last be able to march from the *sanctum sanctorum*, fed and strengthened, in full knowledge of who you are for the first time and ready at last to do serious work upon balancing the wisdom which you offered to yourself as a gift and as catalyst.

You seek to wend your way from the penumbra of articulated thought to the daylight of love. We wish you every good fortune in your seeking and we commend you for your awareness of the basic situation.

May we ask for the next query, my brother?

J: Can you speak of the response on the inner planes to those who choose to relinquish their status as spiritual achievers and surrender their proudly held, imbalanced acquisitions for the common good?

We are those of Q'uo, and are aware of your query, my brother. The response to one who has at last been able to lay aside pride, break the pottery of intellect, and offer the naked soul, as it is, to the one Creator in all humility, is embrace, inclusion, comfort and support. Indeed, these are the responses of your guidance system and those spiritual forces which surround you regardless of your circumstances.

However, to one who has indeed cast aside arrogance, the voice of spirit becomes quite audible and there is a liveness of interchange that is not possible while the egoic structure of the personality shell retains its knowledge of its self-sufficiency.

We speak as if there is a "we" and a "they," a "you" and an "I." And this is not precisely correct. For there is an ever-flowing movement of energy along lines of force which are created by your thoughts and feelings rather than there being a dynamic of two.

You are experiencing ways of structuring the self so that it may be known to the self. We do not wish to take away every structure of your thoughts in an instant. Rather, we would that you would conceive of this journey as a dance. It is a dance in which your movements express a gradual increase in your ability to be naked and without personality.

In the privacy and the intimacy of your silent meditation, allow all to fall away as it will and sit with that which is left until it, too, falls away. And then sit with that which is left until it, too, falls away. Repeat this process until when you sit, you simply sit.

May we ask for the next query, my brother?

J: I find in myself a strong affinity for higher-density planes of both polarities and information about them. This and other things have led me to believe that I have wandered through higher-density planes, both positive and negative, and then chosen to hop back into the maelstrom of third density. Could you please verify this and discuss the phenomenon of individuals exploring both polarities into higher densities? Could this be merely a grand way of deferring true polarization?

We are those known to you as the principle of Q'uo, and are aware of your query, my brother. We tread close to the limits of free will as we respond to this question. In our opinion—and we offer it for what it is worth—the pattern which you describe is that of a sixth-density wanderer whose fifth-density experiences were felt by the sixth-density entity to have too marked an effect upon the basic ground of being which is represented by the pallid word "love" and by the activity of the student of fourth density in realizing fully …

(Side one of tape ends.)

(Carla channeling)

… the depths of that ground of being. The Thought that created all that there is was not a thought of wisdom. It was pure, unconditional, love. Consciousness is a Thought which creates and destroys the universe. That consciousness is a consciousness of love.

It is difficult to bring into focus within third density the function of wisdom. Perhaps the most skillful thing we could offer at this juncture is that which has been noted by all, we feel sure, and that is the difference between the thinking of the intellect and the thinking of the heart. Each entity knows people who seem to think with their hearts. Whether their intellects are great or modest, the solutions to the catalyst within their lives seem to involve the creative aspects of love.

Practices which aid an entity in becoming more aware of his own heart are those practices which are very momentary. It is difficult to discipline the self to use the present moment. But it is in the present moment that you may practice opening the heart.

Stop and think about your facial expression. Are you smiling? Are you frowning? Place upon your face the beginnings of a smile and each time that you become aware of your expression, curve up the edges of your lips into a slight smile. Over time, examine the results of this seemingly completely superficial practice.

When you become aware that you are entering the presence of another, take a moment to acknowledge, accept and admire the perfection of that individual. Naturally, that perfection is not apparent to the outer eye in most cases. Do not let that stop you. You know that each entity is the Creator. Take a moment to establish that acknowledgement, acceptance and admiration.

Before you arise from your bed, call for help. Your guidance system cannot begin to act actively in your life unless you call it, not just once but every day and every moment.

Wisdom has a tendency to create within an entity the feeling that he or she is powerful and self-sufficient. In truth, when power has been wedded to peace and light has been wedded to love, true power emerges. And in that power is rest. In that compassion is wisdom. But the ground upon which you stand in order to do this work of reconciling and harmonizing those factors that blend into who you are is love.

We find that this instrument's energies are waning and we would ask for one more query before we leave this instrument.

J: Why is it that fourth and fifth-density negative beings don't work in conjunction with their higher selves to see where the negative path leads and then switch over to the other polarity? This would seem to be so much more efficient! Is it fondness for the game, the enjoyment of feeling strong, inflowing, apparently fulfilling energies and fear of annihilation or interminable misery that keep them enthralled in their mischief?

We are those of Q'uo, and are aware of your query, my brother. And, indeed, we find that you have offered many fine answers to your own question. Therefore, since this instrument's energies are waning at this time, we would ask for another query before we leave this instrument.

J: Now that the era of service-to-self activity on this planet is coming to an end, are there scholars in the inner planes who are tallying up the lessons learned? What do we do better to understand now about the lure and the explication of violence and selfishness? From observing such difficult passage of a planet to fourth density, how can we better understand the properties of the service-to-self vortex as it reflects to us a distorted image of unending love?

We are those of Q'uo and are aware of your query, my brother. We thank you for the subtlety and the beauty of this question and, indeed, for the great thought that you have put into all the questions for the session.

We truly have no words to offer but only the humility of silence to those who would seek to know the one infinite Creator. When such hopes and desires are expressed, it is time to move to the bare beginnings and to take up with joy a condition of infanthood, and then to surround that beloved, precious, infant spirit self with the greatest of faith that you as an entity may find within your self.

For it is faith alone that cleanses the intellect, that simplifies the abstruse, that brings the flight of fancy back to the most simple and profound truth of the one Creator.

Who is counting the beans, my brother? You are. This instrument is. Each entity does it for the self. And as the self acknowledges, accepts and admires with great affection the self, the Creator harvests all of that complexity and strains it into self-awareness that is without vice.

That which you seek, my brother, is closer than your breathing. Remove the stumbling block of self, with a small "s" and, as you are able to peel away layers of maya,[6] consciousness shall emerge and you shall become transparent to eternity.

We thank each again for the pleasure of this interaction and for the beauty of your vibrations. We leave you, as we found you, in the love and in the light of the one infinite Creator. We are known to you as the principle of Q'uo. Adonai. Adonai.

---

[6] Maya is a Hindu term meaning illusion and used to indicate the earth world.

L/L Research

L/L Research is a subsidiary of Rock Creek Research & Development Laboratories, Inc.

P.O. Box 5195
Louisville, KY 40255-0195

www.llresearch.org

Rock Creek is a non-profit corporation dedicated to discovering and sharing information which may aid in the spiritual evolution of humankind.

ABOUT THE CONTENTS OF THIS TRANSCRIPT: This telepathic channeling has been taken from transcriptions of the weekly study and meditation meetings of the Rock Creek Research & Development Laboratories and L/L Research. It is offered in the hope that it may be useful to you. As the Confederation entities always make a point of saying, please use your discrimination and judgment in assessing this material. If something rings true to you, fine. If something does not resonate, please leave it behind, for neither we nor those of the Confederation would wish to be a stumbling block for any.

© 2009 L/L Research

Sunday Meditation
April 16, 2006

Jim: *(Reading question.)* "Q'uo, many New Age seekers and fundamentalist Christians believe there will soon be a rapture or ascension in which the true believers or chosen people will be whisked away by UFOs or angels, leaving the rest of humanity to suffer the tribulations of these last days. I don't believe that any true Christian or service-to-other seeker would want to leave Earth before their fellow seekers could leave too. Could you speak to the difference between this idea of a rapture or ascension and the [Confederation channeling's concept of a] graduation to fourth density that follows the death of the third-density physical body? What spiritual principles could help us think about these possibilities?"

(Carla channeling)

We are those known to you as the principle of Q'uo. Greetings in the love and in the light of the one infinite Creator, in Whose service we come to you this day. Thank you for the great privilege of being called to your circle of seeking. We rest in the beauty of your vibration.

We are most glad to speak with you concerning the query about the so-called rapture. But before we begin we would ask each of you to guard the gates of your perception carefully. Do not allow our comments and thought to sway you unless they seem to be particularly resonant to you. If they do appeal to you, by all means work with them, but if they do not appeal to you and do not seem lively and helpful, then please leave them behind.

We are no more of an authority for you than you are for us. Please realize that you are the authority for your spiritual journey and use your discrimination well. If you will do that for us then we will not be concerned about infringing upon your free will. We thank you for this consideration.

Before we approach the fundamental query we would like to address a matter that we find appearing frequently in entities' queries when they have to do with ascension or the rapture. We would like to address the thinking of those who were involved in creating the concept of the ascension or the rapture, at the time in which the *Bible* was put together.

At this time in your history your Middle East, as this instrument would call that region of your globe, was the home of many civilizations that shared this area. It was not the native land of [any] but rather a place where many cultures mingled.

The common belief system at that time for many Jewish entities, as well as for the many other religious groups that populated that area at that time, was in reincarnation. The difficulty with a belief in reincarnation, if you are looking at that belief from the standpoint of one who wishes to get the attention of a populace, is that if an entity believes absolutely that he is part of a soul stream that will incarnate many times, then that entity is not particularly concerned with whether or not he is virtuous in this life because he assumes that he shall have another chance to make things right in his next incarnation.

Therefore, the concern of teachers was to focus the student on this life and the behavior that was required in order to create a shift in consciousness from the old ways of doing things to the new way of doing things. For the one known as Jesus, the old way of doing things was the way of the world. The old way was the way of money, power and influence. The one known as Jesus was suggesting that it was time for people to wake up, to turn from their worldly ways and release their concepts of the importance of money, power and influence.

The one known as Jesus had another kingdom in mind than the kingdom of the world. He called that the kingdom of heaven. He was interested in turning people's minds from the world to heaven, from fear to love.

As he talked about the end times, therefore, this entity was speaking in stories and parables, not attempting to teach literally but attempting to create an atmosphere in which the truth would become clear.

Many times this entity said, "He who has ears, let him hear. He who has eyes, let him see. He who has a heart, let him understand." He was asking entities basically to move from the environment of the mind and from one way of thinking to another environment of the mind in which the heart did the thinking.

We cannot address the concerns of those who would read these words from the standpoint of a faith in the literal truth of them. We do not wish any to believe, word for word, in what we say, and we do not wish to persuade those who believe the *Bible* word for word that they are wrong.

We would simply ask that those who believe in that fashion not attempt to work their way through what we have to offer you, for we assure you that the view of your church authorities, though narrow, is penetrating. You will be able to follow the instructions and the teachings of the one known as Jesus the Christ without reference to what we have to say. And for your own peace of mind we would suggest that you not proceed further with any but those sources that are accepted by your leaders, for we truly would not leave a stumbling block before you.

Now let us move on to the basic query of this session.

It is so that the one known as Jesus spoke of the day of rapture, of a time when one person would be left in the field and one would be taken. We have indicated that we do not believe that this is a literal scripture nor that the teacher known as Jesus intended it to be taken literally in terms of space and time.

However, my friends, there are other ways to look at this concept that perhaps may create for you a more understandable story.

There are two ways in which there is an absolute ending to the open possibilities of the present moment. The first is that moment when you, as an incarnate being, pass from this world to the next. At the moment of the physical cessation of breath, as the life leaves your body, so does your consciousness. And that tuning or vibration which you carry at that moment is absolutely the final tuning of your incarnative experience.

It is at that resting point at which you leave the incarnation that you move on in consciousness to that vehicle of light which you have enjoyed as it has interpenetrated your physical body throughout your incarnation. And in that body of light energy you shall move through the process of graduation. That moment in the field is that moment that you may call death.

In a larger sense, and this is from the standpoint now not of yourself but of the planet as a whole, there is also an ending point to the possibility of being able to sustain third-density choice-making possibilities. The third-density energy on your planet wanes at this time. There will not be many further third-density incarnations.

Those who have been incarnating lately, for the most part, are those entities who have volunteered proudly and sacrificially to enter this waning third-density environment as pilgrims of fourth density. They are like unto those led by Moses in the desert. They shall not see the Promised Land, but they shall create the Garden of Eden upon your planet once again to the best of their ability.

Thusly, treasure this incarnation and realize the gift that it represents for each of you. This is your last opportunity to make and sustain the choice of polarity that shall lead you through graduation and into your taking up higher-density work. Those who do not make a choice of polarity and sustain that choice until polarity is built up to the point where you are able to bear the light of higher densities shall experience another cycle of third-density incarnations upon another planet and shall once again take up the lessons of love.

We emphasize that in our opinion there is no true downside to this equation. If you are not ready to make that choice, you have all the time in the world to consider it further. If you are ready, then this is the opportunity to seize the day, to take hold of the direction and path of your spiritual evolution and to invest your walk into the light with every fiber of your being, every hope and every joy and enthusiasm. Give thanks, my friends, for these are wonderful days for those who wish to make that choice and to walk that path towards the light.

In terms of what physically is going to happen upon your planet, we are not able to tell you precisely how the possibility/probability vortices will work themselves out. Your people are waking up at a phenomenal rate. It seems to be spreading exponentially, not only in the area of the world of which this instrument is aware, the United States and North America, but in every continent; in every culture, and in all peoples, no matter what their circumstances.

Indeed, my friends, those whom you would think would know the least about these troubled times—that is, those indigenous tribes and natives in various parts of your globe—are fully aware of the situation and have not been distracted from direct and intuitive communication with all of the densities, both inner and outer, by the distractions of civilization. It is actually the civilized nations, so-called, that are the furthest from a direct apprehension of the situation as it exists at this time.

We do feel that there is little or no danger that the Earth herself, in her movement into full fourth-density existence, shall need to express a global catastrophe that would cause a physical rapture to occur. As we have said before through this instrument, what we see as we gaze into the mind and the heart of your people as a global tribe is a troubling tendency to seek aggression and war instead of diplomacy and conversation. This tendency multiplied throughout a power-hungry world could result in your nation-states acting aggressively in such a manner as to set off a true doomsday with their bombs. This is possible.

And we would ask each of you to be aware of this tendency in the human heart toward aggression instead of patience insofar as you are able personally. We would encourage each of you to choose communication over aggression, patience over impatience, love over fear, and hope over exclusion.

What you as a person do may seem to begin and end within yourself. But we say to you that you act not only for yourself but for humankind. The choices that you make, if made purely and with conscious intention, can change the world.

Yes, you are that powerful, that magical, and that influential! You have within you the consciousness that was in Jesus the Christ. It is buried, in some cases, beneath the rubble of a carelessly spent life. Begin this day, then, to live with care, patience and love, being consciously aware that you stand for Earth this day, not only for yourself. Do not let this concern you or weigh you down. But know that your choices truly make a difference.

You have asked what the dynamic or the difference is between this theory or story of the rapture and ascension and the Confederation's teachings concerning graduation and walking the steps of light.

In a sense, the differences are slight because both stories focus upon each individual soul making a choice, of his or her free will, as to how to be and how to serve. Shall you be a radiant servant to others, a servant of light? In that case make each choice with that in mind.

For those few who read this who are dedicated to polarizing in service to self, in terms of your graduation we say to you, my friends, focus carefully each time you choose upon who you serve and how you wish to express your choices.

To those who persist in their choices, graduation is almost inevitable, for you are full of the desire to move on and when you organize that desire into a focus and point your will, nothing can stop you. You can be in prison and you can still make your choices for love, service, devotion, joy and gratitude. You can be on your deathbed. You can be on your sickbed. You can be in any circumstance whatsoever, and as long as you have the will to make these choices, you are already in paradise.

It is those who do not wish at this time to engage with this weighty choice of who to serve and how to serve that shall not graduate. For they simply have not become people of power. They have not chosen. Few there are, however, at this point, who are not aware that there is a choice to make.

You have time to direct your thinking and to pursue your seeking. There are some years yet of third-density energy. We do encourage you, however, to move ahead at this time with your choice-making and to be as faithful as you can to the intention of that first choice. For you enter now into a time, in perhaps six or seven of your years, when you shall no longer be able to make that initial choice. Time is short.

It is not that you shall die when this energy wanes from third density. It is that the vibrations will be simpler and will not contain those energies that mount, spiraling upward. Therefore, life shall be sustained, and those who come into the environment having already graduated, as many of those born now have done, will carry with them that energy of graduation and will not need to be concerned at the end of their third-density existence. Those to whom we speak now, however, for the most part have yet to graduate. Therefore, we speak to you, not with a sense of urgency but with a desire to share the information that will help you make skillful choices in your present and in your near future.

In terms of the way we see what shall occur in your next few years, we do see the difficulties and the inconveniences which are involved with the Earth moving through the changes that it must make in order to achieve a stable balance within fourth density. This is calling for third-density Earth to realign itself. That realignment is well advanced.

The work of this group and many, many others like it, as well as many individuals working alone in terms of physicality, have created a grace period. Since 1998 in your counting, you have been living on grace alone. This grace continues. It shall not continue beyond a certain point. For you see, at a certain point it is as though there were energies mixed in a glass of water.

We apologize for the oversimplification of this figure, but we are using a non-scientific instrument.

The energies are all mixed in a glass of water and to a certain extent they continue to be melded within each other, but at a certain point, the heavier elements sink to the bottom and the lighter elements rise to the top and there is a separation between the two levels. That point is coming for third density on planet Earth. This is not a tragedy. This is not the rapture. This has nothing to do with ascension. It is the natural, evolutionary process by which spiritual evolution of people and of planets occurs.

Your Earth shall become, in the fullness of time, a fourth-density positive planet. However, there is a golden period that is coming for your people. It is a time when those entities who have graduated third density and who are very concerned with the karmic patterns of their past are going to be able to create a time of restitution on planet Earth.

It will be a difficult time. It will be a challenging time. For the technology that you have currently created will not be adequate to the needs of the future. You will be creating new ways to do things. But the energy that is among you will clear tremendously from that which you are experiencing at this time. Those entities among you at this time that are attempting to graduate service to self will have moved on. Those entities who remain upon the planet shall be those positively-oriented entities whose concerns involve restitution to this planet.

There is another group of entities who shall be upon your planet for some time into the future if they so choose. These are entities who are not able to graduate into fourth density, or higher densities if they were wanderers, but who yet feel that karmic pull and wish to make restitution. Those include many who are alive at this time, and you will find that many entities will be attempting more and more to refocus upon the needs of the planet and its resources. They will be wishing to clean its water, its air, and its soil.

These entities are hoping not to graduate but rather to go to a kind of summer school, if you will, where they can free themselves of the habit of carelessness. For it is a careless thing to misuse the environment. It is also a careless thing to misuse people, relationships, societal entities and groups.

So this is a time of great excitement and hope upon your planet. Many are attempting to graduate. And many who do not feel that they can graduate at this time are attempting to make restitution so that they are free of the karma of having destroyed or hurt the planetary beings upon which they lived in the past.

This is how we see your present moment, not as one in which there will be a sudden change but one in which the changes are continuous and metaphysical in nature rather than physical.

We thank the one known as Jim for asking what spiritual principles are involved in thinking about this question, for that allows us to ponder with you that great and central spiritual principle of unity that governs the outworking or manifestation of spirit in the world.

We said earlier to you that if you could consciously make your choices knowing full well that you choose for Earth, you would indeed be part of the creation of a shift in consciousness for planet Earth.

Unity consciousness is very powerful. When you see people making distinctions between those who belong and those who do not, you see clearly the marks of service to self.

(Side one of tape ends.)

(Carla channeling)

No matter how logical the explanation for leaving out certain entities in any grand design, the underlying truth is that such thinking carries delusion and error. To the Creator, all of us—we, you and everything that there is—are one being. The concept of rapture has within it the seeds of service to self, for it chooses some and not others, and condemns those who have not made it to this final destination of heaven to a final destination of hell.

And we say to you, your heaven and your hell lie in the present moment. You make of your world a heaven or a hell. He who approaches life from an attitude of love creates a heaven wherever he goes. We find in this instrument's mind the example of an entity named Dietrich[7], who in the Second World War was condemned for preaching the gospel and put in prison. These entities were on starvation rations and were expected to die. This entity knew code, and he would tap out prayers and encouragement on the bars of his cell and other entities who knew code would carry on and pass the word. He would do this every day. He would create services and prayers that sustained an entire prison block of entities through the Second World War. He did die a natural death, but not before he had carried with his love and with his faith an entire community of imprisoned souls into light and love simply because he kept talking, the only way he knew how, about the only thing that mattered to him, which was love.

Let your lives be about love and you shall make of your world the heaven it surely is. When you walk through the gates into larger life you shall only see more of the same, my friend, for you have been there all the time. This day you are in paradise. Believe it and act on it and let the word spread that heaven is on earth today. It is in your hands. It is on your lips. And it is in your heart.

Is there a follow-up query at this time, or would you wish to ask another query at this time? We are those of Q'uo.

Jim: We have another question: "In order to choose the light we must first acknowledge and understand the darkness. That is the only way we can consciously exercise our free will. The question concerns the nature of the darkness. There has been much given about negative entities that bring disease and disharmony to those seeking the light. But is there a separate class or type of negative entity that brings disease and disharmony to service-to-self beings as well? Are the service-to-self beings themselves what have been called dark angels or demons that have been cast out? Could you offer any spiritual principles that would help me to think about this?"

(Carla channeling)

We are those of Q'uo and are aware of your query. My brother, we would untangle your question a bit before we respond fully, for we find that there are two questions where you intended only one. Therefore, we would remove one question from the other so that we may answer cleanly.

The situation in which an entity might help to create illness within a spirit in incarnation is rare. There are such situations. However psychic greeting is able only to accentuate preexisting faults, or as this instrument would say, chinks in the armor of light.

---

[7] Dietrich Bonhoeffer. Please see www.dbonhoeffer.org for more information.

For instance, in this entity the chink in her armor that created the possibility of a rash of unfortunate falls and difficulties that have resulted in this instrument having a broken ankle and other difficulties, bruises and so forth, was her tendency to be forgetful and not to be aware of where she is or what she is doing because of the fact that she is thinking about something.

It is a habit and a pattern of absent mindedness that this instrument has carried since birth and has accepted because it actually has physical roots in birth defects that have to do with her amygdala. Her eye was pushed into the amygdala at birth and therefore the connection between long-term and short-term memory was severed at that time. She has compensated well, but she has an inborn tendency towards faulty memory and absentmindedness.

And so when she was indeed greeted lately in an attempt to distract her from those good works in which she was engaged, the target of opportunity was her physical body. And so she has sustained what she calls "dings" to it. It has not dismayed her or distracted her. Nevertheless, this is a good example of the kind of ingress into physical health that an outside force has. It is not great.

The general cause of disharmony within a body system is disharmony within an entity's thoughts. There are very toxic thought patterns that can be guaranteed to result in a less than optimal physical configuration.

Thoughts of fear drive out peace. Thoughts of love build up inner peace. It is as simple and as challenging as that. As your mind, so shall your body go.

That which you worry about, that which you fear, you call to you. We would encourage you to watch your thoughts like a hawk. When you find them becoming toxic, ask yourself to stop thinking along those lines. Ask yourself how your highest and best self would approach the situation that has you in worry and fear.

When that thought comes to you of what the highest and best would be, try it on, my friend. See if it feels more comfortable to you, more profitable, more skillful, and more helpful than your fearful thoughts. This is the kind of choice which does not look like a choice of polarity, but it is. The choice of fear is the choice to have life be about you. The choice of love is the choice to have life be about the one infinite Creator.

Is there another query at this time? We are those of Q'uo.

Questioner: *(Mostly inaudible. The question was about whether the inner and outer densities are the same as the inner and outer planets.)*

(Carla channeling)

We are those of Q'uo, and are aware of your query, my brother. It is so that the inner and outer densities are the same as the inner and outer planets. This is so, my brother.

Questioner: *(Mostly inaudible. The questioner asks something about a break point.)*

(Carla channeling)

We are those of Q'uo, and are aware of your query, my brother. There is no difficulty in having both. There is no break point, as it were. There are inner planes in each density. All densities have all densities within them in sub-density form. In third density you have all densities, one through seven, in the inner planes. They are inner-plane densities as opposed to outer-planes densities in that they are time/space in configuration rather than space/time in configuration.

May we answer you further, my brother?

Questioner: *(Inaudible).*

(Carla channeling)

We are those of Q'uo, and would ask for a final query at this time.

Questioner: *(Mostly inaudible. The question has to do with how the Q'uo group sees the group gathered on the internet from around the globe as it sits for this circle of seeking.)*

(Carla channeling)

We are those of Q'uo, and are aware of your query, my brother. We give this instrument the image of the planet itself, with the kind of view down from a height that this instrument has seen from an airplane flying across the continent from one big city to another.

As she looks out the window at night she can see the lights that twinkle such a far, far distance below. From miles up, she can still see the lights of the farmhouses and the little towns in the smaller, less populated areas of your country. And so we see your lights as you exist about the globe.

And yet at the same time we see you that are absent from this group as it sits in Kentucky, those that sit in one room, being together in one locality. This is because by opening up the group to non-local members, you are truly acquiring time/space characteristics in the midst of your space/time, real-time presence.

It is a very exciting experience for us to have this time/space component which is created by the non-local entities joining this local group. It is a beautiful grouping in which, although you are probably not aware of it, your auras are interpenetrating and so you are creating dynamics that are inexpressibly subtle and yet quite ineffably beautiful. The coloration as one entity's soul stream touches another, that touches another, that touches the next, is perfectly marvelous and we feel very lucky to be a part of this group.

We greet all of you and we thank all of you for taking the time out of your very, very busy lives to seek the truth in this circle of seeking. This instrument's energy wanes so we would at this time leave this instrument and this group in the love and the light of the one infinite Creator. It has been our privilege and our pleasure to be with you and we thank you for calling us once again.

We are those of Q'uo, and we leave you in the love and the light of the one infinite Creator. Adonai. Adonai. ✣

L/L Research is a subsidiary of
Rock Creek Research &
Development Laboratories, Inc.

P.O. Box 5195
Louisville, KY 40255-0195

L/L Research

www.llresearch.org

Rock Creek is a non-profit
corporation dedicated to
discovering and sharing
information which may aid in
the spiritual evolution of
humankind.

ABOUT THE CONTENTS OF THIS TRANSCRIPT: This telepathic channeling has been taken from transcriptions of the weekly study and meditation meetings of the Rock Creek Research & Development Laboratories and L/L Research. It is offered in the hope that it may be useful to you. As the Confederation entities always make a point of saying, please use your discrimination and judgment in assessing this material. If something rings true to you, fine. If something does not resonate, please leave it behind, for neither we nor those of the Confederation would wish to be a stumbling block for any.

© 2009 L/L Research

Special Meditation
April 18, 2006

Question from J: In the *Law of One* series, Ra mentioned several people: Jesus of Nazareth, Edgar Cayce, Taras Bulba, Genghis Khan, and Rasputin. I found out there's a common trait of these entities, that is, regardless of their polarity, they all learned their ability via the remembering process. This remembering process seems to have a accelerating effect on these entities' learning and growing process. Is my thinking correct?

If it's correct, I wonder if there are some effective methods to help us to activate such a remembering process. For example, Edgar Cayce's self-hypnosis or some special type of meditation.

And I wonder if Q'uo can describe the practicing details of these methods and also any precaution that we need to be aware of?

(Carla channeling)

We are those known to you as the principle of Q'uo. Greetings, in the love and in the light of the one infinite Creator, in Whose service we come to you. It is a privilege to be called to your circle of seeking and we thank you. To be able to share our humble thoughts is our chosen service at this particular time and you greatly help us by giving us the chance to perform that service. It aids us in our evolution to serve the one infinite Creator in this way. We thank you for taking the time out of your extremely active lives to form this circle of seeking and ask for truth to be shared. As always, we would ask you to monitor your reactions to our thoughts carefully and discriminate between those thoughts that resonate to you and those which do not. Please leave those thoughts that do not resonate behind—they are not for you at this time. If you observe this discrimination then we feel much more comfortable in sharing our thoughts freely, for we would not intrude upon your evolution.

We are aware of the query of the one known as J concerning the various entities who remembered facets of their soul stream's history and are aware that you wish to know more about what you call the remembering process. We would offer some general thoughts before we respond to details of your question. The purpose of third density existence is not to penetrate the veil of forgetting or to know anything of a worldly nature at all. Certainly, there are times when it naturally comes to entities to remember this or that detail of a past life or to get a general impression concerning the background of that entity that you are that has come into incarnation in this lifetime.

However, it is unnecessary in terms of preparing the self for graduation from third density to penetrate the veil of forgetting. Indeed, it is far more important, in preparing for graduation from third density, that one come finally to the understanding that one knows nothing and can know nothing of the mystery that is the one infinite Creator. Reaching this level of humility and emptiness offers to the seeking student a peace and a confidence that are lacking when one is striving to know more and seek more deeply into the history of the self before this incarnation.

The veil of forgetting was put into place not in order that it may be penetrated but to set up the conditions for a life in which the choice of polarity and the continuing choices of polarity that follow such an initial choice might be played out without any possibility of proof. The choice of service-to-self or service-to-others polarity is intended to be made against the backdrop of unknowing so that one must literally take a leap of faith in order to choose how to respond to the catalyst of everyday life. In each situation where there is a decision to be made that has ethical overtones, the whole point of that veil of forgetting is to clear the canvas of any paint except that which you wish to apply in the present moment. Your choices, then, are made very cleanly—not because you feel there was karma from this or that previous lifetime or because of any other fact that you feel that you have come to know but because, by faith, you wish to choose your manner of being in a way that expresses your heart's desire.

Therefore, while we are glad to speak with you concerning ways to penetrate the veil of forgetting, we do so with a careful warning to those who wish to do this. That warning is that that which you know or feel that you know about the larger picture of your soul's history and its business within this incarnation creates a heavy responsibility. If you know something, you are responsible for that knowledge. Decisions that you make, then and thereafter, need to be made carefully and with utmost focus upon who you are and why you are in incarnation on planet Earth at this time. Any information you feel that you have gained needs to be carefully remembered and carefully applied, for you have gained in responsibility.

We call to this instrument's mind the story of Adam and Eve in the Garden of Eden. They were asked not to eat the tree of the knowledge of good and evil. They chose to ignore this request and to eat this fruit. Their eyes were opened to issues about which they had been blessedly unaware of previous to the eating of the fruit of this tree. They became aware that they were in a natural state but that they were not simple beings, free and innocent like the animals and plants—they were entities with an awareness of ethics, morality, good and evil, as the story goes.

They immediately began judging themselves; they decided that their natural, naked state was not acceptable. Modesty was born, repression was born, they became responsible for the knowledge that they had acquired. It is a heavy burden to have knowledge and it is not necessary to have this kind of knowledge in order to make the choice of service to others or service to self and to persevere in continuing to maintain that choice and that focus throughout the remainder of incarnation, thereby gaining polarity sufficient to graduate from third density.

Further, in general we would suggest as a focus for gaining information of a certain type that is helpful within incarnation, we would suggest that a more skillful focus for gaining information is an attempt to get in touch with your guidance system. We have in other sessions discussed in some detail methods for doing this and would refer the one known as J to the information contained in such sessions.

We would now move to a discussion of the details of ways to get in touch with more information about the self in previous incarnations. There are two basic ways which you may find efficacious in getting in touch with the information concerning past incarnations. The first way is organic and slow. Usually it involves simply expressing to the self each day the intention of coming—we correct this instrument—of becoming more aware of the experiences that have occurred to the self in other parts of the soul stream before and after this incarnation. It may be helpful to express this intention by looking at the self in the mirror. You may look into the eyes or you may simply look out of focus at the face. Either technique is efficacious for some entities. You may indeed find the image of your face in the mirror beginning to change into different faces as you gaze into that mirror for some time—we would suggest five of your minutes as the appropriate cutoff point; certainly between thirty seconds and five minutes at a time is enough intensity for you to experience at any one time. We would not suggest doing this more often than once a day. Such work as this may seem slight; however, it is substantive and powerful. When you harness your will and focus it, you are a person of magic and power and that which you desire will come to you.

If you desire to work with this information in a quicker way, the second technique would appeal to you. That technique involves using a professional and highly trained hypnotherapist. The technique involved is to ask the hypnotherapist to take you back, once the hypnotic state has been achieved, beyond birth so that you are not in this incarnation nor are you in any other incarnation. You will have instructed the hypnotherapist to ask you to make contact with your higher self. You will also have offered to they hypnotherapist the question that you wish to ask your higher self. The hypnotherapist may then ask those questions that you would wish to explore and the higher self, then, will respond through you to the question that the hypnotherapist is asking on your behalf. Since you as a person may well find it very difficult to recall what your higher self is saying speaking through you, it is well, if you pursue this avenue of investigation, to use a tape recorder or a CD recorder so that you have a record of that which was said.

Your remaining query had to do with the dangers that might possibly be involved in penetrating the veil of forgetting. We believe that we have expressed a sufficient degree of caution concerning this avenue of exploration. It is entirely up to you as to whether you wish to move forward with this investigation. Certainly it is fascinating to discover details of past lives and to muse and ponder upon the information that you have gained. There are times that spontaneous information will come to you—we correct this instrument—there are times when such information will come to you spontaneously. When it comes to [you] spontaneously and organically, it is part of the flow of your natural process of spiritual evolution. It is an indication that your higher self feels that you are capable of being responsible for this information and putting it to excellent use.

If you persist in speeding up the process of penetrating the veil of forgetting, please recall that you need to be very careful to use such information in a spiritually mature way, not judging yourself or spinning tales [of] adhering karma and dire consequences. We ask that you refrain from moving through such judgmental patters. Look at the information that you may have gained as a kind of story that will help you to have a larger and a more informed point of view and remember that it is not what you know that is important but how you respond to the present moment. This incarnation of yours, my brother, is not about acquiring information or wisdom, it is about opening your heart and becoming able to share and carry the maximum amount of light and love as it flows from the Creator to the Earth and through y our physical and metaphysical bodies. If you can open your heart in this moment, you are doing the maximum amount that you can do to serve the Creator and the creation.

May we ask if there is another query at this time? We are those of Q'uo.

J: When one activates his remembering process, does he accomplish via experiencing some things or is he guided by higher beings in the time/space?

We are those of Q'uo, and are aware of your query, my brother. There is always guidance coming into your aura, my brother, from what you would call higher beings. Your guidance system is always with you and many entities other than your higher self are attracted to those who are seeking and attempting to experience the truth as they understand it. This kind of metaphysical activity alerts many entities within what this instrument calls the unseen realm or plane of existence. You have within your aura, shall we say, many helpers waiting to be asked for help. It is truly written, "Ask and you shall be answered; knock and the door shall be opened; seek and you shall find".

Information cannot flow to you unless you open the door to it by asking for it. When you do not know that for which you should ask, simply ask for that which your higher self sees fit to share with you in the present moment. We encourage you to ask for this help before you arrive each day, and during the day when you have a moment to reflect, ask again that the spirit may speak to you. When you ask, you open the door to the potential of the present moment and spirit will find many ways to give you hints and inklings. Watch for repetitive numbers. When you see them, ask yourself what were you thinking? Whatever you were thinking at that moment, it would be helpful for you to move further with, to seek more deeply and more profoundly.

Watch for curious coincidences. This also is an invitation that the thought that you were thinking when the coincidence occurred is worth exploring more deeply. Or, if it is indeed a repeating thought that is the coincidence, examine that thought ever more deeply. Sit with it and see how your deeper self responds too.

In terms of the experience of discovering more about your soul stream's history, it is not the activity of higher beings, precisely, that is involved. If it happens organically and spontaneously, it is the action of your higher self, which in concert with that portion of your consciousness that exists between incarnation is responding to the conditions of your being as you meet the present moment. There are times in your life when you become aware of an entirely new level of the self and it is often at such times that your higher self is particularly active in responding to your needs because a great deal is happening at such times. These are usually times when you have been through a dark night of the soul and as you come to the dawning that lights up your life at the end of such a difficult period, many epiphanies and realizations may hit you like waves coming in from the ocean. It is at those times that spontaneous, new information about your larger self and its history may come to you. Otherwise, what you learn about your soul stream's history is likely to be because of your focus, your will, and your desire.

May we ask if there is a further query at this time?

J: During the remembering process, would one see some images in his visual screen or inner eyes?

We are those of Q'uo, and are aware of your query. It is usual in cases of the spontaneous penetration of the veil of forgetting that you will come to the information in a non-threatening manner. This usually takes place during the dreaming portion of your sleep. You will have a dream that seems particularly vivid and it will constitute the discovery of the way a previous incarnational experience feels or felt. Within the dream, you are simply in the other incarnation and experiencing life from that point of view.

The characteristic experience of one who is learning through this bleed-through experience of dreaming is that the dream will seem preternatural vivid, colorful and detailed. It is rare that such information streams into the conscious mind while you are awake. Although, certainly under the pressure of a sustained request for such information, it may be that such information will come as in a vision, or in the case of one working with the mirror, seen dimly or with increasing detail in the mirror itself during the experience of looking into the mirror with the eyes out of focus.

May we ask if there is another query at this time?

J: What requirements does one need to activate the remembering process? What is the maximum possible degree of total remembrance that one can achieve?

We are those of Q'uo, and believe that we grasp your query, my brother. The requirements for penetrating the veil of forgetting are a sincere feeling that this is an important piece of information that will help you in your spiritual evolution. If the desire is pointed in the direction of this information, then that activates the process of coming into possession of more information of this type. The maximum degree of penetration of the veil of forgetting is variable. Different entities will be able to bear different percentages of the full weight of the experiences that have been embraced and assimilate by the soul stream.

The density and weight of such information is incredibly great. You, my brother, would find it difficult to believe the amount of information and the kind of information that you have accreted to your soul stream during the very long and busy history of your beingness. You must realize that you have existed since before the planet upon which you now draw breath was created. You are a portion of the Creator Itself. You have experienced all densities within this octave of creation. In the non-local or metaphysical sense, you are even now in all of the densities, accumulating information to yourself to offer up as a gift to the one infinite Creator. Consequently, to know even one percent of your total history would be far too much information for you to bear within incarnation.

May we ask if there is a further query, my brother?

J: If one wants to open the gates of intelligent infinity, is it necessary for him to remember all things in his past lives?

We are those of Q'uo, and are aware of your query, my brother. Indeed it is not necessary at all to remember any of the details of your past lives. In order to achieve harvestability within third density, it is necessary only to intend to love and to allow the self to be loved in return. Loving and being loved are the activity that shall open your heart and create in you a cleanliness, a peace, and a power that expresses the love and the light of the one infinite Creator in its truth and its beauty.

We thank the one known as J for these queries and for seeking the truth. We thank all of those in this circle for the privilege of being allowed to share our thoughts and for the beauty of your vibrations.

We leave you as we found you, in the love and in the light of the one infinite Creator. We are known to you as the principle of Q'uo. Adonai. Adonai. ✤

L/L Research

L/L Research is a subsidiary of Rock Creek Research & Development Laboratories, Inc.

P.O. Box 5195
Louisville, KY 40255-0195

www.llresearch.org

Rock Creek is a non-profit corporation dedicated to discovering and sharing information which may aid in the spiritual evolution of humankind.

ABOUT THE CONTENTS OF THIS TRANSCRIPT: This telepathic channeling has been taken from transcriptions of the weekly study and meditation meetings of the Rock Creek Research & Development Laboratories and L/L Research. It is offered in the hope that it may be useful to you. As the Confederation entities always make a point of saying, please use your discrimination and judgment in assessing this material. If something rings true to you, fine. If something does not resonate, please leave it behind, for neither we nor those of the Confederation would wish to be a stumbling block for any.

© 2009 L/L Research

Sunday Meditation
May 7, 2006

Group question: "I would like to ask the Q'uo for your thoughts on the spiritual principles involved in the process of disease and in the process of healing disease both in ourselves and in our serving as conduits for the healing of other selves, such as in Reiki healing."

(Carla channeling)

We are those known to you as the principle of Q'uo. Greetings in the love and the light of the one infinite Creator. We come to you this day in the Creator's service. Thank you for calling together a circle of seeking and asking us to join you. Thank you to each of you, both in the room physically with this instrument and in the world at large. Truly, in the temple that you have made together by creating this circle we are all in one time and one metaphysical space and we are honored to be among you.

We would ask, as always, that each guard well the gates of perception and discriminate between those thoughts of ours which hit the mark and those which miss it for you. Be very careful before accepting any of our thoughts to work with. Be sure that it is truly a resonate thought for you, for we would not wish to lead you astray. We thank you for this consideration.

You have asked this day concerning the principles involved in the process of disease and in the process of healing—whether the healing is done upon oneself or whether the healing is done for others. The two are two sides of one coin and that coin is the mystery that you behold before you in the mirror: your physical vehicle, its energy body, and all of the attachments thereto.

Let us look at the model which we would use to talk about you as a physical being that has something called wellness or health.

The body that is your physical vehicle is the outward and physical sign of your consciousness. It is not your consciousness. The physical body, left to itself, is as any animal among your many species of animals upon your planet. It has an instinctual life and it owns a brain which you generally experience as that brain that makes decisions. That is what your physical body's brain was created for, as a choice-making tool. It makes choices on a hierarchy of priorities, the first being survival.

When you took upon yourselves the ambition of entering incarnation, you agreed upon a process that would inextricably bind you to this physical vehicle which you now enjoy, for the duration of your incarnation.

The consciousness that you possess as a citizen of eternity moved into interpenetrative intimacy, body upon body, so that the body of your consciousness—which some call a light body, some call the energy body and others call the chakra system—interpenetrated the physical form and connected with it in a very careful and specific way.

We give this instrument the vision of a plant which grows up within a pot. The pot has the soil necessary for the growth of the plant. The energy which creates the ability for that plant to grow is found in the soil of the pot. That is what your physical vehicle is. It is a clay vessel.

You, as consciousness, made an agreement with that body or physical vehicle, before incarnation. That body agreed to carry you. In a sense you may see yourselves, all of you, each and every one, as a walk-in, to use the New Age term familiar to this instrument. You, as a human species are a species of walk-ins.

Into the natural physical vehicle your consciousness walked in, made its connections with each of the various facets of your energy system that connect directly into your physical body along the line of the spine and you settled in for a shared experience together where the physical vehicle would have the privilege of carrying consciousness and you, as consciousness, would have the privilege of having an incarnation in flesh. It is a beautiful and a carefully made collaboration which you enjoy.

Left to the choices of the physical body, the kind and degree of illness which you experience as human beings would not exist. You would be healthy until your physical vehicle became weary. Given that you had food and water and the things that you needed for life, you would undoubtedly remain healthy until that illness which offered you the opportunity to leave the incarnation presented itself.

The drama of stress and tension that you experience and all of the emotional and physical aftereffects of such difficulty within the so-called energy body would not be experienced. Yours would be a life as natural as that of a cat, a horse, or a grizzly bear. In your environment you would thrive if there were enough food, enough water, enough salt, and so forth. Life would be simple.

For the human being the simplicity of that life becomes hidden. You cannot reconnect with the animal body and become a simple animal. The nature of your consciousness militates against such a choice.

No matter how deeply you attempt to bury your faculty of judgment, you as a human being are all about judgment. It is a judgment that is carefully created as a kind of instinct within consciousness which propels you forward in a metaphysical sense. As you form opinions and make choices, consciousness, which has links in the inner planes and throughout the universe, creates a reverberating sounding board which bounces your decisions, your choices, and your judgments back to you for review.

Until you begin to grasp the power and the responsiveness of this system, you may well experience a wide range of catalyst. As you become more skilled at realizing the dynamics of the natural system in which you are involved, energetically speaking, you will begin to realize that there are attitudinal choices that you can make that create within your experience much more of a feeling of participation in the process of experiencing catalyst and choosing to respond to it.

Until you grasp just how powerful a being you are as one possessing consciousness, you will be completely at the mercy of catalyst. Conversely, once you grasp the rules of this game of incarnation you are playing and begin to apply the rules of the game, which are relatively simple, you may well find yourself in a process of transformation.

Things may begin to simplify themselves for you once again. But the simplicity will be the simplicity that moves in a spiraling fashion up to the unified level of body and consciousness. This is not precisely the same thing as the psyche and the soma or the mind and body, as psychology has it, for you are more than your psyche and your body. Health [and] the process of illness as well have a great deal to do with that "more than" that you are.

In a way, you may see yourselves as pilgrims who carry their packs not over their shoulders wrapped in a kerchief, as the mythical hobo figure does; rather, you may certainly see yourself as that pilgrim on the road, the journey of spiritual evolution. The pack that you carry lies within. What is metaphysical food? What does your pack hold? The answers that you offer to that may well indicate the true nature of your wellness.

We would, in passing, distinguish between health and wellness. It is well to realize that no matter what the age or health of the physical body, by examining such things as the eyes and the general feeling that being around a person may give you, you may discover that many seemingly physically healthy people are not well. You may also discover that many seemingly frail people are extremely healthy.

The actual state of wellness within your organism is a function not only of the state of your physical body and not only the state of your mind, it also contains an element that is difficult to quantize.

In consciousness there is a ground of being. That ground of being is love. You are an expression of the one original Thought. That is the gift that you carry in your physical lifetime. You don't carry a little love. You carry the love that creates and destroys. It is at once your glory and your biggest woe because when you do not focus and direct the awesome power of your personality, your character, and your belief system and instead you allow it to follow its impulses without giving them particular thought, you may find yourself in the situation where life experiences are occurring to you that do not make sense and to which you do not know how to respond.

This being said, your basic health is like a default setting. If you were born with radiant health, then that is your factory setting—that is how you came from the manufacturer. Your light body, your energy body, or your chakra system copies that group of settings before birth as part of the integration process of soul or spirit and physical vehicle or body. The memory of that default setting, which is health, radiant and unblemished, is retained by every cell in your body and by every iota of energy in your energy body.

The process of disease occurs when the balance that is the default setting for wellness in your particular physical vehicle and energy body becomes upset. Such balances can become upset because of purely physical and mechanical reasons. If you fall and break your bone, there may be no higher interpretation of such an event. You simply had an unlucky accident. However, if you are a seeker on the path, it is well to open up your mind and your thinking to the possibility that some imbalance in your energy body threw you off so that you were literally out of balance and so you fell.

If you look at health as strictly physical, you will go with an unlucky accident. You will go to the doctor, follow the doctor's orders, and eventually you can get well. You will not have learned anything. Your physical vehicle was damaged and then it repaired itself.

If you go with the latter explanation, that there were imbalances within your energy body, you may still go to a medical doctor for help with healing the body, but you may also go within to that divine healer that lives within your consciousness. When you choose to examine your thinking, your actions, and the possible ways to look at the balances of your energy system, you open yourself up to a whole level of powerful possibilities that are not there if you stay strictly within the physical parameters in your thinking.

Consequently, when entities decide to work with the game of incarnation at a deeper level than the physical body, [they] have made the choice to move into a faster lane as far as the pace of spiritual evolution because the sufferings and the woes of the physical existence are created as part of the work which lies before the consciousness you carry. That consciousness will use every bit of the suffering that you are able to penetrate [with] your faith. It will use it to learn how to return to the default setting. Many supposed miracle healings have been done simply because of the depth of an entity's faith.

In general, when there is a movement away from perfect balance in any part of the energy body, the key word in looking for cause is fear. There has been a contraction away from the relaxed and peaceful default setting of the emotional and mental part of your physical vehicle. That contraction has pulled some part of your energy body into imbalance. That contraction was in one way or another caused by the faculty of fear.

If you see the perfect body and wellness itself as a state of love, then you will see that fear is a choice which turns one away from the face of love. Therefore, the choice for healing is a choice to lose fear and choose love. Because it is sometimes difficult to drop all fear, healers exist which work with the energy body rather than the physical body. What they do is to offer to the entity who seeks healing the opportunity in a neutral atmosphere to drop fear and choose love.

We realize that we have barely, barely looked at the top layer of an enormously profound subject and we have a desire to speak further with you at a later time. However, this instrument informs us that there are other queries that she would like to focus upon to some extent this day, and we, too, would like to respond to the great privilege of having this wider group that is non-local. And so we would also like to turn from this query for now in order to field some of these other queries.

May we ask the one known as Jim to read from the sheet which the one known as R has given him?

Jim: "I'm interested in knowing what transition may be like for a dual-activated person. Will the transition between third and fourth density bodies be seamless or is it more abrupt, like the death process? If so, exactly how does it work? Is it more of an individual process or is it more of a process done by the social memory complex?"

(Carla channeling)

We of those of Q'uo, are aware of your query, my brother, and we thank you for it. Third density is third density. And while you are in a third-density physical vehicle you will primarily be a third-density entity. The fourth-density activation, however, enables you, far more than those about you, to be tough. We think that is perhaps the simplest way to put that.

The interpenetration of third density with fourth-density energy in the time/space sector of this development is bombarding the Earth with wave after wave of a denser kind of light that brings all entities' worst fears to the surface and plays them out.

It is a separating device, if you will, between wheat and chaff, in biblical terms. There are tares sown among the harvest of good that you have created in your life[time]. These waves of energy call for the truth from you, and, so, many of you are facing parts of yourself you never wanted to see and at which you don't want to look.

The fourth-density-activated entities or dual-activated beings are tougher at looking straight in the mirror of the self, seeing the weeds, and deciding on a form of weed control.

It is up to you to decide how you want to deal with this judgment of self. We especially want to indicate that in our opinion it is not well to judge the self in the way of this instrument's experience of the Old Testament. We do not want you to condemn yourself. We want you to see that when a plant is not wheat, that plant is a weed.

Do you want to pluck it out by the roots? You may, but it will take time. Do you want to snip it off so that it may grow again but for today it does not show? You may do that. That is your choice. But the dual activated body will unerringly give you the toughness of mind to go for the root and to do the work in a timely manner.

In terms of what body will be activated when: they are both activated now, but you are in a third-density physical vehicle. You are living on a third-density planet. You are here for a reason. Many, many others are here for the same reason.

Those with dual activated bodies have graduated and have come back. Just as the Elder Race, when it graduated, chose to return, so have you returned. You do not want to go on to the exciting and even thrilling prospect of fourth-density existence, with its greatly enhanced options for learning and for service, until you have done your utmost, not only to help others of the human tribe to move on into fourth density with you but also to restore and reconstitute the health of Gaia,[8] of planet Earth, in her living form.

For many of you in dual activated bodies there is a feeling of great and passionate desire to connect with the Earth and to love and be a good steward to the Earth. For there is that within your consciousness as a person and in your consciousness as part of a race of beings that you have, in the past, been part of the destruction of a planet, a continent, a city, or family. And that destruction has caused the Earth to grieve, to mourn, and to become disoriented.

By the time you leave this planet, the planet will know that it is loved. That is a very large factor in many of those who are dual activated and is their primary reason for being on the Earth at this time.

Of course, because of the fact that you chose to come into third-density incarnation, you are always subject to the basic rules of this game. You need to polarize in this lifetime towards service to others to an extent that enables you once again to walk the steps of light and walk into a higher density.

Otherwise, you shall simply move on with those still in third density at the end of this time to another third-density planet where you will continue to be of service and to gain in memory of who you are and why you are here, until such time as you once again get yourself on the right road, the road of your own

---

[8] Gaia is a name for planet Earth which comes from Greek mythology, in which Gaia is goddess of the earth and mother of Cronus and the Titans.

deepest choosing, and then walk that walk, step by step, in great thanksgiving and joy, every day that you are privileged yet to be alive and breath the sweet air of [planet Earth].

May we ask if there is another query? We are those of Q'uo.

Jim: The next query is: "I, for one, would like a nice summation from Q'uo on this whole transition phase, how the pieces come together, if we are allowed to know.

"As I currently understand it, a convergence of the dark brown companion star comet cluster and wave or energy surge ushers in the shift or realm border crossing for planet Earth from third to fourth density and all kinds of service-to-others and service-to-self spectators are coming to watch the show. The Ra and Q'uo groups have mentioned the cessation of third density around 2012. Is this correct? An aspect of service-to-self entities aren't agreeing to this or accepting it. So after that is supposedly a thousand year transition period on this service-to-self and service-to-others choice.

"What does this thousand year period entail, a weeding out process between the two polarities? Perhaps a last chance for those newly awakened; those whose choice is not quite firm enough to allow full entry into fourth-density form? Or how does this change in classrooms apply to the various groups such as service-to-self, service-to-others, wanderers, indigos, dual-body activation, etc., etc."

We are those of Q'uo, and are aware of your query. There are portions of your query that do not make sense to us and about which we will not comment except to say that in attempting to imagine those things which bring about the harvest, there are sources which use information which may be seen in a non-literal sense with much more helpfulness from that construction than attempting to make literal sense out of some material.

Concerning the basic setup of the transition, there is a moment of transition in terms of the planet itself. That moment of transition is at some point near to the winter solstice of 2012. It is fairly set—cut and dried, as this instrument would say.

For the human tribe that inhabits the surface of Planet Earth, things are not so cut and dried. The time of choice is greatly limited now among your peoples. This is not a cause for great concern for most of those, if not all of those, who shall make that choice for graduation have already made the initial choice of service to others. There is still time to make that initial choice, but you may do the calculation necessary to see that the time is short. [The year] 2012 is within [the] lifetime [of] each of those to whom we are speaking. This is something that you may choose and you may do completely and well in the next few years.

For most of you, indeed, as we said, the choice has been made. You have decided to be of service to others. Let these next few years that remain before 2012 be a testament to your stability, your spiritual maturity, and your ability to persevere. Bloody mindedness and sheer guts is sometimes part of what it takes to make the choice of love.

You have to look beyond your own feelings and your own first responses and ask, as this instrument has heard often from us and from those of the Ra group, "Where is the love in this situation? Where is the light in this moment?" When you are prompted to ask this query of yourself, you may well find that you are the only source you can find in that situation of love and light.

(Side one of tape ends.)

(Carla channeling)

Yes, my friends, you! You are only one being, but you have within you consciousness. That consciousness is what this instrument would call Christ consciousness. It is the consciousness of unconditional love.

Go looking for that consciousness. Ask for help in finding that consciousness. Your guidance system is just waiting for you to ask for help. The angels that surround you are breathless with anticipation that you will remember them and call for them. They love you with a love that we cannot describe to you. It is the love of the one Creator. They are bits of that consciousness; uncreated, sent forth in purity, unable to enter incarnation and able only to help when asked by incarnated beings such as yourself. Remember to ask for that help.

After these years of choice have been lived through, you may well live for quite some time thereafter. You will not notice changes in your own ability to breath and eat and do the natural functions of a human being. You will be able to live out your life.

The one known as Jim was saying that in *The Ra Material*, the period of transition was suggested to be perhaps between 100 and 700 of your years. The reason it is so approximated is that we do not know who shall inspire whom with love and with the daring to make courageous choices at difficult moments. Every choice that you make for love extends that transitional period. And it is good to have that time, simply to work with the earth energy and to reconstitute and restore the health of the planet.

For those who graduate in a positive sense, their next incarnation will be on planet Earth, unless they are wanderers and have chosen to move after graduation into other realms or densities for further work as a wanderer.

For those graduating in the negative sense, they will go to a negatively oriented fourth-density planet unless they are wanderers, in which case they will be able to, after graduation, move back into whatever they feel would serve them the best.

For those who have not chosen either service to others or service to self as a polarity, there is still work to do in third density, the density of choice. You shall have some more time to make that choice and it shall be upon another planet.

Once third density winds down on planet Earth, it shall be inactive for a time. This is due to the need of new fourth-density entities to learn the ways of invisibility. There is no desire in fourth-density entities to disturb or surprise third-density entities. If fourth density were visible to third density, you would find yourself in a charming but very crowded universe made up of elementals, nature spirits and devas, totems, fictional entities who have gained inner-planes life because of the continued thoughts of many and so forth.

It would be an enchanting and diverse experience but it would be too much for you to bear. You are veiled from fourth density and all other densities that would give you these experiences because you are here in third density to discover who you are—that is, an ethical being—and to decide what you want to do with that troublesome consciousness that you have found.

May we answer you further, my brother, on that question? We are those of Q'uo.

Jim: No, but we do have another question, Q'uo, if you have time. It is from A: "We third density humans tend to categorize things—the time of the year, the races and classes of people, the species of animals and even the flavors of ice cream.

"As we've been told many times, fundamentally, all things are one. Does the need and purpose of categorization diminish as we advance toward the higher densities? Do we eventually lose all differentiation between ourselves and all that exists?"

(Carla channeling)

We are those of Q'uo, and are aware of your query, my brother. We find this to be an interesting query in that it assumes almost the direct opposite of what is true, but it does so because of the logic of third density. We do not operate according to that logic.

As one rises in densities, one becomes aware of the tremendous, unimaginable array of information. Each density has a quantum leap of information involved. It is as if the light had more facets so that it could carry more information.

As your souls crystallize in the way water is a crystal, they become much more easily magnetized and you become a much more fluid and responsive being. In higher densities you are aware not of less organization but of more, for you are not veiled and shielded from the dance of creation as a whole. That dance is endlessly, beautifully, rhythmically, gracefully organized. All parts of the creation are aware of all other parts of the creation.

You are familiar with this kind of dance because you see it in the second density and first density about you all the time. The trees, the air, the oceans, and all of the energies of nature are responsive in one holistic system, of which you are a part, but a bumbling, awkward and unknowing part. For the most part, you don't catch the rhythm of existence and so you don't celebrate life. You just accompany it. You're missing out on the celebratory aspect of this wonderful dance of life.

So, my brother, in brief, as you rise in densities, you see the details in much more full array than you do now. But you also see the organizing principle of love that drives the dance. This overarching love is the consciousness of which we were speaking earlier. Each of you possesses it and as you rest back into both yourself and the essential nature of the world around you, you will be led closer and closer to the immediate apprehension of the beauty of this dance.

We would encourage you, my brother, to try, as an experiment, the experience of resting within a natural environment, far from clusters of people, and drumming or beating upon a piece of wood with your hand or anything that enables you to begin to express the rhythm of your being. For you have this dance within you. Allow civilization to take a back seat for awhile and just beat the rhythm of the beat of your heart for a while. It does not have to be a terribly long time. It is a way of putting you in touch with the part of you that is in rhythm and dancing with all of the rest of the unified creation of which you are an integral and loving part.

May we ask if there is a final query at this time? We are those of Q'uo.

Questioner: What would Q'uo recommend that doctors, nurses and family do in hospitals to reduce or eliminate the fear of their patients?

(Carla channeling)

We are those of Q'uo, and we are aware of your query. We find that our first response may be impractical but we will offer it to you anyway.

In the first place, if it is possible to avoid an institutional setting when you are ill, it is well to do so.

The one known as Norman, whose last name this instrument requests us to give—it is Cousins—wrote a book which this instrument read, in which he spoke of being given a terminal diagnosis. And what they suggested to him had a great deal to do with hospitals, radiation and so forth. He decided that he did not wish to heal himself in this way.

He figured out what it would cost him to enter a hospital for these machinations by the medical community and realized that he had a fairly large budget. He chose to put himself into a good hotel with room service, which happened to be a very good room service. He installed a video player so he could watch movies. He watched all of the Marx Brothers movies, all of the old Jerry Lewis movies that are part of this instrument's memories as a young girl, all of the Three Stooges movies, and any other comedies he that he could lay his hands on. He laughed himself well.

Rather than focusing on the illness and his fear of dying, he decided to focus on his wellness and his love of life. In this entity's case, it worked well because this entity had done the work before he was given this diagnosis to be able to come up with this scheme.

Therefore, our first suggestion is if you can find a way not to enter an institutional setting for healing, I encourage you to do so.

If you are going to take the institutional setting in order to accomplish things that need to be done and you have become convinced that this is an appropriate thing for you to do, then we would suggest that you remember that you can create your own environment wherever you are. You can override the environment around you. But you must know that and know it very well before you enter such an institutional setting.

The institutional settings of so-called "health" [industry] are cesspools of negatively-oriented energy. In the first place, my brother, there is the fear of the patients. In the second place, there is the stink of the physical setting itself, which is by nature and by necessity cold, easy to clean, cleaned often and never quite cleaned to the point where the distressing odors that have been cleaned away go away. There is always the remainder of the various waste products of the human body that is ill that remain within the physical olfactory senses of all those who enter it. It is a depressing place to be, simply physically speaking, esthetically speaking, and so forth.

Thirdly, there is an aspect to doctoring, as you call it in your culture, which is heavy and dark because of the overwork of the doctors involved in the system and because of the completely needless attitude of utter dependency that many patients employ in relating to doctors, nurses and other authority figures within the health industry. This creates an irritability and an impatience within those supposedly attempting to heal you.

And lastly, there is the metaphysical atmosphere of a hospital or other health facility. Inner-planes entities and outer-planes entities find fear and suffering to be excellent food and so they congregate in such places looking for targets of opportunity.

All in all, it is a very unhealthy place to be ill and it is obviously to be avoided if possible.

If you cannot avoid these places—and certainly this instrument has often, time and again, been placed in the middle of a hospital situation—it is still possible to create your own healthy, light-filled environment. This instrument and the one known as Jim have, in the past, used the Banishing Ritual of the Lesser Pentagram[9] in order to cleanse the space of a hospital room or an operating room. This can be done for the self and it can also be done, if permission is given by the other entity, in absent healing for another person who is perhaps too weak to create this cleared space herself.

We find that this instrument's energy wanes. We realize that we have barely touched upon these queries and we welcome refinements of them in the future.

Meanwhile, we thank each of you for the beauty of your beings, the harmony of your coming together and the depth [of] character that it takes for entities as busy as each of you are to make a special time to seek the truth. It has been a pleasure and a privilege to share our humble thoughts with you and we would leave you at this time, as we found you, in the love and in the light of the one infinite Creator. Adonai. Adonai ✛

---

[9] This ritual and the explanation of why it is effective are contained in William E. Butler's book, *The Magician; His training and His Work*.

L/L Research

L/L Research is a subsidiary of Rock Creek Research & Development Laboratories, Inc.

P.O. Box 5195
Louisville, KY 40255-0195

www.llresearch.org

Rock Creek is a non-profit corporation dedicated to discovering and sharing information which may aid in the spiritual evolution of humankind.

ABOUT THE CONTENTS OF THIS TRANSCRIPT: This telepathic channeling has been taken from transcriptions of the weekly study and meditation meetings of the Rock Creek Research & Development Laboratories and L/L Research. It is offered in the hope that it may be useful to you. As the Confederation entities always make a point of saying, please use your discrimination and judgment in assessing this material. If something rings true to you, fine. If something does not resonate, please leave it behind, for neither we nor those of the Confederation would wish to be a stumbling block for any.

© 2009 L/L Research

Sunday Meditation
May 28, 2006

Question from A: *(Read by Jim.)* Our question today is this: "You've mentioned before that the harvest of this particular sub-logos, planet Earth, is not typical. You've said that other sub-logoi have had considerably less difficulty at their times of harvest. Would you consider our sub-logos' use of combined free will, together with strong veiling, to be an inefficient combination? And can you compare that to the harvest of third density on Venus? Both Mars and Maldek had warlike societies, and we were wondering what the third density was like on Venus and what major factors and catalysts went into their societies to bring them to a service-to-others choice. They must've done something right. So could Q'uo speak to the harvest that is now happening on planet Earth and perhaps contrast it with the harvests on Mars, Maldek and Venus?"

(Carla channeling)

We are the principle known to you as the Q'uo. Greetings in the love and in the light of the one infinite Creator. It is our privilege and our pleasure to serve the Creator by offering ourselves to groups such as this one which may have an interest in material such as is channeled by this instrument. It is a great privilege to be called to your circle of seeking and we thank each of those who have taken the time and the space out of their very busy daily round of activities in order to create a sacred space in which to seek the truth.

As always, we would ask of each the care with the discrimination in listening to what we have to say. We may not hit the mark for you. If our thoughts do not resonate to you, please lay them aside without a second thought. We would not wish to be a stumbling block in your way. Sometimes, if the wrong thought is held in stubbornness, when resonance is not there, it can do harm. So we would appreciate your being very careful about those thoughts that you allow past the gates of your perception.

Your query this day is about the differences between various planetary entities' take on third density and what was done differently on the planet you call Venus that allowed that planet to have a more harmonious and far more successful journey through the third density.

The one known as A asked whether the combination of very clear and starkly delineated free will and the fairly profound veiling that is apparent on Earth's third density, or the Density of Choice[10], was a combination that spelled a difficult and challenging third density for those of planet Earth. And we would agree with this assessment of factors involved in the creation of a somewhat challenging Density of Choice for planet Earth, especially in regards to comparing it to the Density of Choice on the planetary energy called Venus.

---

[10] These two terms are used interchangeably by the Confederation sources.

For indeed in that third-density environment, there was less of a heaviness involved in the veiling. The free will was as marked as is the factor of free will upon your planet. However, there was, for the entities of Venus, a transparency in the veil which was just transparent enough to allow processes which you know as envisioning, journeying and dreaming to have a more robust life within the conscious processes, as well as the subconscious processes, of the entities in third density upon the planetary influence you call Venus.

This is, in fact, the one difference between the third density of the planet known as Venus and the other planetary influences of which you are aware.

The problem with the somewhat transparent veiling process upon third density is that the choice is not made in an atmosphere of boot camp. Therefore, when the third-density entity becomes a fourth-density entity, and then a fifth density entity, the energies move along with utmost smoothness until fifth density, at which time the lack of challenge in penetrating the veiling process shows up as a dynamic that is negative with respect to being able to work well with the opening of those energies of wisdom which seem dark to the naïve and unsophisticated seeker.

Consequently, the work and challenge came for those entities experiencing the [higher] densities on Venus' influence instead of in third density. Those who graduated into sixth density from the influence of the planet known as Venus, then, have often, in coming back into third density on your planet to serve as wanderers, been faced with a very challenging, self-given agenda of learning. That agenda is in rebalancing love and wisdom in order to value them in such as way that they are able to interpenetrate each other in true sixth-density unity.

The benefit of the more impenetrable veil is that it creates for the third-density entity attempting to choose between service to self and service to others a stark and seemingly profound experience of suffering which this instrument would call Golgotha.[11] The third density of your planet calls forth from the seeking entity a purity of humility and surrender that is, in our humble opinion, a far more favorable plinth[12] upon which to build the character that will move through all the densities of your octave than the third density where there is always seen the benefit of teachers and the benefit of taking another entity's word for something. Third density with a lighter veil creates a wonderful [place] for entities to put themselves in the teaching situation. And the system of guru and chela, as known among your Buddhists, is very similar to the kind of enjoyment that third density upon Venus created.

However, it was found, in this early third-density experience, that indeed there were difficulties in higher-density work that were engendered by the seemingly quick and easy move through third density. What this has to offer to those asking this question is our assurance that those within Earth's third density at this time have received a powerful gift. In receiving such a difficult and challenging third-density atmosphere, you have faced those shadows that await you, if not in third density, then in more subtle work [in higher densities] where those shadows are more difficult to deal with. Your present environment is a powerful environment; powerful, that is, just as a loaded gun is powerful. The question is, "Where do you wish to aim this experience when you pull the trigger on tomorrow?" Where would you like to be headed? Because the choice of heading is indeed yours.

You are in a position, each of you, my friends, to make powerful and life-changing choices this day and every day because you must deal in faith alone. When you do choose to move in faith, the planet moves with you. You take the power of your being and focus it upon your intention, and that which you choose is chosen. We cannot express to you the power that you have over your destiny. We cannot express it, nor can anyone, because that which you choose must be chosen in faith alone.

What we can say to you, my friends, is that there is ample companionship for you. It is unseen, but it does not have to be unfelt. Ask for your guidance to be with you in these difficult days and in these difficult moments. For each of you has particularly difficult moments either at this time or in the near future.

---

[11] Golgotha is the small hill outside Jerusalem upon which it is said that Jesus the Christ was crucified.

[12] plinth: a flat or slab-like member at the base or bottom of a column, pier, pedestal, architrave or other architectural vertical member.

That is the nature of these times, my friends. That is the nature of these somewhat inconvenient times. Nevertheless, they are times extremely fertile and rich in learning and in service. Please do not be concerned that you shall be responsible for some learning or for some service, for all has been, is and will be attracted to you as you are ready to express it.

Therefore, allow the spirit to move through you when you feel that it is your time to speak, your time to envision, your time to pray, or your time to heal. For when you sense the resonance of that moment and act upon it, all of the heavenly worlds support you, my friends.

Is there a follow-up to that query at this time, or another question at this time? We are those of the Q'uo.

Jim: We have another question. The question is: "As a practicing Reiki master teacher, I'm interested in what Q'uo has to offer about Reiki energy. Specifically, I'd like to know what can be shared about the nature of the physical and spiritual characteristics of this energy that, in my experience, can bring about profound improvements. What are the mechanisms by which Reiki energy can heal? How are the physical cells in the body affected by Reiki energy? Is it necessary for the recipient to believe in and accept Reiki energy for healing to occur? What's the source of Reiki energy? Is Reiki energy protected or guided by higher spiritual beings?"

(Carla channeling)

We are those of the Q'uo, and are aware of your query. We would ask the one known as Jim, after we have responded through this instrument, to review the questions upon this subject and to re-ask any which we did not touch upon in the first response. We thank the one known as Jim for this aid.

We are not aware, because this instrument is not aware, of the roots of the meaning of Reiki. We do not know this word as such. However, we examine the physical vehicle of this instrument which has experienced a great deal of Reiki energy given through various practitioners and masters of that art. There are, indeed, some strictures upon what we can say concerning this energy. However, we may touch upon some of the queries that were asked.

We would say that this energy is the energy of the one infinite Creator which is modified by its travel through the chakra system or the electrical body of the practitioner who is offering healing. It is not at all an energy which comes from the practitioner. However, it is helpful when thinking about offering Reiki energy to think about the concept which we have suggested through this instrument before in other applications of the being or soul as a crystal.

Each of you, both in the physical body and in the electrical body, has some of the characteristics of a crystal. Physically, in your watery body, you contain a great deal of that crystal substance known as water. And therefore your entire body may be easily tuned and magnetized to whatever vibration you wish to tune it. This instrument carefully tunes its physical body as well as its energy body before each session of channeling by singing hymns, offering prayers, and protecting the self by various means; calling the Archangels and focusing down into a more focused state within the physical body, the emotional body, and so forth. So does each entity have this ability to focus the energies of the physical body as if the body were a crystal and it could be tuned.

Now when the physical body is well tuned, it then may choose what kind of energy it will pick up—it chooses the radio station that it wishes to play, let us say. For a channel such as this one, the radio station is us. The channeler tunes the body, tunes the spirit, prepares itself, and then calls for the highest and best radio station in its capacity to receive. We show up. The instrument offers its faculties to us, and we speak through the instrument.

For a healer, it's a slightly different contact, but it is the same kind of result. The practitioner tunes itself by aligning itself to open up its truest, deepest and most honest self. It tunes to its own highest and best self. This is one of those areas into which we cannot probe because of the fact that Reiki teaching is of a certain type, and we would not wish to infringe upon the teachings of this particular kind of energy work. Nevertheless, there is tuning involved, and it is a freeing kind of tuning where much of the self is dropped away that is irrelevant to the essential or core self, and that core self is freed from its normal strictures and allowed to become the dominant part of the mind, body and spirit.

This tuned being, then, this crystal, is now ready to carry energy. The energy that it receives comes into the crystal self as the entire spectrum of energies of the one infinite Creator. This power source is infinite, and the amount [of energy] that may be given at any given time is also infinite. The Creator is endlessly generous.

Now the nature of the activity within the crystal before the energy flows through the hands and from the body of the practitioner and into the energy system and the body of the patient, shall we say, is most closely approximated by a discussion, in brief, of the act of Holy Eucharist, or Holy Communion. In that rite of worship in the Christian Church, the body and the blood of the one known as Jesus the Christ is called into being either in literal or in symbolic form, and then is drunk by the communicant who receives the strength and the energy of Christ Consciousness.

In the Reiki energy exchange, infinite love comes into the physical and electrical body system of the practitioner of Reiki. That practitioner breaks itself open, blesses its unique vibrational characteristics, and offers them to the energy that is coming through. The energy that is coming through is then particularized and colored by the crystalline properties of the Reiki master, and the Reiki master blesses the resulting energy that is moving through it, and releases it in its altered form to flow into the energy system of the patient. Thereby, an impersonal, universal energy has been particularized and personalized by the genuine love and the open-hearted compassion of the practitioner.

This is not done in any kind of intellectual way. In fact, when intellect is applied to this art, it falls apart. It must be done from direct feeling. That is the way the heart thinks. The heart knows and then immediately it produces that which, in thinking, would be a process.

May we ask the one known as Jim to repeat the portions of the query about Reiki upon which we have not touched? We are those of the Q'uo.

Jim: "How are the physical cells of the body affected by the Reiki energies? And is it necessary for the recipient to believe in Reiki energy?"

(Carla channeling)

We are those of the Q'uo, and are aware of your query. The energies of Reiki move through each cell, and their information is coded so that each cell may pick up the energy involved. Let us be clear in stating that there is no push or pull to Reiki energy. It is not something that is given. It is, rather, an environment that is created. For the time that the Reiki work is being done, the patient lies in an increasingly Edenic environment. The distortions that create illness are suspended. The crystalline nature of the energy pouring through creates an alternative environment, and if the person chooses to accept the new environment, healing may occur. If the person chooses not to accept the healing environment, then it is as if it never occurred. No harm has been done, but also no healing will have occurred.

It is not at all necessary for an entity who is being healed to believe that anything is occurring. However, it is necessary for the entity to accept the new configuration of energy. Some entities are completely able to do this without believing at all in the entire exercise. They are able to say, "Given that such a thing occurred, then I accept the healing." It is not belief that is necessary, but the willingness to accept a new environment that is required.

We are those of Q'uo, and would ask if there is another query at this time.

Jim: We have a series of questions about names of various entities. What can you tell us about the original Yahweh, now a name. Is it a social memory complex? If so, what density did Jesus come from?

(Carla channeling)

We are those of the Q'uo, and are aware of your query. The entity known as Yahweh is an inner planes entity, as opposed to an extraterrestrial entity. It is an essence native to this particular sun system which has been involved in the guardianship of the Earth sphere for thousands of your millennia. It is a combination of energies which are male and female. Rather than creating a hermaphroditic entity, however, this entity holds the energies of male and female in a sacred dynamic. One might as well call such as entity Adam and Eve, but it is both Adam and Eve. And it is not in any way, shape or form that which has been incarnate, but rather, it is of the angelic realm.

It is ironic in the extreme, we feel, that it is this entity which is responsible for creating conditions under which the male aspect of the species has become so unbalanced in its dominancy over the female aspect of deity, which in the original Yahweh energy was in perfect balance.

May we ask if there is a follow-up to that query, my brother?

Jim: Ra refers to this entity as unnamed, as Yo-Heh-Shin-Vau-Heh, and its meaning as "He comes." Can you explain the abundance of names and non-names? And finally, Arcturus also means "He comes" and is an Egyptian name. Is the positive Yahweh from Arcturus?

(Carla channeling)

We are those of the Q'uo, and are aware of your query, my brother. The entity Yahweh is not from Arcturus, but rather, as all angelic entities are, is part of the energy involved in your sun body. However, this entity has been involved with Earth, as we have said, for a great deal of your time. The naming of entities, and its seeming confusion, is due to the fact that in both lower and higher densities, naming does not necessarily occur. It is not necessary, for each thing has an unique vibration. Your vibration is a much more eloquent signature of your character than a name that has been given to you by someone who is not aware of the sacred nuances of your character.

The attempt to name essences and energies is generally done because there is a third-density being involved who feels more comfortable and more in control knowing the name of an entity, and not just how that entity feels.

The energies involved in Yahweh became aware that the work that they had done in creating an enhanced DNA signature for the human species had not had the results which had been hoped for. That entity moved into a time and space of deep and devotional meditation and prayer asking how it could begin to make amends for the mistakes that it had made.

The addition of Shin to Yod-Heh-Vau-Heh was chosen by Yahweh in order to adjust the vibrational nuances of its name in order to indicate Christ Consciousness. It is as if Adam and Eve changed its name to Emmanuel. There was a move from the feeling of the Old Testament to the feeling of the New Testament. That was a move from worth by being chosen people to worth by a certain level of consciousness which was love. This was indeed, for this entity, a valuable adjustment and one which has reflected down from the heaven worlds into the Earth world as that environment into which the one known as Jesus the Christ came.

Is there a follow-up to this query, or is there another query? We are those of the Q'uo.

Jim: I think R may have some questions from the internet group.

Internet questioner: *(Inaudible).*

(Carla channeling)

We are those of the Q'uo, and are aware of your query, my brother. And may we say parenthetically what a joy it is to be in touch with you and with all of those who visit with this group from a non-local location. It is a treat to us, indeed, to work with this non-local group and the enhanced energies that it offers for communication and for fellowship.

Anything that affects the physical body will have a rippling effect upon the non-physical or form-making or electrical or chakra body. However, it is impossible for us to pinpoint how physical effects ripple over into the non-physical, electrical body. It is completely the product of how each person's chakra body is wired. Each entity is wired in a unique way. We do not mean that simply some entities have stronger red ray than orange ray, or stronger orange ray than yellow ray, and so forth. It is not only that to consider. There is also to consider how the chakras are wired within themselves and between themselves. The complexity of this, and the many, many different ways that people do set up their energy flow, make it impossible for us to discuss how diet and exercise and so forth would affect the energy body.

What affects the energy body most is the thoughts that one has. Therefore, if one is improving one's diet, and is happy about it, the information of the improved diet moves into the chakra body as good news. If, on the other hand, an entity is plodding through a dietary regimen that is prescribed for an illness, but that entity is unhappy and feels constricted by this regimen, then the information that is given to the chakra body will be quite different. It will seem like a negative thing to the chakra body, rather than a positive thing, for the chakra body is not listening to the doctor nor is it listening to ideas that contain the word "should." It is only listening to the feelings and the thought forms involved in the translation of physical effects into the feelings and the sensations of the body. A happy heart is more helpful to the chakra system than a good diet. A peaceful mind is more helpful to the chakra system than exercise.

There are times when it is wise to follow the needs of the electrical body and the chakra system rather than the needs of the physical body. We encourage all of those who must guard their health by means of diet, exercise and other regimens of this kind never to let duty press out the joy from the life. No matter how essential it is that the right things are eaten, and the right things are avoided in a diet, or how important various exercises are, in looking at the health of the entire organism, the faculty of joy is primary.

Find a way, if you must follow a regimen, to inject joy into it, and then even the bitterest of herbs, even the most stringent of diets, even the most aggravating of exercising routines will be part of that which makes you joyful, peaceful and strong. No matter how essential it is that you take care of your health, remember always that your health begins with thanksgiving, praise, joy and the open heart that embraces the Creator, the self, and all other selves as one beautiful, perfect, interrelated pattern of love and light.

May we ask if there is another query at this time?

Internet questioner: How may we increase the positive polarization of our connection?

(Carla channeling)

We are those of the Q'uo, and are aware of your query. The key to increasing positive polarization with the Earth is to realize that the Earth is already positively polarized. You are not attempting to do anything to the Earth when you attempt to polarize positively with regard to it. You are joining it in its dance.

The Earth is dancing a dance of love and joy. Every flower and tree waves in harmony and ecstasy, dancing perfectly with all of the other elements of Creation surrounding it. We feel that many of you have had experiences where you tapped into this dance, the song of nature, the wonderful jig of Creation. Some of you have seen the mountains clap their hands, and the seas and the oceans leap for joy.

Enter into the joy of the dance of Earth! It is already ongoing. You have only to cast aside every doubt and every thought that would keep you from being purely an elemental part of Creation and join in its dance. Many have attempted to make this a complicated thing. It is not at all complex. It is a matter of shedding complexity and embracing what is.

We find that this instrument's energy is beginning to wane. Thusly, we would ask for a follow-up to this question or for one final query at this time.

Internet questioner: Is a non-local group better than a local group?

(Carla channeling)

We are those of the Q'uo, and are aware of your query, my brother. We would not use the word "better," as in saying that a non-local group is "better" than a local group. We would say that there is a difference. In a local group, there is a certain level or grade of energy which is possible for that group. It is that which is created by the members sitting in the circle, plus their unseen friends—their guidance system, angels that are with them, the rest of the social memory complex that overshadows wanderers and so forth.

When you create a non-local group, it is as if you've raised the energy or the plane of the group by one level. It is as if a flat circle has become a sphere. The non-locality of the group creates a more complex and intricate family system that is backing up the entities that are sitting in the group. Further, the fact that you are not local means that there is a global aspect to the group that is not obvious to the group when it is a local group. That is, a local group represents the planet, just as a non-local group represents all of humankind. However, it is not self-perceived as a group that represents all of humankind.

Whereas, in the perceptive web of each of those attending this session, there is a self-awareness that they are part of a planet-wide circle of seeking that is seeking to know the truth. This activates an enormous amount of energy on the inner planes of your planet and, indeed, in the surrounding families of those who serve to guide or offer angelic assistance to the members of the group. Consequently, it is a larger entity. It is an entity of a different level or quantum, and that difference is such that we are far more able to surf on the energy of the group in working with this instrument. So there is that aspect of a smoother and more universal channel which is opened through this particular instrument. So, as you can see, there are differences between a local group and a non-local group that cannot be accounted for simply by the numbers being greater in a non-local group.

Is there a follow-up to this query, my brother?

(No further queries.)

In that case, having greatly enjoyed each and every moment of our time together, we would at this time take our leave of you. We leave you in the love and in the light of the one infinite Creator. We are known to you as the principle of the Q'uo. Adonai, Adonai. ✴

L/L Research is a subsidiary of Rock Creek Research & Development Laboratories, Inc.

P.O. Box 5195
Louisville, KY 40255-0195

www.llresearch.org

Rock Creek is a non-profit corporation dedicated to discovering and sharing information which may aid in the spiritual evolution of humankind.

ABOUT THE CONTENTS OF THIS TRANSCRIPT: This telepathic channeling has been taken from transcriptions of the weekly study and meditation meetings of the Rock Creek Research & Development Laboratories and L/L Research. It is offered in the hope that it may be useful to you. As the Confederation entities always make a point of saying, please use your discrimination and judgment in assessing this material. If something rings true to you, fine. If something does not resonate, please leave it behind, for neither we nor those of the Confederation would wish to be a stumbling block for any.

© 2009 L/L Research

Special Meditation
July 7, 2006

Question from A: What guidance can you offer for my spiritual seeking? What spiritual principles would you recommend that I take thought on in my development?

(Carla channeling)

We are those known to you as the principle of Q'uo. Greetings in the love and in the light of the one infinite Creator, in Whose name we come to you this day. It is a great pleasure and privilege to be called to this circle of seeking. We would thank each of you in this circle for carving out some time in your very busy lives to seek the truth.

As we experience this instrument slowly relaxing into a more penetrating clarity of focus, we realize the tenacious hold that the details of the day have upon each of you and we congratulate that effort to move to a more spacious point of view and to spend that precious coin of time in attempting to move to the center of your self, your being, your purpose, and your nature.

As always, we would ask each to use discrimination in responding to those things which we may have to say this day. Be aware that we do not always hit the mark with our comments and be guided by your own perceptions of relevance and interest. Look for the resonance of those thoughts that we share. If our thoughts are not resonant, we ask you to lay them aside and move on until you find something that truly opens your heart or engages your mind.

You ask this day concerning the situation of being in the midst of an incarnation and looking at the spiritual principles that may aid you at this point.

We find that there is much of the past which has been very productive in one way or another, my brother, in your seeking. There is a substantial amount of information which you have become fairly well able to call upon and to use.

We find, further, that whereas in many cases among your people, there is a lack of passion and determination to persevere in the spiritual life; this is not true of you. Your interest in seeking the truth is stable and you have won through those energies that test one's decision to be of service to others.

We would say that there is much progress that you at the soul level and your guidance system will be very pleased to observe when you next meet after incarnation. You are at a point in your maturation spiritually, my brother, that you share with a great many others. You know many things and you have had some real success in applying those principles that you have learned so far.

Perhaps the principle we would suggest for you to consider at this time is that simple principle of oneness, the oneness of the system of which you are a part. It is easy to focus upon details, and in a way it is reassuring to focus upon details. If one is concerned with meditating, for instance, at the correct time, meditating in the proper posture, and so forth, there is a quantity of things to work on and a product that you can admire at the end of it—a finished meditation done properly.

However, my brother, you are at a point in your development where it is profitable to you to go deeper than the form of the meditation. It is time for you to become aware of yourself as part of an enormous, indeed, an infinite pattern. You are one with the Earth. You are one with humankind as a tribe. You are one with the Creator. You are one with truth, and the values of that system in which truth is a living being, that system of time/space, or the metaphysical universe, in which your soul and your spirit live and move and have their being.

It is time to move beyond what you know and what you can know, and to keep a part of your consciousness free to observe as much as you can of the larger picture into which all of the details of your life and your thoughts fit.

When one begins the spiritual search there is a tremendous eagerness for new information. There are many interesting and fascinating subjects which seem to pertain to the spiritual walk—and we use that term, walk, advisedly. The process of spiritual evolution is a journey and it is taken one step at a time.

It is not about progressing or chalking up accomplishments. Rather, it is about finding the grace to allow those things about you that are not serving you to fall away.

It is about beginning to penetrate your own outer self, that self that so fascinates the psychologists. Beneath that personality shell lies consciousness itself. You share that unified consciousness with every iota of the Creation. You put your own spin on it as it comes through you but you participate in the dance of being. You are not cut off from the pattern and its so-called implicate order.

Therefore, we would suggest that the principle that is most helpful to you at this time is that great principle of oneness which underlies and makes possible the universe and your own unique place within it. The adventure of seeking the truth can be seen profitably as caving. Remember, as a spelunker, to carry your lamp and keep it burning brightly. Hold faith itself to be your safety lamp, and replenish your battery by dipping into the silence of your own sacred space within your heart.

May we ask if there is a further query, my brother? We are those of Q'uo

A: I believe my son, Seth, has an activated fourth-density body. In thinking about this, what spiritual principles would I consider?

We are those of Q'uo, and are aware of you query, my brother. We can indeed confirm this dual-activated nature of your son. This entity experiences life slightly differently than do you because of this double activation.

In the short run, such double-activated entities have a difficult time, from time to time, in the growing-up process, as this instrument would call the process of developing into a mature physical being. The sense-awareness matrix of such entities allow more sensory input and as this instrument would say, it gets noisy in there from time to time, more so than an entity who is activated only in the yellow-ray physical body.

While this is inconvenient both for the child and the parents, there are advantages to being wired for both densities: the density that is now being experienced upon your planet and the density that is interpenetrating it. As this entity becomes a mature being, physically as well as emotionally, the inherent stability and toughness of the basic structure of the double-activated body will be of great help to this entity.

As the interpenetrating energies of green ray buffet this planet more and more, the challenge to all entities is to be able to face the truth of themselves clearly and straightforwardly. Double-activated entities have a head start in being able to become completely honest with themselves. This creates an atmosphere in which they may be more calm and serene under conditions which may seem challenging.

The forces of evolution create a forward movement which is the response of nature itself, shall we say, to the rapidly changing environment of planet Earth. We encourage you therefore to relax into an awareness of the rightness of such changes. They may sometimes seem to be those changes that are inconvenient. However, the overall plan is a good one and your child's hope to serve as this entity desires to serve within this incarnation he is experiencing is not in vain.

May we ask if there is another query at this time?

A: Do you have any suggestions for establishing and maintaining an optimal working space, metaphysically speaking, for teaching and learning in a high school classroom?

We are those of Q'uo, and are aware of you query, my brother. The conditions of an environment do not end with the dynamics of the dimensions of the room, the heat of the room, and so forth. A classroom is far more than a physical space. It is in some ways a cocoon where the larva enters to find a little quiet and time for thought so that he may ultimately emerge as a butterfly.

In some aspects a classroom is a sacred space. It is filled with souls. They have been thrown together by circumstance, and there is a rough influence from authority figures, such as principals and other entities which create curricula and give textbooks and so forth their place. Yet, at heart it is a place where the teacher and the students shall create together their environment, their experience in their path of learning and service together.

It is as much of a work environment for the children as it is for you, my brother. This is the practice that entities receive as children that is intended to train them to take their place in society as entities with a good work ethic and a good moral ethic in the ability to participate in their democratic environment as citizens.

Yet these are also flowers who need sunshine and rain. They are living entities with hopes and dreams; they suffer as much as any grown person. They struggle and they deal with a tremendous amount of incoming catalyst, just as do you, my brother. Yet, because of your situation you are the leader of this little band of souls. As an ethical person who is desirous of serving, we know that you wish to start with the first distortion[13] in considering how to move on in creating this environment of classroom.

The first distortion of the Creator's universe is free will. In considering how to handle situations with your students, recall that principle and attempt to apply it to the situation at hand. All entities are deserving of respect, and their rights are in your hands. See what you can do to maximize their experience of personal freedom without minimizing your experience of a comfort zone for yourself and for the whole class.

The second distortion of the creation is that Thought which chose to create the universe that you experience at this time, and that the rest of those parts of the Creator that are we, this instrument, those in this circle, and everyone else, experience also. Remember, this love was so powerful that it set into motion those forces that have created all that you see and all that is unseen as well in endless and amazing order.

Find the springs of love within yourself that are not attached to any students or any personalities whatsoever, but are attached only to the Creator, so that you are seeing the Creator in these flowers of the field that have come to you. No matter what they are doing, their nature is love. Let the love within your soul respond always to that same love which lies within them. They may not have become acquainted with that portion of their personality, but as you look deeply within them, past the misbehavior and the personality quirks, and see them clearly, so shall they then see themselves as in a mirror for the first time and perhaps even begin to recognize their own true worth.

The third distortion is light, that light that manifests all things. A great part of your function, in terms of the teach/learning aspect of a classroom, is involved in this illumination. Information is the light of the mind; it is the food of thought. Encourage entities to think. If the curriculum as you look at it does not excite you, how shall you make it exciting for them? Therefore, as you prepare for your students what you do not find illuminating, move to one side and instead venture forth into those aspects of what you are teaching that you do find interesting and that you feel your class may find interesting as well.

Indeed, we would encourage you in this regard to pay close attention to the questions that you are asked, and to those subjects that are brought forward. There are often opportunities for teaching that lie completely beyond the bounds of any subject. Be bold at laying aside your textbooks and your lesson plans and saying, "Today we are going to talk about what you just said, because this is something that you need in life. You need to think about this."

---

[13] This terminology is typical of Confederation information. The Creator is a mystery without distortion. The first distortion to this mystery is free will. The second distortion is unconditional love or Logos. The third distortion is light.

There is much that we could continue to say to respond to this question because in being a teach/learn learn/teacher, you are entering into a transaction that is of the most deep and profound character. When you, yourself, look back upon those forces that shaped your life, you undoubtedly recall special teachers that told you that you had worth and that sparked your interest, so that you wanted to know more. What were the characteristics that you loved about them? Think about that, my brother, and develop within yourself those characteristics that you most admired in your own favorite teachers and inspirers. For you are a voice in the wilderness to which they will listen. Circumstances have brought you together. Take this opportunity to maximize that environment for freedom, for loving, for learning, and for exploration.

Why is it that entities must go from their homes out into the world and engage in work? What is it that pulls people together for goals and ambitions that lie beyond the needs of survival? What is it to be human? What is it to learn? As you shape this environment for yourself and your students, ask these questions without having to answer them. Let them be those questions that open the windows and let fresh air into your own thoughts in the processes of your own professionalism as a teacher.

May we ask if there is another query at this time?

A: Does the curvature in my spinal column indicate an energy blockage or imbalance which I will not be able to correct in this incarnation? If so, what is my best metaphysical response? Or does it indicate a condition which I set in place before incarnation? If so, what was the plan? Any thoughts which you would find helpful to share about my mind/body/energy and suffering I would appreciate hearing.

We are those of Q'uo, and are aware of your query, my brother. There are aspects of this query which lie beyond the boundaries of the Law of Confusion.[14] This is an active question in your own metaphysical development at this time, my brother, and so we will step lightly around part of your query and focus upon the response, which is the same regardless of the details of why you are suffering at this time.

In many cases, before incarnation there is set up a fail-safe system that kicks in if during incarnation if you as a personality shall forget to focus on that which you as a soul wished for the incarnation to be focused upon. In other cases there has not been a preincarnative arrangement made, but there has been sufficient difficulty within incarnation that there has been illness that has occurred.

In either case, when the suffering is part of your environment, the most skillful first assumption to make for a seeking soul is that it is a good plan. It is a plan to get your attention and it has succeeded. Therefore, you may give thanks that you have awakened within the dream of life to one of the aspects of this experience.

It is not usually a one-to-one or linear relationship between pain or suffering and the metaphysical reason for the pain. It is a comfortable and easy thing for outsiders to look at someone with a bad back or an ulcer or a cancer and say, "Oh, that person may be carrying too much, and that's why the back hurts," or "Oh, that person must be worrying too much and that's why the ulcer is there," or "That person must be feeling great anger inside and that is why the cancer is there."

My brother, this is often not at all accurate. It is less linear and more filled with grace and charity than that. Being in pain or being ill is a way of narrowing your attention. It is a way of distracting an active and energetic soul from loitering on the playground of life when there is work to do in the classroom, for life itself may be seen profitably as a school.

The density of choice[15] is a certain type of classroom. Before incarnation you had a plan for this incarnation. You wished to learn certain things—not linear things, but rather qualitative things. And you wished to be of service.

You brought grist for the mill with you so that you could learn. You chose your parents and other relationships. You chose many more relationships than you actually needed, because you knew that you would move through relationships. So you have a great deal of redundancy in that system. You will

---

[14] The Law of Confusion is another way which Confederation channeling has of expressing the primal nature of free will. To invoke the Law of Confusion is to say that a question which has been asked cannot be answered by them without their violating the free will of the questioner.

[15] Third density and the density of choice are both terms for consensus reality, the life we are living now on planet Earth.

not run out of good catalyst that will help you to learn.

You gave yourself gifts to share. You packed those in your bags when you came into incarnation. For this instrument, it is a singing voice, and she has sung throughout her incarnation. Everyone has little things that they can do that make others smile: a special dish that they can make or the way they greet you and obviously are enjoying your presence. Some people have that gift of hospitality. There is no end to the gifts that you can bring with you. Some are dramatic and others are not noticed, really, by those that are looking for accomplishments out there.

Trust that you have these lessons to learn and these gifts to share and that if your physical vehicle is acting in ways that limit your movement or your abilities, that part of the plan is not random. Part of that situation is for your profit as a soul. Upon what has this suffering caused you to focus? Upon what have you concentrated as a result of this catalyst of pain and suffering? Have you given thanks for it? Have you trusted a seemingly negative situation enough to offer honest and heartfelt thanks? We encourage thought along these lines, for it is in an atmosphere of gratitude and thankfulness that the beginning of the solution to the particular tangle of this puzzle will come to you.

When you assume that it is a helpful condition that is for your benefit as a soul, you shall begin to see the great gifts that illness offers. In the first place, to those who are overactive and overly distracted, it offers rest and the opportunity for leisurely thought and contemplation.

It offers you the opportunity to experience a tiny portion of the suffering of humankind as a whole. In your suffering you are one with the entity in Biafra who is starving to death, the entity in Iraq who is being tortured, the child in New Orleans who is being beaten, and the wife who is being brutally raped within the sanctity of her marriage. The suffering of the world is shadowed in your pain and you are a part of that dark beauty, a part of the whole that contains those dark notes. Rejoice, for you know the cost of living more profoundly than a healthy, comfortable person.

It is interesting that entities among your peoples know that they shall die and yet they fear it. Face that which is implied in suffering, that is, death itself, and know that this is a part of the experience of incarnation. Gaze firmly into the eyes of death. And when you have realized fully your mortality, open your eyes to the sunshine and the beauty of the night sky and know the privilege of living and suffering and sharing all things in this experience called living.

It is so intense when one is within incarnation and cannot see the greater pattern clearly, but we encourage you to find the very center of self that exists most triumphantly through any pain and suffering and so focus on that center of self that you are able to move into an environment that is free of anything, any sense input or intellectual input of any kind, and that simply contains the love and the light of the one infinite Creator.

This instrument has at times been in a great deal of pain with rheumatoid changes to her skeleton and musculature, and the effects of those changes can be very limiting. Because this instrument is a Christian she used some of the holy words that she had learned as a child from her *Bible*. The phrase that she used over and over during this period was that which is found in the writings of the one known as Paul who said, "If I live, I live in Christ and if I die, I die in Christ, so whether I live or die, I am in Christ and Christ is in me."[16] Substitute the words "unconditional love" for "Christ" and know that this is the reality of your experience, in or out of incarnation, in or out of pain.

You are unconditional love. You have poured that love into a package that carries you through this incarnation, but this is your nature. Use this experience of suffering, for it is there in order for you to use it. As you use it, you may find your situation changing. Your first job then, is to embrace this opportunity.

May we say that you are never alone when you are attempting to do something like this. Your guidance system is very close to you and you need only ask for it to begin responding to you. We, ourselves, are glad to be with you and mentally requesting us will bring us to you immediately. We are there to underscore your meditative efforts and help you to feel that feeling of support and encouragement that is so precious to the growing soul.

---

[16] The accurate quotation, from Paul's Epistle to the Romans 14:8, in the *Oxford Annotated Bible*, reads, "If we live, we live to the Lord, and if we die, we die to the Lord; so then, whether we live or whether we die, we are the Lord's."

We thank you for this opportunity to speak through this instrument. The energy of this instrument begins to wane, and so we would suggest at this time that we end the session. We thank each and leave each in the love and in the light of the one Creator. We are known as the principle of the Q'uo. Adonai, Adonai. ✺

L/L Research

L/L Research is a subsidiary of Rock Creek Research & Development Laboratories, Inc.

P.O. Box 5195
Louisville, KY 40255-0195

www.llresearch.org

Rock Creek is a non-profit corporation dedicated to discovering and sharing information which may aid in the spiritual evolution of humankind.

ABOUT THE CONTENTS OF THIS TRANSCRIPT: This telepathic channeling has been taken from transcriptions of the weekly study and meditation meetings of the Rock Creek Research & Development Laboratories and L/L Research. It is offered in the hope that it may be useful to you. As the Confederation entities always make a point of saying, please use your discrimination and judgment in assessing this material. If something rings true to you, fine. If something does not resonate, please leave it behind, for neither we nor those of the Confederation would wish to be a stumbling block for any.

© 2009 L/L Research

Special Meditation
August 25, 2006

Question from J: My main question has to do with knowing and understanding more about what I am and why I am here. Am I on course in fulfilling my highest potential as a wanderer and as a soul? My greatest desire is being of service to others. Please offer me any thoughts.

(Carla channeling)

We are those known to you as the principle of Quo. Greetings in the love and light of the one infinite Creator. We come to speak with you through this instrument this evening. May we saw what a great privilege it is to be with you and to be called to your circle of seeking.

We appreciate you, this instrument, and this group taking this time to seek. The honor is ours. We are most grateful to share your meditation, and enjoy the beauty of the harmonies of your flower-like auras as they blend and form a sacred temple that towers high above this physical dwelling. It is a service to the one Creator that we greatly appreciate. We thank you for sharing. We thank the one known as J for her very thoughtful query.

When we hear one whose focus is so crystal-clear, it is far more easy to express our thoughts without fearing we will interfere with your free will. The very questions that you ask, my sister, concerning who you are, why you are here, and what you have left to do define for us your ethical clarity and your character as a personality. We would not have to examine you further than that question to be able to tell you that you are on task, not only as a soul, but also as a wanderer.

As a soul, my sister, you are on track because you are alive.

As a wanderer, you are on track because you are remembering who you are. You have awakened to the possibility of being here for a purpose. You are beginning to believe that you shall flower and bloom in the service of the one infinite Creator in the time left in your incarnation,

As part of the creative principle of this planet and a steward of the spirit of this planet, and of its people, you have the rest of your days to pursue the infinite subtleties of your incarnational lessons, those things which keep repeating in your life, and discovering that which is acutely new to your consciousness but which has been coming together in your subconscious mind through time in incarnation.

The great advantage of being past the first blush of youth is the sheer repetition of patterns that constitute the material from which you draw catalyst, as well as your opportunities for evolution and service.

When an entity within incarnation awakens and grasps the basics of choice, that entity becomes a magical being. And so you have become a magical being, my sister. The challenge for you now lies in your ability to persevere with utmost dedication and focus on service while simultaneously releasing your expectations, so that those things which are new may flow into your pattern with the least possible resistance.

We do not say this simply to you, my sister, for you are part of a very large group of entities. And we should say we talk about not one group of entities but groups of such groups that have all come together as planned to help to shift the consciousness of this beloved planet which you have so enjoyed, and which you so dearly, dearly wish to serve at this time.

That which shall freely shift consciousness upon this planet cannot be found in the patterns of your culture. Although a listening ear may hear them in the patterns of your religions, the public and overt side of religion has left those voices out. Those voices of love must be your voices and they must sing a new song. And they must not do this singly. They must do this globally.

And so it is occurring. As more and more entities awaken, you and many others shall conspire, in the name of love, to create an increasingly powerful paradigm that is new. How shall that novelty be shaped, when that which you already know has proven to be effete?

Where do you find your sturdiness? Where do you find the heart of meaning?

We ask you these questions, because it is in your hands, rather than ours. It is in the hands of the people of this planet rather than in the hands of those who would serve and help you to make the choices that open you to becoming a being capable of creating outside the cultural box.

We lift to you a beacon and that beacon is yourself. We ask you to see yourself for the first time, clearly and lucidly. Light courses through you, my sister, not from you. There is no effort to being who you are. There is only the removal of blockage from the passage of light.

And you do not have to move the furniture of your life out of the way of this light. You have only to check and be sure that it has not gotten rumpled and thusly has obscured the passage of this light. Make sure that chimney which goes through your heart and out into the waiting world can open very safely, very clearly, and very cleanly.

As that energy flows through you, allow it to rise. And note and observe that which keeps it from rising. When you have a chance, sit down and look at that again and see what you think. How can you nudge that rug or that chair, or that little side table or emotion, or opinion, or judgment, out of the way? Don't manage it. Love it! Appreciate it! You spent years coming to those opinions. Value them! Just don't let them block the light.

My sister, you share with this instrument a tendency towards earnestness. This is not a bad thing. It works well in a culture which tends to pacify and patronize women. You are proof against such things. You will persevere. You will keep on with that seeking which is the heart of your heart. And that is good.

Remember always, and we say that also to this instrument, to lighten up. To relax. To enjoy. To cherish and relish the tiny things that seem silly and make you smile. For these too give you power. Rest your soul. And create balance in your life.

May we ask if there is another query at this time?

J: The second question is, how can I remember more authentically who I am and where I come from?

We are those of Q'uo, and are aware of your query, my sister. We pause in considering which direction to take in responding to this query because there is almost an equal balance between one level of information and another.

We will begin then, my sister, with the level of information that is closest to the surface. You may know more about who you are and where you're from by accessing resources within your mind which are not usually available to the conscious awareness. Methods for doing this include keeping a dream journal, creating a workshop and a safe place for journaling and the awareness of [consciousness.][17]

You can also consult a hypnotherapist to move through a carefully constructed method of asking these questions of your higher self while in an hypnotic state. Because of the fact that we have answered other queries of this kind in recent years, we will allow you to investigate that which we have said to others on this subject, using the website

---

[17] Carla: I think the Q'uo group were saying that being aware of one's own consciousness from moment to moment is as helpful as keeping a journal, doing dream work, or creating an inner workshop.

which belongs to those at L/L Research. There is a search function on that which will give you that information which you seek.

To move to that which we feel a pull to express, we move into deeper waters, my sister. And we must ask your forgiveness in advance for being relatively unable to be clear in talking about this deeper level. However, we feel that in the end it is more satisfying for you to investigate this deeper level than to find out from hypnotic regression what you might have done in a previous lifetime or other things of that nature.

When you move into that part of yourself where the seeds of these questions truly lie, and from which they grow into that bloom which is yourself within incarnation, you move into common ground. You move into nested realities of who you are. You are you, of course, within incarnation. You are the only you that ever was and ever will be. But you are nested into your soul stream along with all of the "you's" that you have created in many blooming incarnations. You are a full garden of beings in one. You are nested into your soul group, which is nested into the entire societal clan which decided to come to planet Earth to be part of the light and the love of the one infinite Creator.

And this is nested into your being a part of Earth itself, the tribe of Earth which you became when you took flesh and laced your soul carefully into the substance of the mind, the body, and the spirit of that entity which sits within our room this evening and is able to share energy with us.

And all of this is nested into order of magnitude after order of magnitude, until you are the one infinite Creator. All is run not simply from the top down but from the tiniest iota of being upwards. And each iota of that universe of the creation contains the creation within it.

When we translate that reality back into your question, we say that within you lie rivers and oceans of purified emotion that constitute an archetypical world. You can touch into emotion that has moved through all of its more shallow expressions and into that which is beautiful and pure of its kind, leached of pity and impurity, sorrow and anger, until the emotion you experience is the essence of sorrow, the essence of pain, the essence of impatience.

When you move into those archetypal rivers of purified emotion, you become more and more aware of what kind of being you are. What an exotic, complicated and unimaginably complex, multilayered being you are! It is stunning! And when you can see how stunning you are, you see that all of your imperfections add power. You begin to see how beautiful everyone else is because you have forgiven yourself for that imperfection. And now you are ready to see the beauty of everyone else too.

As you get to this level you begin to see that who you are changes, the deeper that you go. At the bottom of that digging is a place in your heart where you are unconditional love. In that place, the Christ waits for you. To some entities the Christ is a being, a person, with eyes and hands and a voice. To some entities Christ is the energy, the creative principle that created the world, wrapped into a cloak which any entity may choose to prepare the self to wear.

The cloak of love that is unconditional may be seen as a crown. It may be seen as a mother nursing its child. It may be seen as the figure of the Christ washing the feet of his disciples and saying, "Follow me and be the servant of those you love."

It is difficult to discuss being itself. Words fail. And we can use only metaphors, stories and well known and even clichéd figures to describe the world in which that energy resides. Who you are and where you came from are things that evolve into your conscious awareness very naturally, little by little, throughout an incarnation, if you are interested.

Except for those whose karma it is, shall we say, to discover specific information, generally that information level is not given to you. What is given to you is the resonance, when you're ripe, when you sense into something that is most deeply you and expresses where you may have been.

Look then for that resonance. Wait for that feeling within yourself. The energy within yourself will move when you run into something that speaks to you. When it does, take yourself seriously. If you can't think about it right away, note it down and think about it later.

We truly are all one and you shall find that one of the great advantages of third density has been to block you from the knowledge of all of that so that you may pursue the heart of your seeking in a much more focused way.

May we ask if there is another query at this time?

J: The third question is how can I develop and improve my inter-dimensional communication techniques?

We are those of Q'uo, and are aware of your query, sister. We find that we have basically communicated the information to you about this question in the previous answer. The simplest way to become more able to work with inter-dimensional communication is to practice silence. We find that we are repeating, yet it always bears repeating. Go ever deeper into that silence but without any expectation. Follow your heart. Follow your practice. Experiment when you sense that something is not quite alive within you. Kick the energy when you feel it has stopped. But, in general, enter that silence knowing how sacred that quality and faculty is and how infinitely much it contains for you.

We would also suggest that from day-to-day you retain a consideration as to what the very center of your seeking is, so that you may ask and form an intention as you move into the silence, not because you expect to hear a voice telling you what to do, but because silence is a place wherein the Creator is communicating with you, and you with the Creator.

The Creator has no problem communicating within Its silence. Those within incarnation have less sense of the power of their thoughts, and so it is helpful to form an intention consciously, in the same way that you would form a list when you go out to do errands. Or form a short list of topics in your mind, as when you're going to have a conversation with someone on the phone.

We greatly enjoyed the music before the meditation this day and that image that the one known as Joan had of the Creator at the end of the phone, the only person with enough nerve to actually use the telephone being the Pope in Rome.[18] We hope that you will use that telephone very often and with great effect. The minutes are free.

Is there another query at this time?

J: How do I fit into the Confederation? If this question falls beyond the threshold of free will, please tell me what you can about the spiritual principles involved in looking at this question.

We are those of Q'uo, and may we say, my sister, that your adding that last sentence was our only hope of answering your query with anything more than, "We find that we are unable to speak of this particular question because of the fact that it is part of your active seeking process at this time."

We cannot learn for you. We can only be a good resource for you, if we can, as a teacher. To take over your lesson and explain it to you would be an infringement of free will for which you would not thank us, once you looked back upon this exchange from a time in your future.

These mysteries are very good to ponder. We encourage you to ponder them, this one, especially. See where it takes you.

In general, the spiritual principle involved in looking at questions like, "Where do I fit into a group?" is that if you have a resonance with fitting into a certain group, then there is probably a connection. So it behooves you to investigate it further.

That principle of resonance is the one that we would suggest to you, my sister, and certainly not just in this wise, but in many ways. There are many, many times during every day when the spirit is attempting to speak with you in one way or another. And the first obstacle to hearing that voice is, as we find, there are many people who do not catch the drift. The first job is to know that the spirit world is

---

[18] Q'uo refers to a song written and sung by Joan Osbourne, the lyrics to which are:

> If God had a name, what would it be
> And would you call it to his face
> If you were faced with him in all his glory?
> What would you ask if you had just one question?
>
> And yeah, yeah, God is great! Yeah, yeah, God is good!
>
> What if God was one of us;
> Just a slob like one of us;
> Just a stranger on the bus
> Trying to make his way home?
>
> If God had a face what would it look like
> And would you want to see
> If seeing meant that you would have to believe
> In things like heaven and in Jesus and the saints and all the prophets?
>
> And yeah, yeah, God is great! Yeah, yeah, God is good!
>
> What if God was one of us;
> Just a slob like one of us;
> Just a stranger on the bus
> Trying to make his way home?
> He's trying to make his way home
> Back up to heaven all alone,
> Nobody calling on the phone
> Except for the Pope maybe in Rome

talking to you so that you pay attention to the street signs and the little birds and animals that visit and so forth during your day.

The second thing that keeps people from hearing spirit is that they do not value their own awareness. A passing thought will sneak into their mind and they think, "Now why did I think that?" And then they'll go, "Oh well," and then move on.

When a thought sneaks into your mind next time, stop and say, "Why did I think that? Let me put that aside for a later time when I can ponder that." Write it down. Look at it again. Follow the pattern, the thread that goes into the weave somewhere. And in that weave are interesting and eye-opening details of context.

Is there another query at this time?

J: How do my daughter C and my husband L fit into my purpose? If this specific information is beyond the threshold of free will, please tell me what you can about the spiritual principles I will find most helpful in looking at these relationships.

We are those of Q'uo, and are aware of your query, my sister. And again we are very pleased that you thought to ask about spiritual principles because, naturally, your family members are indeed an active part of your process at this time. You chose them specifically. The question is always, why did you choose these entities?

Naturally, you chose them to serve and to learn from. Therefore, you gave yourself some challenges with them that are only outcroppings of incarnational challenges which you set for yourself because you wish to come more into balance. We will leave it to you to decide which way the balance goes. Are you more wise and need to open your heart or is your heart too wide open and does that make you too naive to do the loving thing sometimes? Because the truly loving thing is Solomon-like and involves some wisdom. Think of Jesus-meets-Sophia[19] and you begin to have the good balance there. When you look at your life, see what you think.

And then that gives you more of an idea as to where skill lies in responding to circumstance. You know that you want to offer the highest and best response that you can, no matter what the catalyst is. The challenge is always to find that sweet spot where your heart is fully open but your wisdom has been engaged as well.

We would ask at this time if there is another query.

J: Is there anything specific I can take with me tonight to begin from this point to be more focused?

We are those of Q'uo, and are aware of your query, my sister. And we would say to you, my sister, that if you can take this moment with you in memory, some memory of the way it feels, the joy, the elation, the peace, the power of this holy place that you have created, not with your hands but with your hopes, your intentions, and your desire to serve and to know the truth, you will have a place where you can do your work.

And that is all you need, my sister. For your heart will lead you to the rest.

Know that you are never alone. Your guidance is with you. Many angelic presences surround you. The world of nature is very aware of you and responds to every heartbeat and every footfall of your life.

It is an interactive universe, my sister. And all of it is in love with you. And all of it thanks you so much for loving it. Keep that feeling. Remember it and let it bring you home to yourself.

We find that this instrument's energy does wane at this time and so we would leave this instrument and this group in the love and the light of the one infinite Creator. Adonai. Adonai. ☥

---

[19] Carla: I believe they intended it to mean, "Think of the energies of Jesus the Christ and the feminine principle of wisdom, Sophia, to feel how the combination would balance planetary energies."

L/L Research

L/L Research is a subsidiary of Rock Creek Research & Development Laboratories, Inc.

P.O. Box 5195
Louisville, KY 40255-0195

www.llresearch.org

Rock Creek is a non-profit corporation dedicated to discovering and sharing information which may aid in the spiritual evolution of humankind.

ABOUT THE CONTENTS OF THIS TRANSCRIPT: This telepathic channeling has been taken from transcriptions of the weekly study and meditation meetings of the Rock Creek Research & Development Laboratories and L/L Research. It is offered in the hope that it may be useful to you. As the Confederation entities always make a point of saying, please use your discrimination and judgment in assessing this material. If something rings true to you, fine. If something does not resonate, please leave it behind, for neither we nor those of the Confederation would wish to be a stumbling block for any.

© 2009 L/L RESEARCH

Sunday Meditation
September 3, 2006

Group question: The question today is, what work is necessary to be done by the seeker upon the chakras or the energy centers in order to facilitate the raising of the kundalini and of what value to the seeker is this raising of the kundalini?

(Carla channeling)

We are those of the principle of Q'uo. Greetings in the love and in the light of the one infinite Creator. It is a great privilege and blessing to be with you this day, to enjoy the beauty of your vibrations, and to be asked to share our humble thoughts on what work is needed to do by the seeker upon the chakra system in order to encourage or advance the raising of the kundalini, so-called, by those students of seeking in the oriental tradition of Yoga. It has also been asked what value that project is and it is that with which we would start.

However, first, we would be careful, as always, to request your cooperation as we speak. Please reserve and retain the quality and faculty of discrimination. You are responsible for your universe, for the thoughts that you think, and for the progression of those thoughts. For us to be speaking to you from a position of authority is not an option. We need for you to see us as fellow seekers; those who have had more experiences than you which we remember at this point and therefore those who may be able to share helpful thoughts. We cannot guarantee the accuracy of our thoughts nor their appropriateness in your process and it is important to us that you be able to place the thoughts that do not resonate to you to one side and move on without feeling that you have somehow missed the point.

If nothing resonates to you about one of our thoughts, it is not you who have missed the point, it is we. Not every thought is going to work for everyone. If you will be the guardian of your thoughts, accepting only those thoughts of ours which seem resonant to you, then we will feel free to speak without being concerned that we will infringe upon your free will. May we say how much we thank you for this consideration.

The purpose of the raising of the kundalini within the system of study and worship known as Yoga is to aid the seeking soul in its progression towards perfection. It is a particularly Oriental concept and not one in which the Western religions spend much time or consideration. Consequently, for most raised within the religious systems of the West, the concept of perfection is puny or paltry. The West seems rather to want to focus upon the humbling of the self by the realization of its imperfection and then the experience of rebirth in cleansing through the intervention of a manifestation of the divine.

Redemption is not the same thing as the progress towards perfection, even though the activity is the same. Let us explicate. In, for instance, the Christian crucifixion ritual, the sacrificial victim takes upon himself the sins of the population on whose behalf he is being sacrificed, just as in olden times when sacrifices were burned to the gods. As the fires burn his flesh and dry his bodily fluids to ash, that benediction of blood and flesh absolves and redeems the imperfect entities of the congregation. That is the illogical but spiritually viable goal of the crucifixion. The resurrection is a new twist upon the sacrifice of the slaughtered animal and represents that which the one known as Jesus, as well as many other crucified saviors, desired to bring into the concept of sacrifice and that is the resurrection and new life of the being that has been sacrificed.

That which Jesus suggested was that each entity take up the cross and follow him. When the one known as Jesus took up the cross, he was walking towards his crucifixion and eventual resurrection. In taking up the cross, you take up the nature of the cruciform reality in which you live—which is called consensus reality or space/time—and you walk with it to Golgotha. When it is your time to learn the nature of sacrifice, you place yourself upon that cross. You experience suffering. You experience your dark night of the soul and you experience the resurrection into new life. You do this not just once in an incarnation but in a repetitive and cyclical fashion, gaining the experience of winning through to new life each time that you experience these small deaths of transformational change.

It is never described to the Western religious seeker that the goal of such suffering is perfection. It is, however, implied that the experience of one who has won through following this directive of following the steps of Christ will experience an enhanced or expanded awareness after the sacrifice has been made. This is as close as the Western religious system can come to the Yogic concept of perfection.

It is a handicap of this particular distortion of a way to study the one infinite Creator. However, in the rich coloring of the story of sacrifice and resurrection, the emotive qualities of the story create an atmosphere in which it is far easier to understand the nature of redemptive love. Consequently, this is the glory of the Christian faith: that one glyph of a suffering and fully conscious Creator, perfectly willing to go through the pain of death in order to demonstrate its illusionary quality and thereby offer the realization of larger life to those who are able to view the stunning reality of the transformation of the light-struck tomb and the empty grave.

The glory of the Yogic system, however, is that concept of perfection. The Yogi is not afraid of becoming the Creator. The difficulty with that system is the opposite of that difficulty with the Christian system. Some may say that the system lacks a certain amount of color. It is more difficult to achieve an iconic representation of unconditional love from studying the systems of Yoga. It is not impossible. It is simply not as easy to choose that central icon and say, "This is unconditional love."

The Yogic system is far more complex and far more accurate. It therefore appeals to those who are wanderers from fifth density or who simply have within this incarnation a more intellectual or mind-driven seeking process.

We cannot say that a mind-driven seeking process is superior to or inferior to a heart-driven seeking process. We simply point out, number one, that one is seeking in one or another wise, primarily, and, number two, that whichever way you are seeking, part of your consideration of moving forward may well be to reach into that part of the seeking process which you are not using and encourage balance within yourself, so that you are seeking not only with the desire of your mind but with the desire of your heart. They are two different things and there is a tremendous power in bringing those two together.

What you do when you bring the passion of the heart and the desire of the mind into harmony is to yoke will and love into a working pair of creatures that can draw the cart of your seeking process forward and engage your will, the faculty of your purified desire.

Desire drives the chariot of progression through spiritual evolution. The most precious faculty in the seeking process may be said fairly to be desire that has been well realized; that is, desire that has been harnessed to passion and purpose. To bring body, mind and spirit into union is to activate a very powerful force of nature. For you are one step down from being a sun. You are a co-creator, and to the extent that you begin to realize this, you begin to see the possibilities inherent in the human condition.

The work that one does upon the chakra system in order to raise the meeting point between the incoming love and light of the one infinite Creator and the downpourings that are called forth by questions and in prayers, creates the point at which work may be done. Normally the untuned and unconscious entity is not capable of effectively desiring in a focused manner in terms of spiritual things. The prayer or regard for the infinite Creator expressed as devotion that drives mystics tends to be missing in the makeup of the unawakened soul

Therefore, the energy within the energy pipeline flows at a variable rate and with variable efficiency. Work in consciousness cannot be done with any degree of stability underlying or undergirding the effort. There may be flashes of great inspiration and clarity in anyone, because of special occurrences that catalyze a moment of clarity and an opening of that faculty wherein the guidance system of an entity may pour in love and inspiration. And there may be long periods wherein there is no apparent connection betwixt the guidance system and the self.

When an entity awakens to the realization that there is more to life than what is seen by the naked eye, this opens the potential for that entity to seek to know more about the unseen. Such a seeker enters an area that is very mysterious in any rational sense. For spiritual seeking the rules are completely different from scientific seeking. The experiments are done within the self and only subjective criteria can be used.

It is nearly impossible to obtain scientific data that proves the existence of spirit. It is carefully designed to be very difficult to prove what faith is in any way, shape or form, what desire is, what the will is, or any other metaphysically viable tool and resource for hastening or accelerating the pace of the evolution of mind, body and spirit.

This is because the only actual progress made in polarization and the seeking of truth is made in an atmosphere of unknowing. If it is known that such and such a thing is true, there is no risk in setting out to reach that truth. It is important, indeed, it is centrally important to the seeking soul that he realize that he is risking everything with the potential for gaining nothing. He may be on a wild goose chase.

Faith requires that you walk off the cliff of known things into the mid-air of unknowing and it is in that mid-air that the seeking soul who decides to activate his desire and use it to fuel his seeking must do his work. Therefore, the only solid ground beneath such an entity whom we may call, for convenience's sake, an adept, is the knowledge of himself, who he is, why he is in the process of seeking, what he is living for, and what he would die for. That is that upon which one stands in metaphysical seeking: not physical ground but the ground of being.

Therefore, the use of the chakra system is that use which, firstly, clears the pathway through which energy flows from the soles of the feet and the base chakra at the base of the spine through all of the chakras, one after the other, and finally out through the top of the head.

Now, this basic flow goes on all the time in everyone. When one attempts to improve the flow, one is not simply tinkering with the physical system. One is working with the metaphysical system. The model of the energy flow through the energy body in space/time that is comfortable to look at is that of a self-contained system. However, in the metaphysical view of this pipeline, while on the level of consensus reality or space/time it is indeed a self-contained system, on the level of time/space it is an open system. At each point it is open to the density that equals that color and to the entities that people that true color.

Further, when entities are working on a certain difficulty, as the one known as M pointed out, they may be working in two or more chakras at one time. The one known as M gave the example of having low self-worth, which is worked within the orange ray as well as in the indigo ray and, indeed, to some extent, that low self-worth shall be worked on by each and every one of the chakras in one way or another.

Consequently, when one takes up the goal of clearing the chakras, one is doing a great deal more than clearing a physical system. One is doing more than clearing a pipeline. One is asking the self to perform the mental actions necessary to create a change in the way one sees the self.

If one is blocked in a certain way in one of the chakras, one is seeing the self in a certain way. One is giving honor and respect to that issue which is blocking or overactivating the chakra. In working to clear the chakra, then, one becomes vulnerable to the need to rest and examine that blockage; to sit with it and to gaze into the workings of that blockage. When does it occur? How does it arise? What was the first thing that you thought of that made you realize you were caught? How have you experienced this before? What pattern surrounded this thought when you had it before? What about the time before that? Can you find the first time that you were blocked in this way? What was the exact circumstance of that blockage?

The closer that you can get to the source of your blockage or your overactivation, the more chance that you have of unearthing the ore that contains this gem of information, this piece of crystallized pain. When you do this, you hold in your hand the gift of much suffering. Wash it! Polish it! It is a gem you have earned, but it is not a gem that you need weighing you down.

There comes a time to lay down a piece of crystallized pain that is emotional in nature, mental in nature, or spiritual in nature. You will know when that time comes. We do not encourage you to hurry yourself. However, it is indeed a wise person who harvests such crystallized pain, realizes it, thanks it, and moves on. It is not necessary to carry behind you that great sack which bears the accumulated pain of your incarnation.

The process of doing this work is a process which clears the chakras and strengthens their integrity. As you clear yourself of those blockages you experience in each ray, you are doing an exercise that, upon repetition, becomes easier. Eventually you will find that you are hungry for clearing your chakras and you wish to do the clearing as quickly as you can after you experience blockage. This is because the experience of wellness—speaking emotionally, mentally and spiritually—is a wonderful elixir compared to that murky, unwell experience of being confused or caught within the details of whatever drama has caught you away from the free flow of the present moment. You are here to get caught in the free flow and stop the flow so that you can examine the catalyst that you have just caught or that has just caught you.

Nevertheless, when you are caught the appropriate reaction is not self-pity or floundering in despair but rather the realization that you have been given a gift. You have been given a puzzle to solve and in the solution of this puzzle you will come across a version of yourself whom you have not yet met. The working out of the puzzle may involve suffering, especially if one is new to the practice of the discipline of examining one's thoughts and responding to them as if they had worth and honor, but repetition makes every attempt to do this easier than the one before it and as you gain results from doing this work, that too will give you the courage to make even bolder attempts to understand yourself and to allow to fall away those distortions which do not serve you.

Inherent in the process of the raising of the kundalini is the concept of the possibility of perfection. One must be able to accept one's creatorship or one will never be able fully to utilize this whole concept of the raising of the kundalini. For when one has attained the supposed goal of the raising of the kundalini and the kundalini has settled at the brow chakra, the gateway to intelligent infinity can swing open—but only for the one who is able to consider himself a creator.

Now, what is the use of this process of the raising of the kundalini from the indifferent movement in the lower three chakras and occasionally the opening of the heart to a steady rise up into the indigo ray? For many people there is no use in it whatsoever. It is a highly individual, personal and even intimate decision for each as to whether they wish fully to utilize this powerful resource of the human mind, body and spirit.

We find it difficult to put into words what motivates an entity to have the ambition fully to use the resources of his incarnated soul energy to attempt to become, in a word, an avatar. Yet, this is the potential for any. Christhood is as a cloak or a crown that may be worn by choice by the one who wishes to walk in sacred symmetry. It is a choice that is highly personal. If chosen, it is a choice that will consume the rest of the incarnation. Yet it is a choice with tremendous advantages for the entity who values the possibility of moving forward in polarity and in moving forward as well in the learning of those structures of knowledge that enable an entity to be of service in a more efficient way.

The signpost of magic is the slogan, "I desire to know in order to serve." The entity who chooses to work with the kundalini is an entity who is choosing to become a magical being and whose motto is to use that knowledge that is gained only in service to others.

Naturally there are negatively oriented magical beings and their desire would be to know in order to serve the self. We are not those who discuss service-to-self practices, for we are service-to-others oriented and do not have the ability to teach in any other way. However, since we are speaking exclusively to those who are service-to-others oriented in this circle, we feel that we are in good shape in being able to express that which you would wish to know.

This energy that comes from the central sun into the sun of your planet, into the center of the Earth, and from there into the soles of your feet and upwards through your energy pipeline and out of the top of your head, is in infinite supply. As much energy as you can run, that energy is available. As high an amperage as you wish to run it, that energy intensity is available. Therefore, the portion of the raising of the kundalini having to do with the clearing of the pipeline is a matter of an infinite journey into discovering how to clear yourself, for the more that you are able to clear and drop away from your personality the more wide open that you may run that energy that's pouring into the base of your spine.

The energy that comes down through the gateway to intelligent infinity, down through indigo and then from indigo to green or to blue or staying in indigo, is that energy you have called forth by your desire and your will. Therefore, hone your desire with every fiber of your being. Keep the edge of appetite keen for the truth. Call upon the energies of justice, fairness, beauty, truth and equality. Bring to mind the qualities of compassion, mercy, hope and faith. Know that these are the elements upon which those who wish to serve cut their eyeteeth These are the structures—or beings, if you will, for they are living structure—that stand like sentinels along the path of light, through your body and through your spirit.

You are capable of embodying that which you can pull through from above by your desire. If your desires are for lust then you shall leave your kundalini in red ray. If your desires focus upon personal relationships, then you shall raise your kundalini to the orange ray. If your true desire is for marriage and a good work situation, then you shall raise your kundalini to the yellow-ray level. If your deepest desire is to open your heart, then you shall raise the kundalini to the green-ray level. If your deepest desire is to learn how to love with wisdom and to know what it is to have compassion while invoking justice, then you move into those energies of acceptance and of justice that are invoked in blue ray. And when you finally desire above all things to be devoted ultimately and completely to the one infinite Creator and live in the precincts of faith, then by your desire you have pulled up the energy into indigo.

But you cannot simply desire to love the Creator and expect to have full energy into indigo. You must keep the pipeline clear while keeping your desire clear. It is a true discipline of the personality to pursue this goal and it is one which is like housework: it never ends. There is always, in the moment after a fully experienced perfection, something that pulls you back into the world of maya or illusion. And there, you must get a grip upon your new situation. Then you assess it. You sit with it. And you use it in the way that you feel is the highest and best.

Naturally, it is always important to ask for help in making these decisions. Invoke your guidance as often as you can. However we would advise you, in order to have a balanced invocation, to spend time daily focusing not on what you need but on your thanks, your gratitude, your joy, and your devotion to and love of the infinite Creator. Do not be reactive but proactive in this regard. For it is not the entity who waits to have a conversation with the Creator until there is a need to whom realization is given but rather it is to the one who goes to the Creator as to his lover because he cannot stay away, because he cannot stop thinking about the beloved One.

(Side one of tape ends.)

(Carla channeling)

It is this hunger that is the key to the raising of the kundalini. You will have to judge for yourself whether this is an asset you wish to develop within yourself. There are simpler ways to envision service to others. There are simpler ways to achieve a harvestable polarity. However, the concept of pulling your energy upwards from the grosser to the finer aspects of your body, then your mind, and finally your spirit is a concept that has a tremendous amount of power and certainly its structures are stable to those who seek truly.

This instrument is informing me that the principle needs to let this question lie as it is. Certainly, it is a question that could be developed and we apologize for moving on but we are sure that there are other queries that entities within this group would like to ask at this time and so we would like to ask if there is another query at this time or a follow up upon what we have said so far. We are those of Q'uo.

S: I have a query. Many of us begin our seeking with great flames of enthusiasm and desire to serve and proceed quite rapidly at the beginning until we find that which somehow matches our seeking and feeds us. And then we carry on upon our chosen path for a substantial time finding eventually, however, that the vicissitudes of life and the struggles that we get caught up in have somehow diminished that original desire and we find ourselves in a position where it can even be the case that our perceived requirements of service seem to be militating against the desire to seek itself. So I wonder if you could speak to how one might keep that flame alive or attend to it in such a way that a balance between the seeking and the service results and enables the seeking to invigorate itself as it finds it needs to.

We are those of Q'uo, and are aware of your query, my brother. Certainly we cannot respond in a way that is specific but, in general, we might suggest two avenues of procedure.

Firstly, it is well, when the outer circumstances of one's life militate against the outer expression of seeking, to build an ivory tower, shall we say, within one's heart of hearts that is a safe place in which one may seek the Creator. It is well to keep this place a secret and to cherish it as a treasure deep within one's hidden treasure house. There is no one to ridicule or disturb that entity who has built for himself a sacred space within.

Once that sacred space has been built according to the precise desires of your heart, then it is available for you to go to, to enter and to rest. If you are too tired, spiritually and emotionally speaking, to seek further than simply basking in the presence of the Creator then you may rest and be fed, and this is a positive step. Perhaps it is all you may do for a while but you are gaining in battery strength, shall we say, until you reach a point where your light is able to be switched on and in that light you are able to descry some of the mystery you seek. Even a tiny rune of the great tablet of wisdom and love available to the seeking soul is often enough to recharge the inspiration that has gone lacking for lack of exposure to the process itself.

It is not encouraged to jump into seeking in an attempt to jumpstart the process. Rather, it is encouraged to respect the self enough to create an inner place, a place in time/space, within the inner planes of the self, to which one may repair for rest and for learning when enough energy has been built up.

The second thing that we would suggest as something to consider as a resource for rebuilding desire and inspiration is fasting. The process of setting an intention is a very subtle process but a simple one at the same time. The group today has been talking about analogs and whether or not they are real. Working spiritually it is possible to work upon an analog to something and have the analog itself become real. Because the body is the creature of the mind, that which is capable of being thought, exists, once it is thought, and will continue to be real until there is no one that thinks that thought.

Therefore, if one wishes to set an intention for a new life, one can use the body as an analog for the mind and the spirit. It is difficult directly to cleanse the mind or cleanse the spirit and if one sets an intention of cleansing the mind and the spirit before a fast, then when the feelings of hunger and then lack of hunger and increasing lightness are experienced and the body is obviously cleansing itself, the mind and the spirit become cleansed by analogy, shall we say, by the intention of the doer of the fast. Therefore, it is well several times in the day to do that which is necessary and beautiful to the seeker as a way of reminding that seeker of what he is doing, therefore keeping that intention sharpened and that desire fresh.

At the conclusion of a fast, then, it would be well for such a seeker to give thanks and declare the goodness and the efficacy of this process, stating the faith and the hope of new life and the certainty that the potential has now been prepared and the student is ready for the transformation that is at hand. Then whatever dawn breaks, it shall break upon a conscious soul, a soul conscious of its work, its worth, and its readiness for new consecration.

We thank the one known as S for this question and would ask if there is another query at this time.

(No further queries.)

We are those of Q'uo, and if there are no more queries at this time we shall take our leave of this instrument and this group, thanking each of you for the beauty of your vibrations and thanking you as a group for the combined beauty and the towering nature of your combined sacred space. It is an honestation to the one infinite Creator and we thank you for our ability to be a witness to it and a part of it in our humble way.

May we say that a great cloud of witnesses beholds this meeting, for each of you carries with you unseen friends and family members, some from other densities and some from the inner planes, whether they be angelic or devic. It is a glorious gathering. We are happy to be a part of it.

My brothers and sisters, we leave you in the love and in the light of the one infinite Creator. We are known to you as the principle of Q'uo. Adonai. Adonai.

L/L Research

L/L Research is a subsidiary of Rock Creek Research & Development Laboratories, Inc.

P.O. Box 5195
Louisville, KY 40255-0195

www.llresearch.org

Rock Creek is a non-profit corporation dedicated to discovering and sharing information which may aid in the spiritual evolution of humankind.

ABOUT THE CONTENTS OF THIS TRANSCRIPT: This telepathic channeling has been taken from transcriptions of the weekly study and meditation meetings of the Rock Creek Research & Development Laboratories and L/L Research. It is offered in the hope that it may be useful to you. As the Confederation entities always make a point of saying, please use your discrimination and judgment in assessing this material. If something rings true to you, fine. If something does not resonate, please leave it behind, for neither we nor those of the Confederation would wish to be a stumbling block for any.

© 2009 L/L Research

Sunday Meditation
September 17, 2006

Group question: The question this week, Q'uo, has to do with the state of the world as perceived by those of us who are in it. We were wondering if you could give an idea, just in general, of the types of energies that are available now for people who wish to grow and how people who are able to open their heart in some degree can accept these energies and what you could expect in your daily life, your pattern of growth, the amount of catalyst, the ability to deal with it, and then contrast that perhaps to people who are having difficulty opening their heart, maybe not being able to do that at all, and the types of experiences they might expect from being unable to open their hearts to these energies. Could you tell us about the energies and how people are able to experience them with harmony and without harmony?

(Carla channeling)

We are those of the principle known to you as Q'uo. Greetings in the love and in the light of the one infinite Creator. It is our great privilege and pleasure to be with you. We thank you for calling us to your circle of seeking. You enable us to be of service to you by this request to share our thoughts with those who would seek to know them. That is our humble desire.

We assure you that we are very well aware that there is no way in which we can be an authority for you. We can only share our opinions and we must ask of you your most carefully discrimination as you listen to our thoughts. Please take only those that have resonance to you personally and leave the rest behind. We would not wish to be a stumbling block before you. We are, as you, fellow seekers, and are glad to share our experiences and our opinions. In order for us to do this in a free manner, therefore, we would ask you to be careful in your discrimination of what you accept to work with in your process. It is a very sacred thing to us to maintain integrity and freedom of will in our relationship with you. We thank you for this consideration.

To give you a complete and detailed description of the energies that you meet on all of the levels of orders of magnitude in your experience would be an exhaustive and lengthy process. Suffice it to say that the universe is a universe of vibration. The physical vehicle within which you experience life at this time is a fairly dull instrument compared to some of your other animal species in receiving those things that may be heard and tasted, sensed by the sense of smell, and so forth.

These very simple vibrations are not to be ignored. The temperature and the comfort of your physical vehicle has a sometimes powerful impact on the thinking processes of your being, keeping you focused almost entirely within very simple energies.

Overlaid to these purely physical experiences, like how warm it is and whether the wind is blowing, whether it is raining and so forth—all of which have very characteristic vibratory bouquets to offer your physical body, as well as your emotional and mental bodies—there are the metaphysical energies that are native to your planet and are not particularly swayed by the end of the age or considerations of that kind. You have a certain vibratory structure in this particular density of your universe as well as the other densities within that octave of densities that creates the universe that you know and see, and, as well, that reciprocal universe that is unseen and yet is felt in terms of its effects upon you, more and more.

These energies connect with you where you are working within your energy body. The infinite love and light of the one Creator flows through your body system continuously. The energy is caught by weakness or over-activation within a chakra or ray within the energy body, or perhaps a chakra is simply blocked completely because of serious distortions within that particular kind of energy.

Therefore, before one even moves into considerations of the so-called end of the age and its specialized waves of vibrations, one is already living at the center of a personal vortex of energies: energies that are incoming, energies that are flowing through, and energies that you are blessing by your thoughts, your intentions, and your actions, and allowing to go forth from you. Are you a lighthouse? Or do you turn out your own light? That is for you to decide and it does not have anything to do with the end of the age.

These are the energies of every day and they are indeed challenging enough. They are set up to aid you in receiving that catalyst that you need in order to create choices that move you forward. You have the opportunity at any time to accelerate the pace of your spiritual evolution by using the resources of your mind, your emotions, and your body in a disciplined way. And we always encourage each to look at each day with that sense of creation and authorship that you would if you were looking at a blank canvas and deciding what to paint.

There is a great deal of life as you experience it that seems to be intransigent and unable to be dealt with in any way except to accept what is. However, there is always a creative way to find the love, the thanksgiving, and the joy that are inherent in that pattern, however difficult it is.

It may be that you see the love in that moment coming from the beauty surrounding the situation, whether it is physical or whether there is something about it emotionally which is touching.

It also may be that you are the only love in that moment and that creates for you a tremendous opportunity to settle into your true vibration and share that with the situation. It may not change the outer situation, but your use of energy, your expenditure of energy at that time, has made a difference, not only in the local atmosphere surrounding the situation in which you applied love without judgment, but also because such energy expenditures are added to the fund of love upon planet Earth. For your energy expenditure, when it reaches the level of ethical choice, redounds to the tribe of humankind, not only to your own spiritual evolution.

In addition to these normal energies which buffet you as though you were a small craft in a very large sea, each and every day of your life, planet Earth and the surrounding planets as well are being buffeted by galactic energies which have to do with the fact that Earth, as you call this living being, is rotating and spiraling as is its sun system, into a new area of space/time into which it has not rotated previously.

It is time, in space/time and in time/space, for a new age to begin. It is an age with a different kind of energy and while it is not to be physically linked with the idea of fourth density or the heaven worlds, it contains more light than the light particles that you know of as the photon. Therefore, there is more information in this incoming energy from the new age.

To simplify this discussion, we will focus strictly on the time/space age which we would call fourth density. Trying to bring a physical body and a physical way of understanding transformation into the discussion is impossible for us. You will have to take it as given by us that our opinion of the process of physical death and transformation is that it is a natural occurrence which is very easy to do when the natural time for transition comes. Dying, as this instrument has said several times, is difficult, but the actual death is very easy.

We ask that you not concern yourself with such fear-based thoughts as what might happen to you that is difficult or challenging or causing death in the event of the interpenetration of third-density vibrations by fourth-density vibrations. This is not an occurrence that we see happening in your Earth world. We do not see a possibility/probability vortex at this time, in terms of the natural run of things in the metaphysical world that would cause a planet-wide catastrophe. Your planet has received enough love and understanding from the many, many groups around your planet that are attempting to communicate that love and concern and sense of stewardship and partnership with the Earth.

That which we do see as a possibility, and that which we would encourage you in all ways that you see to be helpful [to respond to], is the blocking of the pretensions of some of your leaders who are drawn by energies that they cannot explain towards the act of conflagration which would be a physical Armageddon.

Nature does not need a pole shift, so-called, at this time because the Earth's people are waking up quickly at the grass roots level. Many of them cannot explain it. They cannot talk about it. They are not confident enough to be able to say anything about what is occurring to them to the world around them.

But what is occurring to them is that they are waking up and realizing that the goodness of themselves and the goodness of other people cannot depend upon governance but can only depend upon the self and the other selves in the local area about the self, so that more and more, people are becoming awakened to the possibilities of cooperation and peace done somewhat under the radar of government and the larger culture.

We believe that there is a tremendous possibility that these pockets of love and light and cooperation will begin to proliferate as loving people find other loving people and form local groups to solve local problems in all of the different areas of life.

However, the picture, regardless of the possibility of some man-made Armageddon, at this time is a picture of a time of graduation and harvest that is already occurring. Many of your people have already graduated. For the last thirty years, you have been receiving—as children coming through the normal processes of procreation—wanderers from your own fourth density who have graduated from your present third density [and who have] realized all of the many options available to them now that they are dwellers within fourth density, and have decided, naturally enough, that what they want to do in terms of service to others is to come right back to planet Earth and help the rest of the planet shift their consciousness to the value systems that are compatible with fourth density energy.

As you begin to settle into a fearless attitude towards the incoming vibrations from fourth density and the many waves of energy that are hastening the process, shall we say, or helping it mature appropriately from what this instrument knows as the central sun, there are increasing probabilities that, for each entity, the experiences that are to come will be substantial. They will not necessarily be heavy, for heaviness depends on how you emotionally react to the incoming catalyst. However, the nature of the fourth-density energies is one of the most transparent honesty and truth.

Under the light of this energy, or shall we say, under the influence of this energy, that which is within the mind and has been shut away as unworthy or undesirable, shall move from the shadowed recesses of that inner closet into outer manifestation. There will be a situation in your life or a person in your life or just an inner thought process that will show you the shape and the basic feeling that you have about this hidden part of yourself. That's the key to understanding how to work with these incoming energies.

Resistance, as this instrument remembers the Borg saying many times in *Star Trek*, is useless. These energies have an intended effect of helping individuals who are attempting to awaken to see the shape, the texture, the odor, and the nature of those parts of the shadow self that have not yet been recruited to be a part of your round table of white knights.

Remember that knighthood is that which is attained by warriors. In working with these energies, see yourselves as warriors for light and truth, let yourself become fierce. Do not be afraid to gaze at the murderer within, the liar within, the adulterer within, the lazy person within, or whatever other distortion hits your attention with all of the power of a harsh wind or a severe rain. Stand in the wind, glory in the rain, and give thanks.

When you are giving thanks for this catalyst, you are releasing from yourself pride and pretension. You are emptying your mental pockets of all of the tools that you have in the everyday world that are supposed to fix things. You empty yourself of these tools because that which is hitting you is not to be dealt with from the level of third density. It is to be dealt with from the level of fourth density. There is no concern as to what this means, my friends, for you have heard it many, many times, in many different ways. You are love. You are light. You are all that there is. You are not going anywhere. You are never at risk.

When you begin to get a sense of the eternal and infinite nature of your soul stream, and when you realize that you are here at this time specifically to be hit with this truth and this shining light, that realization may help you to firm up your determination to take advantage of this opportunity. You are not responsible for what you see coming in. Your area of responsibility is in how you respond.

This is not a call to martyrdom, my friends, but rather it is a call to ethical behavior. It is an encouragement to make of life a spiritual, sacred, game in which you attempt to move yourself from the still point where you neither love others greatly or yourself greatly. We encourage you to make a choice. If you wish to polarize in service to others, start gazing at others with the realization that you are here to help them just as they are here to help you. Open your minds to the creative question of what seed might you plant that may be helpful.

You also asked concerning the experience of the energies as felt by those who do not at this time find it possible to move through those actions which open the heart. Those entities are divided into two very distinct categories. We would first speak briefly of the category of those who simply have not awakened. They have not polarized and therefore they are not experiencing the same level of life as this group which has asked this question. They are completely involved in the local cultural processes of moving through life.

It is quite possible for such entities to make graduation and harvest, for the energies of graduation and harvest have to do with unconditional love, it is not a book-oriented test. It is not an information-oriented area. The final will simply be your vibration at the time of your death. If it is a fourth-density vibration, you will graduate. If your vibration is still involved in the earthly things from the standpoint of Earth, you will continue to spend time on an earth-like planet until your eagerness and your hunger for more has driven you to move beyond that particular so-called box.

Those who have not awakened, however, may well be experiencing a good bit of illness and shortened lives because of the difficulty of dealing with energies that are full of truth hitting body, mind and spirit when that body, mind and spirit complex is not able to bear the truth or even realize what the truth looks like.

This is, in a way, unfortunate, and yet in another way it is the natural concomitant of an entity who has decided at some level not to do conscious spiritual work at this time. When an entity has decided not to move forward, it is inevitable that the entity starts moving backwards.

And you see, my friends, in many of those who are fundamentalist in their beliefs and very rigid in their dogma and doctrine, in whatever religious and political system to which this applies, the contraction into fear and the tendency to see all things in very black and white tones, when in truth it is truly a rainbow universe with not only black, white and shades of gray, but the most outrageous combinations of bright and creative colors, as entities have emotion, express suffering, and find in all sorts of energy exchanges more and more truth, more and more light, more and more grace, so that which they understand or feel begins to be coherent and they begin to achieve a metaphysical stature. This is the kind of work which begins to equip one to deal in fourth-density ways with third-density catalyst.

The last category, of course, is those service-to-self oriented entities who have decided that their way to the Creator is to love themselves more and more purely and to attract to themselves those entities which will help them and then put them to work as, shall we say, slaves or very obedient servants. You may see this kind of structure in place in organizations like your armed services and some of your churches.

The truth of the service-to-others polarity is just as viable as the truth of service-to-self polarity: no more and no less. Therefore, it is not surprising that some entities choose the service-to-self polarity. We are not of that polarity and have never been drawn to approach that polarity. We have found that the Creator of this particular sun system, of which we are also a part, has a bias towards service to others.

And we find that it is a straighter and more muscular path, one that is more fun to work with and one that yields a much greater harvest as one moves on. It is straighter, my friends, because one does not at some point have to switch polarities. For the negative polarity can only go just so far. Nevertheless, from the standpoint of an entity choosing between service to self and service to others, it is a very viable choice.

For those who have not opened their heart because they refuse to do—and that is the conscious choice of a service-to-self entity—the incoming vibrations will not be particularly troublesome. Such entities have long chosen to put themselves under the most rigid discipline. Emotional affect does not serve them. Being out of control in any way does not serve them. Consequently, they cope very well with a surprising amount of difficult catalyst because they really have to be firm in their desire to love themselves and very confident before they can make any progress whatsoever in that very difficult polarity.

We do not see a great deal of the global surface being filled at all thickly with those who have made the service-to-self choice. However, those who make the service-to-self choice have a tendency to seek earthly power as well as inner power and consequently they tend to create systems of governance which tend towards the enslavement of some beings for the benefit of others. We would ask entities who wish to think about this further to gaze at the world scene with those particular thoughts in mind.

The query asked what the state of the world was from the viewpoint of the people on planet Earth. We cannot answer that very well. We do not have the viewpoint of people on planet Earth. We have a somewhat detached viewpoint. We have the viewpoint which sees the perfection of the pattern.

We see the economy with which this time of inevitable transformation is progressing. We encourage each to realize that they are powerful. Each and every one of you is a sun, radiant, infinite and loving. As you sit in this circle in the gathering twilight, feel the power of your combined love and let it bless the world from your open hearts.

We thank this group for this query and would ask if there is another query at this time. We are those of Q'uo.

Questioner: I had lung surgery a little over two months ago and I am in extreme pain all of the time. I am going to my doctor weekly. I've been to an acupuncturist and am going back this week. I'm going to start going to a social worker who specializes in pain management and I have an appointment with a pain specialist doctor in three weeks. I'm doing everything possible. Is there any other suggestion of what I can do to relieve this pain?

We are those of Q'uo, and are aware of your query, my brother. We thank you for this question and would offer our sympathy as you experience suffering, as we offer sympathy to all who suffer. We shall not insult you by suggesting that your pain is not real. What we do suggest is that there are ways to think about what you are feeling that are helpful in terms of becoming able to remain untouched internally by the discomfort that you are experiencing, no matter how fell and intense it may be.

The first asset that we would encourage you to consider is the strength of your own love of life. If you are glad to be somewhere, the discomfort involved in being there is less. Therefore, in your mind, ask the witness that is within you to pay more attention than you have been to the little things. For it is in the little things that sacredness most often shows its face.

Gaze at a blade of grass. Gaze at the shape of a leaf. Look at the quality of the sunlight as it dapples through the forest and touches your skin. See the color of something that creates in you a feeling, whether it be in a painting or a color on a wall or a point of decoration. Note that moment when you responded and know that you are part of the dance of all that is and what you see is only that part that awaits what you give back to it.

Feel yourself not as an entity in pain but as an entity that is part of an incredibly complex and yet harmonious dance. Let your spirits move outside the limitations of your body. The more spacious your universe, the smaller a physical pain.

Secondly, develop for yourself an intention. When this instrument happened to be in a great deal of nerve pain from the shoulders, spine, neck and arms, after a good deal of searching for a good focus for intention, this instrument, because of her Christian background and because of her love of science fiction, chose two points of focus. One was intended to take away physical fear. The other was intended to take away mental fear.

To take away physical fear, this instrument used a quotation from the *Holy Bible*. The sense of that quotation was, "If I live, I live in Christ and if I die, I die in Christ. So whether I live or whether or die, I am in Christ and Christ is in me."[20] This always allowed this instrument to return to a state of fearlessness. Fearlessness is the key to working with pain. That is most helpful.

The other point of focus was a short phrase taken from the first edition of *Star Trek* and that was, "Faith, the final frontier."[21] It helped to remind the instrument to pick up faith, jump into it; throw yourself at it and don't wait to be convinced. That is emotional fearlessness. It sufficed for this instrument. It would probably not suffice for another human being. We use this example because this instrument gave us permission and because it shows the kind of work that you do in order to toughen the mind and become an athlete in dealing with pain.

The remaining resources simply have to do with recognizing that some pain is important to note and other pain is simply noise and not signal. That pain management approach that you are now investigating will offer you many helpful resources, we are sure.

Is there another query at this time? We are those of Q'uo.

Questioner: We have several major cultural traditions here on Earth and they've evolved over some time but some trends are rather constant. Was most of our culture developed here on Earth or was it brought from the main places that humans have come from on other third-density planets?

We are those of Q'uo and are aware of your query, my brother. Your use of the word "culture," my brother, makes it difficult for us to be accurate in our discussion. We shall perhaps answer a question that you had not asked and for this we apologize.

The underlying and fundamental nature of all of the various planetary groups that have come to Earth are enough different that they constitute a certain dynamic which, if played wrongly, is a clashing tone cluster. If played correctly, it is a triumphant symphony. Your peoples do indeed have aspects of their archetypal minds that are significantly different, one racial or planetary group from another.

The unfortunate state of affairs among your many peoples is that one particular racial and planetary group, that which came from Mars, worked in Atlantis, and is now, through many repetitions of history, experiencing power upon the globe at this time, [and] has held onto its place in the world scene far beyond its natural time of rulership of the way planet Earth feels and thinks. We cannot call it a culture because your planet has not allowed culture to progress to the point where the various archetypal minds of planet Earth begin to collaborate with their many common points, since all are citizens of planet Earth and all have come through the gates of incarnation.

You have not realized, among the many planetary entities and resulting racial groups, the possibilities of collaboration, the choices of the Atlantis bunch, shall we call them, being heavily involved in the masculine virtues of aggression and the ability to make war and conquer, which have distorted the gifts that all entities upon the planet have to offer.

The culture that does exist upon your planet is in little spots here and there where you will note that there is a radiance and a positive energy that is discussed by many. Such centers of spiritual aliveness can be found by those who begin to seek for direct experience with such energy. It is truly said that when the student is ready, the teacher shall appear.

We encourage you to consider being part of the creation of a culture. Examine what you know of your own family culture, of the culture of your city, of the culture of your geographical area, and of the culture, such as it is, of your nation. What has been lost that could be again found? What songs that are not listened to could again be sung? What pictures could be drawn that have not yet been encouraged by teachers and authority figures? What creative possibilities are latent within the archetypal minds of your people when they are not deadened by giving up their creative nature in order to belong and to spend time involved in those things which are not creative but rather comforting?

May we ask if there is a final query at this time?

---

[20] The quotation is from Romans 14:8: "If we live, we live to the Lord, and if we die, we die to the Lord; so then, whether we live or whether we die, we are the Lord's."

[21] The opening credits of the original *Star Trek*, as well as *Star Trek Next Generation*, began with the words, "Space! The final frontier!"

Questioner: I don't have a query. I wanted to say thank you for your words in the past and for the energies and for all of the help with the painful situation I've been dealing with. I very much appreciate it.

We are those of Q'uo, my sister, and the pleasure is all ours.

Is there a final query at this time? We are those of Q'uo.

(No further queries.)

If there is no further query at this time, then we shall take our leave of this instrument and this group, leaving each of you in the love and in the light of the one infinite Creator. Adonai. Adonai. ✣

L/L Research

L/L Research is a subsidiary of Rock Creek Research & Development Laboratories, Inc.

P.O. Box 5195
Louisville, KY 40255-0195

www.llresearch.org

Rock Creek is a non-profit corporation dedicated to discovering and sharing information which may aid in the spiritual evolution of humankind.

ABOUT THE CONTENTS OF THIS TRANSCRIPT: This telepathic channeling has been taken from transcriptions of the weekly study and meditation meetings of the Rock Creek Research & Development Laboratories and L/L Research. It is offered in the hope that it may be useful to you. As the Confederation entities always make a point of saying, please use your discrimination and judgment in assessing this material. If something rings true to you, fine. If something does not resonate, please leave it behind, for neither we nor those of the Confederation would wish to be a stumbling block for any.

© 2009 L/L Research

Special Meditation
September 26, 2006

Question from M: In this situation in which I find myself, I can see a fundamental pattern. I see some fear and resistance around becoming more determined! I fear to trust in the use of my own talents in music, business and other things. Therefore, I remain in a threshold zone, repeating experiences until I destroy this deep fear. By experiencing this situation of the lack of a job, the feelings of uncertainty and hazard, and the load of the responsibility to support and provide for my family, how can I process this experience to transform the inner chains I still have as fear and pride?

(Carla channeling)

We are the principle known to you as the Q'uo. Greetings in the love and in the light of the one infinite Creator, in Whose service we come to you this evening. It is a profound privilege and pleasure to be called to this circle of seeking and we express gratitude and thankfulness that you have given us an opportunity to share our opinions with you. It would be helpful to us if you are very careful, as you listen to our thoughts, using only those thoughts that resonate to you and feel alive and useful. Those thoughts to which you do not respond in this way are thoughts that miss their mark, and we will ask you to leave them aside.

If you will discriminate with care, that will allow us to speak freely without concern for possible infringement of free will. So we thank you for this consideration.

My brother, the query that you place before us is rich in thought and depth of insight. There is in the query itself a great deal of useful self-knowledge, an overview that is often not seen in those who are seeking the truth.

It is easy to become involved with the seeming chaos that occurs when one's outwardly physical concerns are not as you would wish them to be. It is easy to become deafened by your own self-doubt when things have gone awry in the outer world. It is a more mature spiritual being who is able to see underlying themes and repetitive energy expenditures that have not served as you would wish your energy expenditures to serve you. For that we commend you, my brother. It is far easier to speak with one who sees more clearly into the ways of the self.

Now, let us look at that word, self. This instrument has been reading a book entitled *New World* by Ekhart Tolle. This material, which she and the one known as Jim have been reading in their Morning Offering sessions, center upon the nature of the self. It is synchronistic that your query happens to involve this concept deeply.

My brother, you are aware that in our way of thinking all things are one. The Creator and you are the same. Yourself, therefore, at the deepest level, is the self of the Creator. Your I is the I AM of the godhead principle.

Moving a bit closer to concensus reality, moving down from an infinite Creator who is a complete mystery to the half-revealed mystery of that expression of unconditional love that this instrument call Jesus the Christ, it may be seen that you are one with the unconditional love and compassion which Jesus the Christ carried upon his human shoulders as the regal robe of kingship that was his.

You also, my brother, are royal. Every soul in the infinite reaches of the creation is heir-apparent to creatorship.

So, what is this self that you think that you are? It is an interesting question, for there is a part of you that is asking the question of the rest of yourself. It is interesting, my brother, to see how the personality begins to disintegrate upon careful examination.

Indeed, your culture is not oriented towards helping you to move deeper into the nature of the self. The somewhat materialistic culture of what you are part tends to identify the self by various things about the self.

Each entity chooses distinguishing characteristics which are their favorites. They can include sexuality, racial origins, types of skills, whether at work or at play, and so forth.

Your culture does not have an interest in your moving deeper into who you are. It would be happy to see you define yourself by how well you are doing in the eyes of the world.

There are, in your own patterns and structures of personality, favorite quirks and things about the self that feel important. It is a rich round of characteristics to examine in a contemplative fashion, looking at the nature of each quirk, what its possible origin might be and what it shows, the way a scar can show an injury under the skin.

You spoke of using the catalyst that you are now receiving, which is trying to find a job and being concerned about taking care of your family, in order to work on those areas you feel are the most significant, namely fear and pride.

We are speaking now of pride. Pride is the self which is aware that the self has virtues. It is not that it is incorrect to be aware of your virtues, any more than it is wrong to be completely aware of your weaknesses. However, when there is an emotional charge to the awareness of one's traits, that emotional charge creates something to defend.

The one known as Eckhart commented upon this concept, saying that was characteristic of the unconscious or egoic self, that it liked to be right and, therefore, it identified others as being in the wrong. Structures which include pride, no matter what the source, are structures that tend towards splintering the light and dividing the power of love into smaller and smaller fractions.

It is difficult indeed for an entity that is more intelligent, more creative, and with a more mature spiritual point of view than most to avoid feelings of satisfaction at the distance traveled so far. However, often it is that times of difficulty offer the positive effect of bringing one to one's knees and making one realize that of oneself, one can do nothing.

The humbling of a proud man is a gift that is difficult to receive, we are aware. Yet at the same time, there are gifts at the end of the process of emptying your pretentions. One gift is that you are indeed empty, with nothing to prove and nothing to defend. In that state of emptiness, you then may ask to do the will of the one infinite Creator, to serve with love, compassion and a far more directed will.

When one does not distinguish between tasks and when one does one's tasks with love, all tasks are equal. Pour your pride, then, into a new vessel and let it be transformed into the will to serve at whatever lies before you in this day.

If you are able to find an exalted place of employment that stretches your creative abilities and offers you a great deal of the world supply, then do that work with absolute love and passion, do your best.

And if fortune sends you labor that you feel is beneath you, yet you can do it, and it can pay the bills, then find the love and the pride that you would take in that exalted work and apply it with utmost integrity to the work that lies before you to this day.

Do not distinguish between kinds of work but rather focus, in all that you do, on creating a poem of your love and your movements in the work of your hands, your mind, and your heart.

Speaking of fear is a different matter, my brother. Fear is that contraction which occurs when one feels that one is at risk. Since life itself is a bad risk, ending surely in death, it is the human condition to experience fear. The universe is unfathomable and uncontrollable. Why should there not be fear within the heart of all beings who are able to watch while difficult and challenging situations occur all around them? It seems a dangerous place to be, planet Earth, does it not?

And yet fear is not greatly to be desired by the seeker of truth. What is there to fear? This instrument immediately responded to our question with thoughts of the fear of going hungry; the fear of being without four walls to call your own, and other fears that are concomitant to not finding a job, and finding it difficult to make ends meet.

These are very real and substantial fears. And yet we sense in your query a deeper fear, and that fear we can address, in such a way that perhaps it affects the fears within the outer world.

In truth, there is nothing to fear.

You are dwelling within a certain kind of illusion and your consciousness has created about itself a physical vehicle which moves this consciousness around. It offers a great deal of benefit to the consciousness inhabiting the physical vehicle.

When something occurs that creates an unviability to the physical vehicle, your consciousness will move onward without a break. You shall continue.

At heart, then, there is nothing to fear. For any circumstance whatever is as it is, until it changes. The changes are inevitable. The only question is the timing. You shall always, in this density of choice that is the Earth world, find yourself in the process of change and transformation.

If the fear that you feel is at heart a hollow thing, it is a matter of becoming more aware of the dynamic to fear. The dynamic to fear is love. Fear and love do not coexist, any more than light and dark coexist.

And just like light, love cannot be killed by fear. It shines even in the most hostile environment, just as does light. Even the light of a tiny candle creates a significant glow and illumination to the eye. The love within you is waiting for you to embrace it. It is something that you can do quite consciously. However, there is a significant amount of discipline involved in availing yourself of the catalyst that is incoming at this time, and using it in a positive manner.

When you sense fear within yourself, do not devolve into an inner atmosphere of self doubt and upset. Look at that fear. Intensify that fear. Become fully aware of your fear. And then ask for its opposite. Allow yourself to become aware of love, that love that flows all around you at all times; that love of the one infinite Creator which is without any limit.

Let that feeling of unconditional love lift you and help you to glow as if you were a lighthouse carrying this wonderful Pharos[22] of love and light that express through you. Feel that glow, and know that it is as real and as true about you as the fear that you are carrying.

You are not attempting to destroy your fear. We encourage you, rather, to think of it as a balancing mechanism. The human condition will always include fear, but it can at the same time include an equal and balancing amount of love, so that you as a being are one of 360 degrees, the light and the dark, the difficult and the easy, the sorrowful and the joyful.

You can allow yourself to continue to work with those things about yourself that you feel need work: the pride, the arrogance, the fear, the concern, the awareness of risk and hazard where you would far prefer to be competent. The details of your personality will take time to show themselves to you.

We encourage you, as you do this work, to remember that you are the Creator. You are the Redeemer. You are all the roles of godhead. Therefore, it is up to you to judge yourself or to refrain from judging yourself and to look to the purity of your intentions to asses your true worth. If the voice within you condemns you, who, then, shall save you?

Let the voice within you be a voice of encouragement, strength and grit. Let all of those deeply anxious feelings be turned into perseverance and the determination to live well. When your focus is on living well, serving in as beautiful a manner as you can, and remembering the one infinite Creator in all your devotions and all your days, you will find

---

[22] Pharos is a peninsula in northern Egypt near Alexandria where Ptolemy built a lighthouse that was considered one of the Seven Wonders of the World in ancient times. Any lighthouse can now be called a "Pharos," through long usage.

it less and less easy to waste time doubting yourself. For you shall be focused on the goal of serving in such a way that when you look back upon your life, you will see a poetry and the grace and the symmetry of your intentions, your thoughts, and the projections of your creativity.

We would encourage you, my brother, to bolster this work with a gift to yourself: sacred time. It is sometimes fiendishly difficult to carve out for yourself a true experience of inner silence. And yet, in whatever way is most meaningful to you, we would encourage your securing for yourself those moments to be alone with your seeking, your quest, and your hopes and dreams.

Nourish and encourage yourself with silence. Wether it is the silence of nature or the silence of some form of formal meditation or whatever your choice may be, give yourself that strenghtening gift, for in that silence are connections to your personal guidance system and many, many other sources of inspiration and comfort within the inner planes as well as elsewhere.

We ourselves are always glad to be part of your meditation in order to strengthen your basic meditative state. You may ask for our presence by mentally requesting it.

It is well to remember that while this work is extremely solitary, in that it is inner and subjective, nevertheless, you are never alone. The hosts of the unseen worlds vibrate in sympathy with those who seek the love and the light of the one infinite Creator. Your hopes and your seeking and your persistence draw increasing numbers of helpful souls to you.

We would leave you with encouragement to believe in yourself, to have confidence in the worth of your thoughts, your being, and your dreams. You have before you a pattern that is challenging indeed. See what you can do to cooperate which that which you find before you, always pulling back for a wider view, a view that sees the curve of the Earth rather than the streetlamps, the trees, and the houses.

You live in both worlds. The key to living in this one is to live well in the unseen world of your thoughts, your intentions, your insights, and your integrity in seeking the truth.

May we ask you at this time, my brother, if ther is a follow up question, or another question?

(Transcript ends.)

L/L Research is a subsidiary of Rock Creek Research & Development Laboratories, Inc.

P.O. Box 5195
Louisville, KY 40255-0195

L/L Research

www.llresearch.org

Rock Creek is a non-profit corporation dedicated to discovering and sharing information which may aid in the spiritual evolution of humankind.

ABOUT THE CONTENTS OF THIS TRANSCRIPT: This telepathic channeling has been taken from transcriptions of the weekly study and meditation meetings of the Rock Creek Research & Development Laboratories and L/L Research. It is offered in the hope that it may be useful to you. As the Confederation entities always make a point of saying, please use your discrimination and judgment in assessing this material. If something rings true to you, fine. If something does not resonate, please leave it behind, for neither we nor those of the Confederation would wish to be a stumbling block for any.

© 2009 L/L Research

Sunday Meditation
October 1, 2006

Question from J: *(Read by Jim.)* The first question today is from J. It is this: "Exactly what is the central sun of our galaxy around which all the stars revolve? P considers it to be a super-dense mass equivalent to thousands of our suns. It is constantly emitting powerful, omnidirectional rays, punctuated by periodic mega-bursts that flow out to all parts of the galaxy.

"He feels that these travel just below the speed of light. Do any emissions, these so-called trigger points, travel at the speed of thought, in other words, instantaneously?

"I've considered that the central sun was another name for a black hole. Are they or are they not the same thing? Can these be compared and discussed as to the role that each plays in creation and the evolution of consciousness? I want to know what the central sun is. Does it have anything to do with black holes? And what is the effect of the central sun and of black holes upon the evolution of consciousness?"

(Carla channeling)

We are those known to you as the principle of Q'uo. Greetings in the love and in the light of the one infinite Creator, in Whose service we come to you this day. It is a great privilege and pleasure to be a part of your circle of seeking. The beauty of your vibrations is stunning and the combinations of energies, as your auras blend in your sacred circle, is a wonderful bouquet of sight and texture and tone.

It is indeed a privilege to be called to this circle and we thank you.

It will aid us greatly in offering our opinions if each of you would take responsibility for discriminating between those thoughts which we offer that seem helpful to you and those thoughts which we offer which do not seem helpful to you. Please take those that seem helpful and leave the rest behind.

If you will use this discrimination then we shall be much more comfortable with the concept of sharing our thoughts with you. Our concern is to preserve your free will. We are not those of your planetary influence. We do not have the right to infringe upon your free will as would, say, a family member or a close friend. It is important for our own preservation of polarity that we be very sure that we remain those who share opinions and not become those who cross that line into telling people what to do. This we would not wish to come close to doing and we thank you for this consideration in this regard.

We thank the one known as J for this query. We must proceed with exquisite care in our response. There are several reasons for this need for care. We will enumerate them.

Firstly, as this instrument said to the one known as Jim before the session, the request that is specifically placed before us for information is not a request for spiritual principles but rather a request for information on how things work in the physical illusion. This constitutes, in the normal run of

© 2009 L/L Research

77

questions, a question that we are unable to answer. The substantive difficulty here is that this represents an active phase of a seeking entity's learning process at this time. Rather than asking for spiritual principles which would be helpful in approaching this question, the query was simply to explain the situation as regards the central sun and to compare and contrast this central sun or the idea of this central sun with the idea or concept of black holes. That is our first problem with this query as it was asked.

Our second and equally substantive challenge in responding to this query is that the instrument which we use at this time has virtually no scientific background and therefore we would be completely unable to fulfill the parameters of your query, my brother, in that we cannot say anything exact through this instrument having to do with scientific questions. The concepts and the vocabulary for such exactitude are missing in this instrument's make up. Therefore, our response shall be inexact and shall contain that flow of information which we are able to offer which we feel may be of use to you, my brother.

The concept of a central sun is one which many sources, including us, have used in discussing the energies that pour from the center of a galaxy or the creation itself. It is a challenge to discuss this concept of the central sun because of the relationship of the space/time or physical world, which is that which houses your consensus reality, and the metaphysical universe or time/space which houses your consciousness, infinity, eternity and the great mystery of non-locality.

In the space/time universe, there are layers of physical laws which, to some extent, work in order to create information which is helpful in making the gadgets that your civilization enjoys.

In a time/space universe, the work done is unseen. The values are not local and one is freed from the relativity of space/time. Nevertheless, as the creation presents itself to the physical eye, especially that physical eye that is enhanced by those instruments that enable you to see farther and to see closer, there are an increasing number of ways in which scientific eyes have been able to see things that they cannot explain.

In some part, this is eternally the situation in any expanding universe of knowledge. That which is not yet known is that which has perhaps not even been imagined Or, if it has been imagined or dreamt, there may be no way to measure or test the concepts and structures involved in the theories that are created to explain observations that have been made.

In the case of the concepts of the great central sun and the black hole, you are looking at a phenomenon that is partially within the world of space/time and partially within the world of time/space. This may be seen to be logical in the same way that a circle is round. The circle is round; therefore it has no beginning and no end, except that it does!

Each creation of the Father has a beginning and an ending. However, because of the fact that the beginning and the ending are firmly in the precincts of time/space, what you are gazing at as you gaze at the central sun and at the black hole are the alpha and the omega of an unending circle.

There is within this instrument's mind the concept of the Big Bang that supposedly began the creation. Through this instrument in the past we have spoken several times of the beating of the great heart as a model to use when thinking of the creation. Certainly, when the heart beats, there is that moment when the pumping action of the heart occurs and blood is moved forward, not only through the heart but through every vein and artery in the body. And each heartbeat is, in a way, a new world, a new situation for the circulatory system of that body.

The great central sun, which is gaining a great deal of attention within your scientific world as instrumentation becomes more sophisticated and more details and facts are able to be gathered by your scientists, is that portion or phase of the Big Bang that exists after the heart has first pumped; that is to say, after the Creator has decided to found and furnish a creation so that It may know Itself.

The so-called black hole, similarly, is that shadow of a time/space event that exists in space/time which marks the progress to and the point from which there is no exit from the return to the one infinite Creator.

This arrangement of energy expenditures is a part of the structure within which all of those parts of the Creator which you represent may move through the dance of the densities, seeking the truth, learning what it is to be, to be aware, to be aware of the self, to be aware of love, to be aware of wisdom, and to be aware of unity. To attempt to understand the Creator by understanding the Creator's house is, in our humble opinion, an indirect attempt.

Before we leave this particular query we would simply say that there are points of energy throughout the creation which are created by thought when a galaxy, a sun system, or a planet such as yours is at a particular stage of evolution. Some situations or cruxes within the evolution of an entity, a planet, a sun, or a galaxy, call for the availability of certain kinds of information and you may, in some cases, see these pulses as being filled with information.

May we ask at this time if there is a further query?

Jim: J2 asks if you could tell us what crop circles are. Why does no one seem to see them being made? Is there a spiritual principle behind crop circles?

We are those of Q'uo, and are aware of your query, my brother. The phenomenon of crop circle is just as the great central sun and the black hole phenomena: a phenomenon that has its roots in the world of time/space rather than space/time.

The energies of evolution move from thought. There are planetary entities, which we have before called social memory complexes, whose mode of service it is to create points of coherent mystery.

The same energies are involved when an entity or a group of entities creates a notation such as the Celtic runes. Such a notational system blends the mysterious and unknowable with everyday shapes, designs and images. A rune may be a series of simple lines. It may be associated with a certain kind of tree. It may be intended to indicate a magical energy of such and such a vibration.

When a system of such notation is worked out, it creates a kind of language. Your alphabet is such a notational system. The modern way of writing down music is such a notational system. And crop circle are a rudimentary notational system that is being created, not by a person but by an entire planetary group of entities who attempt to serve as those who alert the people of your planet to the fact that there is more of a mysterious and unknown quality to existence than could be surmised by an examination of the physical world.

UFOs or unidentified flying objects, themselves, in some cases, are the result of the precise same energy. However, in the case of the unidentified flying object, when it is in fact an image rather than a flying object, it has been created by thought; that is, the deeper thoughts of an entire planetful of entities.

Interestingly enough, when a certain amount of the awareness of a planetary group of people such as yourselves reaches a critical mass of consciousness, the people themselves, from their deep unconscious minds, begin to collaborate without knowing in their conscious minds that they are doing so. The result of these collaborations is a tear or a break in the continuity of the illusion of consensus reality. And in that hiatus[23], images may appear that bring forward into outer expression the hopes, the dreams, and the fears of an entire culture or population of a planet.

Crop circles, for the most part, are created not by planetary consciousness but by the consciousness of planetary groups from elsewhere who wish to help the people of Earth to wake up at this time from the sleep of consensus reality.

May we ask if there is another query at this time, my brother?

Jim: I and P sent in this question: "In July of this year, the British Study Group took part in a sweat lodge ceremony in Forest Row, England. The ceremony included the gathering of natural materials from the immediate environment, the building of the structure, a statement of intention, and several hours of silence and contemplation prior to entering the lodge.

"Into the lodge was placed hot rocks. Water was poured onto them, creating a great deal of steam. In this uncomfortable environment, each member took turns to express gratitude, ask a question, sing with the leader, and enjoy silence during a series of rounds of indeterminable length.

"We found this to be a powerful experience which felt like a death of sorts and a rebirth into which our group merged together on some level. The man leading the ceremony commented that it was one of the 'hottest' lodges he had ever taken part in. A lot of energy had been released by the group.

---

[23] hiatus: a break or interruption in the continuity of a work, series, action, etc.

"Would Q'uo please comment on the metaphysical implications of the sweat lodge and what energies were put into motion? Was there any unseen help? Did our ceremony have any effect on the lodge and the land around it?"

We are those of Q'uo, and are aware of your query, my brother. As we respond to this query, we would ask the one known as Jim to re-ask any parts of the query that we have not covered at the time that we finish that which we have to say. We would appreciate this aid, my brother.

When entities are conscious, awake and aware of their true nature and they wish to create a change in consciousness—their consciousness and the group consciousness—they have various ways to create a ritual that will embody their desires for transformation.

One line of movement of energy in this regard is known as the tradition of western ceremonial white magic. It creates a structure for transformation that is essentially mental and it intends to connect to the emotional and heart-centered part of the seeking souls that use rituals of white magic by the use of profoundly moving, poignant icons or images, thus making this an essentially mental path to open the heart. It is extremely effective for a certain type of personality.

For many other types of personalities, it is inappropriate. The way a sweat lodge is created moves much more from the heart than from the mind and consequently it is much more accessible as an instrument of transformation than is the creation of a magical ritual. Instead of occult patterns, the circle builds the sweat lodge. They are not drawing symbols in the air. They are using stones, wood and fabric and creating a building for their transformation.

The choice of the heat is an excellent choice for moving seekers out of consensus reality. How does one move the mind from consensus reality? One changes the parameters so that an entity is no longer comfortable. It is the same kind of technique that is used in a fast. Instead of giving up food and thereby becoming uncomfortable, the seeker of a sweat lodge places itself in excessive heat and thereby becomes uncomfortable.

Now, the discomfort by itself would be meaningless. But the mind sets an intention and thereby creates a pattern that is metaphysical in nature and gives meaning to the discomfort.

What the circle is doing as it enters a sweat lodge is telling its deeper self that it is ready and willing not only to seek the truth but to accept and act on the truth. The truth is generally not something that can be expressed in language. The truth that is sought in a sweat lodge, in a magical ceremony, or in any seeking to find the truth of the self, is a truth without words. The truth of the deeper self has no words. It is an essence. It is.

The structure of this particular illusion that you call life in third density is a structure that is designed with many secret places. They are tucked into the folds and the pleats of your everyday. These folds are bursting with truth and many are the entities who have come upon these little pockets of truth and realization in the midst of the most mundane and everyday chores. Usually, however, the seeking soul must alert itself as to how serious it really is about accelerating the pace of its own spiritual evolution. And that is the basic function of a sweat lodge.

Indeed it is very true, my brother, that there is a death and a rebirth involved when this ritual is done correctly. There is that giving of the self to the heat, knowing that the heat will destroy and burn away all the dross and the chaff of the being, leaving only the shining, glowing, glorious essence of unconditional love. That is the truth of your nature.

The problem of everyday life is that it so blocks your senses with detail that you cannot find your way to the truth of your being. It is well, in whatever way seems good to you, to form these intentions to grow and then to create a structure that will manifest that intention and alert your deeper nature to your seriousness.

Any time that a group of people create an event that is metaphysical in nature and focused upon the Creator, that event does indeed have an impact upon the environment around it. To the creation—to the trees, the wind, the Earth itself, and the sunlight—all is one. You are dancing with them. There is no sense of separation.

So naturally, when a group event occurs that has a profound effect, such as yours did within the group of which you are a part, that process of energy sharing and energy expenditure was taken out and made part of the dance of the land, the sky, the elements, and the flora and the fauna of Gaia in that local area in which you offered your ritual.

We are those of Q'uo, and would ask the one known as Jim if there are parts of this query to which we did not respond at this time?

Jim: Was there any unseen help that was present during the ceremony?

We are those of Q'uo, and are aware of your query. My brother, there is always unseen help, and that is not simply when there is a sweat lodge. There is unseen help in every breath you take. It is said in your holy works that the Creator knows when a sparrow falls. This is true; this is abundantly true. For the Creator is everything that there is. It is a system of reportage that is unparalleled.

If the Creator is in all parts of the creation, how shall It not know all of the rhythms and rightnesses of the patterns of the dance of creation?

As to what types of unseen help that you have there, we would ask you to consider all of the various kinds of help which are available in creation. There are the forces of nature that were contacted and alerted by the ceremony of the sweat lodge. Many of those energies you call devic were dancing with you at that time.

(Side one of tape ends.)

(Carla channeling)

There are those energies of the primeval land as it existed at the beginning of its time and those entities who lived upon that land when the land was new and of whom you and your kind are descendants. They were as elder brothers, standing like trees about you, a forest of witnesses.

There was the guidance system of each of those present. And there was the higher self of the group as it is beginning to form, that higher self that is formed of the higher selves of all in the group. And yet in that gathering of higher selves, another entity is born that is a resource for the entire group, and, indeed, much more than the sum of the parts.

And because there are those in the group who come from elsewhere, there is the family connection to the social memory complex from that culture which was left in order that the wanderer might come to Earth and serve as a light bringer at this time.

So, my brother, there was a host of witnesses and there always will be, not only for positive things but for negative things and all things in between. Whatever you do in the manifested world attracts the attention of those unseen energies that are complementary to or attracted by that vibration which you are exuding at the moment.

May we ask if there is a final query at this time?

Jim: What effect did the ceremony have upon the land on which the lodge was built?

We are those of Q'uo, and are aware of your query, my brother. We addressed this partially, previously, when we stated that whenever entities create a change in their consciousness, it also creates a corresponding change in the environment around them. Let us simply say that, as you were recreated, so the Earth around you was recreated as well and received the blessing that you received of new life, new hope, and new awareness.

We find that this instrument's energy wanes and so we would take our leave of this instrument and this group, thanking you once again for the privilege of this conversation and the beauty of your beings. We leave you in the love and in the light of the one infinite Creator. We are known to you as those of Q'uo. Adonai. Adonai. ❧

L/L Research

L/L Research is a subsidiary of Rock Creek Research & Development Laboratories, Inc.

P.O. Box 5195
Louisville, KY 40255-0195

www.llresearch.org

Rock Creek is a non-profit corporation dedicated to discovering and sharing information which may aid in the spiritual evolution of humankind.

ABOUT THE CONTENTS OF THIS TRANSCRIPT: This telepathic channeling has been taken from transcriptions of the weekly study and meditation meetings of the Rock Creek Research & Development Laboratories and L/L Research. It is offered in the hope that it may be useful to you. As the Confederation entities always make a point of saying, please use your discrimination and judgment in assessing this material. If something rings true to you, fine. If something does not resonate, please leave it behind, for neither we nor those of the Confederation would wish to be a stumbling block for any.

© 2009 L/L Research

Sunday Meditation
October 8, 2006

Group question: The question this week has to do with balancing our energy centers and continuing on the path of seeking when it seems difficult. When we feel despair, doubt and darkness, it feels like there is really no good reason to continue. Is there some way that the spiritual seeker can even out these high spots and low spots? Is there something that is a signpost of when we're seeking in the right direction? Or should we just wing it and take it as it comes and do the best that we can with seeking and balancing? What could Q'uo tell us in the way of spiritual principles to which we should be attending as we try to balance our energy centers?

(Carla channeling)

We are those of the principle known to you as Q'uo. Greetings in the love and in the light of the one infinite Creator, in Whose service we come to you this day. Thank you for calling us to your circle of seeking. It is our privilege to be so called. We would ask, as always, that you preserve your powers of discrimination in listening to our ideas and thoughts. If they are not for you, please discard them and move on. This will enable us to speak freely without being concerned about infringing upon your free will. We thank you very much for this kind consideration.

We give to this instrument the vision of an open and empty road. The road has a kind of aliveness to it. It almost sings with energy. As you appear on this road, you can feel the energy of it and you know that you are in contact somehow with magic.

This is a theoretical and mystical road, not a road in a location near you. This is a road of energy. That energy, that long and empty road that sings with potential, is the system of chakras that aligns with your physical body and is the form-maker for that physical body. It has enough power in its make-up that healing can be done using this energy and offering to the form-maker body or the chakra body the opportunity to choose a different arrangement of vibrations as the typical chakra setting.

In this vision of the energy body as a road, one cannot see the colors of the chakra centers. And so, perhaps we could place the various [nexuses] of points of energy ingress by saying that here and there along the road are a series of linked power stations. The energy into the red power station, if blocked, will go no further. If unblocked at the red power station, it will move along the road in full and free fashion to the orange-ray chakra power box. And if all is well within that nexus of energy, the energy will move forward freely and fully into the yellow ray. And if indeed that energy is free, it will move into the open heart.

As energy reaches the heart, it undergoes a powerful transfiguration. The center of spiritual work is in opening the heart. It is this point upon the road from which we believe this question most appropriately may be viewed.

First of all, let us complete the description of the chakra system with which this instrument is familiar. The center that is next in this line of power [nexuses] is the blue-ray energy center, in which one practices and begins to be able comfortably to inhabit realms of trust, honesty and communication and the ability to feel true compassion which is blended with wisdom. This creates in the entity working in blue ray a tremendous feeling of safety so that others feel that they can speak their minds without being judged harshly.

The indigo-ray energy center is the next nexus of energy along this road. It is the seat of those who are attempting to find rest from weary searching. It is the chakra in which faith is the characteristic attitude and in which work in consciousness may be done. Once the typical spiritual seeker discovers the possibilities of becoming more advanced spiritually, it begins to set goals for the self. It begins to wish for the self a certain degree of spiritual maturity.

From this expectation of the self comes a wealth of catalyst. The self, judging the self, can sometimes be very harsh, especially if the self is judging the self unfairly or harshly in the first place, so that justice is not part of the judging.

The typical goal, then, is to do work in consciousness, and one plunges into that work desirous of becoming far more aware, far more well realized as an entity, as a soul. However, the energy that flows along this energy road is part of the creation as a whole. It does not start with you or end with you. You are in the flow of it and your energy body takes in energy from the red ray and moves it through all of the chakras, up through the top of the head, and back out towards the infinite Creator in an endless loop of energy that is infinite and eternal.

It is not for lack of life's energy that you shall go through the gateway of death. It is because it is time for your physical vehicle to retire and for you to take on your energy body and move forward as a consciousness and a soul in that body.

However, the physical body is anything but unimportant. The most common error made by those who are attempting to progress spiritually, in our humble opinion, is to attempt to move faster than the physical, the mental, and the emotional organism can move. To the spiritually awakened neophyte, there is a boundless enthusiasm for new techniques that open up the inner world that has now been glanced and that now has become an object of desire. There is the tendency to reach and to push.

We would ask you to consider that you may cease the pushing and the reaching and be more effective because of a lighter, gentler and more patient attitude towards the self that you are asking to move through these hoops. Because in a way, when an entity is beginning to alter his lifestyle to include work with the silence and the attempt to become aware in each passing moment of that moment in its infinity of possibilities, the body, the mind, and the emotions all object.

It was comfortable being spiritually asleep. Now the self is asking the body to sit and do nothing for periods of time in meditation. The body reacts, sometimes violently. There may be feelings of nausea, headaches, rushes of tingling in the body or a feeling that the body is swelling. The body is restless and does not understand what it is being asked to do. It is not looking at anything. It is not doing anything. What's going on?

So, at the very beginning of a practice of meditation, one has to deal with the body itself. Eventually the body will become comfortable sitting quietly in meditation for periods of time. Indeed, the body may eventually come to depend on the rest of these quiet moments and this communion with the divine.

The mental aspect of starting a practice of meditation and awareness can be harsh, also. The usual track is for the mind to find reasons not to practice on a certain day or at a certain hour. Or it may, when you sit down to meditate, conjure up images that are disturbing. This is because, just below the surface of consciousness, there lies a large area of half-digested emotions, feelings and thoughts. When these feelings and thoughts are replicated and repeated in your inner behavior, speaking only of mental thoughts and images, those ideas and thoughts that you have repetitively entertained become thought forms.

And when you go into meditation, these thought forms can rise into your consciousness as shadowy images. If all of your repetitive thoughts be positive, then you shall be greeted by cherubs and angels. If, on the other hand, your repetitive thoughts have been fear-based, then you shall see fearful images. We know of no quicker way to explain to you how important your thoughts are than to share this particular fact.

Feelings of despair, depression and darkness are absolutely necessary to the seeker who wishes to go through the refinery and get that refining fire to cleanse the surrounding dirt from the gems hidden within the ore. Each of you has programmed for yourself times of intense suffering, culminating in various choices. As you approach such difficult times, what really helps to regularize your response is the memory or the remembrance of the gift that this represents. You and your guidance system created this difficult moment. Suffering was expected to be a part of the pattern that would shake you loose enough from old habits of thought that you would be able to perceive options other than those which have been repetitively your experience in the past.

When such suffering comes to you, then, we would encourage a turn of the mind so that the difficulty is embraced and thanked. Once you realize that you have a gift, then you can open it with a feeling of anticipation and an eagerness to see how the highest and best part of you might react.

Despair is often a blockage within the very lowest of chakras but it seldom is as simple as a one-chakra problem. Despair at its heart is a judgment against the self. The entity who is caught in the web of despair looks at the world and sees nothing beautiful. It is unable to get out of the bell jar[24] of an internalized existence. There is no air inside a bell jar. When an entity does not feel that there is any beauty in life, the blockage occurs immediately. The solution is so simple that we are apologetic about offering it. The solution to being in a bell jar of selfhood is to leave the bell jar.

Earlier this weekend, the one known as R took a day and a night to go and soak up the country and the wisdom of the land, the trees, the wind, the sun, and the stars. Talking around the circle this day, this entity spoke of how he has no idea of why it works for him to go into retreat for a day but when he comes back, somehow the land has healed him. And we would say that it is true that there is healing in the land but we would also say that one known as R and the land known as Avalon healed each other.

Getting outside of the bell jar of an internalized consciousness is a very freeing experience and each entity hungers for the ability to escape the self. The solution to such hunger is to start releasing the hold that you have on yourself. What is important to you about your identity? Examine it, because it may be a blockage. Or in the future it may be an occasion for it to be a blockage. When you are concerned about what people think, it stifles that freedom of thought that considers all options.

We have talked mostly about the negative side of a swing from negative to positive to negative and so forth because of the fact that most entities do not object to feeling very positively inspired or ecstatic. However, it is a valid question to ask about the swing between extremes and what that might indicate and how it might be brought back into more of a disciplined and balanced configuration.

To a certain extent, it is perfectly natural for there to be a variance in mood. Whether it is simply part of a natural cycle of living, where some days there is a stronger spirit in one than another or whether other factors are involved, it is natural and normal for entities to cycle from feeling very positively to feeling somewhat negatively and back again.

And we do not believe that this is what the one known as M was asking. She was concerned, we believe, that too much extreme experience in a person's flow indicates that there is perhaps something toxic that needs to be brought into more control. And we would say to the one known as M that it is well to go very gently and quietly in attempting to harness the self. We would encourage an attitude of observation and companionship with the self that is acting out these moods.

Each entity is a complex entity made up of a consciousness that is the observer of the life and various surface parts of the personality shell which behave. The goal of the observer is not necessarily to change the behavior. The goal of the observer is to understand the behavior and to experience the effects of that behavior.

You are not simply the doer. You are the entity that has asked the self to do this or that. You are the critic that observes how you do this or that. You have many roles in terms of how life happens to you, because it is truly a feedback system and it is in that regard that we would encourage the awareness, when you are *in extremis*, that [it] is especially important to

---

[24] bell jar: "A cylindrical glass vessel with a rounded top and an open base, used to protect and display fragile objects or to establish a vacuum or a controlled atmosphere in scientific experiments."

remember to observe and be a companion to that entity that is containing all of those dark and difficult emotions.

When you are good company to yourself, you have a feeling of being far more able to move through the energies that you are experiencing. You are not helpless. You are not a victim. You are an entity observing the sweep of a tremendous storm that is moving through your emotions and your chakras. Your job is to observe and experience, not to judge and not to change anything.

As you observe yourself from a standpoint of unconditional love, you will begin to self-correct the extreme behavior because you will have been able to interrupt the old pattern that acted as a trigger for the despair. We cannot say what that pattern is. It is different for each entity and in each situation. We simply encourage you to note carefully those moments when extreme feelings are triggered.

As you begin to collect data, you will begin to see the pattern of your particular distortion. You'll be able to see more about how you are blocked and where that energy is getting stuck.

One last thought before we leave this subject and that is that it is not particularly helpful to apply the intellect and the powers of analysis to self-examination until you have found that self within you that is loving, insightful and compassionate. Many are the entities who simply feel deep inside themselves that they are not worthy to move beyond a certain point. Be aware that you are worthy. You are a part of the infinite Creator. When you get these feelings that you are not worthy, sit with them, be a companion to them, and bring your spirit home in peace and in love.

When you come into difficult times, see yourself as a person who is broken apart. There has been no iota lost, but you are in pieces. So, gently, the awareness that carries the personality shell walks about and picks up the pieces and then that consciousness that you are waits for time and the Creator to glue it all back together again and make it better than before.

You are tougher than you think, my friends. You are very powerful, magical beings. We honor you. We offer you our love and we leave this question with love, for it is not a question that can be answered fully, perhaps no matter how many times we would attempt to discuss it.

Bringing the self that appears to be the self to the point of meeting the self that has been there all the time is a delicate business. One doesn't want to wipe out the personality. The personality is the interface with the world. On the other hand, one does not want to be that personality when one can be the essential self that is consciousness.

We would ask if there are other queries at this time. We are those of Q'uo.

R: I have a question, Q'uo. I would like to ask if there are many readers of the Law of One books and readers of many of the channelings that you have helped to transmit that try to make a system of seeking and spiritual work out of the various readings. Since you are an outer-entity contact, you are limited by the law of free will and how much detail you can offer. I have always felt that another teacher called Aaron that you have worked with is able to offer greater detail on directions of working with emotions on the personal level. So I wanted to ask if you agree that what Aaron teaches is very compatible with what you are trying to do and if actually those seekers who look for more direction can try to combine those two approaches, Aaron's and yours, or if it is more accurate to say that there is enough guidance inside one's seeking that any outer sort of directions are really not necessary?

We are those of Q'uo, and we believe we understand your query, my brother. We would agree that the one known as Aaron is far more able than we to offer specific information and indeed we have enjoyed each and every communication that we have shared with the one known as Aaron and the one known as Barbara.[25] We would say that it is a help to suggest sources to people that they may find helpful. The only error, my brother, would be if you expected them to heed what you had to say. One drops a seed and one does not look back.

And lastly, we would agree with you that the basic drive towards evolution lies within one. The seeker will, without any prompting whatsoever, eventually come across every piece of information and inspiration that he needs. It is, however, a service to others to keep an ear out for times when you feel

---

[25] Barbara Brodsky, channeling Aaron, and Carla L. Rueckert, channeling Q'uo, have co-channeled a series of sessions together from 1991 to 1996. To find the sessions, you can do a search on the www.llresearch.org site for "The Aaron/Q'uo Dialogues."

that someone has a need concerning which you may offer a helpful thought. It is not an infringement on free will for you to share ideas when asked, it is only inappropriate to expect entities to respond to your thoughts in any particular way. There is a way for everyone and certainly not the same way for any two people.

May we answer you further, my brother?

R: I thank you for that. I think what you are saying is that I have taken something that has been true for me and I try to extrapolate it for a large group, which is not necessarily helpful unless you consider the law of free will and lack of expectation as to how the others would react. Is that correct?

We are those of Q'uo, and that is correct, my brother.

R: I also enjoy that you were able to use what I had said during the sharing before we started channeling. It is a great joy for me to offer something like this so any time you see a thought or experience that you can use that has been mine, feel free to do so.

We are those of Q'uo, and we thank you, my brother.

T: Why is Aaron able to give more specific information than those of Q'uo?

We are those of Q'uo, my brother, and understand your query. The planet upon which you live is not one Earth but many, interpenetrating each other at various levels of fineness of vibration, so that there are actually seven inner Earths to one physical Earth. Entities who live on Earth and have incarnations upon your planet move into the inner planes, the "heaven worlds," upon death, and live in whatever niche they have earned by their vibration.

We searched for a word other than "earned" because it is not a matter of studying hard and passing a test. It is a matter of that absolute honesty of self that your violet ray is. Whatever your violet ray expresses, it will bring you to the appropriate place in the inner planes where everything is vibrating in harmony with your vibration at that time.

Entities move from the inner planes back to incarnation, then back to the inner planes. Sometimes they stay in the inner planes for quite some time and decide not to take incarnation. This is the case with the one known as Aaron. The one known as Aaron describes himself as a former Buddhist monk and because of the fact that he achieved realization when the one known as Barbara stepped in front of him and [defended] him, he vowed to be an inner guide to the one known as Barbara until such time that she also received realization.[26]

This entity has lived on Earth. He has worked and eaten and sweated and died. This entity has a belonging. He is part of the tribe of humankind on planet Earth. Those of a tribal family may speak to each other. They may give advice. They may share any information that they have available. They have the right to interfere with the free will of others of their family.

Those of us in the Confederation of Planets in the Service of the Infinite Creator have not had incarnations on Earth. We are not part of the tribe of humankind on planet Earth. We come from elsewhere. We do not have the right to interfere with your decisions. That is the difference between an inner guide and what this instrument calls an outer source, meaning that it is from elsewhere rather than from inner planes.

May we answer you further, my brother?

T: No, thank you very much.

We thank you, my brother. Is there a final query at this time?

R: I have one more question, Q'uo. When I try to imagine Earth in seven interpenetrating layers, and then I add inner and outer planes, are you talking about inner and outer planes for those seven different Earths? And why is the inner plane called "inner" and the outer "outer"?

We are those of Q'uo, and are aware of your query, my brother. The term "inner planes" is misleading in that the inner planes are planes in time/space or the metaphysical world as opposed to space/time such as your planet is with solid rock and water and so forth. Therefore, the inner planes do not have a physical location except tangentially because they belong to the planet Earth. This instrument calls them inner planes because she has read other writings that also call them inner planes and also because they are inside you.

(Side one of tape ends.)

---

[26] Aaron says that the incarnation 500 years ago was his last physical incarnation.

(Carla channeling)

They are not inside creation. You are the center of a consciousness that is local and is also non-local. The locality of the consciousness is that connection with the physical body that happened at some point between conception and a few weeks after birth.

May we answer you further, my brother? We are those of Q'uo.

R: You have answered the second part of my question and that was very illuminating. The other part is this. When I think of inner and outer planes I think of them being somehow related to the seven Earths that were spoken of during this channeling and I try to create a visual image for myself to see what it looks like. I think you are saying that these planes exist in time/space so that there is no physical equivalent in space/time, and that inner and outer are simply words that were chosen to point particular aspects or qualities of these planes rather than their location. Is that correct?

We are those of Q'uo, and we thank the one known as R for this question. My brother, you are correct in realizing that these heaven worlds do not have a physical location. They do have an arrangement in orders of magnitude, perhaps we would say, so they nest together without disturbing each other. There is in each focus of the Creator, which is you and each other human being upon your planet, a gateway into those inner planes. And again it is one of those situations where, unless you are very, very experienced and sophisticated, if you are able to penetrate the gateway and move into the inner planes, you will pretty automatically be taken to the location which matches your needs or your desires the most.

The solution of each of the seven inner planes being connected to a corresponding locality is not correct, as far as we are aware of the situation. All of the inner planes are connected back into the one physical locality of the influence of planet Earth.

Does this answer your query, my brother, or would you like to follow up? We are those of Q'uo.

R: No, thank you, Q'uo. It does answer my question. And even though this is asking about the "furniture of heaven," I thank you for indulging my curiosity.

We are those of Q'uo, my brother, and we are most glad to do what we can.

Dear ones, it has been a most enjoyable time. This instrument's energy is truly running out and we shall have to take our leave soon. But we do wish to share with you the joy that we feel in your beautiful presence. Thank you again for this experience of a shared meditation and a sacred time together. The energy exchange we have had with you has been most blessed. We leave you in the love and in the light of the one infinite Creator. Adonai. Adonai. ☥

L/L Research

L/L Research is a subsidiary of Rock Creek Research & Development Laboratories, Inc.

P.O. Box 5195
Louisville, KY 40255-0195

www.llresearch.org

Rock Creek is a non-profit corporation dedicated to discovering and sharing information which may aid in the spiritual evolution of humankind.

ABOUT THE CONTENTS OF THIS TRANSCRIPT: This telepathic channeling has been taken from transcriptions of the weekly study and meditation meetings of the Rock Creek Research & Development Laboratories and L/L Research. It is offered in the hope that it may be useful to you. As the Confederation entities always make a point of saying, please use your discrimination and judgment in assessing this material. If something rings true to you, fine. If something does not resonate, please leave it behind, for neither we nor those of the Confederation would wish to be a stumbling block for any.

© 2009 L/L Research

Sunday Meditation
November 12, 2006

M: Ever since 9/11, I've been concerned that this planet may be heading towards a catastrophic war. I feel a sense of failure, helplessness and hopelessness. I feel myself heading towards complete despair. I'm beginning to question whether all is well with the birthing of fourth-density Earth. Has the planetary experiment gone awry? If so, what spiritual principles are involved in transmuting despair into hope and doubt into encouragement?

(Carla channeling)

We are those known to you as the principle of Q'uo. Greetings in the love and in the light of the one infinite Creator, in Whose service we come to you this day. Thank you for calling us to your circle of seeking. It is a great privilege to share in your meditation.

As always, we would ask your kind consideration in being very careful what thoughts of ours you use as you move through thinking about your spiritual process. Please disregard any thought that we offer that is not immediately helpful to you. We would not wish to be a stumbling block before you. We thank you for that consideration, for it allows us to speak freely without being concerned that we might infringe upon your free will. We are emphatically not authority figures but rather travelers with you upon a certain kind of path that goes on forever.

This day you have asked about feelings that you have about the society and culture in which you live and about the government which rules your particular part of the world. You express feelings of deep concern, despair and hopelessness. You express a feeling that you are not able to help the situation by anything that you can do. And you ask what the spiritual principles are in dealing with these thoughts and in looking for ways to transform the inner landscape of your thoughts.

My sister, we thank you for this query. Our response must be somewhat indirect as we cannot make a frontal approach to your query. We are those who come on a vibration of unconditional love. Our contact, and our type of contact in general, does not have the facility with detailed, earthly information of a practical nature that, say, an inner-planes entity might have. It is not our place to interfere with the governance or the affairs in general of planet Earth.

For good information on how to affect your government, your politics, your economics, or your society in general by practical and worldly means, we would strongly suggest that you inquire from other sources than we. We are a carefully tuned contact that focuses upon spiritual principles. From that level, my sister, we may answer you, but it is perhaps an answer other than you would have wished.

And for that we can only say that our ability to speak through this instrument is based upon her preserving a certain tuning. Were she to slip out of this tuning range, we would be unable to continue offering her information. However, she might be able to continue receiving information from an entity of a negative nature that was able to ape or imitate the vibration of those of the Q'uo group.

We say these things to you so that you will understand if we do not roll up our sleeves and dig into the cleaning up of planet Earth. Indeed, my sister, we do not see that picture. Let us talk a bit about what we do see upon your planet at this time.

Firstly, you were concerned that there may be a conflagration caused by humans setting off bombs in a nuclear holocaust that would strip the planet of its atmosphere or, were it not so horrendous a conflagration, would simply cloud the atmosphere so that life upon planet Earth would become extinct from its inability to function in the new environment.

There are many peoples upon your planet who have access to such bombs and weapons of mass destruction and there are more who have the capacity to acquire them if they see the need. Therefore, my sister, your concern is valid. What shall you do then with that concern?

This instrument recently read an article which described an Hawaiian healing technique called oponopono.[27] In this healing technique, the healer never touches the patient and may not even see the patient. He may simply be told about the patient. This healing technique is intended to be used in healing mental illness, emotional distress and the criminal mentality. The healer receives all the information concerning the patient. He then looks within to discover that condition within himself. When he has found that condition within himself, he sets about healing that condition within himself. When he has healed himself, quite often the prisoner or mental patient is found to require no more medication or to have been healed of criminal tendencies.

The spiritual principle that is behind this healing technique is the very basic principle of unity. All things are one. It is interesting that we see all of you, individually and collectively, as enormously greater in substance than any other details of your Earthly environment whereas you see yourself as the smallest portion of an environment that towers above you, beneath you, and on all sides of you, making you insignificant, helpless, hopeless and full of despair.

We would encourage those who wish to make a difference on planet Earth to gaze at the planetary dysfunction and then to internalize that gaze and find the dysfunction within. It is not difficult for most humans to do. Both the one known as J and the one known as T were talking *(during the round-robin discussion that typically precedes a Sunday Meditation)* about how easy it is to move from a mental and emotional attitude of unconditional love to an attitude of irritation and hostility when the catalyst of an unhappy and abrasive person breaks into the peaceful world of home and family.

What dysfunction is there in the world this day that might lead to the self-destructive and utterly irrational decision to set off nuclear bombs? What is that distortion but the belief that there is separation between people? How often, my sister, do you think that you will be able to work on healing that sense of separation between yourself and others that you see in the world's dysfunction?

We ask you to realize that we are speaking on the level of a causality that is far beyond the causality of worldly things. We are not saying that if you heal your sense of separation today, the world will change tomorrow. We are saying that when individuals who belong to the tribe of humankind choose one, upon another, upon another, to serve the love and the light and to refrain from fear, that attitude will spread. That emotional safety net will begin to spread out. And the more people that are doing this kind of work within themselves, the more the environment will shift on the inner planes in such a way that those who come after you will be able to do this work in consciousness more and more easily.

It is understandable that entities gazing upon the world scene would feel helpless, hopeless and despairing. Certainly, my sister, we, too, see the broken bodies of the children and other innocents carelessly killed by those who do not see that they and their brothers are one. We do not intend to downplay or shrug off the suffering of the world.

At the same time, we do see from a point of view which encompasses a larger pattern than you can see from within incarnation.

The fourth density is being born normally and in a healthy way. The efforts of many groups, including

---

[27] Two good web sites for learning more about this healing technique are www.hooponopono.org and http://tribes.tribe.net/hooponopono.

this one through whom we speak this day, have spoken of light and love and the word has been passed, more than perhaps you might realize, at the grass-roots level, at the level of indigenous peoples; and at the level in civilized worlds of the first fumblings and reachings for something that has substance.

We see the world waking up to love. We see it beginning to identify the hunger that it has. We see it beginning to respond, love being reflected in love. There is great hope at that grass-roots level, below the radar of politics and empire.

We cannot tell you not to be concerned about politics, society, economics and culture. Depending upon your own judgment and your own free will, we encourage you and all entities to follow your heart, to define those gifts that you might feel to share with your society and your culture that might make it better. This is your free will and your good work to do if you wish it. What we are here to speak with you concerning is something far simpler and at the same time something far greater.

We come to tell you a story about love: love unconditional, love unlimited, love that creates and destroys. It is a simple concept: this one great original Thought of unconditional love creating the universe in order to know more about Itself.

If you can look at your experience in the context of the Creator's desire to gather experience and information about Itself, then you will see that the Creator is perfectly happy with you whatever you are doing and especially delighted with you when you are attempting to know yourself at an ever deeper level.

If a third-density experience ends not with a bang but with a whimper by humanity polluting its air and its water until it can no longer find a way to live, this will not overly trouble the Creator, for the Creator is gathering the information about the entire range of experience that is had by this population or tribe of humanity on the third planet from your sun. Indeed, if you were to destroy your planet, as has been done elsewhere in this solar system, on Mars, for instance, the Creator would still feel that it had received good information from you. Consequently, to the Creator you basically can do no wrong as long as you are authentically acting and gaining experience.

Now, to your own consciousness and conscience, you have much more accountability. For you sent yourself forth into incarnation with a plan. And there is a part of you that is hoping day by day, as you go through your entire life, that you are on track with your mission, your plan, and your purpose.

There are those who attempt to nail down the nature of that plan. Yet you as a spirit did not plan specific activities. You planned opportunities and relationships. Those are the keys.

When you are tempted to feel helpless, hopeless and despairing, we would encourage you to remember that you do not need to relate to some idea of the Creator and please the Creator. Neither do you need to relate to the world and in some way please the world. In terms of your spiritual work, you have only yourself to please.

When you see before you your own statement, "I feel helpless; I feel hopeless; I feel despair," how [do you think] your highest and best self would respond to that complaint?

You see, my sister, the answers lie within you already. By merely encouraging your own process a bit, we believe you may see the answers flowing into place before you.

You are not helpless. You are a person of infinite power.

You are not hopeless, unless you choose to take that pose and stand as a statue, ignoring the movements of life.

You may well be despairing because you have allowed yourself to identify the illusion as the realest portion of your life. In actuality, in terms of spiritual evolution, that which occurs outside of your mind is food for the mill. The pay dirt of spiritual seeking lies not in circumstances but in how you choose to respond to them.

There are always reasons to despair. There are always reasons to be intimidated. That which this instrument calls the loyal opposition would be delighted to see entities give up those faculties of hope and faith that make people unreasonably optimistic.

We, on the other hand, would encourage you to see that if you choose to stand knowing who you are, your feet planted upon the soil of your life and your experience and your arms stretched in praise and thanksgiving to the Creator of all things, you are a person of great power.

If you so choose to adopt and embrace faith, no suffering can break you, for you choose the truth and all else is illusion.

If you choose hope, those wings shall fly you where you need to go.

For each entity, morale and attitude are a matter of choice. There is no limitation which can keep an entity from grooming and settling his own mind and his own heart along the lines of peace and joy and thankfulness if he so desires to seek those levels of being within himself. And, my sister, as each entity does these things, so the world will change.

May we ask if there is another query at this time?

M: We see a lot of lies and corruption in government in these times. What spiritual principles are involved in holding a vision of peace in the face of rampant corruption?

We are those of the Q'uo, and are aware of your query, my sister. There is a saying among your people, "Power corrupts and absolute power corrupts absolutely." This tends to be a true statement.

You may see power in one of two ways. You may see power as coming from the outside in or you may see power coming from the inside out.

The power that comes from the outside in is the power of government and authority, the usual suspects in your world. There are many ways in which people can be persecuted by authority figures. You have seen evidence of many of these kinds of persecution. You recoil before the stink of empire. It is understandable that you would see this power as being very vast and hanging over you somehow. This is the way of things upon the level of consensus reality.

We are witnesses to another kind of power. It is not the power that changes governments or topples armies. It is not a power that has weaponry or clever disguises or plans and protocols.

The power that comes from the inside out is the power, firstly, of knowing who you are and, secondly, of emptying out the content of who you are to the extent that you are able to follow the changing currents and eddies of the present moment.

We would encourage you to see yourself as a lighthouse. The lighthouse lights its lamp and keeps its windows transparent. It gives to that lamp the power to turn in endless circles, so that those coming in from the open water may see the rocks and avoid them and come to a safe harbor. A spiritual lighthouse has its own kind of light and when you become aware of the power of your beingness, you may, if you wish, consciously become that kind of lighthouse that radiates love and light into the spiritual space around you.

All the speaking that you might do is not one-thousandth as powerful as the focus of your very nature when it is focused upon unconditional love. Let your answer to fear be an openhearted, sunny, carefree, joyous, confident feeling of love and rightness. Develop that environment within yourself: lightening up, looking for the laughter, looking for the fun.

And although the world may seem to wag on as before, no better and no worse, do not be deceived. What you do within the precincts of your own sacred heart and mind affects your world. Please know, my sister, that people by the millions are asking these questions, coming to this same kind of conclusion and taking up the power that is theirs by spiritual birthright.

May we ask if there is another query at this time? We are those of Q'uo.

M: I am concerned that people on planet Earth do not have good information and that their ignorance could jeopardize the entire planet. Ra said of those unawakened beings in their third-density experience that, "To those who wish to sleep we could only offer those comforts designed for the sleeping." What if Earth's sleepers endangered the entire planet by creating the conditions which could precipitate nuclear war by failing to counteract the control that the service-to-self leadership exercises on such a wide and pervasive scale?

We are those of Q'uo, and are aware of your query, my sister. We have no pat answer for you in this wise except to assure you that there are avenues of information available globally to those civilized entities who are equipped with electricity and computers. The amount of information available to those who have access to your internet is astronomical.

The information is available for those who seek it. The Earth is not being threatened by those who do not seek. The patterns which present themselves to your eyes at this time are strong patterns that have repeated within your history quite a few times. They are patterns of empire: the gathering of resources, the subjugation of peoples, and the turn of the wheel, so that the conqueror becomes the conquered, and another world balance of power is set up. This wheel has turned before. It shall turn again. We would suggest, my sister, that knowledge is not the problem. Indeed, there is only a problem within the illusion.

It is difficult to communicate in words how helpful it is to release worry and concern. These energies are energies of exhausting power. They rob you of your natural optimism and confidence. It may seem that we are suggesting that you turn your back on the facts and dwell in an ivory tower. We do not intend to suggest this. We intend rather to suggest that you love the world and accept it as it is.

Once you have chosen that fundamental attitude of loving the world no matter what, then it is not going to unbalance you to investigate as much as you wish into the structures of politics, economics, social living, culture and the formation of myth. Learn all that you can.

Absorb and consider and mull over information as long as you wish, as long as you are able to do this within the context of loving that which you understand ever better. Understanding is a positive thing. When you gather information so that you can find more things about which to worry, then you have begun to take the world too seriously.

May we ask if there is another query at this time?

M: I want to alert people to the information they don't have, but I am concerned about preserving their free will. What spiritual principles are involved in desiring to share information which may open their eyes to the reality of the planetary game without a prior request to do so?

We are those of Q'uo, and are aware of your query, my sister. The spiritual principle involved in communication of ideas is what this instrument would call the Johnny Appleseed Principle. All thoughts that you feel are helpful and useful for others remain so only in your own mind, just as other people may tell you all manner of things which you do not find relevant or interesting. So you may talk until you are, as this instrument would say, blue in the face without ever making sense to anyone else or doing them any good.

Spiritual information is sensitive to context and environment. You cannot simply take the world by the throat and say, "Listen to me. I have information that is helpful." Those who force information on others are acting in a way that they feel is helpful, yet, in effect, it is service to self, for they are teaching what they believe is good for you without regard to what you think about it or how you react to it.

The Johnny Appleseed Principle is one of dropping seeds. This instrument, for instance, and the research group with which she is associated, maintains a website with thousands of transcripts and speeches that this instrument has created through her work throughout several decades. It lies there, waiting to be found by those who have a spiritual impulse. Many, many other beautiful and inspiring sources of information also lie waiting. There is no shortage of information.

We ask you to rest your concern and internalize that desire to help so that you see the very living of your life as an emblem and a symbol of the living of the life of the world.

Consciousness is not yours alone. You share the innermost identity of yourself with all that there is. Walk, my sister, out of the small rooms and dim hallways of fear and come out into the outdoors of wind and water and fire and earth.

Come from the local to the infinite.

Come from the world of detail to the world of the four directions, the elements, and the powers.

Come to the great cross of life: the vertical reach to the infinite; the horizontal reach within incarnation to loving and being loved.

And know that it is in the little things that you shall create a new heaven and a new Earth.

May you do each little thing as if it were a great honor and privilege!

May you shine as the lighthouse you are!

May we ask if there is another query at this time?

Jim: Not from here.

If there is no further query, then we shall leave this group and this instrument in the love and in the light of the one infinite Creator. Adonai. Adonai. ❧

Special Meditation
November 16, 2006

Question from W: I believe that my child is an indigo child. Can you confirm this for me?

(Carla channeling)

We are those known to you as the principle of Q'uo. Greetings in the love and in the light of the one infinite Creator, in Whose name and service we come to be with your circle of seeking this day. Thank you for the privilege of being called to this circle. We are very glad to be able to respond to the queries of the one known as W.

As always, however, before we begin, we would ask, not only of him but of all those who may read or listen to this session, that you use your powers of discrimination in deciding which of our thoughts you wish to consider further. Look for resonance and that feeling of a half-recognized truth that you know is for you. If you do not feel that resonance, then please leave our thoughts behind. We thank you for this discrimination as it will allow us to speak our thoughts freely without being concerned for infringement upon anyone's free will.

My brother, we may confirm that your child is an indigo child. May we ask if there is further query? We are those of Q'uo.

W: The main question is, I'm seeking to understand the dynamics involved in relating to my indigo child. It seems to me that my child has such a powerful psychic link to me that even slight variations in my mood and in my ability to tolerate frustration are reflected in my son's sometimes challenging moods of anger and frustration. Is this an accurate perception? If so, are there metaphors, fields of inquiry, images, analogies or spiritual principles which come into play in this developing relationship, which will help me experience this relationship and treat my son in the most loving and skillful way?

(Carla channeling)

We are those of Q'uo, and are aware of your query, my brother. In some ways, my brother, the image that comes to mind is the image of Daedalus and his son, Icarus.[28] When you ask about the relationship between yourself and your son, and the tight interconnectedness of your energies, the myth of Daedalus and Icarus comes to mind.

In that particular story, the son was so ambitious that his father created for him wings to fly, but he flew too close to the sun and thusly fell back to Earth, burned to a cinder. You are Daedalus, hoping to help your son not to soar too high or to crash too low. We do not by this, however, [mean] to suggest that you are a policeman. Indeed, your sense of being very connected with your son is accurate.

---

[28] This Greek myth is told on this web site: http://thanasis.com/icarus.htm. It is a classic story of a father helping his son to fly high while attempting to guard against his flying too high. Icarus' wings were made of wax, and flying too close to the sun melted them.

The indigo child is a third-generation wanderer, if you would wish to use the language or terminology with which this instrument has some familiarity.

The first generation of wanderers was made up of those such as this instrument, which responded to the call of Earth by coming from a higher density to move into incarnation and share the love and the light of the one infinite Creator with those of this planet in an attempt to shift the planetary energies more towards the light.

The second generation of wanderers was comprised of those who also were interested in helping planet Earth. However, this second generation of wanderers is characterized by more confidence than the first generation of wanderers, but also less of a dedication of service to others in that their chief motivation for coming into incarnation at this latter hour of your third density was to use the boot camp like atmosphere of planet Earth to do what they would consider "quick and dirty work" in adjusting the balance of their energies between love and wisdom. For some, this means emphasizing the heart and the opening [of] the heart. For others who already have their hearts opened, it means emphasizing wisdom and asking the open heart to receive that highest and best self's wisdom which comes from guidance and informs loving compassion in such a way that there is equanimity to match the passion of your dedication to service.

The third generation of wanderers is made up of what this instrument and many others call the indigo children. There are many other terms for these children. However, in general, they are the first graduates in this harvest from the third density of planet Earth. These souls have moved through the gates into larger life. They have dropped their physical bodies and entered into a healing process with their guidance and with all of those forces which protect and nurture entities in the inner planes who are moving through the processes of death and rebirth. Further, they have moved through the steps of light and have passed their graduation test. These are fourth-density wanderers, whose first act, upon choosing what would please them the most to do next, was to return to their beloved home planet in order to assist not only the people of planet Earth, but also, and perhaps more principally, the planet itself.

These entities are characterized by a thinner veil, which enables them to remember more about who they are and why they are here. The sense of mission or destiny is very common in third-generation wanderers. Your son and all of the indigo children like him are people who, when they have achieved a mental and emotional maturity to match their spiritual gifts, will be far tougher by nature than many among your people, able to deal with difficult times and situations and able to absorb rapid change. These abilities are appropriate for these indigo children. However, there are side effects to being built in such a way. These side effects are those times of difficulty and difficult emotions upon which you have remarked.

In dealing with indigo children—and indeed, most of those being born into your Earth at this time are indigo children—it is well to keep in mind that these entities, though wise in their way, are indeed children. There is as much need in them as in any other child for good, stable, consistent guidance. However, you are also correct in noting the extreme interrelatedness of yourself and your son in the terms of the motion and rhythm of your moods and the behavior that stems from such moods.

We would ask you to imagine a rolling sea. The storm lashes the top of the sea and drives the winds onto shore, bringing waves and storm in their wake. Below the surface of that stormy water lie riptides that tend to pull entities away from their moorings and out to sea. Beneath that level there lie calm waters: stable, ancient and beautiful.

It is a naturally stormy atmosphere in the everyday of planet Earth for most people. Unless entities are working especially carefully to stay in the present moment at all times, the flow of living includes many abrupt stops and hasty turns, many changes of attitude, and many alterations in the flow of what is happening which call forth many new and unexpected emotions.

We are not suggesting that you alter this natural run of stormy weather in the everyday of your and your son's existence. What we would suggest is not so much a metaphor as a kind of game. We ask that you see your energies and your son's energies as part of a dance. You and your son are creating this dance. You are dancing a kind of mirror dance. What you do, he imitates, and what he does, you imitate.

When you and he are doing loving and positive things, the dance is a happy dance, or so it seems to your judgment. When there is challenge, upset and hostility, then it seems to be an unhappy dance. However, in order to play your game more skillfully, we would ask you not to label your various moods as good or bad. We would ask you not to label the exchanges of mood between you and your child as good or bad. Rather, we would ask you to see the whole of the pattern as an ongoing dance.

In a dance, my brother, there are many missed steps. This does not mean that the music stops playing or that you have in some way failed to dance properly. Rather, we encourage you to dance with lightness of heart and with as much clarity of observation of which you are capable at any time.

This is a game in which attention to detail is very helpful. As you said, even in the smallest things, your son and you seem psychically connected. Indeed, all entities have this psychic connection. In the case of indigo children, however, there is allowable more awareness to be brought into the incarnation. So, such children are often much more sensitive and aware of their parents' moods and unspoken feelings than would have been children of days gone by, shall we say.

It is not that you are responsible for smoothing out your son's moods, any more than your son is responsible for smoothing out your moods. It is that you are presently engaged in an intensely intimate relationship with an entity whose powers are greater than his ability to control those powers or even to understand them or be able in any way to express them. When a child has trouble expressing all that is within him, he may become very frustrated, and this is often the case with an indigo child.

We are not encouraging you to find some method of teaching this child. On the other hand, we would ask you to be quite responsive to any questions or comments shared by the child with you. Such expressions are your invitation to tell your stories, share your wisdom, and embrace the child in an atmosphere of acceptance and love.

Above all, my brother, we would ask you to explore the concept that you and your child are one and that, indeed, the mirror that the child holds up to you enables you to work upon yourself. This is the attitude that will serve your child and you the very best. When you use the mirror, use it to work on yourself. See what is there, find it within yourself, and work upon that energy in yourself.

Your child will feel that you are doing spiritual work responsibly. He may not consciously or intellectually be able to express this understanding, but as you stand calmly and with sureness upon the ground of your own being and do the work that has come to you to do, your child will see and feel that there is a stable and supportive atmosphere which accepts him and accepts the images that he is offering. Therefore, as you do this work, you present to your child a mirror of a certain kind. In that mirror, the child will see positive issues, not preached to him but expressed to him by the unspoken manifestation of silent beingness.

As you work upon yourself, you shall be creating for your child the best possible supportive structure. As you accept yourself, your son will feel accepted. As you see the unevenesses within you and accept them, so your child will feel accepted in his unevenness.

There is no question but that, occasionally, if a child is disrupting the family, and the child cannot be coaxed into altering his behavior, the child must be shown the limits of acceptable behavior. You may choose your own way of doing this. We give to this instrument the picture of her disciplining her cats. Her cats cannot understand language, but they can understand the word "no" connected with water. Therefore, the cat can be trained to avoid behavior that will elicit the word "no" and the wetting.[29] We do not know how you would emphasize that the word "no" occasionally has a firm and limiting meaning but we do encourage you to think carefully and speak with your mate concerning the rules of the house, so that there is a stable and consistent set of limits beyond which behavior is not acceptable.

This instrument calls removing a child from an environment for discipline a "time-out." We would suggest that time-outs are appropriate. Also appropriate are any other means of non-violent expression that underlines the word "no" without doing violence or physical harm. Sometimes, it seems a cruel thing to set a limit. However, it is helpful in terms of the incarnational experience of a child that, from the beginning, the child is aware that, indeed, there are limits and that there is not a

---

[29] The Rueckert-McCartys keep spray bottles of water handy at appropriate places in the house for such discipline. They are filled only with water, so the cats never get hurt.

chaotic existence with no meaning, but rather, a meaningful existence with order, ideals, peace and beauty. If you do not give your child a certain sense of limits and order, the child will be left in chaos, not knowing how to value his feelings, his thoughts, and his dreams.

As we finish answering this query, we look at that word "dream." You have dreams, my brother, and so does your child. You are those who dream together. And so are we all. But you and your child have special dreams known only to you. Forget all except loving, being loved, and sharing your dreams.

Let imagination wing its way through your relationship with your child. Let your creativity blossom as you surround this child with the essence of your unspoken love. People his kingdom with your fairies and gnomes and archangels to keep him safe. These are all the creatures of your honest and heartfelt love, and they will be good companions for your child.

May we ask if there is another query at this time?

W: I believe the viability to act as a loving parent to a son depends on how open my heart is to love. My intention is to use this relationship as an opportunity to know myself and to expand my capacity for forgiveness, levity, compassion, faith and healing. Which archetypes would you suggest which might clear up all the dynamics that work within my family, especially in relation to my son?

(Carla channeling)

We are those of the Q'uo, and are aware of the query, my brother. The archetypal energies surrounding your relationship with your son are those energies between the master and the pupil. You are teach/learner and your son is learn/teacher. Although your son's gifts are astonishing in some ways, they are not developed. You are that entity who has a spiritual maturity which has been hard won.

It is fortunate, my brother, that life has not been able to dim your light. It has wearied you, and we see in you a desire not to be so weary. But it has not caused you to lose faith or to relinquish your dreams. Therefore, you are a good master, a good teach/learner, for your child. Rather than holding to the dynamics of teacher and student, however, we would encourage you to be open to the subtleties of the teach/teaching's becoming learn/teaching and vice versa, for your child has things to teach you as well as your having things to teach him.

You stand for your child in some ways as an agent of the unconscious. Your child is not born knowing which way to move in terms of metaphysical principles. Therefore, allow the things around you—your books, your papers, those items that you love—to be meaningful to your child as well as to you. Invest time in responding to even minor questions, knowing that your child's unevenness of personality will cause him to move at things roundabout and in a serpentine and indirect fashion. Move with those energies. Operate with him in his rambling so that you may come with him to a place which you have not expected.

He is seeking in a way which moves from level to level. Therefore, your beingness rather than your behavior is going to help him the most. This, as you said, will cause you again and again to move from the doing to the being. It is not what you do with your child that matters nearly as much as your attention to your own state of awareness. Are you aware, conscious and alert to the now? Or are you caught up in what the one known as Eckhart called "content"?[30] Move always from content to essence, from detail to essence, from facts and this and that to essence. It will often seem to be an impractical move. But in terms of helping both you and your child to be refined by the fire of planet Earth's atmosphere of learning, it is the most skillful choice.

Is there a further query, my brother?

W: My son has issues due to being different from his classmates. I would like to shore up his self-esteem but I am concerned about interfering with his free will. Should I think about setting the stage for his actions on planet Earth when he is grown? What are my chief spiritual concerns in raising my son well?

(Carla channeling)

We are those of the Q'uo, and we are aware of your query, my brother. Your chief spiritual concern in dealing with any relationship is to bring to that relationship your true self. Thusly, we move the energy back from "what shall you do with another" to the consideration of "how shall you be." How shall you create an atmosphere that will provide you

---

[30] The Q'uo are referring to the writing of Eckhart Tolle in his book, *New Earth*.

with a good environment for pursuing your spiritual process?

We would suggest—as we often have suggested before for others, my brother, so it is not personal to you—that there be a daily period of silence that is observed by you in a consistent manner. We suggest the circadian[31] rhythm because your body has that daily rhythm. If you make a habit of seeking the silence at the same general time each day, within the first month of your making such a habit, your body will move through all of its objections [to] the sitting or the resting in the silence that it can throw up, and it will begin to be able to rest in the silence. It takes a certain amount of training simply to quiet the body so that it does not feel threatened by sitting without doing anything, whether watching the television, listening to the radio, or something else.

When there is no content, the mind and the body become anxious. It takes time to create a habit of solitary silence so that your body welcomes it, expects it, and is not disturbed by it. Once you have trained your body, your mind, and your emotions so that you are able to sit in the silence without interference from them on the gross level of twitching, developing symptoms of headaches, and so forth, then you have the chance, at last, to rest in that powerful silence that offers you what words never can. The love and the light of the one infinite Creator are completely expressed within the silence.

To try to translate that silent expression into voice, words, music, poetry of any kind, is tremendously difficult. The easiest way to approach the Creator is through unexplained, unmanifested silence. Let that be a part of your being, and that shall, in time, place you in a state of mind which is far more likely to alert you when you have gone away from the present moment and have become distracted by detail.

You cannot hope to be undistracted. No entity in third density is expected to remain undistracted. The purpose of incarnation is consistently and cyclically to be distracted. Each distraction teaches you about yourself and who you think you are as opposed to who you are. Work on that, and that shall be the safe place for your child. As he sees you in praise, meditation, in prayer each day, he shall know that there is more to this life than the play, the work, and the sleeping. He shall see for his own self, without being taught a word, that those entities whom he values, value spiritual life and seek it out. And so he will be curious as well, for children, by nature, are imitative. By your being, by your seeking, you shall offer him the opportunity to see how that tune goes, and he can try that out. Children try things out that they see and work with them in their own way and in their own time.

We would suggest that you always respond to questions, but that you do not attempt to teach unless questions are asked. The times will come, as you love and care for your child, when it will be natural for him to ask along the lines of this or that spiritual concern. At that time, my brother, share your truth as straightforwardly and lovingly as you know how, knowing that there are many mistakes but that love wins through.

We would ask if there is another query at this time?

W: Sometimes, I believe that I am a wanderer. Can you confirm this, please?

We are those of Q'uo, my brother, and we are aware of your query. We can confirm, my brother, that you are a wanderer. Is there a further query at this time?

W: I feel called to manifest inspirational, devotional music. Sometimes I find that I feel it is appropriate to express pure sound with music instead of words. Could you talk about this? Please offer any suggestions as to what spiritual principles are involved in this outer work of my lifetime.

(Carla channeling)

We are those of Q'uo, and we are aware of your query, my brother. The work of any artist is a work of translation. An artist translates concepts into a manifestation that is flat, shall we say. The concept is a very round and living entity. It is infinite in its content and is a whole. The human intelligence does not work with concepts, it works with words. Intelligence puts words together to make ideas and sentences. Intelligence struggles to go from point A to point B to point C and to learn. The artist is an entity whose other intelligence has been somewhat awakened, for there are two intelligences in any human being.

---

[31] circadian: an adjective meaning daily or "noting or pertaining to rhythmic biological cycles recurring at approximately 24-hour intervals," to use the definition given on www.dictionary.com.

There is the intelligence which came with the body that you enjoy in this incarnation. That intelligence is a choice-making intelligence. It gathers facts and it is geared to make decisions. It does that very well. However, it is not a kind of intelligence that is capable of dealing with concepts. Yet it yearns for that which is beyond its intelligence.

On the other hand the heart, yours and all those of planet Earth, lives and dwells in the land of concept. It does so in silence. The heart works with feelings, insights, inspiration and hunches. Artistry comes through that non-local, non-linear part of your intelligence. So what you are doing, as you work with your music to manifest it, is to catch that ball of concept that is the creature of sound that you wish to make. And then you set about clothing it in its details, the words and forms that express the feelings with which you began.

When the feeling and the emotions run far ahead of that part of you that is harnessed to translate concepts into words, what you get is melody and not so many words, which is what you are experiencing. We would note, in this regard, the sound that you make instead of the word more accurately expresses the feeling that you are attempting to convey than does any word. Consequently, we would recommend that you open your mind to the concept of tones with vowel sounds as part of your music. You are only attempting more purely than language allows to express a certain quality or essence that lies in the underground, purified rivers of emotion that are part of the archetypal mind. You are attempting to bring these deep melodies up into conscious awareness. And indeed, as you do so, it shall be of service to others of some note, shall we say.

However, such work cannot be rushed. Consequently, when you feel that there is a lack of some kind in any composition on which you are working at a particular time, we would suggest that you take it into your heart and let it sing itself to you while you listen to it.

It may help if you move while you are doing so, as in going for a walk or doing some rhythmic activity such as the chores of the day, the mowing of the lawn, the picking up of the leaves, or some mindless, repetitive task. See that as a dance that accompanies your unfinished song. Dance to it and let it sing itself to you. And in that state of no stress and no worry, that which is at the heart of what you are attempting to catch will come to you.

If it is not in words, then let it be without words and trust in your sense of the appropriate vowel sounds that bring up certain emotions in certain configurations from the unconscious mind.[32]

Underlying our advice to you is the simple encouragement to trust yourself. Believe in yourself. Do not judge yourself according to what you have accomplished. Judge yourself not at all, except to know that you and the Creator are one and that your whole desire is to be a part of that creative principle. This is your heart and it is a good heart. You are worthy. With that confidence and that calm that goes with the knowledge that you, imperfect as you are, are worthy, then you shall be open to receive the gifts of the present moment. And, my brother, when you can relax and lift yourself to the simple joy of being, you have just created for yourself the best possible environment for receiving inspiration.

May we ask if there is another query at this time?

W: I feel a procrastinating energy around manifesting this music. What is happening here, spiritually speaking? Please talk about this seeming blockage that comes and goes in my creative work.

We are those of Q'uo, and we are aware of your query, my brother. Procrastination occurs when there is a portion of the self that feels unready to move forward. There are always riptides, as we have said, beneath the surface of the water. It is easy to splash through the surf, and even to enjoy the surf with a surfboard, but in your life there are many triggers that have been set for you by your experiences and by the fact that you have not balanced them in the past. They are like riptides that catch you and toss you away from your center, so that you are no longer communicating with your muse, shall we say. You have lost touch with your guidance.

In many people, this feels more like depression than distraction. However it comes to you, it is a sign of your lack of focus. You are working against yourself.

---

[32] It is interesting to note that the British rock group, Genesis, created music in just this way, with Phil Collins singing pure tone only at the start, then finding more accurate vowel sounds to express the felt emotion and only at the very end of the creative process creating lyrics for their songs.

Part of you wants to create and part of you does not feel ready. In order to resolve the impasse, we would encourage you at such times to go into the silence once again and to offer up the frustration of creativity gone awry. What will come out of that silence is unknown. You may receive a real jolt of energy so that you are able to create. You may, instead, receive a feeling that it is best to move on to something else, to move away from that which is not coming easily and to give that part of yourself that is not quite ready time and space to do what it needs to do beneath the surface.

When you are working with subconscious energies, you do not have the luxury of seeing what you are doing. You must take a lot on faith. You must have faith that the creative process in you will complete itself if you keep your instrument tuned. That is what the silence is for. That is what the attentiveness is for. You are an instrument of the Creator's and you wish only to be used. Consequently, keep yourself in tune and ready to respond when the wind of spirit blows across the strings of your instrument.

May we ask if there is a final query?

W: What archangel or other spiritual essence might aid me in coming into a place of inspiration where music and lyrics flow into the most beneficial form?

We are those of Q'uo, and we are aware of your query, my brother. This question treads too closely to the bounds of free will for us to respond directly. We would ask you to trust and to know that you do indeed have a muse and that muse is focused entirely upon supporting, encouraging and inspiring you. What is the shape of that muse, my brother? What name shall you call the source of your inspiration? What helper have you yearned for from the beginning? Name it. Claim it. Use it. For us to name that guidance and that inspiration for you would be utterly fruitless. This is your active process and we wish you happy hunting!

We thank the one known as W for this session, for this time together. We thank each of you in this circle of seeking for the beauty of your vibrations and the beauty of the combination of them that has made this a surpassingly lovely experience for us. It has been a true pleasure to share our energy with you and to experience the beauty of each of you.

We leave you, as we found you, in all that there is, the love and the light of the one infinite Creator. We are those known to you as Q'uo. We leave this instrument and this group in love and light. Adonai. ♣

L/L Research

L/L Research is a subsidiary of Rock Creek Research & Development Laboratories, Inc.

P.O. Box 5195
Louisville, KY 40255-0195

www.llresearch.org

Rock Creek is a non-profit corporation dedicated to discovering and sharing information which may aid in the spiritual evolution of humankind.

ABOUT THE CONTENTS OF THIS TRANSCRIPT: This telepathic channeling has been taken from transcriptions of the weekly study and meditation meetings of the Rock Creek Research & Development Laboratories and L/L Research. It is offered in the hope that it may be useful to you. As the Confederation entities always make a point of saying, please use your discrimination and judgment in assessing this material. If something rings true to you, fine. If something does not resonate, please leave it behind, for neither we nor those of the Confederation would wish to be a stumbling block for any.

© 2009 L/L Research

Saturday Meditation
November 19, 2006

Group question: *(Read by Jim.)* The question this week has to do with the conflict between what we project as a personality in our daily round of activities and our soul essence that moves with us through various incarnations and really has the basic plan for evolution in mind. Frequently, our personality seems to be at odds with this deeper self that knows what we need to do. When we are in catalyst situations in our daily round of activities and we'd like to punch somebody out, there's this little voice that says, "That's probably not a good idea."

We were wondering if Q'uo could give us some information on how we can deal with our personality. Because it is our personalities that we would use to deal with it. Do we need to refine our personalities? Do we need to get rid of our personalities? Do we need to balance our personalities? How can we most skillfully deal with what seems to be a conflict between the personality that wants to do certain things in this illusion and the deeper soul-self that really knows what we ought to be about and what we ought not to be about.

(Carla channeling)

We are those of the principle known to you as Q'uo. Greetings in the love and in the light of the one infinite Creator, in whose service we come to you this day.

It is a delight to be called to your circle of seeking and we are most glad to share our humble thoughts with you concerning the dynamics between the personality and the soul or spiritual essence.

As always, however, we would preface our remarks by the request that you not take them too seriously. We offer our opinions hoping that they will be of use to you. We cannot know what of our thoughts will prove useful to you and what of our thoughts will not prove of any use at this time. We would ask of you to use your discrimination and carefully and consciously select those thoughts that you wish to follow up, using those thoughts as resources. We would ask that you forget all of those thoughts with which you have not specifically felt resonance. In this way we would have the opportunity to speak freely without being concerned that we shall in some way infringe upon your free will and the rhythm of your spiritual process. We thank you for this consideration.

Perhaps you have seen a type of mollusk that creates a shell that is called the chambered nautilus. The animal that creates this shell first creates one shell which is in the nature of a scoop or an amphitheater. As it lives and gains in time and experience it gradually creates a second, larger amphitheater for itself. As this sea creature matures and gains in age, it creates house after house after house, always spiraling into a larger area, always creating a vaster domain, always bringing the self into a more spacious point of view or range of view.

The personality, as you have termed it, can be seen to be this kind of being. It must have a house. It must create and form and erect and maintain a façade of some kind. That is the nature of what you call the personality.

Now let us talk a bit about the personality. In its own way, your essence has a personality. There is a flavor to the vibrations that are uniquely your own. However, this flavoring of sweetness and spice is extraneous to the basic vibration of your being. In contrast to your personality on Planet Earth—that is, your earthly personality—your soul essence does not have that kind of personality.

For the moment we are focusing on the personality because, as the one known as Jim said in his query, one must deal with this concept, this perception of a dynamic between the personality and the soul, with the personality itself as a conscious being, in a third-density physical vehicle, living a life on Planet Earth. The personality is that which gives voice even to the most deep and profound of spiritual truths.

Indeed, that is why artists, prophets, priests and other visionaries so often cry out in anguish. For they can feel and test the truth, but to move it into words is more work than many can ever encompass. Therefore, one must work with the personality in order to aid the spiritual seeking of the self.

One cannot simply work within silence and allow that to be the spiritual practice. There needs to be a structure of thought that is able to hold and order the concerns of the lifetime. The house or chamber of the nautilus that you are born with is a small house. Its structures are simple. When you are a very small child you gain the concept of "me" and "mine" and the nurturer and the one who is loved and the one who loves you. These are very simple structures, but they are very meaningful.

You barely begin to realize that there are other entities in the world—until you are first told to share. That is perhaps the beginning of your career of one who grows on Planet Earth. For that concept of someone else to whom you are kind makes a shift and a change in consciousness that moves you to a larger house, to a larger point of view.

Throughout your life then, cyclically, when you have prepared to move house, spiritually, emotionally, and mentally speaking, you shall find yourself in a more spacious palace and a more panoramic view shall be yours as well. Such houses are not built of nothing. In the case of the personality upon Planet Earth, the move from a smaller to a larger house, a smaller to a larger point of view is costly. You pay the price in whatever suffering you do as you work on what you conceive of as your spiritual process. You also work upon it with every consciously received moment of thanksgiving and joy.

This instrument has said to herself and others many times that if she can focus on giving thanksgiving and praise for what is happening, she finds there is less of the difficult work to do that seems to involve suffering, either mental, emotional, spiritual or physical.

The pressure to grow is indelibly etched into your very essence. You are, by your very nature, a life form in the midst of an evolutionary process. You may dig in your heels and attempt to resist growing and you will slow the rate of growth, but you cannot stop growing.

What entities can do, and often choose to do, being unaware of a spiritual dimension to their lives, is attempt to remain as deeply asleep as possible, softening the blows of life with pleasure, distraction and sleep. We are not speaking to those who wish to sleep. Therefore, we sympathize with you! For you are awake; you cannot go back to sleep. You truly do wish to grow and you truly are weary at times of the amount of suffering that seems to be involved.

And the catalyst, as the one known as C, as the one known as Carla, and as the one known as Jim all said, does not stop simply because you become aware that it is catalyst. You do the work of becoming grateful for the good catalyst and thankful for the good work to do. You can only manipulate your true feelings so far.

This instrument was speaking earlier, for instance, of how she must remove from her consciousness all of the details of her present moment before she can come to that formless awareness of self that is the real self, the consciousness that is shared with the infinite Creator and with all the forces of love and light within her world.

It is possible to become that emptied, open vessel, but it takes work. It takes a deliberate and ruthless willingness to release pain and, more than that, to release the resentment that grows up around having to feel the pain. We realize that we are talking to a wide range of entities. For some of you, the pain is emotional. For some of you the pain is physical. And for some the pain is spiritual. In all cases there is a mixture of each, but always there is an emphasis on one of those three.

Whatever the kind of suffering that you are experiencing, it has the same function within the growth processes of your soul. It is designed, as the one known as C said, to target specific issues which you came into this incarnation fairly determined to balance. You had to give up the memory of all this good planning, so the actual agenda of your life only comes to you little by little unless you are very lucky and it strikes you all at once.

If you receive a whole vision like that, almost nothing can stop you. But for most entities, the vision is acquired slowly and in stages. And there is a lot of self-doubt. There is the wondering if you are on the right track. Could you be doing something better? Could you be doing something else? Could you be more honest with yourself? And so forth and so on. [These are] questions that are good to ask, questions that are needful to ask, but questions that distract you from the process of letting faith be your keel and hope your rudder.

You can only go so far with your chamber, given that we continue to use the image of the chambered nautilus. The most marvelously expansive palace with the widest point of view possible will give to you everything right up to the limit of the rational and the known. You will look upon physical things from this personality shell. You will see stars, but they will not live. You will hear the wind, but you will not hear it speaking to you. You are trapped, as a personality, in a world of thought and form.

You cannot see that the forms and the thoughts are common to you all. You cannot see beyond the uniqueness of your body and its obviously physical separation from all other bodies. You cannot see the dance of your auras as they dance upon each other and form harmonics and combinations of woven color that are quite remarkable in their beauty.

You cannot see all of the entities of Earth—the flowers, the trees, the animals, the water, all the elements with their characteristic vibrations and their characteristic auras, all merging and flowing in and out of each other in an endless harmony and a beautiful symphony. That is the limitation of that entity that you are when you use the word, "I."

You moved into incarnation in this very limited physical vehicle with its very limited instincts and mentality because you as a soul had work to do. It may well help, when you are in the midst of suffering, to remember and validate for yourself the simple fact that you chose the work you are about now in the world. You wanted it very much. You wanted the opportunity badly. Not only did you want to help others, you wanted to work on your vibration.

Some of you felt that you were overbalanced toward love and tended towards becoming martyrs rather than applying the wisdom that balances martyrdom and creates of it continued life and continued teaching and an expansion of possibilities.

Some of you came into this incarnation with the opinion that you had far too much wisdom and that it was keeping you from coming into the full openness of heart that you truly wished for yourself. From whichever dynamic you are approaching balance, you will be drawn to certain lessons. Those who wish to gain wisdom will be offered opportunities to use wisdom. Those of you who wish to become openhearted will find those themes of catalytic event occurring again and again that challenge you to open your heart at the expense of rationality and the perceived wisdom.

Realize that when you do this work, your responsibility is to form an intention and to offer it up to the spirit within you. There is much that is hidden in mystery about your guidance. Do not attempt, then, to reason out these moments of suffering and learning. Certainly, apply the wisdom of analysis as you wish. But realize always that skillful work with the personality involves moving back into the silence, allowing the personality to fall away, becoming empty, as this instrument was talking about doing earlier, and receiving in that silence things that are and will remain a mystery but which will, nevertheless, create for you the possibilities of new structure, a larger home, a more capacious and compassionate personality.

We would say, "No," to the question would we suggest for you to lose the personality. You do not wish to lose the personality, although as various parts of it fall away naturally, it is a wonderfully freeing experience. Your personality is a perfectly good structure. You are, however, working to refine your personality.

Now the word "refine" means to purify, and it calls up images of the fiery furnace and being reduced to your liquid components of this metal, that metal, and so forth, and the dross being drained off and the good part being made into some fine steel or creating something metallic. Yours is not that kind of refinery. If you will notice your physical vehicle, it is a chemical refinery. It takes in raw foods. It uses the good, and it excretes the waste.

It may help you to think of your mental and emotional appetites in the same way. You're going to be eating a lot of raw food when it comes to food as experience. It will hit you sometimes like a French *au cuisine* dinner, sometimes like an unfortunate trip to a greasy burger place, and sometimes somewhere in between.

Some of the experiences that you receive will be sweet to your tongue and delicious to process—your lover's touch, the cry of your baby, those wonderful times when you see the beauty of the moment in the sunshine and shadow. Treasure and store up those moments of pure awareness.

The kind of refinery you are as a soul is one who takes all that hits the self in the present moment and gazes at it with an eye to response. If you are too quick to respond, then you have quickly used up that opportunity. If the response is not complete or well thought out, or on the level you would have preferred if you thought about it further, then you have minimized the effectiveness of this particular catalyst.

Consequently, in terms of dealing with difficult catalyst, it is helpful that you become aware of your resistance to it. It is understandable for you to resist by instinct anything that will make you uncomfortable. Whether it is a physical discomfort because of a physical condition or an emotional discomfort because of a difficult relationship, the discomfort is there and the instinct of your physical vehicle with its intellect is to resist it.

You wish either to change it or to eliminate it. The last thing you want to do is accept it, appreciate it, bless it, and use it. Yet for those who have the presence of mind to go through that process of separating the self from the immediacy of the catalyst and becoming that self that is aware of the catalyst and wishes to choose how to respond, such catalyst can begin to be seen as the gift that it truly is.

It is the work of a lifetime to learn not to resist seemingly difficult catalyst. Yet as each of you has at times discovered, when you release all resistance and embrace the situation your environment lightens as if dawn had just broken on a new day. You are able to say, "All right, I see this and I welcome it. Help me learn how to receive this gift. Help me to have insight into its purpose in my life. Help me to look in the mirror of this discomfort and see the face of the infinite Creator."

We believe that this is a good stopping place for this particular topic and we would, at this time, ask if there are other queries that this group may have. We are those of Q'uo.

(No further queries.)

We are those of Q'uo. As we seem to have exhausted the questions in this group at this time, we shall thank you once again for calling us to your circle and for allowing us the privilege of sharing your vibrations. We leave you in the love and in the light of the one infinite Creator. We are those known to you as the principle of Q'uo. Adonai. Adonai.

L/L Research

L/L Research is a subsidiary of Rock Creek Research & Development Laboratories, Inc.

P.O. Box 5195
Louisville, KY 40255-0195

www.llresearch.org

Rock Creek is a non-profit corporation dedicated to discovering and sharing information which may aid in the spiritual evolution of humankind.

ABOUT THE CONTENTS OF THIS TRANSCRIPT: This telepathic channeling has been taken from transcriptions of the weekly study and meditation meetings of the Rock Creek Research & Development Laboratories and L/L Research. It is offered in the hope that it may be useful to you. As the Confederation entities always make a point of saying, please use your discrimination and judgment in assessing this material. If something rings true to you, fine. If something does not resonate, please leave it behind, for neither we nor those of the Confederation would wish to be a stumbling block for any.

© 2009 L/L Research

Sunday Meditation
December 10, 2006

Group question: The question today has to do with discrimination. How or what is the root cause of the prejudice that various groups of people have against other groups, whether it be because of race, creed, color, national origin, religion, the place where they live? Whatever the reason, everywhere around the world there are groups of people that discriminate against other people because they are different. Q'uo, could you give us some idea about what really are the roots of this type of discrimination and disempowerment of other people by majority groups? And what can we do about it as individuals?

(Carla channeling)

We are those known to you as Q'uo. Greetings in the love and in the light of the one infinite Creator, in Whose service we come to you this day. May we say what a privilege and a pleasure it is to join your circle of seeking. We are most happy to share our humble thoughts with you on this subject of prejudice and its roots and what people can do when finding that situation in their environment.

But first we would, as always, request of each who is aware of our words the careful and conscientious use of your discriminatory powers. You and you alone know what thoughts are helpful to you. If our thoughts are not helpful to you, please cast them aside and move on, for the thought that is helpful to you is right around the corner. If our thoughts are resonant to you, then you are welcome to them. We thank you for this consideration. It enables us to speak our mind clearly without fearing that we shall infringe upon your free will.

My friends, in speaking with you about prejudice and its roots, we speak with you about two main levels of thought. Those levels of thought are the dynamic between love and fear and the dynamic between unity consciousness and the consciousness of form. Before we move into those thoughts, however, we would talk just a bit about the traps of your Earth world and how they came about.

When this creation was younger and worlds closer to what this instrument calls the central sun were maturing, the work done by a planetary population was a work done by a population of one kind or race or being. In the course of many graduations from many planets, there gradually began to build up populations from Earths such as yours which had finished their third density, the density of choice, and had not been able to graduate into the density of love. These population groups then needed to move to another third-density experience to take up once again the lessons of making the choice. This choice is a choice of polarity. It is a choice between choosing to love, include and accept, with compassion [for] all things and beings as part of one Creator, and the choice of seeing all entities as those who may be able to serve you. It is a choice of service to others or service to self.

It is a simple choice. It is not an intellectually staggering thing to determine when you are being kind, inclusive and compassionate, and when you are being unkind, un-inclusive and non-compassionate.

As simple as this choice is, it is not a choice that many of your peoples have found easy to penetrate with a stable determination to follow either the ways of service to others or service to self.

Therefore, as the creation has matured and consciousness has spread throughout the infinite creation that you see in the starry night sky, planetary population after planetary population has found a portion or all of its tribe unable to graduate when the harvest of their third density came due.

At first, the answer was simply to move through another time of harvest on the same planet. However, planets also have their periodicity. Each planet is different. But each planet has a limit to the amount of third density that is available. It is as if we were to say that there are a certain number of 30-watt bulbs for each planet and when that supply runs out, they must put in 40-watt bulbs. The light changes when a stronger bulb is put in. That stronger light will not support third-density life.

Consequently, the creation began to move planetary populations to a second-chance planet where they would mix with the native third-density population and together those two tribes would seek to learn how to make the choice of service to others or service to self.

This is the situation upon your planet. You have a very, very small population of native third-density Earth entities. Virtually all of your tribes are tribes who have come to this second-chance planet to have another try at the school of third-density life.

Each sun or sub-Logos, as this instrument would say, has made choices in how the fundamental consciousness of the planetary population will express itself. We are not talking about the level of conscious choice, but rather the level of the archetypal mind and the roots of consciousness. For each planetary tribe, there is a unique flavor and quality to the archetypal and mythical aspects of that tribe. When coming to the second-chance planet of planet Earth, those populations carried the uniqueness of their archetypal minds, their roots of consciousness, with them.

When you look at races upon your planet, those who look a certain way and are called Caucasian, those who look a certain way and are called Hispanic, those who look a certain way and are called Native Americans, and so forth, you are looking at entities that don't simply look a bit different on the surface. They are different, at the roots of their consciousness, in ways that they can never consciously express except by art or music or some craft which escapes the bondage of words and the intellectual or analytical mind.

Consequently, upon planet Earth at this time you have many tribes who are having their second chance at making the choice between love and service to others or that love which is turned into fear and service to self.

We offer this thought as prelude to those principles of which we spoke because we do not wish simply to say that all are one, which is true enough. We also wish to celebrate the differences in myth, culture and archetype which create ways in which each tribe has a unique perspective to add to the simmering stew of harmony and unity which may blend all the tribes of Earth into one while retaining each excellence of each planetary population.

Let us now look at the dynamic between love and fear. There is the surface tendency in many entities' minds which seeks to call something right and something else wrong. Whence does this stem? It stems from the fear of an individual who is not at peace with himself. He is not secure within his own sense of self. Rather than being able to rest in that love which sees all things as one, he feels fear because of the differences between himself and others.

This fear is natural. It is not to be condemned. It is to be seen as the first step of many. When you are an infant, your world is bound in fear. You are thrust forth from the unity and the peacefulness of the womb into the cold air which you have not yet learned to breathe. You are more than terrified. You are sure that you are going to die. Your first experience is likely to be terror. This is a difficult start to an incarnation but it is part of the very nature of incarnation itself. It is built into the structure of the human experience.

Naturally, in most cases, the parents reassure and protect, cuddle and rock the infant and the baby becomes peaceful. But terror awaits at [every] door in every hour, for the baby is unable to care for itself. When it is hungry it must depend upon the kindness of others. When it is wet it must depend upon others giving it a new diaper and a bath. When it is in pain with colic or cutting teeth, it does not know why it is in pain. It knows only that it cannot get away from the suffering that it feels.

Gradually, oh so gradually, the human leaves infanthood and enters childhood and the fear recedes somewhat. A child has learned to speak. It can ask why. It can defend itself with words to some extent. But the patterns of fear are deep. They are not evil. They are natural. Throughout the lifetime of an entity in third density, fear is around the corner, outside the door, under the bed, in the closet: the boogeyman. Yet the true location of this fear is in the experiences of being born and of being helpless.

What child has ever had all of its needs met? What growing teenager has ever been able to plumb the depths of its own passage? My friends, you arrive at adulthood battered by the experiences you have undergone. Some, indeed most, entities cover their pain with that thin veneer of civilization: the clever words, the appropriate actions, the right clothing.

But within the deep mind of each entity lies many a doorway into fear. And fear has many friends. Fear can produce anger. It can produce unworthiness. It can produce guilt. It can produce many difficult and dark emotions and feelings.

When we greet you in the love and in the light of the one Creator, we are greeting the heart of you and the heart of you is love. We penetrate through the shell of conscious experience garnered by your personality and we see your souls. You are beautiful. You are beautiful beyond any words. You bloom in the air of faith. Your roots are fed with the rain of hope. And you stand up strong because you are. You cannot be denied in your essence. But these qualities of you are those that come through the surface disturbances of personality and prejudice and fear.

We can say that you are creatures made of love, but in so many cases your experience does not feel like that. In so many cases you experience yourself not as the perfect flower that you are but as a weed, or at least as something to be groomed and done unto. So in a way, finding yourself to be a creature of love is an act of faith which has no proof of being the right choice.

It is into this environment of entities living in their own private suffering and fear that the challenges and the lessons of third density are aimed and experienced. The Earth experience is a refinery. Again and again you receive catalyst that causes you to question who you are and why you are here. These questions and these feelings can pound and shake you until eventually you begin discovering that the process has uncovered some of the gem-like beauty of your deeper nature.

And so, for the first time, as you move through this refining fire of incarnation, you begin to have a sense, a genuine sense, of who you really are, and it does not sound so foreign and alien to say, "I am a child of love. I am a being of light. I am a creature of infinite power because I am part of the one infinite Creator."

What a journey it is from the beginning of life to that moment when you first awaken to the unitary nature of consciousness. What a joy it is when you first feel at one with another person. What an accomplishment it is, my friends, when you are able to move from feeling at one with another person to feeling at one with groups of people and finally with all of the people that make up the very variegated tribe of humankind.

At every turn, there will be that call to fear what is happening. And why is that, my friends? It is because there is a tendency towards inertia in the mind of humankind, whereas there is an implacable tendency towards progression in evolution in the energy of the planet itself. People tend to fight change and yet change is the essence of the incarnational experience. The body changes continuously, shedding its cells so that in seven years there is not one cell in the human body that was there seven years ago. The outer look of the human body changes, if not continuously, than rapidly, from infanthood to toddler-hood to childhood to teenage-hood to young adulthood to middle age and then to those varieties of old age that entities wish not to label so as not to acknowledge.

In the end, each entity is transformed from the womb through the bloom to the grave. Change is inevitable and yet change seems to be feared. And if one is identifying oneself with one's body, then there is every reason to have fear, for the death of the body is inevitable. Thusly, it is easy to make fear-based choices when confronted with change.

One way that things change for an entity is that they are placed in new contexts, meeting different kinds of people. If one has already made the choice for service to others, then one tends to see others as an opportunity to be of service. The well polarized entity sees all entities as opportunities to be of service.

That entity which is polarized in a negative sense also has no prejudice because it sees all entities as equally useful in serving the self.

It is to those who have not yet made the choice that prejudice seems a good choice to make. If "they" are correct and acceptable, then the way they are is the way things should be. When entities come into their environment and express differences, then the fear-filled entity is simply going to feel that those other selves need to conform to the way they think.

Now let us look at the other leg of this two-legged entity of prejudice, that is, the dynamic between form and formlessness, or unity and diversity. It is entirely understandable that entities at all times and in all places should be seduced and swayed by the appearances of form. The five senses of which you are aware consciously have to do with form. You see form. You hear form. You touch, smell and taste form. There's nothing on the surface of things that would tell you that there is anything other than form in your universe.

It is very helpful to call upon the knowledge that each has of the scientific nature of form. Each form which you may consider is almost entirely made of space. You as an entity are a collection of energy fields holding cells together in a certain configuration. Each cell is almost entirely space. Your body looks like the Milky Way to an entity that is able to look into the microscopic structure of your world. The chair upon which you sit is mostly space but its energy field holds it together so that you do not fall through the chair or the floor. And so the illusion remains intact.

And yet who you are has nothing to do with your form. What you think as a soul has nothing to do with forms. Again, this is not obvious on the surface of things. It is no wonder that you begin your incarnation completely beguiled by form. "Am I pretty?" "Am I rich?" "Am I smart?" "Am I strong?" "Am I good?" "Am I powerful?" These questions are asked and answered on the level of the illusion and no wisdom comes from the questioning and the responses as long as the questions remain on the level of form.

In form there is always relativity. If you are smart, someone is smarter. If you are rich, someone is richer, and so forth. In order to penetrate to the level of the school of third-density life where the lessons are truly learned, you must penetrate through form into consciousness.

Consciousness has its home in all of the spaces that we have mentioned. Consciousness interpenetrates every cell of your body and every cell of everyone else's body. It penetrates the Earth itself and the heavens and it is all one thing. You, as a spark of the infinite Creator, are a focusing spark, an observation point. You are a witness to the love and the light of the infinite Creator. You are here to bear witness, to experience, to collect those experiences as you would a bouquet of flowers, and then to offer that bouquet to the infinite Creator.

When we see you, we do not see form. We see a different level of illusion which we would call vibration. We see your vibratory display as if it were the petals of a flower of infinite beauty unfurled for us to see. Every quirk, every imbalance that colors you in this or that way, we see not as mistakes or errors in thinking but as your own individual beauty. To us you cannot make a mistake. To the Creator you cannot make a mistake. For just as you are, exactly as you are experiencing, you are gathering up information to offer to the Creator.

In terms of using the environment of planet Earth, of third density in general, however, it is well for you to gather these various descriptions of self and to form an intention to penetrate the more shallow levels of perception so that you may begin to stand upon the good Earth of who you are as a spirit.

(Side one of tape ends.)

(Carla channeling)

In terms of what you can do in the outer world to alleviate the forces of prejudice, the impact of information is great. This instrument was saying before this communication began, in the discussion around the circle of seeking, that she would like to learn Spanish and has planned on taking a course in Spanish because of the fact that there are more and more Spanish-speaking people with whom she comes in contact.

When something is different, the way out of prejudice is to collect information and begin to understand the differences. And we do not leave this idea of differences to include simply racial differences, although certainly race and language seem to be barriers of otherness that stop many entities cold in fear.

We would suggest that there are many, many ways of experiencing fear when faced with differences. The dynamic between men and women, for instance, is often the occasion of fear and the acting out of that fear in cruelty of various kinds.

Always, though, the inner workings of prejudice depend upon your continued seduction by fear and by form. When you choose to live in faith that all is well and that you are where you need to be, then you may drop whatever fears that you may have and you then have the freedom and the space in your mind and heart to consider the needs of others around you.

What are your gifts, my friends? How can you be a lighthouse to others? It is in first knowing who you are and gaining confidence in your own power as a person and then in turning to the infinite Creator, dropping to your knees, and saying, "Infinite Creator, how may I serve the greater good this day? Show me your ways. Teach me your ways."

Open your eyes after saying that prayer and behold a world made new, sparkling with opportunities to serve, to include, and to embrace.

May we ask if there is a follow up to that question or another query at this time?

R: I have a question, Q'uo. As you were describing the different tribes that came to Earth as their second third-density planet, you said that these groups bring their own archetypes and consciousnesses from their first planet. How does that mesh with this planet having its own archetypes put into place by the Logos of our galaxy? Can you speak to that? I have a difficult time making it more clear than that.

We are those of Q'uo, and are aware of your query, my brother. When there is one archetypal system in place, it is a system of waterways in the deep mind which are calm and serene. Even the darkest of emotions runs along a channel that is simple.

When entities from another planet enter into the archetypal energies of Earth, carrying with them the archetypal energies of another sub-Logos, another sun, it is as if there is the same basic waterway system. However, each sub-Logos has made differences here and there. They are small differences, but, all taken together, they add up to a rich array of rivulets, small streams and sometimes so many streams that there are swamps or morasses where dark emotions of different cultures have developed into less of a clear form and more of an amorphous or unembodied form.

This entire creation contains one basic blueprint of the archetypal mind of its people. It is up to each sub-Logos, however, to tinker with that design a bit so as to increase the variety of experiences available to the infinite Creator. So when an entity on its first planet falls into the emotions of suffering or joy, those waterways move smoothly and the myths are of a piece. When there is superimposed upon the basic plan of waterways, shall we say, that the archetypal mind represents in the roots of consciousness, the archetypal mind of another sub-Logos, you see the enriching and the somewhat interesting rapids and morasses that occur with the overlay of more than one sub-Logos.

It is as if when you sink into an expression of deep feeling, you as a second-chance Earth being have the capacity for more different kinds of emotion and each subtle difference in emotion is authentic. You have richer choices of ways to feel your authentic essence and the Creator has an enhanced opportunity to know Itself as these tides and rivers of archetypal emotion sweep over streambeds made uneven by the pebbles of different archetypal influences.

It does not muddy the experience but rather enriches the experience of positive emotion. Because of the nature of darker emotions there is the tendency to find a muddying effect in emotions like anger and fear. Consequently, those working on the path of service to self have a real disadvantage at this time for they must, with exquisite care, find the true heart of those purified emotions. However, for those on the path of service to others, the differences are seen as articulations or waterfalls or linns or cascades. And as you watch the water flowing from these linns and catching the light, you may see the rainbows of different effects as they fall through you and you become one with these purified rivers and streams of emotion.

May we answer you further, my brother?

R: Thank you Q'uo. There are no more questions from the online circle members, so I will ask one. The last question I have is if there are entities who choose to continue their third-density experience on planet Earth because of the muddying and the possibilities it offers? Or is the assignment of the second-chance third-density planet something that the entity itself does not actively partake in?

We are those of Q'uo, and are aware of your query, my brother. Your latter supposition is correct. The placement of a planetary population in a second third-density environment is made at a level where the guardians responsible for that entire planet make that choice of placement. The individual is moved as a part of the planetary tribe.

We find that this instrument's energy wanes and so we would take our leave of this instrument and this group, thanking each for the incredible beauty of your vibrations. We are humble before you, you who have the veil covering your eyes, keeping you from the clear sight of the Creator. Yet you move forward, gracefully, courageously and gallantly, never giving up, but always, as the ones known as T and R have both said, just giving it another try, starting over tomorrow morning.

Day by day your beauty astounds us, your courage amazes us, and we cheer for you and love you. We are always here if you would ask us mentally to deepen your meditations. Again we thank you for calling us to your circle. We are known to you as those of the principle of Q'uo. We leave you in the love and in the light of the one infinite Creator. Adonai. Adonai.

L/L Research

L/L Research is a subsidiary of Rock Creek Research & Development Laboratories, Inc.

P.O. Box 5195
Louisville, KY 40255-0195

www.llresearch.org

Rock Creek is a non-profit corporation dedicated to discovering and sharing information which may aid in the spiritual evolution of humankind.

ABOUT THE CONTENTS OF THIS TRANSCRIPT: This telepathic channeling has been taken from transcriptions of the weekly study and meditation meetings of the Rock Creek Research & Development Laboratories and L/L Research. It is offered in the hope that it may be useful to you. As the Confederation entities always make a point of saying, please use your discrimination and judgment in assessing this material. If something rings true to you, fine. If something does not resonate, please leave it behind, for neither we nor those of the Confederation would wish to be a stumbling block for any.

© 2009 L/L Research

Sunday Meditation
December 17, 2006

Group question: The question this week, Q'uo, has to do with teaching and learning. We're wondering just how teaching actually occurs as the result of our desire to teach and our attempting to teach certain subjects or topics. Much occurs by the very nature of our being, of who we are and how we are. Could you speak to the topic of how teaching and learning really occur?

(Carla channeling)

We are the principle known to you as Q'uo. Greetings in the love and in the light of the one infinite Creator, in Whose service we come to you this day. We thank each of you for calling us to your circle of seeking and, indeed, for taking the time and the attention in your busy, busy lives to spend this time seeking the truth. We are most privileged to be able to offer our thoughts.

However, before we begin, we would, as always, ask for your discrimination in listening to our words. We encourage you to be very real as you move through thoughts, sensing deeply into whether or not these thoughts help you, whether or not they resonate to you and seem useful. If they do not, my friends, drop them.

The energy, the information, and the inspiration that you need is close to you. If it is not we who offer it to you, please be assured another source will come to you, for that which you desire always comes to you, one way or another. If you will use this discrimination and listening to what we have to say, it will enable us to speak freely to you without being concerned about the issue of free will. We thank you for this consideration.

You ask this day about teaching and learning, how one teaches and how one learns. That is a question of enormous subtlety. And there is a wide variety in the ways in which we could approach this subject. We shall focus upon those aspects of the question which we sense are at the heart of the interest of those who have created the question. We wish to acknowledge beforehand that our response will be incomplete.

The universe in which you and we and all that there is experience consciousness is a unitary universe. When you are teaching, you are teaching yourself. When you are learning, you are learning from yourself.

We wish to start with this very deep level of truth about teaching because, unlike many who ask about the teaching process, the energy companioning this query feels deep and spiritual in nature. Therefore, rather than focusing upon the surface of teaching, we would start at the very foundation.

You are all teachers. You cannot help but be teachers. Even if you were alone for your entire lifetime, you would be teaching yourself. Indeed, you do teach yourself. From the very beginning [of] your incarnation, you are teaching yourself what you like and what you do not like. Each observation about your preferences creates for you a more and more complex structure of opinions about yourself, in effect, by your instinctual reactions to that which is occurring in your environment. You are building intelligence as to who you apparently are.

Because of the culture in which you live, this intelligence is composed almost entirely of the things that you learn when you are conscious and alert. However, much teaching of the self by the self occurs beneath the level of alert, waking consciousness. Those levels of teaching occur when you are asleep and dreaming.

You receive a tremendous amount of material that has been processed to a certain extent by your conscious mind as you release your conscious mind and move into the deeper levels of the mind to take your rest. You also are able to open the door to those deeper levels, which are unable to communicate in words. The deeper levels of the self communicate in images, concepts, colors and various aspects of feeling. On the surface of your life, you might be experiencing a very muddy picture. It may seem to be a very chaotic present day experience. Beneath the surface of consciousness, however, there are tremendous resources available to you.

They are, in the sense of dreaming, quite automatic to a certain extent. That which is on your mind have been important to you one way or another. That day registers like a knock on the door registers to someone in the house. By the focus of your waking concerns, you knock on the door of your deeper consciousness as you gain experience in working with your dreams. And you may even remember to ask, when you are knocking at the door unconsciously by your emotions and your feelings, for good guidance, for clear guidance, for the highest and best guidance. These create a strident and focused knock upon the door that elicits clearer dreams or symbols, clearer images, and clearer feelings that come from the dreaming.

Other ways in which you teach yourself are achieved also when you release consciousness. Time and nature walking silently, and gazing at the world around you frees up the mind, because no one is talking to you; you are not guarded, nor do you expect to comprehend, sense or make sense. And so your mind goes slightly out of focus, which is precisely the intent of such contemplative nature walks.

This instrument—we correct this instrument. This instrument would call this process letting the brain sag in the middle. When you let the brain sag in the middle, the usual connections that you make when you think thought "A," may not be the ones you come to, because your flat mind has become a mind of curves, hills, valleys, hidden places, unexpected things touching. And so you receive new connections. New combinations of thought. New positions of feeling and emotions. And so often, you may surface from such an experience with a feeling of wonder and discovery, because your brain has not been the dictator that it likes to be and something has crept in through this door from the unconscious mind into the conscious mind. And suddenly, one particular pattern of your experience may fall into place for the first time, so that instead of chaos, you begin to perceive the implicate order.

There is a vast and comprehensive order. It is not fixed. The order of your creation is flowing. It flows because of your feelings, your thoughts, and your desires. However, each moment is an opportunity to release the dictatorship of the intellect and begin to become aware on more levels than the intellectual levels of your environment. In such ways may you teach yourself.

Other uses of silence and the releasing of the mind are those we have mentioned to you many times. The reading of inspirational works and then the contemplation of what you have read. Silent meditation. Meditation following the breath. Meditation staring at a white wall. Walking meditations, and so forth.

This instrument's use of the services of her church is another good example of how one who has begun to perceive the way learning actually takes place may use what to another person would seem to be a fairly random and close to meaningless series of readings, prayers and so forth which make up the church service. When one is allowing one's brain to sag in the middle, when one is not insisting that one make sense at all times, one may suddenly see a connection that helps on a level far beneath the surface of life.

So, when an entity decides to offer itself as a teacher, it is offering itself in addition to the subject matter that is being covered in the class that is being taught. Even in the case of scientific courses, where a large amount of detail and specific information must be understood in a certain order in order to be able to become facile in working with that particular discipline, it makes a great deal of difference, as any student will tell you, as to what teacher has taught that course. Every student remembers teachers that lifted subject matter from the conscious everyday level of "learn these facts" and "take the test" to a level which let the student see into why the teacher loved that particular discipline and why that teacher was teaching that particular class.

Love, passion and affection are catching. When a teacher loves the subject he is teaching often he is able to excite others because of his love, his affection, and his passion for his discipline. So even when you are simply trying to memorize the facts of biology, chemistry or astronomy, a good teacher will motivate you through his love of the subject to create a sense of adventure in learning that is lacking from an uninspired teacher's presentation.

When one becomes a spiritual teacher, the subject matter of the class becomes less important [and] the character and nature of the teacher becomes more important. There are practices of Buddhists and Hindus, for instance, in which the entire learning experience of the guru or the teacher and the chela or the student is conducted in silence. The teacher sits and rests in his essence. Within the essence, there is affection, compassion and all the gifts of the spirit which have been granted to this teacher. Implicit in his silent meditation [are] his acceptance, true love, and all of the environment which points the student toward his own essence. It is as if the teacher is a star, twinkling in the night sky, that by its clarity and lucidity of essence creates in the student the ability also to become such a star, twinkling, lucid and clear.

The teachings of the guru do not have content in this preference, that is, because the essence of spiritual teaching does not have content. Let us refine upon this thought, because it is a substance of one. When one is teaching how to understand what makes Herman Melville's book, *Moby Dick*, a good book, one can rely upon the book itself; one can talk with the student about the characters in the book; one can discuss what historical era that historical book was written in, and how that might have affected the writing of the book, [to] deepen the understanding of this or that aspect of the writing.

When one is attempting to teach spiritual maturity, one is in a pure sense teaching entities how to be themselves by being themselves—we correct this instrument—by the teacher being himself. It would seem impossible for this to be an accurate or productive teaching technique, except for the fact that many, many generations of highly evolved spiritual seekers have used this technique in order to learn. The basic feeling in this type of learning is resting in the affection of the teacher. All the cares of the world fade away. Resting in this safe environment. Loved, cherished, supported and encouraged. The student is then able at last to release all expectations except the experience of being with the teacher. And so the student humbly empties his mind of all except for his affection for his teacher. And in that trust, faith learning is passed from heart to heart. From soul to soul. It is an energy exchange. The student and the teacher are sharing awareness. At the moment that the student is allowing this connection, the teacher and the student become one. Why is this possible? It is possible because all entities are one. The teacher has simply found a way to help the student become aware of that blessed unity that underlies all the seeming separation and detail of the awaking human experience.

Many teachers who attempt to teach spiritually are greatly hampered, though often they do not know it, by their restrictions and limitations of their form of belief. We do not speak strictly of religious belief here, although religion and their dogma are the most common sources of restrictions and limitation of being able to share the awareness of oneness and essence that is at the heart of spiritual teaching.

Many wonderfully mature spiritual beings are nevertheless hampered greatly by the need to justify dogma. However, you will find that in that every religion there are teachers who have been able to transcend the structures of dogma, so that as they work within the structures of their religion they nevertheless are able to make connections that lie so far out of the box of that particular religion. Such entities have the impulse to create connections with other religions and to form spiritual relationships that go beyond any one dogma.

We would offer the example of the one known as Thomas. This instrument is aware of the one known as Thomas Merton for she has visited the gardens of Gethsemane, where this entity was a monk for many years, and has listened to the sweet solemn sounds of the chanting of the monks as they move through one of the six daily services, blending the [anonymity] of the monk's robes with the ultimate idiosyncrasy of their individual voices and then blending all those individual voices into one instrument of worship such as this entity's environment when he was teacher of the new arrivals to Gethsemane.

This entity created bonds between the East and the West because he felt called to go to India and to Tibet and to create relationships with those in similar vocations in those places, and his work studying what is common to the East and to the West is greatly helpful [to] those who are caught in dogma, as is the work of the one known as Krishnamurti and many others who have done this combining and harmonizing work, trying to break the bonds of dogma.

Unlike chemistry, unlike literature, unlike any intellectual pursuit, the pursuit of the spiritual is the pursuit of mystery. You cannot understand a mystery. However, you can become the mystery by inviting in that mystery, by embracing it, and by being willing to be changed by it. Entities come to a spiritual teacher not because they wish to add to their learning, although that is what they think they are doing. Entities come to a spiritual teacher because they wish to subtract distractions of their worldly life from the essence of their being until only the essence remains.

So, the great spiritual teachers are those who are content to be. They do not have an axe to grind. They do not have a pet topic that they wish to lecture to you about. What they have in common is the quality of their own realization of self. This is the secret ingredient in all teaching. And therefore, if one wishes to be a teacher, one needs to engage in a style of living that leads one ever closer to honesty, self-acceptance, comfort within oneself, affection for oneself. These gifts of the self can only be given by the self. You cannot become compassionate by studying. You can only present yourself to your innermost heart as your own student and say, "Dear heart of self, dear Christ consciousness within me, teach me your ways, help me to become."

This instrument has been reading a book called *Handbook for a New Paradigm*, and one short prayer is suggested by this particular book, "Lord, I am a human being. Help me to become." When you know who you are, you are then free to change. When you are self-accepting, you are then free to evolve. Spiritual learning is not getting all the information needed and then having a degree in learning. We correct this instrument. In spirituality, spiritual learning is a mystery that occurs as the student begins to realize who he is, what his nature truly is. This instrument has over and over again in her life become tremendously excited and passionate, because she has experienced herself. And in that experience the self no longer contained the tired, drab garments of everyday personality. The self—any self, each of you, all of us—is a focal point in an infinitely complex and yet unified universe in which the Creator may learn about Itself. So you, as a teacher, are responsible, basically, for being that focused light through which the Creator shines. You are getting your surface personality out of the way so that the Creator may shine through more clearly.

Now, no entity in Western culture can teach in this silent way. There is always some content that is expected of a teacher in the Western culture. And certainly there are many, many good things said about many good subjects. Each teacher in his own way decides what the important facets are of spiritual evolution, and attempts as he talks about these things to open doors for the students. What this instrument was saying earlier was that—we correct this instrument. This instrument was saying earlier that when she is working with someone who is trying to understand a spiritual principle and how it applies to situations which may concern the student in everyday life she does not lecture. She asks the student to talk about his feelings, his thoughts, and his confusion. She stated that usually she is able to weave together from what the student has as the same material, in a slightly more focused form, by asking the student questions or by making comments on that which the student has said, asking the student for a reaction. What this instrument was attempting to express is the principle of that respect that a teacher has for the student when the teacher realizes fully that the student and the teacher are one.

What is happening when teaching a course in your schools is varied depending upon the teacher. If you have a merely competent and adequate teacher of the material the student will hear the explanation about the subject [and] will study what the teacher suggested. It will bring into mental organization a certain amount of awareness of that topic, which is aimed at passing a test and getting a grade. One might call this kind of learning "rote learning," learning by memorization. If this memorization is followed by a long period of repetition, that brief amount of learning gained in one class then deepens and true awareness takes place, where the student now is capable, not just of repeating what the teacher said, but of understanding the whole of the subject and how it all fits together, so that there is then in the student's awareness a livingness to that body of material.

When the teacher that teaches those same subjects is alive and aware of the subject, the element of inspiration is added to the subject and the students find it far easier to undergo the learning curve of rote memorization and so forth. But when the teacher, in its own spiritual journey, has reached a point of view which sees all things as one and sees the student one with itself there is added an ineffable deep level of support and encouragement that is completely unspoken and has to do with the essence of the human being that is sharing information. The best teachers are those whose chief delight is to learn from their students. Love is reflected in love. This is the spiritual principle upon which you may depend.

This instrument says, "What goes around, comes around." If you wish to teach, be the person that you are. Do not allow yourself to be distracted for long by the seduction of your own personality, by the concerns of your day, by the difficulties, the sufferings and the limitations that you may experiencing. If you wish to a good teacher always go back to the center of self and be yourself. You are a window. You may open upon the creation of the Father and through you entities may see light and love. When you offer that quality to your teaching, you [are] maximizing your role. And remember, it is a role. There is no end to the roles that you may play as you dance through the patterns of your life. Let your dance be grounded in self-awareness. And let yourself move to the music that you hear in your innermost heart.

May we ask, is there another query at this time?

Jim: S was wondering if the translations that she was making of our sessions into Italian contain the same energy in Italian as they do in English.

We are those of Q'uo, and are aware of your query, my sister. This question has seemingly one direction [and] our answer must contain two levels. What we mainly wish to assure you of, my sister, is that because your translation is done in love and because your offering is a labor of love you not only carry the vibrations of the original but you enhance it by the addition of your special [offer] of energy so that there are two translators. We are translated into English from concept communication by this instrument and you are translating from us to this instrument and then through yourself to reach those who would seek who live in a different language.

Consequently, you may rest assured that you lose nothing of the vibration of love and light which you yourself feel as you receive this information in English. Indeed, you may be encouraged to know that you add to those vibrations richness and depth by your love and light and your dedication to service.

The other level which we would touch upon briefly is simply this. Each language is idiosyncratic. There are, generally speaking, straight translations for the basic things of communication. Let us call it tourist communication. One may ask directions, one may say thank you, and one may order from a menu and do the things that are needed in a foreign land and trust the translations are accurate, because these are very basic conversations. When one is talking about spiritual principles, one is reaching into myth, archetype and mystery. And in these ways it is sometimes difficult to catch the flavor of English in another language. Just as an Italian, you could see that it would difficult to say some things that you say in Italian and have them translate directly into English. In each culture, there are unique perspectives, stories, myths and backgrounds that feed language. And so there is from time to time a difference in the way the concept maybe presented.

However, we celebrate the difference. We are limited by this instrument's culture, her language, her preferences, and so forth as we use this instrument. Because this is conscious channeling we use those things that are familiar to this instrument in order to convey concepts that are completely beyond this instrument's understanding. This is always the nature of spiritually based communications, because [you] are not talking about apples and pears, you are talking about truth, justice, beauty, compassion, unconditional love, realization and enlightenment.

Relax, my sister, and know that your part in serving others is fully acceptable and greatly appreciated by us.

May we ask if there is a query at this time? We are those of Q'uo.

R: I will ask a question Q'uo. And it concerns the translations. My question is when someone reads a transcript of one of the sessions and they try to understand the message that you were transmitting are you aware of this, are you able to join that person at a metaphysical level and help them understand?

We are those of Q'uo, and are aware of your query, my brother. When an entity reads something that has been channeled through this instrument our social memory complex is not informed of this. The entity that is involved is a more localized part of the guidance system of which we are also a part that is your personal guidance. It is your personal guidance system that is fully aware of any efforts that you may be making to understanding spiritual principles.

We are what this instrument would call a universal contact. You guidance system is what we would call an inner plane contact. You inner plane contacts are very intimate and personal to you. And your guidance system is indeed yourself, in a form that has been refined by higher density learning, so that you have a powerful helper that is always aware of you, always aware of what you are seeking and very responsive to any request that you may make of it.

If an entity who is reading our material, however, desires to involve us, it is immediately and instantaneously possible for that entity to do so. However, we must be asked. We have no right to have an energy exchange with you without your knowledge, it is part of the same restrictions under which we always ask you to be guardians of your own thoughts so that we do not have undue influence over you. We attempt always to remain completely aware of the supremacy of each entity's free will. And each entity is right to learn for himself. We would only weaken spiritual seekers were we to begin learning for them and telling them what to do. However, we are fully willing to be with any who asks us to be with them. It is a mental request that is necessary. Simply mentally think to yourself, "Q'uo, I would really appreciate it if you could be with me right now." And we will be there. We will be there to love you, to support you. And when you go into meditation and contemplation, to help you find the heart of yourself so that you may deepen that level of focus and that level of contemplation, that level of awareness of the silence. We are most happy to do this and are only a thought away.

Does that answer your question, my brother, or do you have a follow-up? We are those of Q'uo.

R: Thank you, Q'uo, that does answer my question. Thank you for being willing to be with those who requested and for enunciating with such beauty of the importance of observing the free will.

And we are those of Q'uo, and we thank you, my brother. It has been a supernal loving experience for us being with you this evening. We thank you once again for calling us for your circle of seeking.

We leave you as we found you, in the love and light of the infinite Creator. We are those of the principle of Q'uo. Adonai. Adonai. ❧

Year 2007
January 7, 2007 to December 29, 2007

L/L Research

L/L Research is a subsidiary of Rock Creek Research & Development Laboratories, Inc.

P.O. Box 5195
Louisville, KY 40255-0195

www.llresearch.org

Rock Creek is a non-profit corporation dedicated to discovering and sharing information which may aid in the spiritual evolution of humankind.

ABOUT THE CONTENTS OF THIS TRANSCRIPT: This telepathic channeling has been taken from transcriptions of the weekly study and meditation meetings of the Rock Creek Research & Development Laboratories and L/L Research. It is offered in the hope that it may be useful to you. As the Confederation entities always make a point of saying, please use your discrimination and judgment in assessing this material. If something rings true to you, fine. If something does not resonate, please leave it behind, for neither we nor those of the Confederation would wish to be a stumbling block for any.

© 2009 L/L Research

Sunday Meditation
January 7, 2007

Group question: The question today, Q'uo, has to do with how the seeker that desires to be of service affects both the service and him or herself by either doubting the service, doubting the self, or feeling a little bit too good about it, like maybe he or she did a really good thing. How does the attitude of the one who seeks to serve affect the server and the service?

(Carla channeling)

We are those known to you as the principle of Q'uo. Greetings in the love and in the light of the one infinite Creator, in Whose service we come to your circle of seeking this day.

We thank you for taking the time and the energy to create a circle of seeking. We thank you for calling us to share our thoughts with you. It is a great blessing and privilege and it fills our heart with joy to be asked to offer our opinions on the subject of the effect on service of attitudes such as pride and doubt.

We, as always, first, however, would request for all of those listening to these words or reading them, that you be aware of how powerful a person that you are. You are the only person capable of distinguishing for yourself between those things that are useful for you in your spiritual process and those things that are not useful for you at this time, no matter how sensible they may be or how well they sound.

You are the guardian of the temple of your process. Please guard well our thoughts as they come to you.

If they resonate then by all means take them and use them as you can. If they do not resonate please do not attempt to make use of them but simply lay them aside and move on. We thank you for this consideration for it will enable us to speak without being concerned that we might infringe upon your free will or impede the directness of your progress.

We thank the one known as R for this query. In order to respond to the question about the effect of attitude on service, we must take many steps backwards from the specificity of that question. For such a question begins with the deepest question of all philosophical questions, "Who am I?"

Who are you, my friends? Are you the entity that thinks? Are you the entity that sits in a chair in this room, has clothes on, looks a certain way and has come to this moment of pondering with a personality, a history, and an incarnation's worth of memory?

Are you the roles that you play? Are you the things that you say?

The one known as D pointed out that in the metaphysical world, our thoughts are things, so that that which you do in the world is not at all, metaphysically speaking, the whole of [who] you are, when you have thought upon thought upon thought that has been generated by you, followed by you, and either dropped or used as a tool for transformation or cyclical worry.

Who are you? Who are we? My friends, you know that we are messengers of unconditional love. Our message is not that we come to you in love but that we and you are love. Because we are all one. So your question is asked against our background of being aware that all of us are one interacting, interpenetrating union of various foci or points which the Creator may use to observe, to process, and to harvest experience. Therefore, when you serve another, you are serving yourself.

However, in a sense of being able to use that information to work spiritually, we realize that there needs to be more discussion. And so we move a step closer to the question and talk about you and those with whom you interact. We have just noted that you and all others are part of a unitary creation. However, as with all good spiritual principles, there is a paradox involved. That paradox is that each of you exists in his own universe. You are the Creator of that inner universe.

Therefore, it is as if you were a sun, radiant and unimaginably full of the love and the light of the one infinite Creator. Others are also suns with their own radiance and effulgence.[33] Between you, just as there seems to be a great distance between suns, there is a great distance, shall we say, a sea of in-between.

Each who is incarnated in a physical body such as you are is deeply aware of that great water of otherness that seems to exist between one person and another. While it is true that all of this "otherness" is an illusion, nevertheless it is also true that the sense of being different from the rest of creation was carefully set up for you in order to create an atmosphere in which you could do spiritual work.

The Creator has attempted creations in which each entity in third density was aware of the truth of unity. It was discovered that in this atmosphere of being completely aware of who they were, entities were not motivated to seek further. The veiling of this awareness of the unitary nature of all creation was discovered to be an improvement on the design of, shall we say, the schoolroom of third density.

Your particular creation, then, is a creation in which you are veiled from that stunning awareness of your identity with all that exists. And it is as though you live in a body which is a barrier or a defense and certainly a limitation and a demarcation between you and the rest of the world.

When you come into contact with other people, it is as though those two stars become two ships that are sailing closer and closer together. Naturally, they do not wish to run into each other. They navigate around each other with some care.

There is that within each which yearns, however, to come into right relationship with others. There is a deep desire to find harmony, peace, relaxation and mutual affection when you reach out to another person.

How you think about yourself does impact the way that other people see you in a subconscious manner. This is because actions speak louder than words. Your body language, your gestures, your speech, the expression on your face, the look in your eye, all come across to other people in ways you cannot imagine looking in the mirror.

You do not see the self that others see when they look at you. You shall never know how beautiful some people think you are and hopefully you shall never know how unattractive others think you are. You are encased in your own opinion of yourself and while others' opinions of you may batter against that bastion, they cannot bring it down. What you think about yourself is what is in your creation and in your universe.

There is a moment in the seeker's life when the seeker chooses his way of life. When that moment comes—and, indeed, for many entities upon the surface of your planet at this time, that moment has not yet come and may not come at all—something changes about the way you see yourself. When you decide you wish to be of service to others and you wish to polarize in that sense, you create an expectation, a hope, and a goal.

Naturally, you cannot imagine precisely what being of service to others will entail. But you set your intention. And with that intention your ship has now formed a rudder. Your star has now formed its orbit. You have created in your universe a Pole Star[34] of hope.

---

[33] effulgence: radiant brightness.

[34] The Pole Star is also known as the North Star and is the brightest star in Ursa Minor. Pole stars are often used in the navigation of ships because the pole stars' position in the sky doesn't change throughout the night and thus dependably indicates north.

This creates, metaphysically speaking, a passage from the spiritually immature person to the spiritually mature person. This is not to say that there is not always work to do in ripening the fruit of self but that until you take yourself seriously enough to make that life decision to offer all that you are in service to others, metaphysically speaking, you have not yet awakened from the dream of incarnation.

When you have taken yourself that seriously and dedicated yourself that completely to the hope of being love within the world that you experience at this time, you become a magical entity. You know who you are to a greater extent than anyone could who has not yet come to the point of making that choice.

As you go about your life after that point, there may be no obvious difference in the services that you render to others. Nevertheless, to you there is a difference! There is a profound difference in that you have taken responsibility to seek resources and materials that will help you to investigate how to be of service and how to be of service more skillfully.

So, in a way, you put yourself under the gun. We use that idiomatic expression because in a way the decision to be of service to others is like the starting gun of a race. It is a marathon. It is more than a marathon. It is a lifetime. And you seek to move steadily, running a "straight race with God's good grace," as this instrument's hymn has it.

This same hymn brings us to our next point. The next words of that particular poem are, "Lift up thine eyes and seek His face."[35] You are under grace, my friends, when you choose to be of service. A tremendous amount of help surrounds you in that choice. Grace abounds, for when you choose to love, you choose to express the nature of the creation and the Creator. Your choice is in direct alignment with the truth, that truth that is such a great mystery that no one has ever been able to articulate it.

When you lift up from gazing at your own thoughts, your own processes, and the details of your conscious existence, you lift yourself into a goodly company. You lift yourself to a level of concept.

Now let us look at that a moment. Selfhood is in itself a concept and you are asking about this concept when you ask about how attitude can change your service. Lifting up from the concept of self is not looking away from the self, it is seeking a deeper and more informative and helpful kind of awareness of what that self is.

So, as a servant of the light who wishes to serve others, you have a dual awareness of self in that a part of yourself is aware that you are one with all with whom you interact.

The other part of yourself is self-conscious, self-aware and self-bounded by the limits of the thoughts within the brain, the shape of the body, and the shape of the concept of the physical self that you have.

Both of these concepts of self are useful and accurate and you play with them your whole life long. For, when you are moving out the front door to get the paper in the morning, you are moving not only as love itself, incarnated in physical form, you are also moving as a sleepy human who is noticing the weather and the state of the morning and so forth as the paper is fetched from the mailbox. You are at the same time sublime and endlessly and tediously detailed and worldly.

Letting those two concepts of self harmonize themselves is an art. And we encourage you always to make room for the sleepy one who is going out and fetching the morning paper to see the news of the day. As you progress spiritually, do not scorn the everyday and the ordinary. For those are moments of sacredness also.

Indeed, our answer is couched in the concept of allowing the self to become aware, slowly and gradually, of the depth and the richness of your own self. Not shunning or eschewing any part of the self, any part of the veneer of civilization and culture, or the slightly deeper natures of race and teaching and culture. Never shunning sexual differences, but embracing them and acknowledging them. You incarnated just as you are for good reasons. Do not turn your back upon them but appreciate them and see what they have to give you in order to help you be of service to others.

---

[35] The second verse of J. S. B. Monsell's 1863 poem, "Fight the Good Fight," is:
  Run the straight race through God's good grace.
  Lift up thine eyes and seek his face.
  Life with its way before us lies.
  Christ is the path and Christ the prize.

Service to others can be seen to consist of two parts, simplistically speaking. That is, the service you intend to give and the service that you give. In addition to those two parts, there is a third part which is entirely private and important only to yourself.

The service that you intend to give is in line with your decision to be of service to others in the first place. You have set your intention for your lifetime in that cornerstone decision. Each time that you repeat that decision in choosing consciously to be of service to another, you are doubling your polarity. You are creating a more and more powerful self, a self more and more capable of achieving changes in consciousness at will.

You are becoming a magician in the most high sense of that word. You have left your mailbox and your home town behind and you are relating directly to the star of hope. How glorious and how beautiful that upliftment is as we see you repeatedly attempting to set your intention and to serve. Those intentions cannot be taken away. What happens in the world "out there," shall we say, is of no consequence, in terms of what is happening metaphysically.

Service to others' second part, shall we say, is the service itself. When you serve another person it is as if you gave a gift. You cannot help but wrap that gift in a certain kind of paper with a certain kind of ribbon and a certain kind of bow. You are who you are. Your gifts are generally wrapped in biases that constitute the wrapping of the present. That person's reaction to the package will, to some extent, affect his use of the present itself.

We do not say this so that you will be concerned about it. We say this so that you will understand that you are not responsible for the way people take what you offer with a pure and good heart. You are responsible only for the offering and for crafting that offering to be as beautiful as possible.

When you have given that service, whether it be a word, a gesture, a gift of money, a gift of time and attention, or whatever your service to others is, it is completely out of your hands. Your baby has left the dwelling place, never to return. And in someone else's universe, a gift has been given.

What that entity does with your gift is of no concern to you. Many, many times that which you intend occurs, and there is rejoicing between the two of you. Many other times, my friends, your gifts will not be recognized for what they are. They will be trampled into the dust. They will be taken for the opposite of which you intended. Or any other number of things may occur to that gift.

You have to let that be all right. You cannot be chasing after your service to others and shaping it up, altering a bit here and spiffing up there. You must let it go.

If you find resistance to your gift, we suggest that you study that, sit with that, as the one known as R said earlier. Allow that to be part of your awareness as you ask yourself, "How may I better serve?"

That third and inward part of service to others has to do with the attitudes with which you approach service. As long as you remain within your personality shell, you will always be second-guessing your service. You will always, according to your nature, either be concerned that it was not enough or proud of yourself because you have done such a good job of serving others.

This has little to no impact on the service itself. The service itself has been moved into another entity's creation. You cannot affect your service by doubting yourself. The service continues unimpeded. You cannot affect the service that you give by being proud of it.

However, everything, my friends, is grist for the mill, including the thoughts that you have about what you do, what you think, and what you say. In the intellectual reaches of your creation, you can chase your tail in an endless number of ways. You can doubt yourself, congratulate yourself, feel guilty, wonder if you could have done better and any number of other emotions, thoughts and feelings which, in turn, become that at which you are now looking.

If you simply continue to watch yourself think and become conscious of the process, you shall eventually achieve realization. We always encourage each to spend time in the silence and to sink down into that silence to receive its riches.

Part of the sinking down into the silence is letting go of your self-concept. With us now, visualize yourself, each of you, in a small room. It is bare, monk-like, and yet when you go to that room, you are happy. For it is the room where you pray and ask. It is the room in which you are fed in that muscular silence of the inner heart. Kneel down upon that bare floor and remove from yourself the concept that you have of who you are. Take it down, my friends. Take every concept away and just allow yourself to kneel before the love and the light of the one infinite Creator.

As you allow yourself—the concept of yourself—to melt away, you become an empty vessel, shaped to hold the love and the light that you find pouring into you in that inner room.

Who are you then, my friends?

When you have emptied yourself so that you can hold the gift of love and light, you are in the position of the one known as Jesus the Christ when he knelt down in the garden of Gethsemane and said, "Not my will but Thine be done."

And when you rise up and go out again from that inner room, you will find the Earth a sparkling place, bursting with joy. You will sense the air humming around you as if to welcome you to the world.

And you will know who you are.

You will feel that livingness without the need to identify it, define it or describe it. Because you are no longer your personal self when you rise from your knees in that inner room. You are a very impersonal self, that self that all entities truly are beneath the many layers of self that have been taught, the poses that have been struck, and the decisions about details that have limited you this way and that until you have painted yourself into the corner of who you describe yourself as being.

You have burst free of all of that when you become the "I" that serves. And then, my friends, you do not have to wonder how you did. You do not have to doubt yourself and it will not occur to you to pat yourself upon the back.

You cannot stay within that state of mind on a continuing basis if you are like most of those upon your planet. And you are not intended to stay there. For you have work to do that you gave yourself to do, that did not have to do with service to others as much as it had to do with growing your own mature balance of self.

Balance is a very helpful word when it comes to attempting to envision and focus your energies and spend them wisely. There is always a dynamic balance that is going on in your life, no matter what issue you take up. Look for the balance, not for the right or the wrong. Look for the resonance and the sense of deep confidence within that says, "Yes, this is where I should be. This is how I wish to serve. This is my best environment."

When you feel that you are in the right place at the right time, then there is a relaxation within you.

(Side one of tape ends.)

(Carla channeling)

And you do not strain or stretch in the space which the world has for you. You have made your space by identifying yourself as the "I" that serves. Take your Christhood upon you. Wear it well. Wear it humbly. Wear it proudly. You shall serve, my friends, with excellence.

We are aware that we have but scratched the surface of this topic and yet we are also aware that this instrument is suggesting to us that we move on, and we would ask at this time if there are further questions that you have or a follow-up to the query that has already been asked. We are those of Q'uo.

S: If you wish to serve with unconditional love and yet seemingly those around you do not wish what you have to offer, where do you go with that?

We are those of Q'uo, and we believe we understand your query, my brother. We said earlier through this instrument that when you have offered a service, it is no longer your own. This is a harsh truth sometimes, because sometimes your offering falls upon stony ground.

This has nothing to do with your offering, my brother. For that which you have offered with a full heart and a pure intention is as it is. It cannot be scorned or taken down in the world of concept and metaphysical truth, although in the illusory world which you call consensus reality there is no guarantee that anyone will ever understand any gift that you may give.

We believe that this is the kind of situation about which the one known as Jesus the Christ was attempting to talk when he was speaking of the blessings of being poor in mind, of being in grief, of crying, of being in so many difficult situations and yet before every description of a sad situation—sad seeming to the world—the one known as Jesus said,

"Blessed are those…" We believe that the one that meets your needs at this time is, "Blessed are the meek in heart, for they shall inherit the Earth."

The blessing of not being understood or accepted for precisely who you are is that it moves you to a deeper place where you offer that self to the lover of your soul that is the infinite Creator. In your grief, there is a beauty that is unmistakable. And all we can suggest to you, my brother, at this time is that you focus on the blessing of this situation and allow it to sweeten you as it humbles you.

Out of that humility and sweetness come the sprouts of new hope, new life, new energies to meet, new loves to greet.

May we answer you further, my brother?

S: No, thank you for that.

We are those of Q'uo, and we thank you as well, my brother. May we ask if there is another query at this time? We are those of Q'uo.

T: Yes, I would like to ask a question. We spoke earlier of meditation and the difficulties of sitting in meditation and finding the time or just going and doing it and I have been working with programming before I go to sleep at night with thoughts that I want to explore or just various things. I guess that I would like to have some comment on the efficacy of doing that. I feel it's beneficial but I would just like to have some comment on that if you would please.

We are those of Q'uo, and believe we understand your query, my brother. It may seem an unspiritual thing to say, but in truth, a good deal of what is processed through your instrument as a spiritual seeker is much like work on the computer. There is programming involved. You have a set of defaults, in general, in your life. You were born with some of them. Others of them were taught to you by those who wanted to tell you who you are. This constitutes the original programming for the kind of query the one known as R was asking earlier, about how does your attitude affect the service.

When you ask yourself to program for a certain intention before you get to bed at night, you are overriding the original programming and making it your own. This is an excellent thing. As you set your intention, then, set your intention truly, mean it sincerely, ask it humbly, and release it.

Now, it is very important that you release it. Because it will grow if you allow it to grow. That programming alerts other programming deep in your bio-computer, shall we say, programming having to do with accepting help and becoming more sensitive and attentive to guidance. And as you continue to move along one line of intention, you are accelerating the rate of your spiritual growth greatly.

To balance the excellence of this we would simply offer you the corresponding and balancing dynamic to all intentions to accelerate the pace of your spiritual growth. That is, that the more skillfully you program yourself for opening up to transformation, the more change will seem to occur in your life. Change is often very difficult to process. And so you may feel, if you contemplate this, that you have done yourself a disservice. This is not true. You have simply asked of yourself that you move more quickly than the earthly part of you might perhaps feel comfortable in moving.

So, as you move into doing this programming before sleep as a steady and stable practice you may well find that various things in your life seem to jump up at you and say, "I am a problem. I need to be dealt with." Yes, you have asked this of yourself! These are the little ten-minutes quizzes you get when you are in the midst of transformation. This does not mean that it is not a good idea to do what you were doing, it is simply that it is well to mention that there is a corresponding dynamic when you are being the most successful, shall we say, at becoming more what you would wish to be, in that each effort in that direction is balanced by the challenges or catalyst that will appear in just such a shape and form as to be sure that you meant what you said.

May we answer you further, my brother?

T: No, thank you.

We thank you, my brother. Is there a final query at this time?

Jim: The instrument is attempting to write articles to explain the archetypes to people who would like to study them. What would be the philosophy concerning archetypes that would be the most important to get across?

We are those of Q'uo, and are aware of your query, my sister. In this effort, my sister, your art, pallid though it may be, is the art that must be used; your words, inefficacious that they may be, must be the words used. As you are attempting to learn how to teach and as this information is very active in your life at this time, we cannot infringe upon your free will be attempting to make decisions for you.

We know that you understand and that you were aware that this may be the outcome of such a question. We may, however, share with you our encouragement and encourage you further to relax your mind and to pray before you begin to write each day. There are times that you have forgotten to do this, my sister. Do not forget it. Opening to that guidance is doing a good deal more than you can possibly imagine.

You have an excellent mind, as do many artists. And yet the burden that you wish to sing is beyond your instrument, as it is beyond all human instruments. Therefore, open yourself to the inspiration and the intuition that come from that movement towards prayer, that movement towards the asking, "How may I serve?"

At this time, we would take our leave of this instrument and this group, with great regrets, we must say, for we have greatly enjoyed your company. Your beauty astounds us. The sacred space you have built together houses us too. Thank you.

We leave you in the love and in the light of the one infinite Creator. We are known to you as the principle of Q'uo. Adonai. Adonai. Love and light. Light and love. ☙

L/L Research

L/L Research is a subsidiary of Rock Creek Research & Development Laboratories, Inc.

P.O. Box 5195
Louisville, KY 40255-0195

www.llresearch.org

Rock Creek is a non-profit corporation dedicated to discovering and sharing information which may aid in the spiritual evolution of humankind.

ABOUT THE CONTENTS OF THIS TRANSCRIPT: This telepathic channeling has been taken from transcriptions of the weekly study and meditation meetings of the Rock Creek Research & Development Laboratories and L/L Research. It is offered in the hope that it may be useful to you. As the Confederation entities always make a point of saying, please use your discrimination and judgment in assessing this material. If something rings true to you, fine. If something does not resonate, please leave it behind, for neither we nor those of the Confederation would wish to be a stumbling block for any.

© 2009 L/L Research

Sunday Meditation
January 21, 2007

Group question: We saw a movie last week[36] where the hero gave his life to save a friend from a gang of bad guys but he killed a number of bad guys in the process. His intentions were pure to serve and save his friend but his actions were mixed. We would like to ask Q'uo how our polarity is affected when our intentions are good but our actions are mixed.

(Carla channeling)

We are those known to you as Q'uo. We greet you in the love and in the light of the one infinite Creator, in Whose service we come to you this day. Thank you for asking us to join your circle of seeking and to share our thoughts on the workings of intention, action and polarity. Certainly today, my friends, you ask a rich question and we will attempt to mine this lode of questing as best as we can.

As always, we would ask for you to be guardians of your own temple, to be the lions at the gate that do not accept information unless it resonates. If our thoughts resonate to you, then they are yours to work with. If they do not, my friends, please leave them aside. In this way you will safeguard your own free will and make sure that we do not have an undue influence upon your spiritual process. We thank you for this consideration as it allows us to rest in the knowledge that we are not infringing upon free will.

You ask this day concerning the motion picture which this instrument calls *The Ninth Configuration* and the issues which it raises. Many are the times, when violence is involved, that the intention is relatively pure, as was the anti-hero's in *The Ninth Configuration*.

Most entities involved in violence, whether personally or on behalf of a group such as a nation-state, are not habitually in a state of rage, anger or other violent emotions. Most have responded to the need to defend that which they hold dear. In the end, many involved in violence on behalf of their nation-state die attempting to protect their loved ones at home and the safety of the home environment.

While there are those who delight in violence and look for opportunities to be cruel and destructive, by far the majority of entities upon your planet strive towards goodness, truth and beauty and do not love violence or the dark emotions that surround the physical acting out of aggression against fellow human beings. Your entire planet has a population with ideals and intentions that are far purer and

---

[36] "The Ninth Configuration," written, directed and produced by William Peter Blatty and starring Stacey Keach, was originally released in 1979. It was one of Don Elkins' favorite movies and we screened it so that Gary could see it. The title reflects the film's thesis, which is that the very presence of life on earth, which required such a specific set of conditions and molecules in the scientific "ninth configuration," must imply the existence of some higher force or purpose.

more positive than the actions which they undertake might lead one to believe.

In this regard we would note that your culture, with its menu of television shows and motion pictures which demonstrate and even glorify violence, is not geared to aiding its population in the ways of spiritual seeking. Your young ones have violence shown to them in their toys, their programs and movies, the stories of heroism and valor on the battleground and their video games, in which they are able to achieve a sense of invulnerability as they pretend to kill target after target after target, thereby predisposing their growing minds to the numbing affects of the acceptance of violence as a way of behavior.

And indeed, how many of you have seen violent acts? How many of you, my friends, have had parents who abused either you or those near to you? How many of you in your school days have experienced the bullying on the playground or the less obvious but equal violence of words, meanness, pettiness and rumor spread with delight by those who enjoy victimizing the outsider, the one who does not fit in?

This adds up to an atmosphere or environment which is pervasively accepting of violence. We do not wish here to move into discussion of a nation's right to make war in order to defend its principles. This is not the place for that discussion. We look at violence here from the standpoint of the soldier in the trenches and the person on the street, not the society or the governing institutions which help to create the environment which you find yourselves enjoying at this time.

Into this atmosphere and this environment you came, as the one known as William said, "trailing clouds of glory,"[37] from a place of perfect love into the violence-strewn environment of Earth as you find it this day. The clouds of glory depart, the veil falls, and the young child begins to wend its way from absolute unawareness, unconsciousness and ignorance towards consciousness, awareness and understanding.

You are not your environment. Your heritage is not only Earthly. Your genealogy is not only of the blood of Earth. You are citizens of the starry heavens. You hold within you the truth you seek. Safely is it buried beneath the drifts of memory and habit that you have accumulated in this incarnation.

Some of you have investigated yourselves enough to have become aware of who you are and why you are here. Some of you have scented that prey of understanding and awareness that you seek and you are after it like a dog on the scent of a fox.

We would encourage all of you to persevere in your seeking, taking each day as it comes and letting wisdom and understanding drip into your environment as the dew of heaven falls upon the grass, just as manna fell upon the grass for those who followed Moses.

You are not your surroundings or the ideas of those around you. You are one who can take nourishment directly from spirit. You do have a plethora of what this instrument would call bad information. Some of you wonder if there is any possibility of an entity being a truly ethical human being, so compromised is each soul in his own estimation. However, you have sources of good information as well. And so we ask you to take heart.

There are several ways to look at ethics. There is the Rhadamanthine[38] way. It is severe and stark. In that system of judgment, which is completely earthly and not at all taking the characteristics of consciousness or infinity, a man who has murdered another is guilty.

In this Rhadamanthine system which informs your present system of courts, justice, checks and balances and so forth, there would be a representative from the victim stating that this man was guilty because he had committed murder. There would be another

---

[37] This quotation is from a poem by William Wordsworth, written from 1803 to 1806, entitled "Intimations of Immortality from Recollections of Early Childhood." The quotation above is from the fifth stanza, which begins thusly:

> Our birth is but a sleep and a forgetting:
> The Soul that rises with us, our life's Star,
>   Hath had elsewhere its setting,
>   And cometh from afar:
>   Not in entire forgetfulness,
>   And not in utter nakedness,
> But trailing clouds of glory do we come
>   From God, who is our home:
> Heaven lies about is in our infancy!

[38] Rhadamanthys, in Greek mythology, is the son of Zeus and Europa. He exemplifies justice during his Earthly life and after his death is made a judge of the underworld. His name has been given to systems of justice which are inflexibly just or severe.

entity defending the rights of the man on trial saying that this man was acting in self-defense. In this system of justice, the twelve good men and true, as the jury in your legal system is often called, would weigh the sin of murder against the extenuating circumstances and call the entity either guilty or not guilty.

In your Earth world, such questions must be settled one way or another, even if there is truth on both sides. And so a judgment would have been made, the entity undoubtedly being imprisoned for his crime and perhaps himself being killed as part of the severe justice of this type of system.

There is a second way of valuing: intentions versus actions. The one known as Jim was speaking earlier of that segment within the sessions of this group with the one known as Ra where the Ra group stated that the one known as Jesus the Christ was only absolved of his childhood violence when he forgave the thief on the cross beside him and said to him, "This day shall you be with me in paradise."

At this level of looking at the workings of polarity, the one known as Jesus the Christ was in karmic debt from the point in his boyhood where he had done violence to another human being, however unintentionally. Because he had not forgiven himself for that action, he was karmically tied to that action and that entity because of his unwillingness to release himself from the burden of guilt. He was unwilling to forgive himself of his sin. And we use that word "sin" advisedly. That would be a topic upon which we could speak in and of itself! Perhaps you could substitute the word "error" in order to create a more neutrally emotional word for a lapse in judgment that results in unfortunate consequences.

When the one known as Jesus was faced with this self-confessed thief and murderer who asked him for forgiveness, Jesus the Christ not only forgave him but he realized with a flash of insight that pierced his very heart that he had the ability to forgive all others in the world but he was holding himself away from the redemptive power of the forgiveness that he himself came, in his own intention, to offer to the world. And so, finally, joyfully, thankfully, he released himself from his mistake. He forgave himself and he was free.

Note here that we are not talking about the level in which some things are right and some things are wrong and the wrong things must be punished. That is the Rhadamanthine system of justice upon your planet. We are talking here about the world of karma where bonds are made between people when they interact in an unbalanced way and do not work out that imbalance. The workings of karma are only very partially outward.

In other words, the entity known as Jesus could go to the family of the entity whom he hurt in his childhood and ask them to forgive him. It would be hoped that they would find it in their hearts to do so. But the wheels of karma are stopped not by the forgiveness of another but by the forgiveness of the self by the self.

There is a curious unwillingness in entities to let go of their guilt. What is past is past and what was wrong will never be right in the earthly sense. But it is fear that keeps the soul from standing in the light of ethical day and confessing that error, that darkness within, to the infinite Creator and asking forgiveness. That is an externalization of the process in which you ask yourself for forgiveness.

It is helpful to have that outer machinery of the structure of the Creator above and you below so that you can lift your hands up in supplication to a forgiving and loving Father and ask for forgiveness. Yet, in truth, this process is internal and the Creator you ask for forgiveness dwells already in your heart of hearts.

Thusly, on this level of karma, the disposition of this anti-hero who had striven with all of his heart to be totally positive and yet had, in the end, acted out tremendous violence and done murder, would hinge upon whether he forgave himself as he died. He had condemned himself by refusing to allow anyone to know that he was hurt. He wished to die for that which he had done. Thusly he drew down judgment upon his own head in the Rhadamanthine fashion, in this instrument's mind, at least.

The film did not make it clear whether or not the anti-hero forgave himself. If he did not forgive himself, he remained tied through karmic bonds to those whom he hurt and killed. If he forgave himself, karmically speaking, he was no longer in karmic debt, for such debts are put "Paid" when forgiveness offers its redemptive value to the equation.

There is a third level upon one which may consider intention and action and how that affects polarity.

And this is perhaps closer to the crux of your query than either of the other two levels we have discussed. This level of consideration is entirely metaphysical.

At this level of consideration, one is not looking at the facts on the surface. "Who did what to whom?" is not a consideration here. For at this level, each entity is dwelling within its own completely whole and three-dimensional creation.

It is no shadow world, this world that you are in, metaphysically. It is indeed an environment more real than the consensus reality of planet Earth in terms of your being a citizen of eternity.

In the environment of consciousness and the heart, we are looking not at manifestation but at energy expenditures. We are looking at the vibration which an entity has. This vibratory complex is as your fingerprint or your DNA, on a metaphysical level. Let us explain this briefly.

Consciousness is, at base, precisely the same in all of you. And as you move into more and more maturity, spiritually speaking, you will begin to discover that consciousness is impersonal, carrying the nature and quality of the Creator Itself which is the Logos or unconditional love. Each of you has this consciousness and works, either fitfully or steadily, with this consciousness in moments of insight, in dreaming, and so forth.

That which you are doing at any particular moment may be affecting your vibration. You have the ability and the capacity to change your vibratory nature, to lift it up. Indeed, you will gradually change in vibration through the effects of life experience, whether or not you intend to progress. If you do intend to progress and take steps to focus in on your energy body, the expenditures of energy for which you are responsible, and the decisions which have ethical implications, you are accelerating the pace of your spiritual evolution.

The more ways that you can find to bring ethical considerations into your thinking, the more lucid your ability to evaluate situations will become. The more you ask for guidance in looking at ethical questions, the more accurate your web of perceptions can become.

Yet in the end you are responsible only for doing your best. You cannot entirely corral or control your own vibrations. They are like your breathing or your heartbeat. You can consciously stop breathing for awhile but unconsciousness will soon come and you will begin breathing again. You can race your heart until it is beating as fast as two hundred times a minute by doing intense physical exercise but when you stop that exercise it will find again its own level.

However, if you hold your breath repeatedly you will eventually develop that system of lungs that will therefore be stronger because of your practice. And if you exercise regularly, running your heart up and letting it cool back down again, you'll find that your heart is pumping more efficiently and is able to move the blood around your body with fewer beats of the pump of that heart per minute.

So you have some effect, as a physical person, upon how your body works. But you are cooperating with nature. You do not have the final decision as to whether your heart shall beat and your breath shall respire. It is the same kind of situation in your energy body. You can be attentive and watchful and look as the hunter for his prey for situations that can be considered for their ethical values. You can ask your highest and best self, your guidance system, to help you make ethical choices that lift you from where you were to a new level of acting out the thoughts that you understand to represent virtue.

You are able to walk your talk. And this exercise, too, strengthens and changes the energy body so that it more efficiently is able to allow the love and the light of the one infinite Creator to flow through into the heart chakra, where lies the stunning mystery of the one infinite Creator.

In this system of judging the dynamic between intention and manifestation, it is not precisely that intention is all. It is that intention is the only metaphysical portion of the equation. So intention figures into the vibratory nature of yourself as a result of the action that you have done.

In this system of evaluating the anti-hero's situation, we would say that this entity was clearly vibrating in service to others at the time of his death and would guess that the screenwriter intended to portray an entity who was extremely service-to-others oriented by nature. So dealing with this hypothetical and fictional anti-hero, we would say that, undoubtedly, as he was represented by the author and the actor that acted his part in the motion picture, this entity graduated in service-to-others polarity.

And indeed, again, it was not simply his intention that moves into that estimation by us but rather his entire being as it vibrated naturally beyond his control, expressing the truth of himself, including all of the mysteries and the secrets that he had not discovered yet about himself or had discovered and then buried.

It is a relativistic ethic indeed that we offer you for consideration this day. Pure ethic, that Kantian search for the categorical imperative where, if something is right once, it is right always, cannot work either in Earth or in the starry heavens.

Certainly, ideals themselves are pure. But ideals are called ideals because they are not earthly. They are the thoughts that lift us up and inspire us. They are those fields of purity that attract us and enchant us but their nature is such that they are entities, living entities. Living, certainly, not as humans, but as the angels or fairies or gods and goddesses of myths. They are ideas and concepts. And in their own world they are living beings.

You may dip into truth, dip into justice, dip into fairness, and so forth, to take on the energy of that pure idea. But as it moves into your energy body, it is colored by your presuppositions and biases, the distortions that you have made in this consciousness that is common to all.

It is good, in terms of lifting your vibrations from day-to-day, to ponder and remember these wonderful ideals of truth, unconditional love, beauty, hope, charity, justice and fairness. It is good to invite them to be through you a beacon unto the world.

But it is well to realize that in a very complex series of energy exchanges, the finished product of what you have done by praying is a minute but significant adjustment in the balances, the clarity, the amount of energy, and so forth in your energy body. And it is your energy body, specifically the read-out of the entire energy body that is seen within the seventh chakra or energy center, that determines your polarity at any given moment.

You cannot bank polarity. You cannot do so many good things and so many bad things and add up the difference. You are involved in an illusory progress through time. The one known as Thales[39] said, "You cannot step in the same river twice." And we say to you [that] you cannot step in the same action or thought twice. It happens and you move on. It is gone forever. That chance that you had to think, to pray, and to act is gone forever. In its place is an equally precious present moment. And so this continues throughout each heartbeat of your incarnation.

You are always experiencing the final moment of your life and then discovering that you have outlived that moment. But it is well to act as if each moment were your final moment. For this points out the gravity and the substance of your ethical choices and how important it is to pay attention to them. For only by making these ethical choices, one upon another upon another, so that you get the habit of fielding the ethical implications of the present moment, can you maximize the use of your time.

(Side one of tape ends.)

When you go to graduation you shall not have a grade of 100% of service to others. However, the Creator seems to grade on a curve here. If you even have 51% of service to others, you are ready to graduate. Each time you consciously choose to serve others, you have moved above 51% and into positive polarization comfortably sufficient to graduate from planet Earth. The more habitual your realization of choices is and your determination to choose the highest road, the most compassionate and loving response, the more positively you will be able to affect the tuning of your energy body so that it vibrates more and more in service to others in terms of polarity.

You shall never be able to untangle the good from the evil within humankind, my friends, because you, as a member of the human race, are both good and

---

[39] Wikipedia: "Heraclitus is famous for (allegedly) expressing the notion that no man can cross the same river twice: *We both step and do not step in the same rivers. We are and are not.*"

Q'uo attributes the same notion to Thales, who lived seven centuries before the time of Christ in Miletus. He was the first recorded Greek philosopher and was considered one of the Seven Wise Men of Greece for his exhortation on Unity. He was the first man to attempt to explain the nature of the physical world philosophically—by the natural processes of human thought—rather than mythologically—by the supernatural. Thales' basic theory is that everything in nature is one thing. He thought that one thing was water; hence the significance of this statement attributed to him by Q'uo.

evil. You contain all the shades of virtue and vice within one global entity.

By a series of choices, you have found ways to be yourself to the outer world and to yourself. You have shut much of the shadow side of your nature away because it is unpleasant to see and it is very difficult to bear. Unusual situations such as occurred in the case of this anti-hero in *The Ninth Configuration* create situations that take us all by surprise, as this fight took the anti-hero by surprise.

We ask you, then, not to dwell in judgment of yourself or others. You cannot help being judgmental and we do not discourage the practice of judgment. We simply ask that you begin with the judgment that is inherent in your nature as a human being, but that you do not stop there. Move forward into the blessed light-strewn fields of the Creator and invite the sunshine of wisdom and unconditional love as you find ways to spend your precious energy and your precious time within the school of planet Earth.

This instrument is informing us that we need to move on. We must admit that we are sorry to leave this interesting question! As so often we are sorry to get off of our soapbox, tuck it under our arm, and trundle out of Hyde Park.

May we ask if there are any follow-up queries or any other queries at this time?

R: Not from me, Q'uo.

(Pause)

We are those of Q'uo, and we find that we have exhausted the curiosity of those present in this circle of seeking for now. We reiterate that it is a blessing to us to be with you. You help us in our service to others at this time by asking for our humble opinions and it opens our heart to be able to share thoughts with you.

We share also a great love and affection that passes between each of you and us, and that, too, is a blessing to us for which we are most thankful. And the blessing of being with you and of seeing the beauty of your articulated energy is wonderful. We are amazed at the courage and the goodness within each of you.

We leave this instrument and this group in the love and in the light of the one infinite Creator. We are known to you as the principle of Q'uo. Adonai. Adonai. ☙

L/L Research

L/L Research is a subsidiary of Rock Creek Research & Development Laboratories, Inc.

P.O. Box 5195
Louisville, KY 40255-0195

www.llresearch.org

Rock Creek is a non-profit corporation dedicated to discovering and sharing information which may aid in the spiritual evolution of humankind.

ABOUT THE CONTENTS OF THIS TRANSCRIPT: This telepathic channeling has been taken from transcriptions of the weekly study and meditation meetings of the Rock Creek Research & Development Laboratories and L/L Research. It is offered in the hope that it may be useful to you. As the Confederation entities always make a point of saying, please use your discrimination and judgment in assessing this material. If something rings true to you, fine. If something does not resonate, please leave it behind, for neither we nor those of the Confederation would wish to be a stumbling block for any.

© 2009 L/L Research

Sunday Meditation
February 4, 2007

Archetypes Gathering II

Group question: Q'uo, today the question concerns the study we've been doing for the past weekend on the archetypical mind. These are concepts that are very intellectually challenging and we would like to know, as we go back to our daily round of activities and our normal lives, how best to apply these concepts in our daily lives. How can we attempt to use them to better open our hearts and to understand the Creator and each other and ourselves? What's really happening in our space/time environment, our daily lives, and what's happening in the metaphysical realms, in the spiritual realms, as we attempt to apply these principles to catalyst and circumstance that comes our way?

(Carla channeling)

We are those known to you as the principle of Q'uo. Greetings in the love and in the light of the one infinite Creator, in Whose service we come to you this day. We thank you for the privilege and the pleasure of being called to join your circle of seeking.

Indeed, we thank each of you for somehow finding the time, the attention, and the room in your very busy lives to turn from all other pursuits and seek the truth. In humbleness and in sincerity have you come to form this circle and your beauty is astounding, my friends.

We would appreciate, as always, your using your powers of discrimination in listening to our thoughts. If they are resonant to you then they are yours to work with as you wish. If they are not resonant to you for some reason, please assume that we have missed the mark and lay those thoughts aside so that you may go forward to meet the resonant information that is coming your way. For we are not the only source of useful information and inspiration. The entire universe speaks to the one who has the listening ear and the understanding heart.

You ask this day concerning the use of the archetypes, and the archetypical mind in general, as you move from this sheltered and protected environment wherein you have been able more deeply to study and ponder these things than is possible within the helter-skelter of your daily routine. There are many approaches in answering this question and we see virtue in several of them. So, if you will allow us the rambling, we will approach this question from several different angles. Perhaps in that process you may find useful material at various levels of your process at this time. That indeed is our hope.

Become aware of yourself at this moment, as you are resting against your chair. Feel your lips, your eyelids as they are gently closed over your eyes, the lashes resting on your cheeks. Feel the relaxation and comfort of this seated figure that you are. Feel the articulation of your fingers and your toes. Be aware of yourself as a being poised in this moment of the present.

Who are you? Why are you here? Rest and ask. We pause.

(Pause)

(Carla channeling)

We are those of Q'uo, and are again with this instrument. Our desire was to bring you to a point of focus wherein you were exquisitely aware of the reality of yourself. It is something that is easy to take for granted, for you are always with yourself, waking and sleeping. Yet you are a miracle and a wonder.

My friends, you are a focus within which the Creator can know Itself. You are precious. Think of the value of a rare gem and then realize that there is only one of you. How precious are you, my friends? How exquisitely beloved and dear to the one infinite Creator you are. Feel the love that surrounds you and interpenetrates every cell of your body.

You are an instrument. Each of you has a tune, a melody, an air that you play the best. And you share that lilt with the world. There are other melodies within you which you wish to discover and become able to play with the instrument of your beingness. You are not satisfied with that which is yours at this moment, for there is a seeking in you that wishes to go deeper, to become more aware and to open to that which can not be known but only experienced of spirit in manifestation.

Because you wish to seek further, go deeper, and look with more intensity, you have come together to help each other, to encourage each other and to support each other with the respect and the validation that you give to each other. Beneath the clothing of the behaviors of society, my friends, you have experienced within this weekend true charity, true affection, true friendship, and as you have expressed as you talked about the circle before this channeling, a true feeling of home.

Strengthened from this time together, you are ready now to soar upon your way. For each of you has unique items to address in your personal agendas, both in the inner world of seeking and in the outer world of manifestation, work and play.

Gather your wings! Indeed, my friends, feel them! Feel the wings of spirit that help you to soar. Feel them knit themselves to your very flesh, for you are spirit in manifestation and you have both the Earth and the starry heavens in your makeup. You can indeed claim your wings and fly.

And whither shall you fly but to do the will of the Creator? "And what is that will?" says the flesh that does not soar. "Tell me what shall I do? Where shall I soar? What is my mission?" And we say to you, take wing, knowing that all has been prepared for you this day and henceforward.

When you ask yourself what to do, open your eyes and see what it is at which you look. What you see before you is the gift of the present moment. And as this instrument often asks, "Where is the love in this moment?" This is the starting place for everything, this present moment. And not just this one as this circle sits in focused sacredness but every moment of every day.

We ask you to move in mind now with us to a larger point of view, for we wish to create a context in which you may see the workings of the archetypical mind and mind in general both against the backdrop of the everyday and the backdrop of eternity.

Each of you has limitations that distract your mind from perfect awareness, perfect peace, and perfect focus. The distraction may be physical. It may be emotional. It may be buried in mental distortions inherited from other lifetimes or from periods earlier within this lifetime when certain relationships of energies became entangled, so that there is a seeming difficulty in separating out the strands of being and doing.

For any entity within third density there is every expectation that you shall experience these limitations in an ongoing fashion; not necessarily continuously but nearly constantly, throughout your incarnation.

Take a moment to give thanks for these limitations and distractions. They move you by their creating in you discomfort and hunger. They keep you from being placid. And most of all they awaken you to the song of the bird, the rush of the wind, the glow of the stars, and the heat of the sun.

It is easy to feel that you are living an inconsequential life because of these limitations. And it is well if you encourage yourself when you feel that you are beginning to drown in your own banality, to lift yourself up from that point of view and refocus your attention upon the beauty in your environment. This refocusing awakens you in a sense in which spirit, mind and body function together. Allow yourself to be the enlivener of yourself.

As we suggest that you do this, we are suggesting that you spend time with archetypical energies. We realize that each of you has struggled with the concept of invoking the archetype or becoming the archetype. So let us look more carefully at what it is to awaken oneself up from the dream of life and to become alert to the listings[40] of spirit.

You dwell in a universe in which all things whatever are connected and knitted up together in love. That which you know that you are is interpenetrated and surrounded by that which you know not that you are; that remainder of your whole self that ultimately includes every iota of consciousness in the universe.

In a very deep sense, that point of light and love that you are, metaphysically, is the realest thing about you and the realest thing about all other points of energy masquerading as human beings that you shall meet in your lifetime.

Were you all clever and full of fourth-density's lack of a veil, you would see the dance that you dance together. But in fourth density, my friends, you would only be able to do the dance that you created for yourself in the third density that you now experience. Now, in this lifetime, at this moment, you are creating for yourself the choice of polarity and the balance of the energies surrounding that choice which shall be your starting point for all of the evolution that you shall experience as a soul for the next densities of experience. This time is most precious and we encourage you to embrace it with gusto and joy.

As you move into the everyday activities of your daily life, leaving this domicile and going back to your own, moving on with those patterns which are in progress in your life, encourage yourself to continue to feel the connection between yourself and all other consciousness, especially the points of consciousness with whom you have had moments of real connection during this weekend together. Let that feeling of family, validation and support linger and be a part of your heart. Know that you are loved and allow yourself as a point of consciousness to continue to drift and observe your feelings, your thoughts, and your biases.

The archetypical level of mind is a level of consciousness in which you become exquisitely aware that you are the link between the everyday of space/time—morning, afternoon, and evening, the rising and the setting of the sun—and utter infinity and mystery.

Because of your unique vantage point, you are able to dip up into the ocean of consciousness that is common to all of you in such a way as to receive from that consciousness gifts that no one else has ever received or ever will. With your colorations and your biases, you do not go further away from perfection, but closer to it. The shades and the colorations of your feelings, your thoughts, and your actions create for you a unique experience of dipping up into that common river system which is the archetypical mind.

We have never been able fully to describe the archetypal mind because it is an infinite, ever-shifting ocean which is fed by all the rivers of all the energies that are possible to expend in creation. When you seek up into an archetype, you are attempting to join the creation itself as it dances its dance of creation. You are slipping into an already proceeding dance and moving into the flow where you can feel where to whirl and where to turn and where to leap and where to bow. For it is a stately dance at times, and at times a merry jig, and at other times the saddest of dirges with the most deeply expressive woe.

Dance all of your tunes, my friends, and dance them with all of your heart. The difference between the everyday and the magical is the difference between the entity who sees and hears no music and feels no desire to dance, and the entity who, hearing and seeing no music, and feeling no urge to dance, nevertheless rises up and invokes the dance.

There will always be entropy[41] that will encourage you to stop and not go further today. There will always be inertia that encourages your wheels to grind to a halt. You can always say, as this instrument said earlier, "I am weary. I am exhausted."

---

[40] This usage is quite archaic and means the "tendencies or leanings" of spirit, much as a ship or boat lists to one side or another, to port or starboard.

[41] Entropy has several meanings, the most general of which applies here: inevitable decline and degeneration.

Seek beneath those feelings for the will and the faith that is yours. Who are you? Ask and continue to ask. The answer is not half as important as the question.

In a way, life is a puzzle. There is often a feeling of pieces missing, as if the fellow who ran the jigsaw finished cutting the picture up into its component puzzle pieces and then slipped off with two or three of them in his pocket. You shall always be missing a few pieces of the puzzle until you call upon that which you know not.

In choosing to call, you join the dance.

In stopping to pay attention, you join the dance.

In becoming aware for a split second of the beauty of your own self, you join the dance.

We do not ask you to dance beyond exhaustion. We encourage you to rest when it is time to rest. We also encourage you always to lift up your heart and listen for the new song, the new energy, the new moment, the new life. You have a new life every moment if you will claim it and if you will direct it. You do not run out of chances to work spiritually. You may work in prison, in sickness, in any limitation whatsoever, to enlarge your ability to allow the energy of the one infinite Creator to flow through you and out into the world around you.

To touch up into the archetypical is to ask for the generality, of which you are a specific case, to inform you of your own nature. This incarnation, this third density in which you have enjoyed so many incarnations, and this day are all about choosing the point of balance in your life and then choosing it again and choosing it again.

Different people have different ways of describing what it is they seek. This instrument asks for the highest and the best. She will say, "What is the highest and the best way that I can meet this catalyst?" Find your own way to place yourself in that powerful position of one who chooses. This is the dance of the archetypes. Your third density is about choice.

There are many levels of choice. The fundamental level is the choice of polarity. And in the choice of polarity, as you were studying this weekend, you may see the figure of the Two Lovers or the Transformation of the Mind with the tug present—not one tug greater than another but two equal choices.

You know which way you wish to go. Each of you here is deeply committed to seeking how to become more and more polarized in service to others. This does not mean that the choices that you make are simple. Third density is very good at presenting you with complicated polarizing choices, choices in which part of your choice is to polarize towards service to others and part of it is polarizing backwards towards service to self.

As you rock back and forth in choice, find your sweet spot of surety and choose your own version of the highest and best. And then move off to court the feminine principle of nurturing, healing and pure affection that you are invoking by making this choice.

Allow yourself the encouragements of energies too deep for words. Listen for the brush of angel wings. For as you know that you are choosing, you become the magician, or as this instrument would [say], the Hierophant. You become the actor and the chooser.

We greet you, citizens of eternity! We, as you, are stars that twinkle in the Creator's eye. We, as you, are points of focus within the infinite vibrations of the Creator's universe so that the Creator may know Itself.

As you attempt to bring home with you the blessing of those feelings that you have enjoyed in this workshop, in this time together, know and rely upon the truth of what you have experienced and your complete ability and capacity to move forward with grace and intelligence, pursuing your polarity, pursuing your lessons and pursuing your service.

(Side one of tape ends.)

(Carla channeling)

And if your energy feels dim, call upon those who wait to be asked to encourage you, love you, and help you. For your guidance is ever with you. But it cannot speak with you until you ask. If there is one thing we would leave you with as we leave this subject, it would be the importance of asking, for help is ever near and your guidance is ever with you.

As always, we are sorry that we need to leave this fascinating question. Yet this instrument has asked us to close that particular subject for this day and ask if there are other questions or follow-ups that you may have at this time. We are those of Q'uo.

T: I do. My question is, if two entities are committed to deepening the relationship in seeking each other and the Creator to be a service and a light, what is happening metaphysically in the process of that third entity between them in the Creator? And then please discuss any practical ways to facilitate growing consciously in everyday life.

We are those of Q'uo, and are aware of your query, my sister. When any two entities who are aware that they are spiritual beings choose to seek together, there is created immediately an oversoul made up of their two incarnate energies connected to their guidance systems. In many cases, also connected to the entities and their guidance systems are the families or social memory complexes with which they have traveled to be of service to this planet. Consequently, even a two-person oversoul may involve an enormous family gathering if you look at the structure that has been created by the dedication in love and service to others of two beings who are aware of their opportunity to choose.

This may be seen not only to be helpful in and of itself but also to constitute a gift to the planet, to those about the self upon the planet and to the Creator. This is because it is a reflective and interactive universe and when two entities vibrate together in love, that vibration awakes a resonance within those not only in the seen realms but in the unseen realms which are vibrating at that level. The end result of entities forming connections with each other and with larger groups is the shift of consciousness of the entire planetary population. Therefore, it is big work that you are speaking of doing when you ask this question.

It is very helpful in everyday life to have made a conscious commitment to working spiritually as one being. There is no ducking away from the responsibility to treat each other as the Creator but the embracing of that challenge. And each time there comes the inevitable uncomfortable energy exchange, there is the opportunity boldly to go where few people have gone before upon your planet and that is into the thick of the disagreement between you, into the very thing you least want to look at between you.

Because in that very thing at which you least want to look is the gift that you have given yourself to unravel, that gift where you may untangle the ribbons of self and find how the energies can flow again. You find tremendous rivers of forgiveness and understanding flowing where there was dry land before and thirst and desert simply because you have turned and faced that seeming disharmony.

It may only be a small thing, yet the smallest of disharmonies is worth the attention, the respect, and the honor. It does not matter that the disagreement may be about nothing. It does not matter about perceived rightness and wrongness. When you, working together, allow light to shine through both of you as one, you are moving beyond yourself and entering a deeper portion of yourself which is ultimately impersonal. Yet it contains all of your heart and all of your soul.

It is a misapprehension that as you go deeper and become more closely allied to the Godhead principle that you lose yourself. You cannot lose yourself. You are part of the Creator. You are here to stay. Yet, in letting the boundaries drop and asking for healing and understanding, you find yourself growing in strength, in courage and in that feeling that you have in your heart that may be called respect for yourself. For you are taking yourself seriously and you are attempting to expand the energies of this incarnation in a profitable and efficient way for the service of the one infinite Creator.

This is true of any two people, but when entities are mated, they have awakened and shared with each other one of the most primal means of expressing the unity of the one infinite Creator that is available to the incarnate being within third density. And as they allow the harmony between them to be absolutely primary in their concerns, they are creating an energy pathway which leads to not only a mutual experience of sacred oneness as the Holy Eucharist of the red ray is shared and brought up into the heart in green-ray energy exchange, there is also that which stems from such substantial energy exchange, that being the ability to offer understanding, compassion and shared worship.

Worship, my friends, devotion, those deep levels of feeling that is purified: these things explode into a blooming of energies that is as the light upon the hill. And those mated entities who are able to sustain the challenges of the ever-advancing ego and its self-centered concerns will find themselves able, without even intending to do so, to be a light for others that is very helpful to them.

It is not that you are preaching to them, "This is the way to live life." You are simply radiating the love and the light of the infinite Creator, Whose pathway you have made straight and clear and flowing in the transparency of your personalities.

May we answer you further, my sister?

T: That was perfect.

We are those of Q'uo and we thank you. Is there another query at this time?

(No further queries.)

We find that we have exhausted the supply of questions that entities are ready to ask at this time and this is well, for certainly the energy of this instrument wanes and it is a good time for us to say farewell to this instrument and this group.

We say again what a pleasure and a privilege it is to behold your beauty and to share your meditations. We are known to you as those of Q'uo. We leave you, as we found you, in the love and in the light of the one infinite Creator. Adonai. Adonai. ☥

L/L Research

L/L Research is a subsidiary of Rock Creek Research & Development Laboratories, Inc.

P.O. Box 5195
Louisville, KY 40255-0195

www.llresearch.org

Rock Creek is a non-profit corporation dedicated to discovering and sharing information which may aid in the spiritual evolution of humankind.

ABOUT THE CONTENTS OF THIS TRANSCRIPT: This telepathic channeling has been taken from transcriptions of the weekly study and meditation meetings of the Rock Creek Research & Development Laboratories and L/L Research. It is offered in the hope that it may be useful to you. As the Confederation entities always make a point of saying, please use your discrimination and judgment in assessing this material. If something rings true to you, fine. If something does not resonate, please leave it behind, for neither we nor those of the Confederation would wish to be a stumbling block for any.

© 2009 L/L Research

Sunday Meditation
February 11, 2007

Group question: Our question this week, Q'uo, is: Each year, for many years now, we see at least one channeled source that says, "This is the year that the big changes will happen in consciousness." Some now say that 2007 is when this age will change instead of having to wait for the year 2012. We want to know what spiritual principles could help us look at this situation when channels get this kind of information.

(Carla channeling)

We are those known to you as the principle of Q'uo. Greetings in the love and in the light of the one infinite Creator. We thank you so much for inviting us to join in your circle of seeking and to share our thoughts with you this day on the subject of these predictions of the shift of the ages and how they cycle.

However, as always, before we begin we would encourage each of you to take responsibility for your spiritual process. It is not wise to accept any information without examining it closely to see if you resonate to it personally. Many are the true thoughts that help someone; few are the true thoughts that help you. You need to distinguish those thoughts that are truly helpful to you at this time and those which are interesting but do not resonate. If you will take the time to do this, it will reassure us that you are taking responsibility for your own process and therefore we need not be concerned about infringing upon your free will. We thank you for this consideration, my friends.

You ask this day concerning the repetitive predictions of transformational times either immediately following the channeling or predicted within the channeling to take place within the near future, usually between two and five years. You ask how it happens that this information is repetitively offered, always with good rationales and always with interesting and supporting material offered by the channeled source.

There are a couple of different levels to the response because there are a couple of different spiritual principles involved in why this happens and what kind of information you truly are receiving.

In the first instance, the spiritual principle involved is that any spiritually oriented entity, once awakened to the situation of the present moment, has consulted those questions so important to spiritual seekers:

"Who am I?"

"Why am I here?"

"What should I be doing?"

There comes a realization, either slowly or quickly, that the time for equivocation has passed and the time for spiritual work is now. This is a non-local feeling of urgency, not connected with time and space. And yet you, as third-density entities, dwell in space/time. Naturally, you as a human being are going to think about these sensings that you have from your meditations or your contemplations and feel that they indicate an event.

In the largest sense, this event has been building since well before the time of Jesus the Christ. This entity came to help the shift of the ages more than 2,000 years ago and this entity was already feeling the urgency of taking up the work and moving forward on choosing service to self or service to others as a way of life.

The one known as Jesus the Christ felt a sense of urgency, as did the one known as John the Baptist. The apocalyptic content of their messages is substantial as it is given in your Holy Bible in the New Testament. That is how long people have been sensing the need to alter and shift their consciousness and the consciousness of the planet which is the location of their beloved home and of the tribe of humankind of which they are a cherished part.

At that level, you may see that it is an archetypical energy, when an entity awakens, to project his own awakening upon the world at large. And this is a legitimate and valid viewpoint from a certain point of view. Each entity is the author of his particular creation. Admittedly, there are points of reference which are common to most people's creations, including data about the society and the culture in which they live.

Yet each entity's creation is his own. The biases that he encourages in his life become the biases of his world. Entities are people of great power. They are part of the godhead principle. All entities, even the elements, the animals, and all of nature, have this power. But they do not know that they have it. And consequently they use it effortlessly and without any impurity, being incapable of altering their nature and only capable of fulfilling it.

You, as self-conscious entities, have far greater ability to create because you are conscious of yourself. You are aware that you are a being that is seeking. You have an observer function. Indeed, many entities have a very complex observer function, where the observer is watching the observer who is watching what's happening. You can create a lot of complexity in terms of how you perceive things and what you choose upon which to focus.

Consequently, your particular creation has sometimes a dramatic difference in coloration from the creations of some about you as you walk through your everyday experience. When you have achieved a sense of your own power and are dedicated to using that power rightly, you become a force beyond the normal run of human energy. Because you have awakened to your potential as the creator of your universe and because you have begun to enter into creating the universe as you feel you would wish it to be by acting in an ethical manner at times of choice, you begin to develop an energy about you that is the energy not only of your personality but of the creation which has become imagined into being within your life.

Consequently, insofar as you have entered into this conscious development of yourself and your creation, you work not only for yourself but on the level of planetary energy. The situation is not that what you think becomes something others think. It is that that vibration which supports your work radiates as would the light of a lighthouse shining out across the dark and stormy sea.

As you allow your light and your universe to shine, you are, in your beingness, fulfilling one of your deepest purposes: you are changing and shifting consciousness at the planetary level. We would emphasize that, at this level of perception, we are not speaking of those things which can be pointed to and spoken of in words. We are talking about the shift of a point of view.

There is a point of view with which each entity looks at the world. Before the awakening process has begun, that point of view is reliably somewhat limited. The concerns of the instinctual animal that you are, as a descendent of the great ape family, are concerns about your family and your tribe. You want them to be safe, clothed, warm and fed. You want to gather those resources which you will need for them and not run out. And if you feel that they are threatened, you want to defend them.

These are the big bones of the skeleton of the typical concerns of one who is unawakened and functioning as a member of society at large without regard to any spiritual aspects of that life or those thoughts that the entity has. Therefore your work, while done privately, and not necessarily ever spoken into words, is magical, powerful work and well worth the doing.

There is an entirely different level which is a transition between the first level and the third. That transition level is that point at which the situation as regards your planetary dealings has become noted. As this instrument and others in the circle of seeking were speaking in the round-robin discussion that precedes these meditations, they were discussing the repetitiveness with which our most basic observed themes repeat. Those themes are those themes of empire which have dominated this particular planet's history for its entire run of recorded history.

And indeed, paleontologists and archaeologists indicate that, long before history was being written, the energies which aim towards empire were alive and well in one of the earliest pre-human bodies discovered. The entity had been killed by a blow to the back of the head.

The energy of solving problems by means of resorting to violence is an old one upon your planet. It indeed predates your particular planetary energy, for you have, in the course of the last 75,000 years, received entities from several planets which have been unable to complete their own third-density school or classroom because of creating changes in their planets by means of violence on a mass scale which rendered the planet uninhabitable or because of outright destroying it by blowing it up. All of these entities are here, now, and are working to break old habits.

So there is a spiritual entropy[42] that happens when progress is not made. Energies become less and less organized and more and more chaotic because the energy is unusable after a certain point. Further, there is the energy of inertia, which means that even those who are not particularly involved in the tendency to resort to violence to solve problems yet still do not have sensors that send up the red flags of warning when they hear thoughts of empire being discussed.

They know that something is off when they hear discussion of how we should all be living in fear upon planet Earth. At the same time, they have no defense against what sounds like reasonable prudence. This seeming reasonableness can be attributed firstly to the fact that each of you upon planet Earth has gone through this cycle several times and has become used to it and secondly to that inertia within you which does not want to wake up because awakening is uncomfortable.

When you awaken and you see that things are not as you thought they were, you then feel that you wish to respond to that awareness. And the more that you make responses with the dedication in intent towards becoming more aware, more yourself, and more a part of the godhead principle, the more you are asking for change to occur at the deepest levels of your personality.

When you ask to awaken, to transform, and truly to serve at the deepest level of which you are capable, you are asking for the forces of transformation to come into your life. The one known as M was talking earlier concerning the efficacy of water used as a cleansing mechanism. And we would note that many are those entities who have found the use of water or other cleansing protocols helpful and useful because, as you change, you are dumping a good deal of toxic spiritual, emotional and mental material.

And whether it comes through the physical body, which some of it does, or whether it comes through the energy body, as some of it does, it needs to be processed and allowed its natural flow through you and out.

When entities do awaken and do realize that it is an urgent matter for them to shift their consciousness, they can feel that it is needed for others also to shift their consciousness. There comes into play a tendency towards what we might call spiritual materialism, in which you want everyone to form up and live in a new way.

In this regard we would suggest that the skillful choice is always to work on the self without regard for working with other entities. Service to others, working upon what you perceive needs to be done in the world, begins and ends within yourself. Until the point at which you are asked specific questions that you may answer in what you hope is a spiritually helpful manner, the work you do on yourself is sufficient and more than adequate in terms of how you may affect the consciousness of planet Earth. Change yourself and you change the world. That is how powerful you really are.

---

[42] entropy: "A doctrine of inevitable social decline and degeneration." In thermodynamics, the word means, "A measure of the energy that is not available for work during a thermodynamic process. A closed system evolves toward a state of maximum entropy."

The third level that we would address is a level in time/space and space/time where these changes are actually occurring for your planet. And here we will need to take some time to discuss the mechanics of your situation, insofar as we can express them through this instrument. We hope you will bear with us as we work with a non-scientific channel in this regard.

There is a point early in your third density at which it was observed that the harvest of third density upon planet Earth was far behind schedule and indeed was not developing at all well. It was seen that the introduction of entities from other planets, and further introduction of changes within some of the templates improving upon the human genome, created unforeseen consequences that deepened the power of entities to use free will without the spiritual ability to see where that free will power was headed.

Another consequence was the enhanced ability to amuse and enchant the self by means of stories of power and empire. The culture as a whole, then, by its use of free will, had moved into a situation that concerned the guardians of this planet enough that it created for this planet a time lateral, a kind of track parallel to the main track of time and space as it is naturally developing in your physical environment.

You have never experienced life in your totally natural physical environment because you have been on a time lateral in quarantine for thousands of years. It was hoped, by quarantining the planet from further outside influences of any kind, that the free will of the body of the tribe of humankind would gather itself and would begin to address realizations of how ethical choices might be made in a way that progressed from the basic feeling that, when threatened, the proper response was likely to be violent, for that got the job done—and right quickly.

Consequently, riding upon this time lateral as you have, you have experienced repeated waves of empire as they have flourished and fallen only to see another empire rise and fall and another and another. If you look at your outer environment you may see these forces at work even now, moving in a repetitive manner, satisfying that portion of the tribe of humankind's deeper mind which is used to these energies and feels comfortable with them, not because they are good but because they are what planet Earth is all about.

The breaking forth of new life into this dark world is a common occurrence because the light cannot be put out by darkness. And person after person after person has moments of brilliant insight in which they see that responding to violence with violence is not a wise move.

More and more of your entities are investing time, talent and treasure in finding different responses to the surrounding darkness based not upon the darkness itself but upon the light that comes from within the darkness and which the darkness cannot extinguish. Entities focus upon that first candle of light. And that tiny illumination illumines more. And then that illumines more. And a process of lightening the consciousness of yourself begins.

The time is coming and indeed is nigh at hand when something you might call a tipping point is imminent. And indeed it stands before you at this time. What is that tipping point? That tipping point is a straw vote, shall we say, an informal poll, if you will, of the tribes of humankind, to see if the majority of entities want to separate themselves forever from any path except violence or if they want to progress into fourth density and beyond.

There are entities from fifth density on the service-to-self path that are attempting a coup, shall we say, of this train of humankind running along this parallel time track. They would like it not to rejoin the main track. The guardians of this planet and those light givers within your planetary forces, both seen and unseen, have all moved heaven and Earth, literally, to create a slowing of the forces of time so that every possible instant may be given to the development of planet Earth's human population to the point where the vote of the straw poll is for service to others and not for service to self; for radiance, peace and harmony rather than contraction, war and hostility as a background to the everyday life.

We are very hopeful. If that last moment were this very day, the straw poll indicates that your planet will rejoin the typical, normal progression of space/time. What the negative entities would like to do is to have that tipping point go the other way and to have people say, "No, no, it's important to war because we want to gain resources, because we want to defend our family," and because of the whole laundry list of those things that the great apes are instinctually bound to consider priorities.

At that level, there is almost no time/space or space/time wherein a third-density entity may make that primal choice for service to others on third-density planet Earth. Your density has now become fourth density. It has not waited until this year or even several years before this but has been vibrating in fourth density to the exclusion of creating more third-density light.

Therefore, those third-density entities who now walk the planet are more and more sensitive because they do not have the support of third-density light which hides most of the truth. Rather they have fourth-density light interpenetrating their third-density understanding of their world, creating an environment where it seems and indeed is happening that wave after wave of truth and light and understanding is washing over this planet.

The fourth density is the density of love. But it is also called the density of understanding. What is happening to entities now is that that which is in their thoughts and in their unexamined assumptions is being mirrored out to them in everyday life for them to see clearly. They no longer have so much of a cushion of easy untruth because if they are awakening spiritually there are forces within them that have determined and intended to challenge those unspoken assumptions which are not serving the greater good.

So, insofar as you as a third-density entity are unawakened, you will simply find life getting harder. It seems that more extremes are taking place. You are not feeling as well. You lose more jobs. Whatever it is that you are working on [in] this life, there become problems with it that seem harder than they used to be. This is because you are not protected from your truth as you once were.

Now, entities who are awakened are experiencing the identical situation, are experiencing an increase in suffering and are experiencing more difficult times. However, what they have on their side is that they have set their intention to serve others and to know the truth in order to serve others. This creates a fourth-density support system that is powerful indeed and can take the place of the previous comforts of the unawakened.

However, when you become awakened and set your intention to be an ethical being that is worthy of fourth density, you also ask of yourself that you begin to live the life that reflects those fourth-density values that are implicit and explicit when you think about service to others.

The principles involved in service to others are implicit in all that is done in that when you meet the moment, you are meeting it as one who serves. That is a general standpoint and that basic viewpoint brings to you a wider point of view which is based upon the guidance that you are receiving which is activated by your desire to serve. When you ask for the truth, the truth is there before you. Ask and you truly shall receive.

And then you are responsible for your actions in a way which was inconceivable when you did not know and had no knowledge of how the spiritual forces of evolution work. That of which you are ignorant, you cannot be held responsible. When you become aware of the spiritual principles involved in natural evolution, then you become also responsible for acting upon that knowledge.

This is not an easy time because of these factors. As the song before this meditation says, entities may often be standing knee-deep in the river of love and light and dying of thirst[43] because they do not know how to scoop that life-giving liquid up into their bodies, their minds, and their spirits. How do you crack up an earthly life and let the sun shine in?

Fortunately, my friends, it is not a matter of cracking open your life to let the sun shine in. It is a matter of cracking open your personality to become aware of the sun that is already shining, in an infinite supply, into your heart, your mind, and your consciousness, into every fiber and cell of your being, both physically and non-physically.

To sum up this third level, we would say that to the best of our knowledge—which is not without error but is only opinion—the timetable of your planet is a set one. The planet itself, minus the time lateral,

---

[43] The song played is by Lacey J. Dalton. The lyrics to which the Q'uo group refers are as follows:

> If the game's getting old,
> and you're cold and exhausted and maybe
> You'd just like to cop-out and crumble,
> or lay down and die;
> If you come to a time when you need to decide,
> Friend, you might want to ask yourself first,
> "Am I standin' knee deep in the river and dyin' of thirst?"
> 'Cause a great river runs from the heart of the sun
> Through the soul of the whole universe
> From the limitless light that brings order and might
> To the substance of Heaven and Earth.

will completely shift into fourth density at the winter solstice of 2011.

There is an area around this time that is not clock time because the change is not in space/time but in time/space. That penumbra, shall we say, of the time of shift began approximately in 1998.

As we give this instrument dates, be aware that we are not particularly good with numbers. There was in the planetary energy system an adjustment made at one point that would simply remove the planetary population through natural means because it was failing to come to harvest. This pole shift was averted in 1998 by many groups such as this one [that] were aware that consciousness needed to be lightened and [that] spent a good deal of time and energy as light bringers and those who spoke about these energies, these times, and the spiritual principles involved in evolution.

This work has enabled this planet to have the added physical space/time for those entities within incarnation at this time to come to harvest on their own and also in order to give entities who graduated early the opportunity to come back into this planetary environment you call Earth and help accelerate the shift in consciousness. They, more or less, shall we say, have stacked the deck, making the tipping point ever closer towards rejoining the main line of space/time.

We confidently believe that your planet will rejoin that natural movement and progression of your planet into fourth-density space/time.

(Side one of tape ends.)

(Carla channeling)

We do not believe that the entities who attempted this coup will be able to convince the majority of entities upon planet Earth that a fear-based and violence-ridden solution is the correct solution to the ethical dilemmas of this time.

If entities convinced themselves that the forces of war are the correct forces in which to invest, your planet would be lost and would become a feeding ground for fifth-density entities who feed off of fear and suffering. This would be a slavery which all the slaves agreed was needed.

We believe that your people will throw off the yoke of slavery to violence and begin to sustain responsible efforts to become truly free, to evolve, and progress. It is, as always, the choice of those of planet Earth and none other may vote in this particular referendum.

So, it is in your hands. There are waves of energy coming at this planet that you so lovingly enjoy each and every day, every month, quarterly, yearly, and at times which are irregular but based upon time/space events rather than space/time events. In an irregular manner, however, they also offer unique and sometimes highly discomfiting waves of energy.

These are energies of the shining, glorious, honest truth. Embrace them insofar as you can. See how you might cooperate with these energies. If they bring things up in your life that you have not wanted to face, give yourself a smile, because you need it, and then sit down to do your work, my friends.

Remember who you are and why you came here. Remember what it is that you think you want to do in order to serve. And then look that shadow side of yourself, that has been flung up against your eyes, straight in the eye, thanking it for the gift that it is, and realizing that it is not the truth of you but it is a portion of the truth of you that you have not examined and therefore that you have not brought into the light and the love of your heart.

Do not allow yourself the easy way of projecting that concern onto other people or a situation that is beyond you. Bring it into your own life. Bring it into your own heart. And take responsibility for dealing with that energy that disturbs you.

You are fully capable of doing this, my friends. You have every faculty available to you: your intellect, your intuition, your support system, however you see that to be, and your choices as you move through life. You could say indeed that 2007 was the year of shift and you could be right. You could have also been right in 1962 when this instrument first became aware of a channeled group that predicted Armageddon and the need to get to safe places, and every year since then.

At every point that is now, there is a branching off into an infinite number of possibilities. The world you make is the world you choose at each of those moments of now. You have accumulated a good many of them in your lifetime but they are as nothing compared to the choices that you make once you become aware that choice is a very blessed and central way of embracing your truth, your progression, and your acceleration of your evolution, spiritually speaking.

Let the time be now. Come to the river, as John the Baptist had it in the New Testament, and offer yourself to his rough ministrations. Make straight in the desert a highway for unconditional love. Repent and return. Repent of your ignorance and return to the truth as you see it, know it, ask for it, and seek it.

You need never be satisfied with where you are nor need you ever be unsatisfied. You are on a long, sometimes arduous but always powerfully exciting journey. Once you realize that you ride forth as a knight for the light, may your banners shine. May they speak of love, beauty, truth and compassion. May you polish your metal, that armor of light, with every decision you ever make to try to do your best and to serve the one infinite Creator.

And then go forth. Do not see yourself as one who fights against anything, but one who stands for the light. And let all of the gifts that are yours flow through you and out into the world. The time is now. The time has always been now.

This instrument is asking us if we would please move on, for there is limited energy and perhaps there are queries at this time that we may answer. We would ask if there is another query at this time. We are those of Q'uo.

R: I have a question, Q'uo. I am curious about how the process of the time lateral rejoining the main path of Earth happens. Is it something that the guardians watch over after this straw poll that you have mentioned is taken?

We are those of Q'uo, and are aware of your query, my brother. It is indeed the design of the guardians. However, it is automatic. Given that the energy of this planet is one which yearns towards love and light, there will be an automatic cessation of the time lateral, as we said, around the penumbra starting in 1998 and going well past the precise moment when the planet itself transits into a space/time position which is different in the emission of light it receives.

It is automatic and what occurs is what you are seeing now where more and more entities have become aware that something is happening, that this planet is not functioning as it had been used to and that it is suffering from [humanity's] uncaring ministry and stewardship of its resources.

Therefore, the energy for a pole shift or some other natural kind of disaster cannot be ruled out to express the roughness of the transition over to the main line from the parallel line. Any time a fast-moving vehicle such as a train moves through a shunt from one track to another, there is a bobble in the environment of the people onboard the train. And certainly your people are feeling that bobbling already. And it will continue. And at its end, those who remain upon planet Earth are those who are at least partially capable of dealing with fourth-density energy.

Many entities have already been removed from the Earth scene because of the increasingly powerful bursts of truth that have been bombarding the planet, creating ways to see the truth out in front of the eyes. Those who have reacted with the most distress to these energies are those who have been brought through the gates into larger life because of illnesses that hit them when they were relatively young. These illnesses include everything from heart trouble to cancer to many of your designer diseases, shall we say, like sexually transmitted diseases and other diseases that were designed to be agents of removal of certain energies from the Earth scene.

May we answer you any further, my brother? We are those of Q'uo.

R: No, Q'uo. That was interesting to hear. And I wanted to say that the Confederation speaks of these things without fear. Fear is often heard, so I think many of us who listen to the messages appreciate your efforts at fidelity.

We are those of Q'uo, and we thank you, my brother. We indeed have absolutely no fear, for we see from our vantage point that each spirit is legitimate, sacred and worthy, regardless of how that spirit is acting at this particular moment that you experience in space/time upon your planet. At the soul level, all entities are the Creator.

When the time lateral ends and those who are still breathing third-density air upon Earth are still around to pick up the pieces—which you are already doing, my friends—those who were not able to make the transition with you will all have been picked up as they enter larger life through the gates of death and with infinite care, cherished and supported through their own process of discovering what lay behind the veil of forgetting. They will be given every chance to consider their lives and what they wish to do next. They will go to a third-density planet somewhere that is not Earth and they will take up the third-density classroom once again, attempting to learn to make that choice and to set the intention not just for third density but for so many densities to come, all the way through the middle of sixth density.

What you are doing here is so important in terms of your extended work. You set here the benchmark of choice which you cannot do in fourth density, fifth density, or sixth density. We would not wish for any to be lost and indeed it is impossible for any to be lost. There is no hell deep enough to lose the love and the light of the infinite Creator. There is no prison whose bars can keep you from the love and the light of the infinite Creator.

Momentary difficulties loom large if the viewpoint is short. We see that all are cared for. Every consideration is given equally to those who are striding forth to seek the light in fourth density positive and, just as importantly, to those who have chosen to stay longer at these lessons and learn them better. These are also completely provided for in that they have all the room they need to make every choice with their own free will.

There is no cause, in our view, for any fear. This is simply what is happening upon your planet at this time. How it will play out in the Earth scene, in the manifested world, we do not know. Each and every one of you has the say in that. And we know that you are setting your intention, setting your sail on this journey of the waters of spirituality and asking for the wind of the spirit to be behind you and to send you where you need to go.

May you rejoice, my friends, in this moment. We are always with you. If you would wish for us to deepen your meditations, simply ask mentally as you sit down to meditate and we are glad to help you to deepen the state of your consciousness.

We shall leave this instrument and this group at this time, for the energy wanes rather dramatically. We leave you, as we found you, glorying in the beauty of each of you, your courage, the love in your hearts, and the color of your passions. Never could we see a more beautiful sight than all of you together, blending colors and making harmonious palettes of beauty for us to behold. Thank you for asking us to be with you once again. It has been a pleasure and a privilege. We leave this instrument and you in the love and in the light of the one infinite Creator. We are known to you as the principle of Q'uo. Adonai. Adonai.

L/L Research

L/L Research is a subsidiary of Rock Creek Research & Development Laboratories, Inc.

P.O. Box 5195
Louisville, KY 40255-0195

www.llresearch.org

Rock Creek is a non-profit corporation dedicated to discovering and sharing information which may aid in the spiritual evolution of humankind.

ABOUT THE CONTENTS OF THIS TRANSCRIPT: This telepathic channeling has been taken from transcriptions of the weekly study and meditation meetings of the Rock Creek Research & Development Laboratories and L/L Research. It is offered in the hope that it may be useful to you. As the Confederation entities always make a point of saying, please use your discrimination and judgment in assessing this material. If something rings true to you, fine. If something does not resonate, please leave it behind, for neither we nor those of the Confederation would wish to be a stumbling block for any.

© 2009 L/L Research

Sunday Meditation
February 18, 2007

Group question: The question this week has to do with the various religions that we have on planet Earth. They all seem to have a center of truth, but each religion also seems to have a number of adherents who interpret it their own way and who become fanatic in one way or another, trying make the religion into a dogma, to say this is the way and the only way. Is this a human trait? And how can we really know what is the true path for each of us? It seems like each of us has that spark of the Creator in us that recognizes truth and we are more reminded of truth than informed of truth. Can Q'uo give us some general principles as to how look at the various religions and how to find what is "the way" for us?

(Carla channeling)

We are those known to you as the principle of Q'uo. Greetings, my friends, in the love and in the light of the one infinite Creator, in Whose service we come to you this day. Thank you for creating a circle of seeking. Thank you for inviting us to join that circle. Thank you for the excellent question concerning how each seeker may find his own way amidst the welter of seemingly disparate theories of who God is and what the nature of creation is. It is our privilege to share our thoughts with you on this interesting subject.

As always, we would ask that each entity listen carefully for resonance, not only in the things we have to say but in listening to all opinion from whatever source. You are fully able to feel that resonance and that spark of interest and we would encourage you to wait for that resonance and that spark rather than taking everything that we have to say as being equally useful.

We thank you for this discrimination on each of your parts. It allows us to speak our thoughts to you without being concerned that we will inadvertently infringe upon your free will or disturb your sacred process of evolution in mind, body and spirit.

You ask this day concerning how to wend your way amidst the amazing array of religious and philosophical opinion concerning the nature of the godhead, the nature of creation, and the nature and purpose of human life. In former days we would not have been able to have such a simple beginning to a discourse upon this subject. The progress of your science has enabled us to have a fairly straightforward entry into the doorway of the nature of the created universe.

Investigation has shown that which seems to be solid matter is actually made up largely of a plenum[44] or a space in which there is no mass, very thinly populated by energy vortices. These energy vortices are the atoms and molecules that make up the cells of your body as well as the material of all other things that you can see, feel, touch, taste and smell.

---

[44] plenum: the whole of space regarded as being filled with matter, as opposed to a vacuum.

These energy fields cooperate together and nest within one another in various ways according to the nature of attraction and repulsion, forming the universe that you see. Scientific inquiry has proven that all parts of the universe communicate and are connected with all other parts of the universe, so that the universe is one thing. This is not given to you by priests or prophets but by your scientists, who have become the priests and prophets of your culture, if we may give it that name.

What is the nature, then, of these vibratory patterns that arrange themselves hierarchically so as to create orders of magnitude, creating everything from the atoms and molecules within the cells [of] your body to the star systems within your galaxy? We of the Confederation of Planets in the Service of the Infinite Creator have identified the nature of these hierarchically unitive and harmonious energy fields as being that of love.

The energy that created the stars is that of love. The energy that created you is the energy of love. That does not define love, for if love is all that there is, there is nothing to which to compare it. There's nothing from which to contrast it. In its undistorted form it is forever a mystery, unable to be plumbed by centers of consciousness which are aware of themselves. The truth of the universe lies most profoundly in the unknowable reaches of the mystery of the love and the light of the one infinite Creator.

Yet the universe is unitive. And it is unitive in a certain way. It is unitive holographically. Any one spark of the infinite Creator contains the entire nature of the one infinite Creator. Every cell of your body sings the song of the one infinite Creator. The suns in their courses sing the song of the one infinite Creator. There is fullness to the universe that is intense, as if every particle and iota of the universe were stuffed to bursting with the love and the light of life.

You experience life as you breathe in and breathe out. And you ask what this experience is, for you are aware of yourself. And certainly you have many, many voices in your ear, happy to explain precisely what life is and how to live that life in a good way.

Please understand, as you look back over some of your more difficult experiences with authority figures who have attempted to tell you what to believe, that every entity who seeks to serve the infinite Creator can fall into what the one known as T called "the trap" of teaching in such a way as to constrict the energies of those listening to his words.

Let us look at that energy of the authority figure who wishes to teach well, in order to come into a more compassionate and charitable understanding of what drives such an entity.

An entity who is moved and inspired by whatever agency, personality or inspired writing becomes aware of himself in a special way. He becomes aware of how alive he is, and he thinks, "I must give this gift, this wonderful life I feel, to others! I must pass on this wonderful inspiration that is given to me!" There is generally no intention of doing anything other than the purest of good. However, the trap of dogma is always waiting for the teacher.

It is a wise teacher indeed who is able to differentiate between his personal experiences with the divine and that which is helpfully expressed concerning seeking the divine. In a world that wishes to codify, organize and arrange life in an orderly manner, the mystical view, which is found at the heart of all religions and many philosophies as well, while greatly appealing, is found cumbersome and awkward to teach. When you're speaking of something that is indescribable and ineffable, words fail.

The human tendency, then, is to apply an organization to the mystery of the one Creator. And different religions have had different reasons to create different structures of belief, which have hardened into dogma.

If the Creator is infinite love and infinite light, and if the creation is evolving continuously forever, then there is continuously more of truth than there was before. Consciousness is continuously expanding. The problem with any dogma, then, is that it cannot re-form itself to hold the new truth that is flowing forth at every moment from the creative principle.

As the seasons change, as the grass blooms and withers again and again, so the consciousness of humankind evolves and grows. You are a point of that consciousness. You have access in your very nature, in every cell of your body, in every thought that you think to the one infinite Creator in its undistorted form.

Yet that truth lies deeply protected in you. It is protected from your casual thoughts. It is protected from the stormy seas of your daily, conscious experience. It is protected by its placement within your heart. The mind and all of its intellectual forces cannot storm the bastion of the open heart.

Entities, then, seeking to share bits of their truth with others, become invested in this codified, formalized, organized structure of thoughts that add up to a way to seek the one infinite Creator. With the gift of hindsight, scholars have often pontificated as to where a certain religion went wrong or how a certain religion has everything right. Yet as soon as the seeking for the one infinite Creator becomes codified and organized beyond a certain point, it can be a delimiting influence rather than an expansive influence.

Many churches and many different religions decide to bypass the intellect and rest upon the opening of the heart. They engage in song after song that praises the one infinite Creator within the language and clothing of that particular religion. Their members are perhaps encouraged to pray out loud and to become ecstatic. And in the surging of the rhythmic cadences of the songs, in the prayers and the praise, the love and light of the one infinite Creator seem palpable. And therefore the experience of those seeking the Creator in these ways has a certain amount of purity to it which is missing from those more intellectually organized religions where the mind is the tool used to probe at the meaning of life, of what it is to be a human being and what it is to serve the one infinite Creator.

Interestingly enough, love is the one great force that all entities know intimately, but which resists definition completely. And indeed, to attempt to use words to describe love is to attempt to build a great edifice out of pebbles.

Love is all that there is. That one Thought is the creation. And you have a port on the ocean of that Thought in your heart of hearts. Therefore, you are as equipped as any entity in the universe to seek the one infinite Creator. You have primary access to the direct experience of the Creator.

And indeed, it was for that purpose that you came into this illusion. You are gathering information. You are working with that information according to the biases of your personality and your desires. And as you gather your life experiences, each of you makes choices which open to you a way to move forward and to progress.

And each of you has had this experience of awakening and coming to the realization that you are a truly powerful entity, able to question and able to seek.

Once an entity has awakened and has begun to ask the deeper questions, a rhythm begins to occur between Creator and created. The asking and the answering becoming as entwined as a heartbeat, in and out, pulsing, pulsing, pulsing, so that as you ask, so you receive; as you ask, so you receive.

It [is] instantaneous and constant in your life. You have at each heartbeat, at each breath, the opportunity to ask and the opportunity to receive an answer. The sticking point here is that that answer comes within the mystery of silence. And it oozes up into your conscious experience almost as a surprise to you. You have learned by osmosis. You have soaked up the truth.

And as you live out your life you discover what you are learning as it shows up in your thinking. And many are the epiphanies and "aha's" of a spiritual life in which the seeker is content to let this teaching occur mostly in the silence of meditation, contemplation and the deep resting in whatever practices create for you personally a sacred chamber in which to tell the secrets of your heart to the loving ears of the one infinite Creator.

You are consciousness. It is not something you possess. It is not a characteristic of you. Consciousness lives your life to the extent you can get the details of your personality out of the way. And yet the details of your personality are all valuable. Therefore, the perfectly natural desire of the intensely devoted student to cast aside the personality and devote the self entirely to the silence is, for most entities, a solution that shall not be satisfying. For most entities, each coloration and quirk of the personality is there for a reason. Each seeming challenge, difficulty and sorrow that occurs in the life has been placed there not to make you stumble but to help you learn.

Entities who give themselves over to a religion and accept its dogma simplify their path in a certain way. And if they are able to dwell within that simplified structure of thought without falling into the trap of judgment of the self and other selves when they do not believe as do you, they are very likely to be able to use that religion as a way to the infinite Creator that works well. For each religion teaches the basic love of other people and the love of the one infinite Creator. And if an entity loves the Creator and loves the neighbor as the self, however that is put, the path to graduation from third density is clear. The choices to serve others has been made. The work is good.

More and more, however, as entities have matured after many, many incarnations within third density, entities find themselves unable to restrict themselves to the dogma and the canon law of a particular religion. And when entities find themselves unable to do this, then they are set on a new path, a path of their own choosing, a path which they will create themselves. Any entity can create within himself a way, a truth, and a life if he begins and ends with love.

We would not for all the world criticize or undermine those who are in any religion or believe any philosophy. The paths to the one infinite Creator are as many as the self-conscious beings who seek that Creator. Your way will be unique to you, just as everyone else's way is unique to them.

It helps to see religion for the kind of powerful influence that it is. If you may see the forces of religion to include that of the world as well as that of the starry heavens, then you may see how quickly the energy of a new religion can become heavy and bogged down with dogma and politics.

Look at the religion that this instrument understands the best, for it is her own: the Christian church. It began in the mysticism of the Essenes. The one known as Jesus the Christ was trained and trained in the Essene way as well as in the scholarship of the Jewish religion.

This entity's stories and parables were about simple things: being a peacemaker; understanding that he who loves the prisoner, the orphan, the widow, is loving Jesus the Christ; understanding that he who feeds the hungry is feeding Jesus the Christ.

Jesus asked entities to care for each other and to hold all things in common. There was not in any of his teaching instruction on making a church. Indeed, this entity had no home, and during his peripatetic[45] ministry, he walked on dusty trails with very little of worldly goods at all.

In his name, and in his memory, humankind has created a monstrous, rich, arrogant, political organization with many beautiful buildings which reach to the heavens with their spires and their crosses. Yet within them there is no virtue, except in the hearts of those who still seek the infinite Creator and use those sacred spaces to do so.

Look at any new idea and it is alive! It has a dynamic energy to it that excites people, and people want to capture that and pass that on to their children and their children's children. And so they make another building, another religion, another code to try to capture that which cannot be captured.

At the same time you must appreciate what religion has done for entities on planet Earth. It has given the intellect something to gnaw on. In many different ways it offers people a chance to meet the Creator.

Whether you seek within the bounds of a religion or whether the path upon which you walk is one you have created yourself, your very nature demands that you will meet the Creator, again and again. Things will happen to you that are meaningful to you personally and that move your consciousness from one point to another. Whether you are an indigenous entity that has never read a book, an auto mechanic, a college professor, or the most rarified mystic meditating upon the roof of the world in Nepal or Tibet, you have an equal opportunity to meet the Creator upon the road of your everyday life.

Appreciate religion for what it has offered, to you and to all. In the mystery of the one infinite Creator there are no roads. There is no way to think upon the sacred. The only opportunity you have is to be the sacred, and therefore to know it from the inside out.

Within churches and temples and synagogues and mosques the world over, you have entities and groups of entities who are dedicated to preserving a certain structure which has been helpful to many entities in their search for the infinite Creator. This instrument, for example, chose long ago, in her childhood, to live a life of faith within the Christian church as the path of her life.

As she understands it—as she understood it then and as she understands it now—there was a particular virtue to dedicating her life to Christ. This entity was a devotee in a religion that does not usually have

---

[45] peripatetic: walking or traveling about; itinerant.

devotees, of that particular kind which this entity is. That is, she was not hungry to soak up the dogma, but rather hungry for the mystery that she felt bursting the bonds of dogma.

(Side one of tape ends.)

(Carla channeling)

And she understood that, in any sacred writing, there is a database of inspired thought which bursts the bonds of words when heard again and again in different circumstances of life. And so this entity lives her "rule of life." She continues to study the same database, the *Holy Bible*, which she has studied for her entire life. And yet she has rejected all dogma by conscious decision.

Now, each entity can make this kind of choice for himself. And indeed it is necessary to look carefully, and with the artist's eye, at how to live a rule of life. We do recommend that each entity create a kind of rule of life for himself. What we cannot recommend is how that rule of life goes. You need to walk your own path, paying attention for that which the moment brings to you.

Some entities are drawn irresistibly to the Christian faith. Some entities are drawn just as irresistibly to the Buddhist faith. There is a path for just about every personality type. And yet all of these paths hold the barest skeleton of truth in its ineffable and mysterious form. All of those structures of thought that religions represent fail. None of them satisfies that thirst to know the truth.

This instrument is informing us that we must stop this discussion at this point, so we would end with this thought: you are the possessor of truth, but you do not know that you are. However, the Creator is generous in arranging for you within third density an illusion in which nothing can be known, and yet in which you can come to know with a particularly resonant awareness what your path is or what your truth is.

You cannot make it happen. What you can do is to set yourself up in an environment which is capable of holding *gnosis*, or knowing. Therefore, trust in your own senses, sensings, thoughts and feelings. As you seek to awaken, to seek and to serve, listen and look for the resonances that tell you that you are on the path that is for you. Once you start looking for resonance, you will find that the creation is full of information for you. And the more that you practice listening, the more that you can hear of the voices that are speaking to you in every moment.

We lift you up and honor you in our thoughts and in our hearts. For you have the courage to probe the darkness, knowing that there is nothing but light. We wish you well on your seeking, and thank you for the opportunity to share these humble thoughts with you as you go upon your way.

May we ask if there are other queries at this time? We are those of Q'uo.

(No further queries.)

We are those of Q'uo, and find that we have exhausted the questions of this group at this time. This leaves us only to say what a pleasure and a privilege it has been to be with you this evening. Your beauty astounds us. Your love of the Creator encourages us. And to be a part of this circle of seeking is a great blessing to us.

We leave this instrument and this group in the love and the light of the one infinite Creator. We are known to you as the principle of Q'uo. Adonai, my friends. Adonai. ✤

L/L Research

L/L Research is a subsidiary of Rock Creek Research & Development Laboratories, Inc.

P.O. Box 5195
Louisville, KY 40255-0195

www.llresearch.org

Rock Creek is a non-profit corporation dedicated to discovering and sharing information which may aid in the spiritual evolution of humankind.

ABOUT THE CONTENTS OF THIS TRANSCRIPT: This telepathic channeling has been taken from transcriptions of the weekly study and meditation meetings of the Rock Creek Research & Development Laboratories and L/L Research. It is offered in the hope that it may be useful to you. As the Confederation entities always make a point of saying, please use your discrimination and judgment in assessing this material. If something rings true to you, fine. If something does not resonate, please leave it behind, for neither we nor those of the Confederation would wish to be a stumbling block for any.

© 2009 L/L Research

Sunday Meditation
March 18, 2007

Question from Carla: *(Read by Jim.)* The question today is from Carla, and it states: "Q'uo, I have been writing a book about Confederation principles. It is about how third density works. In discussing these principles, I have found it helpful to offer them as information helpful to playing the 'Game of Life.' It is a sacred game yet it is definitely a game.

"The issue of self-worth and dignity has been much on my mind of late. In a way, one could say that in framing life as a game, I have taken away its dignity and taken it lightly. I do not mean to do so. I believe this game to be most worthy. Could you offer me any spiritual principles that may aid me in finding the best way to talk about the worthiness of the game board?"

(Carla channeling)

We are those known to you as Q'uo. We greet you in the love and in the light of the one infinite Creator, in Whose service we come to you this day. It is, as always, a blessing and a privilege to be with this circle of seeking. We appreciate your calling us to be a part of your meditation and we are happy to share our thoughts with you at this time.

As always, we would request that each who hears these words uses his powers of discrimination to distinguish between those thoughts that are helpful and those that are not. We appreciate your consideration in this regard.

Your query this day is an interesting one. There is a certain amount of care which we shall need to take in responding because of the part of the puzzle that must be worked by the one asking the question. We do not wish to infringe upon the free will of the asker of the question and we will refrain from doing so. However, there is, because of your asking about spiritual principles, much upon which we can comment. We shall do so in ways that do not infringe upon the free will of this instrument, who is the asker of the question.

The concept of games is indeed normally associated with some form of amusement or entertainment. However, the entertainment and amusement value of a game is only part of its appeal to a player of a game. There is in humankind a tendency to wish to associate in groups. Once a group associates, it will spontaneously develop at first a rough and then, as time goes on, a more and more refined set of rules to govern the interactions of the members of that group.

Your third density is a relentlessly social density. There is literally no way an entity can avoid interacting with other entities of your species. Living upon the third density of planet Earth requires a society.

There is an inevitable tendency within the mind of humankind towards creating games; that is, groups of people who are attempting to win something or to gain in some way and who are attempting to do so together. When this instrument chose the image of the game and extended it as a metaphor throughout the writing of the book, the fit was good because of the fact that, in terms of winning a common goal—that is, graduation from third density to fourth density positive—there is a process which follows a certain set of rules in which an entity can succeed in penetrating the game by means of learning, understanding and applying the rules of the game.

Therefore, from our point of view, using the image and the figure of the game is a good decision in terms of communicating, by means of familiar and comfortable structures, the massive structure of the Game of Life, as this instrument has termed it in her book. If one looks carefully at the great systems of thought that have attempted to describe the nature of life on planet Earth, the nature of humanity's place in the cosmos or the nature of being itself, one may find in many different authors of many different systems of thought a structure emerging which defines the rules of the game which that particular philosophy set out to solve.

There is a stigma attached to the word "game" because of its association with amusement and entertainment. And yet it is likely that each entity who reads these words will have systematically played games with himself as a means of coping and moving through life.

For instance, in school a student may decide that if a paper is ten pages long and is due in two weeks, the student will do a certain amount of work each day, fulfilling the game plan of being ready to write and then producing the paper on time. The strategy of how to get the paper written is a kind of game and yet it is a quite serious game with a firm intention which has no aspect of entertainment or amusement in it. Rather, it is that which needs to be done in order to fulfill the requirements of the class.

One can look at certain situations in life in the same way. For instance, to extend that particular situation, say that the student who is taking that class in college is also a parent and is attempting to work and go to school and take care of a child at the same time. In order to fulfill all of her duties, she will need to arrange her time carefully and if she is wise, this student, mother and adult will create a game plan where there is a certain amount of time for this and a certain amount of time for that.

Using the figure of the game, the author enables the reader to slip into the story of what this game is about. We can not estimate how entities will respond to the finished product that is streaming forth from the instrument's cyber-pen. We cannot know precisely how spirit and she will interact. What we do know, in a sturdy and certain way, is that the worthiness of the game board will be expressed in the way the author and spirit present the material.

Coming from a place of infinite respect and devotion to the infinite Creator, it is, in our humble opinion, extremely unlikely that whatever is written will fail in the end to inspire entities with the sense of the sacredness of the game being played.

Sometimes a creative entity can become too close to a project and can begin to question and doubt that which has gone into the creation of the project so far. We encourage the instrument to plow right into any doubts that come her way. And indeed, in general, when there is a second-guessing of a situation, when there is a wondering if something was the right thing to do, by all means give that concern its due. Give it time. Rest with that thought and see where it takes you when you are calm and serene in your mind and in your heart, so that whatever you discover from examining and reexamining an idea will not seem to be a negative thing but a positive thing, even if it causes changes.

We are not suggesting that this instrument should change anything. We are simply suggesting that if she is concerned, or indeed if any who create are concerned, that rather than quickly erasing and deleting and doing things over, there is a time allowed where the entity simply rests in the silence.

Indeed, if there is one thing that is most helpful to any who attempts to create spiritually uplifting material, it is to embrace and use the silence. There is a tremendous amount of information that streams into each seeker's mind and heart every moment. When the intention is set to hear that silent information, the result is instantaneous and enhanced guidance is immediately with the entity who is asking for that silent information. It does not necessarily result in an immediate and conscious realization of something specific that needs to be done. Rather, the nature of spiritual information and insight is that it balances and sets into perspective the events and situations that are being examined.

The making of the choice of polarity, either service to others or service to self, is indeed the central aspect of what this instrument has been calling in her book, "The Game of Life." There is a common goal for all of humankind and that goal is to make The Choice. It is a simple concept and indeed it is such a simple concept that it has escaped serious consideration except in those institutions which this instrument would call religious.

Therefore, in our opinion, the use of this construction is a positive thing. We believe that the worth of that game, in the end, will speak for itself. For in the end, one sees a majestic, rainbow-colored structure of spiritual evolution that begins with this choice. Making this choice is the key to the spiritual development of each seeker for many, many lifetimes to come. And when this instrument chose to create this book, her desire was to get the information across in a simple manner. Consequently, we would encourage this instrument to persevere, without doubting the self, to strive for excellence and to tell the story truly and honestly. The story of love is worth the telling.

We would note before we leave the subject that although it is excellent for this instrument to write this book and for all who wish to serve to share their vision of helpful information, we feel that underlying all such efforts is one's spirit. If it did not come through this instrument, it would come through another and another, for we do not speak any words that are unique to us except in the precise arrangement of the metaphysics of the information we offer.

All of those concepts which are part of stating that the universe is unitary in nature and that, at this point in the development of humankind, it is time to make the choice of service to others or service to self, can be found in many different repositories of inspirational knowledge.

Consequently, we suggest working through inspiration, rather than through any heavy feelings that there is an urgency or that time is short. These energies will not serve a spiritually oriented project, for they are the energies of fear. We would instead suggest, to all who wish to serve, serenity and acceptance of any given limitations in an absolute determination to see the project through to its natural end, in order that the baby that has been created may be birthed and shared with the world.

May we ask if there is another query at this time?

Jim: D asks: "I read a little of Walter Russell's work and he mentioned in his treatise on light that our universe expands and contracts in 14-billion-year cycles. Could Q'uo comment on this?"

We are those of Q'uo, and are aware of your query, my brother. May we say that it is good to touch into your wonderful energy.[46] As to this time period suggested by Walter Russell, it is certainly accurate and is a portion of the cyclical energies that create the heartbeat of the one infinite Creator.

We would also note that time is a slippery and plastic thing when it is being applied to spiritual time as opposed to physical time. The inadequacies of such measurements are due to that factor.

Is there another query at this time?

Jim: Just one more. A lady by the name of F was asking: "Why have I developed a sensitivity to electromagnetic fields? Is the sensitivity associated with spiritual growth or healing? Can it be used to assist others? Are there any spiritual principles involved which would help me contemplate this question?"

We are those of Q'uo, and are aware of your query, my sister. That which is occurring to you, my sister, is a result of what we might call the thinning of the veil, as you have made the choice to awaken and to live life consciously if you can. When such a decision is made, and then when the decision is followed by a persistent series of ethical choices that bolster this decision to be alive, to live from the heart, and to espouse the values of unconditional love, in time this creates an entirely different inner environment within that entity who was before comfortably asleep and is now wide awake and alert.

Spiritual work is expressed in each seeker's physical body in different ways. Some people experience electrical energy moving over their body. Some people experience similar sensations but rather than the sensations being electrical, they are those of being much larger than they actually are, as if, seated in the chair, their bulk became balloon-like and almost floated in the room.

---

[46] D has been a long-time meditation group member and supporter of L/L Research, and the Q'uo group was acknowledging him.

There are as many reactions to increased awareness, and therefore increased energy, as there are people. Your response to the constant bombardment of third-density Earth with fourth-density waves of energy has caused you to have this particular reaction. There is no particular spiritual credit or debit to such sensations. They are a fairly mechanical part of your consciousness waking up and beginning to investigate who it is, who you are, what you are doing here, and so forth. We encourage you, my sister, to move right along with your investigation and not to be dismayed by the variations in your awareness of electromagnetic energies.

You will of course need to find out how to be comfortable with these sensations but we would suggest encouraging cooperation in a fearless and joyful way with the symptoms when they occur.

As to their being useful, this is something which we cannot discuss other than to say that it is a good question for you to ask yourself. It is a good avenue of inquiry to pursue in your personal process.

We wish you and all of those who are awakening and feeling somewhat disquieting symptoms of this type the courage to move forward without fear. For these are momentary and light symptoms of an awakening heart and nervous system, shall we say. It is as though, when you awaken spiritually, your energy body gets a chance to stretch and breathe and bloom. So you are in the process of helping your energy body to achieve a real maturity and many-petaled beauty. And we encourage you, and all who would seek, to serve and to learn.

Is there a final query at this time?

(Pause)

If there is no further query at this time, we will take our leave of this instrument and this group, leaving each in the love and the light, the power and the peace, of the one infinite Creator. We are known to you as the principle of Q'uo. Adonai, my friends. Adonai. ♣

Sunday Meditation
March 25, 2007

Group question: By the physical construction of the male and the female, it seem like in sexual intercourse there is a bias towards the male having an orgasm and the female not having an orgasm. Is there a metaphysical reason for this seeming difference?

(Carla channeling)

We are those known to you as the principle of Q'uo. Greetings in the love and in the light of the one infinite Creator, in Whose service we come to you this day. It is our pleasure and our privilege to be called to your circle of seeking and we greet those who are non-local in creating a global circle of seeking as well as a local one.[47] We thank you so much for creating time in this day for seeking the truth and we are humbled by your hope that we may be helpful in our thoughts. And we will share them gladly.

As always, however, we would ask that each of you be responsible for his own perception of these thoughts. If you wish to use them and they are resonant to you, then by all means, follow the path of that resonance. If they simply seem to you to be fair words but those which do not move you particularly, then they are not yours. For when you come across information that is subjectively helpful to your spiritual process, it sets up a kind of resonance. If you will follow the path of that resonance when you are receiving information, you will find that you cannot go wrong.

We thank you for this discrimination because we wish for you to reject the thoughts that we offer that do not help you. In this way we can be sure that we are not infringing upon your free will.

Free will is very much the lifeblood of the human experience, shall we say. In perfect free will, you have placed yourselves in an incarnation which is a heavier kind of illusion than that illusion in which entities who are part of the creation of the Father generally dwell. It is more difficult to know the truth because the truth is carefully hidden by the veil between the conscious and the subconscious mind. You do not remember why you came, or how to complete the lifetime that you hoped to complete before you took birth. You are in the position of having complete free will and yet finding that that means that you are responsible also for defining the game that you are going to play with your life, its rules, and its rewards.

Coming into heavy chemical bodies that reproduce by means of sexual relations, sexual congress, or sexual intercourse—these three terms being used interchangeably—you have come into a world of intense emotions, desires, expectations and fears. The tendency of people with free will who do not have the desire to create families is to avoid the

---

[47] This channeling meditation was broadcast live on the internet as part of a six-month trial of offering this service. The other sessions in 2007 are April 8 and 22 and May 6 and 20. There is a webcast navigation button on the L/L Research site.

experiences of sexual intercourse with partners who do indeed wish to become mated and to raise a family. Through your early history upon this sphere, there was a very clear-cut and definitive rule: if you had sexual relations, you were prone to have a child as a result of that sexual congress. If you wished not to have children, you did not have sexual congress.

The technology which your science has given you has created ways in which the function of bearing children is avoided during sexual congress by means of birth control. This creates a different situation in terms of energy expenditure. In the first instance, when there was no birth control, if you wished to treat a woman well and you were a gentleman, defined by the culture of the times, you wooed the woman, married the woman, and created a family with that woman. It was, in fact, in many early cultures part of the measure of a man that he could maintain a happy family.

Similarly, in those early times, the defined position of a female in society was that of a mate who was to be the helpmate of the male energy, the husband, the provider, the go-getter. The archetypical organization of male and female was kept fairly close to the archetype in conscious living by virtue of the male going forth and hunting and gathering and bringing home what was needed while the female energy of nurturing and inspiration kept a happy home, raised children, and created that atmosphere which produces a happy body, a happy mind, and a happy spirit.

The reason that this seemingly unbalanced situation worked so well for the spiritual benefit of all was simply this: that which male and female lost by playing the roles that they played was balanced by their mutual enjoyment of a happy home and the awareness that they had created that happy home from their affection for each other and for the Creator.

The times which you experience now are times in which birth control is generally available. Consequently, the attraction between male and female, whatever their seeming gender physically, is between those who care for each other. This is a potentially good impulse that could create energy exchanges that are of service to each other and of service to the Creator. When there is no need to be concerned about conceiving children the atmosphere of sexual congress changes in that it is known to be shared by two people who simply wish to create an exchange of energy rather than by two people who wish to have a family. Those vibrations are quite different, one from the other.

In the first instance, when there is always the awareness that a sexual congress might result in the birth of a child there is an instinctual awareness of the power of sexuality. Man and woman together in sexual intercourse know that they are using the power of their sexuality to create life. This creates an atmosphere that is potentially more conducive to transfers of energy which approach sacredness.

The playing field now has been leveled. Those who wish to have sexual intercourse may do so without fear of creating children. And consequently that first reason for valuing sexuality is gone. You are not using your power to create life, at least not physical life, if you are using birth control or have, by some other means, rendered yourself sterile. What are you, then, doing in terms of the exchange of energy that entities experience, without a doubt, when they do have sexual intercourse?

What they experience, potentially, is the right use of power and, to be specific, the right use of the power of sexuality. Now let us look at this from a couple of different angles, for this is not a simple subject.

In the first place, the reason that you have power is that you are a portion of the one great original Thought, a spark of the original fire, a glint in the Creator's eye. You are a focuser and a station which receives and transmits vibrations. You can receive from the world of space/time and you can receive from the world of time/space. You are very sensitive instruments, holding tremendous power, the power of unconditional love, that love which created all that there is, which created you, and which would create children through your use of sexual intercourse if you so desired it and made it possible through your own sexual intercourse with your mate.

The power of sexuality does not go away because there is no intention to reproduce the species. That reproductive function is an helpful function to a certain extent but it is not that with which spirit has anything whatsoever to do. That instinct of reproducing the species as thickly as possible is a pure red-ray instinct. When you begin talking about the power of sexuality and you are not talking about having children, then you are beginning to talk about the possibility of sacred sexuality.

There is no function for the woman having an orgasm during sexual relations if the desire begins and ends in the sacred mission of creating a child. Therefore, the easy access, shall we say, to stimulation which would result naturally in orgasm, was covered over by folds which one could think of as petals of a rose. They are not defensive but they are protective and in an archetypal way. Just as the archetype of the potentiator[48] has a cover over the book of wisdom that she holds to her heart, so a woman's womanhood has a veil that protects it from the casual stimulation of sexual congress.

In order to create a female orgasm, it is most often necessary for the mated pair to go about that in a careful and conscious manner. You have heard the phrase about pearls before swine, and we do not mean to insinuate or in any suggest that your physical bodies are swine. What we do mean to suggest is that the energy of red ray is an energy that cannot function as an energy transfer in the same sense in which we speak when we are talking about sacred sex.

Indeed, for the untutored entity who may indeed be fond of this lover, or even have decided to marry and take a spouse, these orange- and yellow-ray activities of personal relationship and legal relationship are not yet enough to create a true energy exchange. The only kind of energy exchange that is possible at this level is a one-way exchange from one entity to another. This has been experienced by many within personal relationships and within marriages.

And we feel it is safe to say that, in most people's experience, this kind of sexual intercourse, left at the level of the relationship and without opening the heart to a great deal more than is suggested by the simple running of orange or yellow-ray energy, results in the typical exchange of energy, where one entity manipulates, uses or otherwise dominates another entity. Therefore, one is indeed giving energy to the other and the other is accepting that energy. It is an exchange of a kind but is tremendously prone to being abused and becoming a toxic kind of energy exchange where the honor, dignity and self-worth of the entity that is being controlled and manipulated comes into question by both mates.

Consequently, when we speak of true energy exchange, we must consider that the energy between two people has moved a very long way from that beginning red-ray attraction which eventually initiates sexual congress. It has gone from lust to a personal relationship and then often to a legal relationship or a committed relationship which is mated. And then the couple has the opportunity to ask for the Creator Itself to enter the sexual relationship through the open heart.

And so the couple that wishes to express sacred sexuality and to become entities who serve in a certain way in the environment of planet Earth agree together, very consciously, to set forth on a journey together in which they woo each other with true affection and patience, in which they see the Creator in each other, and in which they feel the power of the Creator's love and the Creator's light. Each mate dedicates itself to loving the other unconditionally.

This is green-ray affection and it is at this point that the female orgasm becomes useful. There are more miles to go indeed in exploring sacred sexuality, but this is where it begins.

When true affection has been established in a sexual relationship and when that sexuality has been dedicated to the Creator, to each other, and to planet Earth, then the path of progression, for a sexually maturing mated pair, is to spend a good deal of time working with the blue-ray energy of communication. Each entity that is involved in personal relationships and sexual relationships is an oddity, a one-of-a-kind item. That is why entities are so specific about whom they love. They become used to a certain flavor of being that this entity exudes or vibrates. And so they prefer that entity's company.

Therefore, in communicating with each other, history is shared. The reasons for this quirk and that quirk become available, either because the mate understands herself or himself, or because you observe and become able to understand your mate all on your own.

Every piece of intelligence that you have, then, you see, is a kind of piece of power, as this song today

---

[48] Q'uo is speaking of the Potentiator of the Mind, one of the twenty-two archetypes of the Egyptian tarot. in this image or "concept complex" the woman who is the potentiator-figure is holding a book of wisdom to her bosom. The book is only partially seen, as she is wearing a veil over herself and the book as well.

was suggesting, "a golden feather, a heart of stone"[49]. What shall you do with this knowledge of each other? Shall you use it kindly or shall you use it to make points the next time you become upset over a trifle?

When working with sexual energy, it is very important to realize that you are dealing with enormously powerful forces, and therefore, as you become more intimate with your partner, you need to become ever more careful, ever more affectionate, and ever more thoughtful about how you say things as well as what you say. For you have become a powerful person to your mate and you wish to treat this mate with all the honor and respect that you would give to the Creator Himself or Herself.

You see, if you are a man, your mate is the feminine energy of the Creator. If you are a woman, your mate is the male energy of the Creator. Together, you make the full 360 degrees of Creatorship that takes in all the polarities that you both express. You have shared all that you are and you have become one with the Creator.

How can you, then, value the female orgasm? You value it by creating a safe atmosphere in which such a thing can take place. You value it by continuing an atmosphere of gentleness, honor, romance, if you will: those small things that, to the feminine temperament, indicate a genuine and deep interest and not simply the red-ray sexual energy of lust.

If you are a woman, you treasure yourself. You do not worry about having an orgasm, as if it were the same thing as a man's orgasm for, my friends, it is not. Certainly it can be made rough and primitive. It can have the energy simply of sexual congress in the red ray. However, it is far more likely for the feminine temperament to appreciate what's going on when that orgasm happens to her. For a woman tends to have more of a connection with the unseen world. So, she is actually more aware of the kind of energy that is pouring through her when she is expressing an orgasm physically.

Consequently, a woman in that position is a priestess, just as a man is a priest, in sexual intercourse when they are working together sacredly. But to the man goes that kind of energy that is called by this instrument "yang," to the woman goes the energy that is considered by this instrument "yin," so that, in the sexual energy exchange that is sacred in nature, from the man comes that powerful energy of physical wellness and vitality—that which you think of when you think of the word "masculine."

What the feminine offers is the inspiration from spirit. That is the other portion of that male expression of strength, power and virility. The woman is expressing acceptance, unconditional love, and the energy of the Creator Itself. For you see, the woman, unlike man, is possessed of a direct route or connection to the womb of, shall we say, Mother Nature or the red-ray energy of planet Earth.

The woman has that sea of infinity and eternity flowing through her. She is much closer to her priestliness because she must tend to the circumstances of her menses monthly and she feels the pull of the moon, the tides, and her passions in a way that, generally speaking, men are not encouraged to do in your culture.

Consequently, if two entities choose to become magical in their sexual practice, they have the ability to become great ambassadors, if you will, of light. For as they consciously call up this power that they have together and give it to each other, when they are completely saturated and filled up with this energy of orgasm, they then allow that orgasm to shine, both into the world of time/space and the world of space/time.

In the world of time/space, it is a kind of birth of created light. You have, in your own way, lightened that expression of the Creator that is occurring upon your Earth at this particular moment. You have energized and healed, with your magically offered energy, the natural function of your sexuality. It is a long way from the red-ray disturbance of the senses that adds fire and color to the life by creating sexual desire and by giving a way for it to be fulfilled to the work in indigo where entities become sacred to each other in a very formal way, so that what they offer to the Creator and to the world is very consciously offered.

---

[49] This Robbie Robertson lyric, in part, goes like this:
> In the autumn night
> When there's no wind blowing
> I could hear the stars falling in the dark
> When you find what's worth keeping
> With a breath of kindness
> Blow the rest away.
>
> I gave my love a golden feather
> I gave my love a heart of stone
> And when you find a golden feather
> It means you'll never lose your way back home.

This female orgasm, then, is hidden on purpose from easy access and it is immediately available to the mated pair who chooses to value the creation of the female orgasm as something that is not simply a add-on, shall we say, to the experience of sexual intercourse, but is part of an extended, romantic and affectionate time together in which the Creator is very much present.

Is there a follow up to this query? We are those of Q'uo.

Jim: We have another question, Q'uo. As this month marks the birthday of the Prophet Muhammad, peace and blessings be upon him, and we in the West have so little unbiased information about him and his way, I was wondering if you could add to what those of Ra said about this entity being a Messenger of the Law of One. I also would like to ask about the nature of his spiritual transmission, which is still so evident within the many Sufi orders today.

We are those of Q'uo, my brother, and we believe that we are aware of your query. The one known as Mohammed is one with the same energy that created Moses, Elijah, Nahum, Jeremiah, Isaiah and all of the other prophets and priests that responded to the call of that entity which we may call Yahweh, the "name" of the Creator that cannot be said because it is too sacred.[50] This Mohammed also was a prophet of this one God.

The problems resulting from the Koran are the same problems resulting from a good, solid reading of the Old Testament and those two works should be considered together when forming an opinion concerning these matters, for there is much in all the literature, not only of the Koran and the Old Testament but in those books and writings which did not make it into the final versions of those sacred works but had a good deal of information along those lines to share about this creation of the "One God" which, instead of being the one infinite Creator, was a kind of artifact made up of those of one of the groups that were guardians of your planet in an attempt to create a more spiritually capable human being.

---

[50] The formal "name of the Creator" to Jews is "Yod Heh Vau Heh," which is never spoken. For the sake of convenience, the Name is rendered Jehovah or Yahweh when spoken.

Those whom they altered genetically, prior to placing them upon this planet in times gone by, they felt the need to follow. It is ironic, indeed, my friends, that those in your Middle East—the followers of Jesus, the followers of Yahweh, and the followers of Allah—are in a state of mortal combat. They are all of one blood. They are all of one teaching. It is a mark of the inefficacy of making physical changes in order to create more viable spiritual workers that this is so. That which was created to improve the genetic pool of gifts of the humans thus altered were the mind to be more intelligent, the body to be more strong, and the will to be more powerful. What no entity can put into a gene is any code that has to do with spirituality, for this is that which can only be chosen by free will.

Free will is where we began in this discussion and free will is where this question also takes us. By free will, entities following these teachers have chosen to focus upon judgment and justice: an eye for an eye and a tooth for a tooth; and someone being right and someone being wrong; someone being the holy people and the rest of the world not being the holy people. Followers have focused upon this rather than the inclusive gifts of the spirit that are equally obvious in the holy works themselves.

There is no more hospitable a book than the Koran or the Old Testament. The fatted calf is offered in many, many stories; not just one but sometimes thousands of them, because of the glory and the joy of certain meetings and certain occasions. Hospitality, indeed, to this day is a very, very important part of the culture of these entities who worship this "One God."

We would suggest that it would be helpful to look for the positive gifts of the one known as Mohammed in the mysticism of the Sufi's, just as one may most likely find the most positive aspects of the Old Testament writing and prophets in that small circle of entities who have worked with the Kabala to develop the Tree of Life. In both cases the outer husks of religion, the dogma, the exclusiveness, and so forth, have been cast aside to get to the heart of the fruit of spirituality which is the same in any religion or system of worship. And that is simply the adoration of the one infinite Creator by the creation that has been made. The Creator responds with Its adoration for that which It has created. This combination creates an infinite atmosphere of unconditional love. Those who focus down to this point from any road, whether it be Christian, Jewish, Islam or any other, are doing the same good work.

Is there another query at this time?

Jim: Concerning the same time of evolution within the religious practices of humans here. Ra said that the Hebrew sounds had a special meaning or a very natural way of falling from the creation into use by humans. Is that because the Hebrew sounds are associated with the light spectrum or are they encoded with any human genetic code? What makes the Hebrew alphabet so special?

We are those of Q'uo, and are aware of your query, my brother. We apologize for not being able completely to respond to your query. There are two problems that we have with this query. Firstly the instrument herself is not a scientist and in order to speak in a way that would be helpful to you technically we would need to be able to use her instrument with her having embedded some terms and simple awareness about how light works which she does not have. What we generally do with this instrument when talking about light and the use of sacred sound is to call upon this instrument's experience as a singer.

We will say, this being understood, that sound is song. Any song an entity makes has a certain vibratory signature. However, each has perhaps experienced the difference between singing a popular song and singing a sacred song when you are attempting to worship.

When you are using sacred words and sacred language, and when you produce the sound consciously, aware of the sacredness of that sound, the voice brings to life underlying time/space-oriented or non-local energies that alert certain areas of vibration throughout the infinite universe of the one Creator. You can look at these simply as vibrations or you can look at them as Cherubim, Seraphim, and all of the other designations of unseen but very powerful and very real entities which are involved in the worship of the one infinite Creator.

These energies have been built up since the beginning of the energy of this octave of creation, with thousands and thousand of lifetimes and thousands and thousands of repetitions of various sounds.

(Side one of tape ends.)

(Carla channeling)

Certain sounds are therefore more sacred than others. The Lord's Prayer is a good example of this type of constantly repeated set of words.

It is interesting to note that perhaps the most deeply felt prayers, by those who have worshipped in the past in your Roman Catholic churches, have been those words that they did not understand but that they knew to be holy, the vibration of those Latin words by priests who did not even understand what they were saying, nevertheless, by their sheer repetition in the ears of the faithful, generation after generation, [they] became magical, and the use of them was powerful.

When an entity uses language consciously, he becomes a priest. And indeed, we say to you: everything that you say may be seen to be sacred or deliberately chosen not to be sacred, because the default setting of speech of any kind of utterance is that it is sacred. Yet that beginning nature of sound itself, when involved with the human breath, is not used by most entities in most applications. Most people are not aware that, when they open their mouth and speak, they are people of power, and so they do not concern themselves precisely with what they say. And they may throw away many, many words which mean very little, simply having a good time communicating small facts and enjoying life.

However, in the case of two languages, the Sanskrit and the Hebrew, those involved in the early creation of the tongues and the writing down of them into a form of notation which you would call writing were working from the premise that their sounds were sacred. And this makes them sacred.

It is not that there is a code involved or that there is some statistical relationship betwixt the genetic code and certain vowels or syllables. It is that the intention of those who created and notated those two languages was to create a set of sacred vibrations.

These were unique in the creation of languages upon your sphere because of the fact that most languages have been created by those who wish to do business. And therefore the whole vibrational energy of words in most cultures is not that energy of sacredness, at least not consciously. Certainly, when these sounds are brought together into inspiring speech or ineffable singing, once again the human heart can begin to hear the sacredness of sound and the power of the human breath to express the love and the light of the one infinite Creator.

It is well to sense the self as a priest and to know that each time you open your mouth, you have the power to judge and you have the power to love and forgive. Using your voice sacredly is a great service.

Is there a follow up to this query, my brother?

Jim: No more questions here.

We are those of Q'uo. Is there a final query before we leave this instrument?

R: Not from me, Q'uo.

We are those of Q'uo. It has been a great pleasure to be with you this afternoon, my friends. The beauty of your vibrations is astounding and we thank you for sharing this time with us. We leave you in the love, the light, the power, and the peace of the one infinite Creator. We are known to you as the principle of Q'uo. Adonai, my friends. Adonai.

L/L Research

L/L Research is a subsidiary of Rock Creek Research & Development Laboratories, Inc.

P.O. Box 5195
Louisville, KY 40255-0195

www.llresearch.org

Rock Creek is a non-profit corporation dedicated to discovering and sharing information which may aid in the spiritual evolution of humankind.

ABOUT THE CONTENTS OF THIS TRANSCRIPT: This telepathic channeling has been taken from transcriptions of the weekly study and meditation meetings of the Rock Creek Research & Development Laboratories and L/L Research. It is offered in the hope that it may be useful to you. As the Confederation entities always make a point of saying, please use your discrimination and judgment in assessing this material. If something rings true to you, fine. If something does not resonate, please leave it behind, for neither we nor those of the Confederation would wish to be a stumbling block for any.

© 2009 L/L Research

Sunday Meditation
April 8, 2007

Easter Sunday

Question from D: I feel as though something is out of order as far as time and the perception of time. The days don't feel like they are supposed to be. It is as if something is out of sync. We are wondering if Q'uo could give us any information about the energies that affect our illusion at this time. Is there any particular reason why people who are sensitive to such things might be feeling that there is something not quite right with the way we are perceiving time; with the way time is being experienced in our illusion? Are there any spiritual principles here that Q'uo could speak to that might help us understand this situation?

(Carla channeling)

We are those of the principle Q'uo. Greetings in the love and in the light of the one infinite Creator. It is a pleasure to be called to your circle of seeking and a privilege to be asked to share our humble opinions with you on the subject of perception of time at this time.

As always, we ask you to be governors and guardians of the temple of your minds and hearts. Listen to our words with an ear for that thought which reverberates and resonates to you. That thought would be the one most likely to yield results if you work with it. If the thoughts that we share do not have that resonant feeling, we would suggest that you lay them aside and move on. For that which you seek is waiting for you to discover it. Pay attention, therefore, to the path of resonance rather than to your high opinion of any particular speaker. We thank you for this consideration, as it enables us to speak freely without being concerned that we will infringe upon your free will or disturb the process of your spiritual evolution.

You ask this day concerning time, or the perception of time. It is indeed so that there are various ways in which the stream of time is plastic, and we would discuss them without giving one distortion priority over another in terms of whom they affect and so forth.

By far, at this time, the largest proportion of entities experiencing variation in time are those entities who are experiencing a simple speeding-up of time. Hours don't seem to be hours and days don't seem to be days. And the year goes by too fast. There is nothing metaphysical about this time distortion. It is, rather, an artifact of the changes in your environment over the last two hundred years.

Over the last two hundred years, a great deal has changed in your environment as a species, and we speak to those primarily in the first world, shall we say, and the new world, who have the conveniences of civilization in its corporate glory at this time and have come through the process of the industrial revolution. Two hundred years ago, if one wished to travel from Philadelphia to St. Louis, one boarded a wooden wagon, sprung on wheels and pulled by horses or oxen, or one traveled by horse, by cart, or on foot, in real time, to those places where one wished to go.

Naturally this made everyone think carefully about where they wished to go, because they would have to devote whatever time it took to walk there, do the business that was to be done there and walk back, or alternatively to ride a horse there or harness the horse to a buggy of some kind. All of these things slowed down events. They had to happen at the speed of the human body's ability to move, or, at the very most, at the ability of a horse or ox to move.

A hundred years ago, things advanced considerably in that century. You were now able to travel by getting on a train. You were able to traverse the distance from Philadelphia to St. Louis in a thirtieth of the time it had previously taken. Nevertheless, you were earthbound. You gazed out the window and saw every speck of country between Philadelphia and St. Louis that lay along that track. You were still in real time, in terms of being in a tactile, sensual relationship with that which came between one place and another.

At your present time, if you traverse the distance from Philadelphia to St. Louis, you can get upon an airplane in Philadelphia and you can, in the same afternoon, land in the airport at your destination in St. Louis, having had no actual experience of travel, except that which is related to the peculiar experience of riding on an airplane which, at least in this instrument's mind, does not count as actual travel, for there is, besides a beautiful sky, no sense of where one is, no sense of the land between point A and point B.

Looking at another aspect of life two hundred years ago, if you wished to write and communicate with people, you took your pen and your foolscap[51] and you carefully wrote out that which you wished to say in a fair hand. You then gave that letter to the postal carrier who was working by horse and eventually that letter would be received. In local letter writing, entities simply sent messengers from one house to another with notes, and those notes were returned by those same messages on foot. Eventually, plans were made, associations were formed, and business was conducted.

---
[51] foolscap: a type of inexpensive writing paper, especially legal-size, lined, yellow sheets, bound in tablet form. It got its name from its watermark, which in the seventeenth and eighteenth centuries was, literally, a fool's cap.

A hundred years ago entities communicated by typewriter and could send the speedily written documents to their destinations on the train. The telephone was in its early days at that time and so people could communicate from place to place in certain areas where there were telephone systems. The cable and the wire were also ways of communicating rapidly and business and communication had sped up.

In your day entities tend to go through life with their cell phones on so that they are completely available at any moment from any where in the globe by anyone who has the telephone number of their cell phone. Computers send information using light as their medium. Needless to say, this communication is fast. Entities now are completely overwhelmed with information, communication and an intimacy that is global. The irony of having such massive communication is that entities feel more isolated than they did a hundred years ago, just as entities then feeling things speed up around them felt isolated by the change.

This is the major experience of people, and as we said there is nothing metaphysical about it. It is that which happens when people have too much to cross off their lists before they can rest. As life has gotten more assisted and entities are free from the drudgery of washing by hand, scrubbing on their knees the floor, having appliances, and so forth, more and more options have opened up. There are more and more expectations in more and more areas.

And the center that there was to life in a simple survival mode has been lost, because there are many assists to survival these days. Food is prepared for you and you can buy it ready-made or take it home frozen and zap it in your microwave oven. Yet at the same time you have lost that feeling of connection with the land and the crop growing from the land, going out in the dawning to harvest your crop, preserving it carefully, and enjoying the food that is yours, that grew on your land and that is for you. This has been lost. This kind of center has been lost in many different areas, so that entities are flying high and doing a great many things, but there is a tendency not to have a center that makes sense of existence or is the pivot around which the wheel of your life can turn.

The solution for correcting this distortion is to remove from yourself the necessity to respond to all of the different facets of possibility within modern life as you know it. And when you do each thing that you do, do it with that feeling of a center to things.

What is your center? From what center are you working?

This instrument prays every morning, *"Send us now into the world in peace, and grant us strength and courage to love and serve you with gladness and singleness of heart.*[52]*"*

When your mind is on serving the one infinite Creator, then you can slow life back down, because you have a center. You can take the time to dedicate your efforts, no matter how humble or how grand, to the one infinite Creator. And this normalizes your time. It may still go quickly, but you have more of a sense of being there and being an active and conscious part of your own life. Without that center there is a tendency to feel that life has overwhelmed and overtaken you and you can never catch up.

There is another way in which time is being distorted, and we can only touch upon this generally because of this instrument's lack of knowledge of science, especially physics.

Two densities of Earth are existing simultaneously as they have always. However, up until approximately fifty years ago, by far the more powerful of the two densities that were shaping time/space was the third density, the density you now experience. At about that time, fifty years ago, the fourth-density planet Earth began to activate.

These things come in stages, coming from the very highest realms of manifestation and filtering down through the tree of life, shall we say, to individual galaxies, individual sun systems, and individual planets. But just as the turning of wheel that moves the clock from one o'clock to two o'clock, the hand of time began waking up fourth-density olanet Earth, to activate and become, in its turn, the manifesting density of this particular planet.

So, you exist at this time in a between-time, where third density's energy is all but gone and fourth density's energy is bursting forth. However, this is still a third-density experience for each of you who is experiencing Earth on what is called a time lateral.

The nearness of fourth density to third at this time means that there is a bleed-through. When one is operating on default third-density values, such as protecting the home and tribe and being the winner and that sort of value, the experience of this intermixing of vibrations is simply a feeling of being weary, cranky, sick or in some way "out of kilter." Rather than beginning to welcome these fourth-density vibrations they simply seem to be toxic.

The reason for this of course is that entities vibrate at a certain level. It is not a simple matter of the electromagnetic properties of your body. Your thoughts are very powerful and there is a kind of vibration that you create by your thoughts.

When you are tuning your thoughts towards thankfulness, joy and worship, your vibration is moving upwards. Your frequency of vibration is increasing. When you allow thoughts of depression, disappointment, grief, anger, resentment and other such negative emotions to persist in your consciousness, and especially when you allow them to become habitual, you begin to vibrate at a lower rate of vibration. You simply cannot enjoy fourth-density vibrations. They seem to be attacking the body.

Those who are conscious, awake and on the path of spiritual seeking do not feel these vibrations as toxic. They do not feel them as that which makes them sick. However, they may well feel them as challenging. For these vibrations are vibrations of shining truth. They demand truth. They live in truth.

You may say, "What is truth?" And we say to you that to each person it is something different. What the fourth density does is make transparent everyone's truth. One may see not only one's own center—which one cannot see now in the third density in which you live—one may also see the center of each other person.

It is a wonderfully normalizing thing to be at a fourth density level and to see the Earth populated

---

[52] These words are part of a closing prayer in the Episcopal Church's Holy Eucharist Service, Rite Two, found in The Book of Common Prayer, page 365. In that Eucharist, the words, "through Christ our Lord" immediately follow that text. In our Morning Offerings the closing prayer, of which this is a part, has a lot more to it and other thoughts of praise, prayer, devotion, thanksgiving and requests for guidance intervene before the closing of the prayer. However, our prayers are always concluded in the same manner, "through Christ our Lord" or some variation of that phrase.

by flower after flower after flower of the Creator's sons and daughters who are coming into bloom in incarnation. That is the true nature of each of you, and that is how you would see each other, were you living completely in fourth density.

It is not that you would be better. It is that it would be transparent as to who you are. And it would be transparent to you as to who everyone else is. All the imperfections that now hold you back and pull you down into self-judgment mean nothing. Because it is obvious that every attempt is being made not to err. And yet error is inevitable. For when one is learning, one learns from one's errors. One must make the errors in order to progress.

Therefore, there is an inclusive feeling of one being one tribe when one is gazing at the other selves around one. Entities within third density often come very close to achieving this kind of fourth-density experience in special moments such as this meditation and such as the Easter services and the Passover feasts and all of the other holy occasions that mark this time of the year, for many there are, different religions and spiritual practices such as Wicca, which take this time to observe the rites of spring.

At these moments entities can almost see the promised land of utter equality, utter compassion, and the utter embracing of each other. They can almost taste that desire to move forward as a tribe and not to play off against each other but to serve each other, becoming the least in order to lead, as the one known as Jesus taught so well.

But for the most part it remains a challenging kind of vibration where you, in third-density bodies, with the third-density veil still down, are asked to look at everything that is keeping you from becoming a fourth-density being, everything that is holding you back from polarizing more and more towards service-to-others.

What is holding you back? It isn't going to be the same for any two people. In general what holds entities back is that which causes them not to pay attention to who they are and why they are in incarnation. It is easy to lose track of the big picture. If you can maintain a hold on the big picture and when you discover that you have strayed from it, move back to it, you will have the best chance possible of being able to cooperate and enjoy the revelations of truth that this fourth-density energy is bringing you.

If you see that which do you not like, take special care to embrace and examine it and research that which you are seeing. Do not say, "Oh! That could not be me!" Rather, dig deep and find out, within yourself, which is the echo and the shadow of what you are seeing in the mirror of someone else or some relationship of which you have heard that horrifies you. Do not turn your back on that and say, "That could never be me!" Rather, find that portion of yourself that resonates with the dark side of that which you have seen, and bring that dark image of yourself up.

When you face the darkness within you, you can ask it to work for you. You can say, "I need you. I need you, anger. I need you, grief. I need you, all seemingly negative emotions, because I need to persevere. I need to keep going. And you are my grit. You are my resolve. You are the iron that strengthens my will and encourages me to return to my faith. Come with me on this journey. Let us, dark and light side, worship and love the one infinite Creator in its mystery."

These actions will bring you ever more peace and serenity within yourself. As you acknowledge and embrace your imperfections and task them to help you be better and to help you become that which is ahead of you to become, what have you in mind to become if not that entity which is ever more polarized; more full of the love and the light of the one infinite Creator?

We do not say these are easy times for anyone, but they are interesting times. And each of you is here because you wanted to incarnate at this time very badly. You wanted to make a difference. You wanted to serve. And you want now to graduate at the end of your incarnation here.

Use these odd feelings of time being perceived crookedly to remind you that you are in this period of shining truth, which is being rained down on you in a sideways and circuitous manner because of the interaction of third density and fourth density. Their space/times are enough different that there is a challenging dynamic to the times.

There is another way in which we may look at time at this time, and we mentioned this earlier in passing. Because of the fact that your Earth is on a time lateral, time has deliberately been slowed in order that there would be more opportunity for members of the tribe of humankind to reach graduation with a polarity that will enable them to move on to fourth density. And we may honestly say that many, many entities have literally moved heaven and earth in order to maximize this possibility.

It is not only those from outside the planet or the planetary influence which have contributed to this effect of time dilation. It is also the many, many light-workers who, for the last half century and more, have joined the ageless community of those who meditate for the good of planet Earth, with very specialized agendas having to do with their being wanderers coming into Earth incarnation in order to help shift the energy from one vibration that is third density to a higher vibration that is more full of light, denser with the love and the light of the one infinite Creator.

And those wanderers have infected and spread the light so that many, many of those who are not wanderers at all have also awakened and become wanderers themselves, shedding and spreading light in turn on others, who in turn catch it and pass it on. This also has greatly ameliorated the severity of this shift from third density to fourth density.

And lastly, there is an experience which is very rare, but about which we feel that the one known as D is inquiring. When entities focus into the world of spirit past the point in thinking in words, generally they are entering into silence. So the one known as D is atypical in that she has not come into the heart of the mystery by entering the silence so profoundly that the doors open. This entity has done so by sinking down into the roots of language, almost as if she were able to take an electron microscope to the human voice or the human breath and discover what sacred act may be achieved by the use of symbol and breath.

And so this entity, too, has broken through a kind of barrier that, once broken through, opens up a vista that is infinite. When realizations of this nature occur, there is a mark left in the pond of local time. It is as if each realization is a pebble being dropped into that local, personal time experience, so that there are waves and ripples and disturbances. They are local. They are not dangerous. But they are definitely there. And they will only be found or be perceived by entities who are able to tune into the warp and woof of space/time.

Space/time is due to a mismatch; there is a bit more of space than time in space/time and a bit more of time than space in time/space, which is what creates, in both space/time and time/space, the ability of certain entities with certain organs designed to do this to be able to make sense out of vibration. Thusly, the mismatch between space and time in favor of time brings your illusion into focus. Your eyes are then able to interpret bits of information that they collect about that which is in front of them. They send it to a place in the brain which forms it into a kind of guess at what they are seeing and they are able to move forward as if they were seeing everything perfectly when in fact very little of a person's environment is usually in focus, and entities eyes are generally in focus upon the face of the person to whom they are talking, or some object which is the center of attention, and everything else is more or less seen but not seen.

When an entity is able to penetrate this mismatch, there is a still point, an astonishing experience which is full of possibility. And when this particular time distortion occurs, we encourage the entity that experiences it to pay very close attention to that which occurs and to ask for that which is one's heart's desire.

We thank you for this query and would like to know at this time if there is a follow-up to this question? We are those of Q'uo.

(Pause)

We are those of Q'uo. May we ask if there is another query at this time?

R: I have a question, Q'uo, that is somewhat personal, so I ask you to comment as you are able. The question is about my perceived lack of questions for entities such as the Confederation. As I keep learning my spiritual lessons I have noticed that when I was new to the seeking or consciously new to the seeking I had lots of questions. And as I have spent more time in silence I seem to have fewer and fewer questions, even though I am still just as grateful for the information and contact from the Confederation as I was in the beginning. Others have observed a similar process. My question is: is this the normal progress of spiritual seeking, which is turning inwards?

We are those of Q'uo, and are aware of your query, my brother. Indeed, it is normal for entities who begin to seek to be very active in the constant process of questioning everything. In spiritual seeking the first thing an entity must do is tear down a good deal of misconception that has limited his growth without his even knowing it. As an entity begins to awaken he discovers many things that did not occur to him before because he is not ready for these concepts.

It is an exciting time and it is an important time for entities—that beginning, that waking up! And it is to be encouraged. Then there is a longer period in which, as you say, there are fewer and fewer questions, but you continue having questions and it almost seems as though you finish one layer of questions only to find a deeper layer of questions.

And then, my brother, finally, as one continues to seek, one reaches a level where there is a great appreciation for the information that is within the silence, and the tendency is to be hungry not so much for words, which are the creation of humankind, but for the concepts that are full of the mystery of the one Creator, that can be communicated from heart to heart rather than from mind to mind.

My we ask you have a follow-up query, my brother?

R: No, thank you for your comments, I appreciate that very much.

We are those of Q'uo, and we always appreciate your vibrations as well. Is there a final query at this time?

(No further queries.)

We are those of Q'uo, and since we have seem to have exhausted the supply of questions at this particular circle of seeking, we shall take our leave of this instrument and this group, thanking each for the true pleasure of being a part of the beauty of this sacred gathering of souls.

We are known to you as the principle of Q'uo. We leave you in the love and in the light of the one infinite Creator. Adonai. ✥

L/L Research

L/L Research is a subsidiary of Rock Creek Research & Development Laboratories, Inc.

P.O. Box 5195
Louisville, KY 40255-0195

www.llresearch.org

Rock Creek is a non-profit corporation dedicated to discovering and sharing information which may aid in the spiritual evolution of humankind.

ABOUT THE CONTENTS OF THIS TRANSCRIPT: This telepathic channeling has been taken from transcriptions of the weekly study and meditation meetings of the Rock Creek Research & Development Laboratories and L/L Research. It is offered in the hope that it may be useful to you. As the Confederation entities always make a point of saying, please use your discrimination and judgment in assessing this material. If something rings true to you, fine. If something does not resonate, please leave it behind, for neither we nor those of the Confederation would wish to be a stumbling block for any.

© 2009 L/L Research

Special Meditation
April 14, 2007

Jim: The first question from T is: "What exactly is the time lateral of Earth? Does it indicate an illusion within a more real illusion? Or is it like the holodeck on Star Trek's fictional world? Then are all the stars and planets except Earth all holograms because Earth is in the time lateral? Or, on the other end, if there was no such thing as a time lateral in the beginning, what would the third-density Earth be like?"

(Carla channeling)

We are those known to you as the principle of Q'uo. Greetings in the love and in the light of the one infinite Creator, in Whose service we come to you this evening. We wish to thank you for the privilege of being included in your circle of seeking and are happy to share our opinions with you about the queries with which you come this evening.

As always, we would ask for you to use your discrimination, listening carefully and distinguishing between those thoughts that seem helpful and resonant to you and those thoughts that do not. Please abandon those that do not ring true to you and work with the ones that seem helpful. In this way, you have protected your own process of evolution and have used your free will in order to distinguish between thoughts helpful to you and those not. We thank you for this consideration.

As always, when we speak through this instrument concerning those questions which have to do with physics and the whole realm of science, we express the surety that we shall not be able to be precise in our response, for this instrument does not have the knowledge or the vocabulary of mathematics and physics at her command. Nevertheless, we shall attempt to share our thoughts with you in the best way which is open to us.

At the end of the second minor cycle of harvest in third density upon planet Earth, the Council of Saturn became concerned that the solar system as a whole had been able to bring to a normal graduation only one of the planets in this particular solar system that you call the Sun. It decided that it would be helpful to create a time lateral and to place the planet under strict quarantine. It was further decided that all of those entities whose third densities had been interrupted be brought to Earth to join Earth's cycle leading to harvest.

Accordingly, the metaphysical or time/space portion of your third-density Earth was reconnected to the main track, shall we say, of the progression of time/space and space/time in such a way that it was as isolated and protected a hotbed or greenhouse for growing souls as could be devised.

It is precisely as real as the main track of time/space. And indeed, it is equal to the main track in time/space. It is a carefully created alternative track which naturally feeds back into the main track of time/space and space/time progression.

At the conclusion of this time lateral, then, the population of planet Earth shall be ready to take advantage of the opportunity to end the third sub-cycle of harvest and greet the end of that seventy-six-or-so-thousand-year cycle that is a third-density cycle in its completion.

Because this is not a physical alteration but a metaphysical alteration, there is no physical marker for the end of the time lateral. And indeed, this time lateral has been very successful compared to experiments in the past. The accumulation of awakening interest in altering the course of the vibration of planet Earth has been late in starting but has rapidly spread and gained strength in all parts of your globe, in all peoples, cultures and places. Your world is truly waking up.

Again, because of the fact that such activities are primarily metaphysical rather than physical in nature, the effects of the improvement in the vibration of planet Earth are not physically obvious except for the fact that your Earth is still functioning without the need to experience a polar shift. It was thought at one time to be probable that your Earth would, by the end of your twentieth century, have found it necessary, in order to express the heaviness of the vibration of Earth, to destroy the Earth once again in terms of it being habitable for human life, as you call your third-density species.

However, the work of many groups such as this one has created the possibility of a strengthened and lengthened track in the time lateral so that the maximum number of entities may awaken and choose whether to serve others or to serve the self before the time of such choice has passed. Once again, there will be no physical change when this time has passed. There will only be a change in the core vibration of the atoms of your universe, atom by atom, cell by cell, being by being.

You have asked if the experience of the time lateral is like the holo-deck and we would say that, indeed, whether you speak of the time lateral that you have experienced, with its careful isolation and insulation from the full spectrum of thought available in the infinite creation of the Father, or whether you speak of the main track, you have the same material and one single agenda for moving forward and fulfilling your hopes for progress within your present lifetime within third density.

May we ask if there is another query at this time? We are those of Q'uo.

Jim: The second question is: "In such a vast Milky Way, did the time lateral experiment happen in other planets before? If so, are the results always positively successful?"

We are those of Q'uo, and are aware of your query, my brother. Such experiments have occurred from time to time in the past and the results have been checkered.[53] There is, perhaps, nearly an even division between those experiments in which the various groupings of entities upon the planet turned from strife to a more unified view of the planetary population as one tribe and those that were not able to achieve graduation in either polarity.

Some of those experiments succeeded. There have been other attempts at, shall we say, cleaning up the energies of an entire planetary system where it was not possible to bring entities into one united spiritual being that could be called a social complex.

The difference in planet Earth's experiment is that the sub-Logos chose an experiment which was extremely rich in the full play and travel of free will, so that the veil was quite thick and almost impenetrable. This heavy veiling and full play of free will has resulted in entities turning not to the Creator but to their own intellects and to their own abilities to find solutions to what they perceive as challenges or problems.

In previous experiments, the veil was thinner because there was not so heavy a veiling and there was not so much free will. The nature of third-density entities upon your planet is, therefore, somewhat more primitive or has a tendency to remain primitive longer than on planetary experiments where the veil has been thinner and it has been more obvious to entities, by virtue of the thinning of the veil, that all are one.

In the absence of any hint from the outer world that all entities are one interconnected being, the tendency has been, upon planet Earth during this cycle, for entities to find reasons to separate rather than unite and to disagree and come to embattlement rather than seeking with all diligence for points of commonality that become a consensus for gradual and global change. At this point, we can

---

[53] Checkered means marked by numerous and various shifts and changes; variegated or marked by dubious episodes; suspect in character or quality, according to www.dictionary.com.

say that the probability is that your experiment shall, to some extent, be successful.

The outcome which those of negative polarity in higher densities would like to have occur upon planet Earth is that the majority of entities upon planet Earth decide that they are only safe and in proper spiritual alignment if they can live in fear and continuously find enemies to fight in order to express the feelings of winning the day and controlling what is seen as available sources of power, and we mean this not only physically but also metaphysically.

If a planetary social complex became involved in what you could call a "knot of fear," then they might voluntarily choose not to rejoin the main track. This would mean that this particular planet would be locked in a permanent third-density cycle without the third-density energy needed to progress. This would make this planet a slave planet in which entities fought and suffered endlessly and created food for the fifth-density entities who have long eyed this planet with greed and the hope of conquest.

Again, we cannot know the outcome of that which is completely at your free will. We can only tell you that the probability/possibility vortices have greatly opened in a favorable way within the past generation or half century of this planet's history. Things look hopeful, shall we say, that the rapidly increasing awareness of the need to choose a better way than strife for relating to one's fellow beings is needed. And as this realization spreads and as the hunger for true peace, union and love among all people grows, there is very likely to be a positive outcome at the end of this time lateral.

May we ask if there is another query at this time?

Jim: The third question is: "Evolving to the fourth density seems a distant goal. Is there a simple way to measure how close we are to the threshold of the fourth density? Living on Earth by faith alone, we are prone to losing our faith. What spiritual principles are involved? What practical advice can you offer?"

We are those of Q'uo, and are aware of your query. Your question is in two parts and so we would prefer to respond in two separate communications. Therefore, when we conclude our thoughts upon faith, we would ask that you repeat the first part of your query. We would like to respond to your question upon faith first.

My brother, faith is that which is a product of the use of will to choose to know that all is well. It is not faith in anything. It is not tangible. It is not measurable or quantifiable in any way. Yet all entities know what faith is because when they see it, they are drawn to it, transfixed by it, and blessed by the light that is expressed from faithful eyes, faithful voices, and faithful hands.

The spiritual principle involved is very close to the beginning of creation. For the principle involved is a mature understanding of the function of free will and the structure or makeup of your mind, body and spirit in third density. Because of the thickness of the veil, it is indeed not only difficult but impossible to prove any reason for faith.

Faith is truly faith. It is not faith in something proven, no matter how religious leaders like to use logic and words to create an atmosphere where they may convince believers that there is only one tortuous path to follow in order to find salvation.

Indeed, faith is born within each entity's heart as he decides or chooses to rest without varying in the vibration of absolute faith that all is well. It is an activity and a choice which is strengthened as it is used. Like any muscle, it gets stronger with every repetition.

There are those strains within entities which would prefer not to be powerful. There are ways of thinking endemic to the human condition, shall we say, that would like to lean upon an outer support, such as that which religion offers.

And to our way of thinking, all such endeavors are potentially helpful. We always encourage entities to seek amongst the various ways of seeking the Creator that are present upon your planet to find a good fit for outer work, such as attending services with a group, acting as a spiritual community, studying a body of sacred literature, and other ways in which religion attempts to help entities mature spiritually.

However, when entities give their power to others and say, "I must listen to an intermediary. I must cast my hopes upon the kindness and compassion and saving grace of an intermediary," they have not yet grasped and accepted the responsibility for their own power.

This instrument has been reading a work by an entity named Joshiah[54] and this entity's work is very congruent with that point that we are attempting to make. The one known as Joshiah says over and over that each entity makes its own reality.

We agree completely with the one known as Joshiah. You, as an individual, create your reality and you as a tribe of humankind create together a global or Earthly reality. If you do not like your reality, you are able to change your reality.

However, in order to change your reality, you must believe that you are capable of doing so. You must believe in the power of your own choices. As you polarize, choice by choice by choice, we ask you to look for the light that is given to you. Seek out the wisdom that is available. Dig deeply within yourself to discover the heart of compassion that lies within you, inviolate and untouched by any human error.

For you are one with the Creator. And that goodness and love which is the very nature of creation is at the heart of every cell of your body and every atom of each cell. Your very nature vibrates with the infinite love and light of the one Creator and you are a Creator in your own right, not greater than any other Creator but able to choose your reality and to see it into manifestation.

In a minor way, each entity does this. Entities choose to pursue various ends in a worldly sense and are able to see the results of those choices. However, we are talking about power at the level of changing the vibration of your being. For as you tune your thoughts and as you persevere in the outworking of faith within you, you can become a part of the shift of thinking that lightens not only your vibration but the vibration of the entire planet.

It is the hope of many who watch this experiment with interest that entities shall become so on fire with love and so able to share that love in a pure way that does not create exclusion and the tendency to form cliques or to isolate themselves from others who think differently, that, in one sweep of relatively short time, the planet will come alive with the realization that it can, as a whole, find a way to express the love and the light of the one infinite Creator in a way that is more congruent with those fourth-density energies that are already a very big part of your third-density experience.

May we ask at this time for the remainder of the query to be repeated? We are those of Q'uo.

Jim: "Evolving to the fourth density seems a distant goal. Is there a simple way to measure how close we are to the threshold of the fourth density?"

We are those of Q'uo, and are aware of your query, my brother. From the preceding answer, you may perhaps guess that we shall inform you that there is a very easy way to judge as to how close you are to fourth density. You are in fourth density, my friends. You are in third-density bodies and so are not able to see the incredibly beautiful infant fourth-density Earth that interpenetrates third density at this time.

However, far below the level of conscious awareness, you are more and more aware of your power, your truth, and your beauty. The thinning of the veil has been occurring for some time, as these energies interpenetrate more and more. At this time there is virtually nothing of third-density energy left. There is just enough energy left for a few more of your years in which entities can make the choices that will place them in a position to be able to graduate from third density to the density of love that is your fourth density.

May we ask if there is another query at this time?

Jim: "During my recent study I found a small paradox regarding Latwii's home. I'm not being picky, I just want to make sure if dwelling in a sun body indefinitely is strictly a hallmark of sixth-density beings?"

We are those of Q'uo, and are aware of your query, my brother. It is indeed so that it is the sixth-density habit to dwell as part of sun bodies. Those of fifth density cannot sustain the vibratory purity necessary to dwell within the sun body.

However, under the influence of the union of what you would call male and female energies, there is, in that state of consciousness that involves mutual love, each for the other, the possibility of moving into sun bodies in order to express the fusion energy of sexual congress: light to light and love to love. That energy cannot be sustained and so when the expression of love has been concluded, fifth-density entities move out of that level of vibration and into their fifth-density physical bodies, shall we say.

Is there another query at this time? We are those of Q'uo.

---

[54] Bub Hill, *Joshiah—Conscious Creation*.

Jim: "I wish to know the opinions of Q'uo regarding the Oriental wisdom. For example, the Buddhism, Taoism, Feng-shui, Chinese medicine, fortune telling, etc."

We are those of Q'uo, and are aware of this query. There are portions of this query which we must tread carefully in answering, due to our desire not to infringe upon free will. However, in general, we may say that in our opinion the religious practices and folk practices of the Orient are worthy, just as are the practices of the West. You may guess from what we have said earlier concerning churches that we feel that all organized attempts to understand the infinite Creator, the self, and one's place in the creation are worthy.

We would not rate one strain of pursuit of the truth as being more worthy than another. We note that some entities are drawn to intellectual discussion and contemplation, while other entities are more drawn to a pure emanation of love. Other entities are drawn to expressions of power and wish to align themselves with that power.

Each religious practice and folk practice follows one of these three strains of study: either the intellectual and increasingly abstruse consideration of truth, the non-intellectual pursuit of insight, realization or gnosis, or the manipulation of the forces of the natural world for the benefit and safety of the self. Some religions have only one of these strains. Most have two and some have all three.

Lying beneath, above, on all sides of, and interpenetrating all of these structures lies that which may be called the truth. The truth lies within you. It is a creature without words. It speaks in silence. It gives information that is far richer and more powerful then any words. It is to that entity who finds his way to the silence that speaks that realization will come. To us it matters not how that entity forms itself up or follows ways to tune itself in order to seek the truth. The fundamental matter of importance is to reach the heart of the self where the silence speaks.

Is there another query at this time?

Jim: "In our last meeting, we discussed the red chakra and sexual energy. So I wish to ask Q'uo some advice to raise or unblock the energy flow of the red chakra. Since most of my energy is supporting my brain, I think that my lower three chakras are weaker. I wish to boost the energy into my red chakra so that my energy flow can be raised from the indigo chakra to the crown chakra."

We are those of Q'uo, and are aware of your query, my brother. Again, we shall need to tread somewhat carefully in our response in order to avoid infringement upon free will.

There are misconceptions wrapped into the question that has been asked. And so we must spend a bit of time looking at the question from various angles.

Firstly we would correct the misperception that the reason for unblocking the red chakra is to enable the energy to move into the crown chakra. This is not correct. The reason for opening the red-ray chakra is to bring power through into the heart. There is not a direct connection between opening the red-ray chakra and opening higher chakras.

(Side one of tape ends.)

(Carla channeling)

It is something that must be done not once but again and again. Indeed, the chakras can become blocked many times in one day, either by fear or by over-activity of desire.

The second misconception within the query has to do with the comment concerning energy moving mostly to the mind. It is easy to think of the energy body as having some dynamic between mind and heart. However, in terms of the movement of energy through the body, there is not an entity which could be called "mind." Rather, there are various kinds of energy within the energy body. The energy of the mind could be seen primarily to be that energy of the orange-ray chakra and the yellow-ray chakra which together form what is known among your peoples as the ego.

The ego or the personality shell dwells within those two energies. And so let us speak briefly of these two energies.

The energy of the orange-ray energy center is that energy in which the individual expresses its power as an individual. The orange-ray chakra can be blocked by the feeling that one does not like oneself or does not feel that oneself is worthy. It can also be blocked by feeling that other selves are not likeable or are not worthy.

The yellow-ray chakra is a powerful chakra within your system because you are in the yellow-ray density. It is the chakra where you express your power as part of a group and as your humankind is a very social group, interdependent upon one another for the necessities of life, there is the tendency to find ways to think of oneself as powerful in third-density ways, such as religious groups, birth families, and mated families.

When you say that the primary power in your energy body is going to your mind, you are really saying that you are blocking and/or over-activating the orange-ray and the yellow-ray energy centers of your energy body. This means that energy is not getting through to the heart in its full spate.

In our opinion, working with the energy body is working with a structure which is made of feelings and ways of expressing feelings. When you are successful in keeping your rays open, then you become transparent to the energy flowing through. So it is not that you are doing anything when you have cleared your chakras but rather that you have become an instrument, a wind instrument to be exact, so that the Creator may play you, may blow the wind of spirit through your instrument and you then create a song, a melody of love and light from the impression of spirit upon your instrument.

How many times this day have you considered the beauty of a thought? Indeed, how many times this day have you considered your thoughts carefully? We encourage a daily examination of those thoughts and feelings that have changed you this day, that have taken your mood and moved it, either in a positive way, according to your judgment, or in a negative way.

What has attracted you this day? What has repelled you this day? These are the images you wish to balance so that you may see that you are all things and that there is nothing that is foreign to you. Thusly you may gather together your entire self and know its worth, despite surface appearances to the contrary.

We ask that you consider, my brother, the possibility that dwelling within one chakra or another is not the goal of a spiritual seeker. Rather, the spiritual seeker's goal is to serve the one infinite Creator. In doing so, all of the notes of this instrument shall be played. None of the chakras is more important than any other. They are all necessary for the functioning of the energy body. It is just as important to have a strong red ray or a strong orange ray as it is to have a strong indigo ray. It is impossible to do work in consciousness before you have begun to have a holistic view of your energy, valuing every aspect of your feelings.

We use this term, feelings or emotions, in a general way, being unable to dig deep down beneath surface emotion to the archetypal rivers of emotion that are true or hold the truth within their flow. Think of it in terms of vibration. Overall, your energy body vibrates at a certain rate. It is a conglomerate rate and the read-out of that rate is your violet-ray chakra.

What you are attempting to do in opening the heart is not to leap from the heart into indigo ray but simply to find yourself able to use the resources of the heart chakra which make work in consciousness ever more possible. As that heart not only opens but is persuaded by the constant tuning of the individual to stay open, more and more, finally there is a habitual default setting of open heart and dependence upon the concept of love and a need to be a part of the principle of love and light upon planet Earth.

In such a way shall you be able to keep your system open and ready to speak the words of love, to sing the melodies of wisdom, and to reach out, hand to hand and heart to heart, to each other, as you practice being one in love.

May we ask if there is another query at this time?

Jim: No more questions from T.

May we ask then, before we leave this instrument, if there are any queries in the sitting group at this time?

R: Many questions are on my mind but they are overridden by the appreciation of silence, where the answers lie, Q'uo.

We are those of Q'uo, and are aware of your desire for the silence. And so we shall leave you to that silence, thanking this instrument and this group for creating a circle of seeking and for inviting us to join. We hope that our humble words may be of some use to you. We honor you and leave you in the love and in the light of the one infinite Creator. We are known to you as the principle of Q'uo. Adonai. Adonai vasu. ✤

L/L Research

L/L Research is a subsidiary of Rock Creek Research & Development Laboratories, Inc.

P.O. Box 5195
Louisville, KY 40255-0195

www.llresearch.org

Rock Creek is a non-profit corporation dedicated to discovering and sharing information which may aid in the spiritual evolution of humankind.

ABOUT THE CONTENTS OF THIS TRANSCRIPT: This telepathic channeling has been taken from transcriptions of the weekly study and meditation meetings of the Rock Creek Research & Development Laboratories and L/L Research. It is offered in the hope that it may be useful to you. As the Confederation entities always make a point of saying, please use your discrimination and judgment in assessing this material. If something rings true to you, fine. If something does not resonate, please leave it behind, for neither we nor those of the Confederation would wish to be a stumbling block for any.

© 2009 L/L Research

Sunday Meditation
April 22, 2007

Group question: Our question today has to do with catalyst and how we process our catalyst. We are wondering how we could really test our feelings or know our feelings or know when we have worked successfully, and when we have perhaps worked with it on a surface level and then maybe buried some of it that really needs some more attention, and thinking that we've gotten it and then we go on and at some point it seems to come around again and we need to work on it again. So, Q'uo, please give us some direction as to how we can take a look at what's happening in our lives with our catalyst, so we know when we are working with it successfully and when there's really more work to be done because we've either ignored it or buried it in some fashion.

(Carla channeling)

We are those known to you as the principle of Q'uo. Greetings in the love and in the light of the one infinite Creator. It is a great privilege to have been asked to join your circle of seeking this day. We cannot thank you enough for the opportunity of being allowed to share our thoughts with you at this time. As always, we would ask that each of you use your discrimination as you listen to what we have to say, keeping those thoughts that seem helpful to you and discarding the rest. This allows us to feel that we are not likely to infringe upon your free will or to interfere with the process of your spiritual evolution. And we appreciate your courtesy in tending your own thoughts and guarding the temple of your heart, your mind, and your spirit.

You have asked this day concerning catalyst and the responses to catalyst and so we would like to begin by sharing some thoughts about the process of catalyst and why it is even necessary to have catalyst.

As the group was discussing earlier, the spiritual path is a path of transformation. There is an archetypal energy that surrounds and integrates your everyday experience with the eternal, the infinite, and the mysterious. You are that meeting point of two worlds and you are that translator that gradually learns to become able to switch back and forth between the two, sometimes surprisingly different, points of view of the two different worlds: that world of time/space where metaphysical realities like concepts and thoughts have the kind of mass that you would think of a person or a chair having, so that they are very real entities within that world; and then coming back into the everyday world where such thoughts and concepts are not at all solid and seem so insubstantial as perhaps to be useless. You are that integrative element in the design which gathers information for the Creator and offers that harvest to the Creator.

The archetypal arrangement of your third density is a hero's journey, let us say. It is a stately journey which is both very simple and amazingly complex. The simplicity of the journey is that the needs of the doughty knight upon the road of seeking are faith and will. These two energies can fuel an entire lifetime of seeking through thick and thin, as this instrument would say.

At the same time, the shape of this journey is somewhat complex because the energies that you carry are all of the energies that there are. You are a holographic bit of the one infinite Creator, so that in every cell of your body the Creator is at its heart. The Creator is also at the heart of your life, alive, as this instrument would say, and well, waiting in those sacred chambers of the inner heart to be discovered and to be used as the resource and asset that unconditional love always is.

Your journey is a journey from the start of the incarnation, where you are not precisely a blank slate but a very uninformed soul, to the end of your life, where you have made decision after decision and met circumstance after circumstance in ways which develop into patterns, which develop into your identifying yourself as an entity who does things this way.

Your choices build upon themselves until you have built for yourself a house in which you live. This house is made of ideas about what is right and what is wrong. And periodically, you clean that house and you sweep out your old ideas and dust up all of those icons that you click on the desktop of your life to open up emotions and feelings that seem good to you.

One such example of this kind of icon is the cross that this instrument wears around her neck. Many different emotions are possible when gazing at this instrument wearing her cross. This instrument has a certain reason for wearing this cross and responds to that image in a way that she feels helps her to become a more faith-filled and service-oriented person. It is a reminder to her that calls to her each time that she gazes down at it as it hangs upon her bosom or sees it in the mirror when she is passing the commode in the bathroom, for instance. It is a kind of constant tuning mechanism for this instrument.

Many things in everyone's life begin to hold that kind of ability to change the tone or the vibration of the moment simply by being seen, heard, smelled or some such sensual cue.

In this archetypal journey, the self is splayed, shall we say, like all of the colors of the rainbow, across the various types of energy that are experienced within the energy body and the various types of expenditures of energy that result from that which is taken into the energy body.

Your incarnation is in a classroom or a school that this instrument has called a "refinery of souls." You are looking, during your incarnational experience, to create for yourself a personal reality that seems to you to be an improvement in terms of service to others, and other ideals that you may have, from how you were vibrating and, shall we say, who you were or who you saw yourself to be when you first awakened to your desire to move forward on the road of seeking to take some proactive part in attempting to encourage yourself, now that you have awakened, to wake up even further.

You do this by receiving catalyst and then by choosing how you shall respond to this catalyst. This is where catalyst comes into this archetypal journey of every soul that seeks to return to the one infinite Creator and to become aware of who he is and why he is here. Catalyst, therefore, has an archetypal and sacred place in the scheme of this school. You may see each time that you are overly disturbed by an event or a thought as being a time of receiving catalyst.

The nature of catalyst is that it, itself, is not changed. But it provokes or triggers a reaction from those chemical elements around it. This is a term used in chemistry and has a fairly precise meaning. That is what catalyst basically is. The one known as R was saying earlier that he realizes that catalyst is received from the mirroring that he receives from those around him, and we feel that this concept is worth investigating a bit further.

Perhaps you have been told at some point that when you are dreaming, whatever story you are dreaming contains several different characters and they look different than you. However, in terms of analyzing your dreams, you understand that at one level or another all of these entities are a part of you, that you have, in your dream, out-pictured and separated these personas from the rest of yourself in order to look at them more carefully.

In your waking life, the dream goes on. However, the structure of it is different because your subconscious is not directly able to organize the agenda for the most helpful things that could happen to you as a spirit seeking to know itself better.

What happens in everyday life is that that same spirit, hovering over all creation, brings to each seeking soul a rich harvest of people and events that contain the seeds of those lessons that you incarnated partially in order to learn.

You have other reasons for incarnating. You desired to be of service and you desired to be in this particular place at this particular time because of the momentous shift in consciousness that is occurring at this time.

But each time that you look into another entity's face, spiritually speaking, you are looking into your face and the face of the one infinite Creator. Therefore, when someone says something that hurts you or makes you feel happy, life has out-pictured the energies that are moving inside of you so that you can look in the mirror of another person and that person's concept of who you are and see things both happy and sorrowful that surprise you and about which you realize that you need to think, because they are new thoughts. They are the seeds that have been given to you this day by your own temperament.

At the end of each day, therefore, it is very helpful to review the catalyst that you have picked up that day. What has moved you towards the positive? What has made you experience negative emotions, so-called in your society, such as anger, guilt and resentment?

The play of these thoughts within your head is tantalizing because your surface thoughts skate away like little insects on the pond, moving too quickly for their movements to be able to be understood or isolated as they are going by. However, in your time alone, you may choose to contemplate the thoughts that you have thought this day. What reactions have you had to the catalyst that you have perceived?

As you keep doing this asking of yourself and then reviewing your daily feelings and thoughts, you will begin to see a very rich array of patterns, so that you can see that, "Okay, at this level, my pattern is this, and as I go deeper, my pattern is this."

And there are two different ways, two different points of view to take, in dealing with the same circumstance. Generally speaking, entities' surface reactions or instantaneous reactions to catalyst tend towards being fear-based and shortsighted.

Naturally, enough entities in third density are not hit over the head, shall we say, by the catalyst. They are able to rationalize their reactions to various types of catalyst in ways that do not involve the necessity to change or transform the self.

It is the spiritual seeker who proactively chooses to enter into that transformative road of seeking that can begin to move to layers deeper than instantaneous and sometimes instinctual reactions; to seek further into where in the energy body that over-activation or blockage is occurring, why it may be occurring, and how he can clear that blockage.

As you become more experienced at reviewing your thoughts, you will become ever better at finding the precise triggers that have caused your catalyst. However, as you become more experienced, you will also have been practicing seeing what triggers you without judging what triggers you. When judgment enters the equation of feelings and emotions, the natural tendency of the non-thinking person is to judge what has been thought and to put it away in a slot that, while judgmental, does not put it away for good. It places it in a part of the memory where toxic feelings are periodically recycled, again triggered by another piece of catalyst.

Therefore, in general in doing such subtle work, you basically know that you have finally become balanced on that one piece of catalyst when it occurs to you again, or it occurs to you in memory, and your only reaction to the memory or to the occurrence is to smile and say to yourself, "I remember that lesson. I think I really have learned that lesson and all I feel for you, piece of catalyst that you are, is love."

There is a very specific difference between catalyst with which you are not finished and catalyst which you have balanced. When you remember a piece of catalyst and experience something sad or something said to you, and it puts you back into an emotional state that corresponds with the emotion that you felt at the time of the initial incident of receiving catalyst, then you have not yet concluded your work upon balancing that particular kind of energy expenditure.

When instead you recall the instant, or the remembrance of that experience comes to you, and you do not have a feeling of being there but only of acknowledging the presence of that lesson, then you are probably complete in your dealings with that catalyst.

So it is a matter of observing where your triggers are and, when you are triggered, looking carefully at the thoughts that arise and the feelings that come with those thoughts. What you are doing is a kind of prospecting. You are looking for the gold in the ore of your personal, emotional, psychic and mental mind.

The joy of this kind of work is that you find gold at the heart of each learned lesson and it is a lesson that is, shall we say, a heavenly treasure, a treasure of the soul. It is not something that has any value at all in the outer world. All of its value is within that world in which you are a citizen of eternity and a member of the godhead principle.

We are those of Q'uo, and would wish to know if there is a follow-up to this query at this time?

(Pause)

We find that there are no more queries and yet we find that this instrument has energy yet, so with your permission we would like to continue our conversation with you. Would it be acceptable to each of you if we talked a bit, before we left, on subjects of interest to us? We are those of Q'uo.

(Agreement from the group.)

We are those of Q'uo, and we thank you for your willingness to move with us into what this instrument calls potluck.

We would like to ask all of you take a moment now and to become aware, in the silence that follows these words, of the beauty and the perfection of yourselves and of the fact that you are never alone.

We ask you to rest in the silence and experience yourself.

We would also like you to open yourself to receiving information at the silent level. As the one known as Joshiah[55] says, silent communication is by far more eloquent than words, for words are poor attempts to translate the mighty and living power of concept into the flat structures of language.

We shall now pause. We are those known to you as Q'uo.

---

[55] *Joshiah—Conscious Creation* is a book of channeling by Bub Hill.

(Pause)

We thank you, my friends, for moving with us into this space of grace and sacredness. We of Q'uo are most grateful to be able to share with you on these silent levels. And truly there are many sources of positive information which are also glad to interact with you in the silence. It is, however, always necessary for you to ask for the presence of such entities in your meditations. This is to avoid any infringement upon your free will.

We enjoy this instrument's bewilderment, for she naturally has no idea what we are going to say. And what we wish to say does not take so very long. We would simply encourage each to gaze with more and more willingness to be enraptured at the happenings of the day.

It may seem upon the surface that the life experience is made up of bad news around the world, difficult situations in personal and corporate life, and so on. Yet the great secret to life is to look closer, to move past the surface, with its dazzling array of surface catalyst, and into those quiet woods, waterways and caves of your own being.

We are not encouraging you to withdraw from the world. We are not encouraging you to separate yourself from society. But we are encouraging you to come to appreciate yourself in a different way than society shall ever appreciate you.

Your culture is a very disempowering culture, in our humble opinion. It seems to be bent upon removing from your mind any thoughts that do not have to do with maintaining the status quo of life as a consumer. However, my friends, you are at heart not simply a consumer. Indeed, you are potentially a co-creator and a magical, powerful being, capable of functioning in such a way as to change the true core nature of planet Earth, on the metaphysical level.

It is a real challenge to take oneself seriously when the veil is so thick. Further, it is difficult to take oneself seriously when one makes so many errors, at least self-perceived errors. And yet, beneath the thoughts and the judgments and those surface details of your personality lies a part of yourself which you share with every living being in the universe. You share the consciousness of unconditional love.

This consciousness you have in common with all souls. As the one known as A has noted recently, this is a spiritual democracy. You are precisely equal to all other souls. You are all a part of the infinite Creator. When you are attempting to form a rule of life, as each of those present in this room is attempting to do, let the heart and the soul of this rule of life be love. Let the center be consciousness.

What is consciousness? In your spiritual writings, there are various ways of looking at what the ground of being really is. In this instrument's Christian faith the ground of being is embodied in a person, the person of Jesus the Christ. And this entity carries in his story the vibration of unconditional love in a way that anyone can understand, at least in the broad strokes of giving up ones life in order to serve others and to make life richer for others.

Again, you see the importance and the sacredness of this catalyst that you receive in life. Many times within each person's life, there is that feeling of being on the cross and suffering. Remember the rest of the story, my friends, when you feel that way. Christ-consciousness does not stay upon the cross of sacrifice but rather, having accepted that sacrifice which is inherent in growth, transformation and service, the entity known as Jesus the Christ soared to the heaven worlds.

And so may you, as you experience that feeling of being on the cross, that feeling of suffering. Yet you are also consciousness. And consciousness can help you to soar. Consequently, there is tremendous power in your being able to remember, whatever the details of your rule of life, that the very center and heart of your practice is the stunning awareness and constant remembrance of who you are. You are the one infinite Creator in a very young and very untaught form. You are gaining experience. You are beginning to create for yourself, within this incarnation, more and more of a solid feeling of who you are and why you are here.

It is a very good idea to have a rule of life. This instrument's rule of life, for instance, calls her to worship in the morning and in the evening. Briefly in the morning and even more briefly in the evening, this instrument puts down everything else in her mental, emotional and physical life. There is a bell that is rung by pressing the two parts of a gong together to make a beginning to those sacred times. It is a time of remembrance and a time of centering. Such daily devotions are very helpful in a rule of life and we commend the one known as M for stating that he wishes to work further on this.

It is a good technique in working with a rule of life, also, to reflect upon those moments that come to you where you feel that something important or momentous has occurred in a vibrational way rather than in a verbal or conscious way. When you sense these moments, take the time to move into them more deeply, to rejoice in the gift of the present moment, and to use that moment of inspiration further to dedicate yourself to the love and the light of the one Creator and to being agents for that love and that light.

When there is a good deal of intellectual capacity in a seeking soul, the times in the silence—which is anti-intellectual and profoundly moving into zones of mystery and paradox—are very helpful in order to balance and make more flexible that personality which carries you through this experience.

It is a definite gift both to take the self seriously, seriously enough to do the work of spiritual seeking, and to take oneself lightly, so that one is not burnt out by the rigors of the road. As you ask yourself to become more disciplined, retain the ability to let all of the discipline go and to enjoy the moment.

You are not a machine. It will not serve you, in the end, to force yourself into devotions which to you are empty. Instead we encourage you to follow, as this instrument often says, the line of resonance in your experience. You shall receive many, many chances to work with your process. They will come at you every day if you let them.

Let yourself also have times of leisure, times when you are a butterfly on the wind, a cloud blowing by, a bubble on the ocean. This instrument enjoys a chant by Paramahansa Yogananda whose words are, "I am a bubble, make me the sea". This is your journey.

We thank you for allowing us to speak further. It has been our privilege and our blessing to share with you our devotion to the one infinite Creator and our intense desire to be of service to entities such as you, whom we greatly admire for your persistence in seeking the truth.

We are those known to you as the principle of Q'uo. We leave you, as we found you, in the love and in the light of the one infinite Creator. Adonai. Adonai. ✤

L/L Research

L/L Research is a subsidiary of Rock Creek Research & Development Laboratories, Inc.

P.O. Box 5195
Louisville, KY 40255-0195

www.llresearch.org

Rock Creek is a non-profit corporation dedicated to discovering and sharing information which may aid in the spiritual evolution of humankind.

ABOUT THE CONTENTS OF THIS TRANSCRIPT: This telepathic channeling has been taken from transcriptions of the weekly study and meditation meetings of the Rock Creek Research & Development Laboratories and L/L Research. It is offered in the hope that it may be useful to you. As the Confederation entities always make a point of saying, please use your discrimination and judgment in assessing this material. If something rings true to you, fine. If something does not resonate, please leave it behind, for neither we nor those of the Confederation would wish to be a stumbling block for any.

© 2009 L/L Research

Sunday Meditation
May 6, 2007

Group question: The *Bhagavad Gita* and many other positive spiritual teachings speak of self-control as a beneficial and necessary element of the positive seeker's path—self-control in the face of temptation and in directing the will for the purpose of spiritual pursuits versus worldly pursuits. Yet Ra offers an alternative understanding in negating control in favor of acceptance and overall balance. Is there a positive use of control? Does control play any useful role in the discipline of the personality? Can one control, for example, through acceptance, meaning that that which has become accepted is able to be controlled or directed?

(Carla channeling)

We are those known to you as the principle of Q'uo. We greet you in the love and in the light of the one infinite Creator, in Whose service we come to you this day. It is our great privilege and blessing to be called to your circle of seeking and we are glad to share with you our thoughts on the positive uses of control. As always, we would preface our remarks with a request that each of you use your powers of discrimination, choosing those thoughts of ours that are helpful to you and leaving the rest behind. This will enable us to speak more freely and be less concerned with interfering with the process of your spiritual evolution. We would not wish to be a stumbling block in your way. We thank you for this consideration.

The word "control" has a sometimes negatively-oriented feeling behind it, as when one may say a person is too controlling or something of that nature, and yet it is clear that, from the beginning of the life of a human in third density, the learning which you undergo has a great deal to do with control. The infant must learn to control the movements of his mouth and the breath that comes through his voice box in such a way as to reproduce the language that he hears about him in his crib and in his cradle, so that he may ask for food, comfort and relief from wet diapers by doing something besides crying. It is not too long before parents are asking their young children to control their bladder and their bowels so that they can come out of diapers and be free of the need for changing their diapers. One thing after another that the young child meets in his life becomes a matter of learning how to control various parts of his body. He learns carefully how to form letters with his hand and to do other skills that are done with the hands and that promote a more deft and agile use of the fingers.

The mind is asked at a very young age to begin to take in data and organize it into banks of information that can be used readily. The alphabet is learned and the numbers are learned, then words are learned and reading begins. And for the entire travel from childhood to adulthood, skills are taught that the child learns to take in and use. And all of these skills are learned by the student controlling and focusing his mind so that he may wrap that mind around these new thoughts and these new skills.

It is not perhaps thought of as a matter of control and yet all of an adult's preparation for life has to do with control and we do not mean to suggest that there is a negative or a positive spin to this control. The culture in which you live is one in which these skills are considered quite necessary for survival and enjoyment of the finer things of life, such as indoor plumbing and the comfort and convenience of life as you are aware of and are used to living in.

Certainly, the idea of control can be very negative. The tendency of entities in third density to manipulate and control the circumstances around them can turn into a very dark way of handling life. And each of you has perhaps known those whose life is spent in plotting and scheming ways to control the outcome of events that are important to such people. Usually such control is over small things and yet the sum of one person controlling another over a period of time is a very strong negative polarization towards service to self and it is definitely a service to self energy to think of or to contemplate the self as a person setting out to control circumstances that have to do with other people and indeed are not, in terms of positive polarization, available for such control. On the other hand, there are indeed very positive uses of control and this instrument would call it self-control.

There is a nuance in the term self-control that we wish to explore. For, as the one known as T1 said, there is a, "Which came first?" question here. There is a chicken and an egg. Is an entity controlling the self and therefore learning more about how to control the self? Or does the person wait for some wisdom as to precisely how to control the self? And in order to remove ourselves from this conundrum, we would like to take this idea back a bit and look at it from a wider and perhaps a more spacious point of view.

The one known as G is quite correct in saying that, in the view of those of the Confederation who speak with you this day, the universe is a self-generating system whereby there is no need to control circumstances whatsoever in terms of your incarnation being fruitful for you have set up a system of redundant possibility/probability vortices so that if the incarnational lessons that you have chosen to ponder in your particular incarnation do not gel for you in one instance and you may have perhaps missed that catalyst, there will be another circumstance that will come your way very soon that will offer you the same kind of catalyst, the same kind of challenge, and the same kind of questions that you may ask yourself about, "Why is this happening to me and what should I do with it?"

You do not have to control your life in terms of knowing that you will be fed with spiritual food at all times. This is not a cause for concern. And this perhaps can rest your mind, for when you do not need to reach and grasp for the spirituality of your day or the cogency of the catalyst that is being presented to you, then you can relax and focus simply on paying attention to the present moment.

Let us go further back than this, for we wish to set you on the stage of your incarnational experience and we have not yet done so to our satisfaction. Who are you? My friends, you are the one infinite Creator. That is the heart of your reality. You are a spark of the infinite oneness of all creation. That spark is your consciousness which has been wrapped into flesh and bone so that you may experience life within this particular illusion.

Therefore, you are spiritual beings dwelling in a material and physical world. Everything that is at the center of your being calls out for the Creator and sees life from the point of view of spirit. Yet, you have been brought into a culture which encourages precisely the opposite bent of thought. Your culture encourages you to release thoughts of spirituality in favor of thoughts of functionality, economics, socialization, doing what is expected, and so forth. These two energies are a dynamic that are with each entity within third density to one extent or another for his entire incarnation. The minute that a spirit forgets the heart of his being, he may well be able to convince himself of a number of things. He may be able to convince himself that he may control others for their own good. He may be able to convince himself that those things which he believes are such good beliefs that other entities need to believe that way too and so he may become one who bullies or coaxes entities into worshipping a certain way or believing in a certain system of dogma. All of these are subtlety but markedly negative or service to self in that they are using the power of the human spirit in order to change others.

Yet, an entity which is a part of the godhead principle need be concerned only with controlling himself. The work of the spiritual entity is always upon the self. The seeking of a spiritually-oriented entity is always an inner seeking. It may well be that the processes of seeking bring the seeker into community with those who demonstrate unconditional love, and that is a great gift.

But a part of the godhead principle in actuality needs nothing from the outside. There is no need to reach, there is no need to grasp. All that is needed is already lying within your heart of hearts.

The Confederation talks about acceptance rather than control because, from our point of view, once an entity has come into a full acceptance or awareness of who he is and why he is here, that initial acceptance forms up into vectors: each thought and opinion that occurs within the awareness of being a spiritual entity has a direction to it that is spiritual in nature.

As entities accept completely that they are a part of the Creator, they become aware that beneath the level of constant and unremitting human error, they are worthy. They are as worthy as a star, or a tree, or the wind that blows, or the grass that grows. They are worthy in a final and ultimate way. They have not found the heart of that worth. It takes many densities of experience to refine the self to the point where the self is transparent to the self and that worth of self is clearly seen by the self.

But there are helps to you, my friends, in everyday life. For you see the worth of others and that is a strong help to you. Every time that you see an entity whom you feel is worthy, we ask you to remember that you are looking in the mirror when you look at any other soul. As you look into that entity's eyes, you and that entity are both the Creator. That which you see as good in that other entity, you may stop and mark because you have just seen that particular kind of goodness in yourself. Were you not sensitive to that goodness, you would not have seen it in the other self.

So let your own experiences of the goodness of others about you reflect back to you the truth of yourself: you are infinitely worthy, you are a citizen of eternity. Your stay upon the Earth plane is a short one and you came to give yourself the gift of learning and worshipping and being a part of the movement that is taking place upon the planet at this time: to lift and transform the energy of planet Earth. And you are worthy to do this.

Control helps you—or perhaps we would use the word discipline—discipline helps you to maintain the focus of who you are and why you are here. It is not that this discipline is a judging discipline or an attempt to whip yourself into shape. You are not here to judge; you are here to love. And so the work of each and every seeker is primarily and fundamentally the work of being.

We find that this is a very difficult concept for your people to grasp. What is it to be? To breathe in and to breathe out? What is the worth of simply being? And yet the universe as a whole is one great, interactive being of which you are a focal point in a vast array of other sentient, intelligent points of awareness that are gathering experience for the infinite Creator that It may know more about Itself.

This gift of being is always your most fundamental work as a spiritually-oriented seeker. For the doing is at the surface of things; it is the being that gives the doing depth, breadth, meaning and strength.

Control is definitely necessary, for without self-control and discipline, the spiritual seeker may constantly find itself forgetting to keep the focus. Let us talk a bit about that focus that we would encourage you to keep.

Each of you around the circle this day has discussed feelings concerning one's place in life and in some cases the incredible rapidity of time fleeing past almost too quickly to grasp. Yet there is within each of you a center. And there is great skill in finding ways to remind yourself to move back from the outskirts of truth and beauty in your life, always in towards the center again. Life will spin you out constantly. Catalyst will hit you—strong catalyst, illness, the loss of jobs, all of those difficulties that challenge entities who breathe in and breathe out and must find a way to keep a roof over their heads. And your job always is to see yourself spinning and gently, very gently, encourage your spirit to spiral inward again to the place of power that lies within, to the place of comfort that lies deeply within, to the one infinite Creator who waits patiently for you in your heart of hearts.

The more time that you put into resting in your beingness, the more you will become aware of who you truly are and how powerful a being you truly are. And when you sense that power, then of course you want to use that power rightly and that calls for every discipline of the personality and makes such disciplines attractive to you. When you find the center of your power, that creative energy that made all that there is, then truly you wish to use it well and to use it wisely and to use it lovingly.

And so you turn to those disciplines that have served you before: meditation, prayer, contemplation, inspired reading, walks in nature, and all of those ways in which you can come back to the truth that truly does set you free.

So, the question of acceptance or control, in a way, is a question of how you wish to look at who you are. Our approach to the awakening seeker is simply to ask that seeker to become aware of who and what he is. And to become aware of the fact that he is creating his own reality.

When an entity has been on the spiritual path for a while, he may well begin to sense that there is one particular outer work that he has the cluster of skills to accomplish. And that may spark in him the desire to ask for guidance and when an entity asks for guidance, that guidance is there instantly, there is no lag time. You may not be able to hear the voice of guidance but the energy of that guidance and the gentle pressure of that vibration is with you from that point on. This instrument opens her day by asking the one she calls Jesus the Christ, "What would you wish of me this day?" This is her way of centering and offering her day. And if that question seems to be answered by something that she did not expect, that is alright, that is acceptable.

But it is always within the choice of the seeker as to how that seeker shall proceed. In a society which has a tendency towards loudness, meaninglessness and chaos, it is perhaps well recommended that the spiritually-oriented seeker gaze within into the mystery that lies between every cell of your body, and gaze without, not at the creations of humankind, but at the creation of the Father. For there you see not control but a plan that is so vast that it is inconceivable and yet complete and perfect so that the organism of planet Earth as a whole and all of the biota upon it move in a dance of rhythm and harmony in which all needs are met.

We offer to this instrument the vision of the rolling tide. It does not seem to be controlled, but rather it rushes in abandonment towards the shore and then pulls out again towards the deeps of the ocean. Yet if you think about the tides and the moon, you begin to see that there is an order and a balance which keeps the moon in its orbit and the Earth in its orbit; which keeps the sunlight and the stars moving in their cycles. And this moon energy moves through everyone's blood so that your blood wanes and flows just as do the tides. You are a part of something that is in exquisite balance. You are in touch with the spirit world and the highest energies and at the same time you are in touch with the Earth and its heaviest energies. You know of everything from angels and cherubim to the degradation of war, murder, torture and the evil that entities can do to each other. And your gaze is that gaze which orders things in your world.

So perhaps we would say that your most creative means of control is to create the world that you would like to see and live it. For you truly are a co-creator and you truly can create the reality that you wish to see.

May we ask if there is a follow-up on this query? We are those of Q'uo.

Jim: No follow-up, Q'uo.

Very well, my brother. Then we would ask if there is another query at this time?

T2: I'm feeling a very strong connection to you right now and I'm wondering if there is a way that I can carry this connection when I'm on my own because I'm not in Kentucky all the time and I'm not sitting in this room all the time. I feel that there is a lot that I can gain to working to reach and touch you in a manner similar to what I feel right now.

We are those of Q'uo, and believe we are aware of your query, my sister. There is indeed a way that you can take us with you. There is a way that all entities may take us to their hearts and that is simply to ask for our presence. We are not bound by time and space as you know them in this illusion. We are in the now as far as relating to your time and space, for we are metaphysical entities and time to us is unified and circular. Consequently, at any time that you ask mentally for us to interact with you, we shall immediately be there.

We shall not speak. We shall simply be with you and you will feel the unconditional love of our vibration. But there is more to it than that, my sister, as you well know. There is in the world of spirit an enormous amount that can never be said in words and while we are using this instrument to create words that hopefully will have some small use to you, we are at the same time doing a much larger job and that is simply to communicate with you in silence—in the silence between the words and underlying all speech. We are sharing with you in that silence those concepts that cannot be brought into words and language without a tremendous amount of loss. As if you were trying to give someone a beautiful gift and it was this round ball of beautiful concept and yet, when you attempt to bring that concept into words, it is as if you have taken the string that has made that ball and pulled it out, so, in a linear fashion, you can see the thread that made up that ball. It is a long and tedious process compared to the wholeness of concept communication. And that is what we hope to offer those who call upon us any time.

Yet always, our first gift is that of loving and being loved, for we feel your love of us also. So love is reflected in love and the Creator's concepts flow from metaphysical instruments such as we into your heart. We hope that you will enjoy our company for we assure you, my sister, we greatly enjoy yours and are privileged to be called to you at any time. And this goes for all who would call upon us or the entities of the Confederation in general. By all means, make use of us for we are here for only one reason and that is to interact with you at this time when you are trying to get your spiritual feet under you and to make the difference that you came here to make. And may we say, my sister and all, you cannot fail, you cannot err, because as long as you breathe in and breathe out and love, you are doing what you came to do and you are doing it very well.

May we ask if there is a follow-up to that query, my sister? We are those of Q'uo.

T2: The only thing I can say right now is thank you. Thank you.

We are those of Q'uo, and we thank you, my sister. Is there another query at this time? We are those of Q'uo.

(Side one of tape ends.)

(Carla channeling)

It would seem that we have exhausted those queries that entities wished to ask at this time, and that being so, we shall leave you as we found you, in the love and in the light, the peace and the power of the one infinite Creator. We are known to you as those of the principle of Q'uo.

We thank you once again for the pleasure of your company and the beauty of your sacred space that you have created by your interwoven auras. My friends, we wish you could see how beautiful you truly are. You lift our hearts and we praise you for your courage. Again, we leave you in love and in light. We are those of Q'uo. Adonai. Adonai. ⚘

© 2009 L/L Research

L/L Research is a subsidiary of
Rock Creek Research &
Development Laboratories, Inc.

P.O. Box 5195
Louisville, KY 40255-0195

L/L Research

www.llresearch.org

Rock Creek is a non-profit
corporation dedicated to
discovering and sharing
information which may aid in
the spiritual evolution of
humankind.

ABOUT THE CONTENTS OF THIS TRANSCRIPT: This telepathic channeling has been taken from transcriptions of the weekly study and meditation meetings of the Rock Creek Research & Development Laboratories and L/L Research. It is offered in the hope that it may be useful to you. As the Confederation entities always make a point of saying, please use your discrimination and judgment in assessing this material. If something rings true to you, fine. If something does not resonate, please leave it behind, for neither we nor those of the Confederation would wish to be a stumbling block for any.

© 2009 L/L Research

Special Meditation
May 19, 2007

Jim: The first question today from N: "The question is about this new spiritual path that I am on. I would like to know how I got where I am in this place in time, why it took me so long to get here, and where I need to go now to move forward to make the most of things I'm learning and to fully awaken my spirituality to be most useful in service to others and in fulfilling my own spiritual needs."

(Carla channeling)

We are those known to you as the principle of Q'uo. Greetings in the love and in the light of the one infinite Creator, in Whose name we come to you this day. We wish to thank the one known as N for arranging to have a circle of seeking to invite our humble opinions concerning some questions that she has concerning her spiritual development and her situation at this time. It is our honor and our privilege to interact with you at this time and we thank you for this opportunity to be of service. That is a great blessing to us.

As always, however, we would ask both the one known as N and any others who may hear or read this material to take full charge of your powers of discrimination. You may not think that you have an adequate power of discrimination. Yet, my friends, you do. What is right for you now, today, will resonate to you in a certain way. It will not seem simply interesting. It will seem almost as though we were helping you to remember something that you already knew. For insight trembles upon the brink at all times for all entities who are paying attention.

If something does not resonate to you then, please, lay it down and move on to the next thought. And if what we offer does not help you, please move on to the next source of guidance, the next source of inspiration. For truly the Creator has many voices, of which we are only one. That being understood, it will help us to be able to be assured fully that we may offer our opinions without infringing upon the free will of the one known as N or interfering in any way with her sacred spiritual process.

For those who feel that they have come only lately to the spiritual awareness that they have now, there is always a feeling of needing to catch up. And this is a feeling that we would address before moving onwards, for in the anxiety to catch up there lies a lack of rest, quietness and peace of mind and we would not wish for you to lose these. And so we would share with you our opinion that the present moment finds each seeker in the perfect place to receive new information.

There is not a starting load of information that you somehow need to learn, for spiritual growth is not a curriculum in the sense of there being an intellectually satisfying procession of lessons which, when learned, suffice to sustain the spiritual seeker. Indeed, this is not the case.

No matter what spiritually inspiring entity you may bring to mind, we assure you that if you asked that entity, when that entity was alive, if he had been able to achieve full realization, so that nothing more needed to be learned and nothing more needed to be done or undone, that entity, beloved of you, would laugh and say, "I am the least of all the people that I know. I am the most foolish. I lack the most grace."

In a way, it is the way this instrument experiences working with computers. At one time she had the idea that if she could learn enough, she would be able to do whatever she wished to do on the computer. She went to school and took classes on the computer and at the end of all those classes she finally realized that, because of the way this particular electronic gadget works, there will always be more to learn. There will always be new light and new life coming into the world of computers and computer science.

It is precisely the same with the spiritual life. The moment of awakening finds one both a spiritual infant and a very mature and savvy person with life experience and hard-won knowledge about feelings, situations and relationships. Therefore, we ask you and all those who are still feeling a bit new to spiritual seeking to wake up each morning with the knowledge that this is the day, the one day, the one moment, that is before you now.

The American Indians felt that the dawning of a new day was the dawning of a new life for each and every member of the tribe and we would suggest that this is exquisitely true. You of the tribe of humankind can start anew and afresh every morning of your life. For just as the sun rises with new light and new glory, so do you bring all that has happened to you in this incarnation up to the present moment to the unfolding of today.

And that which you have is sufficient for you to be able to pay attention to the happenings of the day and to pick up on the synchronicities and the themes of the day. For somehow it seems that catalyst comes in patterns, and blessings and beauties also come in patterns. You may see the patterns of your suffering and the patterns of your delight.

The one known as N wonders what took her so long to awaken, as she now has discovered late in life, when she is no longer youthful, those remarkable awarenesses that would have indeed transformed her life had she come upon these awarenesses in her youthful years. And we say to you, my sister, that the one known as Paul caught a piece of the truth when he said that it is a long and winding road that leads you to your home.[56] That road is no less sure for being serpentine. Every bend in your road has taken you to a place where you needed to collect experience, feel deeply felt feelings and undergo catalyst, balancing these feelings, ordering them, coming to understand more about yourself and learning how to love yourself.

If there is one key upon which awakening turns, it is that moment of coming to love yourself enough to feel that you are worthy of being taken seriously by yourself. The culture of your people does not encourage awakening or, upon awakening, the commitment to a rule of life that offers time in every day for silence, prayer and devotion.

Do not think, my friend, that those years in your youth are wasted years. For there is nothing in life that is not sacred. There is no action, feeling or piece of suffering that is not sacred. Indeed, you cannot make a mistake in the spiritual path. For every time that you take a turn that was unexpected by your higher self and you walk into a realm of country that you have not seen before, spiritually speaking, there too the Creator has gone before you to offer you chance after chance after redundant chance to pick up that piece of the puzzle that is your next object of seeking.

The one known as N spoke of feeling anxious to move ahead, to learn what there was to learn and to obtain the riches of knowledge that would lead her to insight. We feel that we understand completely the source of this entity's anxiety. It is, in fact, an eagerness to grow, to share, and to be. And that is a good thing.

However, the energy of anxiety is an energy that buys into the thought that there is little time left. Yet indeed, my sister, the present moment is infinite. It

---

[56] The lyrics to "The Long and Winding Road, by John Lennon and Paul McCartney, are:

> The long and winding road that leads to your door
> Will never disappear. I've seen that road before.
> It always leads me here—leads me to your door.
> The wild and windy night that the rain washed away has left a pool of tears crying for the day.
> Why leave me standing here? Let me know the way.
> Many times I've been alone and many times I've cried.
> Anyway you'll never know the many ways I've tried,
> And still they lead me back to the long and winding road
> You left me standing here a long, long time ago. Don't leave me waiting here, lead me to your door.

is well to ponder the difference between the time progression in space/time, as your everyday life experiences the running of time from past to present to future, and metaphysical time or, as this instrument might say, the Creator's time.

In the metaphysical realm, where thoughts are things and you as a spirit are a citizen of eternity, all time is one; all time is now. Therefore, from that point of view, each spirit or seeker within incarnation exists in two worlds at once. Each soul is an interface between the world of time/space—infinity and eternity—and the world of space/time, which is an illusionary reality much like your television programs, where the Creator has set up for you a school in which you may study the lessons of love.

In this schoolroom, there is a heavy veil between the conscious and the subconscious mind. This means that there is no real awareness in the everyday, waking self of one's true identity as a spark or a piece of the one infinite Creator that is holographic in nature.

This aliveness is present in every cell of your body. Your very cells' hearts are love. It is the action of light upon love that has created this illusory, third-density school of souls. And you have entered this refinery, this furnace, because you desired to do at least two things: you desired to learn and you desired to serve.

As you undergo suffering and make choices that reflect your desire to be of service to others or your desire to be of service to yourself, you are working to rebalance and to, shall we say, hopefully improve the balance between love, wisdom and power.

This everyday illusion that you experience is an ongoing gift of third density. It is a gift because only in this veiled illusion, when you are intellectually unaware of the rightness of all things and the unity of all that you see, may you make profoundly heartfelt choices. These choices would not occur to you in such depth of emotion were you fully aware of who you are and why you are here, as are those in other densities of experience.

Many times, there is an agenda built into an incarnation in which incarnational lessons have been set up by you, yourself, before incarnation. They may well involve patterns which do not draw you into the intense phase of spiritual seeking until later in life. This is because, in order for you to complete patterns—as the one known as N has said—existing from prior incarnations, it has been necessary to leave personal spirituality on the back burner, so to speak, while the entity that you are within society and within relationships fulfills the patterns of those relationships and creates closure to those happy tasks that lay before the seeker in her youth.

Indeed, much of spiritual worth has been generated, long before the one known as N came into contact with a series of discoveries and events that brought her to a more conscious awareness of the desirability of the process of seeking the truth in a focused and organized manner.

To any who feel that they have come to this study of how to live well late in life, we would suggest that they are not at all late. They are precisely on time for themselves. They have gently persevered until all patterns have been fulfilled and they are now aware that it is time for this study.

There is an abundance of inspired reading that is available when studying to be wiser and move loving. We assure all those who feel somewhat intimidated by this sheer mass of material that books and words are excellent tools. We use them in speaking through this instrument. There is always a new thought or a new connection between thoughts to make when one is looking at new material or re-looking at old material, for anything spiritually inspiring will be new every time you read it, no matter how many times you read it. This is because as you progress in your own understanding, you always hear those same words in a new and different way because of the advances that you have made in your own soul-growth.

Nevertheless, far more proficient and profound than these poor offerings of words are the gifts of information and inspiration packed into the silence. Let us speak of the silence a bit, for many times entities have a cluster of questions about meditation: what is the best way to meditate, how often to meditate, and so forth. And we say to each that this is a resource that is given to you. It will be for you to choose when in your day you wish to mediate; when in your day you wish to contemplate your thoughts and perhaps try to assign to those thoughts a particular energy, a chakra, or an issue so that you may begin to see into the patterns of your own learning, your own catalyst, and your own growth. These decisions are up to you. But we would ask that you consider creating for yourself a rule of life in which you have made sure to include time for meditation and contemplation.

If we could communicate through this instrument by concept, the words that we have to offer would become pale and sickly in comparison. We offer to this instrument concepts telepathically, but this instrument cannot offer the concept. She must then translate the wholeness of our thought into a linear form of words and sentences. There is always a good deal lost when this translation process occurs. Consequently we would suggest to the one known as N and to all who seek that there is a tremendous advantage to incorporating work in the silence into each and every day, because in the silence your subconscious is entirely open to guidance by concept communication.

Therefore, even though you are not consciously aware of having gained this insight, you will find it working itself into your life and expressing itself to you so that you see that you have indeed gained in insight. You have somehow found a broader and more spacious point of view. How did it happen? My sister, it happened in the silence. It happened when you asked. That is a very important key to working with spiritual guidance. Be sure always to ask for the guidance.

There is an issue of free will here where those entities who love you and wish to help you in an unseen way are forever unable to come into your life until you invite them. If indeed you would wish us to speak with you at any time, know that you have only to ask. We shall not offer you any words. We shall offer a vibration that contains many thoughts, many concepts that are tailored to fit into your subconscious processes. That is the way guidance works. Ask, and you shall receive. But whether you shall be consciously aware of that reception is completely uncertain. For the most part, entities are not truly aware of that moment of insight, but only see its reflection in the life as they live it.

We have said earlier in this session that becoming a self-aware and consciously-polarizing spiritual entity is not a process of accumulating knowledge. Indeed, you may begin reading at any point around the perimeter in any of the religions, spiritual systems, or philosophies that offer insight and you shall find it possible to reach that unified center where all things are one as surely from one path as from another.

And you will finally be aware that all in your life is perfectly balanced and that you are an instrument in the hands of the one infinite Creator, ready to play the music that can come through you because of the clusters of your gifts and your desires to serve. This is the situation of all those who seek to serve upon planet Earth.

Your mission is magnetized to you by your intent to undertake it. And many things that at first do not seem to be a part of your mission to serve turn out to be necessary turns in your path: if "A" had not have happened, then "B" would not have happened, and although "B" is unfortunate, you had to get through "B" so that you could move on to "C" and "D" and "E." How can you see the pattern and the order of things in the moment when you are in the process of transformation? You almost never can see the pattern. Indeed, these experiences of the dark night of the soul are wonderful opportunities for you to invoke your faculty of faith.

We do not use the term "faith" in the way people of religion do. We are not talking about having faith in a certain dogmatic system or of having blind faith in the words of prophets, saints or masters. We are talking about having faith that all is well and that all will be well. This is your gift to yourself, to launch yourself out over the edge of what you know to be, in human terms, a fairly chaotic situation and say, "I know that all is well." And those words give you wings and you can soar on them into the abyss of mystery, paradox and unknowing.

You do not have to see the pattern. You do not have to be wise. You have only to invoke faith and to ask yourself to keep your heart open so that you may love and so that you may receive the love offerings of others. For when you love, my sister, the resulting response from a very responsive creation is bread on the waters ten-fold, a hundred-fold, and a thousand-fold.

As you love, you shall be loved beyond all imagining. And indeed, all entities are already loved at the soul level by those from the unseen worlds of your own planet and from other entities in other planetary influences who have been drawn to you because of your nature, your beauty, your gifts, and your hope to serve. Know that you are surrounded by a cloud of angelic and positive beings who love you and wish only to help you to wake up, to learn and to serve with deftness, skillfulness and joy.

May we ask if there is a follow-up to that query at this time? We are those of Q'uo.

N: Yes, I feel that I might be a wanderer and wish that you would be able to confirm that.

We are those of Q'uo, and, my sister, for what it is worth, you are indeed a wanderer, that is that you have chosen to come here from a higher density in order to be of service at this time of the shift of consciousness upon planet Earth that accompanies the planet's own transition from third density to fourth density.

May we ask if there is a follow-up to this query, my sister?

N: Yes. I'm concerned that I've hurt someone deeply in my patterns of change over the past couple of years and I'm wondering if that hurt that I did by leaving my husband was some type of karmic activity or if in fact there will be more karma involved in my action?

We are those of Q'uo, my sister, and are aware of your query. Let us look at karma itself before we respond more specifically to your query about karma in your life. Entities who come together have planned their relationships before their incarnations began. Perhaps during an entire lifetime, the energies between those two entities have not quite come into balance. When there is imbalance, what is holding the balance up is that there is a lack of forgiveness.

Therefore, when we speak of karma concerning a relationship, we are actually speaking of two different karmas. We are speaking of the karma of your soul path and we are speaking of the karma of the soul path of your mate. Now, given that you came into this incarnation, one of your desires being to work with this entity and to find a better balance of love and of understanding than you were able to find in the last encounter with this entity, you have the continuing challenge of clearing your own energies so that your love of this entity is clean and clear, running like the crystal streams of a beautiful fountain.

In order for you to find that fountain of love and light within yourself concerning this entity, you go through a profound process of forgiveness. Now certainly, the beginning of forgiveness is often obvious. You forgive the entity who has ignored you, abused you, or otherwise not met your needs. This is actually relatively easy to do, especially if you persist in forgiving each time that this cycle of memories which you have about this particular entity is activated or triggered in your own consciousness.

Eventually, you are able to gaze with some equanimity upon this other self that was your mate and say, "I have no bitterness, I have only love. I have only appreciation. I have only honor and respect to give to you. I hope that I may help you, whatever it is that you are doing, and if I cannot help you, then I wish you well."

With that closure out of the way, then you start on the real work of forgiveness. Each entity's hardest sell is the self. You can sell almost anyone else upon good ideas, ways to improve the self, and so forth, but when you come to look at your own character, your own secret thoughts and your own tangled and disturbed emotions, you do not know where to start in even grasping the situation entirely, much less forgiving the situation. Yet that is the way you stop the wheel of karma: you forgive.

So we would suggest, my sister, that in order to stop the wheel of karma in your life as it is connected with this entity, it is necessary for you to forgive yourself, again and again and again, every time this trigger is pulled that catapults you back into toxic thoughts concerning your actions. Forgive the thoughts. Forgive the other entity. Forgive the situation. And most of all, forgive yourself.

We do not take lightly the promises that entities make within incarnation. We realize that there is substantial and authentic concern that accumulates around the breaking of a promise such as marriage vows. In another incarnation, in another culture, faced with the same situation, my sister, you might not have had the luxury of freeing yourself from the toxic situation so that you might work out its metaphysical loose ends. You might well have stayed with this entity and your life would have taken a different turning. You still would have found it possible to achieve realization and insight, even in that situation, for entities can learn and can serve anywhere.

Yet, my sister, it is indeed exponentially simpler, when one perceives that one is in an unchangeable and toxic situation and one has done all that one can to no avail, to pack one's bags and remove oneself from the day-to-day friction of such a relationship. Clearly, when you do leave a relationship like that, there is a great relief felt because you are not being buffeted on the daily basis with the suffering patterns that you have previously undergone.

Yet, you still pack yourself in that bag! So you know in your heart of hearts that, because you are not able to balance the pattern with this entity, there will be other relationships that will sound the same theme, that will pop up in your life and offer you the same work again. It may not be a romantic relationship. It may not even be a personal relationship. There are many, many ways in which you can, once again, receive the catalyst for growth that the mated relationship with your ex-husband represented.

However, the key to proceeding forward is to trust in one's judgment and to validate one's own decisions. This is something you felt deeply to do. How could you be wrong? And as we said before, there are no mistakes. For just like the new GPS machines that tell the driver which turn to take, if you miss a turn the GPS resets and then tells you how to get where you want to go from the new location.

You are on solid ground, metaphysically speaking. You have not erred. You have not sinned. You have not done something that somehow needs to be blessed by the other self that is your mate. You need to forgive yourself, the situation, and all aspects of that situation, including your ex-husband. That will stop the wheels of karma between you and this entity in your creation.

The one who is your ex-husband is responsible for doing the same work. You cannot do this work for him. You may never be able to have a satisfactory discussion about this with him, for it is a relatively advanced concept that one may actually move forward and not be trapped for all the life long in the consideration of what one should or should not have done.

So we would suggest to you, my sister, that you do the very serious work of forgiveness and that you then take a deep breath, square your shoulders, and embrace new life.

May we ask if there is a follow-up query at this time? We are those of Q'uo.

N: I don't have any other questions. Thank you very much.

Is there a question from any in the circle at this time?

Jim: Not from me, Q'uo.

In that case, my dear friends, it is time for us to pack our own bags and leave this instrument and this group, glorying as always in the love and in the light of the one infinite Creator. We are known to you as those of Q'uo. Adonai. Adonai. ❧

L/L Research

L/L Research is a subsidiary of Rock Creek Research & Development Laboratories, Inc.

P.O. Box 5195
Louisville, KY 40255-0195

www.llresearch.org

Rock Creek is a non-profit corporation dedicated to discovering and sharing information which may aid in the spiritual evolution of humankind.

ABOUT THE CONTENTS OF THIS TRANSCRIPT: This telepathic channeling has been taken from transcriptions of the weekly study and meditation meetings of the Rock Creek Research & Development Laboratories and L/L Research. It is offered in the hope that it may be useful to you. As the Confederation entities always make a point of saying, please use your discrimination and judgment in assessing this material. If something rings true to you, fine. If something does not resonate, please leave it behind, for neither we nor those of the Confederation would wish to be a stumbling block for any.

© 2009 L/L Research

Sunday Meditation
May 20, 2007

Group question: The question today for Q'uo is from G. It is: "Though I go about every day as if I am seeking the Creator, I am seeking something that is entirely a concept in my mind, something for which I have no reference, something which I have never consciously seen nor ever truly experienced as an incarnate being. How does one seek that which is so invisible and completely unknown to the conscious self?"

(Carla channeling)

We are those of the principle known to you as Q'uo. Greetings in the love and in the light of the one infinite Creator, in Whose service we come to you this day. We thank this circle of seeking for inviting us to join their search for the truth. It is our privilege and our pleasure to share our humble thoughts with you.

As always, my friends, we would ask that each of you take full responsibility for choosing, out of those things that we have to say, the material you wish to consider. By that we mean that if our thoughts do not seem resonant to you, we would ask you to leave them behind. If you will guard the gates of your own perception in this way, we will feel much more free to share our thoughts without being concerned that you might take our thoughts to be those of an authority and not those of entities who, like you, walk the circle of seeking through infinity back to the source whence all of us came, the one infinite Creator.

My brother, in asking about how to find the Creator when the Creator has no part in intellectual discussion, you pierce through the thin veneer of civilization and culture to the heart of spiritual seeking. The one known as R was speaking earlier of skating across the pond of life, staying on the surface of things and perhaps avoiding the discomfort of the depths of insight.

Even on the surface of life, even in the most limited of awareness, there lies the one infinite Creator. Yet we will readily agree that in order to begin to penetrate the surface layers of illusion that surround the mystery of the one infinite Creator, it is well to think in terms of moving deeper into that mystery which lies within you.

When you say that there is no objective referent for the one infinite Creator, we understand your thought, we believe. For indeed, the Creator is not an entity that can be invited to parties or dressed in a paper hat; He cannot blow a whistle on New Year's Eve to celebrate the passage of time.

The infinite Creator is intelligent infinity, that which, by definition, cannot be thought. There is no conception in the human mind that can compass infinity and eternity. The human mind is designed to work in space and in time, moving linearly in space and time, step by step, along the path of seeking.

Yet there is much more than your mind to the third-density, incarnate human being that you are. Indeed, you have two minds. You have the mind with which your body was born and the mind which is consciousness. This is a key point when working with the idea of seeking the Creator, because one needs both minds. One does not need to discard the intellect, but rather to understand its place and to understand that each of you as seekers is not your intellect but rather is the charioteer that decides where the steeds of your intellect shall go and how fast you shall take the road.

The intellect is a helpful resource for the spiritual seeker. It has those powers to analyze and synthesize and make new combinations and patterns. This investigative and analytical capacity is very helpful in developing your arsenal of discernment and wideness of thought. With the intellect you can read as widely as you wish, until you are familiar with what a number of other people have said about spiritual seeking.

This constitutes a ready and helpful source of inspiration and we would not denigrate or shortchange the value of your intellectual mind. We only ask that you realize that you need to be in the driver's seat. You often need to hold your intellect under very tight reign, for it will tend to plunge around corners of new thoughts and directly into the ditch, fueled by old mind, old memory, and old assumptions.

The intellect is resistant to change. When one becomes a spiritual seeker, one has chosen to accelerate the pace of change and transformation within the life experience. So, although the intellect can move the spiritual seeker into a situation of becoming more aware of who he is and why he is here, it is generally not the intellect or the capacities of the intellect that are able to keep the seeker in balance and on track as the tides and waves of change and transformation sweep over the seeker who is opening like a flower.

Consciousness is the other mind which you have as a mind/body/spirit complex, as the one known as Ra calls a person on this Earth. Unlike the mind which is particularly and solely your own, you share the faculty of consciousness with all beings. We are not simply saying that you share consciousness with all other human beings. We are saying that you share consciousness with every iota within the infinite creation of the one Creator.

This is the second key. The nature of consciousness is not particular to you. Rather, because of your innate nature as a part of the godhead principle, your heart beats with the pulse of the one infinite Creator.

That which created all that there is is a certain vibration of consciousness that, for lack of a better term, we have called unconditional love or Logos. That one, great, original Thought or Logos has created the starry heavens, the vast spaces within each molecule of your body, and you, a unique point of intersection that catches two worlds, that of the everyday, waking consciousness of your people, skating across the pond of life, and that of the one infinite Creator whose Thought is a Thought of unconditional love.

There is indeed no objective referent to the infinite Creator, in terms of your science. There is no way to prove the existence of a ground of being. Certainly scientists and church fathers alike declare the obviousness of the Creator's existence. Scientists move from an observation of the way nature works and find, if they are open to deeper contemplation of the vast, intelligent design of the creation, that there is indeed an author of such meticulous clockwork, such brilliant precision and such unimaginable and far-flung creativity.

Those of the church, whatever the type of church, tend to feel that there is no need to prove that the Creator exists because it is obvious that something made all that there is and something stands behind those creations that He has made. That something is defined over and over and over again, through countless millennia, thousands of approaches to religion, and hundreds of basic approaches that various religions and sects share. But the fundamental tenet of those who focus on religion as a way to learn the ways of the infinite Creator is faith.

In religion, it is by faith that the keys are turned in the locks of wisdom and the doors swing open to offer realizations and insight. All of these words only rap at the door of the deeper truth, which is that the objective referent of the one infinite Creator is yourself.

What do you know about yourself? You know your desires and the strength of your desires. You know that one thing has led to another in your life in a path that has seemed anything but straight, and yet as you gaze back over your life experience, you see how everything fell as it did in order to bring you to this present, immaculate moment of now.

What would you say if we asked you who you are? What is the "I" of you? This is the third key.

One ancient name of the Creator is the Hebrew, "I Am." It is variously interpreted as "I am that I am," or "I am becoming what I am," or simply, "I Am, I Am," and so each of you is an "I Am."

Naturally, you have been taught to ignore such ways of thinking. You have been taught precisely who you are. You have been told that who you are depends on your age, your sex, your station in life, your accomplishments, the roots of heredity which brought you into this life, and so forth. You are endlessly defined by those who do not know you. Even your parents—who would know you more than anyone else, perhaps—tend to fail to grasp the heart of who you are because they are so close to the outer aspects of who you are, as they raise you and help you to move out into the world as they understand it.

And yet, the whole time, you are also existing in a very profound space of "I Am." And this space is held in common with all things. Yet, in the flesh that you have taken on for this incarnation, you are able to embody that mystery and that paradox that is the one infinite Creator.

We ask that you practice, perhaps daily for a while, an exercise that the one known as Ra has given through this instrument before. We ask that you look into the mirror at yourself. Gaze into your eyes, not seeing the color and luminosity of your eyes or the face around those eyes, but gazing into that blackness at the heart of the eye which is letting the light into the internal workings of your physical body. It is through that aperture that your soul shines out.

Perhaps you have known people whose gaze instantly made you glad and happy because of the quality of love in their gaze. The Creator shines forth from your eyes when you allow all of the tensions and the worries of the day to fade away, so that you become empty of all the detritus of human life.

Empty your pockets, my friends. Take out the concerns. No matter how cogent and intelligent those concerns are, for now, for the purpose of seeking the heart of the Creator, let the concerns of this day fade away and open your mind to that level of things where that thing which is important today shall still be important ten thousand years from now. This takes you immediately to consciousness.

You might call consciousness the mind of the heart, for indeed, within the human energy body, the seat of consciousness and the intelligence and insight of consciousness is the inner heart. A great deal can conspire to keep you from knowing, feeling and living within your own sacred heart.

Therefore, the seeker may need to restructure his day in such a way as to make time for that reckoning with the deeper self that brings an entity living on the surface of things down into the regions of truth, beauty, virtue and all of those values that are worthy ten thousand years ago, ten thousand years in the future, and in this very moment as well.

It is not that you must cut things out of your life in order to do spiritual seeking. It is rather that you invite that which is not your intellect but that which is consciousness to take its proper place as the other resource that is pulling the chariot of your seeking. You do not have to depend on your intellect alone. Nor do you have to abandon your intellect and depend upon faith and consciousness alone. Rather, the two are yoked together, just as your spirit is yoked to your body for the duration of this incarnation.

There is a purpose for your being here now. Indeed, you have created the lifetime which you are enjoying in terms of choosing the relationships that shall be important to you within this incarnation, choosing the cluster of gifts and skills that you have brought with you to share with the world on the outer or manifested level within this incarnation. And you have chosen those blindnesses, seeming faults, and ways of being uncomfortable that shall offer you catalyst, so that in this valley of the shadow of death that your short life is, you may make straight in that desert a highway for the Creator.

Each time that you encounter a tangled pattern that calls out to you to be solved, remember that this is grist for the mill. This discomfort and suffering is valuable, for in the fiery furnace of this suffering, this very situation that seems so difficult shall shake you and break you open so that the gems hidden within the ore of your personality may be harvested and you may suddenly, for the first time, see a jewel-like and utterly beautiful aspect of your consciousness that you never knew was there. It was only through this catalytic action, this shaking and stirring of the self, that you are able to see more clearly the choices that lie before you.

When you seek the one infinite Creator, we ask you to remember that you have entered the precincts of mystery and paradox. All things are one, yet every single being is different. Even every snowflake is different. That is the kind of paradox that lets you know that you are on the track of the one infinite Creator. Do not be satisfied with easy answers and the seamless arrangements of thoughts that go into religious, spiritual and philosophical edifices of thoughts. For these are edifices of the mind and the intellect. They shall not bring you to the infinite One. They shall only make you very good at moving symbols around in your mind so that you feel that you have thought upon the divine.

Instead we ask you, if you wish to know the one infinite Creator, to invite that Creator into your life this moment. Ask, and you shall receive. Can you bear the brightness of the face of the one Creator? We believe you can. And in that faceless face that exists and does not exist, in that place of mystery and paradox shall you find a pleasant land indeed opening before you, a land in which you feel that Creator-ship within you.

Another suggestion we might make to the seeker who is working on this deep question is to move from an assumption that is chosen irrespective of its obvious truth. As the one known as G said, he acts as if he were seeking the infinite One. We would ask him to take it a step further. We would ask him to act as if he were the Creator.

He has created everything in his creation. You all have created everything that there is in your creation. You have named every feeling, every object, and every point of view as you choose. Experiment, then, my brother, with acting as though your thoughts had the power of creatorship. This is not a great stretch, for indeed this is true. You are the creator of your universe and your thoughts have the power to adhere to life as you know it.

Therefore we ask you, what shall you create this day with your thoughts?

What kind of creation have you created?

What environment for spirit have you provided for yourself?

When you speak, are you aware that that which you judge is judged and found wanting and that which you approve is acceptable?

We ask you to move from this point of exquisite accountability. At the end of each day, as you assess your thoughts, see what you think you have created this day in terms of a world in which to live, move and have your being.

Have you created an affectionate, compassionate, sweet world in which your soul may bloom? Or have you brought down the blight of intolerance, prejudice and the acceptance of injustice and lack of love?

Have you been at war this day within yourself or with another?

What are your thoughts this day? For you are the Creator and that which you create within yourself is out-pictured into the world.

As we understand the Creator, my brother, there is no entity or image which is the object of your seeking. Rather, as all things are vibration and constantly in motion, you seek the totality of vibration and motion.

And as you become accustomed to this acceptance of the illusion of that which is solid and the reality of that which vibrates and moves endlessly as does light, you become truly aware for the first time of the unified and integrated nature of all that there is.

And you can at last see that the object of your search lies deep within you, not only deep within some part of your body or your mind or your spirit, but deep within every cell of your body, within every cell and iota of your mind, and within every speck of that shuttle which is consciousness in motion, the spirit of the living Creator.

This livingness of the Creator is that livingness of you and all of those around you: all creators, all mirrors of the sacred for you, that you may see the Creator in everyone, in every bush and tree, in all of the elements, in all of nature, and most of all, within yourself.

We are those of Q'uo, and would ask if there is a follow-up to this query?

Jim: No.

We are those of Q'uo, and would ask then if there is another query at this time?

R: I have a question, Q'uo. Could you comment on the similarity between a religion called in our culture Christian Scientology and the concepts in the Law of One, because one of the readers asked if there are similarities and if Scientology is picking up on the same principles that Ra described in speaking of the One?

We are those of Q'uo, and are aware of your query, my brother. We would compare, then, three ways of thought: the Confederation way of thought, the Christian Science way of thought, and Scientology's way of thought.

The structure of that which is called Christian Science or the Church of Christ, Scientist has a very harmonious connection to the Law of One, in that it sees clearly that all things are illusory except for faith, will and the unity of all that there is.

Certainly, there is much baggage that comes with any world religion, shall we say, yet there are aspects of that way of thought that are profoundly united with the basic concept of the Law of One, which is the unity of all things and the transparency of all things to the will of each individual who holds the godhead principle within his consciousness.

The system of Scientology has not the core principles in common with the Law of One but rather various ways of dealing with the world around one, especially in the attempt to lift oneself away from the heavy energy of unforgiven situations and thoughts in the past during the incarnative period. That is, Scientology and the Confederation philosophy alike suggest that it is possible to release pain and to alleviate suffering by digging through the ore of the human personality until those nuggets of pain that have created patterns of suffering in the incarnation are unearthed.

When those nuggets of ore are seen in the light of day—and by that we mean the light of insight, forgiveness and understanding—it may be seen that the suffering is not necessary, that it is a trouble-bubble, and it needs only to be popped, released and forgotten.

This kind of clarity is helpful to the spiritual seeker and it is this basic tendency and vector of thought which is most congruent with the Law of One philosophy.

May we answer your query in any further way, my brother? We are those of Q'uo.

R: I will extrapolate because I am not familiar with Scientology myself, but you have mentioned that the core principles in the Law of One are not the same for Scientology. Are those core principles the principles of free will, of intelligent infinity, and love/light?

We are those of Q'uo, and, my brother, we would add to these the quality of unity and say that that is completely correct.

Is there a further query? We are those of Q'uo.

R: No, not on this subject. And thank you for speaking to it, Q'uo.

We are those of Q'uo, and we thank you, my brother. Is there another query at this time?

Jim: I have a question from T: "Q'uo, can you confirm the accuracy of the following conclusions: In about 6,000 to 4,500 B.C.E. an agrarian societal population lived in un-walled towns of respectable size, appeared to have a female deity, focused on crops and husbandry, had no weapons of war, and was matriarchal due to women's ability to give birth."

We are those of Q'uo, and, my brother, we would agree, not on the date, but on the fact there have been several agrarian cultures that flourished for a time, beginning with what your people call Lemuria and moving into Europe as well as South America and Africa. The most recent of those cultures has remnants of thought that are still active within your culture and that is the society of Celtic beings who were matriarchal in nature and who saw the principle of godhead as being feminine.

Indeed, you will find in old churches in parts of the British Isles to this day, especially Ireland, the symbol of the Yoni[57] or the vagina and the open legs over the church doors, combining the energy of Christianity with the energy of seemingly pagan celebrations of fertility.

And we would note that it is this feminine principle that is so often missing and is so hungered for in your culture at this time. Rather than embracing the

---

[57] Yoni is the Sanskrit word for the female reproductive organs, while Lingam is the Sanskrit word for the male reproductive organs.

power of the feminine principle that can nurture and create life in her womb and bring it forth in affection and joy, the proponents of the "one God" and "chosen people" religions—which include Christianity, the Jewish religion, and Islam, among others—have tended to demean and denigrate women, denying them not only their spirituality but their worth as human beings. They have consigned them to be second-class citizens. We might note that, in our humble opinion, there is a tremendous amount of fear behind that urge of the male to suppress and control the feminine principle.

Indeed, the opposite needs to occur in terms of your globe's being able to spin itself out of the endless cycles of war and aggression that the unbridled sway of male energy has created within your Earth world.

Is there another query at this time? We are those of Q'uo.

(Pause)

We are those of Q'uo, and find that we have apparently exhausted the queries at this session of working. We thank each of you for taking the time and the space in your incredibly busy lives to seek the truth.

And we thank you for asking us to be part of that search and that seeking. Certainly you teach us every time that we come to your circle. We thank you for that which you have taught us and we humbly hope that we may have offered you some thoughts that may prove fruitful in your own process of seeking the truth which is ever and always the same.

All is one. You are all that there is, including the one infinite Creator. You can fold your tents, you can fold up your life, but you cannot fold up the power and the peace that you carry in your consciousness and in your life.

You can stretch your life out to the heavens and to hell, and yet you cannot compass the power and the peace of the one Creator that lies within you.

We wish you good journey. The trip to the center is a trip of great beauty and upon that trip you are never alone. For entities such as we wait to be asked to partner with you and lend you our affection and our support. Ask, and we shall be there; not with words, but with our love and with that information that goes too deep for words.

We are those of the principle known to you as Q'uo. We leave you in the love, the light, the peace, and the power of the one infinite Creator. Adonai. Adonai. ✤

L/L RESEARCH

L/L Research is a subsidiary of Rock Creek Research & Development Laboratories, Inc.

P.O. Box 5195
Louisville, KY 40255-0195

www.llresearch.org

Rock Creek is a non-profit corporation dedicated to discovering and sharing information which may aid in the spiritual evolution of humankind.

ABOUT THE CONTENTS OF THIS TRANSCRIPT: This telepathic channeling has been taken from transcriptions of the weekly study and meditation meetings of the Rock Creek Research & Development Laboratories and L/L Research. It is offered in the hope that it may be useful to you. As the Confederation entities always make a point of saying, please use your discrimination and judgment in assessing this material. If something rings true to you, fine. If something does not resonate, please leave it behind, for neither we nor those of the Confederation would wish to be a stumbling block for any.

© 2009 L/L RESEARCH

SPECIAL MEDITATION
JULY 31, 2007

Question from T: Dear Q'uo, there are many pious teachers and creators in Muslim, Hebrew, Christian traditions who pray night and day in the Palestine region. I believe they all pray for peace and love. Why are there still conflicts and wars raging in Israel and nearby regions?

(Carla channeling)

We are those of the principle known to you as Q'uo. Greetings in the love and in the light of the one infinite Creator, in whose service we come to this circle of seeking this evening. We thank you for asking us to join you in seeking the truth. It is a great privilege to be with you and we hope to be of service to you by offering our humble opinions.

As always, we would request that you listen with a careful inner ear, not only listening to what we have to say, but also listening to your own responses to these thoughts. If our thoughts seem to resonate to you, then keep them and work with them as you will. However, we ask that you put aside those thoughts that do not resonate to you. In this way we may feel free to speak our mind and know that we are not infringing upon your free will or disturbing the process of your spiritual evolution.

My brother, the prayers, hopes and dreams of those who visualize peace in the Middle East, and indeed in all regions of your war-torn globe, are very effectual in a certain way. They are not designed to intervene in the worldly affairs of entities who do not wish to become aware of the love and the light of the one infinite Creator. They are designed to alert the consciousness of the universe, of all creation, and especially of those forces of unconditional love who are the objects of these prayers, to the fact that there is distress among the nations, distress in people's hearts and a yearning for peace, beauty, truth and a life lived in compassion, comradeship and contentment. These prayers are having the effect of awakening the planet at the grass-roots level of ordinary people. Many are awakening at this time because of the fervent prayers of all of those who offer their deepest beseechments to the one infinite Creator in their own ways.

Metaphysically speaking, your planet is in far better shape to meet the time of harvest than it was thirty or forty years ago, because of efforts within religious circles, and within circles that are not religious but rather spiritual or metaphysical, such as this group. All is well, metaphysically speaking. There is no prayer that is not heard by the one infinite Creator.

We also have heard the prayers of your people, and that is why we are attending you who live on Planet Earth at this time, and responding, when there is a way to respond, with our every effort to provide you with our humble opinions as regards the nature of spiritual evolution.

The governments of your people, however, are not at all focused on peace, contentment or compassion. Those in political power have become able to hold the positions which they hold because they have laid aside what they consider to be naive and overly innocent hopes. They have accepted that they cannot be men of complete integrity, in the usual sense, if they wish to serve the state. The organization and arrangement of power is specifically and universally service-to-self upon your planet.

There are those entities who, vibrating in green ray and blue ray, attempt most sincerely to change the atmosphere in which business is conducted at the level of nation-states. However, these entities are either weeded out completely by their inability to accept a system which is corrupt and to work within that, or they become useless in terms of making a change from within governmental systems because they have become used to the perquisites of power and have begun to think in a service-to-self way, while rationalizing to themselves that all that they do is for the greater good. They become more and more separated from any stream of pure metaphysical integrity by their own choices until they can no longer remember what it feels like to make a purely positive response to challenging catalyst.

Indeed, my brother, the entities who are in power among your nation-states are focused upon those goals that have been the habitual goals of people in power upon your planet for millennia. Those goals are the goals of your great ape ancestors. They revolve around a love of their family and their tribe. When they have defined their tribe, then they attempt to defend their tribe's property and acreage and to gather resources so that their tribe may fare well in a world of diminishing resources. They have been in power before, perhaps many times, and have developed the habit of an unceasing thirst for power. And this they shall not yield in order to make room for service-to-others goals such as true liberty, true equality, true justice, and a truly equitable distribution of the resources of your planet.

We ask that you not be overly concerned with the state of the outer workings of your planet. We ask that your concern be to pray that these leaders may be forgiven, for they do not know what they are doing. They will come to dust, as all dragons must. Even now, they are dying. The energy of the old world is weakening and its hold upon the hearts and the minds of ordinary people, such as are gathered in this circle of seeking, is lessening every day.

Nothing is as it seems when looked at from a metaphysical point of view. Therefore, when thinking of the Middle East and its issues, may your concern be to affirm and confirm that there is peace, love and compassion that is stronger than the dragon which is thrashing its tail at this time. For dragons shall die. But those values of love, unity, hope, faith and joy shall live forever. As you affirm and confirm these values in yourself, you are creating the basis for that which is to come. And in so doing, you are also creating for yourself the ability to live through the shift into fourth density that is upon you at this time.

As you look at the Middle East, know that all is well. And if you wish to explore the details of the politics of violence and aggression that make the front pages red with blood, do this studying and this research not to despair but to know ever more clearly the nature of the world that you came to incarnation to love.

And my brother, we ask that you allow no judgment to enter into this love. Praise and bless those who seem to be persecuting and hurting the common man and woman in these difficult and challenging times that you now experience. Let your mind and your heart rest in peace. The outer world shall not hear you, but all of those in the unseen realms who vibrate in unconditional love do hear you and are called to your prayers to amplify them and to strengthen them. You are doing the good work of compassion and love as you offer these simple prayers and visualizations in order to maximize your ability to serve in this way.

We recommend that, as this group does, you set aside time each day, if only just a moment, to visualize peace, harmony and understanding, not only in the Middle East but in all portions of your far-flung globe. We assure you that you are having a wonderful affect on the inner planes. Allow the rest to fall away, for empires rise and fall. The spiritual evolution moves along without regard to the illusion created by power and breath.

May we ask if there is another query at this time.

Questioner: For many years, the leaders of China have wanted to conquer Taiwan by force. Since those of Hatonn have worked with China's leaders for a long time, may I ask if the leaders of China have a more peaceful mind now?

We are those of Q'uo, and are aware of your query, my brother. Perhaps in thinking about what we have just said about all the nations of the Earth, you may predict the tenor of our response to your query about China and Taiwan.

There is a saying in English, "You can lead a horse to water, but you cannot make it drink." Indeed, members of the Confederation have shared thoughts with all nations of the world. Our thoughts, however, are not offered in a way that would infringe upon free will. And those of the nation-state you call China are in sympathy with and polarized negatively along with the other nation-states who have achieved power in international commerce, politics and economics. They are not interested in that which we have to say. They are interested, as we said, in solidifying those possessions which they now have and in reclaiming any possessions that have gotten away from them.

My brother, this is the way of empire. We ask that you not take personally, or as a slur upon your nation, that it has not been able to receive the message of love which we and so many other voices of love have spoken. Rest assured that the information of love, light and unity is available to all who have the ears to hear and the hearts to understand.

May we ask if there is another query at this time, my brother.

Questioner: Dear Q'uo, I have read a paragraph from The Nine's[58] speeches: "Meditation is not enough. One needs to act!" In this regard, other than meditation, is there any other practical way to promote world peace in our daily life.

Those of Hatonn are very much with this instrument at this time as a part of the principle of Q'uo. However, the one known as Hatonn is not that entity which is speaking. We are those of the Q'uo. Hatonn desires greatly to offer their love and their light to this query. May we request that you re-read this query that we may have a clean beginning of our response.

---

[58] To learn more about The Nine, you can find an appendix of their channeled messages in the back of the book, *Uri*, by Andrija Puharich. Though out of print, this book is still available from amazon.com and other on-line booksellers. Phyllis V. Schlemmer also writes about this body of channeling in her book, *The Only Planet of Choice*. Her web site for that book is www.theonlyplanetofchoice.com/puharich.htm.

(The query is repeated.)

We are those of the Q'uo, and are aware of your query, my brother. It is said in the *Holy Bible*, "By their fruits, you shall know them."[59] Indeed, there is great encouragement from spiritual sources of all religions and philosophical systems, not only to offer inner practices connected with increasing one's spirituality but also to live out the fruits of the spirit in one's daily life.

Firstly, we would offer you the concept of unity here, for you and the world are one. Therefore, if you are able to live the principles of love, justice, compassion and understanding in your life, you have significantly changed the vibration of your entire planet, of which you are an integral and holographic part. If you wish to save the world, work on yourself. That is our main suggestion to you at this time.

We assure you that while it is simple for us to suggest this to you, it shall take your entire lifetime to live out the spiritual gifts, graces and fruits with which you have been blessed and which you shall continue to be blessed. We do not give you a simple task, but we give you a task well worth a lifetime of service.

Secondly, if you wish to promote fourth-density values, such as equality and stewardship of the people, the ideals, and the very land around you, we would suggest that you look around you. You shall not have to look far for things which you can do materially to help those who are needy and oppressed.

There are those in your culture who are hungry. Go to a soup kitchen, or whatever place is in your culture, where meals are prepared for those who cannot pay and who do not have homes. Help to prepare the food. Serve it with love. And as you clean the pots and pans, give prayers of gratitude and thankfulness that those that were hungry have now been fed.

There are old ones in your community that may be lonely and having trouble living out the last days of their lives. If it moves you to think on this, find them, companion them, and give them hope and compassion by your youthful smiles and your eyes

---

[59] *Holy Bible*, Matthew 7: 15-16: "Beware of false prophets, which come to you in sheep's clothing, but inwardly they are ravening wolves. Ye shall know them by their fruits."

full of love. Let them know that you honor their wisdom and value their presence in your life.

There are troubled souls in your culture who have lost their way, and have offered their lives to a substance or toxic idea that is now living their life for them. Encourage them to take their lives back from heroin or opium or cultish ideas which separate them from the rest of the world. And if they are having a difficult time maintaining sobriety and rationality, and if it moves you to see this, companion them, encourage them and be sober with them. Teach them how to laugh and live lightly again upon the planet.

All around you there are those who have polluted and destroyed the Earth, and you experience this perhaps in terms that are local to you—a plant that is emitting toxic emissions. If this moves you, see what you can do in your village or your neighborhood to make a change for the better. Become compassionate stewards of Mother Earth, for Gaia is most grateful to those who help her to become more healthy.

Indeed, we especially encourage you in your stewardship of the Earth. For there is a tremendous amount of what this instrument would call "group karma" having to do with the fact that so many of those who are attempting to graduate from third density on planet Earth have, in the past, on Sirius, Deneb, Mars, Maldek or Atlantis, destroyed their environments. There is great heart-sadness amongst the entire human tribe concerning the destruction of Mother Earth. And it is very healing, in your energy patterns as a people, wherever you live, to become involved in loving and serving your beautiful, fragile island home.

In all these ways and many more that we cannot include for lack of time, you may live that which you have received on the inner planes. It is said in the holy work this instrument calls the *Bible*, "That which you have received in the darkness and in the intimacy of your inner sanctum, in secrecy and silence, sing from the housetops."[60] Express the joy of the saving grace of hope and love that flows in an unending stream through your hearts and, blessed by you, into the world.

---

[60] *Holy Bible*, Matthew 10:27: "What I tell you in the darkness, that speak ye in light: and what ye hear in the ear, that preach ye upon the housetops."

You can indeed make a difference. However, never confuse the outer portion of your walk with your walk. Always and ever it must begin with the silence of your prayers, meditations and thanksgivings.

We are those of Q'uo, and ask if there is another query at this time.

Questioner: Since 2011 is coming very soon, I want to ask about the harvest. What will happen in the transition period? Will our capitalized world collapse totally before 2011? How long will the transition period be? Will it be instantly, a week, or a decade?

We are those of Q'uo, and are aware of your query, my brother. We would have no idea as to the future outworking of outer events upon your planet, for those things have not yet occurred. Perhaps you are aware of the theory in physics that at every moment there are universes of choices that you may make in any of a thousand directions, and that all those possibilities are present until a choice is made. It is so in this case also.

We can assure you that the planet does not need to collapse or fly into the sun or do any of the drastic things that have been prophesied by those who confuse a fear of death with the reception of information concerning the entire civilization. When you hear the doom and the gloom predicted, know in your heart that this is the outpicturing of inner fears concerning the individual facing death. Thusly, since you are inevitably going to leave the physical vehicle in which you now enjoy life, you are hearing predictions that are confused, where those who are receiving psychic impressions are confusing their fear of death with the much larger picture of what shall occur for not only the self but also the planet.

It is those among your people who have power and have the ability to destroy the environment of Planet Earth that might cause you a deserved pang of concern. For those with the habit of empire, having destroyed civilizations once or twice, have gotten a taste for the glory of annihilation. For even that negative expression of power is satisfying for one whose mind is bent on conquest. Do what you can my brother, to guide those whom you elect to power, or who have power over you in some way, in the ways of peace and justice.

As far as Planet Earth is concerned, Gaia itself is moving into fourth density and in fact is all but completely immersed in fourth-density vibrations at this time. The shift that has been such a cause of fear among your people is happening now. It has been happening for some time. It will continue to happen for some time yet to come. We cannot see the way ahead. We would not have predicted that you would be, as a planetary tribe, in such excellent shape as you appear to be at this time.

Masses of people all over the globe are awakening to the rightness of love, unconditional and compassionate love. The forces of life are engulfing with their light the darkness that can never deny light. And so darkness is scurrying into corners and attempting to put out the light by creating an atmosphere of fear. Thusly, you are of great service to the planet and to yourself if you cultivate the habit of fearlessness.

We ask you, my brother, do you fear your death? Or do you see it as the gateway to larger life? When you can see it as a gateway to something wonderful, then death no longer has power over you. When the Earth as a whole can see transitioning into fourth density as a natural step into larger life, death shall no more have dominion over you.

We would suggest that the possibility/probability vortices at this time indicate that each entity to whom we speak shall live out his natural physical life, die a natural death, and then walk the steps of light to see whether he has graduated from third grade or density in this school of souls, or whether he shall have to repeat the grade.

There is nothing to fear in either case. If you are ripe, you shall harvest yourself. If you are unripe, you shall receive an opportunity to spend a significant amount of time in another third-density, Earth-like planet, where you shall once again study the lessons of love.

We would suggest that, rather than this instrument speaking longer on this subject, if you wish to become more fully aware of what we would say upon this subject you investigate other sessions such as this one, for questions such as this one have occupied the minds of many of those who ask the group questions in this circle of seeking and there is a substantial amount of information on this subject that has been received, preserved and made available to you.

We are those of Q'uo, and would ask if there is another question at this time.

Questioner: Does each soul have a soul mate? And if so, what is the meaning of a soul mate to each of us?

We are those of Q'uo, and are aware of your query, my brother. We find that in our opinion the term "soul mate" is very misleading. For it suggests that, out of all the world, there is only one entity who matches your temperament, personality and desire to serve. In fact, every entity with whom you come in contact is potentially a soul mate.

There is, however, more resonance and chemistry between some entities than others. If one discards the outer reasons for chemistry, such as good looks or the possession of money and power, and focuses only on those deeper threads of companionship about which we feel you are asking, then you will find yourself drawn to certain entities.

You may have worked with them once or twice or a dozen times in the past. You may have had many different relationships. In a way that is impossible to define or prove, you feel a connection to certain people. If you wish to develop that connection and if the other entity also wishes to develop that connection, in time, with shared history, deep converse, and mutual meditation and service together, you may indeed become mated at the soul level.

Indeed, many of you have incarnated into groups of those with whom you have incarnated again and again to be of service on Planet Earth and, indeed, for many wanderers on other planets as well. The idea of one soul mate is a romantic myth which stems from the yearning of the soul, the heart, and the personality for the opportunity to love completely and to be loved completely.

We assure you, that potential exists between any two people who come to the Creator on bended knee and who ask that the Creator be a part of their companionship, and that the companionship be more than a simple mating of mind and bodies. Ask that your companionships may always include the soul and you shall find unconditional love in your life.

It takes a great commitment to stay openhearted to anyone whom you do not know well. In coming to know them you will find their clay feet and you will be asked to love without judgment. We encourage you to find the compassion to love dearly, humbly and completely, with no judgment. For in such a way shall you indeed be soul-mates with your companions, your spouses and your family members who are in this incarnation, so that you may support them and encourage them and so that they may support you and encourage you.

My friend, they may falter and so may you. And when that happens we would urge you to start over again without judgment and without concern. In the world of spirit, every day is a new creation.

May we ask if there is another query at this time.

Questioner: When I feel my spiritual level is raised continuously then I find that it's very difficult to communicate with others. It's possible that I am meeting a bottleneck in myself. I feel very lonely. What should I do?

We are those of Q'uo, and are aware of your query, my brother. It is very common in those who have awakened and have tasted the nectar of unconditional love for them to strive to spend all of their time in the harmonious reaches of the upper chakras of the energy body: the heart chakra of unconditional love, the throat chakra of communication and compassion, and the indigo chakra of the brow with its work in consciousness and faith. These are wonderful climes and indeed a portion of you may spend all of its time in those heavenly realms.

However, the key to living a balanced life is the constant rooting of those higher energies in the Earth, and the constant uplifting of all lower energies by bringing them into the open heart. Therefore, we would suggest that it is unwise to remain ever in the higher work, but rather it is well to balance all working in consciousness by moving into the lower chakras by praising and giving respect and honor to the most seemingly base or menial of energies. Praise and bless those grounded and necessary energies of sexuality, politeness, responsibility and all those things that would seem to drag you down. Know and find the way to discover ever more clearly that there is no part of life that is not sacred.

Your body itself is a temple. And as you wash it, tend it, care for it, feed it the right food to the best of your ability, and honor it for all its natural functions, you are bringing the higher energies to bless and infuse the lower energies and are redeeming them by your honor and respect.

If you are cleaning the bathroom or the kitchen or doing the laundry, dwell in joy and thankfulness and bliss and know that this is work worthy of all. It is often said within the Christian faith of which this entity has spent her life, that to be a leader you must wash the feet of those whom you know, humbling yourself and being a servant to them.

In a larger sense you may look at the living of an earthly life as keeping a house that has two floors. Upon the first floor is the kitchen, the bathroom, the bedroom, and the living room: those environments which you associate with all of your lower-chakra desires, needs and responsibilities. It is well to clean the bathroom, scour the kitchen, freshen the bouquet of flowers that welcomes visitors to your living room and do everything you can to honor and bless that lower floor of red-ray, orange-ray and yellow-ray concerns. And only when you have cleaned and scoured and blessed and thanked and honored the first floor shall you ascend the steps to the upper room of meditation, contemplation and working in consciousness.

Above all, keep the light touch and the sense of humor, that your good life may never become a heavy life, but rather that it may radiate and be as light as light itself. Laughter is wonderful medicine for those who are lonely.

And indeed, referring back to a question earlier in this session, we would say that if you are lonely, go out into the highways and the byways of your town. Seek out those who need companionship. You will find, in serving others, that the loneliness is no more and that all is lifted by your capacity to serve others.

And in your genuine realization of them as part of yourself, as you serve them, as you reach out to them, you will quickly find that your life has changed completely. For energy given comes around and is given back to you multiplied a hundred-fold, a thousand-fold, and a million-fold. Love is infinite. However, sometimes you need to initiate the giving of love to those who truly need it before you may begin to feel the reciprocity of loving and being loved.

There is a tendency in all of those who have experienced the joys of living in the higher chakras to draw apart from the world which is so hurly-burly and busy. Yet we assure you that your faith will gladly engage with all of that activity and seeming lack of beauty. For if you bring your love to a situation, that situation shall surely be transformed.

We find that there is energy for one more query at this time. Is there a final query at this time? We are those of Q'uo.

Questioner: Do wanderers ever consider the risks they are taking in incarnating? For example, what's the impact on their social memory complexes and themselves?

We are those of Q'uo, and are aware of your query, my brother. Indeed, the commitment to become a wanderer is not taken lightly. It is thought out carefully and considered for a considerable amount of your time, indeed, centuries of your time, while the commitment to the work is perfected, refined and honed to a sharp edge. It is an act of great courage to be a wanderer.

What wanderers usually do not realize is that that which is so obvious and easy from the other side of the veil is impossible to read and difficult to bear within the thick veiling of the third density of Earth, with its free will and its extremely thick veil. The danger always is that the wanderer will not wake up, or, if it is partially awake, that it will awaken only to complain that it is not comfortable, that it wants to go home, that it must leave this place that is so polluted and dirty.

To those who feel these things, we would suggest that it is precisely because this planet is so in need of higher vibrations that you came to serve at this time, to help lighten the vibrations of Planet Earth. And you could not do this without incarnating and becoming one of the tribe of humankind. Your love was so great that you took that step. And now you have awakened and you know how difficult a step it was to take. We encourage you to take hold of the honor and the duty of being a wanderer.

That which you know of the higher planes, that which you remember in a dim or not so dim way, bring into your heart and let it bless the environment that you see before you, just as it is. You are not here to clean it up. You are not here to make it right. You are not here to fix it. For all of the outer world is an illusion. You are here to love it. Take the world in your arms and embrace it. This is how you came to serve. This is your glory and your crown. Wear it well and rejoice in being here.

As to what occurs if wanderers do not wake up. They, like all of the human tribe, walk the steps of light. If they have learned the lessons of love in this incarnation, they are free to move on. And if so, they may choose to go back to their native density. If they have instead remained asleep within this incarnation, then they shall have a refresher course in third-density living, moving with others who have not graduated to fourth density to another planet where they shall once again become students in third density's refinery of souls.

In either case, all is well. You have all the time in the universe to move through all natural energies and rhythms back to the Creator, who is waiting for you with great delight. And you do not wish to return too soon. For the Creator wishes to know of the fullness of your experiences, your feelings, and your emotions. That is the harvest that you bring to the Creator. Whatever it is, he will love it and you, now and forever.

We are those known to you as the principle of Q'uo. And as we have said, Hatonn is especially eager to shed that wordless and silent love and light that is the essence of the open heart. We pause that you may feel this energy, for it shall be in the vibration upon your tape recording as well as in the energy of this instrument's words.

(Pause)

We are those of Q'uo. Brothers and Sisters of the open heart, you are loved beyond all telling. We leave this instrument and this group in the love and light, the power and the peace of the one infinite Creator. Those of Q'uo wish you love and light. Adonai. Adonai. ✣

L/L Research is a subsidiary of Rock Creek Research & Development Laboratories, Inc.

P.O. Box 5195
Louisville, KY 40255-0195

L/L Research

www.llresearch.org

Rock Creek is a non-profit corporation dedicated to discovering and sharing information which may aid in the spiritual evolution of humankind.

ABOUT THE CONTENTS OF THIS TRANSCRIPT: This telepathic channeling has been taken from transcriptions of the weekly study and meditation meetings of the Rock Creek Research & Development Laboratories and L/L Research. It is offered in the hope that it may be useful to you. As the Confederation entities always make a point of saying, please use your discrimination and judgment in assessing this material. If something rings true to you, fine. If something does not resonate, please leave it behind, for neither we nor those of the Confederation would wish to be a stumbling block for any.

© 2009 L/L Research

Special Meditation
August 7, 2007

Question from G: Q'uo, within this illusion, even with our most certain of hunches, I feel we are doing guesswork in the darkness. I may be fooling myself, but, based upon my own study, some part of me feels that I am currently knee-deep in that phase, point or portion in the development of mystical consciousness known as The Purgative Way.[61] If this is so, is there anything that I could do to accelerate and successfully complete this stage of the journey so that I can more fully realize that which I desire?

(Carla channeling)

We are those known to you as the principle of Q'uo. Greetings in the love and in the light of the one infinite Creator. It is a blessing and privilege to be with you. We thank you for inviting us to join your circle of seeking. It does us a great honor and enables us to perform our humble service, just to share our thoughts.

As always, we would request that you be captain of that which you take in to think about. As the one known as G has noted recently, it is the wolf you feed that prospers. It is the thoughts that you think that create your reality. Think on those thoughts that have true resonance to you. You do not have to explain the resonance to yourself, but only to note it and to follow it. Equally, it is useless to attempt to become interested in a thought that does not resonate to you. No matter how interesting, it is not for you. Take what is good for you and blow the rest away, as the one known as Robbie[62] said.

The creation is, indeed, dark to those who have come through the gates of birth on planet Earth to enjoy a lifetime within the valley of the shadow of death. The veil between the local consciousness of your everyday mind and the universal consciousness of the deep mind is thick upon planet Earth. And a powerful, pure free will has been given by this Logos to your people.

Your experience, therefore, is carefully arranged that it may have all manner of shades of gray and seemingly inky black. Metaphysically speaking, to awaken the light within you is a challenge you take upon yourself in the dark.

The process which you have called The Purgative Way is intrinsic to the light, just as the light is intrinsic to the Dark Night of the Soul. Indeed, that

---

[61] This is an ancient term, used in the Christian church since medieval times, to denote the first of three states which the seeker undergoes. The other two are the "illuminative way," and the "unitive way." St. John of the Cross also calls this stage the Dark Night of the Soul. Gary describes it in his experience as being a stage before illumination takes place, characterized by higher confusion, conflict within, and renunciation of worldly desires.

[62] Robbie Robertson, music CD titled *Music for the Native Americans*, from a song titled "Golden Feather," © Robbie Robertson, all rights reserved. Part of the lyrics are:

When you find what's worth keeping
With a breath of kindness
Blow the rest away.

process of spiritual evolution is a spiral; not simply a cycle but a spiral at which, at the same point in the spiral but higher, you enter the natural, intended, fruitful and challenging Dark Night. And well it is called the Dark Night of the Soul, for both the light and the dark parts of this spiral are designed to ready the spirit within to enter the gateway to intelligent infinity.

We therefore confirm your assumption that those who are new or feel that they are young upon the spiritual path do go through the Dark Night of the Soul. However, there are many witnesses throughout history who have written about the fact that the night will come again and again as long as you are incarnate in third density. This is not a function of punishment or judgment, but of your desire to progress spiritually.

One great resource for being skillful in your dealings with this state of mind, emotions and increasingly spirit is patience. We do not speak of the patience of one who endures. We do not speak of the patience of one who counts the seconds. We speak of the patience of a scientist fascinated with the growth of a flower, who sets himself to watch the flower every day from its bud until its bloom.

And then that scientist continues watching the flower, day after day, so that he may know precisely how it decays, how each petal falls away, how the calyx and the sepal crumble inward and the stem gradually withers until it is brown and dead.

And then that scientist continues watching the empty ground for an entire winter, every day watching and brooding over this miraculous flower, for he wants to know just how every bit of its miraculous life comes about.

And he is rewarded when the flower is pulled up through the soil by the weak March sun and is rained upon by the sweet rains of April and May, until once more its stem is green and strong, its sepals and calyx are firm and out-thrusting, and the bud begins to grow from its nest to burst into bloom once again.

The scientist is not satisfied with one revolution of the cycle. He watches again and again, year upon year, lost in the wonder of every detail, drunk upon the beauty of something so rare and so freely given. This is the patience we recommend.

Another great resource when going through The Purgative Way is a lack of pity for the self. Do not move into that space where you are aware of being bothered and suffering. We do not know how to say this in words but there is glory in the furnace that tempers the soul. If you can find the courage and the fearlessness to thank the furnace for this discomfort, then the fire shall not burn you but shall be your friend, your brother, and your sister.

Another great resource for one who moves through darkness and pain is a sense of humor, or a wider viewpoint that sees the lightness of heavy situations. When a seeker can laugh at the peculiarities of his suffering and embrace them instead of expressing jobations[63] and complaints, that seeker is tuning himself as a musician tunes his instrument or a singer vocalizes before a performance.

Your mind is very plastic and subject to infinite confusion and self-deceit. You do not mean to deceive yourself. We understand that it is involuntary and unintended, but every assumption, every cultural truism, every authority, everything in fact that is not coming to you at this moment needs to fade away from the spiritual seeker.

Certainly meditation, contemplation and all of the rich array of mind tuning techniques can help you. But sometimes the best resource is a good laugh and a realization that not only are you an object of ridicule, silly, wrong-headed and erroneous, but that that is fine; that is funny; that is the human condition. Feel the judgment and the tension fade away.

When you do realize at last the beauty of this completely rounded life you live spiritually, dark side, light side, dark side, light side, then every turn of the spiral helps you to rewire yourself.

In some ways, this rewiring is useful in this incarnation. In other ways, the heart of its use is the moment when you have shifted from this earthly valley of the shadow of death through the gateway of intelligent infinity for one final time into larger life, at which time, these heart-felt, sincerely offered devotions of serving through the dark times with faith shall have created for you your next location in time and space.

---

[63] A jobation is defined by www.dictionary.com as "A scolding; a tedious reproof."

For those who take this purgative way and allow it to shape them, it will certainly result in your graduation. And the fruit of your being shall be delicious to the Creator as you pour out to this source and ending all that you have felt and thought, everything at which you have laughed, and all of those experiences in which you sobbed and wept and despaired. Even your angers, your jealousies, your lust, your greed, and every vice has its information for the Creator.

Allow yourself to rest in the knowledge that, although there are certainly better and less fortunate ways to serve the infinite Creator, as far as being polarized in service to others, even your worst mistake is a gift to the one Creator, adding to Its knowledge of who It is.

As this instrument would say, you cannot go wrong. All that you do is a service to the one infinite Creator and it will be your gift to that Creator, not only in this moment but in the moment of your entry into a larger life, when that personality that you are is released from its stricture and falls away, as the husk falls away from the corn which is then ready to eat.

You shall be ripe and you shall be gathered: not the husk, not the body, not the personality, not the details, but the feelings that were authentic, the services that were given with a whole heart, the intentions that you created and nurtured and polished. Whether you were able to fulfill them completely or whether they remained things of beauty to you for which you strove is unimportant metaphysically.

It is not the goal of the seeker who wishes to be skillful and effectual in his process to accelerate the Dark Night of the Soul any more than it is appropriate for a skillful seeker to attempt to lengthen summer breezes and the good times, the mountain-top experiences and those moments of joy that know no bounds. Rather, we would encourage you to allow yourself to be as even with your process as if all states of emotion were alike to you.

Rejoice equally in the daylight and its bloom and the darkness and its time of maximum chaos, disintegration and eventual fertility, for these things that are broken down within yourself become the fertilizer and soil which allow the seeds of new life and new growth to grow strong and healthy and reach for the sunlight when the day does dawn.

And, my brother, the day always dawns.

We realize that one of the things that is most challenging about The Purgative Way is the chaos and confusion that you experience sitting in the dark, hoping that your ways of dealing with spiritual pain are wise. However, it is helpful to remember that there is an instinctual side to your nature which will stand you in far better stead than that which you know.

This instrument will give a talk in the days to come on the keys to unknowing.[64] My brother, take those keys, stand on your two feet and know that you do not know anything in terms of spirituality. What you receive instead of knowing things is what the Greeks called *gnosis*. That is the knowing that comes from the heart, from its insight and its intuition and the whispers of the wind of spirit.

As your tuning song said, listen to the winds of spirit.[65] The ceaseless, restive, ever-moving energies of spirit shall nudge you in ways you know not, if you but ask—and ask every day and every hour. "Use me, spirit, I am yours, this day, this moment, I am yours."

In the heart of darkness there lies a blessed comfort. You can always ask for the Creator to express Its love, to give you a metaphysical hug. Ask and you shall be answered.

We also would encourage you to seek that comfort that is not of this world nor of the mind nor of the senses, but that lies so deep within your heart that is the very nature of your being. Your exploration is inner and when you penetrate the very heart of darkness, it bursts into light, for the Creator is at the heart of all things.

Lastly we would recommend the resource of fearlessness. The Purgative Way is one way of saying that things are being purged from you. The human personality wonders, "How much more can I lose before I am no longer myself?" In all humility, my

---

[64] For a transcript of that talk, offered at Mackinac Island August 11, 2007, please go to the Library/Carla's Niche section of www.llresearch.org.

[65] Lacy J. Dalton, from her CD, *The Last Wild Place*. The song is titled "Listen to the Wind," © Lacy J. Dalton, all rights reserved. The lyrics, in part are:

> This old world's wild; she won't be tamed.
> The only thing you can trust is change.
> Listen to the wind—listen to the wind.

brother, let that self go. For you truly wish to change, to deepen, and to become an ever more fit vessel for the love and the light of the one infinite Creator.

The Dark Night of the Soul is house-cleaning time for the temple of your body and your mind. You are reforming the way that you think about yourself, the way that you see and view yourself. You are moving from the little "I" of ego to the I AM that is the one infinite Creator.

We have said through this instrument many times that the essence of the faith is that all is well. And all shall be well. When you feel lost, try saying those words to yourself and see how the tuning effect of such reminders brings you to a state of remembrance of who you are and why you are here.

We are those of the principle of Q'uo, and would ask if the one known as G has any questions to follow up with?

G: Yes, I often have massive, instantaneous, knee-jerk resistance to my girlfriend's daughter, without seeming provocation, and at times to my girlfriend herself. I desire greatly to proactively feel love for them rather than react in unconsciously created and sustained resistance, yet no attempt to get to the source and the mechanism of this resistance has borne fruit. My question for you is: Would you be able to direct me to the portion of my psyche responsible for this experience and then would you offer me any counsel as to how I may understand and heal this handicap?

We are those of the principle of Q'uo, and are aware of your query. As perhaps you may have surmised, there is much that we cannot say about something that is so centrally a part of your process at this time, for we cannot do the learning for you. To do so would not benefit either you or ourselves, for you would not truly learn to see through this catalyst and we would lose polarity by infringing upon your free will.

We can talk about the general principles involved in relationships. Some portions of relationships are based upon the difference between yourself and another person, such as the difference in age or the difference in sex. You are older than O. You are a different sex than the ones known as V and O.

It is difficult to look straight into mirrors that are distorted. Mirrors that come across the earthly boundaries of that which you see as gender and age distort the image, as though you were in a fun house with its crazy mirrors and corridors. Other portions of reactions to people can be as shallow as a trick or quirk of the voice or the shallowness of the personality you are watching in certain areas.

But the deeper portions of responses to people often have to do with your being involved with them in other incarnations, in which relationships with them play a powerful part in this incarnational experience. Whether or not your karma with them is balanced or unbalanced, the more you become involved with entities that penetrate the outer shell of personality, the more those energies that have spoken through the ages in other incarnations to yourself begin to speak again, ever more resonantly with ever more good information, good catalyst, good grist for the mill to offer you.

And deepest of all, my brother, you are gazing at yourself. Those things which irritate or upset you or cause you to have a bad chemical reaction to another are those things which characterize a part of your shadow self. As always, the work that you truly do is upon yourself. When you are aggravated or have this bad chemistry, when you have the time, whether close to the event or later in remembrance, sit with that feeling and ask it for the wisdom that lies in its folds.

You may need to be very patient, for the forces of darkness do not like the seeker who is patient with his pain and confusion, for they know that it is to those who are prepared to bide with themselves through thick and thin, believing in themselves and yet asking, "How can I learn? How can I be more when faced with daunting feelings?" that the light shall dawn ever quicker. And meanwhile your faith has made a flame that the darkness cannot put out.

We apologize that we cannot get close to, shall we say, earthly advice, but this is indeed an important, ongoing part of your spiritual seeking and thusly we leave you to it with our encouragement, faith and support.

We are those of Q'uo. May we ask if there is another question, my brother?

G: For the seeker yearning to experience mystical unity, what role does the ability to concentrate for an extended period of time play? Is it critical? And what can I do to further develop this faculty?

We are those of Q'uo, and are aware of your query. My brother, you are already doing one exercise that promotes focus and that is your practice of watching your breath. That in itself is a focusing activity. The practice of the disciplines of the magical personality, as this instrument would call them, are very helpful to one who wishes mechanically to increase concentration abilities. The visualization, for instance, of one shape and color, can be useful. This is a technique of the so-called magical way.

If you can hold the image, for instance, of a green circle or a blue rectangle or a yellow pyramid or a rose for fifteen seconds one day, and if you can repeat that for a week of days, then you may increase the time that you hold that visualization quite clearly in your mind's eye as if it were just before you and commanding your attention. Eventually you will develop that faculty of the mind which is called focus.

It is indeed a useful and helpful practice, however you choose to do it, in that it disciplines the wayward attention. You are already aware of the amazing amount of distraction within the normal daily experience. You are perhaps aware also of the more subtle distractions that stem from the self and the self's distortions. And you may not be aware of how those balancing dynamics of your Earth world—darkness and light—are ever at play within you. The darkness desires you to be dark, for it needs a heavy place to hide. The lightness invites you to soar, but it cannot lift your wings. Thusly, that focusing practice, however you wish to pursue it, is helpful and may bring you more and more into that state of recollection and remembrance of who you are and why you are here.

May we ask if there is a final query at this time, my brother? We are the principle of Q'uo.

G: I don't have your traditional type of nightmares, exactly, but I do have three types of recurring dreams that occasionally haunt me and are, like nightmares, just plain terrifying. In one of the recurring themes, I am locked away in prison, my freedom and rights taken from me in what is a deeply, deeply horrible experience. Would you be able to help me unravel the symbolism to this dream so that I may understand what spiritual principles are being communicated to me about my situation within the incarnation?

We those of the principle of Q'uo, and are aware of your query, my brother. There are aspects of this dream about which we cannot offer comment, but in terms of spiritual principles, we may say that your opinion of your incarnation is not all good! And it is accurate, for are you not in a prison, waiting on the executioner's block for the scythe of death to swish down? And meanwhile, are you not often uncomfortable, driven by the demands of the heavy chemical body and subject to countless irritations and distractions?

There is much more to this than that spiritual principle, but in general, dreams tell the dreamer what is on his deep mind, what is bothering him. They have to tell it in code. It cannot be straightforward. For truth is like a blinding light to one who is in darkness. They cannot open the door all the way, for you would go blind. Dreams crack the door and let in a little light, a little inkling.

We would suggest, my brother, that you begin a notebook, either on your computer or with a pad of paper and pen, and journal through an extended length of time about this one type of dream and, indeed, about the other two as well, building intelligence over a period of years, to find out the nuances and the intricacies. Dreams in a way are like a maze. When you reach the center, then the light dawns and you go, "Ah, okay, I see." But until that point you are going up into and back from many blind alleys.

We are reluctant, my brothers, to leave such delightful company. Yet the energy of this instrument wanes and the energy of the group as well, and so we take our leave of this instrument and this group, leaving each, as always, in the love and the light, the peace and power of the One. We are the principle of Q'uo, and we leave you in love and light. Adonai. Adonai. ♣

L/L Research

L/L Research is a subsidiary of Rock Creek Research & Development Laboratories, Inc.

P.O. Box 5195
Louisville, KY 40255-0195

www.llresearch.org

Rock Creek is a non-profit corporation dedicated to discovering and sharing information which may aid in the spiritual evolution of humankind.

ABOUT THE CONTENTS OF THIS TRANSCRIPT: This telepathic channeling has been taken from transcriptions of the weekly study and meditation meetings of the Rock Creek Research & Development Laboratories and L/L Research. It is offered in the hope that it may be useful to you. As the Confederation entities always make a point of saying, please use your discrimination and judgment in assessing this material. If something rings true to you, fine. If something does not resonate, please leave it behind, for neither we nor those of the Confederation would wish to be a stumbling block for any.

© 2009 L/L RESEARCH

SPECIAL MEDITATION
AUGUST 12, 2007

Mackinac Island Gathering

Group question: Q'uo, in light of the theme about our sun that has developed this weekend[66], we would like to know what our relationship is with our sun and how we as human beings on planet Earth may commune on a deeper level with our sun.

(Carla channeling)

We are those known to you as the principle of Q'uo. Greetings in the love and in the light of the one infinite Creator, in whose service we come to you this day. May we thank you with all our hearts for the privilege of being called to your circle of seeking and of being able to experience the beauty of each of your auras and of your combined auras, which make this place a beautiful temple of light. It is a privilege and a pleasure to be with you and to be able to offer our humble service to you, the sharing of information that you might find useful.

Please know that we are not authorities over you but fellow seekers who walk the path to our source and our ending. Take these words, therefore, not as things that you must hear or things that you must follow, but rather use your discrimination and take from what we have to say only those things that resonate with you. Leave the rest behind without a second thought. In this way we will feel free to offer our opinions without being concerned that we might interfere with your free will or skew and distort your process of seeking.

You wish at this time to know more about your relationships with your sun-body and how you can commune with that sun-body. We are most pleased to share our thoughts on this subject.

The one known as William[67] noted the pun between s-u-n and s-o-n. And we say to you that you are sons and daughters of the sun, just as the sun itself is the son and daughter of the one great original Thought, that Logos which is unconditional love.

The Logos is a distortion of the Law of One. The only thing that is not distorted in our understanding is a mystery. That mystery is the one infinite Creator. Beyond all potentiation, beyond all understanding, all that there is resides forever in that one original Creator, which is that from which all has sprung and to which all shall return.

The first distortion of the one infinite Creator is free will. And the play of free will across the mystery of the Creator created the desire for the Creator to know Itself.

---

[66] This channeling session closed the L/L Research Gathering on Mackinac Island, which took place on August 11-13, 2007. The two speeches which Carla L. Rueckert offered at this Gathering can be found in "Carla's Niche" under "Speeches" on our archive site, www.llresearch.org.

[67] William Henry offered two talks at the Mackinac Island Gathering. To look further into his material, go to his web site, www.williamhenry.net.

And this desire was embodied, if you will, in the one great original Thought, which is the second distortion of the Law of One. And that unconditional love, which is the very nature of the infinite Creator, birthed the mechanism and the way of manifestation of all illusion. For, you see, all except the mystery is some kind of illusion.

So all of that which seems real is the illusion and that which is the mystery is that which is real. You come, therefore, into the land of paradox and mystery. And then you know you are on the right track.

This third distortion of the Law of One is light, and light, in all of its gradations of circulation or rotation, has created all the orders of all the vibrations of all that is seen and unseen, from your point of view.

This Logos, manifesting through light, created out of Itself the suns in their galaxies. And each sun is a sub-logos, an undistorted portion of the one infinite Creator, yet each Logos was given the ability to make the tailoring details of its sub-creation of the one infinite Father. Therefore, your Logos has created for you a certain kind of environment for the growth of your spirit and for the collection of information to be offered again to the one infinite Creator, that It may know more about Itself.

It is well to note that this is a scheme in which all of your feelings, be they seemingly positive or seemingly negative, are equally valuable and precious to the one infinite Creator. Therefore, you are loved beyond all belief by an entity who could never judge you, but only support, encourage and embrace you.

The Logos of your sun, then, has further manifested in its creation the particles of the One. For each of you is a spark of the one Creator, and each of you has, in every cell of your body, the undistorted mystery of the One. Your wisdom lies deep within you. You do not have to reach for it. It will come into your consciousness as you are ready and as you ask. It helps a great deal in this process if you know, beyond a shadow of a doubt, again, as the one known as William has said, that you are in your integrity and can rest in your rightness to ask. All are worthy to ask and be answered.

Therefore, each of you is a piece of the One, sons and daughters and heirs of love, creatures of love. You came into this particular illusion having created for yourself, with the aid of your guidance system, your gifts, your challenges, and your relationships. You and your guidance together have planned the direction of your mission, both in terms of the mission of your being and the mission of your doing.

In terms of the mission of your doing, you have only to consult your gifts, or what this instrument would call your "skill set." Each of you has a cluster of gifts in a particular area. It may seem to be very humble and practical and down to earth. It may be mystical. It may be aesthetic. It may be creative. It may be as simple as the creation of a family. The creation of anything that can be created in this universe is equally worthy if it be created with love.

As this instrument was saying earlier to the one known as J, you are never to be identified with that which you do. Rather, you are love and you happen to be expressing or manifesting in the outer world with a particular kind of service for which, happily, you receive pay and with which you pay your bills.

Likewise, you cannot be contained by others' opinions, by the opinions of your culture, or by any other limitations whatever, for you are love and light. You are all that there is, and you are the sun of your creation. Let us expand upon this for a moment.

It may seem that you are quite a small part of a very large universe, and in the outer world, this is certainly so. As the one known as Don[68] has often said, you are sticking up from the surface of the planet like hair on a head, with your heads reaching towards the stars and your feet pointing toward the womb of the earth. You circle a very insignificant-looking sun, in terms of the brightness and size, at the outer part of a very small and undistinguished-looking galaxy that is part of billions and billions of other galaxies. In that scale of things, you are indeed small.

Yet, in the inner or metaphysical sense, you are the sun of your inner universe. You have created that universe and you can recreate it at any time. That which you judge remains judged. That which you love remains loved. In every thought, in every

---

[68] Here the Q'uo group refers to Donald T. Elkins, co-founder with Carla of L/L Research. Don passed into larger life in 1984.

circumstance, you are the Creator. That which you hold to be true is true.

Therefore, it is well to remain at all times attentive to that which is deepest within you; to that which is truest within you. And as you sense into the "I" of you, remember to ask for help in coming even more fully into the presence of the mystery that lies within you.

It is as if you are approaching, across a vast courtyard, the gateway to your open heart. That courtyard is littered with all of your beliefs and judgments. It is thickly littered with your senses of self: your unworthiness; your dislike of your shadow side; your desire not to know your shadow side. And so the journey into full communion with your own open heart, with that sun that lies within, consists at first of going about this courtyard, taking up the shadow side, the unworthiness, the thoughts and beliefs which limit your viewpoint.

They may seem to be like wild animals when first you take them up, for indeed you have powers within you that are very strong and seem ultimately negative. When they are not developed by the light within you, they may act out as murder, war, jealousy, anger, hatred, guilt, resentment and all the brothers and sisters of these energies.

Yet when you take these wild animals, these fearsome energies, into your arms and love them, that gets their attention. And when you have their attention, then you may speak to them tenderly and affectionately. For you must ask for their help. You must ask them to come into your heart and allow themselves to be redeemed by your sense of their worth and by your honor and respect for these dark energies within you.

And when they kneel before you, you take the sword of truth and you dub them your "white knights" of determination, grit and patience, so that you may endure all, bear all, persist through all, with love.

As you gaze out from yourself finally and see the clean courtyard, you know that you are ready to meet the lions at the gate of your open heart. Because there are lions there, my friends, who will not allow you into that sacred space, that holy of holies, that sanctum sanctorum, until you are whole.

It is not that you become perfect and then enter the open heart. You enter the open heart in all your dirt, just as you are. And yet the secret is to know that you are worthy, just as you are, and give honor to yourself, even within this illusion in which you seem to be quite unworthy in some ways. This surety and confidence is your strength and your salvation, and the lions then sense your readiness for the light within your own open heart and the love that lies waiting to embrace you.

The lions bow, the door opens, and you are finally home. What a joy it is to be home in your own open heart, at the center of your creation, where the lion and the lamb lie down together, where peace flows like a fountain, and where all upon which you look as blessed and being blessed, blesses you back. So love is reflected in love; so that all that you see is loved; so that all that you do is love.

As you open to this upwelling of love that is infinite and infinitely available, the ever self-sustaining resource of the one infinite Creator, you become that which is "I am that I am." And your small ego has melted away before that impersonal self that is at the heart of the personal self.

It may seem to you that there are impediments to becoming the "I am that I am" of what this instrument would call cosmic consciousness or Christ consciousness, and as long as you feel that there are impediments, so there are. Therefore, as you experience the feeling of being impeded it is well to rest in that awareness and to collect yourself to bear witness to this awareness, and to sit with it as if it were an honored guest.

What is it that impedes you this day? What thought has caused you to stop feeling as though you are the one infinite Creator in much shadowed form? Sit with this question until it begins to answer itself within you in whatever way it will. Experience to the fullest the energy of that blocked self. Was it impatience? Was it irritation? Was it the feeling of unworthiness? Was it the hesitation that comes from being confused? Whatever that momentary blockage is, first experience it and intensify it and then allow it to call forth its dynamic opposite.

If your stoppage was due to impatience, allow the feeling of patience to come over you. For it will, if you focus upon this dynamic. Once you have begun to experience that patience, then encourage it to intensify itself within you and to become all of your attention's span. And in that wise you may know true and undistorted patience.

Then allow the two dynamics to come together in everyday life, into the center of yourself, so that you have balanced this distortion within yourself.

It is well indeed if you can practice this on a daily basis. For even within a day you may lose the memory of your thoughts. And each of your thoughts is a creation, metaphysically speaking. This is difficult to understand in everyday life because, in the outer world, things and objects are what seem to be real, and thoughts are the lightening bugs and butterflies and moths and all those little beings that fly about. They are beautiful and they are worthy of their own kinds. And yet, should you take them seriously?

We say to you, yes, my friends, for in the metaphysical world, thoughts are things. What you think is what you create. The one known as G gave this instrument a story recently from Indian lore. It was the story of two wolves. One wolf was everything that was good, positive and beautiful. The other wolf was all that was dark, aggressive, violent and evil. The young man went to his father and said, "What should I do with these wolves? How shall I treat them?" And the father said, "Feed the one you wish to grow and let the other one pass away."[69]

Which wolf will you feed in your thoughts? One great secret to spiritual seeking is to remember which wolf to feed.

We sense that within this group there are many questions. And so we would ask if there is a follow-up question to this main question? We are those of Q'uo.

A: Yes. I have a question about the sun cult that has been in earlier times. Do we have any connection to this and to each other through that?

We are those of Q'uo, and are aware of your question, my sister. We may say without infringement upon free will that there are those among you who indeed do have that connection within the history of your planet Earth. However, in general, we would say that your connection to the sun is from your nature, as those who come from another sun and who have chosen to wander to this planet together. For each in this room is a portion of wanderers of sixth density who chose, in a time very early in the third-density cycle of planet Earth, to enter into incarnation upon planet Earth.

After the first 25,000 year minor cycle of your planetary third density, the Confederation of Planets in the Service of the One Infinite Creator became concerned, for the harvest was very small. And so, in excitement of heart, with great passion and absolute purity of intent, you dedicated yourselves to the travail of Earth. Brothers and Sisters of Sorrow, you responded to the sorrow of Earth, to its cry for light and love. And so you came, bravely, daringly, risking all, risking forgetting who you are, in the hope that you could become those who aided in the lightening of the consciousness of planet Earth.

My friends, you have been about that business for a very long time. And mayhap you have become weary with the labor of Earth. But we say to you to take heart and to know that you have made a difference in a positive sense. And that you shall, as you are activated by such meetings as these, wind up your certainty and courage, that you may go forth ever more firmly, seated in the saddle of your great steed of faith, in your armor of light, with your ribbons dancing in the wind from the lance of your truth. You may joust with some unlikely people, mounted on some shabby, shabby horses as you go through the lists of this tournament of service to others!

There may be many, many times when the chinks in your armor of light are intensified by the natural resistance of what this instrument calls the "loyal opposition." And you may experience difficulties and dark nights. Yet, my friends, is not each dawn a new day? It is indeed. As you awaken on each new day, know that it is a new universe, a new world, and a completely new beginning. Nothing is ever old to those who are awake to love. Everything is new now.

---

[69] The story, in its original form, seen here, is not credited to a source. The text is:

An old Cherokee was teaching his grandson about life. "A fight is going on inside me," he said to the boy. "It is a terrible fight and it is between two wolves. One is evil. He is anger, envy, sorrow, regret, greed, arrogance, self-pity, guilt, resentment, inferiority, lies, false pride, superiority and ego. The other is good. He is joy, peace, love, hope, serenity, humanity, kindness, benevolence, empathy, generosity, truth, compassion and faith. The same fight is going on inside you, and inside every other person too."

The grandson thought about it for a minute and asked the grandfather, "Which wolf will win?"

The old Cherokee simply replied, "The one you feed."

Each of you is wondering! As we listened while you talked around the circle, we heard you say, "What is next? What shall I do now?"

My friends, the operant word is "now." It is not next. It is now. What you shall do now is what is upon your heart. And if, as far as you know, there is nothing upon your heart except love, then let it be. You are now ready for that which comes next in your illusion.

Nor are you responsible in any way for that which comes to you as catalyst. It is not that you draw good catalyst, or poor catalyst, or difficult catalyst by some measurement of deserving or merit. Certainly, that which you are thinking or doing creates the nexus from which more things come to you. As you think, so do you draw things to you. Yet, in that moment in which catalyst occurs to you, you are not responsible for that which comes in. The area of your responsibility is to that which is evoked or elicited by the catalyst. Therefore, you, as creators, are responsible for your responses to catalyst.

What shall be your responses this day to the thoughts you think, to the people you meet, and to the situations which you address? That is your area of creativity. It is a good thing to focus upon the fact that you are all creative. How can a creator not be creative? Therefore, create your creation consciously and do not be dismayed that the outer world does not seem to reflect your creation.

In the world of spirit, in the time/space universe, you are the citizens of eternity, even while within the world of space/time and incarnation. That which you create is powerful. And as you understand that, you can link up with those who are of like mind. Even at great distances you can continue to create light.

This instrument was speaking earlier in this weekend of being instruments, receivers and emitters of vibration. And so you are in the unseen realms. And we encourage you to think of yourselves as lighthouses. It is said in your holy work, "Do not hide your light under a bushel but place it on a lamp stand where all may see it."[70]

Do you feel merely like a candle of light in the midst of all the darkness of the outer world? Then, my friends, know that a candle can be seen a mile away. Just one candle can be a beacon of light to those far off. Those to whom you are a source of light know only that they like to be near you, yet as they absorb the radiation of your love, they themselves are activated to be beacons themselves. And so you pass it on and infect others, who in turn infect others, until the world at last is aflame, united, harmonious and complete.

Shall this happen before the harvest is completely white? We do not know, for it is up to you to be as purely a flame of love as you know how to be. However, look not to the outer things for knowledge of your success. Rather, look to your intentions, your dreams, and your ideals and create them ever firmer, ever truer, ever sturdier. These are the measures of the ability to create changes in the consciousness of your planetary sphere.

Therefore, the most important work that you can ever do is done within yourself, for as you heal, strengthen and arm yourself with love and light, so you change your entire world.

We thank the one known as A for this query and would ask if there is another question at this time? We are those of Q'uo.

J: Yes, I would like to ask about buffeted feelings a little more. How do we get through them? When you're sitting in it, you're still in the negative and these feelings can be very overwhelming. Sometimes you can just get exhausted by them. The issue is how to let them go more fully. I know you say to hold them in your heart and then to intensify them and then to think the opposite. But sometimes it is hard to think the opposite when you don't have that in your head. Would listening to positive subliminal tapes be something worthwhile? I know it's not so much a matter of doing-ness as being-ness and feeling comfortable in your own skin, but I feel like still there's a piece missing. Something is not hitting me right. Maybe you can see something that I can't see.

We are those of Q'uo, and, my sister, we see many things that you do not see. However, we cannot see what you see, so it all balances out.

---

[70] *Holy Bible*, Matthew 5:14-16: "Ye are the light of the world. A city that is set on a hill cannot be hid. Neither do men light a candle, and put it under a bushel, but upon a candlestick, and it giveth light unto all that are in the house. Let your light so shine before men that they may see your good works, and glorify your Father, which is in heaven."

We would offer to you the concept of the "trouble bubble." Troubles arise and they form a bubble, an energy field. Then the bubble is popped and it is no more. You are here to create the trouble bubbles and to wait for them to pop. You cannot pop them, precisely. What you do, if you are skillful, is to become patient, for there are some trouble bubbles with a very thick skin and some with a very thin skin, and who can say in what moment epiphany may create the pin to pop that bubble?

Therefore, you do not think the dynamic opposite of that which you have intensified within you when you realize that you are in the middle of a trouble bubble, or a distortion which you consider part of your shadow side. As it was said so beautifully when the one known as Neo, in the movie "The Matrix" held the spoon in his hand, the one known as Morpheus said, "You can't bend the spoon. That's impossible. All you can do is know that there is no spoon."

Know that there is no trouble bubble, but that you have been given the illusion of a trouble bubble within this system of illusions for a reason. It is a worthy reason even if it makes you vastly uncomfortable. It is part of your seeking process and therefore you call upon that great friend of the spiritual seeker, patience, for it may take a great deal of your time for that dynamic to clear, especially when the dynamic has not been created by blocking the energy by constriction but rather by activation.

It takes longer for that kind of energy blockage to relax and be unconstricted than when there is a fear or a lack that is holding you back, for there are many unwise passions that can constrict the energy that needs to come through your energy body in order for you fully to enjoy being a child of the one infinite Creator and co-heir through hope of all that there is.

Therefore, we encourage you to cultivate the habit of deep patience. Allow peace and confidence to rest upon that process of response or "dynamic response," shall we say. If it does not happen in the time that you have, one day revisit it and ask again, then retain this concern until you are fully satisfied that you have penetrated the meniscus that lies between the first dynamic and the opposite.

It may take a while to penetrate in a satisfactory and full manner certain distortions of mind. But, my sister, you have literally all the time in the world. So remove from your mind any urgency or any desire to see yourself improve. For that is indeed judging yourself.

You are already perfect. Rest in that perfection, knowing that there is little hope of your seeing yourself able to manifest the perfection within, but also knowing that you are on the road to that perfect self, and therefore, through faith in things unseen, you are as good as there, metaphysically speaking.

This cleanses and clears your energy field so that you are not caught up in the process of spiritual evolution but rather are at rest in the saddle as you and your lance of truth ride along the dusty road. This instrument calls that road "The King's Highway," for within her distortion of worship that King's Highway is the way towards her icon of unconditional love.[71]

Indeed, you are all sons and daughters of the King and you are going home to meet your father once again. And we, with you, are on that road and ride with you, glad of your company.

We thank the one known as J for this question and would ask if there is a final query at this time?

J: Regarding ultraviolet and infrared rays of the sun, I understand that some energies from the sun, say gamma rays and x-rays, are harmful. And I understand that UV in some cases is said to be harmful and sometimes not. I feel that there isn't enough information out there about UV and maybe the benefits of it. Is it worthy to accumulate UV into the body? Is there a spiritual, physical, emotional or mental aspect to that? Can you change the DNA in your genes with this UV or even infrared?

We are those of Q'uo, and we are aware of your query, my sister. There are parts of your query which we cannot answer due to the fact that this is part of your active spiritual process at this time and it would be a gross infringement of your free will to do your learning for you. We leave you the joy of your exploration in this wise.

---

[71] This phrase is from a poem written by E. A. Cummins in 1922. It was set to music by A. G. H. Bode in 1941 and is a hymn in the Episcopal Hymnal. It reads, in part, "I know not where the road will lead I follow day by day, or where it ends; I only know I walk the King's Highway. The way is truth, the way is love. For light and strength I pray. And through the years of life, to God, I walk the King's Highway. Through light and dark the road leads on 'til dawns the endless day, when I shall know why, in this life, I walk the King's Highway."

However, we may respond to your concerns about the need for balancing the self as it receives what you may consider toxic levels of certain vibrations.

We would encourage you to investigate the work of the one known as Rudolph, and especially in his exercises to balance in a dynamic way the body complex. This instrument knows this Anthroposophical type of exercise as the "olorono" exercise[72]. It is a series of simple movements that anyone can do who can walk. This instrument, being of fragile body, can still do these exercises, and so can most upon your planet.

They are a simple series of exercises in which you are creating for yourself more of a 360-degree vision and more of a complete balance of the body, and therefore of body, mind and spirit. In the process of doing these exercises daily you shall find that whatever is in excess within your body complex is released and whatever is deficient in your body complex is restored.

This entity, the one known as Rudolph, was very clear, in many ways, about this particular concern, although you will find that you must gaze at that which he said with an eye to the heart of what he was manifesting in his writing as opposed to the literal meaning of words. We leave you the joy of this exploration.

You spoke about DNA. In terms of spiritual principles we say to you that the DNA for third density is as it is. And yet you may change your DNA, as some of you are quite sure and aware at this time, by the way you think and by the way you manifest your thoughts so that you bring forth into third density higher densities of awareness.

Those of you who wish to live into fourth density positive upon this planet, which shall soon completely be descended, not only interpenetrating third density but taking over third density completely, may live as though you were in fourth density now. It is as simple and as nearly impossible as that. But you can penetrate that mystery of love. You can change your DNA so that you create four and then eight and then twelve and then up to twenty-four spirals of DNA. And eventually, as you do create the differences in every cell of your body, you shall, more and more, walk the universe freely.

A: I have one last question. It's about 2012. Would it be an infringement on our free will to say something, here and now, about what the actual process of this work or this change will be?

We are those of Q'uo, and are aware of your query, my sister. However, at this time, both the energy and your time grows, in the one case weary, and in the other case short. And so we would at this time apologize for not being able to move further on this point.

However, my sister, there have been many, many questions to our particular awareness group in the last few years concerning this very subject, and this gives us the happy opportunity to offer to you those things which we have said in the past.

Further, we are certain that if you are to write down on paper or by e-mail this very question, this instrument will be able to address it at a future time, for this instrument's group seeks regularly to contact us in circles such as this one and at a future time in your way of reckoning, we may finally address your query.

We apologize for our rudeness at this time, but it is better to rest the channel and for you to go about your daily business than to answer one more query at this time.

We are those of Q'uo, and we thank you, my brothers and sisters. We leave this instrument and this group in the love and the light, the peace and the power of the one infinite Creator. We are those of Q'uo. Adonai. Adonai. ☥

---

[72] Rudolph Steiner created a body of teachings called Anthroposophy which was quite in harmony with the Law of One teachings. He posited that all of creation is unified. The O*L*O*R*O*N*O exercises are part of his teachings called Eurhythmy. A good web site to seek for further information is www.rsarchive.org/Eurhythmy/.

L/L Research

L/L Research is a subsidiary of Rock Creek Research & Development Laboratories, Inc.

P.O. Box 5195
Louisville, KY 40255-0195

www.llresearch.org

Rock Creek is a non-profit corporation dedicated to discovering and sharing information which may aid in the spiritual evolution of humankind.

ABOUT THE CONTENTS OF THIS TRANSCRIPT: This telepathic channeling has been taken from transcriptions of the weekly study and meditation meetings of the Rock Creek Research & Development Laboratories and L/L Research. It is offered in the hope that it may be useful to you. As the Confederation entities always make a point of saying, please use your discrimination and judgment in assessing this material. If something rings true to you, fine. If something does not resonate, please leave it behind, for neither we nor those of the Confederation would wish to be a stumbling block for any.

© 2009 L/L Research

Sunday Meditation, Homecoming 2007
September 2, 2007

Group question: The question today, Q'uo, has to do with channeling. We have a group of people who would like to learn how to channel in order to be of service to others, starting next year when Carla initiates a channeling circle. They have some concerns about the dangers of channeling, about one's will being affected by a strong channeling source, and about getting holes in one's aura. Are there some spiritual principles which you could share with us that would help those who wish to channel to protect themselves and to be of service to others in this endeavor?

(Carla channeling)

We are those known to you as the principle of Q'uo. Greetings in the love and in the light of the one infinite Creator, in whose service we come to you this day, in humility and gratitude that you have invited us to join your circle of seeking. Thank you for the beauty that you have allowed us to behold in your individual energy bodies and in the beautiful blending and harmonization of auras that has created this sacred space of towering and majestic grandeur.

As always, before we address your good question, we would ask that each of you listen to what we have to say with a discriminating ear, being aware of the path of resonance in your own seeking. Some of what we have to say may hit the mark and some of it may not. If we do not hit that mark for you, please leave our thoughts behind and pick up the ones that have resonated to you, for they are our gift to you, to give you resources and tools with which to work in accelerating the pace of your evolution of mind, body and spirit.

We would thank you for being discriminating and careful in that which you take in, for we would not be a stumbling block upon your path but only a voice upon the wind that may be of service at this time.

We have watched with interest as this instrument has gone about the process of choosing to offer a channeling circle once again. We find it interesting that the alarm bells are ringing on an emergency vehicle in the vicinity of this house[73] as we take up the question of whether or not there are dangers involved in introducing yourself and your personality shell to the service of channeling thoughts from entities such as we.

On one level the answer is unknown, for events fall according to a rhythm that cannot be known ahead of time. However, we may speak in generalities and say that it would be an extremely rare event, and indeed one that has not occurred in the experience of this instrument, that entities working within a channeling circle were vulnerable to any physical, mental or emotional danger at all.

This instrument has always been faithful in creating channeling circles which adhere to our requests and

---

[73] An ambulance drove by as we began this session.

those of our Brothers and Sisters of Sorrow in other portions of the Confederation of Planets in the Service of the One Infinite Creator.

Thank you also for asking about the spiritual principles involved in considering this question. So often, we receive questions that do not have that sheathing of spiritual inquiry, so that the energy of the question itself moves from a place of fear. When we encounter such a query, there is very little information which we can give without infringing upon the free will of that entity who has asked for specific information from a place of fear.

In those cases, we cannot offer specific information. However even the most specific question, when sheathed with this garment of the request for spiritual principles, becomes a question that is grateful to our treatment. And thus we are able to speak on this subject.

This instrument was saying, in the course of this weekend of fellowship and study, that the energy of the channeling is one which is carried into the channeling circle by means of the tuning of each of the circle of channels. So let us discuss somewhat this concept of tuning and what it is that you are tuning as you tune your instruments.

All entities within third density are instruments. Each of you takes the breath of life and, breathing it into your physical body, you expel it, shaping words that create energies that bind and repel each other with your thoughts. Certainly words are limited in that which they can convey information in a rational or mental way bound by the definitions of the words used, their origins, and their implications within entities' minds as they hear the words themselves.

However, as instruments you have a means of sharing the vibrations of your feelings and the love in your heart, even if you are simply asking to pass the salt or offering a greeting to an acquaintance on the street. By your awareness and remembrance of who you are, you may utter the most commonplace words and yet send them forth with the blessing of your heart's love and the deepest compassion of your soul. There is no limit whatsoever upon how intense and pure a vibration of love that you may inject into your simplest communication. You are instruments.

This instrument reminds us of a story told by an actress named Anne[74] concerning her husband, Mel. He touched her in a way she felt was rough and she said, "My body is my instrument!" And he said, "Could you play me a few bars?" You are playing your song and broadcasting the state of your spirit, that essence that would always escape any words, each time that you open your mouths.

Consequently, you do not have to pull in our vibration or the vibration of an entity not within your conscious awareness in order to be instruments and in order to practice being instruments that are ever truer of pitch, ever more mellifluous of tone, and ever more pure in that which goes into the production of tone.

Sometimes we realize that instructions such as these to become aware of your thinking and your thoughts and how they are translated into words may cause you to become self-conscious and be unable to be spontaneous. We do not intend this effect. We do say that the great spiritual principle involved in becoming a better channel is to be comfortable within your own skin, in the knowledge that all is well.

When an entity whose heart is full of faith speaks, there is the brush of angel wings. Those listening to such a voice may simply say, "Oh, you have a musical voice," or "Your voice has such soul or timbre." Yet we say to you that that brush of angel wings carries through into the voices of those who remember who they are and rest in that essence, knowing that all is prepared. There is no need to reach or to pull back, but simply to follow that path of resonance as you move from day to day.

You do not know what may be asked of you in the future. You do not know what shoes you will grow into. And yet you have inklings and hints that come to you, saying, "Yes, you have a mission. Yes, you can perform this function." And eventually you learn to trust that brush of angel wings, that inkling from spirit, that moment of fire as the descending dove brings truth and insight into the inner heart to take root and to grow there.

As we continue to speak about being instruments, please realize that if you are not interested in joining this channeling circle, yet still our words are equally

---

[74] Anne Bancroft and Mel Brooks are the couple to which the instrument refers.

appropriate. For all are equally instruments of the one infinite Creator. We cannot say that often enough in preparing entities to channel.

There is our understanding of that great spiritual principle of unity. From that principle of unity stems long lines of logic and insight which end up suggesting that you are precisely where you need to be at this time. You shall continue to be in an excellent state in which to serve, no matter what the outer picture may appear to be. Thusly, the appropriate attitude towards this service, as you enter the beginning precincts of learning that art of translation which is called channeling, is that you are perfect beings, in the right place and at the right time. All striving may cease. All feelings that one should be "better" in order to channel may cease.

We are aware of how you see yourselves in the foreshortened lenses of personality. You do not necessarily give yourselves credit for your grace and courage as you follow your impossible dreams. You see only the suffering, the seeming lack of success, and the feeling of unworthiness to bear so magnificent a burden as the cloak of Christhood. You ask yourself, "How could I presume to be an instrument of sacred revelation?"

And we ask you in turn, "Do you imagine that you are more error-prone than any other entity upon your planet?" We are not looking for the perfect person, whether by our estimate or your own. We look for the vibration of your instrument. There are some entities that are not vibrating within the range of vibratory energies with which we may interact. With those entities we will never be able to establish a contact. Therefore, allow yourself to be your true self as you come to thinking about yourself as a channel. For it is your true self upon which you must build—not an idealized version of yourself, not a self in Sunday best, with hat and gloves, as this instrument would say. The self that you are in your shorts and your tee is adequate to this task.

This instrument has talked to this group about the dangers inherent in opening a channel to outside energies such as we. And so we would speak about this to a certain extent.

Each of you is, as we said, a crystal, an instrument capable of receiving light, transducing[75] light, and emitting light. In the metaphysical world, light is information. Indeed, your computer scientists shall agree readily that light is information, for it is light that is used to produce the information that your computers manipulate. Just so, you are a receiver, a transducer, and a broadcaster or radiator of light.

The crystal that you are may be tuned. As a new instrument begins to try its wings, shall we say, it quickly becomes familiar with the feeling of that particular contact which it has been able to receive. The danger lies in assuming that because an energy coming in feels right, that this energy is necessarily the energy which you wish to receive. This is why this instrument's use of the challenging process is effective. And it is that which we shall discuss with those who wish to learn to be instruments for us in some depth and detail.

Suffice it to say that when an instrument challenges a spirit in the name of its most dearly held principle, that principle which is the fulcrum of that entity's life, that negative spirit who is able to use the same love and light of the infinite Creator as the positive source, and therefore is able to feel the same as the positive source, cannot succeed in remaining within the aura of the channel.

Challenge in the name of love. An entity who does not vibrate in love must leave. It may seem that this is a very wispy and insubstantial thing to trust and to rely upon, and yet we say to you that all of that which is involved in being an instrument will be likewise wispy and insubstantial from the viewpoint of consensus reality. For your scientists have not yet created instrumentation to measure the vibrations that are used in channeling. Were they able to have that instrumentation, there would be a much more scientific and therefore trustable way for people who trust science to understand channeling.

In the absence of such instrumentation, we can only say that as you tune, you are tuning past the radio channels that are not those channels which you wish to receive, and when you have tuned yourself to the highest and best that is within you, when you have crystallized that, and when you have opened to channel, then you may stand firmly upon metaphysical ground in challenging spirits who may wish to speak through you.

It is to be noted that this instrument does not ever seek to channel outer sources without a supporting group. It is further to be noted that this instrument

---

[75] To transduce means to convert energy from one form into another, according to www.dictionary.com.

has been channeling for thirty-three years, and that no harm has ever come to this instrument. The safety net, for balancing and regularizing the energies involved in channeling outer sources such as we, is the principle of batteries in series. One battery is not enough to sustain a universal contact such as ours. There needs to be a minimum of two batteries in series linked to the third battery in series which is the instrument itself.

To a certain extent, the more batteries you have in series, the more energy that can be developed and the more powerful a signal the channel itself may pull in. However, as you expand the number of your group, if you are not careful to preserve the unified quality of your common attitudes of mind and your common desires of heart, you will find that you are actually weakening the battery system.

Some large groups such as this one are magnificent batteries. The vibrations that you have, in your unity and harmony, put forth unknowingly throughout this weekend, have had a tremendous impact upon the grid of incoming fourth density. It has gratefully wound itself about those beautiful vibrations which your mingled auras have produced, and it has woven those strands into the web of love and light that is ever stronger upon your planet.

Another principle that is involved in becoming a good channel is the emptying of one's pockets of those artifacts of ego which, as a group, can call themselves pride. Intellect does not make a great channel. Sophistication does not make a great channel. Knowledge and learning do not make a great channel.

What makes a great channel is a humility that partakes neither of pride nor lack of self-worth. What makes a great channel is that dedication to service that lasts not just today or next year, but every heartbeat until you pass from this illusion into larger life. What makes a great channel is the patience that allows one to wait.

You may have noticed that there are significant pauses as we speak through this channel today. There is, in most entities within your hurried culture, the urge to finish each other's sentences if the other person pauses too long. There is the urge to get on with the conversation or the problem-solving that is being discussed. Yet, there are very subtle and layered forces involved in channeling the best that we can through instruments that are doing the best that they can. And, oftentimes, what is being transmitted through those periods of silence is more necessary for the channel to experience, and more necessary for the circle of seeking to experience, than our words.

Certainly there are times when we say, "We will now have a guided meditation." And then we pause, after setting up an image or a word for you to contemplate. And then the silence does not make you nervous. Yet in channeling, an instrument must be willing to rest.

In music there is a rest symbol, and then there is something called a "grand pause"—it looks like a little bird's eye, usually with a "GP" next to it in the music manuscript. At that point, the song that has been sung by the person or chorus or the choir finishes its phrase, and there is an echo reverberating out into the sacred space in which that song has been sung. Then the grand pause is allowed to allow the last chord to reverberate and die away. And if one is using an instrument such as an organ, before the next word or musical phrase there may need to be stops changed on the organ so that there is a different energy to the accompaniment of the sound of the song, and that too takes time.

When we stop giving her concepts, this instrument does not know when she will receive the next one. Consequently, she has learned to have perfect patience. The art of perfect patience is long in coming for this instrument. And indeed she does not feel that she has perfected it yet. Yet we would say that because of the repetition of her service over many years, she has become undismayed even if our silence lasts two or three minutes—and sometimes it does. The silence is part of the channeling.

This is a subtle and delicate art in which to immerse oneself. We believe that it is a service that is worthwhile. We would not be here if we did not believe this with a passion that is as deep as the roots of our hearts. As far as we know this is one of the most effective ways to insert ideas into the data stream of your people that may be helpful for the acceleration of spiritual evolution.

We know, beyond a shadow of a doubt, that we say nothing new through this or any other instrument. Truly, it has been said, "There is nothing new under the sun."[76] Yet the eternal wisdom of underlying truth is such a simple story that it escapes rational comprehension. How can you internalize the unity of yourself and all beings? How can you internalize the paradox of seeming imperfection and ultimate worth?

In your workaday state of mind, perhaps you cannot. Yet we call all those who wish to improve themselves as instruments to the gradual realization of who they are, for each of you is an instrument. Each of you came here to receive, to bless, and to radiate the one infinite Creator's love.

Each of you came here to accept in full, heartfelt peace the love offerings of others. For we say to you that, as an instrument, you shall need to be able to hear flattering things and simply say, "Thank you." You need to know that you have no responsibility to be a "special" person, only to be yourself, for yourself is entirely adequate and perfect. In fact, as you form your desire to be an instrument, so we match our message to your instrument.

Lastly, perhaps we would say that there is a principle involved in channeling which is acceptance of that which is given. The human that each of you is has a tremendous backlog of life experiences. You have formed many excellent opinions in your time and you have, in the past, perhaps been very effective in offering such opinions to others in times of need.

When questions come to you [as a channel] about which you already have an opinion, it is necessary for you to lay aside that opinion, for that question did not come to you as a human being. That question came to you to be heard by a source which is going to respond through you, not from you. It is an art in itself to lay aside human opinion and to be content with whatever comes through your instrument in that moment.

We would ask at this time if there is another query from this group on this particular question, in order that we may refine this question before we move on to other questions which may be within this group. Is there a follow up to this query at this time? We are those of Q'uo.

---

[76] The *Holy Bible*, Ecclesiastes 1:9-10: "The thing that hath been, it is that which shall be; and that which is done is that which shall be done: and there is no new thing under the sun. Is there anything whereof it may be said, 'See, this is new'? It hath been already of old time, which was before us."

Questioner: Yes, I have one. Is it stressful on the physical body to channel?

We are those of Q'uo, and are aware of your query, my sister. The channeling that we offer through this instrument is of a type in which there is no stress at all upon the physical body, unless the entity who is offering itself as instrument becomes apprehensive and, by its apprehension, would have the normal, human, bodily reactions such as, perhaps, a heightened pulse or heightened blood pressure.

The nervousness involved in being a channel moves through fairly quickly in the learning process of the channeling, so that we would say that there is little to no stress involved in this type of conscious channeling of Confederation sources. We do not attempt to move your tuning to a deeper level, or to move you into trance, as this instrument would say. We are perfectly content with your instrument as you offer it to us. Therefore there is no added stress from the external vibrations of our sending through your instrument.

Further, the battery power of a group, working as a circle and aware of the blending of energies and leaning into that blending with visualization and perfect acceptance, creates a strong additional vibratory stability to the energies both being received and being put out by the various channels in the group.

This instrument has often remarked that when there is a good group sitting, the session of working leaves her feeling not worse, not less energetic, but better and more energetic. This is because the combined energies of a group, working harmoniously, act like the bread and the fishes in the feeding of the 5000, where a few crumbs of bread and a few pieces of fish, broken and shared, create a plenty for all.

There is tremendous strength in moving beyond the solitary vibration of your own aura and having a fearless connection with other auras. Each of you is a powerful light. You would be surprised, indeed, at just what infinite power you hold within the folds of your everyday thoughts. Yet, together, you are exponentially more powerful.

The energies of love always blend well with those who attempt to channel in service to others. Once they have checked their egos at the door, there is a sacred space created by the channeling circle which promotes the rebalancing of health and emotional stability while the channeling is ongoing, so that each of you is receiving the gifts of each others' auras.

Everyone has unique strengths. And those strengths and gifts are those which you pass around the circle. Certainly, each of you passes around those things which you may not consider strengths or gifts. And yet in that sacred space of a channeling circle, those are seen as harmonics that add to the beauty and the timbre of the gifts that you offer each other. Consequently, generally speaking, entities will rise from the channeling circle experience feeling very well indeed, perhaps better than they felt when they began the working.

May we answer you further, my sister?

Questioner: That's all. That was an excellent answer. Thank you.

We thank you, my sister. Is there another follow-up now to that main query to which we just responded? We are those of Q'uo.

Questioner: Yes. The art of channeling, whether it be trance channeling or conscious channeling, has been, as I have understood and seen in my own life, of tremendous benefit. And it has seemed to have progressed, over the last hundred years, to where there are more channelings, especially over the last thirty or forty years. As we are leaving, very soon now, the Piscean Age and moving into the Aquarian Age, do you foresee any noticeable change in the effectiveness of how this particular medium of information transfer might change, moving with Mother Earth into this early fourth density, say up to the next forty, fifty or one hundred years?

We are those of Q'uo, and are aware of your query, my brother. We would agree with you that there has been an up-swelling of awareness of the channeling process within your culture during these past few decades. However, we would offer you the concept that there has never been a time in third density when this process was not ongoing. In other ages, such channeling was considered to be the product of prophets, oracles, seers or fortune tellers. The way entities frame their channeling efforts is heavily dependent upon the surrounding culture. It would be our suggestion that there has been a significant and substantial amount of information offered from sources such as we, as well as from many inner plane sources since the beginning of your density.

The experience upon your third-density world of the channeling process is likely not to change beyond the limits of the changes inherent in those who are progressively born with thinner veils and more of an ability to process subconscious material in a conscious fashion. This means that in days to come, channels may have a more successful time accurately rendering concepts that may be novel to the thought processes of the surrounding culture.

Indeed, we have found, as this instrument has worked with us through the years, that we are far more able to introduce novel concepts through her; that is, those concepts of which she has not yet thought. However, as long as the third-density population of this planet endures there will not be a sea change[77] in the way this particular gift is offered.

Let us speak to some extent about this question of how fourth density comes to planet Earth. It is difficult to imagine something that one has never seen. The closest we can come to explaining fourth-density Earth versus third-density Earth to you is that each density is an illusion. These illusions are nested within the energy field of your planet. Therefore, the second-density Earth is visible to you, as is the first-density Earth, because it would not disturb you to see such as those densities. And, of course, you see your own density.

It would be very dislocating, my brother, for entities of third density to see the full panoply of fourth density as it intersperses with your own. Therefore, there shall not be the manifestation of fourth density until the third-density population of your planet has finished its work here.

It is very difficult for entities to imagine how such a large population, all across your globe, could just shrink and disappear. And yet we say to you that entities moving into incarnation here will more and more be those which are dual-activated until finally, within say one of your centuries by most probability/possibility vortices, you will have no pure third-density entities living upon your planet.

Those with dual-activated bodies are far more able to see whether or not there is the necessity for further incarnations upon this planet. They will begin naturally to refrain from producing children. And

---

[77] A sea change is defined in www.dictionary.com as a striking change, as in appearance, often for the better, or any major transformation or alteration.

so, by a fairly rapid progression after that point, the third-density population of the planet will indeed shrink in a natural and organic way, because there is the awareness that the dusk has come, the evening is at hand, and the work is done.

Those coming to the planet now, more and more, are not interested as much in working with the people of the planet to bring them to their metaphysical graduation as they are interested in balancing the somewhat frayed and tattered garment of earth which your planet wears. There is a great need among your many planetary populations to offer restitution of a planet-wide nature. This is because so many of your population are made up of those who have done damage to their planets in the past and who, because they have not been able to break their habits of seeing the Earth as something to be exploited, have again repeated that tendency to do damage.

Therefore, there is the desire to balance all remaining planet-wide karma by doing such humble things as restoring the quality of the soil, restoring the quality of the air, restoring the quality of the water and finding how to live in such a way that, in every facet of your common life, it is understood that you, your planet and all that lives upon it are dancing one dance together to the glory of the one infinite Creator.

May we answer you further, my brother?

Questioner: Yes, please, but not on that particular subject. You mentioned earlier that there were those of us—and I'm not going to assume whether you were speaking specifically of this circle, or planet-wide or third-density wide—who never will be contacted by anyone of the Confederation, because they fall outside of your vibrations. Can you expand on that a little more as it concerns this group, please?

We are those of Q'uo, and believe we are aware of your query, my brother. There is a very wide variety of radio stations on the air and when you turn on your radio in your car or your home, you may tune from talk radio to classical radio, to your National Public Radio, to rock music, to jazz, to hip hop, to cool jazz, and to all the different genres of music and thought. Similarly, entities upon the planet have a personal characteristic tuning that is as wide in the spectrum of possibilities of those choices we just mentioned.

Because you wish to become channels for the Confederation, you have already created the vibratory levels which we need in order to communicate with you. It is a matter of "like attracts like." Were you not compatible with our vibrations you would not have responded to previous channeling from our sources through this instrument and perhaps other instruments that you may have heard which also bear the mark of this particular type of channeling, that this instrument calls "Confederation channeling."

There are some channeling sources that do not choose to identify themselves as Confederation sources, for instance, those sources which have "channeled through" that body of channeling which this instrument calls *Handbook for the New Paradigm*.[78] Those channels are indeed Confederation sources, yet, because they did not wish to color their channeling even with the identification of a name, such as Q'uo, they have not expressed themselves in that wise. Yet they are vibrating within that Confederation range of energies or vibrations. Therefore, you have already sorted yourselves out and begun to choose the radio station you want and it is radio station Q'uo, or another Confederation source that may fit your needs better.

May we answer you further, my brother? We are those of Q'uo.

Question: One last question—it's a silly question but something that I would like to know. The Confederation of Planets in the Service of the One Infinite Creator, the anagram for that: COPISOTIC. Is there anyone of the Confederation who is offended in any way, shape or form, by that particular thought?

We are those of Q'uo, my brother, and we find that thought copasetic.

(Laughter)

Questioner: Thank you very much.

We thank you, my brother. We are those of Q'uo, and we would ask if there is another query at this time.

---

[78] This book is available on line at www.nomorehoaxes.com. If a reader desires a free copy of this excellent little book, they may request one by writing info@nohoax.com.

Questioner: Yes. In helping to restore the planet, how can we better learn to work with the plant devas and the nature spirits?

We are those of Q'uo, and are aware of your query, my sister. As the energy wanes we find that we cannot offer you the length of answer that this question deserves and would simply say that the devas are already working with you. Their hearts are sore indeed because humans do not see them and feel them and work with them. There is joy that leaps from every tree and bush when humans finally know that those trees and bushes are living entities.

Therefore, we may say simply that as you enter into knowing the reality of these plant spirits, the connections will begin to deepen and your relationship with them shall bloom.

Is there a final query at this time? We are those of Q'uo.

Questioner: Yes, Q'uo. We are attempting to create a group of channelers under the tutelage of an experienced channeler. We are also aware of a large body of work that has been brought through, through this channel. Is there any concern that should be had about expectations of style from that particular channel coloring the channels that are being created?

We are those of Q'uo, and believe we understand your query, my brother. It is inevitable and benign that new channels shall express or translate the concepts given to them in the same way that they have heard the more experienced channel offer those same types of concepts. Indeed, this tradition, shall we say, of a channeling sounding somewhat different that human speech is venerable, for indeed, the prophets of old also spoke in somewhat different style than in their speaking style. And this has been carried down, not simply through centuries, but through millennia of your time. This instrument's formal and somewhat archaic usage is an echo of channeling style, shall we say, or prophetic style that has endured through the ages.

It is more an artifact of the kind of energy that is being accessed than it has to do with the vocabulary and the style of speaking of the channel in daily life. There is a dignity and a feeling of sacredness which surrounds the channeling experience. There is the laying aside of one's whole being in service to the one infinite Creator and the awareness that in that moment, the words that you need to say shall be given to you. And as those words come through, they resonate and feel sacred. And so as the new channel translates into words those concepts received, there is a natural tendency to offer that slightly heightened style that is lifted from the ordinary by that dignity of serving as an instrument for thoughts that are intended to aid in the development of humankind.

There is that awareness that something special is occurring and that human need to offer energy to making that feeling be part of the channeling. We find all of this to be benign. It is to be noted that, indeed, this channel still has a good deal of those artifacts of channeling those phrases and styles that she learned from that senior channel that taught her. However, in the course of many years of channeling, there has been a refinement and perhaps a standardization of her own style so that she naturally repeats many phrases again and again.

As new channels become experienced channels and naturally move beyond their teachers, they too will begin to find their own style, which may include many elements of the style they learned from their teacher but shall inevitably include increasing amounts of novel phrasing and preferred ways of addressing things in certain situations, based upon the natural personality and character of that particular channel.

We would not say from our standpoint that there is a problem with the new channel repeating the style of the experienced channel. Rather, we would say that the difficulty would lie in the new channel's being content to produce what seems to be something that they would know in their human opinion.

It is well to leave such opinions about the channeling itself aside until a point well after the channeling session is complete, for it can cause distress to a new channel to feel that perhaps he is not channeling at all, but is only repeating from his human memory the phrases that he has heard or read so often in other channeled material.

If an entity can remain unafraid of such repetition, then there is no harm whatsoever, and it is merely a natural part of learning to channel.

May we answer you further, my brother?

Questioner: No, thank you.

We thank you, my brother.

We find that the energy of this instrument and of this group wanes and so we would take our leave of this instrument and this group, thanking each for the joy of your company and the questing hearts that bring you to set aside time to create a sacred space in which you may learn and grow and serve.

We are those known to you as the principle of Q'uo. We leave you in the love and in the light of the one infinite Creator. Adonai. Adonai. ✼

L/L Research

L/L Research is a subsidiary of Rock Creek Research & Development Laboratories, Inc.

P.O. Box 5195
Louisville, KY 40255-0195

www.llresearch.org

Rock Creek is a non-profit corporation dedicated to discovering and sharing information which may aid in the spiritual evolution of humankind.

ABOUT THE CONTENTS OF THIS TRANSCRIPT: This telepathic channeling has been taken from transcriptions of the weekly study and meditation meetings of the Rock Creek Research & Development Laboratories and L/L Research. It is offered in the hope that it may be useful to you. As the Confederation entities always make a point of saying, please use your discrimination and judgment in assessing this material. If something rings true to you, fine. If something does not resonate, please leave it behind, for neither we nor those of the Confederation would wish to be a stumbling block for any.

© 2009 L/L Research

Special Meditation
September 7, 2007

Question from D: *(Read by Jim.)* "This is the background to my questions: N is my two year old granddaughter. She is a twin to her brother, M. M was born two pounds heavier than N. They were born August 4, 2005. These are my daughter's only children and she was 46 years old when she gave birth.

"For approximately the last year N has been having blackouts connected with a high fever. These have been labeled "brain seizures." I sent my daughter, E, a book on nutrition for the growing brain but she's not started to read it until recently.

"I've had some indication that the twins are 'Indigo' and that they are here to help my daughter through the coming consciousness shift. I've thought that these blackouts may be some kind of near-death experience and that N may be getting some kind of spiritual instruction during her periods of unconsciousness. I simply hope that this may be true but I have no way of actually knowing in a psychic sense.

"My daughter and her husband, K, both work in the field of corporate insurance. My daughter is a partner and V.P. in her company, which is a nation-wide concern. Her husband was recently hired by the same company but with different duties than my daughter.

"They hired a Mexican nanny for the twins who can teach them Spanish along with their English. My daughter was unable to breast feed them for very long due to complications from the caesarian she had when they were born.

"Each time one of my daughters was conceived, I knew it instantly. This took place 20 years apart and the youngest daughter was raised by her mother and her mother's husband. She didn't know I was her father until she was 17 years old and never accepted the fact and yet there was that spiritual connection between us which has yet to be fully explored.

"She has four beautiful children whom I've never seen but whose photos I found on the Internet. In E's case, although I've had to wait 46 years for her to bear fruit, I've always thought that I might have had some connection to her children on another plane, especially as we approach the coming 2012. That is why I'm seeking clarification from Q'uo."

(Carla channeling)

We are those of the principle known to you as Q'uo. Greetings in the love and in the light of the one infinite Creator, in whose service we come to you this day.

We thank the one known as D for desiring our opinions and we thank the ones known as Jim and Carla for creating a circle of seeking at this time. Above all, we thank all of you for calling us to this circle. It is our great pleasure to be with you, to meditate with you, and to behold the beauty of your auras as they blend and create a sacred place that is common to all three.

As always, we ask that our words be taken with discrimination rather than wholesale. Please listen for those thoughts which appeal to you and seem resonant and leave the rest behind, for we would not wish to be a stumbling block upon your way. We would ask the one known as Jim to read the first query at this time.

Jim: Q'uo, what are the spiritual principles involved in N's brain seizures?

We are those of Q'uo, and are aware of your query, my brother. We find that the spiritual principle involved in this is the preincarnatively chosen distortion which aids the one known as N in becoming more inwardly oriented and finding it necessary to spend time resting and contemplating. Throughout her lifetime there will undoubtedly be ways in which her physical vehicle reminds her that it is well for this particular entity to spend time in inner work, inner seeking and the silence that is so full of information that moves into the intuitional and insightful portion of consciousness.

We would not precisely call that the brain, but would call it the "brain of the heart."

The supposition of the one known as D that this entity may be being tuned for some particular service by this illness is not something that we are able to see at this time. However, our ability to see this, as you well know, is limited. The vibrations surrounding this entity indicate that preincarnative choice was the motivating factor for this early illness.

There is a mechanical or physical portion of this illness. It was not intended to be so severe but was rather intended to be a milder difficulty. However, there is that very mechanical situation in the womb where one entity was able to derive more nourishment from the mother than the other. Consequently, there was a slight amount of difficulty which was involved with the brain tissues not receiving adequate oxygen for a certain amount of time, not very long but long enough to accentuate this distortion.

We would encourage those who wish to nurture the entity known as N to surround her with gentleness and affection, for this entity is most sensitive to those vibrations of true affection which cannot be mistaken for a pose or a mask of proper behavior. We are aware that the one known as D has every intention of creating this very atmosphere and we encourage him to do just that.

We would note at this time that there is a certain amount of information which we do not feel is helpful to share because we would not wish to infringe upon the free will of the one known as D or the one known as N.

We are apologetic about needing to refrain from conversation when it is clearly desired by the one known as D. However, it is more appropriate for us and for the instrument to retain a precise tuning than it is for us to be able to offer specific information. Therefore we apologize for the limitations upon this contact, but feel that it is necessary in order to maintain that careful appreciation of free will. It is always better for an entity to seek spiritually rather than to ask those things which we cannot offer because they would interfere with the learning process.

That being said, we are now ready for the one known as Jim to vibrate the next query. We are those of Q'uo.

Jim: What are the spiritual principles involved in the relationship between N and her mother and father?

We are those of Q'uo, and are aware of your query, my brother. The one known as N seeks to learn to offer love without expectation of return. This is an incarnational theme for many, especially when they are wanderers, as is this entity. The karma between the one known as N and her family is balanced. Therefore, each may be teacher to each.

This entity, therefore, in association with her guidance, which this instrument calls her higher self, chose before incarnation those particular entities who have certain characteristics that might be seen to be difficult in some ways, where there may be high expectations and a tendency toward criticism rather than praise, these energies being acceptable to the one known as N in that it is this soul's desire to become a radiant servant of the one Creator, able to shine like the sun without regard to how she is coming across or what people think.

This entity has set for herself a lifetime of service to others that is very beautiful and the energies that she will be able to process as she grows in spiritual maturity will be of great help in creating that sturdiness and independence of personality that is so typical of what this instrument and the one known as D both call Indigo children.

We find that the life path of the one known as N is well constructed and the choices that she has made of those who will support and encourage her and those who will teach her the discipline of independence and independent thinking are well balanced, so that this entity shall not be bereft of support in her life while receiving the appropriate catalyst that she has chosen for herself.

We find that the one known as N's incarnational lesson is in common with that of this instrument and we feel this instrument's heart opening in sympathy for the one known as N, for this instrument also had perfectionistic parents whose tendency was to explain what was wrong with the picture rather than praising the instrument for being able to draw a picture at all.

However, we find that this instrument is in complete agreement with the one known as N in feeling that there is no better way to become able to stand on your own two feet metaphysically than to find yourself able to love without expectation of return.

We would ask if there is another query at this time. We are those of Q'uo.

Jim: What are the spiritual principles involved between N and her twin brother, M?

We are those of Q'uo, and are aware of your query, my brother. The principle at work in this relationship is one of the right use of power and, indeed, the investigation of what true power is. For the one known as N, while physically weaker and frailer than her twin, is in fact a far stronger entity metaphysically, so there is that play between the metaphysical strength and the physical strength; the open heart and the less sensitive and perhaps not so open heart.

There is also a dynamic of parent and child between these two entities, where the one known as N is as a parent in her very nature, maternal and eager to support and encourage in the way mothers are, so that you may see this entity, as she blooms in her ability to express herself and to act within the physical world, being almost like an older sister rather than a twin.

Also, there is an aspect of intimacy which shall feed both twins in this lifetime. This is often the case with twins in that they are able at the cellular level to exchange information. Naturally, this does not take place consciously. Nevertheless, there is that sense of never being alone and this is helpful to both within this relationship. There are many times in the incarnation to come where the isolation is sensed because of the fact that the one known as N will be operating and looking at life from a standpoint that is several layers more deep into the inner life than those about her. Therefore, she has given herself the gift of this special relationship at this time.

We would say a few words at this time about Indigo children because of the fact that both twins are Indigo children.

It is well to be especially careful, as we said before, to be responsive to questions in an affectionate and open manner, finding ways to speak that tell the truth in a way that a young mind can understand. We do not suggest leaving things out or dodging questions, but simply suggest that answers be given with great care so that the rather rapid intake of information that all entities need, and Indigos need twice as much, may be facilitated.

The role of the one known as D in this setup, shall we say, of the family and the extended family, is that this entity will have a great deal of information that will be helpful to these Indigo children and especially to the one known as N. However, we would encourage the one known as D not to volunteer information, but to await that curiosity of the young mind which will inevitably ask the questions in an organic way at the time it is right, so that this entity may absorb and seat the information. Do not be concerned if there are period of time in which you feel that this entity needs certain information but is not asking for it, but rather be aware that there is a guard upon a young entity's mind which helps it not to ask questions faster than it can absorb the material.

We encourage the one known as D to know that he is very important, indeed central, to this child's metaphysical development. We feel that the one known as D is already aware of this fact, but we are able to confirm it and to encourage the one known as D to speak always from the heart, always from the point of positive and radiating surety that all is well, and to so facilitate this entity's growth of her mind and her consciousness in her young years, that she shall be fearless and able to take up those things that are dear to her heart knowing that she is worthy to work on these interests that she shall develop in the future.

It is well, perhaps, to say also that although Indigo children are overtly and obviously somewhat different than other children, they are still children, in that they have that need for a consistent set of rules by which to live. They have need to learn behavior that is appropriate so that they may, as they grow and mature, be ever able to make others feel comfortable and happy when they are with them.

There is no glamour in being an Indigo in terms of an Indigo's not really being a child or being some kind of wonder-child that already knows everything. Indeed, Indigo children may know a great deal that perhaps less awakened souls may not, but they do not have the instinct for courteous and respectful behavior any more than any other young soul does.

The tendency of the very young mind is to see the world as a very small place revolving completely around the self and it is not helpful to any entity, Indigo or not, to be given completely free rein throughout the childhood years. Discipline is indeed a helpful formative influence. However, again, it is not necessary to discipline this particular child in a harsh manner. There are gentle ways of explaining what is appropriate behavior for being in public and for relating to other entities, and this may be offered when it is appropriate, when the issue comes up for one reason or another.

We are those of Q'uo, and would ask if there is a further query?

Jim: What are the spiritual principles involved as to myself as the grandfather to the twins, N and M?

We are those of Q'uo, and are aware of your query, my brother. There need be no special spiritual principle invoked in the relationship of the one known as D and the one known as M. The typical role of grandfathers in your culture covers that relationship completely. You will be able to share your stories with the small one known as M, so that he will know his roots and all that you have learned in your life, which is rich in knowledge and wisdom, my brother. You will perhaps be able to show him how to throw one of your game spheres or other typical ways of bonding between an older male and a younger male in your society.

Perhaps you may share with him in your gardening if he is interested, or in whatever he comes to you and asks. Feel free to share with him as it is given to you. This entity, M, is also an Indigo child, but his lessons vary in such a way from the one known as N's that you are not the central figure that his higher self has chosen for mentoring this young entity.

The situation is different, as the one known as D as undoubtedly discovered for himself with the one known as N. The one known as D is peculiarly suited to offer a balanced viewpoint to the one known as N as she grows and becomes curious about many things having to do with the inner life, metaphysics, ethics and the great questions about philosophy:

Who am I?

Why am I here?

Why do I feel as though I have a mission?

These are typical concerns of the growing wanderer.

It would be well for the one known as D to prepare for this role by spending time in silence, perhaps with a paper and pen at hand, or perhaps sitting at the computer, so that he may start a session of seeking by asking his own higher self, mentally or out loud, "How may I learn to serve the one known as N?" Then, as thoughts come into your mind, my brother, write those thoughts down so that you have a record of that which is given. For it is easy to receive good information from guidance and then forget it, much as one would forget a dream, so that all that remain are general hazy details. You will find that the one known as N is also your teacher. Therefore, it will help you to have this record which you may look back over as you and N both grow in years and shared experience.

Every life is a puzzle to work, in a way, an apparent chaos that seems jumbled in a maze that sometimes does not seem to have an exit. And yet it is necessary for this factor of chaos and seeming patternlessness to exist in order that entities such as yourself and N may together learn increasingly to think outside the box, shall we say, of societal thinking and assumptions.

You may find yourself learning a great deal in this journaling process as you continue asking, "How may I serve the one known as N." Therefore, we would encourage you to make this either a daily process or something close to that. *(Inaudible)* Part of this pattern is that the one known as D has chosen this opportunity to develop his own inner resources in order to be a better mentor for the one known as N. So this special relationship will be a blessing to both of you.

(Side one of tape ends.)

(Carla channeling)

We encourage you to be unafraid of making mistakes. Allow yourself simply to speak from the heart at all times. And, my brother, if there is at any time any judgment involved with your daughter, we encourage you to refrain from expressing it. For your part in this pattern is to see the love in the moment and to enlarge upon it rather than to engage in any energy of judgment or criticism.

You may keep these things in your heart and work on them by finding that for which you criticize in the other in your own nature, once you have found the corresponding part of your nature that matches the shadow side of your daughter's and in some cases your son-in-law's. Then you're able to do your work in an inner sense without ever having to foul the blue ray of honest communication between you with those things which are judgmental or critical.

Certainly, if you are asked for your opinion, you may give it. But always, my brother, seek to share your shining truth with your heart wide open so that what you say has not only honesty, but infinite tact and compassion.

And lastly, we would encourage you, in this wise, never to defend yourself. For that is unnecessary and might skew the relationships that you so wish to keep unsullied by fear.

This instrument likes to look at such refraining from responding to anger with anger as a Beatitude because of this instrument's Christian background. The Beatitudes are those sentences in the New Testament which have to do with being blessed when you mourn or when you are poor in spirit and so forth.[79] They are blessings because they are grist for the mill for that one who is focused, not on the self but on the Creator; not on fear, but on love; not on maintaining an ego, but on becoming an ever more pure radiation of the one infinite Creator.

May we ask if there is another query at this time, my brother?

Jim: What are the spiritual principles involved in my working with and learning about plants and gardening?

We are those of the Q'uo, and are aware of your query, my brother. Each entity comes into incarnation with a plan of incarnational lessons to learn and incarnational service to offer. It is often a "long and winding road"[80] to find one's way, and yet at the same time one cannot make a mistake. There is a tremendous amount of redundancy built into this system of a lifetime. You have gifted yourself with many more relationships, many more challenges and many more blessings than you need, in order that you may never feel that you have gone astray and that you have lost your way. For you are always on the way to home, that place within yourself where all is well and you are in the open heart which is the home of all entities within illusion, moving always back to the one infinite Creator, resting in that vibration of unconditional love.

The one known as D has moved gradually into more and more of the desire to engage with the planet directly. And may we say, my brother, that you are absolutely on course in your spiritual seeking as you respond to your heart's call to become ever closer to the energies of Gaia and all of the spirit-filled energies of second-density plants, animals and first-density air, fire, water and earth.

---

[79] *Holy Bible*, Matthew 5: 3-12: "Blessed are the poor in spirit: for theirs is the kingdom of heaven. Blessed are they that mourn: for they shall be comforted. Blessed are the meek: for they shall inherit the earth. Blessed are they which do hunger and thirst after righteousness: for they shall be filled. Blessed are the merciful: for they shall obtain mercy. Blessed are the pure in heart: for they shall see God. Blessed are the peacemakers: for they shall be called the children of God. Blessed are they which are persecuted for righteousness' sake: for theirs is the kingdom of heaven. Blessed are ye, when men shall revile you, and persecute you, and shall say all manner of evil against you falsely, for my sake. Rejoice and be exceeding glad: for great is your reward in heaven: for so persecuted they the prophets which were before you."

[80] "The Long and Winding Road", by John Lennon and Paul McCartney, © Lennon/McCartney, all rights reserved, begins:

The long and winding road
That leads to your door
Will never disappear.
I've seen that road before.
It always leads me here;
Lead me to your door.

The overarching principle here is that all is one. However, there is a particular reason that you have chosen at this time to move into a closer relationship with the Earth itself and it has to do not only with your incarnational lessons and service, but also with the one known as N's and to a certain extent the one known as M as well.

The Indigo agenda generally has a large area of concern for the planet itself. This is due to the fact that these entities are natives of this planet, having just graduated from third-density Earth. They have graduated to fourth-density positive and have immediately chosen to return to the Earth sphere in a dual-activated third and fourth-density body. Their physical body is third density but they're wired, shall we say, to be able to absorb fourth-density vibrations of love and understanding in a far less distorted way than those with only the third-density wiring or DNA.

They, and all of those who have come to this planet from elsewhere, from planets that have destroyed their habitat or who come from Atlantis, where they destroyed their habitat, have a great desire to offer to the Earth restitution and stewardship that is based on love and protection rather than on the desire to rape the Earth for its resources.

We would suggest that you create opportunities, whenever it seems good to you, to offer both the one known as N and the one known as M, if this entity desires it, those walks in nature or those hiking experiences or even overnight camping. The purpose of frequent camping or even just moving the bed to the outside in the back yard, where the young entity may rest upon the Earth itself is not only to bond these entities with the Earth but, in the one known as N's case, to have the Earth's healing vibration physically contacting her through the blankets and so forth, so that she is not apart from the Earth but a child of the Earth.

There is a tremendous healing quality to Planet Earth. It truly is Mother Earth, and its love of this small child is such that all of the forces of nature shall be working to help heal the distortions of the one known as N, especially when she is able to contact the Earth itself, certainly with her feet, but also, as much as possible, her torso. She may sit upon the earth while you tell her stories, or you may create for her the adventure of sleeping out under the stars or in a tent.

Naturally, she needs to be protected from the elements with enough warmth so that she does not become chilled, but in general the experience of being part of the Earth's dance of life is a very healing one for this sensitive and positive soul.

Far more goes on, my brother, when one is gardening than the function would suggest. The earth is alive. It is a consciousness that is just as much unique to itself as you are to yourself. It is aware. It is a being. And it is full of the most pure love imaginable for you and for all things that grow and have life within and upon its surface. It is a graceful, rhythmic, pulsating entity.

The awareness it has of you is complete. It is sensitive to your every thought. So often, my brother, it is unable to make contact with those souls in third density upon its surface. And this is a grievous thing to the Earth. It is the unwilling recipient, in many cases, of hostility. And there is a sadness within the Earth because of this. As you appreciate and love the Earth, as you literally put your hands in its dirt, care for it and tend to it and praise its beauty, it is as a young girl who is told she is beautiful. It feels so good to Gaia to be appreciated and to be treated gently and lovingly.

Therefore, you are of great service to the Earth as you open your heart to its beauty and its rhythm. And this too, you may teach the one known as N, for this shall be of interest to her in the future.

We might suggest that the one known as D enter the silence consciously and with intent as he works upon his gardening, letting the dirt's call and the sound of the cricket and tree frog be the music which embellishes the sweet silence of a quiet mind, occupied hands, and an absolute attention to the beauty of the moment.

There are walls within the heart of the one known as D which this sweet ministry shall break down so that the heart may be ever more fully open and so that fear may be a thing of the past.

We thank the one known as D for these queries and would ask if there is a follow-up query of any kind that the one known as D would like to ask at this time before we leave this instrument. We are the ones known as Q'uo.

(The question had to do with D's concern that he lived too far away from his grandchildren to take them camping very often.)

We are those of Q'uo, and believe we understand your concern, my brother. When one is 600 miles away, one cannot precisely share a tent in the backyard. However, my brother, there are times when you are together and it is during those times that we suggest you create those opportunities for a closer relationship with the planet.

We find that this instrument's energy is beginning to wane at this time so we would leave this instrument and this group as we found it, in the power and the peace, the love and the light of the one infinite Creator. It has been a great blessing for us to be with you and we thank you again for calling us to this circle of seeking. We are those of the principle of Q'uo. Adonai. Adonai. ❧

L/L Research

L/L Research is a subsidiary of Rock Creek Research & Development Laboratories, Inc.

P.O. Box 5195
Louisville, KY 40255-0195

www.llresearch.org

Rock Creek is a non-profit corporation dedicated to discovering and sharing information which may aid in the spiritual evolution of humankind.

ABOUT THE CONTENTS OF THIS TRANSCRIPT: This telepathic channeling has been taken from transcriptions of the weekly study and meditation meetings of the Rock Creek Research & Development Laboratories and L/L Research. It is offered in the hope that it may be useful to you. As the Confederation entities always make a point of saying, please use your discrimination and judgment in assessing this material. If something rings true to you, fine. If something does not resonate, please leave it behind, for neither we nor those of the Confederation would wish to be a stumbling block for any.

© 2009 L/L Research

Saturday Meditation
September 8, 2007

Group question: The question this week has to do with the role which personality plays in the spiritual development of the seeker. We'd like Q'uo to give us an idea of the best way for the seeker to look at the personality, to use it or not to use it, and how to use it. What role does the personality play in the work of the spiritual seeker?

(Carla channeling)

We are those of the principle known to you as Q'uo. Greetings in the love and in the light of the one infinite Creator, in whose service we come to you this day. May we thank you for the privilege of being called to your circle of seeking. You can have no idea what it means to us to be able to share our thoughts with you. This is the service that we have chosen at this particular time, and when we are able to speak through instruments such as this one, we feel that we are able to fulfill our service.

Please accept our humble thoughts for opinion rather than fact, for they are our thoughts and opinions. We would not wish to be in the position of authority over you. Consequently, we would greatly appreciate your using your powers of discrimination to sort out the thoughts that are helpful to you from those that are not. We thank you for this consideration, as it allows us to rest easy, knowing that we are not infringing upon your free will.

There is always that danger, when a seemingly advanced entity speaks. One feels one ought to listen. We encourage you not to feel that you ought to do anything whatsoever but follow your heart.

Your query this evening has to do with the use of the personality for the seeker who is doing spiritual work. Oftentimes in your organized religions there is the suggestion that the human being is entirely separate from that entity that may do good works, or who may be acceptable to the one infinite Creator. The things of this world, which include all of those facets of the personality which have to do with this world, are seen as full of sin and the territory which is in the rule of the Devil or Satan or the negative forces.

The spiritual is seen as something separate, something to be yearned for and to be sought through the middleman, whether it be the priest, the Holy Spirit, the Blessed Virgin Mary, Jesus the Christ, or whatever intermediary is taught within other forms of organized religion than those with which this instrument has familiarity.

This is not our view of the use of the personality by the spiritual seeker. We realize that from the level of the personality, it is an unsolvable puzzle to see through the personality. Certainly this instrument has been assailed by many doubts as to her worth, which seems paradoxical in that the cause of this was receiving many, many compliments at a recent Homecoming Gathering. The possibility that she could ever, in a million years, be such as was being described by some of those attending this

Homecoming caused her to feel deep doubts as to her true worth.

We mention this because this is the way the personality works. It is full of quirks and quiddities, often illogical and even contradicting itself in its various facets. The personality shell, as we have called it many times rather than using such pejorative terms as ego, is not a smooth, symmetrical, completely integrated thing. It is, rather, a collection of gifts, challenges and predilections.

Imagine yourself, my friends, before this incarnation began. You and your guidance gazed at the totality that is you, that perfect being that has come through so many waters, so many experiences, and has collected an over-abundance of gifts, challenges and predilections.

You looked at the suitcase that you were going to pack for this incarnation. You had to leave out most of the traits which are part of the totality of your beingness. You chose quite thoughtfully and consciously, attempting to provide yourself with just the right clothing with which to dress your essence. A good deal of subtle and thoughtful consideration was put into these choices.

And so you packed, carefully and with respect, those assets, deficiencies and preferences that you felt would set you up to learn the lessons that you wished to learn in this incarnation and to meet the challenges that you wished would temper your spirit and transform you in this incarnation. You carefully selected your biases and arranged for relationships, or perhaps more accurately the possibility of relationships, throughout the incarnation, the parents, the teachers, the siblings, those who would be your children, your mates and all of those friends that connect with you in ways too deep for words.

In this you were redundant, so that you could never, ever become lost and be unable to find your way back to the proper track that you hoped to follow throughout this incarnation. Some of you packed sparingly. Some of you packed so many gifts and challenges that you had to sit on them to close the suitcase. Therefore, some of you are quiet and some of you are full of energy and bursting at the seams. But all of these things were done with careful thoughtfulness. There was no mistake made in your packing. You did well.

You have come to this incarnation with a personality shell in which there is a loose association of all of these aspects that you packed beforehand. You have taken them out of your suitcase and placed them around you, just as you placed your flesh around the essence of your light body as you took incarnation in flesh. And here you are, a seemingly unified, integrated individual, more or less in control of a busy and productive life.

And yet those are not the experiences from the inside of the personality shell, for the most part. It is quite normal, in fact, for entities to sense that they are not completely seamless in their personality but rather have many shifting elements that can combine in different ways at different times to surprise the seeker at the eye of the hurricane of all of these facets of personality.

So, how shall the seeker deal with its own personality as it seeks to penetrate the surface of life and to go deep into the areas of mind which have real meaning and value, those areas of deep water that call the spirit forward? The one known as C was saying that perhaps it is necessary to put the personality to one side and to release the personality in order to do work in consciousness. And indeed, as we said before, this is the traditional model of organized religion, which sees things human as things sinful and in error.

Our opinion varies from this model markedly. We feel it is well to take the personality somewhat lightly. It is well to have a sense of humor as one gazes at the many quirks and impulses of the personality. One cannot defend the indefensible! One cannot say that every choice made is a good one, when quite obviously there are many, many times when one looks back upon a choice and estimates it as being foolish.

And yet such moments of inner realization teach and instruct the seeker within, so that gradually, as life experiences are collected and spiritual maturity begins to develop in the entity, it becomes more difficult to be thrown off one's balance by the realization of one's folly and one's limitations in general.

We would encourage entities who seek to know the one infinite Creator to spend time developing an affectionate and tolerant relationship with the self. There is no use in dwelling in judgment upon the self, for every day is a new day. Every time you perceive that your personality has led you astray you have the opportunity to begin again. You do not have to carry those mistakes of your past on your shoulders. You do not need to carry old sorrow upon your shoulders. You do not need to retain guilt for those things that you long ago expiated by your very suffering and remorse. It is well to travel lightly, if you are a spiritual seeker, and to release the judgments of yesterday, that you may be entirely fresh this day.

As you evolve, you will discover that there are things about your personality which have begun to become transparent to you. It is not that you lose the personal aspects of yourself at all, but rather that they no longer affect you in the same way. You can see those same impulses and preferences that in the past have been so very powerful, and you may notice that while you see these preferences you do not have great catalyst in choosing whether or not to move with them in a certain circumstance. For your viewpoint has widened. You see through yourself, and this is a transparency that works both in the outer world and in the inner world.

You see through your personality in the outer world, seeing more of the world than just those things that you care about personally. Your viewpoint widens. You are still the driver of your creation but you are no longer necessarily the star player. You begin to sense into the endless mirroring of the world. You become less afraid to contact other people's suffering. And therefore you become more able to rejoice with other people's joy.

The transparency also works within yourself, as you honor, respect and fully acknowledge the quirks of your personality, while becoming able to choose whether or not to indulge your personality at a certain point. It is, indeed, one of the reasons that you took incarnation. For as suffering, pain, loss and limitation temper your spirit and make it ever more flexible and strong, you become more and more an instrument that is transparent to the distortions of the surface personality, allowing them to be declarations and embellishments which do not cover the essence within.

This is not something that can be done on purpose. It is the result of a life lived thoughtfully and consciously. It is a great reward of the spiritual life that eventually you become able to choose to bring into the forefront of your awareness that selfhood of yours which does not partake of any masks, but rather rests in the mystery of the unconditional love of the Creator.

You become an impersonal eye, yet this impersonal eye does not take over the personality. It is not intended at any time during the incarnation that the personality be dropped. It is simply that it becomes that plastic, workable, transparent collection of facets that you brought with you.

Indeed, the sum total of becoming aware of this impersonal center or core to the self is that you fall in love with your foolish, human personality shell. You like yourself. You accept yourself just as you are, for it is this vehicle that has served you so well and offered you so many occasions for laughter, comradeship, love and affection. It is this very personality that has allowed you to open your arms and embrace others and to accept the love of others.

It is this very human, error-prone personality that is one of your glories. It gives your light color and texture, making that light that you welcome through yourself from the Creator have just that certain delightful uniqueness that makes you so very special and so very necessary to the Creator.

Therefore, we would say that the proper use of the personality to the seeker is to respect and honor it, while at the same time realizing its nature. Realize that it is clothing which you have put on to meet the faces that you meet, all of whom are similarly clothed in these ways of looking at the world which are unique to each person.

If you wish to work upon your personality, it is always well to think in terms of balance. There is a tendency in those who wish to be truly devoted to the infinite One to toss aside all things except the highest and best. And yet entities who do this are off balance. They have forgotten how to laugh and to enjoy the transient pleasures of food and drink and the way the air smells on a summer's day when it has just rained and the dust rises off the tar on a country road.

Who would wish to lose the small delights of the personality in order to be ever more devoted, serious, and sober? We would not recommend this approach to seeking the one infinite Creator. For the personality is that which notices and remembers the little things that would mean nothing to the impersonal self. Therefore, open your arms and embrace yourself, for your personality is a sturdy, useful, even necessary garment.

Now, when you speak of garments you also speak of the garment of impersonal life as well. And we encourage you to explore that concept, that even the cloak of Christ Consciousness is a deep personality characteristic. Even the so-called impersonal self, that I AM THAT I AM, is still a cloak with which you clothe yourself. No matter how much you hunger to become completely the Creator's, you shall always, because of the very nature of this density, be that entity which wears the masks and wears the garments, and comes at experience with a certain angle or edge.

Therefore, explore your personality to find those angles and edges that are positive and life-affirming, that bring you to laughter and tears and honest emotion. Encourage those traits within yourself.

And when you find the angles and edges of personality that are life-destroying, look deeply within yourself to find the fear that has caused you to exclude certain activities, people or thoughts from the list of those things which are acceptable.

We find in your settled religions, for instance, that many entities are excluded from belonging to the one infinite Creator, by those who believe in that way, because of not believing as they do. We find other entities that are prejudiced against one or the other sex, against other races than one's own, and so forth.

As you spot these angles and edges in your approach to life and you see that they are destructive of life and denying of the unity of all things, you may well work upon enlarging your point of view and gradually, lovingly, gently bringing these fear-based biases of personality more into the light, that you may develop within yourself a greater compassion for all of life and a greater knowledge and sense, on a personal level, of the unity of yourself and those who you have thought to exclude from your good offices.

Yet, my friends, if you are unable at any certain time to accomplish these things, accept that about yourself as well. There is no hurry. There is no limit in terms of how long it may take you to bring yourself into your best balance. For each moment is a new one. You never run out of the opportunity to see something that will help you to have that epiphany of mind and heart that create in you that wider point of view from which you may, more and more, create the balance within yourself that gives you peace in your heart and peace in your mind.

It is well, in the midst of the confusion and rush of personality, to be single-minded about one thing and one thing only. And that, my friends, is love. Look for the love. When you find it not within yourself, look further, and ask for help. Whoever it is that you ask, whether it be the Confederation, the Holy Spirit, your higher self, your guru, your teacher, inspirational writing, or whatever it is to which you look for aid, seek in all ways to enlarge your awareness of the love within you; of the love flowing through you; of the love that you are able to radiate to those about you.

As always, we recommend the daily habit of silence, one way or another. For there is much transmitted within the silence of a seeking heart, in those energies far too deep for words but enormously rich in information, that goes directly into your subconscious and informs and enlightens your heart.

We would at this time ask if there is a follow-up query to this main question, for we are those of the Q'uo.

(Long pause.)

We are those of Q'uo, and are aware that there is no follow-up query. May we ask if there is another query? We are those of the Q'uo.

Questioner: I have a short question that is very much on the surface. Is the light that you see generated by this circle changed by other listeners who are not local to the room, but are listening to the words somewhere else at this particular space/time? And also, can listeners who listen to the channeling at a later time also partake in the energies or are the energies only present when the circle is present?

We are those of the Q'uo, and are aware of your query, my brother. And may we say that it is far from a surface query. Indeed, it cuts to the heart of that about which we were speaking, in a way. Because it is indeed true that the energies of this circle include those energies of the larger circle of those who are part of the extended group at this time, listening in to the airing of this session in the private chat room.

However, we would go further than this and say that all of those who, in the future, when this session is broadcast, shall listen to this session of working shall also be part of that which is occurring at this time in your illusion. For we operate from time/space, where exist the metaphysical realms of your planet Earth, dwelling in the inner planes or unseen realms that are part of your planetary influence. Therefore, to us, all time is one. And so that which occurs in your future is that which is occurring simultaneously with our discussion at this time.

And, indeed, even those who read this transcript at a later time shall be a part of the energy of this session and shall contribute their love and their light and their interest to the energy that is experienced by the sitting circle at your local time and space.

There is a substantial point to be made in this regard. We say that you are all one. And that it is an intellectual concept that is irresistible in its attractiveness and provable, these days, by the experimentation of your physicists. Thusly, in an intellectual sense, many, many entities are ready to agree that all is one.

Yet there is still that tendency to clutch tightly to local time and space and to see everything as moving in a linear time string. Yet part of that vision that all things are one is the opening of the hands and the releasing of that limitation upon the illusion which you enjoy. A portion of each of you exists in common. That portion is consciousness. Certainly we feel that the one known as C, in asking the main question this evening, was attempting to express her realization of the fact that consciousness is profoundly different from the surface awareness that is the personality's experience of life. For to be conscious is not necessarily to experience consciousness. Consciousness is that ground of being which all entities have in common.

Indeed, you may see that, as you become more comfortable in your own skin or your own personality shell, you may more and more embrace this seemingly impersonal consciousness, knowing that the consciousness within you is identical, as it must be, to the consciousness that is the ground of being for all entities. It is that profoundly unified awareness that allows the magic to occur, that allows the dance to be danced between individuals and groups of individuals, and relating in those groups or as an individual with the plants, the animals and the elements.

And all those forces of love which are a part of your future are, at the same time, profoundly a part of your present moment. All of infinity exists in the present moment. This is a paradox in that it also exists in the next present moment, and the next. And yet it is no less true.

It is such a blessing to be able to share these thoughts! For there is the genuine and heartfelt desire on the part of all those who seek to do so effectively. And so often it is felt that one cannot truly be effective because one is caught up at various times by various stray thoughts and confusions. And yet we say to you that you may look at yourself, as this instrument has often said, as a crystal.

You have, on the outer part of your awareness of yourself, flesh and blood, bones, hands that grasp, and a mouth that speaks. And all of these are very physical things. And yet, driving that physicality and at the heart of that physicality is the essence of your energy body. And in that body you are that which are works with energy. You receive the energy of the one infinite Creator. And as it moves through your chakra system and out through the top of your head, it is colored by that very personality that seeking entities may tend to denigrate.

As you bless, in your own unique way, that energy that moves through you, as you dedicate it to the love and the light of the one infinite Creator and to service in the Creator's name, you color that light with your blessing. So as you radiate out into the world, your radiation is utterly beautiful and unique. There has never been another source of radiation that is just like you and there never will be. For all of those things that have impinged upon your consciousness within your incarnation have added up to this entity that you are at this moment. And even from moment to moment you shall shift and change and make sudden movements, and rest for a long period of time and then make sudden movements that change your coloration again. And at no time are you anything less than perfect.

We are aware that the one known as S was asking about how to work to increase the strands of DNA that are the basic wiring that allows this crystal being that you are to accept and radiate a light of ever increasing density. And we would say to the one known as S that it is in that profound acceptance of the self, that coming to love the self and rest within one's skin in utter peace without giving oneself difficulties without doubting the self, that this transformation of the very cells of your body will take place.

Think of fourth density as you have imagined it, that realm of light and love where you are still playing the card game of seeking and learning, yet everyone's hand is face up upon the table with all the cards showing. Everyone knows everyone else's hand. Everyone sees the struggles, the suffering, and the pain of everyone else. And everyone also sees the beauty the joy and the delight of knowing everyone else.

So there is a far more complex, and at the same time a far more simple, balance of loving and being loved. It is no longer a stretch to love entities at the soul level. For all entities are beautiful when their hands are laid down with the cards facing up, so that all may see all the cards. In fourth density, every entity whom you now judge, you will then see to be a person of infinite beauty. Everyone of whom you thought perhaps too well in third density, in fourth density becomes a very human, flawed and entirely lovable character.

So the fourth density values are those of compassion, acceptance, support, encouragement and resting in love, in all that you see and all that you think. By the time it comes to the doing of things, you are set in your course and your actions shall be those that are imbued with a genuinely heartfelt love.

May we ask if there is a final query at this time? We are those of the Q'uo.

(Long pause.)

We are those of the Q'uo, and perceive that we have exhausted the queries of the group at this time. Therefore, with great thanks for being called to your circle of seeking, we leave this beautiful, sacred space that you have created with your commingled auras. We are those known to you as the principle of Q'uo. We leave you, as we found you, in the power and the peace, the love and the light of the one infinite Creator. Adonai. Adonai. ☥

L/L Research

L/L Research is a subsidiary of Rock Creek Research & Development Laboratories, Inc.

P.O. Box 5195
Louisville, KY 40255-0195

www.llresearch.org

Rock Creek is a non-profit corporation dedicated to discovering and sharing information which may aid in the spiritual evolution of humankind.

ABOUT THE CONTENTS OF THIS TRANSCRIPT: This telepathic channeling has been taken from transcriptions of the weekly study and meditation meetings of the Rock Creek Research & Development Laboratories and L/L Research. It is offered in the hope that it may be useful to you. As the Confederation entities always make a point of saying, please use your discrimination and judgment in assessing this material. If something rings true to you, fine. If something does not resonate, please leave it behind, for neither we nor those of the Confederation would wish to be a stumbling block for any.

© 2009 L/L Research

Saturday Meditation
September 22, 2007

Group question: The question tonight is: Ra says, "Know yourself. Accept yourself. Become the Creator."[81] We would like to know what is the difference between knowing yourself on the one hand and accepting yourself on the other. Could you define these? Is there any significance in the placement of self-knowledge before self-acceptance in this statement?

(Carla channeling)

We are those known to you as the principle of Q'uo. Greetings in the love and in the light of the one infinite Creator, in whose service we come to you this day. What a privilege it is to be invited to join your circle of seeking and to share in your meditation. We thank you for calling us to be with you. As always, we are astounded at the beauty of your vibrations and at your love for each other as you sit in the circle, blending your auras harmoniously and affectionately, creating that sacred space, that temple into which our voice may come. And we celebrate the extended family that sits in the circle of those who listen by webcast or broadcast and thank each of you also for lending your vibrations to this beautiful temple and creating this sacred space.

We are most happy to speak to the query concerning knowing and accepting the self which is before us this evening. But first, as always, we would ask that each use discrimination as our thoughts pass by your ears. Take those which interest you and resonate to you and leave the rest behind, knowing that it is only the path of resonance which is your true path. It is not necessary to consider every thought as equal, for the spiritual walk is very subjective, and what is helpful for one person may be a stumbling block for another. Therefore, please guard the gateway to your own temple of perception. We thank you for this as it will enable us to feel free to share our thoughts without infringing upon your free will or disturbing your spiritual evolution.

You ask this day what it is to know the self, and what it is to accept the self, how the two are the same or similar and how they are different. One way in which they are different is that one precedes the other. One must know oneself before one can fully accept oneself. It is not an authentic concept to accept the self in the absence of knowledge. It is an empty acceptance. Consequently, knowing the self does precede the process of accepting the self. So, we shall talk about knowing the self first.

Recently this group to whom I'm speaking now held its annual gathering, which they call a Homecoming. In this particular Homecoming the theme was, "Who am I?" The entire weekend was spent attempting to approach that question. Those preparing to facilitate this weekend had taken care to

---

[81] Ra, *The Law of One*, Book II, Session 74, October 28, 1981: "The heart of the discipline of the personality is threefold. One, know your self. Two, accept your self. Three, become the Creator."

offer people ways to approach the question that had some structure.[82]

And so the group together looked at the self as a sexual being, as a being who wished to survive, as a being who had personal relationships, and as part of groups such as the family, the birth family, the work family, and so forth. Then it looked at what it was to be within the open heart and how identity was bound together with the ability to communicate clearly and compassionately. And lastly the self was looked at as a magical creature who was capable of doing work in consciousness.

These ways of looking at the self are all helpful in pursuing the self and discovering more of the underlying structure of one's identity. And yet, as our words must, these considerations fell far short of opening up to the seeker the essence of identity.

It is a seemingly simple question to ask, "Who am I?" And yet it is endlessly subtle. For to know the self is to know not simply things about the self, but to know that which holds all of those parts of the self together. Eventually the question of "Who am I?" leads into that spacious and integrated sense of being that reflects one of the names of the Creator chosen by those of the Old Testament times to describe their deity: "I AM THAT I AM."

Part of knowing the self is becoming cognizant of and responsible for one's past. For one expresses oneself throughout an incarnation, from the very beginning of an entity's life in third density, as soon as speech is achieved and communication with others begins. Each interaction discloses the self to the self. And the seeker learns about himself throughout each interaction.

Seekers will find that they have certain characteristics of personality which are persistent and unique to them. And that information is good to know. The seeker will deal with these characteristics of the personality throughout the incarnation, and it is well to be aware of those quirks. Yet, that is just the beginning of learning to know the self. For the personality is as a sketch. It is unfinished. It is in living out the life day-by-day, and garnering that harvest of daily interactions and responses, that the seeker begins to know himself better.

We would distinguish between observing the self and judging the self, for getting to know the self is not a matter of amending the self in order to fulfill a set of guidelines that has been handed down from some source exterior to the self. Rather, getting to know the self is a series of spontaneous realizations, as one looks back upon an interaction that has occurred and realizes that the action that may have seemingly been carelessly chosen was, in actuality, inevitable.

For there are inhering characteristics within each entity's identity that sound the theme of the incarnation again and again. It is as though your incarnation were a film or an opera and, in the soundtrack, the leitmotif[83] of the music would play again and again throughout the incarnation, when the thematic repetition of the pattern would occur.

This instrument was speaking earlier about her inability to grasp how various entities offered so many kind thoughts to her. And yet this is to be expected, since this entity's leitmotif throughout decades of work with those who come to the organization that is known as L/L Research for help has been consistent. There is no grand plan that would support this entity helping others, but only a heart full of love and the intention to support and encourage those about her.

If this is done at random, it does not sound that leitmotif, that thematic melody in the incarnation. Yet if it is done again and again and again, in a consistent fashion, then the metaphysical energy of that consistency sets up a pattern. Love is reflected in love. And so this instrument now has the catalyst of learning how to accept the love offerings of others.

Indeed, to know the self is to begin to become aware of the essence of self that trembles on the brink of manifestation. It is to know that which is the great motivator of the self. It is to grasp, to some extent, that sense of the right use of the incarnation, the right way or ways of offering the self in service to others. Underneath the manifestation of the gifts and the lessons learned there is that underlying and rather vast area or precinct of the self that is beyond

---

[82] The Homecoming 2007 curriculum was based on a study of the chakras. This curriculum and its supporting materials can be found on the L/L Research site, in the "Library" section, under "Homecomings and Gatherings."

[83] A leitmotif is defined by www.dictionary.com as "a theme associated throughout a music drama with a particular person, situation, or idea."

expression, yet which is the foundation for all that is manifest within a seeker's lifetime.

It is easy for us to say to you that all is one and that you are everything and every emotion. It is more difficult to grasp the unitary nature of your being and the being of those around you. The one known as Jesus addressed this unitary nature of all that is when he thanked those who were following him for feeding him and clothing him and giving him supper.

And his disciples said to him, "Lord we don't remember feeding you or clothing you or giving you supper."

And Jesus replied, "Even as you feed and clothe and give aid to the least of these my brethren, so you do unto me."[84]

The question of "Who am I?" extends beyond the precincts of selfhood and into that impersonal portion of the self in which the servant is the master and the master is the servant, in which the giver of love is the receiver of love and the receiver of love is the giver of love.

As the seeker grows to know itself better and presses its search, it begins to learn a great many things which seem paradoxical. For the seeker of identity finds that the self is both loving and unloving; both sympathetic and willing to offer consolation and unsympathetic and willing only to judge. All of these awareness of self, then, can begin to be recognized for the healthful and appropriate paradoxes that are a part of being a human being in third density, of being both sides of the dynamics.

When the seeker begins more fully to grasp the contradictory and paradoxical nature of his identity, he then begins to see the way ahead in terms of the business of the incarnation in third density, which is to choose between those paradoxes and dynamics and opposites, so that out of the welter of all that there is, and within the limitations of the quirks of personality and the cluster of gifts given, he begins to describe to himself the precise dance that he wishes to dance in these few and precious days of human incarnation. He begins to see which song he wishes to sing with the little breath that is given him in one lifetime. And he begins to treasure his time and his opportunity to make choices and to express the deepest and the highest of his ideals, his dreams, his hopes, and his intentions.

As he becomes more and more the master of who he is, he may then choose the manner of his living and his expression. And it is in this wise that the seeker comes to know himself. Certainly no seeker can exhaust the material of the incarnation and conclude that he is now in full possession of the knowledge of who he is. For beingness is a fountain that bubbles up from the depths of each being's heart endlessly. Yet each bubbling fountain of selfhood shall have a unique flavor. Each entity shall sing his own song and dance his own dance.

As each seeker goes deeper he will find the images and the themes of the archetypal mind beginning to have more substance within his awareness of who he is. He may begin to identify himself with beauty or truth or power or love, as he sees within the living myth of his own growing legend the shape of underlying archetype. And these considerations, too, aid in knowing the self. This quest shall always be a work in progress.

Let us gaze know at what it is to accept the self. Accepting the self recapitulates the journey from head to heart, from manifestation to essence, which knowing the self offers. It is easy to accept the self intellectually. There are hundreds of clichés about the business of accepting the self:

"One person can only do so much."

"I'm doing the best that I can."

"I gave it my best shot."

"Anybody would have done the same thing."

With such commonplaces, the mind rationalizes the self to the self. And yet there is no satisfaction in such exercise. An entity may see the imperfection of the self and invoke an outer presence that comes from above to forgive. And there is an

---

[84] *Holy Bible*, Matthew 25: 34-40: "Then shall the King say unto them on his right hand, Come, ye blessed of my Father, inherit the kingdom prepared for you from the foundation of the world: For I was an hungred, and ye gave me meat: I was thirsty, and ye gave me drink: I was a stranger, and ye took me in: Naked, and ye clothed me: I was sick, and ye visited me: I was in prison, and ye came unto me. Then shall the righteous answer him, saying, Lord, when saw we thee an hungred, and fed thee? Or thirsty, and gave thee drink? When saw we thee a stranger, and took thee in? or naked, and clothed thee? Or when saw we thee sick, or in prison, and came unto thee? And the King shall answer and say unto them, Verily I say unto you, inasmuch as ye have done it unto one of the least of these my brethren, ye have done it unto me."

appropriateness to this construct, for the developing seeker has need for ways to ameliorate the effects of his awareness of falling short of his ideals and of making errors which he would take back if he could, but which he cannot take back.

In the song before this meditation began, the one known as Arlo was musing that "footsteps on the water take him back to who he is."[85] So it is for this instrument, for in the figure of the one known as Jesus the Christ, walking upon the water and calming the storm, lies that outstretched hand which the seeker may take to bring him up out of the depths of his shame, his guilt, and his confusion.

Yet accepting the self goes beyond describing oneself as a wretch, as does the old hymn Amazing Grace.[86] It is almost, in this song, as if grace were the Lone Ranger that comes riding into town and saves the wretch from whatever peccadilloes or villains the Western desert has brought forth to threaten or to condemn. There is, in accepting the self, the necessity to move beyond the need for others' acceptance of you and, likewise, to move beyond the need to beg acceptance of a higher power. For if one depends forever upon a higher power to be acceptable or to achieve acceptance or goodness as a spirit, then one can never become the Creator, but shall always remain a beggar at the Lord's table.

And many are content so to be. Yet the intent of the instruction to accept the self has to do with allowing the redemptive power such as a figure as Jesus the Christ to become internalized. It is to acknowledge the oneness between the imperfect self and the perfected self. It is to accept the power of one's ability to judge. It is to accept one's essence as magical and creative.

If all the world accepts you, yet you reject yourself as unworthy, you shall be unworthy; you shall not be acceptable. So the work of accepting the self is the work of gathering these awarenesses of self into full awareness and consciousness and then finding within that self the upwelling creatorship which is able to forgive the self for being its imperfect self.

Accepting the self is a matter of becoming a judge that is not condemnatory but compassionate. We do not argue in any way that each entity has many self-perceived imperfections. However, the nature of acceptance of the self is such that to accept the self is to forgive and to redeem the self.

And how shall that be done? It begins with the bare idea of the possibility of forgiveness. With an upwelling of faith that forgiveness is possible, a seeker may begin to have compassion upon himself. His interest is not in making excuses for himself or rationalizing things done amiss or things not done which ought to have been done, in the seeker's opinion. Rather, it is in the growing willingness to go after the lost sheep of imperfection and imperfect actions and to carry them back into the heart to be loved, respected, honored and forgiven.

It is the work of considerable spiritual maturity to accept the self. Even if every external action in a seeker's life is perfect in the seeker's own opinion, yet still the seeker knows his secret thoughts. He is aware of the mean and petty emotions that churn, unspoken and unrevealed to the world, within his heart. To accept the self, then, the seeker faces these very imperfections and, with willingness to flow into them, he moves into the energy body to the point where those energies dwell: in the shadows of red ray or orange ray or yellow ray; in lust or greed or the desire to persuade, manipulate or control. And he goes after that part of himself that covets; that part of himself that wishes to do murder; that part of himself that wishes to take that which he wants, even though it is not his.

He brings it back as the lost sheep, carrying it tenderly, returning it to the whole system of his being, bringing it into the compassionate heart of hearts wherein lies his part of the creative principle, his spark of the One. For never mistake that the fire of oneness burns within all, known or unknown.

---

[85] From the album, "Mystic Journey," the partial lyrics of the song, "Moon Dance," Copyright Arlo Guthrie, all rights reserved, are:

    As the seabird flies above
    My songs are sung to those I've come to love
    The petals strung into the leis
    The flowering of days I've just begun
    A second chance to grasp a dance
    Beneath the last rays setting of the sun
    Tears along the trail of sand
    Footprints in the water lead me back to who I am.

[86] John Newton's hymn, "Amazing Grace," begins with this verse:

    Amazing Grace, how sweet the sound,
    That saved a wretch like me.
    I once was lost but now am found,
    Was blind, but now I see.

Accepting the self, just as knowing the self, is an unending exploration, for there is always that which is new. New circumstances spring forth and create new situations in which the self has previously been untried. And each interaction in each situation brings its fruit of self-knowledge and its opportunity for further integration into self-acceptance.

The end result of these two processes together is to become the Creator, compassionate, loving and understanding. This is gained by working upon the self. And once one has forgiven and become compassionate towards the self, then that entity becomes that magical person who is able to love, forgive and have compassion on others.

We would ask, before we move on to opening the meeting to other questions, if there is a follow-up to this query. We are those of Q'uo.

(Pause)

(Carla channeling)

We are those of the Q'uo, and are with this instrument. As there is no follow-up to this query, we ask if there is another query at this time. We are those of Q'uo.

R: I will ask a question which touches upon what you described. Would you recapitulate on finding or touching the essence of the self as we go about our everyday activities and feel as if we are doing something right or feel that we are doing everything right, yet we feel that there is a deeper truth of being that is below the surface? Could you comment on that?

We are those of Q'uo, and we believe we understand your query. Do you wish to understand the dynamic between the way in which you feel as you go through a regular day and what is actually happening on a deeper level as you go through a regular day? We are those of the Q'uo.

R: Yes, please speak to that.

We are those of the Q'uo, and we are glad to speak to that, my brother.

As the one known as R was saying before the meditation began, there is a rush and a hurry to the days very often. The days seem swallowed up in detail. There are many things to do. It is the story of Mary and Martha, from the holy work known as the *Bible*, where Martha is attempting to get a meal ready for the one known as Jesus as he sits in the home of Mary and Martha, teaching the disciples.

Martha is ragged with too many things to do and not enough time to serve everyone, so she asks if Mary can come help her in the kitchen. Mary is sitting at the feet of the one known as Jesus, drinking in every word. And Jesus refuses to send Mary into the kitchen to help Martha. Insensitive to Martha's need for help, he simply states that of the two activities, Mary's is the greater.[87]

The hurry-scurry of life for many, many people within your society does not seem to allow time to sit at the feet of the master and drink in the pearls of wisdom that fall from his lips. It would seem that the time must be spent in the chores of kitchen, work, duties, errands, appointments and details of all kinds. Upon the level of the everyday experience it may well be that there is a near-complete lack of the awareness of the undergirding majesty of the moments that pass.

Yet at the same time there is within the one known as R, just as there is within all entities whatsoever, the deeper serenities and lovely tunes of a sacredly lived life. For there is in every seeker a desire and an intention to live life sacredly. Therefore, it is a matter of being able to achieve enough awareness of the self living the day so that there begins to be a transparency to the duties, the chores, the errands, the work, the kitchen, the details of the day, so that one may see, at the same time as one is fulfilling one's duties, the undergirding substance and essence which is sacred.

For it is consciousness which lives the life, whether or not one is conscious of one's own consciousness. Let us speak to that. There are two minds that interpenetrate each other in each seeker's head and heart. One mind is concerned with making choices in order to function well in terms of the needs of the day. That is the Martha-mind. There is another

---

[87] *Holy Bible*, Luke 10:38-42: "Now it came to pass, as they went, that he entered into a certain village: and a certain woman named Martha received him into her house. And she had a sister called Mary, which also sat at Jesus' feet, and heard his word. But Martha was cumbered about much serving, and came to him, and said, Lord, dost thou not care that my sister hath left me to serve alone? Bid her therefore that she help me. And Jesus answered and said unto her, "Martha, Martha, thou art careful and troubled about many things. But one thing is needful, and Mary hath chosen that good part, which shall not be taken away from her."

mind which is impersonal in that it is shared by everyone, and that mind is consciousness.

Each seeker has both of these within him, plaited up as the tresses of a maiden, often indistinguishable from each other and always interwoven, so that seldom is there a completely pure awareness of the Martha-mind. There are almost always little glimpses and glimmers of the Mary-mind as one fulfills one's duties. Yet there is great art and skill in training the self to remember to access the Mary-mind, the mind of consciousness that reveals the Creator in every moment, in every movement, in every humble chore.

For all things whatsoever, done with the consciousness of love, become sacred. Thusly, my brother, when you feel the farthest from any true spirituality in your daily regular life, you are, at the same time, a hair's breadth from accessing the astounding power of consciousness. And when you can access that consciousness and invite it up into the details of your life, consciousness begins to live your life. And you know that there is nothing that you do that is not sacred.

May we answer you further? We are those of Q'uo.

R: Thank you. If one remembers or has the intention of seeing the sacred as he goes into an everyday activity, say, washing the dishes, does the intention actually bring the sacred into everyday activity?

We are those of Q'uo, and are aware of your query, my brother. May we say you are quite correct in saying that remembrance is the key into integrating the sacred into the hurly-burly of a life lived in the fast lane.

How do you remember? Do you tie a string around your finger? Do you write something on your hand? Do you set your alarm on your watch? We would bring it down to the very practical and mundane, my brother, and suggest that you find a way to trigger your remembrance, a way that includes that which is always with you during the day.

This instrument wears a cross, and it reminds her of who she is, and why she is here. And this helps her to remember to live her life consciously. It may be, my brother, that you will find it helpful to write "remember" on the palm of your hand before you begin the day, or to purchase for yourself a bracelet with the word "remember" on it. Or, literally, tie a little string around your finger, or purchase a special ring that calls you to remembrance when you look at it.

It sounds as if it were a trick, and yet at the same time it is far more than a trick, for it aids you to open yourself to that part of your nature for a lack of which you are presently starving.

May we answer you further, my brother?

R: Yes. I would also ask, at the end of the day as one looks at the experiences and attempts to balance them, during this time when one asks for help of the guides or angelic presences to help one to remember the way, does this allow those presences to insert some pointers into the stream of thought to help remember?

We are those of the Q'uo, and are aware of your query, my brother. It is quite so that the development of habits such as the evening time of recollection and balancing of the self acts as a trigger to the remembrance of who your are and why you are here. Any habit that is set in place by the self with the intention of bringing the self to deeper consciousness acts, as the habit becomes ingrained, as a more and more effective call to remembrance.

Is there a further query, my brother? We are those of the Q'uo.

R: One last question. When I think of love/light, and I try to open to it, does the love transform my thought?

We are those of the Q'uo, and believe we grasp your query, my brother. It is so that at any point at which one's heart rises in joy, appreciation and thankfulness at some beauty or blessing of life, one has accessed consciousness. The steady state of consciousness is one of joy, peace and love, and it is a wonderful experience when that sunshine bursts through and one's heart is lifted up in the sudden awareness of the stunning beauty of the present moment.

We find that the energy of the instrument and of the sitting circle begins to wane, and at this time we would, with great thanks for being asked to be a part of your circle, take our leave of this instrument and this group, leaving each in the love, the light, the peace, and the power of the one infinite Creator. We are known to you as the principle of Q'uo. Adonai. Adonai. ❧

L/L Research

L/L Research is a subsidiary of Rock Creek Research & Development Laboratories, Inc.

P.O. Box 5195
Louisville, KY 40255-0195

www.llresearch.org

Rock Creek is a non-profit corporation dedicated to discovering and sharing information which may aid in the spiritual evolution of humankind.

ABOUT THE CONTENTS OF THIS TRANSCRIPT: This telepathic channeling has been taken from transcriptions of the weekly study and meditation meetings of the Rock Creek Research & Development Laboratories and L/L Research. It is offered in the hope that it may be useful to you. As the Confederation entities always make a point of saying, please use your discrimination and judgment in assessing this material. If something rings true to you, fine. If something does not resonate, please leave it behind, for neither we nor those of the Confederation would wish to be a stumbling block for any.

© 2009 L/L Research

Saturday Meditation
October 6, 2007

Jim: The question this week comes from our beginning discussion of Stonehenge and its original purpose, thinking that it has something to do with seasons. We were thinking about the seasons of the seeker. Are there seasons in seeking? Most people start out very much on fire and very excited about seeking and read a lot and meditate a lot and do all kinds of things and then it kind of reduces in intensity and the seeking becomes more of a normal kind of thing, a day by day thing.

So, we referred back to the sessions with Ra where Don's question was:

> It seems to me that the primary thing of importance for those on the service-to-others path is the development of an attitude which I can only describe as a vibration. This attitude would be developed through meditation, ritual, and the developing appreciation for the creation or Creator which results in a state of mind that can only be expressed by me as an increase in vibration or oneness with all. Could you expand and correct that statement?[88]

And then Ra said:

> We shall not correct this statement but shall expand upon it by suggesting that to those qualities you may add the living day by day and moment by moment, for the true adept lives more and more as it is.[89]

And in the following session, Don said:

> You made the statement in a previous session that the true adept lives more and more as it is. Will you explain and expand more upon that statement?

And Ra said:

> Each entity is the Creator. The entity, as it becomes more and more conscious of its self, gradually comes to the turning point at which it determines to seek either in service to others or in service to self. The seeker becomes the adept when it has balanced with minimal adequacy the energy centers red, orange, yellow, and blue with the addition of the green for the positive, thus moving into indigo work.
>
> The adept then begins to do less of the preliminary or outer work, having to do with function, and begins to effect the inner work which has to do with being. As the adept becomes a more and more consciously crystallized entity it gradually manifests more and more of that which it always has been since before time; that is, the one infinite Creator.[90]

---

[88] Ra, channeled through L/L Research on October 21, 1981, labeled Session 73.

[89] Idem.

[90] Ra, channeled through L/L Research on October 31, 1981, labeled Session 75.

So, we would like Q'uo to talk to us about these seasons or cycles of seeking and what we can expect as we continue to seek.

(Carla channeling)

We are those known to you as the principle of Q'uo. Greetings in the love and the light of the one infinite Creator, in whose service we come to you this day. We thank you for creating this circle of seeking and for asking for us to join you and to offer our humble thoughts. As always, my friends, we would ask that you employ your discrimination in listening to what we have to say and if a thought that we offer does not resonate to you, please leave it behind. In this way we can feel comfortable in knowing that we are not infringing upon your free will or interfering with the process of your evolution of mind, body and spirit. We thank you for this consideration.

We would start our discussion with observing the affection of the cat that is in the instrument's lap at this time and purring loudly because it appreciates the energies of the meditation. Indeed, as the one known as Jim reads from the words of the entity known as Ra, there is a vibration or an essence that is more and more, for the maturing spiritual seeker, the identity of that seeker. That vibration is who he is, and many things affect that vibratory rate from moment to moment, from day to day and from season to season.

The seasons of your planet are more than simply those shifting zones of temperature, humidity and weather. They represent the flow of constant repositioning of the forces that impinge upon your planet from the stars near and far, from the moon and from your sun especially. Let us look at these seasonal cycles first.

The culture of those who dwell in cities and who have heated homes in the winter and cooled homes in the summer and who work in air conditioned offices for a living can easily disregard the passage of the seasons. They do not affect him overmuch. He is protected by the civilization and the comforts of that civilization.

Yet the body, both the physical body and the energy body being components of that energy system, is preternaturally aware on a subconscious level, far from the conscious mind, of these shifting seasons and these shifting arrangements of energy that are impinging upon him and upon his body as the seasons roll around from fall to winter, from winter to spring, from spring to summer and from summer to fall.

The equinoxes, one of which you have experienced recently—that is, the fall equinox—offer to you a time of balance. They are the year's equivalent of twilight and dawning, that time when one set of nature spirits and weather spirits, shall we say, are going to sleep and another set are waking up. It is a very magical time. Therefore, it is a good idea to cooperate with the fall equinox and the spring equinox by noting its passing and allowing the self some extra time to rest and reflect upon that which has passed since spring, and then in the spring to reflect upon that which has passed during the long night of winter.

You are a voyager upon a journey that is affected by that "weather of the spheres," shall we say, that your heavenly bodies, your stars and star systems, your planets and especially your moon offer you. The equinoxes are times to reflect on those. And another good opportunity at equinox is to welcome the energies that are coming in. It is helpful to recognize and greet the incoming energies.

The approach of winter brings outer evidence of an altered environment, cold temperatures, precipitation being snow and sleet instead of rain. There is less and less light as one enters into the depths of this long winter's night. And these energies are to be welcomed. It is a good time to take stock as a spiritual seeker of what the daylight has brought through the warm months, to give thanks for those lessons and to settle and seat them in the deep mind, appreciated, honored and respected.

The summer solstice and the winter solstice, on the other hand, are times of power, times of epiphany and insight. At winter equinox one is resting at the very nadir of light. The hours of darkness have completed their march and your beloved planet Earth is at its farthest from the sun.

This is the time to set the intentions, to move into the caves and the depths of your being. This is the time to ask the darkness to envelop and cover the seeds that are the fruit of your past work and to set your intention to embrace those, fertilizing and fructifying those energies of darkness that are needed to incubate and nurture those seeds of intent.

It is at this winter equinox that that great figure of light, the one known as Jesus the Christ, enters the world. So you may behold yourself wrapped in a cradle of darkness and wrapped also in your firm intent to nurture the infant soul within you.

It is a time when it is very easy to slip the bonds of life for those that are marginally living as the darkness descends. It becomes easier to let those tenuous bonds that hold one to life go. This is the cause of there being many elderly entities, especially, who choose the winter months to enter the gates of larger life and leave the world of Earth behind.

This particular group has had a practice at the winter solstice of setting the bonfire and giving to the dark all of those things that they would wish to be gone from their world—poverty, illness, anger and war and all of those difficult and intransigent[91] energies of violence and greed. And this is a good practice, we feel. It is good to mark these points within your cycle of the year and cooperate as fully as you can with the special energies of those times.

The spring equinox is also a time of deep reflection, a time when one is saying goodbye to the night and hello to the dawning of a new planetary day, that long day of spring and summer and early fall when the energies begin to manifest, bursting forth from the seeds which you have planted in the darkness of winter.

In each density of your planet there is that changing of the guard. In the unseen realms this is just as true as in your everyday world. Powers upon powers, spirits upon spirits in the unseen worlds dance their dance and leave at the appointed time, making way for those entities of the new time. And so it is in spring. As the darkness dies, the energies of fertilization and nurturing and deep intent give way to the welcoming of the light and a readiness to be stewards of the energies within oneself which are coming into bloom.

It is no mistake that Lent occurs in the Christian year at this time of the year, nor is it surprising that many a housekeeper chooses spring to clean house, top to bottom and make everything new and fresh again. For the time of manifestation has begun. Summer's heat coaxes bloom and fruit from the slumbering earth in all the glory of spring, and summer bursts into being.

On an inner level as well, warm weather is the time for realizing the fruits of those growing seeds within you. It is an active time, not as the one R was saying, a "rushing" time, but an active time, a time of intensity and brightness. The entities who aided those of your peoples to create that calendric structure known as Stonehenge collaborated in this effort because of the great magical potential for cooperating with the seasons.

We would recommend for those who would like to blend more and cooperate more skillfully with these seasonal ebbs and flows, that reading be done in the area of natural magic. Sometimes this is called "Wicca." It is neither a positive nor negative kind of magic. It is not a polarized magic but rather a unified system of awarenesses having to do with what energies ebb and flow, not only at the equinoxes and the solstices but at the halfway point between equinox and solstice and solstice and equinox. And indeed there are those sensitive entities who have investigated even further refinements, offering suggestions for each of the stations along the planetary year.

Another cycle that can be used by the spiritual seeker is the cycle of the moon. This is subtle work and yet it is well done, for the moon's influence is as the influence upon the ocean. There are tides within your body that ebb and flow according to the new moon and the full moon. It is skillful at the new moon to plant new ideas, and set certain intentions that you wish to set or to reexamine intentions that you have previously set.

At the full of the moon, on the other hand, it is well to rejoice and open and allow those emotions that are within you that are linked to spirit to express themselves, not with a hectic excitement, but with a passionate equanimity.

Seasons for a spiritual seeker are not necessarily totally coincidental with the seasons of the year, for there are deep rhythms within a seeker's life that are expressed throughout an entire incarnation. Each entity will have its own long rhythms of creation, manifestation and rest. Many have written about the various stages of life, seeing the tiny child grow and swell into an entity in its full state of youth and health and vigor, then seeing that entity complete

---

[91] intransigent: (adjective) refusing to agree or compromise; uncompromising; inflexible.

the circle, dwindling down into that second childhood which ends in death.

Within this incarnation's long cycle, there are sub-cycles wherein various learnings are begun, executed and completed. At the end of those times there may be seen to be feelings of part of the self slipping away or dying away and another part of the self coming into bloom.

This instrument is aware of those who feel that these cycles are in terms of seven years, yet we would say that this is not a strict truth. Rather, it is true that for each entity there are cycles that take many years to complete. And while this cycle is going on, from the inside of the cycle the experience is that this is the self and this shall be the self for all of the life long. Yet indeed this is not so.

If you reflect back on various portions of your life you shall see that you have indeed gained so much from previous cycles that you have been transformed by them. We would perhaps call these cycles of learning and growth those which end with the dark night of the soul and then which spring into new life with the revelation and epiphany that the dawning after that dark night brings.

You do not have to look at an almanac in order to cooperate with these very deep rhythms of the self. You can sense the powerful forces of the dark night of the soul coming to bear upon you and you know at that point that a season of learning for you is coming to a close and you are moving through that time when you allow to fall away those things which no longer serve you. So, you let them go with thanks and appreciation.

It is perfectly acceptable for you to grieve for that which has been you but which is no longer. And always, within those dark nights of the soul, it is well to retain the memory, the knowledge, and the faith that morning inevitably comes to banish darkness and new life begins fresh, clean and new.

There is another type of cycle that affects the spiritual seeker, and that has to do with the placement of the self within this time of shift. There are repeated convergences of energies that signal and herald degrees of interpenetration of the new age with the old age, the fourth density with the third density. These are very powerful times for spiritual seekers because the incoming fourth-density energy is an energy of transparency to truth.

You may have noticed that various aspects of your shadow side have been mirrored to you in these last few years and that this effect is continuing and intensifying. We can only encourage you to cooperate with these intense waves of energy as they sweep through your energy body and your awareness. These are magical times for those who wish to craft for themselves an ever more solid awareness of who they are.

It may seem that these energies are inimical. Certainly there is discomfort at times in seeing the shadow side of yourself in a new way and perhaps for the first time. There is, however, no stigma in having a shadow side. There is no embarrassment or shame in finding that your armor of light is not seamless. You may with calmness observe the uncomfortable truths that may face you as you take in these energies of light and truth. We encourage you never to judge yourself but only to love yourself ever more fully as you understand yourself, ever more fully.

We would address that portion of the question that has to do with becoming an entity which is focused in being rather than in doing, in essence rather than in form. Friends, each portion of your physical reality has a form, yet it also has an essence. Every piece of earth, every flower, and every human being is both form and essence. Your outer culture naturally has to do for the most part with form and manifestation. It is not your outer culture's habit even to investigate the essence that lies within the forms.

To the spiritual seeker, forms shall never satisfy. There is always hunger after essence; the essence of yourself, the essence of the creation around you, the essence of who the Creator is. The portion of you that is involved with forms is also involved with those mental and emotional forms or masks that you may call the ego or the personality shell.

(Side one of tape ends.)

(Carla channeling)

There is a great deal that one can do on that surface level to live more skillfully and much more in cooperation with the environment about you.

It is to some extent at this level that you will use the seasons. Yet the influence of the seasons moves into essence as well as form, just as you as a creature move into essence as well as form. As you approach spiritual maturity, you begin to release portions of your surface self. You find parts of your personality shell dropping back or even falling away. And in the place of that personality, you will find an awareness that is deep within you, that is impersonal in nature and that partakes more and more of essence.

This movement from form to essence, from personality to impersonality, from the thinking mind to consciousness is the meat and drink of spiritual seeking. At the heart of each of you there is an identity. You are one with each other, and with all that there is. You share in common the same consciousness that is the Creator's consciousness. It is imbued with and of the nature of unconditional love.

One of the most powerful experiences for any spiritual seeker is to be able to move through the lower chakras into the open heart and from there into indigo and then violet and then the gateway to intelligent infinity. As the seeker does this, he becomes the Creator.

Yet, my friends, we would not say that this is the goal of spiritual seeking. Rather we would say that your aim as a spiritual seeker is to become able to move from form to essence and back to form and back to essence, in an ever more flowing and harmonious manner, neither scorning the surface of things nor becoming overly enamored of the higher states of meditation and awareness.

Your goal as a spiritual seeker is to find where your heart truly lies in terms of polarity. Shall you serve the light or shall you serve the darkness? When you have made that choice, then you have the rest of your incarnation before you as an environment in which to practice being that entity which is a servant and becoming ever more comfortable in that polarity, so that gradually, over time, you become truly balanced.

The dance moves through many cycles and yet always within you, at the heart, is that point of infinite stillness in which essence is all and love rings out to the farthest reaches of the infinite creation.

We thank those of this group for creating such an interesting question. It has been our pleasure to contemplate various facets of it, for it indeed is a large question and could be probed from many different angles.

Before we ask if there are other questions, we would ask if there is a follow-up to this main question. We are those of Q'uo.

(Inaudible)

We are those of Q'uo, and are aware that this theme has been exhausted for the evening. In that case, my friends, we would ask if there is another query that is upon your mind at this time. We are those of Q'uo.

Questioner: *(Inaudible).*

We are those of Q'uo, and find that this instrument would like us to speak to some extent about communication. Recently this instrument completed a chapter in a book she is writing[92] about the issues of the blue-ray energy center, the throat chakra, which is all about communication. This instrument was surprised to find that it was harder for her to write about communication than about any other portion of the energy body. She decided that it was perhaps because she has always been a natural communicator, and so she went back to the work itself upon which she was giving a report—that is, the Confederation material such as that which is being generated at this session of working—and read and studied the Confederation messages about the blue-ray chakra.

Yet what this sparked in her was an awareness that she had not before had. That awareness was how tenuous and vulnerable open communication is to emotions such as hurt feelings and misunderstandings. Her query was to ask us if we could offer some spiritual principles that would enable her to be more skillful in communicating, especially when there were undercurrents and riptides below the surface of communication.

We would acknowledge that many times that communication is layered. There is the voice that is speaking the words that are being used, which represents one level of communication which speaks to the logical and rational mind. Yet also, no matter how skillful the words or how well put the sentiments, there are many unspoken layers to communication which do not yield to the logical and rational mind. This is due to the fact that there are emotions and feelings concerning the words that create layers of either helpful awareness or unhelpful resistance to the words that are being spoken.

---

[92] This book is *Living the Law of One 101: The Choice*.

We could make a couple of suggestions for those times when one is caught upon a moment where one becomes aware that there are unseen elements to the communication and yet this has confused and muddled the communicative energies that are moving between those two or three that are communicating.

Firstly, it is well to remember that you speak with a great deal more than your voice. Each of you has body language which communicates on a level which is below thought. Yet other entities will receive the communication of your body: how you hold it, whether there is tension in it, whether emotions are within you that are causing your facial muscles to change your appearance. It is well to acknowledge those levels of communication and to honor them and if possible to address them within the self.

Secondly, it is helpful to remember that intent is everything, both in the self as it communicates and in the other self as it responds, or in the other self as it communicates and the self as it responds. The same words can be said with various intentions. Therefore we would say, "Look you to your intention!" Is your intention pure? Is it entirely service-to-others oriented? Does it have any aspect of the desire to control or the attachment to an outcome? These are not aids to open communication.

And lastly, we would remind all of those who attempt to communicate that if you hold words in one hand and love in another, love is heavier. Love is more important. Love is the essence; words are the form. Find the love in your heart and let your heart fill the form of words with love, affection, compassion and laughter.

As we have exhausted the questions within the group at this time, we would thank each once again for the privilege and pleasure of your company. Your mingled auras create a beautiful space along with all those positive energies within your universe which have been called to be a portion of this sacred space. We thank you so much for being asked to be a part of this moment. We thank you for seeking and we thank you for being you, for you are truly beautiful. We leave you in the love and the light of the one infinite Creator. We are known to you as the principle of Q'uo. Adonai. Adonai.

L/L Research

L/L Research is a subsidiary of Rock Creek Research & Development Laboratories, Inc.

P.O. Box 5195
Louisville, KY 40255-0195

www.llresearch.org

Rock Creek is a non-profit corporation dedicated to discovering and sharing information which may aid in the spiritual evolution of humankind.

ABOUT THE CONTENTS OF THIS TRANSCRIPT: This telepathic channeling has been taken from transcriptions of the weekly study and meditation meetings of the Rock Creek Research & Development Laboratories and L/L Research. It is offered in the hope that it may be useful to you. As the Confederation entities always make a point of saying, please use your discrimination and judgment in assessing this material. If something rings true to you, fine. If something does not resonate, please leave it behind, for neither we nor those of the Confederation would wish to be a stumbling block for any.

© 2009 L/L Research

Saturday Meditation
October 13, 2007

Group question: *(Read by Jim)* Our question tonight, Q'uo, has to do with how we, as seekers, can deal with adversity. Our third-density illusion has the purpose, it seems, of providing us catalyst and by using this catalyst we hopefully can grow into greater understanding of our place in the universe and of how to be of service. Sometimes, though, the catalyst is either too much, or we feel like we're getting burned out, or it's boringly repetitive and we're getting tired of doing the work, or for some reason, we just feel discouraged and could use some words of inspiration, something perhaps other than, "Well, remember that you're all one," or "Persevere, persevere."

Is there some way that you could recommend that we could look at the concept of catalyst that seems to be a bit much and overwhelming as we deal with it in our daily round of activities?

(Carla channeling)

We are those known to you as the principle of Q'uo. Greetings in the love and in the light of the one infinite Creator, in whose service we come to you this day.

It is indeed a pleasure and a privilege to be called to your circle of seeking and we thank you for the honor. We are glad to speak to you on the subject of difficult times and attempt to share inspiration with you. But first, as always, we would ask that each of you be discriminating in that which you choose to take away from our conversation, for we are not authorities over you and would not wish to influence you unduly.

Please follow the path of resonance in your own thoughts and trust your judgment. If you may do this for us, then we may share our thoughts much more freely, being unhindered by the concern that we may have for infringement upon your free will otherwise.

We thank you for this consideration, my friends. It makes us smile that you ask us to offer words of inspiration. The concept is somewhat foreign to us in that our experience of life in every breath is inspirational, if you would call it that. We are in the fortunate position of having no veil that hides from us the infinite inspiration of the moment.

We find in the mind of this instrument the story of the disciples of Jesus the Christ. It is a story told about him and the disciples at a time after he had gone through the crucifixion and had arisen. The disciples had seen him several times before but it was while they were still in Jerusalem. Now, sad and weary but wanting to go on with the great work which he had left them to do, the disciples decided to travel about and offer the information that Jesus had left with them and also to offer themselves as healers in the name of Jesus the Christ.

They were walking along the dusty road to a town called Emmaus. Part way through the day they were joined by a stranger who joined their conversation. Soon the stranger was offering them thoughts upon the scriptures which they were discussing that seemed most inspiring. It was not until later, when they had stopped for the evening, prepared a fire, and were cooking fish to eat for their supper, that they became aware that this stranger was the risen Lord, Jesus the Christ, among them and speaking with them as if he were still alive, earthly and with them in flesh as well as spirit.

To us, this is a perfect example of inspiration in that the inspiration was with them and unrecognized for a considerable length of time. It was only in the relaxation and perhaps the weariness that heralded their evening meal and the end of the day that their rational minds let go and released them from the limitations of logical thought. In that state alone did they finally recognize their beloved teacher and savior.

Inspiration walks with you, just as the one known as Jesus, the Christ, on the road to Emmaus. Like the disciples and the apostles, it is quite common for you not to recognize or in any way be aware of this Companion of your every thought, word and action. The one known as Jesus said also, "I am with you until the end of the age."[93] The Holy Spirit and tongues of fire leapt upon the disciples' heads and the message was the same: "I am with you."

"Send forth your spirit, says the prayer, and I shall be created and you shall renew the face of the earth."[94]

Can you move away from this Companion of every moment? No, my friends, you cannot. Physically speaking, you can climb the highest mountain or plunge into the depths of the sea and your Companion, unconditional love, shall still be with you. In a metaphysical sense, can any toxic emotion drive away the beloved from your side? No. The beloved presence is with you always in every hour and every moment, day and night, relentlessly, eternally, loving, loving, loving.

---

[93] *Holy Bible*, Matthew 28:20: "Lo, I am with you always, even unto the end of the world. Amen."

[94] From a prayer of the Episcopal Cursillo: "Come, Holy Spirit! Fill the hearts of your faithful and kindle in us the fire of your love. Send forth your spirit and we shall be created, and you shall renew the face of the earth. O God, who by the light of the Holy Spirit did instruct the hearts of the faithful, grant that by the same Holy Spirit we may be truly wise and ever enjoy thy consolation. Amen"

There is, as the one known as R would say, a glitch, a catch, to this infinite supply of unconditional love, and that is the veil of forgetting that divides your mind, so that it becomes preoccupied with that which you can see with your senses, hear, feel, taste and touch. You cannot smell the infinite One as He walks beside you. He is intangible, invisible and usually unheard. Yet unconditional love is your Companion, has been your Companion, and shall be your Companion.

Love is an inextricable part of your nature. It is your founding father and your nursing mother. It is the child at your knee. Any way that speaks to you personally of perfect companionship, that is the nature of your Companion. You may think of this Companion as Jesus, the Christ. You may think of this Companion, as does this instrument, as the Holy Spirit. You may think of this Companion in a structure which we have given you many times before, which is that of a guidance system.

You may think of this Companion as your unseen guru, whose love and affection for you outlasts death, so that even if your teacher is no longer incarnate in flesh, yet still he is the angel on your shoulder and the Companion of every move, every thought, and every word.

How to remember that you are companioned by love is often a great challenge in this atmosphere of heavily veiled experience. Perhaps the slanting rays of sunshine on a beautiful day may give you that hint that reminds you that you are in full contact with love. Perhaps the blessed sound of rain when all has been dust and the rain is needed offers you that chance to recall that you are not alone. But one cannot depend upon a sunny day or a blessed rainfall. Perhaps a beloved face, your mate, your friend, or your teacher reminds you that love walks with you in every step. But you cannot depend upon the presence of a particular person.

In some ways the mechanics of helping yourself to remember that you are practicing the presence of the one infinite Creator seems so very mechanical that it does not seem possible that such mechanical actions could possibly have the results for which you hope.

This instrument is a singer and when she is producing music through her vocal instrument, her thoughts are very often on the mechanics of producing sound and tone. If she speaks the vowel, "e," you will find her in a broad smile because that lifts that vowel into the facial mask and creates a more pure sound. She has to remember to phrase the tones that she produces so that it is not a mechanical or rote expression of praise, thanksgiving or prayer that she offers, but rather is musical, with the rising and falling cadences of beautiful speech.

Sometimes it seems that an entire performance may go by without this instrument's experiencing the gestalt that the choir of which she is a part is producing for those who listen. And yet because of these mechanical-seeming techniques, the instrument is able to maximize her contribution to the beauty of the music sung by her choir.

It is in this wise that we encourage you to go through the mechanical rituals which are the resources of those who wish to break through the veil, as the one known as Jim said, to "break on through to the other side."[95]

Friends, you live in two worlds simultaneously. One world is that world in which you become discouraged and feel that your work is in vain. The other world is a world of vibration, color and texture. It is a world of light without the heavy forms of the physical illusion. You are a citizen of both worlds equally. It often seems that there is a choice to make as to whether to live in one world or the other—the world of form or the world of vibration and light.

It is our humble opinion, however, that it is not necessary to choose. What is needed by the spiritual seeker who wishes to access the joy, the aliveness, and the unconditional love of the world of light is a dedication to the techniques involved in unifying those two worlds.

The seeker begins by realizing that there is another world, a world far more beautiful, real and profound than the everyday world of form. That is the time of awakening and it brings to the seeker a hunger and a thirst for light and love. The seeker wants to find out just how to live in that world. So the seeker begins to meditate or to contemplate. And this is an excellent thing. At the same time it creates within the conscious and rational mind a sense of separation between the person that you are when you are not meditating and the person that you are when you are meditating.

It is often the work of many years of moving into the silence and the meditation and coming back out of it into the everyday world before the seeker becomes aware in a moment that the everyday world is permeated and imbued with the Companion. Everyday things are saturated with the love of the Beloved. There is no nook or cranny within your mind or your emotions and your fears that is not drenched and marinated in love.

This is so in an unalterable and irresistible way because at the heart of every cell of your body is the one infinite Creator, and that Creator has a nature. That nature is love. When your heart beats, it beats love. When you breath in, you breath in love. When you breathe out, you breathe out love.

I have spoken to you many times about the discipline of the personality. It is this discipline of which we speak now again, for the only barrier between your rational and conscious mind that so limits you and creates for you the deadliness of sameness and ennui is the rational mind's basic assumption that that which it beholds is the sum of that which there is.

There are as many ways to help trigger your remembrance of the Beloved that walks beside you and holds your hand and comforts you as there are entities who seek the one infinite Creator.

We cannot create for you the perfect mnemonic. Each person's memory will be jogged by a different mnemonic. Recently we suggested to the one known as R that he wear a bracelet with the word "remember" etched upon it so that each time in his work as a technical expert that he looked down upon his hands on the computer he would see that word and remember who he is and why he has brought himself to this particular moment at this particular time.

This instrument was speaking in the round-robin discussion that precedes the seeking through meditation of this particular group about loving everything that she does and we would comment upon that, for the statement that this instrument made, though she is not aware of it, is not a statement that is literally true. There are many things

---

[95] This lyric is from a song written by Jim Morrison and sung by The Doors on their debut, eponymous album in 1967. It was also released as a single the same year. Partial lyrics are:
> The gate is straight
> Deep and wide.
> Break on through to the other side.

that she does within her day which she does not, with her rational and conscious mind, love. Indeed, she must encourage herself and even goad herself into taking care of many of the details of her day.

Yet her statement was true insofar as it was her honest and sincere experience. Yet this is not because of the work. Friends, it is never because of work that you find your joy. It is because you have accessed or remembered that you walk with a beloved Companion whose name is unconditional love. It is because you have remembered who you truly are and why you chose to be here now.

We would offer each seeker the assurance that, no matter how dreary life may seem at this particular time, everything in your life is moving just as it should. For you are receiving those experiences which you carefully planned before your incarnation began. No matter how dark or seemingly difficult the moment, it comes with gifts in its hands.

The writer of Ecclesiastics said long ago that there is nothing new under the sun. Did this wise entity write those words out of despair? We do not believe so. We believe that this entity wrote those words to pierce the veil. If nothing under the sun is new, then even that which is new to you at one particular time will inevitably be repeated and repeated.

Were you to leave the type of work that you do in order to receive the money that pays your bills, as this instrument would say, and were you to find something that is exciting and new to you, within a matter of days or weeks, months at the very most, your new occupation would seem repetitive and wearisome and you would think fondly of the possibility of lifting away from these responsibilities and of, as the one known as R said, having just two days in which nothing whatsoever was related to that which this entity does in order to earn his daily bread.

One cannot change things around in the world of form and thereby come into one's joy. One cannot change one's circumstances and thereby arrive at a sense of peace and contentment. In seeking otherness, one ultimately finds that every gift one has opened becomes old; every wine, once tasted, becomes stale; every luxury, once repeated sufficiently, pales to nothing. In the world of form there is no escape from weariness and ennui, and this, the writer of Ecclesiastes knew.

When you seek for inspiration, do not seek far, for the inspiration is walking beside you. It is filling your heart. It is the air breathing in and the air breathing out of your lungs. It is the pounding of your blood. It is the rustling of every dry leaf and the song of every bird.

It is not because all is one that these voices speak to you. It is because you are a larger self than you can possibly be aware until you ask for that awareness to become open to you.

There in your workplace [is] that which speaks to you of the Companion. Would it interest you to know that in every key of the computer there is a spirit sitting upon it, laughing and sharing with you the joy of being used, of serving, and of being a part of that dance which you and your computer keys are doing?

Would it make a difference if you could see the angel that is sitting on the edge of your wastebasket or resting, literally, upon your shoulder or placing its head upon your knee, so happy is it to be in your presence?

We speak to you of consciousness that has so many facets and so many levels that there is nothing that is not inspirited. Who lives your life? Who sees through your eyes? Who hears through your ears? Who is it that is you? The request for inspiration when looking at mundane things comes down to the heart of who you are.

Perhaps mechanics are involved in allowing consciousness itself to live your life instead of your personality shell. Yet, my friends, those seemingly mechanical actions and rituals of remembrance and recall yield fruit as you begin to be aware that you truly are practicing the presence of the one infinite Creator in every mood, in every situation, in every moment. There is glory all around you and within you. Open to it, and let joy become your experience.

We are aware that a good deal of the angst which entities feel occurs when they are in a position of working at work that seems to them to be of no great service to others. Then this question truly intrudes and becomes almost an obsession, because there is that enormous desire to serve others. That desire is also spiked and pushed by one's own observation of others who seem to be of more service than you, because of having been born with or having developed more gifts of the spirit, more ways to serve. Yet if your work here upon your sphere of Earth was intended to have to do with outer gifts, then you should have received them. If you do not perceive within yourself the outer gifts that are so obvious in musicians and poets, then your gift here, your purpose here, your mission at this time, is not to sing, or to write, but to be.

That which shall assist you most in cleansing yourself of that feeling of sameness is the ability to release the mind. Certainly many among your people have done this by artificial means. Perhaps they drink an intoxicating beverage. Perhaps they ingest the smoke of some mind-altering substance or they ingest food that creates an alternate reality. We are not suggesting outer substances as a solution for one who chafes under the sameness of the work-a-day world. We are suggesting that that very work-a-day world is full of angels and spirits and guidance and the Beloved.

It is the peculiar nature of those who live with that veil of forgetting that the very last thing that is thought of is faith. Faith is your stoutest ally in becoming re-inspired. Faith is the spiritual breath of life. And sometimes you need resuscitation, spiritually speaking. The great and fortunate thing about faith as a tool and a resource for the seeker is that you do not have to do it well. You do not have to "believe," as it were. You have only to claim it and say, "I have faith," and suddenly your eyes open and you can see that the comrade beside you on the road to Emmaus is none other than love itself.

We are those of Q'uo, and thank you for this query, my brother. May we ask if there is a follow-up to this query at this time?

Jim: Not for me.

We are those of Q'uo, and would then ask if there is another query that we may answer at this time. We are those of Q'uo.

(Pause)

We are those of Q'uo, and are again with this instrument. We grasp that we have exhausted the queries in this circle of seeking at this time. We would say a word or two before we leave you, for we do perceive that there is that hunger and that thirst within this circle this evening. There is a yearning too deep for words to break through to a bright and joyful land where the beauty of life creates meaning all its own.

We would that we could share with you on a steady-state basis our perception of life itself as a miraculous and utterly incandescently beautiful thing, a treasure, precious and rare. We cannot. We can say the words and always we can share with you our love. And you have but to ask for us mentally and we shall be with you, surrounding you and bathing you in our love.

Yet that which comes from the outside, as it were, is never the answer to a spiritual seeker. It is when that which blossoms in the heart then blooms up through all the senses and out into the world that you behold with new eyes.

Remember to relax and release your conscious, rational, fact-driven mind whenever you feel depressed and discouraged by the sameness and the repetitiveness of everyday life. Within the folds of that repetition lie infinite in newness and infinite, sharp pleasure. Open, allow, and it shall come. For it is within you, waiting for you to release the strictures of your rational mind.

This instrument was told by a friend who was a missionary that they were working terribly hard at a hospital which they had founded in a very backward and primitive area. There literally were not hours enough in a day to do that which they felt desperately needed to be done. Each evening they would fall onto their cots exhausted and wondering how they could arise the next morning and do it again.

One of them, this instrument's friend, got the idea to arise even earlier and spend the time in prayer. It was this entity's testimony that this decision completely renewed and revitalized their lives. Suddenly the sun shown brighter, the rain smelled sweeter, the hours flew more gracefully and graciously, and everything felt different. Yet they were doing precisely the same things and meeting the same difficult challenges that they had been meeting before.

The difference was time set aside within an intense desire to see deeper; to see with the eyes of the heart; to experience as the beloved Companion experiences. We commend to you whatever you may do that will help you to combine the worlds of form and spirit, so that you are never without a keen and present awareness of the power of love.

We leave you in that love and that light. We are known to you as the principle of Q'uo. Adonai. Adonai. 🌀

L/L Research is a subsidiary of
Rock Creek Research &
Development Laboratories, Inc.

P.O. Box 5195
Louisville, KY 40255-0195

www.llresearch.org

Rock Creek is a non-profit corporation dedicated to discovering and sharing information which may aid in the spiritual evolution of humankind.

ABOUT THE CONTENTS OF THIS TRANSCRIPT: This telepathic channeling has been taken from transcriptions of the weekly study and meditation meetings of the Rock Creek Research & Development Laboratories and L/L Research. It is offered in the hope that it may be useful to you. As the Confederation entities always make a point of saying, please use your discrimination and judgment in assessing this material. If something rings true to you, fine. If something does not resonate, please leave it behind, for neither we nor those of the Confederation would wish to be a stumbling block for any.

© 2009 L/L RESEARCH

Saturday Meditation
October 27, 2007

Group question: The question this evening, Q'uo, has to do with the indigo and violet rays. The instrument is about to embark upon writing a chapter in her *Law of One 101* book[96] concerning the indigo and violet rays. From the Ra contact we have a good deal of information that describes the various qualities of these rays and the instrument would like to ask you if there are any basic concepts or spiritual principles in relation to these indigo and violet rays about which you could speak that would give her additional insight into these rays as she writes about them.

(Carla channeling)

We are those of Q'uo. Greetings in the love and in the light of the one infinite Creator, in whose service we come to you this day. Thank you for calling us to join your circle of seeking. It is our pleasure and our privilege to do so. As always, we would ask that you employ your discrimination as you listen to our thoughts. Some of them will hit the mark and some of them will go far astray from what you need personally. Savor and use those that hit the mark, my friends, and let the rest go. In this way we can be assured of not having an undue influence on you but only being in conversation with equals.

You ask this day about the indigo and the violet rays or energy centers of the energy body. Indeed, this is a very deep, almost bottomless, subject and we are happy to share our thoughts on this subject.

This instrument is in the process of looking for the keys to these two energy centers in that she wishes to retain the detailed discussion of these higher energy centers for another volume of this series that is being written. Therefore, there is the desire to move to the heart of the higher rays and in particular the indigo and the violet rays [in the present volume.]

The very heart of the function of these two rays has to do with who entities in third density are when they have been able to penetrate the surface of their lives and to move into the essence of their beings.

You could consider yourself as a focal point or an interface in this regard. You have a physical body and a physical mind which ground you, more or less, into the world of the physical, third-density, consensus reality that you enjoy and in which you have your experiences and do your learning. Within you also is the one infinite Creator. In every cell of your body, in every vibration of your thoughts lives the one infinite Creator.

Yet, in terms of process, there is that sensation of needing to move from the outer world through the doorway into the inner world. Basically, you as entities are a living doorway, a living gate, an interface so that the one infinite Creator, in a far less distorted form than you can appreciate with your

---

[96] Its complete title is Living the Law of One 101: The Choice. Carla is working on the next to last chapter and hopes to be offering the book for sale early in 2008.

senses, can move in power into your life. Those known as Ra have described this function as being the gateway to intelligent infinity.

In order to approach this gateway, much work has already been done. For it is impossible to enter the gateway of indigo ray until the entity has gathered the entirety and the wholeness of its integrated self into the heart and has done the work of forgiving and falling in love with this integrated self, with its many perceived faults.

Therefore, we speak of those seekers who have achieved—either by gifts of the spirit or by a process of work in consciousness and the disciplining of the personality—the ability to yearn for and desire that essence of the one infinite Creator that can be pulled through that gateway and into the energy body which is interpenetrating the physical body, thereby bringing infinity and eternity into a finite environment.

The model of this activity is that of what is known in the Buddhist world as kundalini. You have the infinite love and light of the one Creator streaming through the chakra system from the bottom up, feeding it with an infinite supply of light. This is the power and the energy with which you work in getting to know yourself, becoming friends with yourself, and working with all of the various aspects of physical life on Earth as you know it.

In itself, it is a powerful and infinite energy. And yet, as the seeker begins to mature he begins to have a yearning and a thirst for the immediate impact of divine light. Therefore, as the seeker becomes more aware of the true nature of his desire, he begins to be able to focus that desire and to set an intention to ask for the highest and best.

As the seeker does this on a continuing and intensifying basis, that gateway to intelligent infinity becomes clear. As that intensification persists, the gateway opens and the light of inspiration comes through to bless and fructify the fallow and waiting soul.

In the end you might see this expressing as a completed circuit. The bodily energy, having to do with incarnation and carefully enclosed within incarnation, is as the field that is planted and seeded and sown with this fructifying information-ridden love everlasting that, unlike the energy that streams from the bottom of the energy body upwards, has pointed and articulated information in the silence of that inspiration.

The energy coming through from the bottom of the chakras up is that energy which is yours to manipulate or distort, shall we say, in the ways that you find helpful, useful and beautiful. The divine inspiration that you call through the gateway of intelligent infinity is as a massive information-rich fountain that permeates you at the point at which your desire to seek has matched your intention to seek from above, as it were.

There is in this process a kind of self-abnegation.[97] There is the realization that the mind does not have enough words, the heart does not have enough tears, and the being that expresses on the conscious level does not have the capacity, in and of itself, to understand what it is getting through the gateway of intelligent infinity. Consequently, this work is done in a state of unknowing.

That state of unknowing is usually achieved within your density only by a process of self-acceptance that can be lengthy. Self, as it expresses in waking consciousness, simply needs to be put to bed or moved away so that the self is empty and waiting.

This is exquisitely difficult for most intelligent people to do. They have that unspoken assumption that their minds and their insights are going to be adequate to processing the information that comes through the gateway of intelligent infinity. However, this is not so.

What comes forth from this hidden or non-verbal exchange of information is a shadow of the information itself. And yet, the process of making that connection through the gateway of intelligent infinity is akin to splitting the atom, so that even a shadow of that light illumines magnificently the inner landscape of the one who makes that connection.

As you sit in meditation, visualize with us your energy body, with its rainbow of colors: red, orange, yellow, green, blue, indigo and violet. The indigo and violet rays are at the brow and the crown of the head, the very tip of your physicality. Allow the light and the love of the one infinite Creator to flow through the bottoms of your feet, the base of your spine, and up your spine. Feel that energy kissing

---

[97] Self-abnegation is defined by www.dictionary.com as self-denial or self-sacrifice.

and moving through each chakra. Feel it pouring out the top of your head in a fountain of colored light. That is, light which is colored by your working with each of the chakra energies to bring them into your own unique balance. You can see that there is a circular spray, shall we say, of radiated light that moves from the top of your head in all directions.

Now, allow yourself to feel the essence of your desire. What do you desire? Those ready to work with the gateway to intelligent infinity will be saying something like, "I desire to seek the truth. I desire firsthand experience of the One. I seek to know in order to serve," and sentiments of that basic nature which ask nothing for the self except to rest with the Beloved at last and practice the presence of the one infinite Creator.

As you find that desire, my friends, begin to feel the energy within your third eye vibrate. Feel it come alive. Oh, sacred desire! It is vital to be passionate in your seeking. Then, imagine that contact, that moment when that desire is fructified by the inspiration which is focused only for you and adequate in every detail for all that you could ever wish to know or use in order to serve.

See your radiation begin to have weight. You are now not simply radiating out into a void, shall we say, or the area around your head. You have become a fountain. As the inspiration flows into that portion of your energy body it then bursts forth again, but with a weight, so that it is more like water than light in its behavior. It begins streaming in a beautiful circular, symmetrical fountain and coming back under you to catch up again with the energy of the earth, that love and light that comes into the body from the base of the chakras. You sit in the middle of a torus,[98] shall we say, of created light that is your interface with all that there is.

This is the essence of the indigo and the violet rays. Beyond all the techniques of the discipline of the personality, beyond any detail, skill or technique, there is this one overriding essence of connection between energies that are different in a profound way, energies that, when put together, create of you a true and powerful lighthouse.

It is wonderful to be in the presence of an entity with an open heart. That glow, that radiation is so enjoyable to be near! One can always feel the presence of a truly loving heart. There is excellence there of the highest degree. Yet the energy of one who is making contact with intelligent infinity is as the wise man to the youth. The one known as Saint Paul said, "Now I see through a glass darkly; then I shall see face to face."[99] That is the difference.

In both cases, may we ask, "Who is the 'I' who is radiating?" And you shall say to me, "It is 'I' myself. It is the person that I am."

This is the hardest part to perceive. In the case of the opened heart, there is a simple or simplistic degree of selfhood or ego which is an essential part of the radiating form, for it blesses the light that is radiating forth from your heart. It is a very personal thing, although it has great overtones of impersonality as the open heart makes contact with the presence of the infinite One.

Meditation through the gateway of intelligent infinity is impersonal. And so the great work of indigo ray is to move the self, very gently, out of the way and allow only the essence of desire to express the selfhood of the seeker.

We note from the query that the instrument has chosen to speak of these two energy centers together. And while we feel that there are obvious distinctions between the two in form and in function, we would agree with the instrument that this is a sound approach, for the two work so closely together, in terms of the function of penetrating the gateway to intelligent infinity, that it is not necessary to divide the study.

Naturally, it is important, in terms of making a report of what this instrument calls Confederation principles and thought, to distinguish betwixt the two, for there is tremendous movement in indigo ray possible, whereas in violet ray there is a fixed nature to that energy. Yet, as the two work together, they function as that connection to all that there is which

---

[98] A torus is defined by www.dictionary.com as a doughnut-shaped surface generated by the revolution of a conic shape, especially a circle, about an exterior line lying in its plane, or the solid enclosed by such a surface.

[99] *Holy Bible*, I Corinthians 13:9-12: "For we know in part, and we prophesy in part. But when that which is perfect is come, then that which is in part shall be done away. When I was a child, I spake as a child, I understood as a child, I thought as a child: but when I became a man, I put away childish things. For now we see through a glass, darkly; but then face to face: now I know in part; but then shall I know even as I am known."

can make of a seemingly human entity a magical, powerful, impersonal servant of the light.

This may be seen also to have its reflections in sexuality and we would suggest that it is helpful to discuss sacred sexuality as being a part of the function of these two energy centers.

The physical body is a wonderful instrument. We realize that it is a very delicate piece of machinery that is often distorted in various ways and in need of repair. And yet at the same time your bodies are wonderfully adequate to feel the most intense emotions and to sing the most heartfelt melodies of emotion.

In the world of social intercourse, entities use words to connect with each other. And words always are inadequate to convey wholeness, because of their very nature. The body, on the other hand, in sexual intercourse, can communicate without words. It can make connections that can be felt or even seen by some entities as circuitry that is connected with the joining of the mated pair.

And sexuality, of course, goes through all of the chakras from red right straight up through to violet. Each step along the way enhances sexuality. When the heart is penetrated by two entities who are in love not only with each other but with the Creator and love itself, there begins to be possible an energy exchange that is most helpful to the mated pair as well as to the world around that mated pair. Again, there is the creation of fountains of energy because of that spark, that atom that is being split in the orgasm.

When sexuality is a sacred, spiritual activity, that tremendous power is communicated with no words being remotely necessary, but the self becoming that powerhouse that just keeps radiating in fountains of articulated light.

When the mated pair reaches orgasm, regardless of what chakra from which the orgasm is expressing, it is recapitulating the steady state of the creation. It is experiencing the love of the one infinite Creator in a way which it simply cannot deny. It is a wonderfully focusing thing to approach and go through an orgasm.

When the mated pair determines to seek indigo and violet-ray sexuality, it opens a kind of communication with the divine that is otherwise unknown. What a blessing to have a way without words to experience and tabernacle with the one Creator!

We have found that many of your people have so many prejudices against sexuality that it is difficult for them to conceive of a truly sacred sexuality. If there is a desire to make sexuality holy, the tendency is for entities to withhold sexuality from themselves except under certain circumstances, such as deciding to conceive a child. Yet, it is our opinion that the metaphysical nature of sexuality is such that it is one of the most clear-cut and accessible ways to experience the divinity of the self; and yet not the self but the consciousness within the self that you are letting free from all masks and deceptions by the investment of sexuality with your attitude of honor and worship.

As you deal with the indigo and violet rays, you are dealing more and more with things beyond words; with essences. And that is something for which spiritual seekers hunger. The process of moving into indigo and relishing it while you develop your ability to enjoy it is one of the blessings of a spiritually-oriented life, in our opinion. Those in higher densities also retain sacred sexuality and sacred social intercourse, although not in using the words but in sharing whole concepts with each other and collaborating to form group thoughts.

And perhaps what we would leave you with as we leave this subject is the realization that we hope all of you may have: that you have the power to collaborate with the infinite Creator and with each other at this level.

Certainly, sexually speaking, the mated pair collaborates in the most dynamic of all possible ways to practice the Presence of infinite love. But as you meet people who are doing the same sort of spiritual work as are you, and as you talk about that for which you thirst and hunger, you are creating collaboration through that contact point with intelligent infinity, and you are creating thought forms that then have an independence of existence.

You have spoken in this group about the creation of a new paradigm, and certainly this instrument is very focused on that creation of a new paradigm of living and being. Realize, when you have good conversations going between those of spiritual consanguinity, that you are creating changes in consciousness that will outlive the present moment and even your own lifetime. The opportunity for creating this paradigm is just as we have described for sexuality: conversation which achieves the penetration of the gateway. It is the thought that is focused when an intention is made to seek and to know this new paradigm. And then it is released into the emptiness of outer form so that it may reach the essence that fructifies your waking, everyday consciousness.

(Side one of tape ends.)

(Carla channeling)

We would say to the instrument that we feel that she will be fully able to discuss the various techniques of these rays, especially the indigo ray. We do not feel that we need to comment further on those details. And thusly, for this particular time, we have offered you what we hope will be helpful at this juncture.

Before we leave this instrument we would open the meeting to any questions that might be on the minds of those present. Is there another query at this time?

(Long pause.)

As there are no further queries from this group at this time, we will take our leave of this instrument and this group. It has truly been a pleasure to share our thoughts with you and to be a part of your sacred circle. Thank you for the beauty of your vibrations and the sweetness of your interactions, one with another. What a privilege we feel, my friends, to be a part of this!

We leave you in the love and in the light of the one infinite Creator. We are known to you as those of Q'uo. Adonai. Adonai. ♧

© 2009 L/L Research

L/L Research

L/L Research is a subsidiary of Rock Creek Research & Development Laboratories, Inc.

P.O. Box 5195
Louisville, KY 40255-0195

www.llresearch.org

Rock Creek is a non-profit corporation dedicated to discovering and sharing information which may aid in the spiritual evolution of humankind.

ABOUT THE CONTENTS OF THIS TRANSCRIPT: This telepathic channeling has been taken from transcriptions of the weekly study and meditation meetings of the Rock Creek Research & Development Laboratories and L/L Research. It is offered in the hope that it may be useful to you. As the Confederation entities always make a point of saying, please use your discrimination and judgment in assessing this material. If something rings true to you, fine. If something does not resonate, please leave it behind, for neither we nor those of the Confederation would wish to be a stumbling block for any.

© 2009 L/L Research

Saturday Meditation
November 10, 2007

Group question: *(Read by Jim.)* The question tonight is: Conspicuously absent in the philosophy of the Ra contact is any mention of the surrender of the conscious self to a guidance, intelligence or will greater than its own, be it the higher self, love and light, or the Creator. Where is there room for God's grace and surrender in Ra's philosophy? If surrender is suggested in Ra's philosophy, to what does an entity surrender?

(Carla channeling)

We are known to you as those of the principle of Q'uo. Greetings in the love and in the light of the one infinite Creator, in whose service we come to you this evening. Our hearts are full of gratitude that you should call us to your circle of seeking to respond to the question of the place of grace and surrender in the path of the Law of One. We are delighted to share our thoughts with you upon this subject.

As always, we would preface our remarks by requesting that each who listens to or reads these words reserves the right of discrimination as you listen or read, in order that you may choose which of our thoughts you shall pursue and use and which you shall lay aside.

Not all of our thoughts shall be equally appropriate for you and we would ask that, rather than taking our thoughts as a whole and attempting to work with them all, you choose those that resonate to you personally. For the path of truth for each seeker is unique and we would not be a stumbling block in your way by distracting you from the path of your own resonance.

If you shall do this we shall be most grateful, for it clears the way for us to know that we are not infringing upon your freewill or disturbing the rhythm of your process.

The question before us has to do with the place of surrender or grace in the system of philosophy or thinking that we have offered through this channel previously.

Firstly, we shall remark that the philosophy or system of thinking which is sometimes known as the Law of One or the Confederation Philosophy posits a singular, unitary consciousness in which all parts are interactive and all things are one. If all things are one, to what shall any soul surrender? This is why there is no mention of such a surrender within our thoughts which we share with you.

Now let us look at the way of the world, as we might call that world in which it would seem that there is a self that is error-prone and there is a separate Creator which is perfect. This imperfection is contrasted and separate from perfection. The human self of third density is set apart from the Creator of that third-density soul.

There are two basic ways in which those of your culture choose to make the demarcation between the human and the divine. The first is that of the

Christian, the Jewish and the Islamic religions or philosophical systems, if you will, in which there is required of the sinner a repentance and a surrender of the human self in order to worship, adore and be redeemed by the Creatorship of the Messiah or the God named Allah whose prophet is Mohammed. This system of demarcation of human and divine takes its flavor from the male energy of the God-name involved in all three religious systems.

The forerunners to these religions were systems of myth and magic in which there were sacrifices of animals and, in some cases, humans, so that the blood might ascend to the heavens and please the perfect Creator, which then would smile upon the sinning and erroneous human. The human, then, was redeemed to divinity through the sacrifice of an innocent, be it the animal or the virgin human.

In your Holy Bible there is the figure of Abraham being ordered by the Creator to sacrifice his son, Isaac. Not questioning the Creator in any way, Abraham builds a fire, sets the wood, sets the tinder ready to light the fire, then binds his son to the fire to make a human sacrifice as requested by the Creator. At the last instance a ram is found caught in a thicket. Isaac is set free and the ram takes the son's place.

In the New Testament, the son is not so lucky. There is no ram in Jerusalem and Jesus the Christ is crucified upon Golgotha. In both Testaments the figure is the same—one innocent to die in order to redeem all of sinful humanity.

Over against this type of demarcation between human and divine one may gaze at the systems of Buddhism and Hinduism, in which the erroneous human is set over against emptiness, nothingness, release, rest and freedom from suffering. In this figure each entity becomes the Christ, sacrificing its selfhood entirely in order to become free of suffering and thereby free of the wheel of karma and endless incarnations.

What these two systems have in common is a careful split betwixt humanity and divinity or the profane and the sacred. Within the Law of One, no such demarcation exists. Rather, it is posited that each entity within third density has the one infinite Creator at the heart of every fiber of its being.

The mystery of the Law of One is that implicit within the egg of humanity is the full-grown creature of Godhead. And implicit within the Creator is that sending forth of those seeds of self into illusion in order to gather information concerning Its own identity. This does not mean that the concepts of surrender and grace have no relevance to the Law of One, but rather that the process of spiritual evolution is seen, in this model of seeking the truth, to be a journey inward. There is no reaching outside of self but rather the intention to seek the heart of self, which is the one infinite Creator.

This is a model which your culture cannot support and which consensus reality itself finds it difficult to understand. Your culture cannot see the infinite value of the self or assume that perfection lies within the self, which is always seen as prone to error and foolish and flawed in many ways.

Consensus reality has no entrance into a system of thought which posits the perfection of humanity for it is quite obvious, when one gazes upon oneself or another being, that neither oneself nor another being either expresses perfection or contains perfection in some latent state. Being unconscious of the illusory nature of third density, the culture simply has no way to absorb or understand a system in which it is posited that all that is, including perfection, exists within the self.

We have spoken many times about this journey inward. We have spoken about that surface of life that is consensus reality which, rather than being earth, has more of the quality of the ocean, liquid, penetrable, deep, and capable of being entered by the diver who dives deep, perhaps to gather pearls from the ocean's floor and to bring up those precious pearls to store away in the treasure house.

Our consciousnesses have a regular and layered nature. The surface of the ocean of consciousness is that infinitesimal part of yourself that is fully invested in consensus reality. You are as one who floats upon the surface as long as you are content to remain uncurious as to what lies beneath the surface of self. Much of your psychology is content to remain largely upon the surface of self and to work with the structure of the personality.

We have called the personality the "personality shell" to indicate that it is, in a way, a husk which protects the fruit that lies so sweetly within. As long as you feel that you are your personality and are limited by your traits, gifts and limitations of personality, then you shall float upon the ocean of consciousness, never penetrating below the surface disturbances of waves, moved forever by the moon's attraction and washed with the tides that ebb and flow with all the influences on the surface personality.

It is our suggestion that you are capable of diving more deeply within the folds of your personality and penetrating at last into deeper waters which are, although illusory, far less distorted in their ability to express the truth of the oneness of all creation and the beauty, the truth and the Creatorship within each soul.

We can use words like Christ Consciousness or Cosmic Consciousness to help the seeker begin to penetrate the idea that there is an internalized Christhood within each cell of your body and within each iota of your emotions, your mentality, and your spirit.

Thusly, we see a journey that slowly develops for each seeker. The beginning of the journey is the awareness that there is more to the illusion than meets the eye. This awareness rouses the seeker and creates a hunger and a thirst for the truth that is missing from consensus reality.

There is a flatness perceived to consensus reality. Birth, growth, adulthood, working, marriage, children, friends, getting older, failing in health, and then dying are the signposts of the journey across the flat, even if turbulent, sea of consensus reality.

However, the seeker becomes aware that this model of life is not accurate—or not fully accurate. Once the seeker has awakened to the knowledge that there is infinitely more than this life and these details of life, the seeker can no longer go back to sleep. Once awake, the journey has begun.

There are various ways in which the seeker grows as he seeks ever more deeply for the truth about himself. If the seeker uses the settled religions which we mentioned earlier in an attempt to penetrate the truth of himself and his relation to the Creator, he is forever dependent upon an "other."

If the seeker is aware that he is seeking his deepest self, then there is no other, there is only a growing desire to lay aside each mask, each husk, and each trait of personality that veils from him the deepest truth of his nature. Yet this is not a mechanical process. There is no "stairway to heaven"[100] as the song phrases it. There is only the gentle and continuous intention to allow the dropping away of all of those things that keep the awareness from beholding the presence of the one infinite Creator.

And this is where surrender and grace reenter this Law of One. For the surrender is to the deeper self. And in surrendering to the deeper truth of the self, the shallower identifications of self with personality traits, accidents of birth, race, religion, and so forth, melt away. All distinctions blur beside the presence of the Creator within.

It is as though the seeker orbits the self, closer and closer, until finally it is drawn into the heart of self by a kind of spiritual gravity. And suddenly there bursts forth an awareness, a satori,[101] a realization, an epiphany.[102] And in that moment the self is known to the self. And that self is love.

Blessed are those moments of grace when all masks fall away and the naked self stands fearless, beholding its own nature, which is sacred and divine.

We do not object at all to the seeker's use of "otherness." For instance, this instrument works with mystical Christianity and patterns her life after the example of the one known as Jesus, the Christ, whom she calls her Beloved, whom she follows, for whom she would die, and for whom she lives. She is aware of the relative impurity of a model which contains the self and an other-than-the-self. Yet to contain her devotion and channel it in a productive and positive way, she uses the conventions to which she was born in consensus reality as a conscious being.

---

[100] Robert Plant of Led Zeppelin wrote the lyrics to this song and all rights are reserved. Its opening lyrics are, "There's a lady who's sure all that glitters is gold, and she's buying a stairway to heaven." It is interesting, in the context of this session, that the ending lyrics are, "As we wind on down the road, our shadows taller than our soul, there walks a lady we all know who shines white light and wants to show how everything still turns to gold. And if you listen very hard, the tune will come to you at last, when all are one and one is all."

[101] satori: a spiritual awakening sought in Zen Buddhism, often coming suddenly.

[102] epiphany: a sudden, intuitive perception of or insight into the reality or essential meaning of something, usually initiated by some simple, homely, or commonplace occurrence or experience.

It is a way to avoid paradox. For the conscious mind, with its rational and logical nature, has a deep distrust and dislike of paradox. And it is certainly paradoxical to say both that the surface self is real and that the deepest and most unitary expression of self is real. Yet that is what we say, knowing that it is a paradox and a mystery.

There are those among your mystical groups, as well as individuals who do not function as part of a group, who abnegate[103] words and choose the way of silence. Over a period of time the habit of silence decreases the difficulty of absorbing the outrage of paradox. And such silent souls smile at the sophistry of words which separate and logic which delineates and divides to no good purpose, spiritually speaking.

Yet we would not encourage you to become recluses. We would encourage you to embrace paradox and mystery. We would encourage you to continue your journey upon the surface of life, knowing that it, too, is perfect in its way, even with all the masks, all the confusions and all the misunderstandings and limitations of dealing with each other and with circumstances which occur in everyday life.

For third density was not designed to be a quiet and steady dive to the center of self. It was designed to be turbulent, as the shaker that breaks rocks into pieces or large pieces of ceramic into small pieces of ceramic, polishing them and shaping them by friction and impact.

To come at the action intended in third density another way, we could use the figure of the fiery furnace which tempers[104] and strengthens the brittle, callow[105] young soul so that it becomes an instrument of great flexibility and strength.

Your world is intended as a refinery of souls. That catalyst that comes to the surface self is seen by us as a good thing, a useful and appropriate thing, whether it feels comfortable or vastly uncomfortable. Indeed, it is the movement of the self within periods or situations of discomfort which are especially helpful in achieving maturity and a more polished or tempered realization of the nature of the self and the Creator.

Both your physical body and your metaphysical body or your energy body are designed to take advantage of and make use of this catalytic effect of the day-by-day occurrences of life. A great deal of the catalyst of life comes from the relationships which you have, first with yourself and then with other people. And as the spirit grows in maturity, it becomes more able to see through the illusion of suffering. It becomes more able to penetrate the devices and desires of its own surface being to see the patterns of learning that lie within those surface movements of the emotions and the reactions of the mind and the body.

It does not become more in control of what occurs within life. Rather, it becomes unafraid of not being in control. And this is grace. When all about one is pressured and stressful and yet there is that within the heart that remembers the true nature of the self, then that spirit is in a state of grace and may maximize its learning and its service within third density.

What is being refined in the refinery of souls that is Earth? What is the soul within third density? A synonym for "soul" might be "heart." And we have often suggested to you that you are on a journey into your own open heart. Christ is waiting for you within your own heart. As you allow the surface of self to fall away, you become empty enough to fall in love with yourself. You begin to see that all these details of self, wretched though they may be in some cases, and glorious in others, fall away to nothingness before the self's desire to seek the presence of the one infinite Creator.

And so the self within incarnation becomes merry and lighthearted, whether in sunshine or in rain; whether in good times or evil. For the self remembers that it is on a journey whose destination is sure. And thusly, through all the changes and chances of mortal life, that seeking soul may be confident and quiet within, full of faith and knowing that all is well. And this, too, is grace.

There is great power in words. Words can stir up the emotions. Within the power of those who wish to inspire others, there is the ability to manipulate feelings and emotions and to whip up passion, so that an ecstasy of hysteria is achieved in which there seems to be a breakthrough into the love of Christ,

---

[103] to abnegate: refuse or deny oneself (some rights, conveniences, etc.); to reject; renounce, to relinquish; to give up.
[104] to temper: impart strength or toughness to (steel or cast iron) by heating and cooling.
[105] callow: immature or inexperienced; (of a young bird) featherless; unfledged.

however you wish to say that condition of perfect love. And that feels very good. Yet that which is whipped up, dies down.

We would rather not proceed with words that inspire in order to whip up passion and to change rejoicing into an hysterical expression of love for the Creator. Rather, we ask you to use every faculty of your being, your intellect, your will, your body, your emotions, and every fiber of your being to seek, seek, seek to remember who you are.

There are so many ways to work on that question! For all of nature is one with you. And all of nature is full of that information which harmonizes with your desires and sets up patterns of attraction and coincidence.

And all of spirit is one with you as well. All that is unseen and not of nature but of spirit conspires to speak with you in silence, singing into your life those silent melodies of truth and beauty.

(Side one of tape ends.)

There is a wind that blows through you, changeable and sacred. And in every season and mood of your life it brings new life, new light, new power, new information, new expressions of that which is always the same—love, love, love.

We encourage your explorations. However you wish to seek the Creator, we encourage you to follow those preferences and those biases. We simply offer to you our humble opinion of the deeper truth of the process that is occurring within third density. Third density is set up as system after system of opposites. Male and female, light and dark are certainly chief among them. Yet male and female combine to make third density in the sense that it is the male principle and the female principle, attracting each other, which create this illusion that you call third density.[106] It is the very fabric and stuff of third density.

---

[106] It is likely that this is meant not in a literal sense but in the sense in which the Kabbalists and Christian White Magicians mean it. In the Banishing Ritual of the Lesser Pentagram, for instance, the magician begins this purification exercise by envisioning first the downward-pointing triangle of the feminine principle and then envisioning the male principle, an upward-pointing triangle, being drawn to the female principle and covering it. The resulting figure or shape is known in Kabbalah as the Star of David and is the image which represents the consensus-reality world.

And indeed the meat which is chewed in third density is that meat of choice, light or dark, radiant or magnetic, service to others or service to self. There are two paths, both valid and quite opposite in their energy, both pointed towards an eventual unity yet choosing two completely different paths towards that inevitable awareness of utter unity.

In claiming the Law of One, we move ahead to that point in what you would call your future where the positive and negative paths have once again converged and become one for all time, until the creation itself moves from time to the timeless and enters the womb of yet another creation, as the heartbeat of the Creator throbs once more and another creation begins.

You journey homeward. How shall you journey? That is the question of third density. Shall you journey in the light, seeking ever to become more of service, more loving, more giving, more aware of the love within each moment? Or shall you enjoy the dark path where the self is seen immediately as the Creator and all other selves are seen as those who would worship the Creator in you? Thus, the dark path is one where each who follows it attempts to coerce, manipulate, or otherwise use all other selves, to tell them what to do and to make sure they are useful to the self or moved out of the way of self. This also is a valid path, yet it is a dark path and a bloody path. There are those who prefer it.

We are not those. We are those of the radiant path. And so we ask you to re-member rather than dis-member yourself. We ask you to collect all of the pieces of your self and re-member yourself, to gather all of your members together. We ask that you love your imperfections, gather them to your bosom, honor them and bring them into your heart. And then we suggest that you remain in that tabernacle within even as you move upwards into the surface of life once again and experience the turbulence of the surface tides of life.

There is, to our mind, that constant flow of moving from the depths of the truth to the surface expressions of the truth, which in many cases are highly colored but always carry those seeds of the truth which lies so deeply within. All is one and all is love.

This instrument is suggesting that we cease speaking upon this particular topic so that we may use the remaining energy of this group and this instrument to inquire as to whether there is a desire to follow up on this query or to ask another query at this time. We are those of Q'uo.

(Long pause.)

We are those of Q'uo, and are aware that we have exhausted the questions that this group has this evening. And so we would thank you once again, our dear friends, for the privilege of sharing in your meditation and being a part of this session of working. Your circle of seeking is beautiful to behold and your blended auras sing of the love and the light of which we have been speaking this evening. Thank you for allowing us to share in the love and affection that you have for each other and for the one infinite Creator. It is a blessing to be part of your circle.

We leave this instrument and this group in the love and in the light of the one infinite Creator. We are known to you as the principle of Q'uo. Adonai. Adonai.

L/L Research is a subsidiary of Rock Creek Research & Development Laboratories, Inc.

P.O. Box 5195
Louisville, KY 40255-0195

L/L Research

www.llresearch.org

Rock Creek is a non-profit corporation dedicated to discovering and sharing information which may aid in the spiritual evolution of humankind.

ABOUT THE CONTENTS OF THIS TRANSCRIPT: This telepathic channeling has been taken from transcriptions of the weekly study and meditation meetings of the Rock Creek Research & Development Laboratories and L/L Research. It is offered in the hope that it may be useful to you. As the Confederation entities always make a point of saying, please use your discrimination and judgment in assessing this material. If something rings true to you, fine. If something does not resonate, please leave it behind, for neither we nor those of the Confederation would wish to be a stumbling block for any.

© 2009 L/L Research

Saturday Meditation
November 24, 2007

Jim: The question tonight, Q'uo, is what are the key barriers to and requirements for making contact with intelligent infinity?

(Carla channeling)

We are those known to you as the principle of Q'uo. Greetings in the love and the light of the one infinite Creator, in whose service we come to you this day. It is a great privilege and pleasure to be with you this evening, to share your meditation, and to experience the beauty of your blended auras as you build in your circle of seeking a sacred place. The arching light of your circle grows every second and is beautiful to behold.

We thank you for calling us to your circle of seeking. We are happy indeed to share our thoughts with you concerning the subject of the barriers to and the requirements for opening the gateway to intelligent infinity. However, as always, we would ask, before we begin, that each of you use your judgment as you listen to those things which we have to share. It is not possible for all of our remarks to be appropriate for all of those who listen to or read our words. So, as you listen, when something resonates to you, then by all means work with it if you wish. But if something does not resonate to you, then please leave it behind. We would not wish to be a stumbling block before you.

We appreciate your diligence in this discrimination, for it frees us to be unconcerned about whether or not we might infringe on your free will or disturb your process of spiritual seeking. Thank you for your kindness in this regard.

The query places the question about the barriers to using the gateway to intelligent infinity before the question about discussing the requirements for such use. However, we would prefer to discuss the requirements first, so that as we speak of the barriers it will be obvious as to why certain things are indeed barriers.

You are marvelous creatures. Each of you is incredibly complex and at the same time utterly simple. Your energy bodies are those unseen parts of you that have molded your physical body. And the energy body is the essence of you as a person or, as those of Ra call it, as a mind/body/spirit complex. The seven chakras of the energy body are all-important to the functioning of your physical body as well as your finer bodies.

The gateway to intelligent infinity is at the very top of those chakras, involving the indigo and violet-ray chakras. Springing from the open heart, the seeker may open the gateway to intelligent infinity by moving into the violet ray, through the indigo ray, with the desire and will focusing in firm intention and asking that work may be done in consciousness.

So, you open the gateway to intelligent infinity, the door to those specific inspirations which are desired, as opposed to the general and ever-flowing inspiration of the open heart which abides in love itself, love complete and love untouched by any other energy. With the gateway open you become able to work with more specific types of guidance that, though specific, are in general unheard and pouring into the heart itself in concept and essence rather than in thought and in words.

The nurturing and care of the energy body is very important to those who wish to use the gateway to intelligent infinity in their seeking. Indeed, entities who are blocked in the lower three chakras are not able to sustain a full flow of the infinite Creator's energy that comes from the bottom of the chakra system upwards and moves through the chakras exiting at the crown of the head.

The first requirement for working with the gateway to intelligent infinity is that the heart be open. Consequently, although many seekers do not wish to continue to work intensively with the lower three chakras, it is our opinion that it is essential to continue to work with those three chakras, giving them all of the honor and respect that you give the higher chakras.

That which tends to block red ray is a level of depression that argues against life and the joy of life, and difficulties with sexuality. Because of the fact that the red ray deals with matters of survival and sexuality, those who are limping along with no true appreciation of life are going to be limiting the flow of energy into their very first chakra and therefore receiving into the heart only a fraction of the power or the energy that is available from the Creator.

The orange-ray chakra, being the seat of relationships of a personal nature with yourself and with others, is blocked when there is difficulty in those relationships which causes the chakra either to be blocked or to be over-activated. So, it is well to have a continuing focus in each relationship that is your privilege to sustain, watching for the vibrational harmony between you and the other, or indeed the harmony between you and yourself. So often the issues that you have with yourself can be quite toxic in terms of limiting the light that is flowing through that chakra. So, it is well to spend time becoming sweet with yourself and with other selves as well.

The yellow-ray chakra is the chakra of group relationships or legal relationships such as the birth family, the marriage family, the work family, and other groups that create their own energies and have their own, shall we say, oversoul. And in this chakra, too, the usual causes of blockages have to do with difficulties in these relationships. And again, because it is so easy to be blocked, at least momentarily, in yellow ray, it is a wise seeker who tunes his heart and his attention when dealing with these relationships in order that harmony may prevail. And when harmony has been lost from a certain situation, it is well to seek ways to restore it. For this restores the flow of energy through that chakra and into the open heart.

Once an entity has reached the point where the heart is open and energy is flowing freely, he may then choose to move into the higher chakras. If he wishes to do work in consciousness such as meditation, healing, prayer or inspirational reading and reflection, he moves very consciously and deliberately into the indigo-ray chakra, the home of faith.

Here, one is always dealing with unseen things. In the indigo ray, one has left the physical body behind. The indigo ray is physically placed at the third eye position at which the Hindu monk will place a red dot, for in the Hindu system of belief there is a great appreciation of this chakra and it is believed by them, as well as us, that it is the gateway, the door, to direct contact with intelligent infinity, or as they would put it, the Creator.

Dwelling in indigo ray, the seeker begins to approach the gateway by the use of silence. It is necessary that the mind be still to a great extent so that the inspiration which is being sought may have room to flow into the chakra body through the violet ray and then the indigo, and then to be seated in the heart.

Once that connection has been made and there is a downflow of inspiration and information matching the upflow of the Creator's energy, it is possible to work in consciousness simply by allowing that flow to occur and being aware consciously of that flow. For indeed you are seated in the midst of a beautiful fountain of light when the gateway is open and inspiration is moving in.

It is within the blessing of that presence that one takes up the work of that *beau geste* of seeking to know the truth, seeking to feel the insights that only come to a faithful and listening heart.

The barriers to work with the gateway to intelligent infinity are those things that would block an entity in any of the rays up through the heart. Perhaps the most pervasive blockage found in spiritual seekers is a feeling of low self-worth, a feeling of unworthiness to do the work at hand. The one known as T spoke recently to this instrument of the depth of searching that she has gone through since the Homecoming Gathering that this entity attended at L/L Research, asking the question, "Who Am I?"

As she has delved into that question more and more, she has found a great deal of work that she feels the need to do in order to become a more sturdy and stable individual, spiritually speaking. The one known as T said that she found a great deal of self-judgment as she approached the question of "Who Am I?"

We do not attempt to suggest to you that you make no mistakes. To be a third-density human being, my friends, is to be error-prone. You are dwelling within a heavy illusion and your culture has many, many distortions which make it almost impossible to know what the truly ethical or right thing is to do at certain times.

Further, in human nature there is an unevenness of focus that is almost always present to some extent within the personality, so that on one day you may feel that you are doing very well with the catalyst that you have and on another day you may feel that you are doing quite poorly at it, handling things in clumsy ways, saying the wrong thing at the wrong time.

We would encourage you to lift away from self-judgment at times that you feel you have made an error. It is well to observe errors in yourself when they occur. That is how one learns, by making mistakes. As entities become more and more spiritually mature, they find delight in using the fruits of their self-knowledge of the past, and so the heavy burden of self-doubt and a feeling of low self-worth is a little bit easier to dissolve. Yet always there is a disappointment that strikes a seeker when he realizes that he has made an error. He cannot go back and fix it. He simply must begin again and hope to remember the graceful way, the loving way, the compassionate way to handle catalyst of this kind when it comes around again, as it most surely will.

Self-criticism and self-judgment are powerful sources of blockage. There is within many seekers the desire to make a difference in the world, to help others and serve good causes. Yet, in that same general run of seekers there is often a prejudice against working on the self, for it seems selfish to be absorbed in the processes of the self. It is our opinion that it is in healing yourself that you heal the world. It is in learning to love yourself that you learn to love others. It is in finding compassion at last for yourself that you are finally able to have compassion on others. It is in blessing your own suffering by respecting it, honoring it, and forgiving it in yourself that you become able to behold the suffering of the world in its massive and almost infinite depth.

It is necessary, really, for you to fall in love with yourself. Self-judgment cannot be overcome. It must be balanced by compassion. You are bound to make mistakes and come under the possibility of judgment. Yet also do you have within you creatorship, so that you are never in a position of having failed for longer than it takes for you to turn again to the light and start afresh.

There are various techniques for falling in love with yourself. If you are present with yourself and become aware of the wide range of emotions that you feel, that may be the most direct way to become kindly affectioned towards yourself, to like yourself, and ultimately, gloriously, genuinely, truly, fall in love with yourself. Just as you are, you are perfect!

This need not give you any cause for arrogance or pride. All entities are perfect. All entities are the Creator. Yet, you dwell in the creation that you have made. So pamper yourself with good thoughts, good experiences, and frequent dips in the waters of truth and beauty and inspiration in whatever ways appeal to you.

Another very common barrier that closes the energy body down, in whatever chakra it is originating from, is fear. There are any number of ways to be afraid. One may have a condition of chronic fear because of those things which have occurred and have been difficult catalyst to bear. There are ways to be afraid of the future. There may be fear surrounding the very process of knowing yourself for you have a healthy and thriving shadow side and you must acquaint yourself with that as well as with the part that takes your fancy, that part that is in the sunlight and likeable.

However fear does come upon you, it will block the flow of energy through the chakra system. And so we recommend the exercise of balancing to be performed at least daily, in the evening, at the end of your day, when you have a little time to reflect on what has occurred.

Ask yourself what thoughts you may have had this day where your even tenor and your open heart were interrupted even momentarily. And then move to those points of departure from the even keel of an open and flowing energy body. If some issue has arisen that has closed the heart even for a second, it is well to move into that emotion once again, relive it, and even exaggerate it so that you have a very conscious and thoughtful awareness of just what happened, just what it was that caused that feeling of, say, impatience, anger, jealousy or even great joy. Anything that takes you away from the open heart and stops the flow of energy is deserving of an examination.

And once you have thoroughly reexperienced this moment where catalyst became too much for you and closed your energy system down, then allow yourself to begin to experience the dynamic opposite of that emotion. If you felt impatience because another driver on the road cut you off, charging onto the expressway without regard to your car, imagine the situation again, only this time image yourself having complete patience and utter tranquility, and emphasize and exaggerate that feeling until you are swept away by it.

Then release both dynamic opposites of patience and impatience and see how much more balanced you feel. Do this in the case of each of those thoughts or emotions that have thrown you off-balance during the day. Reflect upon each of them, honor them, experience them, balance them, and restore your energy body to a good, even flow.

You may find yourself wanting to tune-up your energy body during the day as well. And it can be done in a moment, if you wish to use that moment.

We do not suggest shaping your thoughts because you know those are the thoughts you should have. "Should" is not a word that is helpful in spiritual seeking. It has nothing to do with the open and spontaneous flow of the love and the light of the one infinite Creator with whom you are attempting to work. Each of your thoughts is appropriate in its own way and true and good, and it is what is. Therefore, it is in that open and spontaneous flow of thinking and acting and feeling that the meat of the seeker's learning lies.

So, when we say to "tune-up the self" we do not mean to alter the behavior but rather to open the self to the awareness of the Creator. When you are able to do this even momentarily, it opens up the chakra body and allows the energy to move freely.

This entity is a mystical Christian and often she has a one-word prayer that she uses. It is "Jesus." That one word can alter her entire attitude. There are key words for each of you. For the one known as R it is the word "remember." Find those key phrases that make your heart smile and that restore the flow of good energy through your body.

We would at this time ask if there are follow-up questions to which we may respond at this time.

Jim: *(Reading from a list of questions sent in.)* "Is a strong and physically fit body, in terms of muscle strength and cardiovascular fitness, helpful in the mystical search for intelligent infinity, assuming that the mental prerequisites of self-knowledge, acceptance, and balance have been sufficiently met within the entity who wishes to make contact with intelligent infinity? Is a healthy and strong body helpful for the channeling of intelligent infinity and intelligent energy? What's the proper role for the body for the entity who seeks intelligent infinity?"

We are those of Q'uo, and we are aware of your query, my brother. The proper role of the physical body for each of you is to carry the consciousness that is yourself as a soul. Certainly a healthy body is helpful in that there are no aches and pains to distract one from spiritual seeking. However, it is in the attitude towards the body, rather than the body itself, that the use of the body is found, spiritually speaking.

If one realizes that bodies are sacred, that they are temples in which dwell the one infinite Creator, then it can be seen that, whether healthy or not healthy, each body is a beautiful servant that has given its entire life over so that you may, as a soul, learn your lessons, offer your service, laugh, love and be loved within this illusion.

Consequently, you want to be very good to your body. It is often an expression of spiritual purity that creates in people the desire to eat a good diet that is respectful to that which the body truly needs. It can be used that way as a vehicle of transformation. It helps to realize how essential the physical vehicle is. You would not be able to experience the school of souls that third density is if you did not have a physical vehicle to anchor you into the vibrations of this illusion. Without that physical body, heavy as it may seem at times, you would have no ability to affect changes, as you wish to affect changes, within your own self at far deeper levels than the surface of life.

It is well, therefore, to have a great appreciation and affection for your body. Indeed, one of the ways to enter the gateway of intelligent infinity is sacred sexuality, in which the body itself experiences that orgasmic joy and power that is the steady state of the one infinite Creator's consciousness.

May we ask if there is another query?

Jim: *(Reading from a list of questions sent in.)* "Billions of entities there are who call out to and seek that which they feel to be the one infinite Creator, each in their own local, unique and distorted fashion. Of those who are truly hungry for the truth, what makes the difference between those who succeed in realizing the divine within and those who leave their incarnation as ignorant as when they came into it?"

We are those of Q'uo, and believe we understand your query.

For all of those millions of whom you speak, seeking in each of their unique ways, if they truly do seek, they have truly found. There is no failure rate whatsoever in terms of seeking not being answered. That which is asked in faith is answered one way or another.

Perhaps, for those who feel that they have never received any spiritual enlightenment, there are continuing blocks which keep that entity from perceiving the answers which are given to the questions asked. Yet those answers have been given and the good of them is locked within the heart for a time when the entity's mind is not deafened by doubting.

Intention plays a tremendous role in terms of whether or not a seeker feels successful in his seeking. It is our way of thinking that the seeking creates its own success, not in terms of results or effects, but in terms of the seeking being the reward. It is not getting to the end of the journey of spiritual seeking that holds the reward, in our opinion, as much as it is the journey itself. It is not the questions that are answered that holds the virtue for the spiritual seeker. Rather, it is the questions that are asked.

Spirituality is a movement beyond words and beyond the crutches of perception that give a limited physical existence its bounds. Without words, without anything but feelings and sensing and the knowing of gnosis or insight, a seeker can be doing tremendous work at the soul level and, because of a lack of perceiving the virtue of that work in and of itself, may shut himself off from feeling that he has made any gains whatsoever.

It generally goes back to the process of not only getting to know the self but becoming willing to fall in love with the self that makes the difference in perception between a seeker who does not feel he is doing well and a seeker who is satisfied simply to be on the journey and have the day's light in which to do his work.

May we ask if there is another query at this time?

Jim: *(Reading from a list of questions sent in.)* "For one desiring the development of mystical consciousness is the ingestion of alcohol or other mind-altering intoxicants inhibitive to growth at any level—mental, physical or spiritual—or does it cause a regression in growth?"

We are those of Q'uo, and are aware of your query, my brother.

The intake of substances that alter consciousness is not recommended as a means of attaining spiritual learning. It is far better to allow a natural development of spiritual powers than to try to attain them by the use of substances which put one artificially in a more pure or refined state of awareness. When alcohol is taken or various drugs are used, depending on the nature of the drug, it shuts down the ability to do spiritual work at that time to one extent or another depending on the substance.

Consequently, if one wishes to have alcohol and become merry, or to indulge in other drug use which seems good to that person, he needs to be aware that he will not be able to have that acuity of mind and that control over the use of the will that go hand in hand with spiritual work. Once the effects of the substance have worn off, the entity is back where he started and is able to use his normal facilities in his normal ways. There is nothing intrinsically negative in the use of such substances.

It may be seen that when one wishes to do spiritual work it is well not to use such substances. Yet one has many moods. And we do not frown upon those who wish to take some relaxation time. Indeed, we feel that the addiction that many of your people have to watching television or playing video games has just exactly the same damping effect on spirituality. One cannot do spiritual work when one is totally involved in a video game or watching a show on television, yet those things are enjoyable and are there for you to use when you wish to use them.

It is a matter of doing that which you wish to do. For that is why you came into incarnation: to experience those things you wish to experience. You may see that it is good to balance the times of recreation, amusement, distraction and social situations of no great spiritual moment, shall we say, with those activities and interests that indeed have a good deal of spiritual work, so that you have a varied menu of things in your day, some focused and highly intense and others relaxed and full of the enjoyment of life.

It is well to have a wide range of things, those seemingly good for you and those seemingly not so good for you but which you desire anyway. Follow your desires, but always be aware that you have the opportunity at all times to choose that which you wish to do and ask yourself, "Is this what I wish to do?" If it is, enjoy yourself. But if it involves the taking of substances that damp down your ability to do spiritual work, then accept that and know that this is a time in your day or your week in which you have laid aside a direct assault on the gateway to intelligent infinity and instead have decided to amuse yourself with some of those distractions that your earth plane offers.

In no case do you need to judge yourself for wishing to have a glass of wine, for instance. All things are acceptable. It is your choice as to when you wish to place yourself outside the pale of work within the gateway to intelligent infinity.

May we ask if there is another query at this time?

Jim: *(Reading from a list of questions sent in.)* "In the case of the pyramid, a technology was used to accelerate the natural growth of the entity to that point at which they would move through the mystical death and rebirth as the resurrected self. Are there any other similar technologies in today's world comparable in function to what the pyramids offered?"

We are those of Q'uo, and are aware of your query, my brother.

The closest analog to the shaman's experience of death which the place below the pyramid offered are the American Indian rituals of the sweat lodge and the vision quest. In the sweat lodge the heat takes one beyond the bounds of human awareness. It feels very much like a death or as if one were close to death and this is often a trigger for new awareness and the epiphany of the moment that has been sought.

Similarly, the vision quest, with its extreme levels of discomfort, offers to that seeker a chance to move beyond the usual bounds of what is considered acceptable. When one is too sleepless for too long, too hungry for too long, and too uncomfortable for too long, there comes a time when one goes beyond all of those limitations. It is forced into a kind of state of abeyance by the very intensity of the discomfort and this also, is a death-like experience.

This technique, however, can be employed on a far less strenuous basis and the one known as G has often made use of these limited fasts. A time of fasting doesn't feel like death, certainly, but it does feel uncomfortable, and when it is fasting with an intention, then it is giving honor to that intention. The result of such a fast is often an enhanced awareness that comes from having sacrificed comfort in order to offer the self a spiritual road to walk.

You may almost see this death of the shaman as a kind of game. For the intention of the shaman in creating within himself the feeling of death or the experience of death is to wake back up into the daylight and to realize for the first time what a gift life is. And this can be realized without the death experience by one who is sensitive and imaginative and who can put himself into that awareness of the place beneath the pyramid or the earth in the sweat lodge or the person on the vision quest who is going without food and sleep and asking for enlightenment.

Indeed, this realization of how sweet and wonderful an opportunity that each day is can be cultivated without the death experience or the analog to the death experience. And we would recommend focusing, each and every day, on thanksgiving for being alive and being able to experience this beautiful creation that you experience each day. When you realize that you are entirely free to seek the Creator this day, it is a wonderful realization and it turns the most dreary of days and the most burdensome of occupations into a dance of delight.

May we ask if there is another query at this time?

Jim: Not from here.

May we ask if there is another query that is not on that page from the one known as G at this time?

G: No, not at this time. Thank you, Q'uo.

We thank you, my brother. In that case, we would ask if there is a query from anyone else in the group at this time.

(No further queries.)

We are those of Q'uo, and since we seem to have exhausted the questions from this group at this time let us iterate to you our thanks, our gratitude, and our pleasure at being asked to be part of your circle of seeking this evening. It has been a true delight for us. You help us so much by allowing us to attempt to be of service to you. And you teach us so much each time that we interact with you.! We thank you with all of our collective heart.

At this time we would leave this instrument and this group in the love and in the light, in the peace and in the power of the one infinite Creator. We are known to you as the principle of Q'uo. Adonai. Adonai.

L/L Research

L/L Research is a subsidiary of Rock Creek Research & Development Laboratories, Inc.

P.O. Box 5195
Louisville, KY 40255-0195

www.llresearch.org

Rock Creek is a non-profit corporation dedicated to discovering and sharing information which may aid in the spiritual evolution of humankind.

ABOUT THE CONTENTS OF THIS TRANSCRIPT: This telepathic channeling has been taken from transcriptions of the weekly study and meditation meetings of the Rock Creek Research & Development Laboratories and L/L Research. It is offered in the hope that it may be useful to you. As the Confederation entities always make a point of saying, please use your discrimination and judgment in assessing this material. If something rings true to you, fine. If something does not resonate, please leave it behind, for neither we nor those of the Confederation would wish to be a stumbling block for any.

© 2009 L/L RESEARCH

Saturday Meditation
December 15, 2007

Group question: The question we have today, Q'uo, is about the meaning of Christmas in our world. Please tell us about the spiritual principles involved in living a life that follows in the footsteps of Jesus; specifically, about living from the heart, living in love. And since this is a season of giving, also please mention the principles about giving with love or giving from the heart.

(Carla channeling)

We are those of the principle known to you as Q'uo. Greetings in the love and in the light of the one infinite Creator, in whose service we come to you this day and always. It is our great pleasure to share this time with you and to be called to be part of your meditation and your circle of seeking. Thank you for this privilege and honor. It is always a wonderful experience to be part of this beautiful array of energies as you combine in one circle to seek the truth, and we are honored.

We are happy to speak with you concerning the Christmas season and the issues of living in the way of Jesus the Christ, and giving as the season seems to request that one does with the kind of love that the one known as Jesus the Christ would have.

As always, we would ask that each of you use your discrimination in listening to our thoughts. Follow and use the thoughts that seem resonant and good to you. If a thought does not seem resonant to you, please leave it behind. We do not expect to hit the target of your own personal needs with each and every thought that we share. We thank you for this consideration.

We wish to say to the one known as R that the part of the principle of Q'uo which is speaking through this instrument this evening is the Brothers and Sisters of the Hatonn group. The subject is unconditional love, which is this entity's native vibration. Consequently, we shall express through the one known as Hatonn this evening.

Winter comes upon the planet in the geographical area in which you live in much the same way as night follows day. It is an inevitable and worthy part of the cycle of life. And yet the loss of the light is a powerful catalyst for those souls who dwell within the more dimly lit wintertime. The long, slow periods of darkness in winter seem very dark indeed and that light which succeeds in shining through the storms of winter is ofttimes pale and wan, for the sun is farther away.

This creates within the third-density entity an inevitable response. In some cases, if an entity is close to the physical death, the lack of light will encourage an entity to move through the gateway into the larger life. The darkness of winter claims many who would perhaps live through the summer and yet because it is winter there is a natural tendency to rest, relax and seek that gateway to larger life. It is a powerful catalyst and we would not wish to belittle those who find themselves distressed at the chill and darkness of this season of the year.

Yet, of course, it is at this very season that the light is desired the most, yearned for and prayed for the most and awaited with the most eagerness. In just such a way does all negative catalyst bring the seeking soul to the point of realizing and expressing the yearning, the hungering, and the thirsting for light, truth and love. It is a natural response to this lack of light to band together and to create a special day, a day that flies in the face of darkness, a day of rejoicing and extra light, a day of abundance of food and drink and generosity of person to person.

And so it has been since long before the one known as Jesus the Christ walked your Earth and took part in this season of darkness. Yet it was the genius of the human spirit that caused the taking of the natural and non-religious observance of the winter solstice and the turning of it into a holy day or a holiday. Indeed, the one known as Jesus the Christ was born in the summertime. Yet it is psychologically right for third density that the birth of this entity was placed in the very heart of the winter's darkness. So, let us look at this moment when light comes into the darkness.

Firstly, we would suggest that each of you is that element which is light born into darkness. Whatever your natural day of birth, you share the birthday of Jesus the Christ in terms of what some among you would call the time of being born again. You are each the infant Jesus the Christ, wrapped in swaddling clothes and lying in the rough manger which holds the hay for the cows to eat.

You are also the blessed Virgin Mary who nurtures this tiny child, this point of brilliant light within the darkness of human experience. And you are Joseph, tolerant, patient and supportive, ready to work as a carpenter to support his wife, the nurturer, and his child, the Christ, the principle of love. And you are the shepherds who come in wonder and awe to lay down their shepherds' crooks and kneel at the feet of Mary, gazing with wonder at this precious, precious infant.

And there is a portion of you, deep within your soul, which has never been separated from the one infinite Creator in any wise. That portion of you is the angels, singing, "Hallelujah, hallelujah, hallelujah! Glory and peace."

It is a poignant moment. And it says a good deal about the human condition. It evokes, as the one known as Jim said to this instrument recently, contemplation of the nature of relationships. For the one known as Jesus, this precious point of light coming into the world, could not have survived infanthood had it not been for the web of relationships he had with his parents and with the owner of the inn that allowed Mary a place to rest her head on the night of his birth, while the shepherds flocked to that manger and formed a deep relationship with this infant.

In the gladsome and free times of summer, with its limitless light, so it seems, the importance of the support and love of that web of support that is called the family and those special relationships that are called friendships do not seem so urgent a matter. The winter night is far more revealing of the importance of these relationships of soul to soul, heart to heart and hand to hand.

Therefore, and quite justly, it is often a time for families to join together to renew old ties, share memories of times long past, and experience the somewhat surrealistic and eerie feeling of time falling away and one's childhood seeming to come back to one, as one experiences these old, old relationships with much shared history that are true of the birth family of mother and child, sister and brother.

It is also a time when it seems appropriate to many to open their hearts in generosity to their friends and celebrate the precious gift of mutual support and encouragement.

The one known as Jim also suggested to this instrument that this is a good time to reflect upon each relationship, asking the self if there is any way in which the self has flinched away from intimacy and the positive nature of each relationship; asking the self, "Could I see anything in which I perhaps failed to express the depths of my appreciation and love for the other entity?"

This is, indeed, that moment in the seasons of the year's cycle where it is especially appropriate to create expressions of apology and forgiveness; apology to those whom you perhaps feel that in your own judgment you held back from offering all of your love. And likewise it is a time to think of those who may have, in your own judgment, done that same thing to you and to offer up a complete and total forgiveness and a reestablishment of that intimacy, as if that flaw that you see has been completely healed.

The nature of unconditional love dwells not only in the one known as Jesus the Christ but in Carla the Christ, in C the Christ, in R the Christ, in S the Christ, in P the Christ and in everyone, the Christ.

The Christ does not come into your world in strength. The Christ does not come into your world in power. The Christ does not come into your world in riches. Indeed, the infant soul comes into the world helpless. With infinite love it gazes with its infant eyes upon a world lost to darkness, despair, disappointment and grief. And it looks upon that lost world with eyes of unconditional love. That light that cannot be put out. That unconditional, everlasting, eternal love gazes from the eyes of a child who cannot speak; who cannot take care of himself; who is in every way needy.

My beloved friends, so are you needy. Your infant soul gazes upon a lost world also, that interior world of your own suffering. It is helpless to speak to it. It is helpless to act. It can only gaze upon you with eyes of unconditional love. And so we would ask you at this time to look deeply within your own self at that infant soul within you that is so beautiful and so pure. Let your heart melt and open and enfold that infant soul of yours as if your love were swaddling clothes.

Pick up that child and rock it and hold it to your bosom and feed it your attention. What does your soul need to grow strong? What shall you offer this infant within you? A baby needs attention. A baby needs support. A baby needs care. And so we would suggest to you, dear ones, to enter into that stable of your soul and dedicate yourself, not for one moment but for all of your incarnation, to nurturing and taking care of that soul within you that is seeking to gain in strength; that is seeking to thrive and find the life in which it may become more and more able to express in ways more understandable than the silence of a baby.

What is it to be a soul dwelling in the darkness of a physical body? What kind of care does that infant soul need? We would ask that you turn your body into a temple, that you fill it with light, feed it the food that makes it be its lightest, offer it the studies and the thoughts that bring it light, and offer that soul the attention that it needs by remembering to embrace that soul nature that is your very heart, not just on a holy day or on a Sunday, but on every day and in every moment of your year and of your life.

For in truth, you are far more the essence of the Christ than you are the essence of the temple which is your body, your personality, and your outer self. Christmas gives you a chance to move through all of the darknesses of self to find, sturdy and strong and ever living, that consciousness of unconditional love that lives at the heart of yourself and is your true essence.

The one known as R asked about the principles involved in giving, and giving with love and from the heart. We would speak to that as well.

This instrument has often noted the mechanical nature of much of the customary habits of people with regard to the conventional ways of expressing friendship or relationship in general, not only at Christmas time. There is a principle of reciprocity. And one can feel very trapped by this principle of reciprocity. For if one goes to a party, then one is expected to hold a party and invite the ones who gave you a party. And so one becomes locked into an endless cycle of giving a party and attending a party, giving a party and attending a party, until one becomes heartily tired of having parties.

Much of this mechanical nature has spilled over into that special season of Yuletide and certainly each of those to whom we speak is aware of the pressure upon each entity to think of appropriate gifts for those whom it holds dear and to purchase them or make them and offer them. Naturally, just as inviting someone to a party is not toxic, deciding to give a present is not toxic either. It is, in fact, an expression of joy, gratitude and thanksgiving that is full of the love and the light of the one infinite Creator.

Blessed indeed is that entity who refuses to be swayed from that intention to express true feelings by the generosity of gifts. This instrument, for instance, truly enjoys giving and receiving gifts, yet it would not occur to this instrument to offer gifts from duty, and we see that as a virtue within this particular soul. Its honesty can be seen to be a rudeness by those who feel that entities should give mechanically and in reciprocity to those who give to them, or give because of a certain relationship even if there is no love there or regard.

What we would suggest, in order to uphold the principle of unconditional love, is that, before writing down the gift list of those to whom you wish to give gifts, you enter into prayer and ask for the gift of sincerity as well as the gift of generosity. Allow yourself the luxury of giving only from the heart, as the one known as R said, only from the depths of a sincerely felt love and never from a duty or from the mechanical routines of a society that does not overly prize honesty and sincerity and genuineness.

We would ask you to be authentic in those gifts that you do give. And as you give the gift, again, pray over that gift, imbuing it with your love, your affection, your appreciation and your gratitude for the gift of relationship. That is how the gift gives to you. For love is reflected in love and that which is given in love blesses you a hundred times over.

Contrariwise, that which is given in the emptiness of custom and habit has a blessing neither for the giver nor for the receiver. There is an energy to the gift that is given well that can be felt by that one who opens the gift, and it makes of any tiny gift a wonderful, abundant present. That which is given without love, on the other hand, remains a thing, an object, that which is not imbued with the spirit.

In the round robin before this channeling, the one known as R asked if it would be all right to ask this particular question because he had so appreciated the work of the one known as Aaron, who makes it a habit at Christmastime to share stories about an incarnation in which he was associated with the one known as Jesus.

As this instrument observed at this time, we cannot do that, for we have not shared any incarnations with any of those upon your planet. Yet, we can share that in every civilization, wherever hearts beat and hopes are high, there lives the personification of unconditional love in one savior or another, one hero or another, one saint or another. And those Christs and heroes and saints are you and I and everyone. Each shall have his moments throughout the long journey back to the one infinite Creator of realizing the self as the Christ, not in any egoistical way but in the sense of giving over the life completely to unconditional love and finding at last the source of all hunger and thirst being filled by embracing the consciousness of unconditional love.

Each of you is on a journey toward that identity and that nature. And you shall not find that identity and that nature by tossing away that which you are at this very moment for something better. Nay, my friends, you are, now, all that you need to be. You are perfect. You may not see as of yet that you are the Christ child, that you are spirit, that you are unconditional love. Yet we say to you that you may trust and rely upon the fact that this is the essence of all of you and each of you, every single one of you.

You may be in prison and have done terrible things. You may be on the road hungry and in despair. You may be angry or hurting or separated from that feeling of love by one thing or another. And yet we say to you that you are the Christ. You are, in your essence, unconditional love. And your journey as a spirit within incarnation may be described as a journey towards that realization and then towards the expressing of that realization when it has become your gift to yourself.

We would at this time ask if there is a follow-up to this question. We are those of Q'uo.

R: I'd like to make an observation and then ask Q'uo to comment. I have been thinking about gifts as Q'uo was speaking, and to me, and I think to others who listen to Confederation entities, it seems a kind of a gift that entities would come and try to speak to us in a way that is uplifting and inspiring. So I always think about giving thanks. Yet I also remember that Confederation entities see that as a service. I want to ask Q'uo if they would like to comment on how they see the appreciation that those who listen give to messages of inspiration.

We are those of Q'uo, and believe we understand your query, my brother.

Indeed, you are correct in that we consider it a privilege to be asked to share our opinions, because we have chosen as our way of service to others to share our thoughts when asked. May we say that your appreciation is a great gift to us. We do not know when we speak as to whether we will hit the mark.

We feel into the vibrations of your particular circle and the dynamics of all of those that happen to be listening to our words and we find various points and various layers of meaning, all of which are sincerely and genuinely requested by the various persons in the circle of seeking.

We are also limited by the fact that we must speak to the least aware of those within the circle, so that we do not leave any behind. And so we create concepts and share them with this instrument, who then shares them with you. And we do not know whether we have hit the mark at all.

So, when we find entities responding to our words in a positive way, it is as though we were bathed in your love. And we are very happy and joyful that we have succeeded in doing that which we hoped to do. It is a joy to have not only attempted to be of service but to have the impression that we have succeeded, at least in part, in sharing our love and our light in ways that are helpful to you and form a resource for your further spiritual endeavors.

Perhaps we should say that we feel as if we were being swaddled in your love and understanding and it feels very, very good.

May we answer you further, my brother?

R: Thank you, Q'uo. I think you hit the mark far more often than you imagine!

We are those of Q'uo, and we thank you for that comment, my brother. May it be true now and ever when you call for us and request our presence.

May we ask if there is another query of this group at this time. We are those of Q'uo.

(Long pause.)

We are those of Q'uo, and we have indeed satisfied the questions of those present at this time. May we thank you for the present of asking us to be with you and to share our opinions with you. You are a blessing to us, indeed! And we always stand in awe of the beauty of your hopes and your vibrations as you create together this sacred space and fill it with your request for the truth, for love and for light.

May you go well, my friends in this Christmas season. May you go well, my friends, through that which buffets the soul at a time when there is tenderness and affection in the air and yet so very, very many are focused upon other things.

Let it not dismay you, let it not distress you. Go deep! Dive into the heart of yourself and of the souls about you, seeing in them not those insincerities and thoughtlessnesses that so often pervade this winter solstice season. Do not let the darkness in yourself or in others keep you from the gladsome light of new life, new growth, new truth, and new light. Let it be summer in your heart. And that light which you are shall make your environment radiant! And light shall abound.

We leave you in the love and the light of the one infinite Creator. We are known to you as the principle of Q'uo and to each of you we say, adonai, adonai. Love, light, power and peace. We are those of Q'uo. ✺

L/L Research

L/L Research is a subsidiary of Rock Creek Research & Development Laboratories, Inc.

P.O. Box 5195
Louisville, KY 40255-0195

www.llresearch.org

Rock Creek is a non-profit corporation dedicated to discovering and sharing information which may aid in the spiritual evolution of humankind.

ABOUT THE CONTENTS OF THIS TRANSCRIPT: This telepathic channeling has been taken from transcriptions of the weekly study and meditation meetings of the Rock Creek Research & Development Laboratories and L/L Research. It is offered in the hope that it may be useful to you. As the Confederation entities always make a point of saying, please use your discrimination and judgment in assessing this material. If something rings true to you, fine. If something does not resonate, please leave it behind, for neither we nor those of the Confederation would wish to be a stumbling block for any.

© 2009 L/L Research

Saturday Meditation
December 29, 2007

Group question: The question this week has to do with being in the moment. We're wondering if Q'uo could give us some information about some of the obstacles there are towards keeping us from being in the moment. Our daily lives seem to be full of things that keep us from being in the moment. Please offer some hints as to ways that we can access the moment and be in the moment. And please give us some ideas about what the benefits might be for the spiritual seeker of remaining in the moment and "being here now."[107]

(Carla channeling)

We are those known to you as the principle of Q'uo. Greetings in the love and in the light of the one infinite Creator, in whose service we come to you this day. We offer you most hearty thanks for asking us to join in your circle of seeking. We find your blended auras most beautiful and the sacred space that you have created by seeking the truth together is wonderful, full of light and hope, and we are privileged to be a part of this gathering.

We are most glad to speak with you about the problems of "slowing down to now"[108], tips on how to do that and the benefits of so doing. However, before we begin to share our humble thoughts with you, we would, as always, request that each of you please use his discrimination in listening to what we have to say. We are not authorities over you, nor should any be, for you are the keepers of your temple. You are those who discriminate between that which is for you and that which is not. If anything that we say has resonance, please follow the path of that resonance as long as it seems helpful to you to do so. If our thoughts do not resonate to you, please lay them aside without a second thought and move on. In this way, we can be assured that we are not interfering with your process or being a stumbling block in your way. We thank you for this consideration, for it enables us to speak freely.

Perhaps we should begin by attempting to describe what we see as the environment in which one does, indeed, have the present moment. Each of you is a spiritual being who is always in the present moment. You have, however, chosen to take on a third-density body which is a heavy chemical distillery in order that you may fare forth into third-density Earth with its characteristics of being both a school and a place to be of service to the one infinite Creator.

The benefits of being in a physical body that works in third density have to do with your not knowing the truth. You have deliberately placed yourself in a situation where the truth is not obvious. It is not obvious that all is one. It is not obvious that this one thing is love. It is not obvious that each of you is a part of the creative principle, an ineffable and inextricably intertwined part of that one thing that is

---

[107] This phrase refers to a book by Ram Dass, titled *Be Here Now*. It was published in 1971 in San Cristobal, NM, by the Lama Foundation, ISBN 0-517-54305-2. It is still in print.

[108] This phrase had been used in the round-robin discussion which preceded this channeling.

all things, the one great original Thought of unconditional love that is the one infinite Creator.

Why would you wish to place yourself in a position of unknowing? My friends, you wished to learn and you wished to serve and above all you wished to choose. And all of these things needed to be done by faith, faith in things unseen and unprovable.

Your world does not give you this faith. There is nothing in your culture which assures you that all is well and that all will be well. Yet that is the discovery that each makes for himself as he wakes up from the planetary dream and discovers that it is a much larger universe, and a much different one, than your culture may have taught you.

What a blessing it is to wake up! And yet, what does one do with that awareness that there is a metaphysical universe that is so much more real than this illusion which is called planet Earth that it creates of the lifetime a completely different experience? Indeed, in many cases there is no one with whom to talk about these perceptions. And there is certainly no support for the awakened seeker within the day-to-day structures of your society.

Each of those in the circle spoke, in the round-robin discussion which preceded this session of working, of those things that are in life that keep one moving and going and doing the work: that which pays the bills, the errands that one must do, and so forth. And yet there is far more in the way of distraction and discouragement in your environment, my friends. There is the characteristic clatter of the media in your lives, whether it be radio, television or newspapers or, as the one known as J said, the MP3 player. There is talk and music and noise that characteristically is a part of your environment on a day-to-day basis.

It is not usually an environment that is conducive to seeking the silence and luxuriating in that silent, voice of spirit in which all is known. And yet, each of you has awakened from the planetary dream. And each now wishes to know how to use that increased and enhanced awareness of the truth more skillfully.

This is your situation. In terms of the world, the consensus-reality physical world, you have no way to prove that which you feel is true. It is as though there was, on solid land, only the ordinary; only the uninspired; only the flat black and white of unenhanced living. And yet the enhanced version of life cannot take place upon the solid ground. Therefore, in order to begin to express a life in faith, the seeker must gather his forces together and choose to leap into the midair of the unknown, embracing the mystery, affirming that which is not seen, and finding his feet only after he has made the choice to believe that, indeed, all is well and all will be well.

Thusly, we say to you, my friends, that there are as many distractions and discouragements that keep one from the now as there are pages in the newspaper, tunes on the iPod, reruns on the television, and above all, my friends, thoughts in your head, thoughts that go around and around without your choosing at any time to get off the merry-go-round and rest.

You as a culture lack restfulness and thusly there is this constant feeling of movement and the need to keep current and up with things and in the flow. And yet, as your world uses these terms, it does not indicate a movement towards unity, peace and enhanced awareness but rather a firmer grip upon the strap of the transit system that is constantly taking you from moment to moment, chore to chore, and job to job.

We paint an unhappy picture, do we not, my friends? Yet, this is the environment you chose. This is the school you asked to attend. And this is the place where you hoped to share, in great joy and radiance, the love and the light of the one infinite Creator. For you heard the cry of Earth and you hoped to hold the light at this time in a dark world, so that gradually, as you allowed the light of the Creator to shine through you, you could infect others with this joy and effortless flow of light and love that is coming through each of you at all times. And yet so seldom is it acknowledged, blessed and given a boost as it goes through your energy system and out into the world.

You indeed came here to do that. Yet this is where doing meets being, for in allowing the light to shine through you, you are not doing anything except giving your will to the one infinite Creator and asking to be used as an instrument of his love, his light, and his peace.

You came here also to balance wisdom and love. In some cases, you also wanted to balance wisdom, love and power. There is a great beauty in being a creature entirely of love, and yet to blend love and wisdom in a more useful way in your energy system is something that each of you is hoping that this incarnation will produce. The catalyst of the day, the grist for the mill that you must grind, those seeming challenges that meet you as you awaken for the day: all of those things are your way of practicing the presence of the one Creator as you go, not segregating moments during your day when it is Creator-time and letting the rest of the day be worldly time. You hoped, when you came here, to find the way to so balance your awareness of love, power and wisdom that you were able to begin to sense the metaphysical world that is inherent in every seemingly passing moment.

You as a soul live in two worlds at once. Indeed, one of the most powerful gifts that you offer through your living of your life is the capacity that you have to be both in time/space, where you are a citizen of eternity, and in space/time, where you are born of woman to live a life within this chemical-distillery vehicle of yours and then allow the vehicle to go to dust while you, as a soul, revert back to the time/space version of yourself which has interpenetrated your physical body and your physical life throughout your incarnation.

You are that entity that can both act in space/time and be fully aware of time/space. You bring those two illusions together, the heavy illusion and the lighter illusion. And yes, we call both the metaphysical and the physical world illusions. As far as we know, all that is seen, touch, felt, tasted and so forth is an illusion. But as well, all that is thought in the worlds that are unseen is also a kind of illusion, each illusion being carefully crafted to give the inhabitants of that illusion those elements which they need in order to experience, learn, serve and grow. For all that you do and all that we do and all that is done in all of creation is harvested to the one infinite Creator, that It may know Itself ever better.

You are, then, that nexus[109] in which timelessness meets time and insight meets intellect. You do not need to let those two separate. You may continue to live a worldly life and at the same time, ever and always, daily enhance your connection with the divine. Remember that you are priests. It is said in your holy works that you are a nation of priests, and so you are, each of you those which conduct the sacred rite of living within the temple of your body, your mind, your emotions, your intellect, and your spirit.

This instrument is fond of recalling a song sung by the one known as Frank in which part of the chorus is "do-be-do-be-do."[110] We encourage you to think of that very wise phrase as you quite seriously, but hopefully with a lightness of heart as well, go about your intention of becoming more and more able to slow down to now, as the one known as W has said.

Now that we have established that just about everything in the life of the culture in which you live seems determined to keep one off balance and unaware of this precious, present moment, as the one known as Rick[111] has called it, we may talk about some ways to trigger remembrance within the self of who you are and why you are here.

This instrument was speaking earlier of the advantages of taking time at the very first of the day to set the intention for the day and to pray aloud—or in the mind, it does not make any difference—to that ear who hears and that heart that understands within spirit, about what your hopes are for the day. If you hope to live in the now each moment of the day; if you hope to realize that Creator portion of yourself; if you hope to enable and empower yourself as a spiritual being, there is no better time than when you first arise to ask for help. Help is all around you. We cannot emphasize that enough.

There are many different kinds of spiritual helpers that are yours. There is what this instrument calls the Holy Spirit, that guidance system that is always with you. There is the presence of the one infinite Creator, closer than your breathing and nearer than your hands or feet. There are angelic presences all around you that have been attracted by your purity of desire and intentions. They wish nothing more than to help you achieve the goals that you have set for yourself this day.

Yet you must ask, for they cannot infringe upon your free will. Therefore, please draw about you that

---

[109] nexus: a means of connection; a tie; a link.

[110] The song to which the Q'uo refers is Frank Sinatra's recording of "Strangers In The Night," a 1966 song composed by Bert Kaempfert, © Bert Kaempfert, all rights reserved. The lyrics themselves have nothing to do with Q'uo's comment. In most printed versions of the lyrics, the part to which Q'uo refers is considered "scat" and rendered "dooby dooby do."

[111] The Q'uo group refers to Rick Pitino. He uses the phrase, "the precious present" in his motivational writing. He takes the phrase from the eponymous book by Spencer Johnson.

wonderful network of loving presence that is always about you. And do not forget to ask nature to help you, for that, too, is a kingdom of the Father. The very ground loves you beyond all telling. The air, the trees, all that there is in the kingdom of the Father is dancing with you and inviting you to join in that wonderful, harmonious rhythm of the dance of the One. For all within nature, not having self-consciousness, is fully aware of the truth and is very happy to be part of the one infinite Creator in its manifestation in this illusion.

It is very helpful to become sensitized to any repetitive sound that occurs in your day. For those who happen to be in school, there is the ringing of the bell in each period. Perhaps it may be the ringing of telephones where you are enjoying your day and perhaps earning your living so that you may pay the bills, as this instrument would say. Whatever sounds are part of your environment, become sensitized to them. Then when you hear the bell ring, the telephone ring, the train whistle blow, the traffic on the road come to a halt at the red light, or whatever noise is in your environment, you will find it not a distraction or something to ignore but that which calls you to remembrance of who you are and why you are here.

The one known as W was speaking earlier of the simple truth that the present moment is that which is. It is the realest focus which a person within third density may achieve. For it is that link with time/space in which all is one, and time goes away, timelessness reigns, and everything occurs now.

In a very real sense, this is the world in which we live, or should we say, the illusion which we enjoy. All that seems to you to be passing by, to us is occurring in a circular now, so that there is no such thing as past and present and future, but rather there is our choice of which place we wish to insert ourselves in this harmonious and rhythmic dance of the One.

For you within third density, life has a very heavy sense of time, time passing, time rushing by, and so forth. This is not something which needs to be resisted. You came here to experience this passing of time. You came to work within these limitations. You came to sleep until you could awaken to the now, to the truth, to the love and the light of the one great original Thought.

Indeed, in a way, you came to be the Logos. And that is a very telling phrase, "To be the Logos." One does not have to try to be a part of the Creator. You are the Creator! You are a holographic spark of the Creator, as is every other portion of this interactive and very much alive creation. But you are a holographic sample or bit of the whole. You contain in every cell of your body that one great original Thought that holds all things together. You do not have to strive or stretch. You have only to allow yourself to be. That is your nature.

It is a tremendously exciting adventure, my friends, to begin to allow yourself to know yourself more fully, to rest in the now and be aware of your being, your essence. You are actually an everlasting part of an infinite creation and this entire experience which you now are enjoying is but one of an infinity of such experiences.

Yet this is the one which holds your attention at this moment. This, out of all the things that you could have chosen to do, is precisely where you hoped to be and here you have every opportunity that you could possibly have to be of service to others, to be of service to the one infinite Creator, and to come ever closer to the realization that you know absolutely nothing. For this is not the density of understanding. And yet you know all that there is to know, for you know love. How precious is this opportunity for you to learn and to serve and to grow.

We encourage each of you to look at the various elements of your day-to-day life and target those repetitive elements that may act as triggers for the remembrance of your true nature and your true beingness as part of the one. Each entity will have different things that will remind him to move back into a balanced and focused awareness of the present moment.

For the one known as R, it is something physical that he can look at frequently, for he works with his hands upon the computer and so can see the bracelet that he wears on the wrist. For this instrument, it is the cross that she wears around her neck. As she moves through her day she is constantly touching it, having formed that habit long ago, for it reminds her that Christ is counting on her and that she has hoped all her life to do nothing more than serve Jesus the Christ.

Each of you will have very idiosyncratic and unique ways of bringing your mind back to a centered and balanced place in which you may rest in the now, even as you gaze with delight and interest upon the scene passing before your eyes.

It may have seemed to you that it has been harder than usual lately, or than it used to be, for you to do this. And we would spend a moment talking about why that is. As third density upon planet Earth draws to a close, which it shall do within the next few years, there is a natural separation of those souls who have chosen to polarize towards service to others and those which have chosen to polarize towards service to self. It is as though oil and vinegar had been miscible[112] for 75,000 of your years but as the time arrives for entities to choose between polarities and to move onto either service-to-self worlds or service-to-others worlds, there is more and more of a tendency for those two to separate, just as oil and water will if not artificially mixed together.

As the times move on towards the beginning of fourth density upon your planet, and as that fourth density upon your planet is a positive fourth density, the vibrations of truth, understanding and love are interpenetrating your third-density world in ever greater waves and convergences of energy. And this means that this process that you have of coming to know yourself, accept yourself, and love yourself has become more challenging.

Because everyone has a dark side. And within your third density it is easy for you to put that dark side in the shadows of self and not acknowledge it. It is difficult for an entity who wishes to be truly of service to acknowledge that shadow side that is the murderer, the rapist, the liar, the coveter, and so forth. Yet, if all is one, are you not all things? Indeed, all of us contain the three hundred and sixty degrees of various kinds of energy that make up the awareness that is the whole of you.

And one of those tremendously difficult jobs for anyone is to go into the shadows and bring out that shadow side to look at, to acknowledge, to come to understand, and to ask if it will join you, if it will cease being part of the dark side and become your grit and your determination and your perseverance.

That is the true function of the so-called dark side. And you can realize all of yourself if you can acknowledge the dark side in the first place. The desire of many is simply to deny that there is anything in the consciousness except love and light and positivity. Yet, there is a whole other side of self to be collected, respected and honored and used.

And this process is becoming more and more difficult because whereas before the end of the age was so prominently close it was quite easy to ignore the dark side of self, in these latter days of third density, when an entity desires to become a truly realized and focused spiritual seeker, he must go collect those shadow bits that he has not acknowledged. And this is difficult now, where it used to be easier, because of the constant barrage of vibrations of truth, so that all of those things at which you least wanted to look are now popping up quite prominently and saying, "Look at me. Acknowledge me. Let me tell my story and please learn to balance me in and make me part of who you are, for we truly belong, we shadow elements of the equation of one."

Therefore, we encourage each of you to take courage and look in that mirror as it comes to you, for all that are related to you by friendship or working relationship or family, all entities that are in your life, are mirroring you to yourself. When you see those things that you like, then you are happy to see those mirrors. Yet some will come to you and mirror those things you do not wish to see. My friends, embrace those things you do not wish to see, not in judgment but with a genuine and whole-hearted desire to integrate that into yourself.

To find it in the first place is very difficult. When one has mirrored something that is distasteful to one, one wishes simply to put it to one side. And yet we encourage you to allow it to come close, to embrace it, and listen to the story it has to tell. Find that energy within yourself. Not that you would murder anyone, but say you gaze at murder; find the murderer within yourself. Go after that murderer and ask it to join you, or to rejoin you. It is as if you are trying to bring all the members of yourself together so that you may be completely integrated as a unit and have no internal divisions where you do not wish to look.

In that way, when you enter your own open heart, you have no strife within yourself, saying, "I am a

---

[112] miscible: an adjective meaning "that can be mixed in all proportions. Used of liquids."

terrible wretch; I don't deserve to be here." Or saying, "No, I am very, very good, I am not wretched." You can let all of that judgment go and bring your whole self into that open heart where the Creator is waiting for you with unconditional love.

You ask what the benefits are of living this life in the now. The first benefit is that it is the truth, whereas all things of time are illusory. The now contains the door through the gateway to intelligent infinity and into the world of time/space. When you are in the now, you are part of all that there is and as the one known as W said, when you are centered and focused in the present moment, you are a natural attractor of those things which may come to you for your benefit in terms of your worldly goals, in terms of the benefit to others of those gifts that you may share with others, and in terms of the relationships that will be most helpful to you in learning and in serving in the present moment, where there is no reaching and no striving. There is a natural law in effect which simply gravitates those entities, energies, essences and relationships toward you which are appropriate for you just this precious moment.

Once one is in this now, one truly can be said to have no ambition and yet to achieve far more than ambitious people achieve, because of the fact that, having moved into this point of balance, all things stem from it very naturally.

The second benefit of being in the now is that it is from this point of presence that the Creator may radiate through you most efficiently and effectively. We do not wish to encourage you to try to beam light into the world, for that would be doing something of your own will.

(Side one of tape ends.)

(Carla channeling)

Consider of yourself that you are a broadcasting unit. You receive energy. You transmit energy. And in some cases you transduce[113] energy. This is your natural state. When you are centered in the now, you are in the appropriate place to receive the infinite supply of love/light energy from the one Creator, to shuttle it upwards through your open energy system, up through your body, through your heart, and out into the world through the top of your head.

That energy just flows like a fountain through you and the radiation from it is something that has caused artists throughout your history to draw halos, attempting to indicate how realized beings who are very secure and focused within their spirits naturally have a fountain of light that is just springing forth through them. That is the secret, my friends, to remaining forever rested and full of energy.

You do not do anything accept bless the energy that comes through you, and see and visualize and intend that this energy is not going to stop with you but is going to shower the world with light through your system. For, you see, you color light in a way that no one else does. Each, as he allows his system to be a lighthouse, has a unique light. No one else in creation shall ever have your light. For the infinite love/light of the Creator is limitlessly white. Yet, your biases and choices and quirks have colored your energy body so that, as energy streams through the chakras and out the crown chakra into the world, you have colored that light in a unique way that is absolutely beautiful.

So, know that you are giving the gift not only of the light but of the light through you, by your choice and by your blessing. This too is that which is not done. It must rest in the essence of your firm intention in the present moment.

This instrument was speaking earlier of that inner work which she feels has helped to support her life in faith, her desire to remain in the presence of the one Creator and tabernacle with the One throughout all experiences of her life whatsoever. We would agree with this instrument and take it further. It is well to support a life in faith with the prayer, with the meditation, with all of those ways to work in consciousness. Yet above all things, we encourage each never to forget or devalue the system as a whole.

If you remain in the upper chakras, working with your heart and your communication and your meditation and work in faith to the exclusion of paying the most exquisite attention to your sexuality, your state of mind as regards whether or not you are happy to be here and full of life and glad to be living; if you put aside relationships so that you may spend more time meditating; if you devalue your work because you wish to be a spiritual person, you've lost your focus. For it is your whole self that is sacred.

---

[113] transduce: to convert (energy) from one form into another.

Your sexuality, for instance, has so many layers to it! Yet it must begin with that wonderful "yes" of lust and chemical attraction. And then you can begin to let it lift, through relationship, to open-hearted relationship, to that love of a legal relationship, and from there to the upper-chakra work of true affection, true communication, and mutual work in consciousness which is sacred sexuality. There is no detail, no matter how seemingly mundane of life, that is not bursting with the sacred and the divine.

Consequently, although naturally we do encourage the meditation and the prayer and all of those beautiful ways of working in consciousness to discipline your personality and become centered more and more on who you really are, we also encourage you to look for the love and the sacredness in washing the dishes, cleaning the toilet, feeding the cat, and whatever it is that you are doing at the present moment. All of it is part of the dance of the One.

We thank this group for asking this query. It has been a pleasure to share our thoughts upon it. We would ask at this time if there is a follow-up to this question or if there is another query before we leave this instrument. We are those of Q'uo.

(Long pause.)

We are those of Q'uo, and are again with this instrument. We appear to have exhausted the queries in this group at this time. Consequently, we shall take our leave of this instrument and this group, expressing again our delight and our amazement at the beauty of your auras, mingled together to form this sacred space. Thank you, thank you, for asking us to be a part of your circle of seeking this day. It has been a pleasure and a privilege. We are known to you as the principle of Q'uo. We leave you, as we found you, in all that there is, the love and the light, the Thought and the manifestation, of the one infinite Creator. Adonai, my friends. Adonai. ✦

Year 2008

January 7, 2008 to May 27, 2008

L/L Research

L/L Research is a subsidiary of Rock Creek Research & Development Laboratories, Inc.

P.O. Box 5195
Louisville, KY 40255-0195

www.llresearch.org

Rock Creek is a non-profit corporation dedicated to discovering and sharing information which may aid in the spiritual evolution of humankind.

ABOUT THE CONTENTS OF THIS TRANSCRIPT: This telepathic channeling has been taken from transcriptions of the weekly study and meditation meetings of the Rock Creek Research & Development Laboratories and L/L Research. It is offered in the hope that it may be useful to you. As the Confederation entities always make a point of saying, please use your discrimination and judgment in assessing this material. If something rings true to you, fine. If something does not resonate, please leave it behind, for neither we nor those of the Confederation would wish to be a stumbling block for any.

© 2009 L/L Research

Special Meditation
January 7, 2008

Jim: First question for S: "All my life I've been dealing with the feeling of not being good enough and with anger. I feel the anger very strongly in [dealing with] my mother and I can feel it in [dealing with] my children too. What are the spiritual principles involved in not feeling "good enough," ending in anger? What am I supposed to learn from these feelings? Does this have something to do with self-acceptance?"

(Carla channeling)

We are known to you as the principle of Q'uo. The speaker this evening is the one known as Hatonn.[114] We greet you in the love and in the light of the one infinite Creator, in whose service we come to you this day. Thank you, my brothers and my sisters, for creating this sacred time for seeking the truth. It is a joy to join your circle of seeking and to be a part of this session of working. We especially thank the one known as S for requesting information regarding feelings of unworthiness and anger. It is a privilege to be asked for our opinion and a joy to offer our humble thoughts.

As always, we would ask each who reads or hears these words to be discriminatory in what you pick up and use from those things which we have to say. Follow the path of resonance and use those thoughts that are resonant to you, leaving the rest behind. That will enable us to feel free to offer our opinions without being concerned that we might infringe upon your free will or disturb the rhythmic process of your own seeking.

Emotions are very, very important in the process of getting to know yourself and of becoming a self-realized person, aware of your own sacred nature. Often those seeking to be serious seekers downplay or disregard the importance of emotions. This is because they see the shallowness and inconsistency of surface emotions and feel that because they are so highly distorted and unbalanced they do not have any virtue, spiritually speaking.

However, it is our opinion that the surface emotions are the beginning of the entry of the individual into its own deeper mind. Each emotion is precious, the heaviest emotion as well as the lightest, the darkest as well as the most joyful.

The two emotions of which the one known as S speaks, unworthiness and anger, are part of what most seekers would call the dark side or the shadow side of the self.

The seeker has a feeling that he is not supposed to be feeling unworthy. He is not supposed to be angry. Yet emotions spring forth without regard to whether they should be felt or not. Emotions tell a truth within the life of the seeker and they are, therefore, great gifts of the self to the self.

---

[114] The principle of Q'uo is made up of three groups, Hatonn, Latwii and Ra. Usually the speaker for the principle is Latwii. Occasionally, Hatonn is the speaker, as in this session. Ra is never the speaker.

Emotions begin with highly colored, impulsive reactions and responses to catalyst. They take one by surprise. They are not planned. This is why they bear truths as a gift. You cannot fool yourself into feeling an emotion. It simply is there and you recognize it.

However, emotions do not stay on the surface for the persistent seeker who is willing to abide with and enjoy the company of these emotions. They begin to have a deeper life. As one feels these emotions again and again, there comes the opportunity, each time the emotion is repeated, to work with that emotion, to embrace it and honor it and to gaze at it to see from what catalyst it has arisen.

When one is persistently fearless with emotions and is able to sit with the self as it experiences an emotion flowing through, there is a gradual deepening of that emotion. Eventually, as repetition and work in consciousness with these emotions begins to yield its fruits, the seeker begins to have glimpses of the refined and purified emotion that started out so highly colored. And eventually that emotion can take one into the archetypical mind, where the deepest of truths may be found.

In the archetypal mind these emotions flow like underground rivers, emptying into the sea of bliss and unconditional love that is the beginning and ending of all that is. As they wend their way through the archetypal mind, they water the myths which make up the roots of consciousness. The stories of your soul are emotional and have a shape and a direction to them. This is the beauty of that highly colored and uncomfortable surface emotion that the seeker first experiences.

Certainly the journey from discovering that one feels unworthy or one feels angry to the place in the journey where one embraces the unworthiness and the anger and loves it unconditionally, is a long journey. Yet, my sister, it is a worthwhile journey and one that has a sweetness to it. For each time you are able to move into a position of greater understanding of your own trigger points and reactions, you have gained part of that fragmented self that has been lost to the shadow side of self. And as you bring it into the light of your own attention, you are able to work with it and to help this feeling to become matured and ripened and begin to have more and more of a clarity and a purity.

You are, in other words, refining the rough surface emotion so that it may penetrate deeper and deeper through the layers of enculturation, previous assumptions and all of the various layers of your surface mind and the gifts that you have been given by your culture, your parents, and your teachers. Generally speaking, personal truth does not lie in the culture, the parents, or the teachers and what they have to say. For the most part, the seeker must discover his own truths and make them a personal credo.

Therefore, these emotions, while not often pleasant to experience, have great value. We say this because we wish to encourage the seeker to work with that which he feels, not judging it, not condemning it, and not being indifferent to it, but rather giving it respectful attention, investigating it, and exploring it. Each emotion, given this honor and respect, will reward the seeker with more and more of a sense of surety as to who he is and to why he is here.

In a way, as you work with emotions you are reclaiming and reintegrating your whole self. You may think of your emotions as treasure. The surface emotion tells you where the treasure lies and then you may sit with that emotion and consider how it arose. What was the trigger? What was occurring when you had that response of feeling unworthy or feeling angry?

Sometimes the answer is very clear. At other times the answer is not at all clear and then you must dig as if for buried treasure, sifting through your memory to find other times when you had the same emotion. What were your triggers then? Compare them with what is occurring in the present, and you begin to see a repeating pattern. You begin to make more sense to yourself and you begin to have more knowledge as to how you came to be the entity who is experiencing right now.

This is true of all emotions, positive and negative. Yet we would now narrow our view and speak of these two emotions in particular and offer some thoughts as to their value and their place in the development of the mature spiritual seeker.

We would take unworthiness first, for it is the more initiatory emotion; that is to say, it is in response to feelings of unworthiness that the seeker often comes to be angry, rather than the other way around. Therefore, we would look at unworthiness first.

It is a very common emotion. Many seekers, especially, have all too much experience, they would say, of this emotion. Certainly, this instrument experiences unworthiness quite often and continues to need to sit with that emotion and embrace it, that it may tell its story and feel that it is accepted.

The roots of unworthiness tend to be found in childhood. Within the upbringing of a seeker there are many times that the seeker, as a young person, hears the scolding and the chiding and is told that it is an unworthy being, that it has not done well, that it could have done better, that it did not do enough, and things of this nature. The young self is relatively undefended. It believes what it hears and it absorbs and takes on this information as though it were the truth.

The fact that it is not the truth, spiritually speaking, is irrelevant to the psychology of how these words, so carelessly spoken by parents, teachers and other authority figures, sink into the psyche and the deep mind.

One grows up physically and the authority figures may or may not still be present to continue to tell the seeker that it is unworthy. However, these voices have been internalized so that even if both parents are gone, as is the case with this instrument, there is still the ability to hear that voice saying, "That is a good effort but it would have been so much better if you had done this and this," or saying, "You are clumsy, stupid, you haven't done enough," and so forth.

Therefore, it is not even necessary for these voices to continue to have any life outside the seeker's mind, for they are internalized so that they spring forth in the situation that triggers the memory of the times when these words have been spoken before.

What generally triggers a feeling of unworthiness is a self-perceived error or mistake. This instrument, for instance, often forgets something, and immediately she has an internalized voice that says, "How could you have possibly forgotten?" Therefore, she is triggered with unworthiness.

There are as many ways to discover that one has made a mistake as there are situations. Any number of things can bring the seeker to the point of being triggered by that feeling of unworthiness.

It is especially painful because a seeker is generally a very service-to-others oriented person and, far from intending to make a mistake, has tried very hard to do his best, and being soft of heart has wished to please the people around him. When the people are not pleased and do not understand the gift being given and instead throw it back in your face and say, "It is not good, it is not enough, it is poorly done, I did not need this," or words to that effect, the triggering is automatic. The seeker thinks to himself, "I tried so hard and I failed."

Now, skill comes in learning how to interrupt the triggering process. One does not wish to repress the emotion of unworthiness. The skillful seeker will welcome it, as it welcomes all catalyst, and take it into the balancing process, paying attention to it, even emphasizing it, and then asking the self, "What is the dynamic opposite of this emotion?"

In the case of unworthiness, the opposite is worthiness and so, after one has experienced the unworthiness, one awaits its dynamic opposite, still in meditation, and asks for it and invokes it, and worthiness then flows into the consciousness with its own information.

Why is the seeker worthy? Because the seeker is part of all that there is. And all that there is is unconditional love. The worth of the seeker, then, is infinite. There is nothing but worth in the seeker's true and deep nature. Yet, if one is not careful, when one has seen the worthiness, one then chooses the worthiness over the unworthiness and therefore makes a judgment about the self. And this is not something we encourage.

Rather, we ask that you see with compassion the full play of unworthiness and worthiness until you see that both are held in dynamic balance within your nature. Both have their goodness, for they are teaching you lessons that you came here to learn. If indeed you have come to discover your true worth, you could not begin to think about that without first feeling unworthy. It is as an alert or a siren that awakens you to this issue within yourself, so that you may work with it to bring it into the balance that it deserves and needs to have within your character.

When an entity is unawakened there is not usually the pain of unworthiness to the extent that a seeker feels when he has awakened and has discovered his true nature. Then, he wishes all that passes through his mind to be thoughts of love and light, peace and gentleness. And yet the dynamics that bring grist to the mill and make the incarnation work are served not by all the good feelings that one can take for granted and feel very good and smooth about, but by those uncomfortable emotions that wake one up to one's imbalances, so that one may then turn, move towards them, gather them in his arms, and take them into his open heart.

We are not suggesting that, over a period of time, work with unworthiness shall cause you to cease feeling unworthy. You may dig up trigger after trigger after trigger and yet it is the general case that there are so many triggers buried in the soil of one's memory from past occasions of pain having to do with unworthiness that there always shall be moments of being triggered and of feeling less than worthy.

If human nature were perfectible, this would not be so. But human nature was designed to be imperfect. This grants to the human the continuing opportunity to go ever deeper to discover ever more fundamental truths about the self.

The energies of judgment have a great part to play in unworthiness. And we iterate that it is not helpful to judge the self. Rather it is helpful to have compassion upon the self and to pay attention to the self. Each difficult emotion is a call for help. It is a call that goes into the self, into that place where you can be your own mother, your own father, your own friend, so that you may heal the wounds of the past and forgive the self and the other self who first offered you these wounds that have given you so much fruit and food for thought.

Anger is generally a byproduct of judgment, and that is why we say it is dependent upon the feeling of unworthiness. We would differentiate between the emotion of righteous anger, which is involved with a sense of justice and fair play, and the anger that springs up seemingly out of nothing in response to something someone says or the small unfairnesses of life.

It is not necessary for a person to experience a relationship with another person in order to feel anger. Anger can be generated by the self all alone, because of the rich array of triggers there are buried in everyday experiences. Say one has a hammer and a nail and one takes the hammer and tries to pound the nail, but instead hits the thumb. Anger arises right on the [tail] of judgment. The first feeling is an instantaneous judgment of the self: "I'm not worthwhile, I can't hit the nail." Then comes the anger. Perhaps the seeker is not even aware of that judgment of unworthiness that has preceded the anger, for anger arises so swiftly. Yet it arises because of the self-judgment.

Do we suggest that one becomes impervious to anger and no longer has that impulse toward anger after working with anger for a long period of time? No, we do not suggest that. Again, the human makeup is such that there will always be those imperfections that remain. There is no virtue in thinking, "I can stamp this out of my nature. I can move beyond this. I can rise above this."

My sister, we would never suggest that you rise above your anger or your sense of unworthiness, for that would be leaving a part of yourself behind. Not that you are an unworthy or an angry being, but that is part of the complete array of positive and negative, light and dark, radiant and magnetic parts of the self. And it is your whole self that the one infinite Creator loves above all telling; not the good self or the worthy self or the peaceful self but the self who is all things worthy and unworthy, peaceful and every other dynamic that can be thought of.

The Creator loves you just as you are, and your hope in working with these emotions is gradually to come into a place where you have compassion, as the Creator has compassion, on those portions of the self that concern you from time to time. They do not diminish you. They should not in any way bring you shame. Your feelings are all equally worthy and deserve to be respected and attended to.

We would ask you to woo yourself as if you were your own lover. At first the self is shy and you, the healer, must say, "Oh, please, I will not be offended. I want to hear about your unworthiness. I want to hear about your anger. Please come and tell me your story and I will listen and I will not judge. I will love you and I will have compassion on you."

Gradually, then, you begin to create for yourself the feeling of being healed, so that when you are triggered you know that you are triggered and you are not swept up in the surface feelings any longer. Your feelings begin to have a depth to them because you have the impulse that is triggered and then you have the awareness that you have worked so hard to gain: "Ah, here is unworthiness. Ah, here is anger." And you love your unworthiness, you love your anger, you love the emotions that make you who you are. And love gradually dissolves the bitterness that is your instinctive reaction to these surface impulses that do not please you as a spiritual seeker and do not seem to ring true.

We assure you, my sister, you will always ring true. Your emotions will always tell you a truth and they always have gifts in their hands. And when loved and understood, they will give you their secrets and show you the places within you that need healing. So take yourself in your arms when you feel unworthy or when you feel angry and say, "I love you anyway. I love you with all my heart. You are my darling. You are my sweetheart. Let me hug you and cradle you." And all of the bitterness can then gradually melt away so that while you understand that you have very uneven and sometimes imbalanced surface reactions, you also have compassion.

The process of working with yourself is very important in the regard that once you have begun to have true compassion upon yourself, then and only then, can you begin to have true compassion for others with all of their mistakes, self-perceived and perceived by you. When you have finally fallen in love with yourself, then you can fall in love with others as well as seeing yourself and everyone else as sparks of the one infinite Creator.

You exist within third density in darkness. It is a place of unknowing. The veil is heavy here. You will make mistakes again and again and feel unworthy. And you will be angry again and again. And yet this too is good. This too is helpful. This too is grist for the mill that creates the refining of your character and your soul, so that you begin to be more and more transparent—not that you have gotten over feeling angry or unworthy, but that you see through these surface emotions to the beauty of your deep self and you begin to have a real confidence in that deep self that goes beyond the tossing of the surface waves of everyday living. This transparency makes of you a better and better lighthouse.

You will never cease to be imperfect in third density, but as you have compassion on yourself you become transparent to these imperfections. Your faith in your deeper self releases you from contracting around these negative emotions. You can let them go.

(Side one of tape ends.)

(Carla channeling)

You can start over. And meanwhile the energy of the infinite Creator that is flowing through your energy body in infinite amounts has a clear path through you, so that you radiate light into the world, not from yourself but through yourself.

This instrument informs us that the turning of the tape recorder is a signal for us to lift away from the main question and to consider other queries. May we ask the one known as Jim to read the second query at this time. We are those of Q'uo.

Jim: *(Reading question from S.)* "I have three children—two grown girls and a boy. What are the spiritual principles involved in my relationship with them?"

We are those of Q'uo, and are aware of your query, my sister. The spiritual principle involved in having children is that of the guardian and lover that sees the beauty of these children that have been gifts to her from the Creator. Children are to the parents an opportunity to share and be of service to another entity in a very special way.

As a mother, my sister, you know better than anyone the utter helplessness of your children when they first came to you. They could not speak or move on their own accord when they first came to you. You had to feed them and keep them clean and warm and offer to them an environment in which they felt happy and safe. And you have learned more about service to others from your relationship with them than probably any other relationships in your life. They have, therefore, been your greatest teachers.

How have you loved them, perhaps you wonder. And yet we assure you, my sister, that you have loved them very well. And you continue to love them very well with all of your heart. Perhaps you feel you have been imperfect in expressing that love. And yet you have always given your very best and your highest to them, and this is your hope at this time in continuing.

Consequently, we say to you that the spiritual principle involved is that of service to others. You have taken entities that made an agreement with you, before either of you came into incarnation, that you would have this special relationship. And you have done and you continue to do your best to offer them all the love in your heart. Your greatest gift to them is this simple unconditional love.

Naturally, it has been necessary to teach them the ways of the culture in order to protect them, so that they would know how to behave when they were with other people. And this has undoubtedly brought you into conflict with them again and again. Yet we assure you, my sister, that one of the ways that love serves a young soul is to indicate where the boundaries are, where the principles that underlie human interaction are.

Had you given them absolutely everything for which they asked, had you said yes to whatever they requested of you, you would not have given them your wisdom. And, my sister, they need your wisdom as well as your love.

It is a very sensitive thing to raise a child. You cannot raise any two children the same way. Every entity is its own entity. What works with one personality does not work with another. And so, there have been many times when you wondered whether you were doing the right thing. And yet we say to you, if you can keep your intention of giving your highest and your best, then you have done the right thing.

Above all, the principle involved in being of service to others is to offer that gift which you do give with love. And my sister, you have done that very well and continue to do that with all of your heart. You cannot help at times seeming judgmental, and we have just said to you it is not good to be judgmental. And yet when you are mentoring a developing spirit, it is well to have those times of saying, "This is not good, this is not useful, this is not helpful," and so forth. But always try, my sister, to say what you have to say and do what you need to do coming from a place of unconditional love and compassion.

May we ask if the one known as Jim would read the next question? We are those of Q'uo.

Jim: *(Reading question from S.)* "Sometimes I have the feeling that my son sees something that I don't see, maybe from the unseen world. He is scared by this and doesn't want to talk about this. Can you confirm this? How can I help him not to be afraid?"

We are those of Q'uo. And yes, my sister, we can confirm this. When a child is psychic, or when any entity is psychic, it can be a disturbing and frightening thing. Others around him are not experiencing what he experiences. He has no real framework for understanding his experience. It is a natural reaction to feel fear when experiencing the unknown.

It may help you to understand how this feels if you think of an entity who has had a drug or who has taken too much alcohol, and because of the alteration in consciousness has had an awareness come to him that would not normally come. This entity would call it a "bad trip."

When an entity has a bad trip he feels fear and he contracts around that fear. It is the fear of the unknown. It is the fear of something that he does not understand. Naturally, on the part of your son and on the part of all of those who by nature are ultrasensitive and do sense into the unseen worlds, it can be a continuing source of unease and discomfort.

In the first place, that which you may do to respond to his need is to be reassuring and to treat these things as normal. When he does not speak of them and does not want to talk about them, then you cannot be verbal in your reassurance. But you can always maintain an even calmness that does not change because he may be experiencing that which he does not understand. And that in itself is reassuring.

If a parent reacts to something sensed in the child by being afraid or being concerned, then that child feels it and projects it into what he is sensing, thereby making his discomfort more severe. But when he senses nothing but a continuing love and peace from his parent, then he knows that everything is basically all right, even if he doesn't understand what is happening to him.

As this young entity grows in years, he will undoubtedly begin to talk more about this, if not to you, then to someone else. If he does choose to begin to speak to you about that which he does not understand, then you may share with him your understanding of the unseen worlds and that they are as real a part of things as the worlds that are seen; they are just the other side of things. There is the physical world of space/time and there is the metaphysical world of time/space, and it is as natural for an entity to experience things in time/space as in space/time.

However, normally the unawakened spirit does not experience time/space. Consequently, this young soul has no one to whom to talk. Be there when he does wish to speak, and continue a silent reassurance until the time when he does begin to communicate.

As this entity is becoming more and more able to use his intellect and to absorb information of this nature, it may be helpful to drop little seeds by having books around and speaking of them, so that he may choose, at a time that feels right to him, to begin to do some reading about these unseen worlds and to begin to explore that which is occurring to him for himself. It may be that he may do the work of coming to understand his gift all by himself. Leaving the books where he has access to them will be helpful.

May we ask for the next query?

Jim: *(Reading question from S.)* "I have a particularly difficult job, one that I don't like, but need it to pay the bills. Since it is not the first time I've dealt with a difficult job, I try very hard to see what my lessons are, but I'm still confused. Can Q'uo offer me some suggestions on how to work with this catalyst?"

We are those of Q'uo, and are aware of your query, my sister. Perhaps, my sister, you are aware of the concept of the energy body with its seven chakras. Each chakra has its own gifts and its own kind of energy. And all of the seven chakras are equally important in the balancing of the whole energy body. Naturally, you want a body to be strong throughout its system. For instance, you would not want your feet to be weak but your mind to be strong. You would not want your hands to be weak, but your shoulders to be strong, and so forth.

You want all of your energies in balance and in a state of health. Therefore, you want your red ray to be strong, with its issues of sexuality and survival. Similarly, you wish for your orange ray to be strong, with its issues of relationship of self to self and the relationships that you have with others, one on one. And you want your yellow ray to be strong, with its issues of group relationships such as the birth family, the marriage family, and the work family.

The issue of the job, then, is that which has to do with your yellow ray. Within your choices before you came into incarnation were included the choice of how smoothly things would go for you in the workplace. You have chosen to strengthen your yellow ray by having situations that are not subjectively perceived as ideal in your workplace. Similarly, you have worked with the energies of the birth family and the marriage family and those, too, have been somewhat difficult from time to time. These difficulties are in place in order that you may work with them and strengthen your being by your persistence in being willing to deal with these difficult emotions that are brought up by the less than ideal situations in birth family, marriage family, and work.

As your maturity has brought you away from direct experience with the birth family and as life has also brought you past having to deal with the more difficult aspects of the marriage family, it is time now in your incarnation for the difficulties to focus on the work family.

How may you be most skillful in encouraging yourself to see these difficulties as the agents of maturity, those agents that will help you become stronger in your yellow ray? Each entity must work with this for herself. And perhaps it is enough for us to say to you that as long as you continue to seek to see the Creator in every entity whom you meet, you cannot go wrong.

This entity often asks herself, "Where is the love in this moment?" My sister, when you ask yourself, "Where is the love in this moment," as concerns your yellow-ray work environment, you may find that the love in the moment must come from you. Therefore, see yourself as a creature of love that is faithful and confident, because she knows that this situation has been given to her that she may grow and become stronger, wiser and more loving.

We realize that there is no way of behaving in an ideal sense at all times, especially when, as was expressed to this instrument in the round-robin [discussion] preceding this meditation, the bills need to be paid, and the work environment has promised to give payment for work done and has not offered the payment. This creates a crisis in everyday life. There are responsibilities to be met. There are children involved.

My sister, firstly, this is a time to be practical and to consider finding a way to pay the bills where, when the work is done, the payment for the work is there.

But secondly, this is a time to invoke faith, for in truth the Creator does provide that which is needed for today, so when there is that sense of not having enough, we ask you to focus on those things which you have so richly, those things which are enough for today. Begin to work at continuing to give thanks, and to rejoice and have the consciousness of abundance. For this, too, is a lesson of yellow ray, that there is abundance, but it is for today only.

In the prayer called The Lord's Prayer by this instrument, there is the request and the petition, "Give us this day our daily bread." Focus upon this concept of rejoicing in that which one has today and praising the abundance of today. And in that way, there will come to you an amelioration of the situation which you now experience, if not in the outer world, certainly in the inner world of your own realization. As a seeker, it is this realization which you are working to refine.

It has been a joy to be with this group and we thank the one known as S and all of those sitting in the circle this day for offering us the opportunity to speak with you on these subjects.

However, the energy of this instrument wanes and we would at this time take our leave of this instrument and this group, expressing once again our gratitude and our pleasure of being a part of the beauty of this sacred space. We thank you and we offer you our love, our support, and our encouragement. At any time that you would wish our presence you have only to ask and we shall be with you.

We are known to you as those of Q'uo. We leave you in the love and in the light of the one infinite Creator. Adonai. Adonai vasu. ✣

L/L Research

L/L Research is a subsidiary of Rock Creek Research & Development Laboratories, Inc.

P.O. Box 5195
Louisville, KY 40255-0195

www.llresearch.org

Rock Creek is a non-profit corporation dedicated to discovering and sharing information which may aid in the spiritual evolution of humankind.

ABOUT THE CONTENTS OF THIS TRANSCRIPT: This telepathic channeling has been taken from transcriptions of the weekly study and meditation meetings of the Rock Creek Research & Development Laboratories and L/L Research. It is offered in the hope that it may be useful to you. As the Confederation entities always make a point of saying, please use your discrimination and judgment in assessing this material. If something rings true to you, fine. If something does not resonate, please leave it behind, for neither we nor those of the Confederation would wish to be a stumbling block for any.

© 2009 L/L Research

Saturday Meditation
January 12, 2008

Group question: Our question this evening, Q'uo, has to do with the concept of transformation. On our individual journeys of seeking, each of us goes through various experiences. And we observe these experiences. And I am guessing that when we observe them with the most accuracy, we don't have judgment for them. We just go through them and let them experience themselves through our lives and in some way or another, cumulatively or individually or at some point, transformations occur. And we would like you to speak to this concept of transformation. How do we come about it? Is there a time within our seeking that is most right for it? Is there a way that we can aid it most effectively? Talk to us about transformation.

(Carla channeling)

We are those known to you as the principle of Q'uo. Greetings in the love and in the light of the one infinite Creator, in whose service we come to you this day. We thank you, my friends, for asking us to join your circle of seeking at this session of working. It is our honor and our privilege to join you. We are most appreciative of the opportunity to attempt to be of service to the one Creator by sharing our humble thoughts with you on the subject of transformation.

As always, we would ask that each of you employs his powers of discrimination as each listens to that which we have to say or reads those words which we share at this time. Follow the resonance in those thoughts that appeal to you and seem full of life to you. If those things which we have to say do not happen to have any resonance, then we would ask for you to leave them aside and continue seeking until you find that which resonates to you, for your powers of discrimination are quite adequate to allow you to sense the rightness of those things which you need to take in to your process at this time.

This applies not only to our words, but to all of those things which you hear or read. Let your natural ability to discriminate between that which is for you and that which is not for you function in the way that it should and follow the law of attraction.

We thank you for this consideration. It will allow us to speak our thoughts freely without being concerned that we may infringe upon your free will or disturb the rhythmic flow of your process.

Transformation is a somewhat overused term among those who seek in the ways of spirit. Both your established religions and your alternative spiritual practices tend to speak of transformation, until it has almost become diminished, as a word, from having been overused.

In its roots, my friends, it means to change form, to cross over from one form to another. In a different word with the same root, transformation often follows an intake of information to form new mental and emotional formations, thus precipitating the deeper self into the need to accommodate new information. By information we do not simply mean that which is taken in through the process of reading books, attending seminars, or listening to inspired speakers. We speak of the whole intake process of a working, conscious, awakened spirit in incarnation on Planet Earth.

There is a tremendous amount of information which flows into the five senses and moves through the awareness and the thought processes of each entity, all things being grist for the mill. So, transformation is a move from one stage or phase of life to another. It almost has the connotation or the inference of being that of a shape shifter, where you actually change your spiritual or metaphysical shape.

There are models of transformation which are helpful in thinking about times of change within the self as it undergoes realizations of accumulated information which have precipitated change. One model is the much clichéd butterfly. And there is some advantage to thinking of transformation using this model. The unawakened pupae and larvae go about their routines, eating and becoming ready to enter into a phase of development that is transformative in a way that changes the form of life from that which crawls to that which flies. And you may see that time of transformation as precipitated by the going into the cocoon of dealing with new thoughts and letting those thoughts marinate within your consciousness.

The thoughts and concepts which you have taken in can come from many, many sources; only partially those of the intellect and intellectual activities such as reading and discussing and pondering inspired thoughts or thoughts that you hope will be inspired. You also are processing the cumulative cycles of your feelings. And you are dealing with the challenges that you are experiencing in all of the various chakras, especially the first three chakras, in terms of those stages leading up to transformation.

And when, in the natural course of time, you spring forth from your cocoon you are indeed a new creature, looking at life from a slightly different vantage point: higher, broader. Little do you know that you also have become beautiful and are flying from person to person and thought to thought with life-giving pollen within your touch. You do not even know you are transmitting it, for the pollen of the awakened spirit is that of being rather than doing, and there is little of intellectual nature in how an entity becomes able to be of service to others by the very radiance of his being.

However, that model of transformation suggests that first you were unawakened and couldn't fly and now you are awakened and you can fly, first you were a slug, now you are beautiful. And such butterfly thoughts will actually get you nowhere.

For transformation is a cycle. It is an inevitable cycle. You will transform. You shall become a new creature. The only question is whether or not you wish to accelerate the process of your own spiritual evolution. Those who are listening to these words and those who read them are those who wish to become more than they have been. That wish, in and of itself, will hasten the rate of speed of change in your life. For by wishing to be transformed and by being willing to be transformed, you make the space for being transformed.

Consequently, we would perhaps rather use the transformational model of the also much clichéd chambered nautilus, which outgrows [his] house and therefore enlarges his house, without ever leaving his house. Just in such a way do you enlarge your point of view as you move through these cocoon-like periods and emerge from them with the sense of having a new perspective which has created for you the self-perceived feeling of being a new creature. You continue to expand your awareness in a cyclical manner until such time as you pass from this environment through the gates of larger life, where you shall not lose a beat in continuing your spiritual evolution.

The rhythm of transformation is linked to several things and we shall look at various of them. Firstly there is the, shall we say, outer or non-chosen portion of transformation which has to do with your life-cycles. There is a natural tendency for each cell in your body to be born, mature and pass. And there is a natural time for each part of the experience of your incarnation to flourish and then to make way for a different experience, based simply upon the accumulation of time and experience in your incarnation. You have little control over this particular part of the cycle of transformation. It is part of your body, part of your mind, part of your emotions, part of the natural phases of life.

There is the part of transformation which is involved in very deep and subtle energies, such as the stars in your sky, the sun especially, and the moon. The monthly, annual and slowly revolving astrological patterns of your life will have some sway over the rhythm of your cyclical transformations.

And certainly the times that now are upon you, where the fourth density is virtually present, interpenetrating third density, has set you awash in energy tide after energy tide, so that you are constantly being washed with rhythmic waves of truth, love and understanding. This has the effect upon anyone who is at all sensitive to these energies of creating a more lucid ability to look at the mirroring that is going on in your particular life at this time.

Each relationship which you have gives you a mirror for yourself. Just as in your dreams, each character represents a portion of yourself. So, in the waking life each interaction with another entity shows you the mirror of yourself, in part, in the actions and behaviors, the thoughts and the concepts offered by that interaction. Consequently, you are constantly seeing portions of yourself mirrored in a somewhat distorted way by those who are in relationship with you.

All of these changes and chances, all of these natural cycles, create a basic default. The human was created to transform. That is the nature of the self-conscious, physical, mental, emotional and spiritual being that you are. That is your potential and that is your destiny: change from one form into another, from one kind of thought into another whole paradigm of thought. You cannot help but progress. So you may feel easy about whether or not you are changing, whether or not you are being successful at transforming. It is inevitable for you to go through transformation upon transformation and you do not have to push or thrust yourself towards transformation. You may relax in the knowledge that it is inevitable.

Then there is the part of the transformational experience which has completely to do with your will, your hunger, and your thirst for understanding and truth. The more passionate that you are about seeking the truth, the more you are able, as a metaphysical entity working in time/space, to have an effect upon the pace of your transformative rhythm. It is entirely possible for an entity who is awake and conscious and aware of the process of change to accelerate the pace of that change by quite a bit.

The fundamental transformation of a human being within incarnation is from that spiritual childhood of feeling that one is tossed about by outside forces and dependent upon luck and chance for the road one is on and the road one may choose to be on, to a more mature spiritual awareness in which the entity has taken responsibility for the occurrences and events of everyday life, realizing that in those very events lies all the grist needed for the mill of transformation.

Consequently, if a seeker wishes to maximize the opportunity for accelerating the rate of spiritual evolution within this refinery of souls which is third density, the seeker may decide to begin to hone and focus his efforts by the focusing and whetting of his appetite for the truth.

The most effective tool in working towards transformation is the self-conscious living of the life. We are not talking about those who mull endlessly over every detail of their life and thought throughout each day, but rather we are talking about the most effective way to work towards transformation. The most effective resource is one's own ability to observe oneself without affecting that which is being observed.

The one known as Jim spoke of being aware that in transformation it was important not to judge. And this is the kind of objectivity about which we are speaking. It is indeed important, indeed central, to refrain from judgment as one goes through the collecting of information about the self that is necessary in order for the self to be offered up and thus become empty enough to have the space in which to transform.

It is ironic, is it not, that in the search for truth the answers lie not in discovering that which can be known, but in discovering that the secrets to the mystery of transformation lie in unknowing and faith. Faith is the most powerful force in the universe, it being another name for realized or positively realized love. You live in a universe made of love. The original Thought was a Thought of unconditional love.

As you transform, the core of your transformation is an awareness that has not been there before about the nature of your central or deepest self as being part of love itself or the creative principle, which is the one great original Thought of unconditional love.

As you become full of new information that brings you to a place of transformation, you suddenly discover that you are no longer full. You discover that this very fullness and sense of new life tips you into the corresponding and balancing awareness of oneself as knowing nothing. It is a devastating portion of transformation, this realization that nothing is known and that nothing can be known within the illusions of the Earth world.

Yet as one moves through that which has been called the Purgative Way[115], one becomes aware that one is utterly empty. And there is a kind of purity in that emptiness that is powerful. You become the Holy Grail which you seek because you are that cup which is now empty or that hand outstretched which has nothing in it, ready to receive that which is new, that which comes from the great original Thought to transform you as a creature so that you have become that which is new.

Then that cycle begins again, where you start from a new place in the spiral of evolution. It is if it were, in a flattened spiral, the same place you have been before in this incarnation. Yet, because it is an upward spiral, you are always moving to that place you were before with a new mind, so that you meet that repeating theme or those repeating themes of your incarnation from a new place of observation and experience.

There are themes to most entities' incarnations, recurring leitmotifs[116] of the music of your life. For this instrument, for instance, the theme is the study of how to offer love without the expectation of return. It is a powerful lesson in that one learns again and again that one's life is not the life of one who reacts, but one who offers from the creative or generative heart that which is given without any expectation of anything in return.

Once one has begun to learn this lesson, one can begin to see how transformed one's life is by the ability to live as a part of the godhead principle; as one who is willing to let love flow through him. It is one of several very common themes for those who have come to this planet in order to be subject to the athanor[117] of experience. Each experience which one has becomes a source of possible catalyst. And as one pays more and more attention to one's catalyst, one becomes more and more able to recognize these recurring themes of incarnational-level lessons that are part of each entity's life in a unique way.

No two entities have the same exact incarnational lessons, for each has chosen those lessons carefully. Consequently, each person, as he transforms and becomes a new person, is offering an energy that has never been offered before in the infinite annals of the creation, for each transformation is from one unique being to another equally unique being.

We thank each for the power and the beauty of the energies which are being run during transformation. The courage of each in being able to go through these dark nights of the soul and to see the magical nature of the self is greatly appreciated by those of us who do not dwell within the veil of unknowing, but have access to the truth in a much less veiled way.

It may help those seeking to maximize their ability to be transformed and transformational beings to look at the essence of the shaman's experience. The shaman, whatever his nationality or culture, is basically that entity who chooses to go through the death experience while remaining alive.

Those of Ra spoke of the shamans of the time of Egypt, who used the pyramid to go down under the pyramid into that catafalque-like place where sensations were numbed and an entity was closed up from all incoming experience, thus mimicking the death process. After days spent within that tomblike place under the pyramid, the experience of death had been well met and the entity was then able to observe life with a delight and an appetite that would not have been available to the one who had not experienced that death of the senses, the death of sensation, the death of stimulation, shall we say.

The great vigor available to the shaman comes from that entirely organic and spontaneous delight which one who has been dead takes in life, after experiencing the deprivation of the dark night of the soul. Whether by the vision quest or by the steam

---

[115] St. John of the Cross is the church figure who most famously wrote about the medieval concept of the three ways or states, The Purgative Way, The Illuminative Way, and The Unitive Way. Another phrase for The Purgative Way is The Dark Night of the Soul. In this phase of development, the seeker empties himself of all the old matter of ego and culture to prepare himself for illumination.

[116] A leitmotif is a theme or melody that recurs throughout a musical piece to denote a character or a concept.

[117] An athanor is an oven used by the medieval alchemist to transform base metal into gold.

and the heat of a sweat lodge, or by any of those transformative experiences that can be found throughout the various cultures of your planet, there is the completely novel experience of new life, new growth, new hope, and new beingness.

With each transformation there is more of an appreciation for the gift of awareness and an ever more transparent ability to allow things to move through one. One becomes a radiant being, not because one has more light within the self, but because one is more able to allow light to move through the energy body and out into the world. It is not that one becomes a more powerful ego, but that one has allowed to drop away from the self many things which were either blocking or dimming the light which moves through each entity within creation.

As entities become more spiritually mature they become more and more aware that they do not know anything. They become more and more aware that they are living in the now, and that this now is a beautiful, magical, wonderful moment, wherein two worlds meet, the world of phenomenal experience and the world of infinity and eternity.

They become aware of themselves as a place where these two worlds may express at the same time. They are embodied spirits and may feel both the day and the night, the heat and the cold and all of the dynamics of opposites that create the world of male and female, the Earth world. At the same time they are able to feel the energies of infinity and eternity move through them and create that consciousness which only time/space and timelessness can offer.

Gradually an entity becomes aware of himself as one who plays in the waters of time, much as an otter plays in the pool, leaping and jumping for the very joy of movement, rejoicing and enjoying water and the sunshine and all that occurs in the rhythmic cycles of play. It is not that one takes oneself less seriously in terms of being willing to spend the life dedicating the self to the infinite Creator and to service to others, but rather it is that the burden of being a serious seeker falls away before the very organic and natural, lighthearted and merry vision of oneself and awareness of oneself as a creature of the one infinite Creator, not striving, but being. The feeling becomes almost one of curiosity. "Ah, I am in this present moment. Creator, where shall you toss me now? What is your will for me this day?"

We would at this time pause to ask the group if there are follow-ups to this central question before we take other questions from you. We are known to you as Hatonn and we now pause.

A: I have a follow-up question. Is Don Juan Matus, the teacher of writer, Carlos Castaneda, real? Can you talk about him as an entity and a shaman?

We are those of Q'uo, and are of aware of your query, my brother. Because this question is part of your active process at this time, we find that we would be influencing you unduly were we to comment directly. We can, however, offer some thoughts connected with this query having to do with spiritual principles, if that would be acceptable to you, my brother.

A: Yes, gladly.

We are those of Q'uo, and therefore are able to proceed in some way. We apologize that our desire to maintain our polarity causes us to refrain from more specific information.

One spiritual principle involved within your query which may be helpful to you is that of truth being untouched by its vehicle. That is, the question of whether one such as Don Juan Matus or Jesus the Christ or Zarathustra was real is irrelevant to spiritual seekers. Each thought that has been thought by any entity in creation has a reality. It has a vibrational nature. Depending upon the intensity of that thought, its life may be tenuous or powerful. And if a group of entities are working with the construct of a Don Juan Matus or a Jesus the Christ or a Zarathustra, then the thought forms connected with this entity build up and have a life of their own, with their vibrational characteristics depending upon the strength of those who come to form themselves by thinking along the lines suggested by one of these great teachers.

Another spiritual principle that is sometimes helpful when gazing at the writings of those inspired entities which have written is polarity.

(Side one of tape ends.)

(Carla channeling)

When an entity who is teaching is purely positive in polarity, there is within the teaching a flow of wisdom and compassion which does not have to do in any way with control over others. The magical systems of many of your cultures, including the so-called sects of the Christian religion, sometimes contain mixed polarity in that there is the attempt, either by the leader of a sect or a type of thought or by the organization that rises up around a leader or a professor of a certain system of thought, which is hopeful of controlling and manipulating entities or situations.

The positive polarity has no axe to grind, but exists in an energy of faith, love, gratitude and joy. Often wonderful teachings that are very positive in polarity are intermixed with teachings that have strongly moved into the energies of yellow ray, where there is the ability to work in groups. And instead of sinking into the group and allowing the group to express its worship and its practices on a spontaneous and radiant basis, there is the negative yellow-ray concern for the manipulation and disposition of its members, or of situations having to do with entities with whom it is in relationship.

We will encourage the one known as A and all of those who read concerning very helpful and interesting ideas such as the one known as Don Juan Matus offers in his system of teaching, to, again, as we said at the beginning of this session, maintain the most thoughtful discrimination so that you slow down the process of absorption of new material to the pace where you can absorb it in a considered and comfortable manner.

There is often a tendency towards impulsivity when one is surrounding oneself with the thoughts of a new source of inspiration. This impulsivity does not serve the seeker nearly as well as the attitude of being one who reflects and then lets go, and then reflects again and then lets go, so that one gradually deepens one's intelligence concerning a particular system of thought.

There are always pearls that are just for you, but there is almost always surrounding material that acts more as fertilizer than as jewel. So there is that process, when working with inspired material, of slowing that self down who is so eager for the fruits of this system to the pace that enables the seeker truly and genuinely to absorb material in a way that does not rush the fences of intellect and toss one into a situation where one is simply beginning to repeat by rote various things that a particular entity has suggested to be true.

May we answer you further, my brother. We are those of Q'uo.

(Pause)

A: If you are asking me if I want more, I'd just as soon hear a question from someone else.

We are those of Q'uo, and therefore would ask if there is another query at this time?

(Pause)

Jim: Not from me, Q'uo.

We are those of Q'uo, and believe that we have exhausted the queries in this circle of seeking at this particular session of working. That leaves us with regret in a way, for we have greatly enjoyed our ability to be a part of your seeking circle and to experience the beauty of your blended auras. Thank you so much for inviting us to share in your meditation. It has been a blessed experience for us and a wonderful opportunity for us to serve the infinite Creator in the type of service that we have chosen.

We leave this instrument and this group in the love and in the light of the one infinite Creator, encouraging each to seek the Creator in all things and to set the mind upon love, for that is that which is the truth. We are known to you as those of Q'uo. Adonai. Adonai vasu. ☥

L/L Research

L/L Research is a subsidiary of Rock Creek Research & Development Laboratories, Inc.

P.O. Box 5195
Louisville, KY 40255-0195

www.llresearch.org

Rock Creek is a non-profit corporation dedicated to discovering and sharing information which may aid in the spiritual evolution of humankind.

ABOUT THE CONTENTS OF THIS TRANSCRIPT: This telepathic channeling has been taken from transcriptions of the weekly study and meditation meetings of the Rock Creek Research & Development Laboratories and L/L Research. It is offered in the hope that it may be useful to you. As the Confederation entities always make a point of saying, please use your discrimination and judgment in assessing this material. If something rings true to you, fine. If something does not resonate, please leave it behind, for neither we nor those of the Confederation would wish to be a stumbling block for any.

© 2009 L/L Research

Saturday Meditation
January 19, 2008

Group question: The question this week Q'uo is: What is your opinion of the use which ritual magic makes of repeated ritualized behavior to seek and serve the Creator? It seems to utilize the doubling effect in that each repetition of the ritual seems to increase the seeker's desire and purity to seek and serve the Creator. Would Q'uo please describe how we, as seekers of truth, can bring this kind of magic into our daily lives?

(Carla channeling)

We are those known to you as the principle of Q'uo. Greetings in the love and in the light of the one infinite Creator, in whose service we come to you this evening. May we express to you our delight at the privilege of being asked to join your circle of seeking and take part in this working.

We are very happy to share with you our thoughts on the devotional life; that is, how to create a life that dwells within the precincts of White Ritual Magic, as the one known as Jim has asked.

However, as always, we would preface our remarks by asking each who hears or reads these words to take responsibility for discriminating as each listens to what we have to say. Take what seems good to you and leave the rest behind. Please do not make the mistake of thinking that all that we say is equally important to you, for spiritual seeking is very idiosyncratic. There will be those thoughts that are helpful to you and those thoughts that do not fit your process as it is. You only need those things that make you feel a resonance and a wish to ponder them further.

If you will discriminate, then that will free us to offer our thoughts without being concerned that we might infringe upon your free will or be a stumbling block in the way of your process. We thank you for this consideration, my friends.

We would further preface our remarks by saying that the basis of all of these thoughts which we offer to you this particular evening is love. One can move into a great many complexities and details in discussing how to live a life that is grounded in love and based upon the awareness that all are one and all things are the Creator. Yet underlying every complexity and every detail is a single, simple truth: the one infinite Creator, and you, and all that there is are one thing. It is a unified creation and the nature of that unity is love. Unconditional love is the one great original Thought that has generated all the seen worlds and all of the unseen worlds as well.

Your question, my brother, moves into that area where the seeker has awakened so thoroughly that he has begun to seek to express the fruits of his new awareness. We do not need to remind each that the prerequisite for working to create a magical ritual of the entire life is an open heart. And the prerequisite for having an open heart is a freely flowing chakra body, with the lower chakras balanced and open and full power moving through into the heart and thence through the upper chakras and out the crown of the head.

When you become aware that this is not the case, in your momentary estimation of your state of mind, then there is the need to relinquish the magical personality and move into that balancing mode where that trigger which has taken you away from an open energy system and an open heart is identified, loved, accepted, embraced and balanced. Then and only then is it wise to move back into the ceremonial dance of the devotional life.

We use the term, devotional life, because it is this instrument's term for a life in which the principles of ritual magic of the white ceremonial kind are brought into the daily life, and it is a phrase that is easier for us to say. Therefore, please understand that when we speak of the devotional life we are not speaking specifically of a Christian life, or any type of belief system that would be behind living a life of devotion to the one infinite Creator. We are simply taking the shortcut of this instrument's vocabulary for describing the life in which the entity sees not only the possibility but the need for imbuing every aspect of the normal, everyday life with magic.

As the one known as Jim has said, the basic work of the magician is to create changes in his consciousness by an act of will. He does this very specifically in order to serve. There is nothing physical connected with the white ritual magical tradition. All the work that is done is work in consciousness. The work consists of invocation. One invokes one's own magical personality and then one invokes characteristics of the Creator or the Creator Itself.

We may illustrate the principles of this type of magic by looking at the ritual that this instrument calls Holy Communion or the Holy Eucharist. The ritual is conducted by a priest. The priest prepares the congregation by reading from holy works, offering prayers and supplications, and then leading the congregation in a general confession of sins. In this confession, all is laid before the one infinite Creator, given away by the self, emptying the self of all that is past. The priest then absolves those in the congregation, reminding them that Jesus the Christ came to love rather than to judge and that all is forgiven.

Thusly he prepares the congregation for the reception of the Holy Communion. He then turns his back to the congregation, or in some churches simply turns his mind and his attention away from the congregation, and he begins to pray directly to the one infinite Creator.

He remembers the actions of the one known as Jesus the Christ in which the Christ is breaking bread and drinking wine with his disciples. He tells them, "Take this bread; it is my body. Take this wine; it is my blood."

And as he remembers this, with his priestly hands hovering over the bread and the wine he is about to give the congregation, he invokes the presence of Jesus the Christ, that it may enter into the substance of the bread and the wine. Magically, then, it becomes a living host, a living carrier for new life. As the congregation takes this bread and this wine from his hands, again he says, "The bread of life, the cup of salvation," and that repetition brings the energy of Jesus the Christ into the awareness of each of the congregation as they eat the body and drink the blood that has set them free to live a new life, unencumbered by past sins.

We describe this ceremony or ritual to you in some detail because we wish you to see the kind of change that a magical ritual is intended to offer. It is intended to create a change in consciousness, or as this instrument would say, a change in vibration. The intent is to lift the natural default vibration of each of the congregation by invoking the presence of the one infinite Creator in the persona of Jesus the Christ.

The everyday life is not spent in church and in the workaday world. Each seeker must choose to be his own priest. Each seeker is fully capable of taking on priesthood. Yet we would suggest to the seeker who wishes to live a devotional life that he become more and more finely tuned to an awareness of this momentary decision to become the priest rather than the lay person. For there is a qualitative difference between the actions of a lay person and the actions of a priest.

When one is a lay person, one is framing the self without any particular power, metaphysically or spiritually speaking. When one styles himself as a priest, on the other hand, he styles himself as an entity who has become able to handle sacred things and to pray directly to the one infinite Creator and be heard.

You are naturally priests. The unnatural frame of mind, in terms of your deeper nature, is that of the lay person. Yet your culture has trained you all of your life to give your power away to authority figures such as priests. Therefore, as you set out to live a devotional life, we ask that you take seriously the responsibility of priesthood. When you do not feel priestly, then it is well for you to refrain from expressing the form of any ritual. It is essential that the essence of the ritual precede and inform the form. Otherwise the ritual is dead and does not have power.

It is not necessary, my friends, to be extremely judgmental or overly critical of the self as to whether or not the self is open-hearted and working with an open energy-body system. Indeed, after a certain amount of practice at remaining in this frame of mind of the priest at all times, it shall become familiar enough to the seeker that there is no longer the concern for whether or not one is in tune. This is due to the fact that once an entity has become accustomed to living in a priestly manner, any aberration from that tenor of mind will be all too obvious to the entity and will constitute that which needs attending as though it were a pain in the body.

It is for the beginner that we offer these warnings. We place them here because it is essential that seekers see the difference between actions and essence. One may speak in ritualistic ways and move in ritualistic motions and yet fail to live a magical life because the heart is not open and love is not flowing. As the one known as Paul said, "Without love, I am a clanging gong."[118]

The most intricate of rituals is always founded on love. That is the prerequisite. Therefore, we encourage each to do the work necessary to support a devotional life. There are all too many of your peoples that have sought the life of a religious recluse because of the great yearning for the infinite Creator, yet because the form remained that which was understood and not the essence, the hunger remained and even grew, despite the monastic schedule of six worship services in each day.

That being said, let us look at some ways to think about the devotional life lived in the rush of the workaday world. In a way, it seems an odd fit to make of the everyday functions of life a ritual, yet each and every portion of the life is entirely prone to and grateful for sacred use. In order to illustrate this, we would take an example from this instrument's own life.

Each day this instrument and the one known as Jim come together at the end of their working day for a bath. This instrument has physical limitations which make it helpful for the one known as Jim to interact with her, far more than most husbands and wives interact when bathing. The one known as Jim draws the bath, opens the oils and lotions that will be needed after the bath and places them ready, and invites this instrument into the bathtub. He helps her sit down and together they enjoy their whirlpool and the cleansing of their bodies.

When they are both clean, before they leave the bathtub, the one known as Jim takes two pieces of ice in holders and for two minutes ices this instrument's back, which alleviates the arthritic pain in her shoulders and spine. When this has been done, the instrument lets the water out of the bath and puts the shampoos and other accoutrements of the bath away and then is helped out of the bathtub by the one known as Jim. He helps her rub oil into her body, dries her off and then puts lotion on her body, working to replenish sensitive skin that is always very dry.

At the end of their bath ritual they are both clean, the instrument has accomplished all that she needs to accomplish with the help of the one known as Jim, and in all of that intricate movement there have been no words. For each knows the dance and each makes of the dance as graceful and beautiful a thing as can be conceived by both of them.

Here it may be seen that the form of the ritual is very homely. There is nothing special about the ingredients of this ritual. They are soap, water, oil and so forth. Yet the love that streams between husband and wife, as the one known as Jim helps this instrument with her daily cleansing, is palpable and powerful and supports and encourages each in his own individual metaphysical life.

There are two things that we would note about this ritual before moving on. Firstly, the one known as Carla, during the whirlpool portion of the bath, actively works with angelic presences, mentally expressing her love, thankfulness and joy and rededicating herself to the service of the one infinite

---

[118] *Holy Bible*, I Corinthians 13:1, "Though I speak with the tongues of men and of angels and have not charity, I am become as sounding brass, or a tinkling cymbal."

Creator. By doing so, she charges the water, acting as a priestess for both, although this too is never spoken.

Secondly, the dance of the bath moves into the succeeding moments of dressing and moving into the next item of the day in ways which link and tie in the energies of love, cooperation and mutual participation in the dance so that the dance does not end when the bathwater is drained.

In ritual, there are two kinds of form. There is the form of movement and there is the form of words. Behind those forms of motion and speaking lie the thoughts of the magician who is speaking and acting. To a magician there is no empty action. The dance is always ongoing. And at the very center of the dance, always, there is love. The magician invokes aspects of love, standing on a plinth[119] of love, surrounded by love, and seeking only finer and more sensitive attunements of that love.

There are a finite number of movements and words within any day. There are a finite number of repeated activities which lend themselves to ritual. Consequently, to an entity whose mind is focused on filling the form of his day with the essence of worship it is not an exceedingly long process of thought to visualize every single repeated action of a normal day.

Each entity's day will be unique to him. However, the work he does in a day will have certain aspects of it that are repeated. Therefore, the seeker who wishes to create the devotional life in the midst of the workaday world shall set his mind to analyzing each action of his day, at work, at home, and on the road.

The one known as Carla, for instance, has in her work environment the computer. All of her work is done on the computer. The one known as J, on the other hand, has in his working environment various types of large equipment such as mowers, blowers and weed eaters. It does not seem to the untrained mind that computers and mowers would be likely targets for a devotional life. Yet we would suggest to you that whatever the nature of your work environment is, you can fill it so full of devotional essence that your workday world positively sings.

Most entities have a transitional environment between work and home, because of the omnipresence of the automobile or other forms of transit. Most entities work in a place that is not their home. And this, too, is a type of environment that at first glance seems inimical to being part of a devotional life. Yet, we assure you that creative thought about the essence of the time of driving or the time of riding shall offer to the mind of the seeker repeated actions which may be infused with the invocation of deity.

All motions may be thought of as sacred dance. All words may be thought of as sacred ritual.

It is in the home environment, however, that most of the fully repetitive actions of the day are performed. The washing of the clothes, the washing of the self, the preparation and eating of food, the preparation for bed and sleep time and the rising from sleep are all inevitable in their repetition. Consequently they offer the deepest resource for one who wishes to live a devotional life.

This instrument and the one known as Jim have long created times of offering and worship at the beginning and end of the day. They have also formed the habit of remembering before food is ingested to thank the one infinite Creator and to thank the food. These are far more outer in terms of type of ritual than the kind of ritual of which we have been speaking, and yet it is helpful in the devotional life to set aside times that are specifically dedicated to worship. This enables the seeker to deepen his base of insight as time goes on.

It is possible in this way to create of the entire life a dance that is an invocation of the one infinite Creator. The element of repetition is a substantial part of a magical ritual. Something that is done once, no matter how beautiful, remains single. When that beautiful thing begins to be repeated, there is, indeed, the doubling effect; that is, each doing of that repetition with full awareness of its sacredness doubles the power of that ritual.

The one thing that is missing in terms of this repetition, when the priest is creating his own sacred life rather than being a part of a group ritual, is that he is not calling a significant amount of the entities who have shared in that same ritual. For instance, in Holy Communion or the Holy Eucharist, many of the words of that service have been expressed in relatively undistorted form for centuries on end. Therefore, when an entity begins to pray in any one of the key prayers of that ritual, such as—

---

[119] plinth: a square base or a lower block, as of a pedestal.

"Holy, holy, holy, Lord God of Hosts! Heaven and earth are full of thy glory. Glory be to thee, O Lord Most High"[120]

—a significant amount of those who have been Christians in incarnation and who are now between incarnations living in the inner planes, are drawn to those words, so that one entity saying that particular prayer can excite and attract a tremendous amount of heavenly help with the repetition of that prayer with heartfelt energy.

Contrariwise, one who is living a devotional life that he has created himself is doubling his own power but not calling a large amount of those who dwell in the inner planes between incarnations with one exception. Angels are not drawn to a particular song or a particular set of words. Angels are drawn to pure essence, having never taken part in incarnation. Consequently, any living of a devotional life will attract angelic help, so that there is indeed not only the doubling effect of amplification of one's personal power, but the supporting and undergirding effect of angelic support and encouragement.

In closing, we would simply say that we cannot iterate often enough the importance of moving from love and from essence in creating a devotional life. If there is not love in the repetition of holy things, then that energy, while not wasted, is diminished in its power to comfort, heal and succor the seeker. Therefore, do not be caught up in the forms of devotional life, but rather be caught up with the emotions engendered by having an open heart and an open energy body and experiencing the self as part of the dance of the One that is ongoing because he exists in that Creation in which all things are indeed one coordinated, eternal dance.

We are those of Q'uo, and would ask if there is a follow-up query on this question, my brother?

Jim: Not for me, Q'uo.

We are those of Q'uo, and would asked then if there is any other query this evening before we leave this instrument?

R: Q'uo, I keep racking my brain for some question because I hate to let you go, but I do not have one, so I'll just say that I appreciate the Brothers and Sisters of Sorrow.

We are those of Q'uo, and are aware of your non-question. Yet you have asked for a little more of our time and because this instrument continues to have energy to offer for a few more of your minutes, we would speak freely, if it is all right with you.

R: Please.

Very well, my brother. There is in this season of the year that is winter much joy in the one known as R, while many others have exactly the opposite feeling about the weather being cold. So there is at all times a multiplicity of people, a multiplicity of opinions, and a seemingly variegated and splintered world where many things seem out of tune and the service-to-self faction of your population dominates the news with wars and rumors of wars, the misuses of power being almost endless.

Yet this appearance is an illusion. Certainly, as the days of third density wane and come to a close, those who are seeking to graduate in negative polarity are working very hard to create as much service-to-self polarization in their lives as possible. These are the entities that gather power for its own sake, that enjoy sending men to their death in the pursuit of policy and that do not blink at lying, stealing and cheating, simply saying, "It's just business."

It is easy for service-to-others entities to become distressed when gazing at what seems to be the way of the world. We would suggest that this seeming way of the world is only large in aspect because of the way your culture values information.

It is as though your mass media functions by a kind of radar which only picks up certain types of vibrations. In terms of your radar imaging, for instances, that which is metallic and magnetic is picked up and shown on the radar as a blip. Many other things are in the sky but the radar does not read them. Radar is set to read the objects which occupy a very small amount of the air and report only on them. Nevertheless, all of the sky is still there.

In much the same way your mass media only pick up as blips those entities which have disturbed the continuum by the misuse of power, whether it be sending entities off to die for policy or whether it be

---

[120] The Sanctus, part of the Holy Eucharist service which comes just before the Great invocation. There are various wordings of this according to the service used. This particular wording is from p. 334 of The Book of Common Prayer used by Episcopalians in America. The same basic service is in use in the Roman Catholic Church as well.

one entity who turns and shoots another. These are the things that create and constitute the blips that are reported on in the mass media. Meanwhile, all the rest of human nature remains unreported.

My friends, you are wonderful people. The vast majority of those upon Planet Earth at this time seek with all their hearts to be good people by their own lights. We ask that each of you take the time to be aware of the good people in your life: the person that sold you something at the drugstore or grocery store, the person that helped you repair something that was wrong with your house or your apartment, the person that let you into traffic on a busy street, and the people in your neighborhood whom you see walking their dogs and chatting in their front yards.

Each and every one of these entities is suffering and yet seeks with all its heart to live a good life and to serve others. We ask that you begin to deepen your appreciation of that which lies below the radar and begin to give less power to the loud voices of your media as they report on that which, if it bleeds, leads.

We would at this time take our leave of this instrument and this group, thanking each for creating this sacred space that we may share. It has been a pleasure to speak with you this evening. We leave you in the love and in the light of the one infinite Creator. We are known to you as the principle of Q'uo. Adonai, my friends. Adonai. ✛

L/L Research

L/L Research is a subsidiary of Rock Creek Research & Development Laboratories, Inc.

P.O. Box 5195
Louisville, KY 40255-0195

www.llresearch.org

Rock Creek is a non-profit corporation dedicated to discovering and sharing information which may aid in the spiritual evolution of humankind.

ABOUT THE CONTENTS OF THIS TRANSCRIPT: This telepathic channeling has been taken from transcriptions of the weekly study and meditation meetings of the Rock Creek Research & Development Laboratories and L/L Research. It is offered in the hope that it may be useful to you. As the Confederation entities always make a point of saying, please use your discrimination and judgment in assessing this material. If something rings true to you, fine. If something does not resonate, please leave it behind, for neither we nor those of the Confederation would wish to be a stumbling block for any.

© 2009 L/L RESEARCH

Channeling Intensive 1 - Session 10 - Channeling Circle 1
February 10, 2008

Carla: The plan is that we are going to go through our tuning processes and when we are done, we are going to put up a hand. Actually you don't have to put it up until you see my eyes open and start to look around. And if you are done, put up your hand because I will go through my tuning process also. Is that pretty clear? I am going around to the left.

Do you want to om to begin or can we just start tuning now?

(Group consensus is to go right into the tuning process.)

Let's just start tuning.

(Carla channeling)

We are those known to you as Laitos. We greet you in the love and in the light of the infinite Creator. We are most happy to be called to your circle of seeking this evening and we thank each of you for calling us to join you. It is, as always, a true privilege and honor to be included in your meditation. It is especially an honor and a privilege to be asked to help train the entities within the circle.

We would apologize to the one known as M for we realize that this instrument was not entirely ready to join the circle and yet we felt that it was well that we move forward while the focus of the other entities within the group was at its maximum.

As always we would ask each to evaluate any word that we say to these instruments, for we are not authorities over you but fellow-pilgrims upon the path of seeking the one infinite Creator. We appreciate your discrimination, for it will enable us to speak freely without being concerned about infringing upon your free will.

The one known as Carla has said that we often use the training technique of telling a story and this we shall, indeed, do at this time. But we would first offer remarks oriented to aiding this circle in its first attempt to receive our contact and express the thoughts that we offer.

First of all, my friends, we are most pleased to be collaborators with you in offering service to the one infinite Creator and to those upon your planet who wish to seek helpful information concerning the process of spiritual evolution. We are one with you in that desire and that particular path of service and it is a joy to work with each of you.

Secondly, we would echo the sentiments of the one known as Carla when we say that we ask you not to be discouraged if there is not an immediate feeling of contact from us. The sensitivity to contact varies from entity to entity. However, it is true that once the contact has been accepted, even if there is only a slight feeling of contact, the acceptance of contact in itself begins to build and strengthen the connection of your channel with our source. Consequently, we encourage you to be fearless. There is no judgment for those who are not able to pick up our communication and there is no judgment for those who begin to receive thoughts from us and yet, for one reason or another, are unable to continue. Please allow this part of yourself which has an ego to die down and be left behind. You are offering your service. You will move as you are able and all speeds are perfect.

We would begin the story with this instrument.

Once upon a time, in a small village at the foot of a great mountain and at the shore of an ocean, there dwelled a young man who had always served in the fields of his father and in the fishing boat of his uncle. His life was a simple one. He hauled the teeming nets at eventide and, when needed in his father's fields for harvest or for especially intense work in cultivating, he walked behind the plow, or behind the reaper or behind the oxen when he was needing to thresh the harvest. He was happy in the sunlight and content in the rain and knew no desire except to live his life out in this small village.

Yet one day, something occurred that brought new thoughts to his mind.

We would at this time transfer this contact to the one known as R. We are those of Laitos.

(Pause)

(Carla channeling)

We are those of Laitos and are again with this instrument. We find that the one known as R has not thought that he is in a position to pick up our contact and so we shall speak a bit further through this instrument and move on to the one known as G.

This entity saw something that he had never seen before. A ship with a sail that he had no knowledge of appeared on the horizon and sailed into his small village, having to moor somewhat offshore because of the shallows. The village rode out in its fishing boats to receive these strangers, and when the strangers came among them, they spoke an unknown tongue.

They were able to make themselves known by gestures and they enjoyed a celebration with the villagers, loading up their water skins, filling the ship's larder with fresh food. And away the strangers sailed. Yet, to the young man there came to be a great desire to know more than he had known before.

At this time, we would transfer this contact to the one known as G. We are those of Laitos.

(G channeling)

We are those of Laitos. We would greet you in love and light. We are having difficulties with this instrument. We leave this instrument. We are those of Laitos.

(N channeling)

We are *(inaudible)* who have a message *(inaudible)* among this group. That message is *(inaudible)*.

(Carla channeling)

We are those of Laitos and are again with this instrument. We thank the ones known as G and N and will continue the story briefly through this instrument.

The young man decided that in order to discover what he should do to act upon his desire to know more than he had known before, he should perhaps scale the mountain and come to the highest place in the area, that he may look over all the lands and the oceans and decide what road he should take to seek further the wonders of the unknown entities who had graced the village with their presence, and had left them gifts before going on their way.

And so, although no one had ever been able successfully to climb to the very top of the nearby peak, he determined that he wished to do so. He said good-bye to his family and set off on the arduous journey, for although the peak looked to be nearby and could be seen by the eye, it was many weeks' journey by foot and there was one obstacle after another in the young man's way. Yet he said good-bye and set out for the adventure to come.

We would at this time transfer this contact to the one known as L. We are those of Laitos.

(L channeling)

We are those of Laitos. The young man in his journey came to a river, one that he could not conceive going across. So he walked upstream, searching another path. Perhaps a tree had fallen across the river and could act as a bridge. Perhaps there were stones that he could reach to cross the river. Perhaps the river came to a place where it was narrower.

However, in his walk up the river he came to a waterfall because the river fell down off of the cliff.

There was no more walking along the river. There was another obstacle in his way.

This instrument may now pass this channel on to the one known as M. He is more capable of receiving our message. We are those of Laitos.

(M channeling)

We are those of Laitos. We are telling this story of this man and his journey. It should be known at this time that this man realized something within himself. He saw a flash over the horizon that brought him back to a time when he was a child. Although he was convinced that the lightening flashed, it appears that *(inaudible)*. Although this man was *(inaudible)* he realized why he was on this trip.

(G channeling)

We are Laitos. This young man surveyed the situation, as you would say among your people. He could see no way to cross. He could go no farther upstream. He went inland and traveled for three times of sleep when the sun did not shine. After three times of sleep when the sun did not shine, he came to a clearing, a large clearing in which there were what you would call dwelling places. There were people. The people looked like him. He was glad to see them. They did not speak as he spoke. He was able to talk to them by making signs with his hands.

He was taken to a very old man who seemed to be one of great wisdom. He stayed with the very old man for several periods of light and times when the sun did not shine. They came to be able to communicate with each other. One way they communicated was by making pictures and signs with a stick. I pass this story to the one called L.

(L1 channeling)

We are Laitos. We greet you all with love. The young man communicated to the old man that he wished *(inaudible)*. The old man told him that this would be very difficult; that no one he knew had been able to accomplish this in all his years. This inspired the young man even more in his quest to reach the top of the mountain. When he appeared so resolute, the old man told him of a path he might take. He gave him a pouch as a gift on his way, and told him that when he was in danger or lost, he should open the pouch. We are Laitos and pass on to the one known as L2.

(L2 channeling)

We are Laitos. We are having difficulty with this instrument. We pass it on.

(Carla channeling)

We are again with this instrument. We are those known to you as Laitos. May we say parenthetically how pleased we are with this band of storytellers who seek to share love and light through their instruments.

There are many, many ways to approach the telling of the story of love and light, and of the journey that each takes when he has awakened to the knowledge that there is more than meets the eye in his otherwise placid life.

This young man determined at last to move back to the point of the waterfall. He did not know why, in order to go up, he must go down, and yet that was what his intuition was suggesting to him, so he bade farewell to his new friend and kind mentor and made his way back to the precipice over which the waters flowed in abundance and beauty, And barring all fear, he spread his arms and leapt into mid-air, offering himself to the quest that awaited him.

As he did so, all of the colors of his vision seemed to change and become more and more luminous. Suddenly he found himself borne up on the back of a beautiful white bird, so huge that he was comfortably able to sit upon this bird's back. Then, as he flew into the land beyond the waterfall, he found that this magical being was able to speak to him. And he had many questions to ask, so his heart was glad.

We would at this time transfer this contact to the one known as S. We are those of Laitos.

(S channeling)

We are Laitos and we are with this instrument.

(Carla channeling)

We are again with this instrument. We are known as Laitos. We thank the one known as S and will continue for a bit through this instrument.

As he flew towards the rainbow that circled the peak that he had been hoping to reach, the young man asked the bird what it was that made him hunger so to know that which he did not know. Yet the bird was silent on this point, only continuing to take him to the rainbow that circled the peak.

And the boy began to muse to himself of all of the wonders that he had seen and of all the new things that had passed before his eyes and accommodated to his experience. He had no answers, and yet he had become something more than he was before. He pondered this mystery of unknowing as he came to the rainbow that circled the peak.

We would at this time transfer this contact to the one known as C. We are those of Laitos.

(C channeling)

We greet you again in love and light. We are those of Laitos. *(Inaudible)*.

(Carla channeling)

We are those of Laitos and are again with this instrument, greeting each in love and light again. We will at this time transfer this contact to the one known as Jim. We are those of Laitos.

(Jim channeling)

We are those of Laitos and greet each in love and light. The young man now felt that the significance of the colors were as a kind of representation of the journey upon which he found himself.

(Side one of tape ends.)

(Jim channeling)

At the ending of his journey, he had learned of the great, bright, red-hot zeal to know what it was that lay beyond his reach at the peak of the mountain, which was barely within his sight. He had experienced great excitation to know, generated by the appearance of those friendly strangers who had appeared in the ship at his village seaside location. As he began his journey, the desire to know became transformed into various hues, likened to the rainbow colors, so that there was a kind of maturation that was tempered by the experience which he was undergoing in each present moment.

Now, as he rested upon the back of the great bird with the pouch given by the elder wise man secured safely across his shoulders, he knew that the journey that he was upon was a journey that would have no end. Though he may, indeed, reach the top of the peak, such a destination was as a beginning, as well as were all destinations. He realized that this journey of seeking upon which he found himself was one which would continue until the day he passed from this illusion and from this life.

He decided that he would open the pouch which had been given to him to see what it was that the old wise man had given to him. As he opened the pouch, he was surprised to find a mirror inside. When he looked into the mirror he saw himself as that which was the seeker and that which was sought. The beginning and end of his journey lay in his hands, in his heart and in his mind.

We shall transfer this contact to the who is known as Carla.

(Carla channeling)

We are those of Laitos and greet each through this instrument.

The young man now burned with a different fire. He burned with the fire of self-knowledge and the keen awareness that all that he sought lay within him. And so he communicated to his feathered friend that he wished nothing more than to go back to the point of his origin. And so it was that the village marveled one day to see the young man walking upon the shore.

"Hey, Uncle," he said. "Do you need some help with those nets?"

"Hey, Father," he said. "Is it time for harvest yet?"

His family and the villagers were astounded to see him again, for they thought he was lost forever. "What have you learned? What miracle has brought you to us? What can you tell us?" they asked him, gathering around him and clamoring.

The young man said, "I have seen that those with different languages are yet kind.

"I have seen that those in other places have wise men as well as we.

"I have seen that when I abandon myself to the quest for truth, the truth itself shall come and give me wing that I may go to the place of the highest and the most beautiful.

"And above all, my friends, my family, my beloved, I have seen that there is nothing more precious than you. I have found my happiness."

We thank each in this circle for working with our technique for beginning to channel that which is not already known. Were we, as we sometimes will with you, my friends, to channel concerning love and light directly, it would, indeed, be an easier thing for you to be able to offer some coherent thought, and yet, at the same time, were we to do this, there would be a far greater doubt in your mind as to whether you had actually received that which is our contact. This is the reason for our technique with you. We assure each that each has, to some extent, felt our presence and yet, as this instrument said as she was teaching before this session, it is a difficult thing to determine whether it is a thought of the mind that is yours, or a thought of the mind that is coming through you. For thoughts are thoughts, and you channel your thoughts just as you channel ours.

As you ponder what you have experienced this night, realize that you are, indeed, channels already. May your channel be one of love and light always insofar as you are able to open yourselves to the heart of yourselves, which is love. Love, my friends, is all there is. You are all creatures of love.

We would ask at this time if there are queries that you may have for us. We are those of Laitos.

Questioner: I have a question. Why did I become so incredibly cold before I channeled?

We are those of Laitos and are aware of your query, my sister. The subjective feeling of cold has long been associated, my sister, with the entrance into your space/time of the spiritual presence of time/space. Indeed, there have been times, we believe, that your scientists have discovered there is an actual temperature differential when there is gathered together a group that is able to accept the presence of that which is a metaphysical presence rather than a physical one.

While it is largely a subjective experience, there is an objective component. The experience of that cold is fleeting and does not continue past the time of initial contact. We apologize if our presence caused you any discomfort whatsoever, but we assure you that it functions as a subjective signal that we are, indeed, present with you.

May we ask if there is another query at this time? We are those of Laitos.

C: I have a question. Carla stated that you are of fourth density. Will you describe what the fourth-density experience is like there?

We are those of Laitos and are aware of your query, my sister. The attempt to describe fourth density is made easier by the experiences of those within this circle of seeking. You in third density have at one time or another glimpsed the taste of that land where there is no need to hide the self in any way or to be defended. You have just barely glimpsed the possibility of being unafraid of intimacy, even to having each and every one of one's thoughts known. It is difficult to grasp, from your perspective within third density, my friends, that there is a comfort and an ease that can be experienced when one is completely and utterly exposed. We assure you that there is tremendous comfort and ease in being fully and wholly known, and knowing others fully and wholly.

Your awareness exists with a thick and heavy veil that separates your conscious and physical self from your largely unconscious and metaphysical self, which interpenetrates your awareness as a human being in third density. We do not criticize each of you for being defended, for in your perception, it is necessary. And, indeed, as this instrument has said earlier within these talks during this channeling intensive, there is a goodness and rightness in the protection of drawing limits and affirming one's seeming separation from those who would overwhelm you and remove your individuality.

That situation is that which you came to experience and use and yet at the same time it is that which to some extent you came to transcend. You have many entities in your life who have given you practice at the defense of self against self, and you have some precious few who have given you the opportunity to experience the joy of being undefended in your intimacy.

The great joy of fourth density is that all is, indeed, known and all is accepted. For there is no opportunity to do else when there is not a veil. For it is seen that, beyond all the colors of the spectrum of the personalities of each that you know, lies the white, limitless light and love of the one Infinite Creator.

You have an intense and powerfully difficult experience as third-density entities striving to know love and light, and to live those values of compassion, understanding and acceptance. You make marvelous strides, going far further in one incarnation than would be possible for those in higher densities in many incarnations. Our work in fourth density, in the density of love and understanding, is to refine upon the choice that you have made in your third density life, that choice of service-to-others or service-to-self. You make the choice. We refine upon that choice.

To us there is also a physical body. To us there is mating, friendship, work and pleasure. Yet to us, the brilliance of intensity with which you, in your unknowing, have experienced life, is not given. To us is given that which is offered when there is no veil, but only the endless mystery of the one infinite Creator, which offers us constant feedback that we may ever more refine that choice for love, that choice for service, that choice to be one with all.

May we ask if there is another query at this time?

G: I have a query. During the telling of the story, I became aware of seeing what I thought was *(inaudible)* on the screen. When someone spoke ahead of me and said that he went through the waterfall, I wanted to cry out, "No. No. He didn't go to the waterfall. He went to the wise man." I would like any information you can give me on what dynamic was going on there. Did my friend perceive one probability and I perceive another probability? Or was it something different?

We are aware of your query, my sister. We are those of Laitos. Your first supposition is correct. The story that we had to tell was not fully formed within our own energies, for we wished to move with the various individual energies of those in the circle. The moral or burden of the story was known to us and the general direction of the story. And yet, we were very willing to move in that direction which first seemed to come into the awareness of that entity who was channeling at the time.

There is the concept of making a mistake. And one might say that, indeed, the one which channeled before you went in a different path than we had originally intended. Yet, there was no mistake, in that we were perfectly able to work with that which had been altered and to recreate the story with the same moral and the same burden.

The accuracy of a channel is certainly valuable and that for which each instrument aims. Yet, at the beginning, my sister, we consider it far more useful to work with somewhat faulty perceptions in giving instruments the opportunity to feel our energy and to become more and more comfortable with the situation of the channeling. Consequently, there is no supposition of error in any of those who have channeled this evening, but rather the adventure of a new experience and the beginnings of a new skill.

May we answer you further, my sister?

G: Yes. I noticed also that at a certain point, shortly after the story began, I saw on the screen what was going to happen next and then after I began telling the story, I saw nothing. It was as though the story was telling itself as far as I was concerned for as long as I was speaking. I wonder about that. During the rest of the time that I was talking, I had a pulsing in my head that I don't have at this time. Can you tell me the origin of that pulsing in my head?

We are those of Laitos and are aware of your query, my sister.

The pulsing that you are experiencing is a variety of conditioning, that which allows you to know in a subjective manner that you are, indeed receiving our contact. We use portions of your brain that this instrument would call the frontal lobes, and in using those frontal lobes, there is, characteristic to this use, a variety of the sensations that this instrument has described, such as the tingling at the top of the head or at the third eye. The pulsing which you experienced, my sister, is a variety or a variation on those sensations.

May we ask if there is a final query at this time?

S: I have a question. For those of us who attempted to channel the story and were not able to, you have a view from the other side than we see ourselves. Is there any advice that you can give to the group, to those in it who were not able to connect or experience the presence strongly enough, or to have the confidence to channel what was seen or felt during their time of being called upon?

We are those of Laitos and are with this instrument and believe we understand your query, my brother.

When a dozen people attempt to do one thing, there shall be a dozen different levels of readiness to attempt the task. For instance, a group of twelve might play with a game sphere such as your baseball and an instrument to strike that game sphere such as your bat. If you toss each of the twelve a pitch, some will not be able to see the ball. This instrument is one of them. She may, by taking courage, swing, and she may, indeed, connect, but her physical apparatus is such that she does not see the ball.

Others may never have attempted to hit a baseball before and so they will be hard put to perform the act with any skill.

Others there are who have varying degrees of experience with hitting a baseball with a bat. They will have varying degrees of displayed skill when they swing at a thrown baseball.

And one or two may have a natural gift for hitting a sphere with an implement designed to make it loft up and go places.

So there will be a seeming variety of responses to our contact, from an inability to perceive it to a facility with it that cannot be explained except by saying that there are some who are gifted.

This does not mean that there are any within this group to whom the ability to channel is not possible. For each does, indeed, have the ability to receive and to transmit our thoughts. Yet, there will be a slight variety in the amount of time it takes each entity to be able to see the ball and swing the bat.

There are many factors involved in being able to channel our words. Some of them are those of personality and natural ability. Others are those of the circumstances of the entity, whether they be fears, preconceptions or opinions, of which, perhaps, those who are working to receive our contact are not even aware.

In all cases, we are thrilled and delighted to work with each and every one of those within this circle as each of you explores this gift, this experience, of channeling. We have a desire to share our thoughts through instruments such as you in order that we may offer the story of love, love unconditional, love unbounded, love eternal, love infinite, to those who are hungry for that message.

They hunger and yet in many cases they do not know that for which they hunger. And so each of you, with your unique personality and gifts, offers to us a different way to tell our tale that is simple and unified. Love is all that there is. And all that there is, is love.

This instrument's energy wanes and so we would leave this instrument and this group in the love and in the light of the one infinite Creator. We are known to you as those of Laitos, and as this instrument has said to you before, we always say, "Do not forget to meditate, even if you only have five minutes."

Adonai. Adonai. We are those of Laitos. Adonai.

Carla: As we let the light that have gathered in the circle go back to its source, let us place in that light our hopes and our dreams and our prayers for healing.

The image goes up. Let the rains fall down. ✣

L/L Research

L/L Research is a subsidiary of Rock Creek Research & Development Laboratories, Inc.

P.O. Box 5195
Louisville, KY 40255-0195

www.llresearch.org

Rock Creek is a non-profit corporation dedicated to discovering and sharing information which may aid in the spiritual evolution of humankind.

ABOUT THE CONTENTS OF THIS TRANSCRIPT: This telepathic channeling has been taken from transcriptions of the weekly study and meditation meetings of the Rock Creek Research & Development Laboratories and L/L Research. It is offered in the hope that it may be useful to you. As the Confederation entities always make a point of saying, please use your discrimination and judgment in assessing this material. If something rings true to you, fine. If something does not resonate, please leave it behind, for neither we nor those of the Confederation would wish to be a stumbling block for any.

© 2009 L/L Research

Channeling Intensive 1 - Session 12 - Channeling Circle 2
February 10, 2008

(Carla channeling)

We are those known to you as Laitos. Greetings in the love and the light of the infinite Creator, in whose service we come to you this day.

We thank you for inviting us to your second practice session of this channeling intensive, as you call it. It is a privilege and a pleasure to come to join your meditation and share your sacred space. May we say what a beautiful thing it is to see the harmony of your blended auras as you create the sacred space for this session of working?

We thank you for seeking the truth and for setting aside the time not only to seek the truth as those who listen but also to seek the truth as those who serve by being channels for sources such as we. You are a blessing to us! You enable us to perform our service, which is to share our humble thoughts with you in hopes that we may create the opportunity for more people to become aware of our simple message.

That simple message is that at this time you have a choice between the ways of love and the ways of fear; between the life-giving radiance of pure love and the darkness of repression, control and service to self.

We cannot thank you enough for enabling us to offer this information through your channels. We shall attempt to work with each of you at this working. As always, we caution each to use discrimination when looking at our words, or any words for that matter. The authority within you is a far better authority than any outside source, no matter how seemingly exalted or spiritually high. You can only know the path of your own resonance, as this instrument likes to say.

Some of you have asked for stories and some of you have asked for information. We are simply those who would use all kinds of ways to help each of you to become aware of our contact. So at this time we shall indeed embark upon another story. That is the story of the beginning of this creation of which we and you are a part.

At the beginning of creation there was the allness of the One. In complete quiet, resting, that intelligent infinity that is the ground of being. Into this intelligent infinity came that first distortion of the Law of One, which is free will.

We will at this time transfer this contact to the one known as R. We are those of Laitos.

(R channeling)

I am Laitos and we are with this instrument now. We are speaking about love and light

(Long pause.)

(Carla channeling)

We are once again with this instrument. We are those of Laitos. We thank the one known as R for moving forward in the attempt to receive our channel. It may not seem sometimes as though there was progress made, and all seems to be confusion.

Yet we encourage the one known as R, and all of those within this circle, to take heart at each mark of courage, that ability to launch the self into the unknown and to attempt to pick up our words.

The first distortion of the Law of One, so called, which is free will, is a shining entity like the flame of what this instrument calls the Holy Spirit, or like the wind of spirit that goes where it wishes. No one can predict its path. It is this free will which touched the complete placidity of the intelligence infinity that is the nature of the Creator's consciousness and suggested that It might, by creating a world, come to know Itself better.

And so it launched forth that one great original Thought which is unconditional love. In that thought lay the potentiality of all that was to come.

We will at this time transfer this contact to the one known as G. We are those of Laitos.

(G channeling)

We are those known to you as Laitos. This instrument asks us where our thoughts are. We reply that his thoughts are our thoughts. We thank you for the contact.

(Carla channeling)

We are those of Laitos and are again with this instrument. We thank the one known as G for working with our contact and are greatly encouraged that the honesty and integrity of each is so careful and that the ability to perceive our contact continues to be more possible as practice is done.

Our thoughts indeed are with each, and yet are a part of all that is, so that they move from the infinite invisible into manifestation as we are able to touch the subtle springs of your own awareness in such a way to transfer information. We would continue with our thoughts about the creation of the universe, for truly it is a magnificent story.

The one great original Thought is unconditional love; love without any hindrance or boundary; love that embraces and includes all that there is. This love is both fertile and creative and at the same time has the capacity to destroy, so that all that arises and all that sinks into nothingness is alike a part of unconditional love.

This unconditional love in its fruitful and fertile state created the third distortion of the Law of One, which is light.

We would at this time transfer this contact to the one known as N. We are those of Laitos.

(N channeling)

(Pause)

(Carla channeling)

We are those of Laitos and are again with this instrument. We thank the one known as N for working with our vibration and believe that as the practices continue, the vibration of our contact will be more and more easily found, not only for the one known as N but for those within this group.

Light, my friends, is an entity of infinite joy and effulgence, full of the love of the one Creator; full of that fertilized and fructifying[121] energy that moves toward manifestation. And in its turn this light has spun out of itself the vast array of time and space; all of the planets in their courses around all of the billions and billions of suns in the billions of galaxies of your infinite Creator.

Is it not amazing, my friends, to ponder the infinite riches of this distortion of the Law of one which is L? For it is endless in its creativity and to its children, the suns, the planets and yourselves, it gives co-creativity, so that each of you is a creator in your own universe.

We will at this time transfer this contact to the one known as M. We are those of Laitos.

(M channeling)

We are those of Laitos. We desire for you to understand the impetus which caused the Creator to decide upon self-expansion. In order to understand this concept we give to this instrument two separate distinct images. The first is of children playing on a summer day. Laughter abounds. There is serenity, no worries and pure bliss.

The other image is of a simple tree, growing in an orchard with no other trees around it. The Creator, feeling the desire for self-expansion, insisted on something occurring. But without the struggles and linear growth, as that of a tree in an orchard, It would gain no self-awareness or understanding.

---

[121] fructifying: bearing fruit; making productive.

We would now transfer our contact to the one known as G.

(G channeling)

I am Laitos. We have been speaking of the history of creation and certain elements of creation have been identified. One element of creation that has been identified was that of love. Another element that was identified as part of creation was light. Another element that has been identified is the element of sound. So three of these elements of which we know, love, light and sound, have created universes over what would be considered to be eons of your time.

Certain globules of material that was not solid eventually amassed into solid forms. Others did not. Certain energetic patterns of attraction were set up which became planetary systems, as you would call them in your language. Eventually certain energies coalesced into forms which contained consciousness. These consciousness forms evolved over many, many of what you have called eons. Eventually there were consciousness forms that developed which had physical bodies. Other forms became what we would consider to be, in your terms, members of the animal kingdom.

I now transfer this communication to L1.

(L1 channeling)

We are Laitos. In that swirling of sound like vibrations, universes were created along with other beings, all extensions of the one Creator. Sounds were able to create different levels. Some were energy forms. Others had more dense forms. These in turn formed other forms, light. On a fourth-density planet each of us is given the opportunity to create new forms, sometimes physical forms, such as children, sometimes animal forms, such as dogs. These in turn shape new ways of thinking and new ways of doing.

These forms created more and more variety of the One, and so there is continual expansion of knowledge, experience and joy. We now pass this contact on to the one called L2.

(L2 channeling)

We are those of *(inaudible)*.

(Long pause.)

(Carla channeling)

We are those of Laitos and are again with this instrument. We keep interrupting our story of the universe because of wishing to compliment and encourage each for their very solid and substantial work in opening their channels to our humble thoughts.

The group of children playing are children of love. The planets are children of the suns and each of you is a child of your planet, being co-creator and ready to produce children of your own thoughts. And yet the plight or the situation of each entity who seeks is indeed like the lone tree who must grow from its own roots and reach toward heaven with its own leafy hands. The other trees cannot grow for that tree but must leave each to its own growth and to its own pursuit of the truth and of consciousness in its most elemental form of unconditional love.

And so each has come through eons and eons of time and space; through experiences of being light, of being sound and of being the elements, plants and animals. Each has those parts of memory that lie beyond the veil within its deepest consciousness; the awareness of all the universe. And yet now, at this very precious moment, each of you has chosen this sun, this planet, and this incarnation to be alive and to seek.

And what shall each seek, my friend. We will at this time transfer this contact to the one known as T. We are those of Laitos.

(T channeling)

We are Laitos. The one known as T is sure that this contact is made; that the sensations in his body are of our doing. And the question has been asked, "What do we seek?"

We seek beyond that which we see before us. We seek always beyond the veil. We seek always beyond ourselves, at whatever level. We seek divine truth. We seek that which is our essence. We seek that which is the Creator, which is, in turn, ourselves.

Our evolution, our movement through time and space, as has been said so many times, is no journey, but yet at the same time it is the greatest of all journeys. We move through this creation. But infinity is beyond all understanding. F foreverness and eternity are beyond all understanding. We give thanks to the One for this most beautiful experience that is most simply called life, and that we don't even understand. We are Laitos. We transfer this contact to the one known as S.

(S channeling)

We are Laitos. In a moment of time there is also the possibility of reaching for another mode of opportunity and light. Following the heart, inside the mind will come new thoughts and understanding and living a life in greater service with the Creator. We now pass this contact to the one known as L.

(L channeling)

We are those of Laitos. This instrument is being shown a picture of a squash and the concept of heart. The squash is representative of the heart. Inside the heart are the seeds of all of us. The heart is the Creator. The heart pumps and the seeds spread across the land. Each one with its own free will may grow as it pleases.

This instrument is having difficulty understanding the concepts that are given. We are still working with her. We would like to pass this contact on to the one known as C. We are those of Laitos.

(C channeling)

We are those of Laitos. We are with this instrument now. Love lies at the heart of all things, all elements of life, of light, of sound. All of the senses have taken eons to create and to culminate. This is the beauty and the intensity of this creation. For it is difficult to show a tree that it is a tree. It is difficult to show a child that it is a child. It is difficult for us to show you that you are the Creator and that you are all things, all together. We see the beauty of the Creation at all levels.

You are awakening to know the deity in your hearts. We see this planet with great joy. We wish to share the joy that we have been given of this knowledge at this time. We will transfer our contact to the one known as D. We are those of Laitos

(Side one of tape ends.)

(D channeling)

(Inaudible)

(Carla channeling)

We are those of Laitos. We would thank the one known as D for receiving our contact and again, we assure not only D but all of those within this circle that in this, as in many endeavors, practice is very helpful. Repetition is very reassuring, as the channel that you have begun to open can then become more refined in its opening each time that the effort is made.

We would transfer this contact to the one known as Jim. We are those known as Laitos.

(Jim channeling)

We are those known as Laitos and are with this instrument. The great work of the one Creator is the work that each of you shares; that is, to know the self, to know the Creator and to know the Creation. All is contained within each portion of your being, and your being is all that there is. These seem like simple truths, yet no more profound statements can ever be made. Your science may explore into the most diverse and obscure regions of any portion of the creation and discover the most amazing truths, laws, theorems and applications of such. And yet at the basis of all such discoveries is the simple truth that all is one; that we all exist in one creation and we are all portions of one Creator. Through each experience does the Creator know Itself and through each experience you know yourself as the Creator. Thus the great work goes onward into infinity, from infinity, in all directions, at all times and in all places.

We thank each for being a part of this circle of seeking and working this day. We are most grateful to each for allowing us to speak through each instrument. It is a great honor. We cannot thank you enough for offering yourselves for this service. At this time we shall transfer this contact to the one known as Carla.

(Carla channeling)

We are those of Laitos and are again with this instrument. It is with joy that we open this session to any queries that you may have at this time. Does anyone have a query for us at this time?

L: What was the concept of the squash. What were you trying to convey?

We are those of Laitos and are aware of your query, my sister. Indeed, my sister, you had the concept that we were attempting to offer. The concept of the squash with the seeds inside is, as you said in your channeling the case for all hearts that are open to the fertilizing influence of the one Creator. You are all parts of the true vine[122], that vine which is of the Creator. As this instrument has learned from her childhood's spiritual teachings, that true vine is the vine of unconditional love or Christ-Consciousness.

And so each of you, in the ripening and harvesting of your own thoughts, can only, through the process of ripening and harvesting and the drying of the fruit, become able to shake the seeds out, that the seeds may then be spread, thought by thought, as you go through your incarnation, offering your thoughts and feelings to those with whom you may have congress and interaction.

May we answer you further, my sister?

L: No, thank you.

We thank you, my sister. May we ask if there is another query at this time? We are those of Laitos.

G: Laitos, I have one. When attempting to channel, my thinking was that I would break the inertia, and as Carla says, put my ass over the line and speak the initial words From there I was hoping to sense the contact and speak what were your words. I did not. Can you tell me what the status of my channel was or what particular blocks I had to receiving your contact?

We are those of Laitos and believe we understand your query my brother. You, in common with every channel in this circle and every human upon your planet has a characteristic restlessness of spirit, a characteristic tendency to flit upon the top of the waves of seeking. The activity that you experience is excellent and of good character. However, that which may perhaps be lacking is that end to restlessness which abides in the One. This abiding is the result of coming to believe with utter confidence in the self, so that there is no longer expectation, impatience or restlessness but only the waiting for the next seed of thought from the one infinite Creator.

---

[122] *Holy Bible:* John 15:1-5: "I am the true vine, and my Father is the husbandman. Every branch in me that beareth not fruit he taketh away: and every branch that beareth fruit, he purgeth it, that it may bring forth more fruit. Now ye are clean through the word which I have spoken unto you. Abide in me, and I in you. As the branch cannot bear fruit of itself, except it abide in the vine, no more can ye, except ye abide in me. I am the vine, ye are the branches: He that abideth in me, and I in him, the same bringeth forth much fruit: for without me ye can do nothing."

The challenge for each who seeks to pick up these voices such as we are, is that of laying down expectation, thought, and all human processes so that the configuration of mind which you enjoy is entirely that of the slate waiting to be filled with writing.

It is a matter of practice, my brother, for each to be able to come through the maze of one's characteristic distortions, such as restlessness, lack of confidence, feelings of unworthiness and the fear of mistaking our thoughts, in order to proceed quite naturally with the automatic and instantaneous expression of that thought which comes into the mind. That is the characteristic skill of channeling; that ability to enter into the speaking of the thought that is given, the image that is given, or whatever you sense is given.

That being said, my brother, it is entirely well that, perceiving nothing, you did not offer anything. That speaks very well of your integrity and your dedication to creating of yourself not simply one who can mimic the part of a channel but one who truly has become an open channel for the love and the light of the infinite Creator.

Always remember that the vocal channeling of our thoughts is a special case of a more general situation. In that special case, you are offering our thoughts, seeking wisdom or inspiration from energies which await beyond the veil, beyond the gateway of intelligent infinity. Nevertheless, in all that you do and say you are already being a channel for love and for light, as you become aware that it is possible for a human being such as yourself to seek the light, to see the light, to serve the light and to share and radiate the light.

May we ask if there is another query at this time or if the one known as G would wish to follow up? We are those of Laitos

G: No, the one known as G would wish to go get the soup ready. That is all.

(Laughter)

G: Thank you, Laitos.

Questioner: I have a question of Laitos.

We are those of Laitos and invite your query, my sister.

Questioner: I'd like to know how you experience us in this channeling circle. Can you see us in physical form or simply in energetic form? And the second part of that question is, are you simply energy or are you currently in an incarnation, within our Logos or without?

We are those of Laitos and are aware of your query, my sister. Firstly, we see each of you as your energy bodies, and more specifically as the readout, shall we say, of your violet ray. That is your identification to us, and that identification is as clear and unmistakable as a physical fingerprint or footprint. Your energy body is your fingerprint, shall we say, in the metaphysical world. Your vibratory rates combine to create one complex vibration that is unmistakably and unutterably unique as you.

As to our situation, my sister, we are those of fourth density and have a physical body which is far lighter and not chemically oriented as is yours. Yet it remains a physical body which we may clothe as we wish, as far as how we look and how our bodies are shaped and so forth. In terms of connecting with you, however, we exist in thought form alone. We have placed our social memory complex's form within the inner planes of your planetary nexus of inner and outer manifestations, chakras, densities and so forth.

We are in the fourth-density sub-density within the inner planes of your Planet Earth. There are endless sub-densities within the inner planes, in which reside those who are discarnate yet part of your planetary population, and also those who come from elsewhere and wish to serve those of your people.

May we ask if there is a further query, my sister, as you follow up on this concept?

Questioner: Not at this time, thank you.

Questioner: I have a query. What spiritual principle would be helpful for me in becoming a clearer channel?

We are those of Laitos and are aware of your query, my sister. The spiritual principle which applies in attempting to become a clearer channel is that principle which may be seen to be quietness or confidence, that realization or assumption that all is well.

There is always the temptation to reach for what you feel is needed in life, whether it is on the physical level or the metaphysical level. And there is certainly much appropriateness to this reaching. For is it not the function of desire and will to reach?

Yet in terms of channeling and in terms of spiritual work in general, it is far better to form the intention, hone the desire, firm the will, and then release all thought of what you as a human being feel would be the way to realize this will with desire, and instead offer to the one infinite Creator all that you are and all that you have. In quietness and confidence know that the consciousness that is at the heart of you knows all that there is to know, has all that it needs to have. It is capable, as you relax and embrace the present moment, of moving into that present moment to express, with the utmost of clarity, that which is able to come through you without coloration because you have relaxed, you have embraced the moment, and you have opened to that which is instantaneously and spontaneously coming through your channel at that time.

There is no need to reach or grasp in the house of the Father. There is no need to hold or conserve in the work of the one infinite Creator. Love is always infinite and fully available.

Is there, at this time, a final query for this instrument? We are those of Laitos.

M: I have a query. Does Laitos hope for or try to convey more detail in the concepts that were given during the channel about the tree and the children.

We are those of Laitos, my brother, and are aware of your query. Indeed, had there been the possibility of moving forward with these images, the hope of our group would have been to develop each of these images in a way which would feed into the flow of the channeled message. Through this instrument, at a point later in the session, the imagines were indeed picked up again and developed, perhaps not as you, with your precise personality and tuning, would have developed them but in a way which was equally compatible with the development of this particular offering of thoughts through you to the world.

There is, however, much to be said in praise for your ability to receive these images and to work with them as you were given the energy and the light to do. We assure you, my brother, that as you repeat these exercises, these various details and transient phenomena of the channeling process shall become more smooth and less utterly confounding. We congratulate each in this circle for moving forward so well, so quickly. Even those who have not been able to channel our thoughts very well, in their own opinion, are moving forward very well in terms of their own natural rate of development.

As always, we would remind each that there is not a common speed of development in this or in any other art, but each entity shall develop perfectly according to his own time-line.

We would at this time leave this instrument and this group, thanking each for the delight of working with you and looking forward, as we see you all intend to do, of speaking through you and with you at a later time.

We are those known to you as Laitos. We leave you in the love and in the light of the one infinite Creator. Adonai, my friends. Adonai.

L/L Research

L/L Research is a subsidiary of Rock Creek Research & Development Laboratories, Inc.

P.O. Box 5195
Louisville, KY 40255-0195

www.llresearch.org

Rock Creek is a non-profit corporation dedicated to discovering and sharing information which may aid in the spiritual evolution of humankind.

ABOUT THE CONTENTS OF THIS TRANSCRIPT: This telepathic channeling has been taken from transcriptions of the weekly study and meditation meetings of the Rock Creek Research & Development Laboratories and L/L Research. It is offered in the hope that it may be useful to you. As the Confederation entities always make a point of saying, please use your discrimination and judgment in assessing this material. If something rings true to you, fine. If something does not resonate, please leave it behind, for neither we nor those of the Confederation would wish to be a stumbling block for any.

© 2009 L/L Research

Channeling Intensive 1 - Session 13 - Closing Meditation
February 10, 2008

Group question: Q'uo, we have two questions. Firstly, thinking about how close 2012 is, and how most of the people in this group are just now learning channeling, we're wondering what we can expect to be our service in these last few years if we're learning channeling and wish to be of service to others via that channeling art.

(Carla channeling)

We are those known to you as the principle of Q'uo. Greetings, my friends, in the love and light of the one infinite Creator, in whose service we come to you this day. It is such a pleasure to be called to your circle of seeking. We thank you for this privilege and pleasure and assure you that your combined auras as you create this sacred space for this session of working are simply beautiful. We are most happy to speak with you this day upon the question of what place channeling has at the end of this third density and the beginning of fourth.

As always, we would ask that you monitor your own reactions to our thoughts and take only those thoughts from what we say that resonate to you, so that it is almost as if we had said something that you already knew but had perhaps forgotten momentarily. That is the kind of resonance that makes for very fruitful work. It is an empty exercise to attempt to learn those things which do not resonate to you. We would much rather that you leave those thoughts behind. For we do not expect to hit the mark with every person, all the time. We only give thanks that we have the opportunity to attempt to share thoughts that we hope will be helpful to you as well to us.

You ask about the channeling that you have been working on this weekend. You ask precisely what use is it, given that there is little time until 2012. And we would answer that in two ways, my friends.

First of all, we would discuss its use within what is left of your third density, those precious five years between 2007 and 2012. You have just begun that five year period as of 2008. In that five years, you will be able to build upon that which has gone before you. That which has gone before you was begun long ago, in the work of Jesus the Christ and those which came after Jesus the Christ who wished to speak of unconditional love. There have been many voices among your prophets, priests and seers, and each voice has spoken to certain entities and helped those entities to awaken.

In this present time, as some of you have mentioned in your discussions moving around the circle before this meditation, this group has been consistently offering a voice of love and it continues to do so at this time. At first this voice was heard by very few. It would surprise this instrument and the one known as Jim to know how far the voice of love that they have been able to offer through their instruments has carried. It has indeed carried to the ends of the Earth. It has done its part in bringing the planetary population of Earth close to a tipping point.

The one known as C has spoken of the "Hundredth Monkey Effect"[123], and we would speak of that as well. From the hunger of a few who wished to seek the truth, there has been given as gifts from person to person and group to group, that same hunger. It is an infectious hunger, and it spreads because the nature of third-density entities is to have that hunger. And so that hunger keeps surfacing, no matter what else is occurring within your culture.

And as the energies of repression and fear have moved heaven and earth—literally—to bring the planetary population to a point of permanent fear and submission, they have, in effect, shot their bolt. They have come to the end of what they can do with fear, violence and war, whereas the voice of love has only just begun. So the purpose of channeling during this last five years is to continue that spread of positively oriented material which may be of help to those who are seeking spiritually in the polarity of service to others.

As the one known as Laitos said earlier in this weekend, each voice that offers to channel our words is unique. Each is as a certain kind of stained glass window that has colorations that to each of you may seem to be defects of character, limitations of spirit. And yet we say to you that those self-same quirks of character and spirit that color your thoughts give a pleasing color to our voice of love. And as you attempt to speak our words through your instrument, you shall create new stories, new ways of saying that one simple statement, "All is one, and that one thing is love."

It is a great blessing to us when there are new entities through whom we may speak. And so we thank each of you for the attempt to open your channels. We thank you also for your courage and your integrity. It is important to offer these thanks to you for you perhaps do not feel very courageous. And yet to break free of the taboos against speaking thoughts without knowing ahead of time what they shall be or how they shall develop is a great departure from those rules of safe conduct of your culture. We hope that as you continue to develop your channel and to serve in this way, you shall find satisfaction in your part in bringing this tipping point ever closer upon Planet Earth.

We realize that it is difficult to imagine what shall happen after the year 2012, since that is when third density ends and fourth density begins. And we can only describe to you that which is to occur by asking you to realize that all of the densities of Planet Earth within this octave, one through seven, are nested together and interpenetrate each other, much as the various channels on your television set are nested together, being picked up by the same transmitters and receivers and being available by the turn of the knob from one to another to another.

Indeed, there are those among your peoples who are able to switch from the channel of third density to the channel of fourth density now, and who can somewhat reliably report on the development of fourth density. Fourth density, indeed, is fully formed at this time. Because it would violate the free will of third-density entities, fourth density chooses not to be seen, not to be visible to the five senses of your human bodies. Yet it is impossible to eliminate or hide the vibrations of fourth density, which are interpenetrating third density at this time.

Indeed, it is not even desirable to attempt to hide or remove these waves upon waves of fourth-density energy. For they are another part of that which is enabling the last of those who would be harvested at the end of third density on Planet Earth to do their work, to proceed, and to polarize to the extent that they shall, with no trouble whatsoever, walk the steps of light that lead into fourth density.

However, third-density Earth has absorbed a great deal of the accumulated neglect that speaks to the racial karma of many, many of those who are upon Planet Earth at this time, who have come to this planet from planets in which their own third density was interrupted by their removing the ability to live a third-density existence on their home planet. In some cases they have even blown their planet to smithereens. In other cases they have simply rendered the planet or, in Atlantis' case, the continent, uninhabitable.

There has been an ever-increasing energy among those who are incarnate upon Planet Earth at this time towards desiring to retake the reins of

---

[123] The "Hundredth Monkey Effect" is a phenomenon in which a learned behavior spreads instantaneously from one group of monkeys to all related monkeys once a critical number is reached. By generalization it means the instant, paranormal spreading of an idea or ability to the remainder of a population once a certain portion of that population has heard of the new idea or learned the new ability. The story behind this supposed phenomenon originated with Lyall Watson, who claimed that it was the observation of Japanese scientists.

stewardship of Gaia, of Mother Earth, and to administer healing and restoration to the planet which has been so loving and so good to them, and has been their home. And this shall continue for some hundreds of your years to be that great work which many who graduate from third density wish to accomplish before they move on into other lessons.

So, at this time there is a tremendous energy of new life and new growth upon your planet, due to the influx of fourth-density wanderers from your own planet. Those of you who have children know that these children are qualitatively different than the children that perhaps you knew as a child, or those children which have lived here in centuries past. These are children who are able to run third-density energy and light and fourth-density energy and light. Therefore, to them the veil is much thinner, and the truth of love is much more obvious.

So, within these days when 2012 has come and gone, information such as is collected and offered for sharing by this group shall be increasingly helpful because there will be far more interest in the spiritual as opposed to the religious. And those words which speak to the stewardship of the planet, as well as those words which speak of unconditional love and the oneness of all things, shall be as meat and drink to those who are searching for the way to be of maximum service at this time.

Many and many are those who are incarnate at this time as fourth-density wanderers from third density Earth. They have come back for the reason of stewardship to the planet, and within this next five-year period, for the lightening of Planet Earth and the maximization of the harvest of Earth.

This is that of which we see as a valuable service, and we are ready to offer our thoughts through instruments such as this one not only until 2012 but as long as there are those entities upon Planet Earth who are devoted to the restoration of the planet and to the healing of the nations.

Shall you in one fine, strong moment be able to change the face of the Earth? Naturally, it is extremely unlikely. It is likely that those who are polarizing towards negative graduation shall continue to hog the news, the headlines, and the avenues of power on this planet. And yet the vast majority of the population of Planet Earth lives without regard to the avenues of power, looking for truth, justice, liberty, beauty and all the fourth-density values within the humble pages of a humbly-lived life.

And it is precisely within those humble pages, within those humble lives that your service lies at this time as a channel. For to those who are seeking, it is a great blessing to find material that speaks directly to that which is on the hearts of those who are seeking. We do not pretend to think we hit the mark all the time with that which we have to offer through instruments such as this one. However, we devote our entire energy to the attempt, and we thank each of you who wishes to aid us in bringing through these words of love, light, compassion, beauty, peace and power.

Many institutions may fall by the way, as various inconveniences continue to occur among your people. That which shall not fall away is the love and the light of the one infinite Creator. And while there is this wonderful tool of what this instrument calls the internet, while it is possible to make things globally available, this is the golden time for material such as this to be developed and shared.

Is there a follow-up to this query before we ask for another question? We are those of Q'uo.

N: Q'uo, with respect to your giving us the date of 2012, is this not considered as specific information? Would this not violate the law of free will?

We are those of Q'uo, and believe we understand your query, my brother. Were there to be no other source of information concerning this date, there might indeed be a concern on our part regarding offering such information as the precise date of the turning of the wheel for your planet from third density to fourth.

However, as it happens, the longstanding and widely respected work of astrologers upon your planet has for many of your centuries offered this date as that in which in one age, the Age of Pisces, turns to another age, the Age of Aquarius. There is also, as you are aware in this group for you have discussed it, the calendar of the Mayans, which also points to this date as the time when the central sun lines up in just a certain way with Planet Earth and the Sun, so that there starts a new Day at that time and the old Day is ended. Further than that, there are other sources, which have targeted this particular time as that time at which there is a shift in consciousness. Therefore, we have long confirmed these suppositions of those who came to us and questioned us as to the centrality of this date.

May we answer you further, my brother?

N: No, thank you very much, Q'uo. I send you my love in the name of the one infinite Creator. Thank you.

We thank you, my brother. Is there any other follow-up to this query before we move on to another question? We are those of Q'uo.

C: I have a possible follow-up to that. You say that in 2012 there will be a shift of consciousness. Will that correlate with the Hundredth Monkey theory? Will what the planetary consciousness comes to depend upon the consciousness of the wanderers who are on this planet and where they are on a conscious level? Will that be where the population goes to when they shift their consciousness?

We are those of Q'uo, and believe we understand your query, my sister. There is a certain amount of confusion and we are apologetic that we have caused confusion. Let us see if we can untangle two different strings of thought.

When we referred to the tipping point and the Hundredth Monkey Effect, we were not referring to 2012. We were referring to the natural spread or infection, if you will, of the planetary population with what this instrument would call a new paradigm: a paradigm of unity and love, a paradigm of peace. This new paradigm is completely outside the box, shall we say, of the culture that exists upon part of your planet at this time. That is, the part of the planet that is as this instrument would say, civilized, although that term could be questioned.

The role of the wanderers in these latter days, beginning perhaps fifty years ago now and coming to this present moment, has been to accelerate the speed at which the consciousness of Planet Earth was lightened and was lifted from the darkness of oppressive and repressive thinking, which focused upon early third-density behavior, such as defense and aggression when resources were considered desirable.

The new paradigm is that in which entities share and share alike, in which entities love each other, become harmonious with each other, and create one world of peace and prosperity. That kind of prosperity does not create huge differences in estate but rather tends toward that happy situation of there being enough of the resources that are needed for all entities.

It is not that this new paradigm can be put into effect and a new fourth-density planet be created in third density. That is not what we are saying. What we are saying is that in third density, the focus in terms of the purpose of third density is upon each emerging self-aware spirit or soul becoming able to make the free-will choice between the polarity of service to others and the polarity of service to self through faith alone.

The role of the wanderers, then, has been bravely and courageously to dare to enter into third-density incarnation, to come through the veil of forgetting, and then to count on their own awakening in time for them to join the lightening of Planet Earth in terms of where they put their energy and their love. Many are those wanderers who have waited until late to awaken, and so as each wanderer does awaken, it makes it ever more possible for other wanderers to awaken. And as the great bulk of wanderers begin to awaken, that makes it possible for the planetary population as a whole to awaken. So there really is a tipping point within the tipping point in terms of the awakening of the planet to love itself.

May we answer you further, my sister?

C: No, that was great, thank you.

We thank you, my sister. My brother, you offered the suggestion at the beginning of your query that there was a second query. May we ask for that now. We are those of Q'uo.

Jim: We're wondering just exactly what are we doing here? It seems to many people who have awakened that we're just trying to get out of a bad situation; get out of a prison; go someplace else. Isn't there something more that we're doing here in this third density than just trying to escape?

We are those of Q'uo, and are aware of your query, my brother. It is very humorous to us that you would describe the planet of your choice as a prison, because each and every one of you in this room, and each and every person upon your planet that is alive at this time, fought tooth and nail, as it were, to get into line to have a body and come here at this time.

When one is not within the incredibly intense atmosphere of Planet Earth in extremely late third density, it looks like the best party in town. There is a unique opportunity that you have here in third density to make rapid changes in your balance between love, wisdom and power. And so many, many wanderers have come here with the desire to serve the planet secondary to their desire to alter the balance within their own deeper natures.

Now, this begs the question of why the planet is indeed such an intensely vivid density, or why third density on this planet is so vivid. And in order to answer that query, we must take a step back and look at the sweep of the octave of creation of which you are now a part. This and every octave begins and ends in the Godhead principle of intelligent infinity resting, utterly asleep in the oneness of all. The vibration of love is all that there is, and yet it is not known to itself, for it is resting. Just as your heart, for one instant between each heartbeat, is at rest, so is the Creator's heart at rest between creations, or between octaves.

At the beginning of the octave, of which you are a part, the creation was resting in timelessness and spacelessness. By the agency of the first distortion of the Law of One, free will, the Creator decided once again to know Itself. And so it became potentiated into a Thought. And that Thought was full of the characteristic of the Creator, which is unconditional love.

The creation itself dwells in a state of ecstasy, much like your sexual orgasm. Yet there is no vector to this ecstasy. It is an ecstasy that rests completely. So, this first distortion of free will caused the Creator to form a potentiated version of Itself, that which could act. And that was the one great original Thought of love. And love in its turn created light, and sent it forth to manifest the creation in all of its stupendously infinite systems of illusion. And so your solar system and your planet and you yourself were created.

In the middle of first density, timelessness began to evolve into time and space. The vibrations that were in chaos began to organize into roughly circular or elliptical forms, creating the coalescing suns, which in turn threw off material that coalesced into planets. And so the creation of the Father was born as a part of first density. Later in first density came the organization of this coalescing mass that you could call a planet into earth and water, so that the elements might have distinct places and habitations within second density. Then the creation further developed the energies from that which had no movement, such as rocks and water and so forth, which may be moved but have no voluntary or independent movement of their own, into life forms which had movement.

This movement, naturally, was that movement towards the light and the love of the one infinite Creator, that which calls all things at all times. Yet these animals and plants that were second-density had no sense of themselves. They had no veil. That is, they knew all that there was to know. They knew that they were one with everything. They knew that destiny lay in harmony and cooperation. Yet other than turning to the light and seeking sources of light, second-density entities did not experience that self-awareness that makes people self-conscious or question their motives or their motions. If you have known second-density entities, such as your pets, you know that they do not question what is occurring to them but rather adapt to it.

Third density is that density that begins the path back to the one infinite Creator. It is the precursor of all that is to come from fourth density through seventh density. It is a bright, brief, intense density compared to all the others, which take millions of years to complete. In contrast, third density on this planet is designed to last only 75,000 years.

It is a period that is long enough for those entities who have come into incarnation at the beginning of the cycle of third density to have time and experience to build their intelligence, their information, to the point where they realize by faith alone that there is more than simply battling for that which is available and then dying. It is that time in which entities may choose the manner of their further progress.

There are many hints that are built into third-density life. Your physical form is created in such a way that you need other people, and you must interact with other people. In order for the species to perpetuate, you must form relationships with other entities. And so the hints concerning service to self versus service to others are built into the human being's very nature, both physical, mental and emotional.

And so as entities begin to lift themselves up from total immersion in the business of survival, they can begin to see that there is a way to live which they prefer. And so they begin to choose to live in love and in harmony with nature and with the Creator. Again, it is part of the human instinct to seek for the Creator. Part of what makes a third-density entity who he is is that instinct to seek for the Creator of his being and to give Him thanks and praise. And so you will not find populations or races or tribes of humankind, no matter how remote or undeveloped according to the earmarks of civilization, that do not have what you would call spirituality or religion as part and parcel of their society.

So, you have a school of souls. It is not a school that pushes entities to make decisions or that makes them at all obvious. Rather, it is a rich environment in terms of potential for choices. And as each choice is approached, there are hints from the positive polarity that a choice for love and service to others is a good choice. There are also corresponding hints from the dark and shadow side of service to self that service to self is a good idea. Indeed, in fourth density, there is what they call in your literature the war in heaven of those fourth-density entities who, in early fourth density, have not yet learned to put down the sword and still feel the need to do battle, the forces of light against the forces of darkness. There is a theme underlying much of the deepest parts of the human spirit which include those thematic notes of struggle.

(Side one of tape ends.)

(Carla channeling)

The positive and the negative are continually in dynamic opposition to each other, offering to the entity behind the veil hint after hint after hint of the nature of the choice that is before each human being.

Each of you has long since awakened. Those in this circle are ready to work beyond the simple making of the choice the first time. Each of you has made that choice. The cornerstone of your life's work has been laid. And yet, you are still behind this veil of forgetting. You cannot know what others are thinking. You cannot sense or see for sure how rich the unseen realms are in those who would help you, and those who love you, and those who wish only to be of service to you as you make your choice.

Oftentimes, entities who are waking up feel terribly isolated and alone. This is not in fact the case, because of the enormous amount of unseen help that each entity has. Yet in terms of that which is apparent to the sight of the physical eyes, it is indeed so that many, many entities are very isolated and must make their choices in isolation and without the comfort and comradeship of groups of like-minded people.

And so you find groups such as this being very helpful as those centers which are available for gatherings such as this one, where entities may find many other compatible entities with whom to talk, that they may find ways to encourage each other and love each other and bring each other home.

In a way, the beauty of this density is its very sharpness of suffering and difficulty. For the extremely harsh conditions create ways in which one may change one's polarity or emphasize one's polarity very quickly, indeed, almost instantaneously. You may do in fifty years, or twenty years, or even five years that which it would take us a million years to do, because of the fact that we see the whole picture. We understand all that there is to understand in terms of the Creator's plan for us. Therefore, it is an open-book test, and that which we learn, we learn in painfully slow increments, gradually refining, and refining again, our choice.

You are making that choice. So the energies of your density may well seem very, very difficult, not so much that of a prison as of a testing field or a fiery furnace, as it is called in the Old Testament of your Holy Bible.[124]

By faith alone is it allowable to know the truth in this density. You hold in your hands the keys of unknowing. There were several during this weekend that said it's not the answers that matter, it's the questions. And my friends, we could not agree more. The answers do not lie within this density. It is the questions that lie within this density. We can offer you the answer that we know to offer you, and that answer is love, love, love.

Yet, how you shall realize that love in your life is completely up to you and your faculties of faith and will. And we wish you every good fortune in persevering until you have managed to find all possible love and light within your heart and within your environment, knowing that that which is in

---

[124] See the book of the prophet Daniel for the story of the fiery furnace.

your heart is that which paints the colors of your environment.

Is there a follow-up to this query before we ask for further queries? We are those of Q'uo.

L: You said that the Creator has come to know Itself many times. This time the original Thought by which the Creator came to know Itself was that of unconditional love. When the Creator comes to know Itself once again, is there a different original Thought each time?

We are those of Q'uo, and are aware of your query, my sister. The fullness of the one infinite Creator when the journey of the density has been completed to the end of the octave, and Its heart beats once more, is succeeded by a fuller fullness. For it has borne the harvest of that which was given to the infinite Creator by each of you, the harvest of your self-knowledge.

Much has been said about the human being the top of the evolutionary ladder, so that it is eat and be eaten up until the human. And the human has no enemy but itself. Yet that is not true. For the Creator eats your self-knowledge, your experiences, your feelings, and your emotions, and learns more and more about Itself from each unique spark of the creation as that spark is collected back to the Godhead principle. Consequently, each new creation is fuller than the last and each Logos is fuller than the last. Yet all Logoi are alike, made of unconditional love.

May we answer you further, my sister?

L: I believe I understand that, and I would like to ask another question. Why do we need the veil of forgetting to make the harvest quicker if outside of this illusion time is meaningless? What does quicker mean? Why do we need to be quicker?

We are those of Q'uo, and are aware of your query, my sister. It is not that the third-density entity needs to be quicker, my sister, but that in order for an entity to make a free-will choice of polarity, it is necessary for it to be made by faith alone. If all of the answers to your questions are obvious, then there is no weight in the choice that you make, and therefore the evolution of mind, body and spirit shall be greatly retarded. The relative quickness of third density is not a feature in terms of quickness. It is a feature in terms of there not normally needing to be a longer period of time/space illusion than 75,000 years in order for entities comfortably to wake up, make their choices, and persist in their choices until they are of a polarity that is able to graduate.

May we answer you further, my sister?

L: That was a very good answer, thank you. I'll pass my questioning on to someone else.

We thank you, my sister. Is there any other follow-up to this query, or shall we move on to other queries? We are those of Q'uo.

T: If I might, I would like to ask a question which I believe might be relevant to this discussion, because it has to do with the creation and this octave. If God or the infinite Creator is all things positive and negative, why is there a mandate that all sixth-density negative entities must convert to positive in order to advance in their evolutionary process in moving into foreverness?

We are those of Q'uo, and are aware of your query, my brother. The nature of the negative path determines its limits, my brother. For the negative polarity is the path of that which is not. The heart of the negative polarity is a lie. That lie is separation. The negative polarity is based upon skipping the development of the heart chakra and developing the ability to use the gateway to intelligent infinity without the use of the heart. This is possible and acceptable to the one infinite Creator. Yet, the creation is as it is. All is indeed one. Therefore, the path of positive polarity is the path of that which is.

The path of that which is not has its ending, quite naturally, in the density of unity. Entities who have denied that they and their brothers are one are able to work with fourth-density light without releasing this supposition. They are able to work with fifth-density light without releasing this supposition. They are able to continue to grow and to develop throughout the densities of love and wisdom by assuming that love is of themselves and of the Creator, and that wisdom is their wisdom and the Creator's. They can still maintain their separateness from other entities.

However, sixth density is the density of unity, and it is glaringly obvious to the negative entity as he moves into sixth density that he is approaching a brick wall. He cannot advance any further. It is the nature of energy to change. It is not the nature of energy to stop. Consequently, there is pressure upon the negatively-oriented entity to continue to evolve.

And yet, he cannot evolve and still hold onto the belief that he is separate from his brothers.

Consequently, just as a convert to Christianity goes from being a hardened sinner, in the terms that this instrument would use, to being the most fervent convert, so the negatively-oriented entity, at one moment of realization, switches polarity and becomes the most fervent follower of the truth that all is one. It is an inevitable reaction to the impossibility of further advancement without making that tremendous change.

May we answer you further, my brother?

T: Yes, as a follow-up to that then, when the Bible says that there will always be wars and rumors of wars, would that be then the limitation to that statement? Because once there is unity in latter sixth density, then there can be no more opposition, because all is recognized as one. But there will be, in the densities from third through mid-sixth, a reality or truth that there is going to be positive and negative interaction. But after that, would wars then, at least from this octave, cease? Would there be peace and unity in this latter sixth and seventh density?

We are those of Q'uo, and are aware of your query, my brother. Indeed, it is even more limited than that. Your Holy Bible is an artifact of third density and is useful only in looking at third-density existence. Although it attempts to project into heaven worlds and worlds of hell, so-called, it cannot do so. For it has only the third-density stuff with which to work. Consequently, it is true in terms of third density that there shall always be the dynamic opposition of light and dark, negative and positive, and so forth. The choice always is betwixt the harmonization of these opposites and the war of these opposites.

The early fourth density, as we said before, often continues to cling to notions that it inherited from its third-density self. And so there is a gradual releasing of this constant feeling of war and struggle, not at the end of third density, but as one moves into the second of seven sub-densities of fourth density. However, this truth of the constancy of conflict is local to your density, my brother.

We would at this time ask for one final query, as the energy begins to wane for this instrument. Is there a final query at this time? We are those of Q'uo.

G: I have a query. A much beloved pastime of mine is doing family history research. And as I learn about the lives of my ancestors, about their joys, their sorrows, their acts of bravery, and their feelings and shortcomings, I have love for them, even though they may have lived 200 years ago and I never met them. And so I see the benefit from this for me, in that I have had a heart opening. And my query is: in doing this research, am I in any way serving those ancestors of mine now in spirit?

We are those of Q'uo, and are aware of your query, my sister. It may be said that any time a heart opens, the entire creation sings. And in that way, you are being of help to your ancestors as you grow to know and love them. But in the main we would say that the advantage of your opening your heart is to your own spiritual maturation and the acceleration of the pace of your own spiritual development.

May we answer you further, my sister?

G: No, that's fine. Thank you.

We thank you, my sister. And we thank you all, and are indeed very apologetic and sad that we must make an end to our discussion for now. If we had our way, we would stay and talk until the evening lengthens and the shadows take over to bring on night, for we have so much enjoyment of your company, and so much of a feeling of being useful as we are able to converse with you. It is a great blessing to us that you have called us to your circle, and we look forward to any time in the future that we may once again tabernacle together in the shadows of the most high.

We leave this instrument and this group, as always, in the love and in the light of the one infinite Creator. We are known to you as the principle of Q'uo. Adonai, my friends. Adonai vasu borragus. ✤

L/L Research

L/L Research is a subsidiary of Rock Creek Research & Development Laboratories, Inc.

P.O. Box 5195
Louisville, KY 40255-0195

www.llresearch.org

Rock Creek is a non-profit corporation dedicated to discovering and sharing information which may aid in the spiritual evolution of humankind.

ABOUT THE CONTENTS OF THIS TRANSCRIPT: This telepathic channeling has been taken from transcriptions of the weekly study and meditation meetings of the Rock Creek Research & Development Laboratories and L/L Research. It is offered in the hope that it may be useful to you. As the Confederation entities always make a point of saying, please use your discrimination and judgment in assessing this material. If something rings true to you, fine. If something does not resonate, please leave it behind, for neither we nor those of the Confederation would wish to be a stumbling block for any.

© 2009 L/L Research

Saturday Meditation
March 15, 2008

Group question: Our question this evening has to do with how extraterrestrial contacts with human beings on planet Earth in third density may or may not infringe upon the free will of the entities contacted. We are wondering about the philosophy that the extraterrestrial entities use in order to decide whether or not to make contact and what kind of contact to make.

For example, during the Manhattan Project, information from positive extraterrestrial sources was given concerning nuclear energy that's very specific. There have been other contacts, such as Billy Meier's contact and the contact with Phyllis Schlemmer from the "Nine" and Tom, which have had more or less specific information to give. We are wondering if this infringes on the free will of the humans who are contacted and what exactly is the philosophy of the extraterrestrials when they make contact with regard to specific information and the infringement on free will.

(Carla channeling)

We are known to you as the principle of Q'uo. Greetings, my friends, in the love and the light of the one infinite Creator. It is our privilege and our pleasure to be with you this evening, to share in your vibrations and to respond to your query concerning the infringement of free will by those of extraterrestrial origin who have been speaking to your people and in some cases meeting them face to face.

As always, before we share our thoughts, we would ask each of you to be responsible for your own judgment and discrimination as regards the things that we say. If our thoughts have resonance for you, then by all means follow the path of that resonance. That is why we are here and we are very happy that we can give you food for thought.

If, however, we miss the mark and do not interest you particularly in what we have to say, we would ask that you leave behind our words and keep moving until you find that information and that inspiration that does resonate with you.

We thank you for this kindness, for it enables us to speak freely without being concerned that we will infringe upon your free will.

You asked this evening concerning the nature of contact betwixt extraterrestrial entities and Earth entities. You asked about free will and how extraterrestrial entities feel about the free will of those upon planet Earth.

We may start with ourselves. We of the Confederation of Planets in Service to the One Infinite Creator have, shall we say, experimented with contact, in terms of face-to-face contact, in your far distant past. We found that the direct communication face-to-face was neither positive nor negative, but only that which the entities of that time felt was part of the natural universe, which at that time was replete with many gods and many unusual things.

What caused us to become more and more aware of the difficulties of clean communication with those of planet Earth was the inability of even the most powerful entity to maintain the purity of the initial contact, once the information we gave had resulted in the pyramids that were built. Instead of the pyramids being used for the purpose for which they were built, they became used for the purpose of the few, the elite, the powerful, and the wealthy.

We became aware of the impossibility of blending physical presence with a lack of distortion. We, those of the Ra group, those of the Hatonn group and those of the Latwii group, chose not to use again any means except the channeling through instruments such as this one as a way of communication of concepts hopefully helpful to the spiritual evolution of those on planet Earth to the population at large.

We are not the only entities from elsewhere which are interested in planet Earth at this time. There are many entities interested in your planet that come from elsewhere. Some of these entities are of the Confederation and have agreed with those of us who have had a relationship with those on planet Earth previously, so that in the interest of retaining positive polarity we have chosen not to appear to your people.

We believe that we are at the apex of that which we can do and remain clear of the possibility of infringement. However, we say in all humility that we are not absolutely sure that, if we speak at all, we are not in some way infringing on the free will of those who may hear our words and be persuaded again their preferences of the truth of that which we have to offer.

It does not stop us from speaking. But this concern is enough to create in us the desire to mention the request, to each who hears or listens to our words, to be very responsible and to discriminate so that none of our words are taken on faith or simply because we say them. The reason for this mention at every contact is this concern on our parts.

The only way that we could avoid any possibility of infringement on free will of those on planet Earth is to stop speaking through instruments such as this one. Yet, the cry goes out from Earth. Many, many millions of you are seeking the truth. Therefore, we come in answer to a call and do not feel that we can turn away from the depth and profundity of this call at this time.

It heartens us to see your planet waking up, metaphysically speaking. We comfort ourselves that surely we could not have done too much damage. For the message is getting out. More and more people have become aware that they are one with their neighbors. More and more people are aware now that love is the only answer.

The energy of this planet is exponentially readier for fourth-density graduation than it was when we began working with this channel thirty years ago.[125]

There are many other kinds of entities who seek to speak with the people of planet Earth, or who seek to influence their decisions. The so-called Orion empire is a kind of confederation of those who are negatively polarized and who are responding to the call of those who wish to graduate in negative polarity into fourth density. Insofar as they come in through the windows of opportunity that are part of the just and appropriate quarantine of planet Earth, they fully intend to infringe upon free will and therefore do not have any ethical considerations to hamper them as they offer their own thoughts for humans of negative polarity who wish to become harvestable in that polarity.

Yet we understand that this is not the kind of contact about which you are asking. You asked about contacts such as that of Phyllis Schlemmer with "The Nine," and the one called Tom, and that contact of Billy Meier with those entities with whom he has spoken.

To respond to that which you have asked, we would take a step back and talk a bit about fourth density, for it is important in our answer that what little we have to say about the fourth density war be understood as background information.

When entities graduate from third density to fourth density, various things occur. Whether or not they have chosen positive- or negative-polarity fourth density, the move from third to fourth density creates a new environment. In this environment there is no veil. There is no veil between the conscious and the subconscious mind of each person and there is no veil between people, between the planet, and between entities of other densities.

Thusly, a fourth-density soul is able to communicate with first density, second density, third density,

---

[125] The Confederation entities began working with Carla in 1974.

fourth density, fifth, sixth and seventh density. It is an open universe. The choices, naturally, are quickly made to shut out most of that which is available to know so that the evolving soul may continue with its lessons. Yet there is that full knowledge of the vibration of the one infinite Creator in all vibrations available to that entity.

However, the graduation to fourth density does not automatically create any improvement whatsoever in the evolutionary status of the soul. Just as a person who has graduated from third grade goes to school the first day for fourth grade knowing nothing more than he knew at the end of third grade, so the beginning student of fourth density has only the harvest of third-density knowledge, awareness and insight as he approaches the lessons of fourth density.

For a great portion of your last major cycle of 75,000-plus years, those who have graduated to fourth density have felt it necessary to defend their polarity from the opposite polarity as if they were still in third density. The entities involved in this war are of the inner planes rather than coming from outside the planet. Fourth-density wanderers are not coming in to carry on this war. Rather, there are entities coming in which, having reached harvestability, have chosen not to go on to fourth density but to remain in the inner planes of third density.

Their awareness is that of fourth density, yet their prejudices remain those of third density. So, they are convinced that they must defend the souls of planet Earth from negative polarity. Likewise, those who have graduated in the negative sense see it as their business to battle the light. They see themselves as those who would use the light for their own purposes, leeching the power of which the positive polarity is full and flipping it so that its power becomes negative.

This situation of war, the so-called "war in heaven,"[126] is a part of your inner-planes environment. Individual entities of both polarities eventually become mature enough spiritually to realize that strife is unnecessary. They finally become free of third-density fear and are able to move on to their lessons, leaving the war behind.

However, there are always people that are new to fourth density who are willing to take up the cudgels of this heavenly war and do what they feel is the right thing to do in protecting the innocent, developing, third-density souls on planet Earth.

It may be noted that in all of this strife, there is nothing but the highest ideals and desires on the part of those of positive polarity, and in their own way, those of negative polarity. There is a good deal of confusion but there is not the goal to spread confusion or to act in any way but a righteous or a good way. It is simply that in whatever density one is, one remains capable of error.

We ourselves, as we have said, feel that we have occasionally made errors. Certainly, the degree of information that we were able to share with some of those involved in your Manhattan Project, also in the work of the one known as Nicola,[127] there was an unwise amount of information shared. The opportunity seemed to be to offer powerful resources that would alleviate the necessity for the people of planet Earth to work so very hard and to use up their incarnational time without being able to work on their metaphysical evolution. Yet these powerfully positive people were not able to control the results of their use of our information.

Is it a concern of ours that this information was used to harm, where we had hoped only to help? Yes, it remains a concern. From each of our mistakes we have learned much. And because of our concern for those distortions that have occurred, we remain within your planetary atmosphere, as it were, ready to speak through such instruments as this one, in the hope of lessening distortion.

When one speaks of such entities as The Nine,[128] one speaks of a kind of entity that has an unusual relationship with some of those within the inner planes of this planet. The entities which make up The Nine are, in fact, those of the entity known to this instrument as Yahweh. This instrument was saying that she felt that this was the designation of that particular contact and we confirmed that information as being so.

As you know, Yahweh has had a long relationship with those of planet Earth, especially those which

---

[126] Read more about this mythological event on Wikipedia, "War of Heaven."

[127] This is a reference to Nikola Tesla.

[128] See the appendix of The Nine's channeling in the book, *Uri*, by Andrija Puharich.

came into incarnation from the planetary influence of the sphere you know as Mars. In altering the genetic code for this large group of entities as they incarnated upon planet Earth, they placed bits of themselves, shall we say, to make a complex story simpler, within the genetic changes that were made, and each of you carries, to some extent, some of these altered changes [in your DNA.]

Consequently, this particular entity contains a host of energies from the inner planes of your planet. There is a legitimate extraterrestrial aspect to this energy, but it is harmonized with inner-planes thought forms which are the templates of the genetic changes made 75,000 years ago when those of Mars came into the Earth's sphere.

This means that these entities which together make up The Nine or Yahweh have never grown past the impulse or desire to interfere—for the good, of course—in the story of planet Earth. There is a tremendous love of the people of Earth from this group and a sincere and genuine desire to help. And yet, because of the distortions that have persisted in their infringement upon the free will of all of those whose genetic codes have been changed, there is a lack of awareness of the distortions inherent in physically presenting themselves before entities or making physical changes in an environment of which they are a part in order to convince entities that they are real.

We deeply understand the desire of those of The Nine to make a difference on planet Earth. We understand, because we have experimented with coming among your people, the desire to make a mass landing and to herald a new day, calling for love and light, with the strength of a massive display of superior insight, intellect and knowledge.

We do not agree that it is a gambit that will be effective in any way in lightening the consciousness of planet Earth and we have, many thousands of your years ago, put away any thought of doing so.

The promised landings, as the one known as Jim said earlier, shall not occur. Yet there is that energy within the psyches or subconscious levels of mind of many upon planet Earth which desire this outcome. And so the desires of those upon planet Earth mingle with the desires of those of The Nine to create a self-fulfilling link in which the information continues to be offered because it is desired.

And this is a point which is worthy of some examination. We find it helpful to work with instruments such as this one, who has no particular need to express its own thoughts, for we are able to channel through this instrument that which we wish to say without this instrument's adding or subtracting information according to its opinions. It is helpful to have instruments with whom to work who have no biases as far as the outcome of their words.

The more need there is on the part of the instrument to channel certain things, the more likely the instrument is to take that which we have to say and to create of our thoughts a little more than we had to say, shall we say. The biases of the channel are always a part of any channeling. The only question is to what extent the bias of the channel has influenced the material produced.

A certain amount of material which is part of the instrument's experience is helpful and we often use stories from this instrument's life or thoughts that this instrument has considered to color our simple message with the various guises of storytelling and myth. For if we offered only the simple truth, without any storytelling, then we would say over and over again, "All is one. That one thing is unconditional love. Love is the Creator. Love is the Creator's house and love is the nature of all beings in that house."

Indeed, we are grateful to have the personal coloration of the instrument to give more variety to our message. However, it is a delicate thing to collaborate with an earthly instrument and produce spiritually helpful material that has a minimum of bias. This is our goal. Needless to say, this is not the goal of all who have spoken with your people.

The one known as Billy Meier is anomalous in that this entity was dealing with unaffiliated entities of fourth-density level; that is, they were not affiliated with the Confederation of Planets in the Service of the Infinite Creator. They, and the one known as Billy, were able to offer some positively-oriented and inspirational material thanks to the catalysis of the one known as Billy.

At the same time, these entities were not entirely positive. That is to say, though of fourth-density level, they had not come through the development into a planetary social memory complex and consequently their actions were, in many ways, flawed according to that rule of non-infringement on free will that is so dear to our hearts.

As you investigate and research non-normal contact between the inhabitants of your planet and extraterrestrial entities, you will find that there is a vast array of experiences that have been had by various peoples in the years of keeping history and writing it down. Some extraterrestrial sources have made compacts with inner-planes sources. Some extraterrestrial sources have become inner planes sources. There is a bewildering array of non-normal contact.

Some of the information in many of these mixed-polarity contacts is useful. Therefore, it is completely up to each seeker to discard information that is not helping that particular person, in his judgment, and to focus on those pieces of information that do seem to be helpful, again, strictly according to that entity's judgment.

My friends, your judgment is adequate to the task of sifting through the variety of messages that you may read. You do have the capacity to follow your heart and to follow the path of resonance.

May we ask if there is a follow-up to this query? We are those of Q'uo.

R: I have a follow-up question, Q'uo. Is it correct to say that entities that are part of the Confederation observe the approach to contact with humans that your group has?

We are those of Q'uo, and are aware of your query, my brother. On the whole, it is fair to say that is true. However, we ourselves have acted other than according to these dictates within your major cycle. Consequently, we cannot say that the Confederation's hands are completely clean, either. However, we believe that we have learned, for the most part, from our mistakes and we hope that we have found the optimal way to offer helpful information without significant distortion.

May we answer you further, my brother?

R: Yes. Is the experience of Earth's having so much extraterrestrial contact towards the end of the cycle the fairly typical experience of planets going through this third density, in this galaxy?

We are those of Q'uo, and believe we understand your query, my brother. It is so that as a planetary population becomes ready to be harvested, it calls for inspiration in such a way that those entities who are sympathetic to that call will come and visit. However, it is unusual for a planet so near to harvest to have visitations from both positive and negative sources. It is more common to see this pattern at the beginning of a major cycle.

By the second minor cycle there is usually the beginning of a planetary choice for the positive or negative polarity. With your planet, contrariwise, the majority of those choosing at all upon your planet have indeed chosen the positive polarity. There is far more positive energy upon your planet than negative. However, there is enough negative-polarity energy to create a dual call, both positive and negative. This has blurred and confused the situation, since instead of having one concerted planetary surge towards the light or towards the darkness, there is this continuing dynamic betwixt the light and the darkness as entities approach graduation.

Therefore, your planetary sphere is anomalous in having dual visitation. And the anomaly is serious enough that this entire planet has been, as we have said before, quarantined for this major cycle in order to attempt to regulate the mix of contact so that those of negative polarity are able to communicate with entities upon planet Earth only at certain randomized intervals.

May we answer you further, my brother?

R: I have one last question on a different subject. But before I say it, I feel that I want to say, at least from my limited viewpoint, that the work that the Confederation is doing with its diligence and attention to free will is deeply inspiring, at least to me, and since I'm part of everyone else it must be so for other people as well.

The question actually is about the nature of the call. You have mentioned that you hear the call. I'm curious about what this call feels like. What is this call to your entity?

We are those of Q'uo, and are aware of your query, my brother. We would thank you for your comments upon our attempts to serve the population of planet Earth. It is, of course, music to our ears to feel that love that you have for us and we thank you, my brother.

Yet it is also worthy to note in this regard that it does not eliminate our questions and concerns as to what that line is between witnessing to our own truth and being persuaders. For we would not be persuaders. We do not wish to pull or push people or do anything except offer hopefully helpful information. At the same time it is obvious from the nature of our information that we are biased towards the positive polarity and that we do rejoice when entities awaken.

The philosophical aspects of our work have never been entirely clear because, as we said at the beginning, the only way that we can be of utterly positive polarity is to cease attempting in any way to influence the entities whom we love so dearly and are calling to us.

Now, to respond to your query on the nature of the call. When one of your human babies awakens in the night and discovers that it is hungry, wet and alone, it cries. It calls out in the only way it knows for help. Blessedly, in almost every case, the parents come and minister to that child, feeding it, drying it, getting a new, dry diaper on it, and cuddling it until it naturally goes back to sleep, content, knowing that it is loved and that all of its needs are met.

Each of you is, spiritually speaking, an infant. And you are crying in the night. You are crying for spiritual food. You are crying to be cleansed of the grime of confusion, sorrow and suffering. And you are crying because you are alone and you do not feel loved.

As entities move through the third density, they begin to become able to address their own needs. As they awaken and become spiritual toddlers, or spiritual preschoolers, they begin to choose to feed themselves heavenly food, to cleanse themselves from spiritually degrading ideas and concepts, and to win through to the knowledge that they are not alone. Because of the intense confusion among your peoples throughout your third-density experience, for the most part entities have not matured beyond the crib. They cry out in the darkness and our hearts go out to them.

There is a great desire on our parts to reach out the hand to steady that baby, to feed that baby, to give that sweet infant soul a new start, a clean diaper, a bellyful of love, and a good rock in the cradle.

We hope that we have become more mature as those who offer help, as we have experimented with ways to answer that call. And we can certainly say that those of planet Earth have begun to become more mature, as it should be. Many are those who have moved from the cradle to preschool, to grade school, to middle school, and finally are ready to graduate third density on time, mature at last, knowing that the food of love is the food for them; knowing that they wish to turn from anything that is not truly love and light; knowing that they are not alone. For as they love, so have they been loved a hundredfold, a thousandfold, overwhelmingly.

The hard part for entities is that first waking up. And it is this effort to which we have come in response. Our love remains unblemished. How far we have fallen short of perfection in our dealings with your planetary population is unknown to us, but we are sure that there are many, many mistakes that we have made for which we humbly ask your forgiveness.

The energy wanes for this entity and this group, so we thank the instrument and leave it and the group in love and in light. We are known to you as those of Q'uo. Adonai. Adonai. ✣

L/L Research

L/L Research is a subsidiary of Rock Creek Research & Development Laboratories, Inc.

P.O. Box 5195
Louisville, KY 40255-0195

www.llresearch.org

Rock Creek is a non-profit corporation dedicated to discovering and sharing information which may aid in the spiritual evolution of humankind.

ABOUT THE CONTENTS OF THIS TRANSCRIPT: This telepathic channeling has been taken from transcriptions of the weekly study and meditation meetings of the Rock Creek Research & Development Laboratories and L/L Research. It is offered in the hope that it may be useful to you. As the Confederation entities always make a point of saying, please use your discrimination and judgment in assessing this material. If something rings true to you, fine. If something does not resonate, please leave it behind, for neither we nor those of the Confederation would wish to be a stumbling block for any.

© 2009 L/L Research

Saturday Meditation
March 22, 2008

Group question: The question tonight is: This planet abounds in a multitude of models, paths and understandings related to the Creator, creation, and the spiritual quest, each susceptible to a wide range of interpretations and most mixed in polarity. There is a vast array of systems of spiritual information that are external to the self, such as the Law of One, Christianity, Buddhism, Hinduism and New Age thought, to name a few, that are printed or communicated in some fashion to the self. In general, what is the ideal relationship between the seeker of truth and information regarding truth which comes from outside the self? How does a seeker situate this information within the self so that it is transparent to the one true authority within and does not become a stumbling block?

(Carla channeling)

We are those known to you as the principle of Q'uo. Greetings in the love and in the light of the one infinite Creator in whose service we come to you this evening. My friends, it is a great privilege to be asked to join your circle of seeking and we are happy to share our thoughts with you on the subject of the appropriate relationship between the seeker and outward expressions of information and inspiration. As always, we would ask each to use discrimination as you listen to our thoughts. If our thoughts seem helpful to you then by all means work with them, but any thought that does not seem particularly helpful is one which we would ask you to leave behind, for we would not be a stumbling block in your way or interrupt or interfere with your process of spiritual evolution. We greatly appreciate your using this discrimination for it allows us to feel comfortable in sharing our thoughts without being concerned that we might infringe upon your free will in any way and we thank you kindly for this consideration.

The question this evening has to do with the proper relationship of the seeker to the various things that he might hear or read coming from all of the different sources which offer philosophical, metaphysical, spiritual or religious systems of thought and, shall we say, systems of proposed belief. You may well guess from what we have just suggested about your using discrimination that we do not feel that it is appropriate for an entity to embrace any system of thought to the extent that the process of seeking the truth stops. The reasons for this are several and we shall be going in a few different directions as we talk about this interesting subject.

As a basic premise we would state that each of you has what you may loosely call the truth safely preserved and carefully stored within your being. You are a creature which is a part of the godhead principle and within every cell of your body lies the truth. The creation within you and without you is full of the truth. You dwell within an environment which is inherently and fundamentally instinct with the truth.

At the same time, from the very beginning of your incarnation the energies of your culture have been busy instilling within you a series of outer truths of the conventional type; that is, the truths of your culture. You have learned how to think of yourself by listening to parents and teachers who offer you a laundry list of standards to which you may aspire and because of which you may feel normal.

We do not deprecate this level of outer truth. Learning the conventions of any society is helpful for one who wishes to move through an incarnation without disturbing the sensibilities of those around him. Yet, these outer conventions of truth do not begin to address the deeper questions of identity, essence and purpose.

The seeker who wishes to move beyond conventions, then, is drawn by those same conventional assumptions to study and read those wise words which have been set down by sages of the past. Again, we do not criticize or demean the study of metaphysics or spiritual subjects—as the questioner has pointed out, there is a vast array of interesting and provocative thought to consider in attempting to move beyond the conventions of work, leisure and family in order to find a deeper purpose, a deeper essence of self, and a deeper knowledge of self-identity.

The exercise, shall we say, of considering the thoughts of philosophers and spiritual writers is often quite helpful in bringing the mind into a series of focuses, each of which expand the viewpoint and deepen the feeling of resonance and clarity.

The use of the intellect is necessary in order to pursue such study and the intellect and intellectual food make a nice, tidy set for the mind. There is the horse to ride, that horse of intellectual thought, and there are places to go on that horse, visits to make at the various interesting thoughts of various entities. We have said through this instrument many times that the intellect is a useful tool given to you to use, not to be ignored or left behind. However, the general run of entities who are involved in intellectual pursuits have a tendency to allow the horse to ride them rather their being the master of that horse. Perhaps it is more helpful to think of modern-day equivalents of horses, like a car. One would not wish the car to choose the place where you wish to go in the car. One would be wise to be the master of the car and to steer that car where one wishes to go at the speed which is most appropriate to the journey.

Therefore, we suggest strongly that the process of intellectual ratiocination be one of which the seeker is quite conscious so that the seeker does not get swept up in the play of words and ideas to the point that the truth is no longer the focus of the seeking.

The seeker has tools of which it may not be aware and we would look at those tools for a bit now. We often suggest that entities follow the path of resonance as they seek. Whether it is our words of any other writer or speaker to which the seeker is listening or from which the seeker is reading, we encourage seekers to follow that path of resonance.

Your path of resonance is unique. No matter how wise your teacher or how inspired the writing, there is almost no chance that everything a given teacher or writer offers to you as food for thought will resonate to you. Ideally, those concepts which you follow will be those concepts which, when first read or heard, awaken within a seeker a kind of recollection as though he already knew that but was happy to be reminded of it once again.

In this search for resonance, it is to be remembered that the nature of language is that it is inherently limited. It is twice limited. First it is limited in that words must be strung together to make sentences and sentences strung together to make paragraphs and so forth. Each word has a little universe of supporting inferences which enrich the collection of words due to the context of each word being placed in its line of the flow of thought. Yet they remain finite and inherently limited.

They are limited a second time because the mind does not function according to words but rather according to concepts. Concepts are infinite. However, they can only be expressed by the human mind and gotten out into the outer manifestation of words by a process of translation which works almost like a cook rolling out the dough of a concept and taking cookie cutters to it and fashioning the flat words which bake up into that translated concept. Needless to say, a great deal is lost in translation.

However, there is a redeeming feature to words and that is that they partake, when being pronounced, in the human breath. The action of speaking is one which can move down into the archetypal mind, bringing forth more than words as the thoughtful focused seeker tries out new thoughts and puzzles over concepts as best he can with his human mind. Therefore, the very structure of words is sacred and the breath is sacred so that there is a blessedness involved in working with words that inspire.

As the questioner was saying earlier, the habit or practice of speaking the name of the Creator seems to be a very powerful spiritual practice which has yielded much fruit. The questioner uses the Creator name of "the one infinite Creator." Other entities might use such names as Jesus, Buddha, Allah, Ram or any of a host of other god names which alike have the capacity to carry an essence and an energy that far outweighs the seeming nakedness of sound and pronunciation. This is because the combination of these letters put together in certain ways to make words and the use of the human breath create avenues deep into the archetypal mind, awakening resonance from very deep places within the roots of mind and consciousness.

There is an old story within Buddhist teaching of a saint who held stones in his mouth for twenty years until he learned to be silent. And we appreciate this effort to arrive at the ability to contain and feel comfortable with silence. In silence, there is no need to take a cookie-cutter to the concepts that speak to the deep mind with that still small voice of spirit. In silence, there is no need to work the machinery of the intellect. In silence, one may rest and allow the truth to rise up into consciousness from the infinite invisible that is the heart of each seeker and the heart of the universe alike.

Because of the fact that there are different sorts of seekers with different habits and frames of mind, we cannot offer one sure way which will suit everyone in terms of finding the right attitude towards words of inspiration and information that have been given. Some entities have a comfortable relationship with philosophical structures and are able to walk down many paths without being swayed by the glamour of beautifully spoken words or ascetically pleasing constructs. Other entities are extremely sensitive to beauty, wisdom or that ineffable quality of profundity that one may feel and so may be overly swayed within his own process of seeking the truth by seductively beautiful constructs.

To the first entity, there is little danger of being swept up in an overmasteringly beautiful religion or spiritual system. For the second type of entity there is the danger of losing the self and becoming instead identified in his own mind with that one way of thought.

It could be argued that is quite helpful to settle into one way of thought and to work within it to the exclusion of all other thoughts or ways of thinking, for are not all paths bound to lead to the one infinite Creator? And is not a purity and focus of seeking easier to achieve using the dogma of a religion or the limitations of a certain philosophical system?

We would suggest that it is entirely possible to achieve harvestability in this third-density school of souls following any of that vast array of spiritual systems. However, your query moves deeper than the question of harvestability. Your query comes to the heart of the nature of spiritual evolution and because of that, we say that the most helpful and appropriate way of relating to all outer words and systems of words is to work with them consciously, at all times creating a spaciousness around the words, the thoughts, the comparisons, and so forth, which gives the soul room for the unspoken, the un—we correct this instrument—the ineffable, the noumenal, for there is much between every inspired word that is unspoken that creates the ambience in which the spoken word rings with truth.

There is great wisdom in taking lightly and with laughter the entire business of study and thought for spiritual seekers. The one known as R was saying earlier that as the decades have gone by and his spiritual seeking has matured he has become less interested in forming questions and getting answers in his search for the truth. It is indeed a mark of spiritual maturity that the intense desire to know the truth becomes gradually transformed into the intense desire to be the truth.

It is not that there is no truth or that there is nothing to seek. Quite the contrary, my friends. However, that which is sought is the heart of the self. The journey towards truth seems as though it is an outer journey, a seeking out there, a winnowing through the harvest of other people's seeking to find one's truth. And yet, in the end, it is as though various things begin to fall away in the seeker's mind and in the seeker's heart and in the seeker's experience until gradually the truth itself rises to the surface of consciousness and realization occurs. That realization that it is a perfect world, it is a perfect environment for unlocking the gate that leads to unknowing.

Within third density, beyond all the things that you come to know and believe, there lies the glory of that final awareness that nothing can be known and that all speaks of the one infinite Creator. Paradox after paradox, mystery and mystery flow and create patterns around one. And powerful and glorious ideas and images move through the awareness and at the end, the seeker has become transparent to himself as he finds at the very heart of himself the consciousness of unconditional love, that love that created him, that love that created the universe, that love with which he and all about him, seen and unseen, are one.

We would encourage, in whatever mode of seeking is desired, a sense of tempo and rhythm for the seeking entity. It does not have to be a set speed of learning or a limit that one puts upon oneself daily or weekly as to how much time is spent on seeking and how much on meditation. For entities fluctuate endlessly. At one time in the life of a seeker, it may be needed and useful to cram the self with new thoughts. At another time, it may be very wise to refrain from study. In general we would say that there needs to be a balance between the use of the intellect and the use of silence. For in silence one may allow the mind—in a focused and conscious fashion—to seat the information and inspiration that has been received.

Certainly daily periods of silence are a strong resource for the seeker who wishes to do more than think about the great questions. For beyond thought lies the truth. Beyond the intellect lies insight. Beyond knowledge lies gnosis.

The seeker's journey is a sacred one, a beautiful one, and often a difficult one. There are many seasons of light and shadow, growth and awaiting, and all are equally profitable. Trust yourself, trust your sense of resonance and then enjoy your seeking, your questions, your answers, and all that goes into a life lived by spiritual means and interests.

May we ask if there is a follow-up to this query before we open this session to other questions. We are those of Q'uo.

G: There is not a follow-up to the main question, Q'uo, from me.

We are those of Q'uo, and are aware that we may now open this session to other queries. Is there another query at this time?

G: Q'uo, I have an excerpt from the *Law of One* material. Ra says, "The measure of an entity's level of ray activity is the locus wherein the south pole outer energy has been met by the inner spiraling positive energy. As an entity grows more polarized, this locus will move upwards. This phenomena has been called by your peoples the kundalini. To attempt to raise the locus of this meeting without realizing the metaphysical principles of magnetism upon which this depends is to invite great imbalance."

I can't quite figure it out, Q'uo. I was wondering if you could define what the "metaphysical principles of magnetism upon which this depends" are?

We are those of Q'uo, and are aware of your query, my brother. The principles of magnetism have to do with polarity. The strength of a polarized field is that strength which appreciates both the positive and the negative poles of the magnet so that it is understood that there is virtue and value in both that south pole, as they called it, and the north pole of information or inspiration sought through the gateway to intelligent infinity.

Oftentimes, entities who are thirsty and hungry for spiritual meat simply keep attempting to move higher and higher and higher within the energy body, upwards into the realms of higher communication, high wisdom, high faith, and so forth, without giving an equal amount of attention to that energy which is coming through the energy body from the south pole, from the Earth itself.

The group known as Ra was suggesting that as one seeks to open the higher charkas it is equally necessary to continue to give full honor, respect and attention to the health and the vibrancy of the lower charkas as well and to appreciate and honor that energy which has come from the one infinite Creator, to the Sun, into the womb of the Earth, and then from the Earth up through the feet and the base of the charka system at the base of the spine in infinite supply. There needs to be a continuing and equal appreciation of this energy and of all that it suggests of mortality and limitation, for indeed mortality is a limitation and the presence of a seeker upon the Earth plane partakes of this mortality and this limitation.

It makes a much sweeter thing of being alive and aware to realize one's limited tenure within the Earth plane. Instead of scorning things of the Earth because they are illusory, then, the one known as Ra is suggesting that one embrace and enjoy and take part in the things that are fleeting, relishing and celebrating the energies of each charka. Sexuality, relationships, group relationships—all of these energies are worthy, all of these energies take daily, thoughtful maintenance in order for each charka to shine and be completely open to the energy of the one infinite Creator as it moves from the Earth in upwards spiraling fashion. Only when this motion upward is fully seated and working well can the seeker then call through the gateway of intelligent infinity for that inspiration which comes from the infinite and invisible world of time/space.

May we answer you further, my brother?

G: That was very satisfactory, thank you, Q'uo.

We are those of Q'uo, and, my brother, we are very pleased to be satisfactory. May we ask if there is another query at this time?

G: Q'uo, I've got another question seeking clarification from the *Law of One* material. In that material, Don was asking about the bent legs of the sphinx in the tarot images and Ra responded said: "The position is intended to show two items, one of which is the dual possibilities of the time-full characters there drawn. The resting is possible in time as is the progress. If a mixture is attempted, the upright, moving leg will be greatly hampered by the leg that is bent."

Could you simply define what "rest" and "progress" in this selection mean?

We are those of Q'uo, and, my brother, it is a long story, shall we say, but there are reasons why this figure is part of your process at this time and consequently we must leave this puzzle for your working. We apologize, but we must pass on this query.

Is there a final query at this time before we leave this instrument? We are those of Q'uo.

R: Not from me, Q'uo.

G: Final one from me, Q'uo. This question comes from a "friend." This "friend" wants to know if the activity known as masturbation expends vital energy that would otherwise be available for higher charka activity?

There are two answers to this query, for there are two levels of masturbation. The physical body of your species is naturally sexual and has a natural capacity for sexuality. If an entity does not masturbate, when the period of time has come in which sexual energy has been built up to the point where there is a need for release, masturbation will take place without any help; it will occur as a night dream or something of that nature. So, on that level, masturbating when there is a build-up of sexual energy and no appropriate outlet with another partner has little impact upon the amount of energy or essence of self that is preserved for metaphysical work.

However, there is a legitimate point to be made in terms of the dedication of the self to spiritual seeking in that there is a magical aspect which can be accessed by the seeker who wishes to dedicate the energy that would otherwise be used in sexual release to the winding of the coil, shall we say.

However, it is equally true that sex itself may be used, whether in masturbation or sexual congress with another, to express positive polarity and the worship of the one infinite Creator. The mind is preeminent in this matter. Depending upon how a seeker feels about his sexuality, he may find it more skilful to work with refraining from sexual expression in terms of how he personally is impacted by the experience of reserving his sexual energy for winding of the magical coil. Or, depending upon the entity and his personality and the way he feels about his body, he may find that it is more helpful to create a spiritually-dedicated masturbation in which the object is to experience that orgasm which is the steady state of the one infinite Creator, that inexpressible and inutterable intensity of unconditional love that is the ecstasy at the heart of the experience of orgasm.

The body is the creature of the mind. We would encourage your friend not to focus upon sex until he has focused upon who he is, how he expresses his essence, how he feels is the most resonant way to manage his humanity in the sense of his red-ray sexuality.

May we answer you further, my brother? We are those of Q'uo.

G: No, the friend *(ahem!)*, thanks you.

We are those of Q'uo, and we thank you, my brother, for these most interesting queries. And we thank each within this group for setting aside the time and the attention and the love. Seek the truth. The one known as R was saying that he did not really understand how we found you to have such courage and such integrity simply because you gather to seek the truth, and yet we say to you, my brother, that it is the rare entity indeed who has come to be able to take himself seriously as a worthwhile and worthy part of the Creator.

Within your dream on planet Earth, it is not at all obvious that there is value in this goal of seeking the truth. We find it a wonderful thing when entities such as yourselves do so and we thank you for this effort. We cannot tell you how beautiful your blended auras are as you have created this sacred space together.

It is time now to leave this instrument and this group with our thanks, our blessing, and our love. We leave you in the love and in the light of the one infinite Creator. We are known to you as the principle of Q'uo. Adonai. Adonai vasu. ☙

L/L Research is a subsidiary of Rock Creek Research & Development Laboratories, Inc.

P.O. Box 5195
Louisville, KY 40255-0195

L/L Research

www.llresearch.org

Rock Creek is a non-profit corporation dedicated to discovering and sharing information which may aid in the spiritual evolution of humankind.

ABOUT THE CONTENTS OF THIS TRANSCRIPT: This telepathic channeling has been taken from transcriptions of the weekly study and meditation meetings of the Rock Creek Research & Development Laboratories and L/L Research. It is offered in the hope that it may be useful to you. As the Confederation entities always make a point of saying, please use your discrimination and judgment in assessing this material. If something rings true to you, fine. If something does not resonate, please leave it behind, for neither we nor those of the Confederation would wish to be a stumbling block for any.

© 2009 L/L RESEARCH

SATURDAY MEDITATION
MARCH 29, 2008

Question from G: In the meditative state, if an entity concentrated upon sending instructions for desired programming to the subconscious or deeper self, would the deeper self respond in accordance to those instructions? For instance, would the self's perception of self begin to be transformed if an entity, through concentration in a meditative state, told the self over and over, "I desire to see through the eyes of love"? What kind of power to effect changes do repeated affirmations have? How can one increase the effectiveness of the mantra?

(Carla channeling)

We are those known to you as the principle of Q'uo. Greetings, my friends, in the love and in the light of the one infinite Creator, in whose service we come to you this evening. It is our pleasure and our privilege to be called to your session of working and we thank you for including us in your circle of seeking. We too seek the truth and we are honored to be asked to share our thoughts with you on the subject of affirmations, mantras and working with the self at that limen[129] between the subconscious and the conscious levels.

There are various aspects to this query which shall cause the flow of our response to be shaped. Our first focus would be upon the query concerning the use of affirmations while in a meditative and concentrated state. We would simply suggest that it is well to untangle the use of affirmations in a concentrated state from the practice of meditation.

The practice of meditation is a practice of silence. The times of visualization, affirmation and other work in consciousness, while equally valuable and worthy of doing, are not the same in terms of that which is required and that which is a good resource for that activity as meditation. So let us simply, briefly state that it is well to retain times within each day when one practices the presence of the one infinite Creator, not by thought, by affirmation, or by any other aspect of the conscious human mind, but by listening to that silence which is pregnant with the one infinite Creator's presence and truth.

It is a temptation to add more into a meditation in order to create desired changes within the self by purposefully and consciously making adjustments. However, while this method of working is certainly useful, we would suggest that it is best done after a meditation or separately from a meditation. This will allow you as a seeker to keep firm those channels of unknowing which aid greatly in maintaining the focus of the mind upon that silence which is so full of information to the subconscious mind.

The questioner's concept of focusing the mind and creating affirmations is excellent. This is work well done, for the personality is, far more than most entities realize, a creature made up of habits, inertia and half-considered ways of doing things that have remained the same for a long time. It is, in fact, a

---

[129] A limen is an entrance or threshold.

loosely cobbled together structure which houses and is intended to protect the sensitive soul within the personality shell. It is indeed pliable and malleable and suggestions are helpful.

There is in this instrument's memory of the work of entities who have created *The Psychology of Perception and the Biology of Change*[130], a video which this instrument has greatly enjoyed, and we would like to use this instrument's awareness of this carefully judged body of information in saying that, for the seeker who wishes to discover in a very systematic way those habits of thought which have been least helpful, the procedures of these particular practitioners, who use the powers of suggestion and intuition and make use of the muscle-testing technique can, within a short period of time for those who wish to move through the material in this video, create the opportunity for a seeker to become aware of the statements which he may be making about himself which are not helpful in terms of his spiritual evolution.

We offer this information not in order to encourage the seeker necessarily to seek in this wise. This area or avenue of investigation is helpful for the seeker who believes that he may well have in his background thoughts that are toxic to him. It is not specifically a spiritual exercise, nor do the results of this particular investigative direction yield specifically spiritual results. However, because this instrument has moved through the work needed to experience the benefits of this particular avenue of investigation there is that awareness within this instrument that this is helpful to some. In a way it is a clearing away of old material so that a more specifically spiritual avenue of investigation can be opened. That being said, we would now like to focus on the concept of affirmations.

We would suggest that affirmations such as the questioner offered are indeed powerful to work with in the subconscious mind. The will of the seeker is carefully focused. The mantra or affirmation or statement itself has been very carefully prepared. The seeker therefore feels that he may trust this affirmation with the whole of his will. He may place the entire burden of his desire upon the realization of the truth of this statement.

There are two particularly good times in which to do this work which occur naturally twice at least during each diurnal period. Those are the moments after one awakens and the moments before one goes to sleep. In this hypnogogic[131] state, your mind is fully collected. It is about to move across that limen of which we spoke earlier, that threshold of consciousness, and enter into the precincts of sleep. Or, it is just arising from sleep, with its mind ready to focus upon the new day but not yet full of content.

During this state in both morning and evening, the repetition of such a statement will be quite effective, for it will penetrate immediately into the subconscious without resistance.

If on the other hand, the questioner would desire to set aside a specific time during the day's schedule for this work, it might be recommended that a period of meditation be followed by the conscious gathering of the forces of self and the repetition of the statement that the seeker desires itself to hear.

We would note that the use of the voice in saying the statements out loud is helpful in terms of creating the maximum impression of the self upon the self using this technique. If a thought remains within the mind, it has its natural limits of power and is of a certain kind. It is a thought form. If the same thought is spoken out loud, and breath has been expended in the saying, it has become sacred. It is not simply a thought form. In the expenditure of breath it is a living thing and the entire effect is greatly enhanced, in that the seeker hears himself.

Indeed, tangentially, we would note that there are many times when it is helpful for seekers to speak out loud to themselves, talking to themselves out loud about their considerations. For in developing the sentences that are spoken aloud, the seeker is able to break the cycles of repetition that occur within the mind when it is thinking to itself. And then the seeker "hears" what he is thinking in a different way.

The questioner, in attempting to create changes in his consciousness by the use of his will, is developing his magical personality. Therefore, we would suggest

---

[130] This video or DVD is by Bruce Lipton and Robert Williams. It is available from web bookstores such as Amazon.com or from the web site, www.psych-k.com/video.php.

[131] hypnogogic: of, relating to, or occurring in the state of intermediate consciousness preceding sleep.

a certain amount of protocol having to do with these periods of affirmation or statement. That is, at the beginning of this period of affirmation or statement, the collected and fully conscious seeker takes upon himself his magical personality. If he wishes, he may invoke it without words. He may make a gesture which indicates to himself that he has taken on his magical personality. Or he may wear a ring or some other form of adornment to the body which is only worn during this particular ritual.

When invoking the magical personality polarity is, of course, all-important. That polarity may be protected by the simple statement: "I desire to know in order to serve." Positive magical workings always have to do with service to the one infinite Creator and, by reflection, to the world and to the self. There is nothing of the worldly self involved in the desires of the magical personality. Consequently, this taking on, in a ritualistic fashion, of this personality creates a cleanliness and purity to the working which it would not otherwise have. At the end of the working, then, the ring or other adornment may be removed, another gesture may be made, or another visualization may be made.

This particular instrument uses the visualization of putting on the magical robes, and of taking them off after the working. When this instrument prepares for channeling, however, the protocol is different. She calls the archangels and asks them to place her on limitless white light to breathe. At that time, she asks the archangels to remove the limitless white light when she is through channeling and place her back on ordinary, everyday air. In this way she protects her magical personality from attempting to maintain its purity when the personality shell has once again taken the stage and life is going on in its usual fashion.

The magical personality is not a mysterious entity. It is yourself at a different stage of your development. We have called it the higher self. It is your highest and best self. It is a completely magical, focused, sacred being. It is your gift to yourself from mid-sixth density across all the reaches of infinite space/time and time/space. Your higher self, or magical personality, offers to you the entire array of resources which its vast experience has gathered. You and your higher self or magical personality created the plan for this incarnation. And your higher self or magical personality is, at all times, as close as your breathing.

The use, in a conscious fashion, of the magical personality is extremely powerful. Therefore, it is well to work carefully and lovingly with these energies as you begin to create the changes in consciousness that you wish to create within yourself. As you seek, the question arises: what do I seek? That which you seek is ever and always a part of yourself, a deeper, more fundamental, more true part of yourself.

We offer a very simple philosophy in saying all things are one. Yes, that statement has implications, and those implications echo and resonate through level after level of awareness. That which you seek, that which all seekers seek is a truer, deeper awareness of the self, of the Creator, of the creation about one. So that use of affirmation or statement in a repetitive, persistent manner is extremely positive in use and well done.

Care and deep love need to go into the creation of the statement or affirmation, the creation of the ritual that surrounds the use of that affirmation, and the choice of how to place this beautiful magical ritual within the coils of the day.

An earlier query by the questioner to this instrument provoked in our response a discussion of the nature of sound and the use of the voice. And in answering the latter part of your query, my brother, we would focus upon that topic once again. Mantras are extremely powerful, as you have already discovered. Like the affirmative statements, they must be well chosen, for they bore deeply within the mind.

When appropriately chosen and full of truth for that seeker, the use of the mantra shall indeed create an immediate change in the vibratory level of the seeker. It is a change in vibration which is not specific. It is a change in vibration which goes to the deepest roots of consciousness. For in the deepest roots of consciousness, the name of every seeker is the one infinite Creator. Whatever god-name that a mantra contains is the deepest, truest name of the self. You are calling to your self across the aeons of timelessness and time, spacelessness and space, moving to that one point where you and the Creator are one. This is meat, as the one known as Jesus the Christ says, of which the world knows not. This is drink, after which the seeker shall never thirst.

Working with mantras is working with the archetypal mind. In a way, this is also a magical working. However, because of the fact that it is without form, not being a statement but a name or principle, there is a safety involved in that the mind cannot do anything with that word, or god-name, or naked principle which is the mantra. And so it lets it go down immediately into the subconscious mind.

As with all magical rituals, repetition is a key to the effectiveness and the power of the ritual. That change in consciousness which is sought becomes more and more easily, even effortlessly, achieved as the habit deepens of using this mantra. It is, as the questioner said in the round-robin discussion before this channeling began, a most effective way of smoothing out the bumps in the personality shell. It brings one to a world where suffering and catalyst, light and dark, day and night are subsumed into a sacred space where all is one and all is well. This being the deeper truth, it informs the lesser truth, so the life is transformed in a way which cannot be explained intellectually but which nevertheless is very effective.

We thank the one known as G for this query and would ask at this time if there is a follow-up to this question. We are those of Q'uo.

G: Q'uo, thank you. There is no follow-up to this question.

We are those of Q'uo, and therefore we would open this session to other questions. Is there another query at this time? We are those of Q'uo.

G: Q'uo, I have one. Is the achievement of what we call enlightenment something that is planned pre-incarnationally or can the entity, with sufficient will and without such a pre-incarnational program, achieve the experience of enlightenment within the incarnation?

We are those of Q'uo, and aware of your query, my brother. In our estimation, there is not the pre-incarnative planning for enlightenment, realization or satori. The pre-incarnative planning focuses on that which shall be sought within the incarnation and those supporting resources needed for the journey of seeking. The pre-incarnative planning includes your relationships, your gifts, your limitations, and what you see as your faults and lacks. From an enormous selection of things that you have been and things that you have done in previous incarnations, you choose for your palette the colors which will paint this lifetime in the most beautiful and useful way.

You wish to have a beautiful incarnation in that you wish to create a sacred journey, a journey which partakes of beauty—ethical beauty, physical beauty, mental and emotional beauty, awareness of beauty. You plan these things for yourself. You wish to be useful, and so you choose for yourself ways in which you may serve, either by being or by doing. And because you also wish to evolve, you plan for yourself incarnational lessons that come up again and again, so that you may practice.

Generally, in an incarnation entities are looking to balance love with wisdom, wisdom with power, or some variety of two or three of those three aspects of the godhead principle: love, light and power. Realization, on the other hand, is that moment out of time, or more accurately, in time/space, when an entity is able to realize and therefore move all of himself through the gateway to intelligent infinity so that he, in the most holistic sense, may be inspired by or be filled with the truth.

There are those who have moments of such realization and yet those moments pass. And there are those who enter that gateway of intelligent infinity never to return, in the sense that the impact of perfection is so powerful that a choice is made to live the life in this awareness even though, shall we say, the wiring of an entity living at this level of energy will burn out the physical body. It is not the goal of the higher self or the self outside incarnation to achieve realization. That is an object of desire which is chosen by those within incarnation and within that veil [of forgetting] which prevents them from knowing that all is truly one.

In terms of your soul-self, shall we say, or the self outside of incarnation, you see the incarnative period as a period of work; work on your balance and work to the service of the one infinite Creator. Outside of the veil, things look different enough that realization seems like the steady state and the incarnation is that wonderful time of unknowing when the entity sets about on the journey of faith.

May we answer you further, my brother?

G: You mentioned the balance between love, wisdom and power. I would like to request what you mean by the use of power—by the word power, that is.

We are those of Q'uo, and are aware of your query, my brother. You have heard us greet you and say goodbye to you in love and in light many, many times. We do not so often speak of power. Power is an aspect of both love and wisdom, yet power is also a thing in and of itself. When you wish to focus your attention, your will or your desire, you are using that power that fuels your attention, your will, and your desire. Physical power is easy to see, and often entities who are metaphysically powerful are also physically powerful. However, the power of which we speak when we speak of balancing love, wisdom and power is the metaphysical power of your will. The focusing of your will is the magical act that creates a change in consciousness for you.

Now, consider how easily an entity who is greatly loving and has a strong will may make numerous and unwise choices for himself and others because there has been an unwise use of power. Perhaps there was great love in a situation and consequently the seeker decides to affect the situation, but does not discover all the parameters of the situation.

For instance, say, a daughter has an elderly parent. Say that this elderly parent is full of years, full of illness, and ready to let the body fall away. The parent is ready to enter the gates of larger life and so heal himself through to a new environment. He is desirous of moving on. And yet, say, this daughter is absolutely certain that the best way to express her love is to keep this entity alive. The unwise use of her will may well keep the entity alive. Yet it cannot be said to be an action that partakes of true compassion or wisdom.

Similarly, a wise entity may easily focus his attention or his will on creating things, making things happen in the physical illusion. Yet he may not have been full enough of compassion to know the just use of his wisdom. In such ways, your lawgivers have sometimes created laws that limit rather than promote fairness.

These are only two examples. May we answer you further, my brother? We are those of Q'uo.

G: First, thank you so much for speaking through example. I love seeing a principle illustrated in a particular circumstance. It helps me to grasp it so much more easily. I don't form my thoughts well without being able to write them down, but the thoughts that I have formed go like this. Based on what I understood you to have said, I would equate will with the capacity to sustain focus and put into action that which one desires, whether internally or externally. And I would see love and wisdom informing the will and equating power with the capacity to sustain and carry out action and seeing that power informed by love and wisdom. Does that make sense?

We are those of Q'uo, and are aware of your statement my brother, and indeed it does make sense, your dangling marsupials,[132] as the one known as Don would say, notwithstanding. You have the basic gist of that which we are trying to express.

There is an infinite variety of ways to talk about selfhood. When one talks of love and light one is grasping two fundamental principles of that in which unity consists: the original thought and the manifestation of that thought. Yet there is power in every atom, in every cell of your body, and in every engram[133] of your emotions.

There is power in every word you think. So, in addition to concerns of learning to be more loving and learning to be more wise there is a concern, as one becomes more powerful, to use that power wisely and compassionately. So, there is a tripod of love, wisdom and power. And there is a just balance for each entity between those three. It is a consideration that goes into each entity's plan for incarnation.

May we answer you further, my brother? We are those of Q'uo.

G: No, Q'uo. Thank you.

We are those of Q'uo, and we thank you, my brother. Is there a final query before we leave this instrument? We are those of Q'uo.

G: Q'uo, how would you relate the concepts of faith and power?

We are those of Q'uo, and are aware of your query, my brother. Faith is a vibration or energy which is far less distorted from the truth than any other vibration or energy which you as a third density entity are able to realize, express or manifest. It is deeply connected with the indigo-ray chakra and is also fully conversant with that process of the indigo

---

[132] Don Elkins had a habit of changing thing slightly as a form of humor. "Dangling participles" became "dangling marsupials."

[133] engram: a presumed encoding in neural tissue that provides a physical basis for the persistence of memory; a memory trace.

and violet ray moving through the gateway to intelligent infinity.

Power, my brother, can move through any of the chakra energies. And in making one's life sacred, one discovers the joy of expressing one's power through the highest possible expression, which is that of faith. An entity which has the faculty of faith well developed is indeed a most powerful beacon. So, we would not equate power with faith, but rather would say that it is a matter of the seeker's journey to find higher and higher expressions of his will, his power, and his focus.

May we answer you further, my brother?

G: No. Thank you so much, Q'uo.

We are those of Q'uo, and we thank you, my brother. We have greatly enjoyed your queries. At this time we would leave this instrument and this group with great thanks for being called to your session of working. It has been a true pleasure. We are so happy to share our thoughts with you.

As always, we suggest that you listen for the path of resonance in all that you hear, whether it is our words or the words of others, taking from us what would be helpful to you and leaving the rest behind. We do thank you for this consideration, as always. We are known to you as those of Q'uo. We leave this instrument and this group in the love and the light of the one infinite Creator. We leave you not only in love and light this evening but also in peace and in power. Adonai. Adonai vasu.

L/L Research

L/L Research is a subsidiary of Rock Creek Research & Development Laboratories, Inc.

P.O. Box 5195
Louisville, KY 40255-0195

www.llresearch.org

Rock Creek is a non-profit corporation dedicated to discovering and sharing information which may aid in the spiritual evolution of humankind.

ABOUT THE CONTENTS OF THIS TRANSCRIPT: This telepathic channeling has been taken from transcriptions of the weekly study and meditation meetings of the Rock Creek Research & Development Laboratories and L/L Research. It is offered in the hope that it may be useful to you. As the Confederation entities always make a point of saying, please use your discrimination and judgment in assessing this material. If something rings true to you, fine. If something does not resonate, please leave it behind, for neither we nor those of the Confederation would wish to be a stumbling block for any.

© 2009 L/L Research

Saturday Meditation
April 12, 2008

Group question: Our question tonight, Q'uo, is: One gets the impression when reading the mystical texts within the distortions of Christianity, Zen Buddhism, Sufism, the Yoga of Hinduism and other, non-codified systems of thought, that the path to enlightenment demands of the seeker a great quantity and quality of time and energy and focus.

What would you say to the seeker of enlightenment whose obligations of service to family, work and society seem to preclude the possibility of devoting the requisite time and energy? Additionally, can sufficient will and faith overcome these daily limits upon available time and energy?

(Carla channeling)

We are those of the principle known to you as Q'uo. We greet you in the love and the light of the one infinite Creator, in whose service we come to you this evening.

It is a great privilege and pleasure to be asked to join your circle of seeking. We thank you for inviting us to share our thoughts with you. As always we would ask you to employ your discrimination while listening to or reading that which we have to say. It will enable us to speak freely if you will do so. For not all of our thoughts will meet all of your needs and it is important to us that we do not infringe upon your free will or disturb your process by suggesting that we are in some way authorities who must be listened to regardless of what we say.

My friends, this is not true. We are those who share our thoughts with you just as you would share your thoughts with us, and just as we would listen to you with discrimination, so we would ask you to listen to us with that same discrimination, using those thoughts that are helpful to you and leaving the rest behind.

We would note that this evening the speaker for Q'uo is Hatonn rather than Latwii. We note this in case those who are aware of our thoughts find a difference in the vibration, finding it more towards the energy of love than towards the energy of wisdom. The query and the constitution of the group require more of a focus on the fourth-density energies of unconditional love and compassion.

Your query this evening has to do with the nature of the spiritual master, or perhaps to use a better word, the spiritually mature entity. The questioner notes that no matter what the religious conviction of the seeker, those who write inspiring material seem to be those who have dedicated their entire lives to the pursuit of the one infinite Creator, not necessarily working for a living or engaging in relationships of a personal nature or the raising of a family.

This is a very interesting query and we shall attempt to look into this from several different points of view.

Firstly, we would look at the supposition that inspiring works are generally written by those whose lives have been set apart from the general run of society. This is true. The works most admired by those who seek the truth are those works that were the product of lifetimes of contemplation and devotion.

Each of the religions has its long list of those entities whose lives were set apart and dedicated in devotion to the one infinite Creator. Out of those dedicated lives have come many books, poems, koans[134], sutras[135] and Vedas[136], and they have been a blessing to many. In the Oriental and Eastern portions of your world and in primitive societies in general, the office of guru, shaman, or priest is an office that is held in high esteem by the tribe or people and each tribe or village has such a beloved and well-supported figure.

This entity is given honor and is part of the very fabric of the tribe or village. The guru or shaman is not precisely set apart from the rest of the population. However it is a full-time role. It is respected, honored and needed. There is no feeling for the Western concept of going to church on one day in a week and not thinking about spiritual matters any other time. Rather there is the sense of the world as a magical and spiritual place altogether; a world of mystery which the guru or shaman may interpret with words or may explicate in his silence.

In the Western or Occidental portion of your world, it is also true that it is those who have dedicated their lives to the seeking of truth who have created the sacred literature that is revered and honored by seekers of truth. However, the society of the Occident is not woven of a fabric in which religious figures are essential. Priests, pastors, and western rabbis are appreciated and honored. However, the office of priest, pastor or rabbi is most usually considered to be a career. It is work done for pay.

The priest generally is given time off, like any other worker, and has vacations from his spiritual career. There is, perhaps, the same degree of devotion in many of those who are spiritual leaders in the West as in the East. Within orders of monks and nuns, dedicated seekers are able to offer their entire lives in devotion to the one infinite Creator. Yet these societies are set apart from the villages, the towns and the cities. They are not an intrinsic part of every neighborhood. They are not a familiar sight within the little area of streets and lanes in which you may live. There is a different emphasis and stress placed on religious seeking or the spiritual walk in the Western world.

It may be noted in this regard that many of the most beloved of writers in the Western world are those of the minority who are monks and have been able to devote their entire life, 24 hours a day and seven days a week, to the pursuit of the mystery.

What unites the East and the West in their attitude towards spiritual masters or teachers or spiritually mature entities is that it is assumed that the rest of the village or the tribe or the city will not be spiritual masters. That job is given to the one entity within the village or tribe who is spiritually gifted and has been chosen to be the guru, the shaman or the priest of the tribe or village in the East.

In the Western world the job of spiritual leader is given to those few who feel called to a special vocation. The rest of the people are content to attend services and listen to the wise words being given from the pulpit. They receive their Sabbath sermons and feel comfortable about moving back into the secular world and not thinking about spiritual things until the next Sabbath.

Indeed, in many cases among the people of your modern culture it is not deemed necessary to think about spiritual things at all, except in the same way one thinks about politics or sports or the latest popular show on your television. It is part of the universe of normal life. It may not be deemed necessary to consult spiritual leaders such as priests, rabbis and pastors except on appropriate occasions such as marriages, baptisms and funerals.

The vast majority of entities then, whether in the East or in the West, are content to think of themselves in non-spiritual terms. They are just people living their lives. Indeed, if one were to suggest to many people that they, too, are priests, there would be no feeling of resonance on the part of those who heard such a thought. They would say, "I am not at all priestly. I am a worldly person. I do not know very much about spiritual things. I could

---

[134] koan: a puzzling, often paradoxical statement or story, used in Zen Buddhism as an aid to meditation and a means of gaining spiritual awakening.

[135] sutra: any of various aphoristic doctrinal summaries produced for memorization generally between 500 and 200 B.C. and later incorporated into Hindu literature.

[136] The Veda: the entire body of Hindu sacred writings, chief among which are four books, the Rig-Veda, the Sama-Veda, the Atharva-Veda, and the Yajur-Veda.

never be a priest. I could never be a shaman. I could never be a spiritual leader. I do not have the time, the energy or the focus that it takes to become spiritually mature."

We would suggest, on the other hand, that each of you is already a priest. Your very nature is sacred. Every cell of your body is full of the love and the light of the one infinite Creator.

The one known as G was saying earlier that there was often the sense that he was very close to this realization of oneness with all. He was often very close to this feeling of all things being sacred and all things being one. And yet there seemed to be a glass wall, a partition he could not see and could not penetrate, that kept him from those realizations of oneness.

We would agree with the one known as G. The one known as A also spoke of feeling walls around his heart, so that he could not be transparent or undefended in his daily life, but rather took care and caution in dealing with a somewhat hostile environment, for so he has found this world to be. And we would say that most entities upon your world find their environment often a hostile one—hostile to their safety, hostile to their comfort and hostile to any sense of true freedom.

The people of your planet have given away their power. For the most part they have lost the conviction that they are priests. They have lost the sense of themselves as magical and powerful entities.

Much has been written within your people's sociology and popular books concerning the feeling in modern society of being cogs in a machine, being less than human somehow. They are asked at every turn, "What is your social security number? What is your driver's license number? What is your passport number? What is your account number?" A name is not unique enough to be satisfactory to the culture which wishes to identify entities carefully.

And so there is less and less reliance upon the quality of a human being and more and more reliance upon that number, that series of integers, that cannot in any way, shape or form express the depth and richness of the personality, character and being of the souls of Planet Earth.

We would suggest to you that it is possible to choose to take back your power; to recover your sense of magic, and to become priests in your daily life once again.

We would wholeheartedly agree that your culture no longer offers you the time to dedicate your life to the seeking of the one infinite Creator on a full-time basis. There are still orders in all religions which offer a limited number of places for people to cast all worldly cares aside and focus on the seeking of the one infinite Creator. But there are very, very few of these places.

And there are even fewer entities who wish to abandon the worldly life and to enter such a restricted and secluded cloister for a lifetime of religious observances and rituals. Your world has become secularized to a great extent. Yet this need not concern the spiritual seeker who wishes to become mature.

The questioner asked about three qualities: time, energy and focus. Certainly most entities do not have time for full-time seeking, in the sense that they do not have time away from the responsibilities of making a living to pay their bills, of tending to the relationships within their family web, or of fulfilling their responsibilities as members of the community and citizens of the world, nation, and region, whether it be a state, a province or a parish.

Yet there remain two aspects to consider besides time. Energy is the second of the three aspects. Certainly, your physical energy is limited. In the worldly sense there is a finite amount of energy and once the physical body has been depleted of its physical energy, it seeks sleep. The exhausted body will spontaneously sleep, given any opportunity, as the one known as Jim noted.

Yet there is an entirely different kind of energy that is not necessarily depleted by the process of earning a living, tending to one's relationships and fulfilling one's responsibilities in the community. That is your vital energy, the energy of spirit, your élan vital, as this instrument likes to call it.

It is certainly easy enough to allow one's vital energy to be sapped. Yet it is not sapped by physical work as is physical energy. It is sapped, my friends, by tolerating cynicism, boredom, and negative thinking within one's thinking processes.

It is extremely easy to become cynical and bored when gazing at an obviously imperfect culture. And such an attitude builds upon itself. If one is not cynical and bored, one may batter oneself against the seemingly impenetrable bastions of power, attempting to change those things which a seeker may feel are not right, not righteous, not appropriate. And many a cynic has been born of youthful attempts to change the world only to find that it was quite resilient and not amenable to change. And so the seeker yields, gives up, and allows a world-weariness to become the usual attitude.

We would point out that this is a choice. There are other choices available that keep the questing spirit alive, enthusiastic and innocent of cynicism.

The one known as Jim said earlier that either one becomes what one hates or what one loves. The energy that brings one towards spiritual material is the energy of seeking to become what one loves. A positive orientation may look at disaster and chaos and yet find hope, stability, and a vector toward place.

Some entities seem to be born with a gift for positivity and cheerfulness. And how such entities are appreciated by those around them! Yet if one were to ask such a seemingly positive entity about his attitude, if he were to become totally honest he would speak of suffering and catalyst that was hard, catalyst that threatened that cheerful attitude. And he would speak of digging deep to find the will and the faith to look beyond the obvious and to seek that energy which is unseen but ever near, that energy of love which is our nature whether we are incarnate, discarnate, of density one, two, three, four, five, six or seven.

This we all have in common. We are made of love. We can access that love through the use of will and faith and this brings us to the third part of the query—focus.

Focus is that which makes up for the lack of time and the on-again-off-again relationships with good and positive energy. In whatever estate one finds oneself, if one can focus and become single minded in the seeking of the one infinite Creator, the world and all that there is in it becomes spiritual. All that one sees becomes sacred. From the least to the most, from the simplest to the most complex, all things speak eloquently of the one infinite Creator. All voices are voices of love.

That focus is the mark of any entity who is able to use the catalyst of Planet Earth in order to achieve spiritual maturity. Whether that entity is a farmer, a mechanic, a factory worker, a teacher, an office person, a technician or any mode of life whatsoever, including being a prisoner or being chained to the sickbed of physical limitation, he can become a priest. Focus is the key, my friends.

We would offer you as an example of this the one known as Jim, who often expresses his feeling of being behindhand in his seeking, for he must spend his physical energy each day doing hard labor. This wears out his body so that it seeks sleep when he relaxes at night. Yet were any of those who know this entity and his work to be asked what their estimate of this entity is, they would express the desire to learn from this entity. They would express the feeling that they perceive this entity to be a spiritual leader. This entity may be riding a mower, yet his very being resonates with the love and the light of the one infinite Creator.

There is no truly spiritualized entity who believes in his own spirituality as being adequate, or who would call himself spiritually mature. That is something that is only part of the self-concept of those who have not yet become mature. The closer towards sainthood a spirit in flesh comes, the more that spirit is aware of the flesh, aware of the imperfection and the impurity, aware of the miles yet to cross to become truly priestly. That does not keep such entities from being priests.

We would suggest to you that it is entirely possible for all entities upon Planet Earth at this time, whatever their station in life are, whatever their schedule, their responsibilities and their restrictions are, to become spiritually mature through the single-minded focus of the desire of the heart on the one infinite Creator.

There are different ways to express that evocation. There are different ways to manifest that single mindedness. Yet all have in common the goal of oneness with the Beloved that is the Creator of all, that great mystery and paradox which we call the one infinite Creator, having no better words to describe the ineffable and indescribable.

And we would suggest one thing more to you, my friends. Were a critical mass of you to take up that single-minded focus on love, your world would be transformed. It would not be necessary for every human being to decide to change their focus for this to happen. Look at the difference made by even one entity that chooses to focus on love. His life becomes sacred to him and he then functions as a priest. Imagine the impact of groups of entities living in the world, yet choosing also to take part in an informal priestly collective, so that love is in the mind and in the heart.

(Side one of tape ends.)

(Carla channeling)

We have spoken before through this instrument concerning the need for a new paradigm, a need for a new way of thinking, for as you think so shall you act. Focus your thoughts on love and see your life become transformed.

It is not that you are transforming anything. It is that you connect with the truth when you focus on love. And that truth carries you where you could not go of your own human will. Your whole concept of self becomes greater and at the same time the personality and the ego become less, as you focus on love and allow the magic of transformation to occur in your life. It will not take you away from your job necessarily, but moving yourself into accord with love will yet transform your world.

We thank the one known as G for this query and would ask at this time if there are follow-up queries to this question before we open the meeting to other questions. We are those of Q'uo.

G: Give me two seconds. I may have a follow-up, please.

We are those of Q'uo, and brother, your time is up. However, we will give you more than two seconds, and therefore we would open this meeting to other questions. Is there another query at this time? We are those of Q'uo.

A: Hi, Q'uo. Thanks for coming tonight. My name is A and I have a question for you. I'll read the question. *(Reads)* "I have a slow and delicate gastrointestinal tract which, together with tension elsewhere in my body, prevents me from sleeping restoratively. Are there spiritual principles that might be helpful for me to think about?

We are those of Q'uo and are aware of your query, my brother. We would note, my brother, that every seeming condition and limitation that would be interpreted as negative has a gift in its hands.

The nature of a wanderer is often sensitive and delicate due to the fact that the spirit comes from elsewhere, where the wiring of the physical vehicle is different. Consequently, the ability to incarnate fully and enjoy the life of third density humanity is limited. Higher-density wiring does not do well in third density. Consequently there is the need to find ways to incarnate more and more into the body and to come to love, appreciate and honor the body.

The challenge of a wanderer then, once he has awakened, is to move through those feelings of dismay and distaste at the necessities of the world. For some it is not particularly pleasant even to eat, to drink or to fulfill bodily functions. For there is the feeling that it should be much simpler and gentler and easier a place than it is. The heavy chemical body requires a good deal of patience and gentleness when the spirit inhabiting it is not comfortable within its own skin; not "a happy camper" as this instrument would say.

Rather, it feels as though one is in prison, looking out through the bars that flesh creates. And one cannot escape the prison of flesh within incarnation. One is trapped for a lifetime, or so it feels to the wanderer. We would suggest, my brother, that it may help you to find ways to reconnect with the earth-energy of this planet which has given you life within this incarnation.

The one known as G was speaking of sitting on a rock in a wilderness forest, letting the sun beat down on him and gradually becoming aware that he was a mythological figure in a story of dawning awareness. Suddenly, he began to hear the voices in the wind, the spiritual nature of embrace and caress that was implicit in the sun, and the thrusting earthiness of the rock which gave him a platform on which to sit within this amazing world which you call the earth life.

As he focused in and focused in some more, suddenly, he broke through those glass barriers that kept him from his own inner heart.

You and many, many others have these barriers that you cannot see. And yet are there. They keep you safe. They keep you defended. But in terms of becoming comfortable within your body, they do not aid. For some, the walking in nature may help to ground and open the doors of spirit within you that create a sense of belonging to this planet, belonging to this earth, of being a part of Gaia. Perhaps that is the door for you, my brother, to a more comfortable physical existence.

There are many other ways of grounding the self. This instrument does this through gardening, which puts her hands physically on the earth, and by a mental practice of feeling down into the earth beneath her chair. It is far away from her chair physically, but the energy of the earth is immediately there if she focuses upon it. Again, it is a matter of focus. It is possible that the simple act of remembering to ground yourself down from wherever you are sitting or standing when you work will aid you in becoming more fully incarnate within your body and therefore making you feel more relaxed, confident and self-assured. For you truly do belong to your Mother, the Earth. You are a child of the Earth And your physical body is greatly helped by this embracing of earth-energy.

May we ask if there is a follow up to this query, my brother?

A: Yes. This is in the same vein. *(Reads)* "I'm experiencing tension, bursitis and tendinosis in my shoulders. Are there spiritual principles that may be helpful for me to think about in addition to what you've already said, or does what you've already said cover that question too?"

We are Q'uo, and are aware of your query, my brother. In a way, my brother, we have already spoken to this in terms of spiritual principles, but perhaps it may help to say it in a slightly different way.

We would repeat, however, the basic tenet. That is that limitations and seeming difficulties offer gifts. Often the gift is to begin to think about and sense into the situation that you are experiencing. The connection between the mind and the body is very close and it is not jejune[137] to connect feelings in the body with the physical things that may cause those feelings. For instance, Atlas carried the world on his shoulders in mythology, and undoubtedly he would have had the conditions that you experience, were he to be human and were he to be speaking of the burden of carrying the world.

When there is a situation within part of the body that would suggest that it comes from carrying too much, then it is reasonable to consider the possibility that in some way you have unhealed feelings of being asked to carry too much. Therefore you are then able to begin to work with those feelings, to look into them, to sit with them, and to begin to penetrate layers of fear and anxiety that may keep you from seeing the pattern of your incarnation.

Sometimes entities come into an incarnation with a pattern of incarnation in mind. And if the pattern is not being fully completed, there may be a series of physical reminders that pull the mind and the feelings back and ask of that entity to respond to this limitation that is sensed. It may be fruitful to consider what such a wake-up call might be about.

You are already perfect, my brother. We are not suggesting that you change in order to feel better. We are suggesting that such feelings may be a signal to you in your inner life that the pattern of your incarnation may be considered in a way that would be helpful.

Gaze back over the life as a whole and ask the self when these limitations come into play the most, and when they are least in sight as far as needing to be handled. And perhaps that pattern may come clear so that you can cooperate with that incarnational pattern and help your body, your mind and your spirit to come into a place that is more comfortable for you.

May we answer you further, my brother? We are those of Q'uo.

A: Yes, Q'uo. Here's another question in the same vein. *(Reads)* "I'm frustrated by my apparent inability to still my mind and to meditate. It makes sense to me that meditation is the basis for much spiritual development. Are there spiritual principles that might be helpful for me to think about?"

We are those of Q'uo, and are aware of your query, my brother. The habit of meditation is, like any other habit, one which is learned through repetition. There is often the concept of meditation as being a complete blanking out of the mind and a resting in heavenly bliss. Yet we would say to you, my brother, that you will also have a fruitful and helpful meditation spending your time in silence, watching you thoughts arise and allowing them to fall, watching them arise and allowing them to fall away, watching them arise and allowing them once again, and once again, to fall away.

---

[137] To be jejune is to be childish, juvenile or immature.

That may be your experience of meditation. That may be your experience of meditation for many years. That does not mean that that is what is occurring in meditation on a deeper level. It means that you have a characteristically active and restless mind and therefore it may take years and years for you to be able to do more on the surface than allow the silence to continue while you interrupt that silence and let it fall away, interrupt and let it fall, interrupt and let it fall.

The seeming turbulence of the surface of the mind does not in any way keep your deeper mind from realizing your intention to focus your will upon the seeking of the communication that is in the silence. And bolstered by this awareness of your intention and the setting of your will, your deeper self will use that meditation time just as it would if your outer experience were completely peaceful.

However, there is another type of repetition which may aid you in achieving silence within and that is that basic practice which the one known as G was discussing in the study group's conversation which preceded this channeling.

Placing something positive for the mind to use as a focus is sometimes very helpful to the meditator. That something may be as simple as seeing your breath move into your body and move out of your body, seeing it move into your body with white light, bringing you new energy, and seeing it move out of your body, blowing away all that is used up and unneeded from your energy field.

The mantra is very useful in this regard for many. Whether it is the name of the Creator or any meaningful phrase, the constant repetition of this God-name or phrase replaces the thoughts that arise and fall away, arise and fall away. You are directing your intention. You are directing your attention. Intention becomes attention and attention becomes bliss.

May we answer you further, my brother? We are those of Q'uo.

A: Yes, Q'uo. I profane God's name regularly in my thoughts. I also have obscene, sadistic and violent thoughts that get mixed into any kind of thinking that I do, including trying to focus or meditation. Are there any spiritual principles that might be helpful for me to think about?

We are those of Q'uo, and are aware of your query. We shall comment.

Thoughts are things in the metaphysical world. The way thoughts make you feel are also things in the metaphysical world. As you think, so you are.

It is your choice as to how you wish to conduct your thoughts. You have learned to conduct them in a certain way and you have noted that you have made these choices. You may also choose to change your habitual patterns of thought so that the energies, rather than being constricting, tightening and tensing, become expansive, generous, loving and joyful.

It may feel, at first, when you substitute an expansive thought for a constrictive thought, that you are faking it. And yet we say to you, my brother, this is an illusion. And in this illusion you are playing with energy. That energy, as it happens within this illusion, penetrates down into physical form and becomes manifested as a physical body and a physical experience. Yet it begins with thought.

May we have a final query at this time? We are those of Q'uo.

A: Yes, please. I've become rather passionate about non-violent communication, a process developed by Marshall Rosenberg.[138] Are there any spiritual principles that might be helpful for me to think about?

We are those of Q'uo, and are aware of your query. We would say to you in this regard that it is well to consider with great passion and enjoyment those thoughts that resonate to you and to incorporate them in your life. In such a way, you are able to interiorize the teachings of others; to make them your own and to begin to become those values and those principles that you most admire.

We are those of Q'uo. We thank each of you for the beauty of your auras and essences and for your dedication in taking this time apart from your life simply to seek the truth in company with those who also have every fiber of their beings pointed towards the great mystery and paradox that is the one infinite Creator, that one great original Thought of love.

We leave you in that love and in that light which is the manifestation of love. We leave you in the house

---

[138] Marshall B. Rosenberg, *Non-Violent Communication: a Language of Life*: Del Mar, CA, Puddledancer Press, c1999.

of the one infinite Creator. We are known to you as the principle of Q'uo. Adonai. Adonai vasu. ✺

L/L Research

L/L Research is a subsidiary of Rock Creek Research & Development Laboratories, Inc.

P.O. Box 5195
Louisville, KY 40255-0195

www.llresearch.org

Rock Creek is a non-profit corporation dedicated to discovering and sharing information which may aid in the spiritual evolution of humankind.

ABOUT THE CONTENTS OF THIS TRANSCRIPT: This telepathic channeling has been taken from transcriptions of the weekly study and meditation meetings of the Rock Creek Research & Development Laboratories and L/L Research. It is offered in the hope that it may be useful to you. As the Confederation entities always make a point of saying, please use your discrimination and judgment in assessing this material. If something rings true to you, fine. If something does not resonate, please leave it behind, for neither we nor those of the Confederation would wish to be a stumbling block for any.

© 2009 L/L Research

Saturday Meditation
April 26, 2008

Group question: The question this evening is, "Would you discuss the spiritual principles behind the creative process of the arts? From a spiritual perspective, what are some of the differences in the creative process between poets, novelists, sculptors, painters, composers, songwriters, actors and playwrights?

(Carla channeling)

We are those known to you as the principle of Q'uo. Greetings in the love and in the light of the one infinite Creator, in whose service we come to you this day. Thank you for calling us to your circle of seeking. It is a great privilege to be called. We shall do our best to share with you some of our thoughts upon this most interesting subject of the spiritual principles behind the creative process.

As always, we ask each who reads or listens to this material to retain your keen sense of discrimination, so that you take that which is useful to you from this conversation and leave the rest behind. We would be most grateful for you to do that, as it allows us to speak freely without being concerned that we may infringe upon your free will or disturb your process.

The spiritual principle behind the creative process is that each entity is the Creator. Each entity has the innate ability to create things that never were and to think thoughts that have never been thought. Each entity upon Planet Earth in third density is equipped with all of the tools and resources for creativity.

You may ask, then, "Why does not everyone create?"

The challenge of being creative is to retain or produce a way of seeing and perceiving that is original to the Creator. Your culture does not encourage original thought. Your culture does not encourage inner-directed behavior and attitudes. Your culture has a consensus reality[139] which is endlessly materialistic. It is as though, with a sea all around you, your culture stands upon a tiny island and says, "This is the world. Do not go to the sea. Do not dive deep in unknown waters. Here in this garden where there is food to eat and work to do, live your life. Question nothing, accept authority, and make no waves. Do not paddle at the shores of the unknown."

The culture and its consensus reality, in our point of view, is the illusion and the water, the reality. The creation of the small island is the pulling together of some gross physical matter upon which to stand and it is built by fear.

At each instant of each of your lives upon planet Earth, infinity and eternity are as close to you as your breath; as near as your heartbeat. Each moment upon this seemingly solid earth and its seemingly

---

[139] Consensus reality is a phrase which asks the question, "What is real?" and answers it by stating that what we agree is real, is real. The film *The Matrix* is about consensus reality, for instance. The implication is that consensus reality may bear little resemblance to reality, which is the inference which is intended by the Q'uo's use of the term.

mundane concerns can open up in an instant to reveal the stunning complexity, paradox and mystery of the infinity of the moment. Land falls away and the waters invite, encourage and attract the seeking heart to escape the island of consensus reality and plunge into the waters of the noumenal[140], the unknown, and the wondrous.

It is to be noted that the artistic impulse exists in some way, shape or form in each person. However, in some cases, the environment of childhood is such that there is too much fear built into knowing new things to make it possible for an entity to explore his creative impulse.

In other cases, an entity may have great appreciation and delight in portions of the creative process and yet be unable, for lack of native talent, to manifest that wonderful artistic vision that is in his heart and in his soul.

There is a certain percentage of your peoples, many of them being wanderers, whose nature is such and whose preincarnative choices of talents are such as to support the creative process. Artists and creators of what this instrument would call "intellectual properties" are not a different breed than other human beings upon planet Earth. They are those whose gifts include a sensitivity to beauty which calls them away from the island and into the water.

We use this metaphor because the difference between that which is non-magical and that which is magical, or that which is non-creative and that which is creative, is the flatness and the two-dimensionality, shall we say, of the earth at the feet, and the figure walking across the earth at a 90-degree angle to it at all times. There is no roundness. The life is shaped in squares.

In the water, if the water separates out, every drop of water is a globe. It is a circular universe, appropriate to the circular energies of time/space and metaphysical things.

We would switch to a different metaphor now in talking about the gateway to intelligent infinity, for the second part of your query, my brother, has to do with possible differences between various types of artists and creators.

We would distinguish at the beginning of this conversation between artists and those entities who are moving from an intellectual perspective and are not involved in the artistic impulse but rather have found that the gifts produced by him are well accepted and can offer him a good living. We are talking about those with the spontaneous and irresistible urge to create. Those who are playing a role and seeing artistic production as a kind of career or work limit themselves by remaining within the lower chakras in their expression of material offered by them, or to them if they are singers or actors.

We speak, as we believe you intended us to speak, strictly of those artists who must express that which is within them and who are irresistibly drawn to perform and to share their gifts. Whether or not such entities would think of offering their gifts in a spiritual sense, it is, indeed, a spiritual exercise by its very definition. For in order to make contact with the creative impulse, the entity must move into the open heart or green-ray chakra and thereby move upwards into the ray of communication, the blue ray, and the ray of faith, indigo ray, and thenceforth to move into the violet ray and the gateway to intelligent infinity.

An artist is moving his attention into a place where he is able to draw from beyond that gateway the inspiration and information needed in order to be able to express the visions that he has seen and the perceptions he has garnered in his own way. He is as the treasure hunter who finds treasure and then must share it.

This instrument is fond of a musician known as Willie[141]. This singer and songwriter was once asked how he created so many beautiful melodies. The one known as Willie said, "There are melodies moving through the air at all times. It is just a matter of picking one out of the air and putting words to it." This entity was accurate. The infinity of possibilities flows through that gateway to those who access it at all times. There is no end to the creative impulse.

We would note that the great and universal difficulty which artistic entities face is that they become overly fond of remaining in the chakras we have just

---

[140] In the philosophy of Kant, the noumenon is defined as "an object as it is in itself, independent of the mind, as opposed to a phenomenon. It is also called a thing-in-itself." Kant's term, in German is "ding an sicht." So the noumenal is that which has a real existence apart from our minds. Again, the inference is that consensus reality is not as real as true reality apart from our minds.

[141] Willie Nelson.

mentioned—the heart chakra, the throat chakra, the brow chakra, and the gateway chakra. They prefer to remain completely in the upper chakras and not to take care of or honor the lower chakras. Therefore they become untethered to the earth, shall we say. They are not grounded into their lives and their incarnations.

This is the temptation for those who love beautiful things, not realizing that beauty begins with the stench of birth, the blood, the wailing, the sharp light, and the terror. The creative process must move down, daily and consciously, into those very beginnings of life, into red ray with its survival and sexuality, into orange ray and yellow ray with its relationships, and work with the entire energy body in order to have the strength and the sheer energy flowing through the energy body in order to make the most of the spiritual gifts of creativity while not destroying the body, the emotions, or the mind, quickly or gradually, because of inattention to the lower chakras and their issues and concerns.

Various artists have chosen before incarnation to bring with them into life various creative gifts. One may sing. Another may be a wonderful actor. One may write. Another may paint. The differences between the different kinds of artistry have to do with the personality or character of the individual who is striving to express artistic feelings and concepts.

Some there are who like to remain within the heart and are expressing from the heart. These, in many cases, are performers. Those who create music, shall we say, or create operas or ballets, move from the heart chakra.

Others there are who have the pronounced blue ray. Those with this particular character will find it irresistible to attempt to communicate in new ways and many of these are writers, playwrights, poets and inspired teachers, for teaching is, in itself, an art form.

Many there are whose character and personality are such that they are drawn to the realms of faith, will and magic. A mixture of these energies is unique to each artist and therefore the mode or manifestation of that art within him will also be unique. Certainly too, an artist may move in his life through various phases in which he is coming from the heart or the desire to communicate or from the desire to express the magic of life. But these are the waters in which the artist plays.

We ask if there is another query, my brother? We are those of Q'uo.

Jim: Are numbers, ratios and arbitrary rates a helpful spiritual lens for understanding the creative process and the creative product?

We are those of Q'uo, and are aware of your query, my brother. Indeed, mathematics and ratios are intrinsic and absolutely necessary to the creative process and if an artist is having difficulty focusing, it may be very helpful for such an entity to work with mathematics, especially sacred geometry.

If one looks at language itself, it is sacred geometry. Each letter in a word has a certain energy. Each word, made up of certain letters, has a certain energy. The study of not just language but alphabets and symbols is endlessly fascinating and it can be seen that through the doorway of letters and words an infinite amount of energy may flow. Such tools are necessary for the artist.

In music as well, it may easily be seen that there is a series of mathematical ratios betwixt the twelve tones of the western scale. There are mathematical ratios betwixt various chords, duads and triads within that system of octaves which musicians use to create the beauty of a melody and the richness of harmonization and symphony.

May we ask if there is another query, my brother?

Jim: In order to bring us full-circle, would you discuss the spiritual principles behind the attraction of art, literature and theater for non-artists and the population in general from a spiritual perspective, being sensitive to how different types of art may uniquely tweak the creative process? How does art affect us?"

We are those of Q'uo, and are aware of your query, my brother. As we said previously, all entities are creators but not all entities are drawn to express their creativity. They are solidly attached to their little island of consensus reality. They want the ground firm beneath them and the sky above. They wish their feet not to sink into the unknown.

And yet, that creative impulse dwells within all. It is part of being part of the Creator. Each entity is a sub-creator. Each entity has magical ability. Each entity through faith and will can change his world.

But there is such a deep acceptance of consensus reality in many that there is no potential outlet for creative expression in the sense of original creativity, although you may see the creative impulse moving through any entity's life in a collection of Barbie Dolls arranged just so, or a beautifully decorated Christmas tree, or meals that are prepared with love, or children that are raised with genius.

Many people, left to themselves, will not enter into intellectual creations, shall we say. They will not let go of the box in which their lives are bound, for they feel safe there. Yet, how wonderful it is to be able to step into a theater or a movie house, an opera house or a place where a ballet is being offered and to sit in the audience and let the performers take you into the water! They aren't steering the boat but they can appreciate the trip. And they know that this delicious dose of mystery and paradox will end and they will be back safely upon the shores of their island once again.

It can be thought of—and this is a shallow statement but helpful, perhaps—as a left brain/right brain difference, saying that the left brain has to do with living on the island and making good use of time within the box and the right brain then goes begging and does not have its needs fulfilled. It is not exercised. It lies dormant. Art, therefore, can take one out upon the water and lift that dormancy into activity. And suddenly the right brain is working. It feels very good. It makes the attendee or the appreciator of art feel as though he is also creative. It is contagious.

Looked at another way, an artist could be described as an entity who is able to compress the vastness of human experience into an offering small enough to view as a whole. In this compression into image, metaphor, melody and so forth comes an intensification of power, so that an artist may punch through fear and bring the attendee or the audience into a place of freedom or love.

The artist has a tendency to tell the truth that has either escaped the multitudes around him or has become too dreadful to contemplate and therefore is ignored. Further, an artist is able to bring a people, a nation, a world through the process of grief and sorrow by creating beauty within that grief and sorrow and despair.

May we answer you further, my brother?

Jim: Finally, from a spiritual perspective, what is the significance of the rise in interest in creativity in almost every cultural domain?

We are those of Q'uo, and are aware of your query, my brother. Perhaps you have heard the expression, "There is something in the air." "Spring is in the air." "Christmas is in the air." At this time, my brother the New Age is in the air. The veil rends. The gateway to intelligent infinity is more easily entered. Vibrations of truth are bombarding planet Earth at this time. Waves and waves of clarity and true perception are interpenetrating with the third-density vibration of consensus reality in a way that cannot be ignored.

If an entity is deeply asleep, he may simply feel these waves of energy as experiencing that things are getting more difficult and he must shut down more and more and focus on just surviving. This is due to the fact that he has not yet welcomed himself, gotten to know himself, come to accept himself, and finally seen the Creator within himself. However, every entity upon planet Earth today is capable of breaking through to a standpoint from which these energies are used in a positive way.

It takes tremendous courage to open up to these crashing waves of perception and say, "I'm in for the ride. I will use this energy to see more deeply into myself, to accept myself more fully, to love myself more dearly, to see the Creator within me, and honor that spark of Godhead."

These are wondrous times. For your people approach graduation day, shall we say, that point after which each death from life on planet Earth shall be entirely open to the possibility of moving forward into fourth density. And not only is the planet and the solar system as a whole receiving these incredible waves of energy signaling the end of third density and the beginning of the dawning of a new age of fourth density, but also at this time there is tremendous interest in helping those of planet Earth who wish to move forward in a service-to-others manner to succeed.

So the inner planes are rich with those who come to experience this time of shift with the incarnate entities of planet Earth. Angelic entities are everywhere. Nature devas and nature spirits are everywhere, all wanting to play, to sing, to dance with you, with each, with all, inviting each to dance this dance into the sun, into the light, into the dawning of the new day.

We, ourselves, are among those who have been drawn to your planet at this time so that we may in our humble and modest way offer ourselves to those who might find our information useful or helpful.

You may expect to see more and more of the artistic impulse within the children of your planet as they are born within the very specific confines of entities who shall live a part of their lives in fourth density. They are wired for both third density and fourth density within their DNA. Consequently, they can accept far more creative information. For them the veil is much thinner.

At this time we would ask if there are any follow-up queries to this initial series of questions? Is there another query from the one known as A? We are the ones known as Q'uo.

A: Yes, Q'uo. Would you discuss the relationship between empathy and the creative process?

We are aware of your query, my brother. There is a profound difference between empathy or the ability to feel fellow-feeling for another entity and the individual creative process. You might see it as the difference between a horizontal action and a vertical action.

When an entity is so open-hearted that he is able to put himself into another's shoes and to walk a mile in his shoes, he has indeed performed a creative act. He has accepted his brother as himself. He has taken on his burdens. He has experienced that which he could never experience within his own individual life. This indicates a magical and loving personality with a spiritual maturity that is unique to those who have awakened and who have become able to be magical persons.

Yet that exchange of energy in empathy is horizontal. It is from person to person. Each of the two offers the dynamic of the Creator between them.

(Side one of tape ends.)

(Carla channeling)

However, the Creator is not something for which the empathic person is reaching. Empathy is person-to-person, eye-to-eye and heart-to-heart.

In the creative process of an artist who is working with his imagination, there is a vertical energy where the artist is opening to higher energies, higher perceptions, and transformative and magical nuances that he senses and then goes hunting for, just as we said, like a treasure hunt. This is a vertical energy. It is that which moves one very decisively out of the box of consensus reality and into that awareness that the ground upon which you stand is merely an illusion and that in truth, there is infinity below and infinity above and eternity on both sides.

May we answer you further, my brother? We are those of Q'uo.

A: Yes, Q'uo, you mentioned that *(inaudible)*.

We are those of Q'uo, and are aware of your query, my brother. An artist's sense of esthetics is as unique as his personality. An artist tends to create from perceptions that make something new of the familiar and take that which is known into places where it becomes something unknown.

This instrument, to give one example, has recently seen the work of an artist who takes everyday objects such as plastic water bottles and creates photographs that have a surface beauty to them but which also have the deepest expression of concern for planet Earth. "Look at all these water bottles," the artist says with his photo. "Look at this sea of water bottles that we, as a nation, have used and discarded in just one day." A vast sea of transparent bottles fills the picture frame to frame, and beneath the undulating waves of crystalline beauty there lies the message.

To move further back for another example, in a time of horror and war, the one known as Brueghel[142] painted what he saw and to this day entities are able to look at that painting and have an immediate insight into the nature of human suffering.

It is not that dark things, in and of themselves, are beautiful, any more than it is that positive or light things are in and of themselves beautiful. It is the perception that the flat postcard of vision can explode into an infinity of concepts that drives beauty.

May we answer you further, my brother?

A: *(Inaudible)*.

---

[142] Pieter Brueghel was a Flemish artist of the 16th century. Some of his canvases, such as "Massacre of the Innocents," "Fall of the Rebel Angels," and "Triumph of Death" work with dark subjects yet are beautiful paintings.

We are those of Q'uo, and are aware of your query, my brother. We believe you are already aware that this is part of your active, personal process at this time. We would not wish to do your work for you. For there is great joy and discovery awaiting you as you move through your process on your own. We can only say to you that your efforts are positive and loving and we wish you every good fortune with them.

Is there a final query at this time? We are those of Q'uo.

R: In looking at the nature of negative polarity and karma, there is the assumption that when one polarizes in the negative sense, for example, as a slave master, then the karma would draw to him the opposite experience of being the slave. When you are in the position of one who suffers and is on the receiving end, will you still polarize in a negative way?" Could you comment on this question?

We are those of Q'uo, and are aware of your query, my brother. It is entirely possible and quite probable that an entity, as you say, on the receiving end of power; that is, being powerless, can polarize very greatly towards the negative.

If you think about the nature of the negative polarity, the negative polarity has to do with seeing all others as objects to be used and to feeling of oneself that one is the king of creation. When such an entity, with this basic turn of mind, is in a position of powerlessness, he is free to spend the entire incarnation honing the edge of his rage. He can use every slight, every insult, in order to make himself more finely sharp as an axe-blade in his distain and distaste for all but himself.

And talking of negative polarity metaphysically speaking, you are not looking so much at the outer estate as you are looking at the possibilities of employing the path-that-is-not. Employing the path-that-is-not means denying that you and the other are one. Whether a negatively polarized entity is on top or on the bottom in terms of the estate he enjoys in society, he is equally capable of honing the edge of his anger and his separation from all others.

We are those of Q'uo, and are aware that the energy of this instrument is waning. We would at this time, therefore, with great reluctance say, as did Romeo, "Parting is such sweet sorrow."[143] We leave you, as we found you, in the love and in the light of the one infinite Creator. Adonai. Adonai. ☙

---

[143] This is Juliet's line in Act 2, Scene 2, Line 184 of *Romeo and Juliet* by William Shakespeare. The couplet ending the scene goes: *"Good night, good night! Parting is such sweet sorrow, That I shall say good night till it be morrow."*

L/L Research

Channeling Intensive 1 - Session 14 - Channeling Circle 3
May 4, 2008

(Carla channeling)

We greet you with a great joy in the love and in the light of the one infinite Creator. We of Laitos are most pleased to be called to your circle of seeking and to work with each of you who desires to become a more open channel for the love and the light of the one infinite Creator.

As we move around the circle to each of you, we shall attempt to make our conditioning vibration apparent to each of you. Although we realize that each has some concerns or apprehensions about being able to develop as an instrument, we do assure each of you that, as this instrument has often said, each of you has the innate ability to receive our thoughts. It is far more a matter of how long it takes each entity to develop this ability to receive and to transmit our thoughts than any question of it being impossible.

When we work with the newer channels, it is our tendency to move into the realm of storytelling, for we find that the exercise of telling a story has more of the ability to feel comfortable to the newer channels and not to present the difficulties that might arise if there was simply a discussion of a point of our philosophy, which you may have heard many times before.

With storytelling, on the other hand, each story is a new one. So there is more of a feeling of confidence that can be created as the channel is passed from person to person, in that the content of the story is not known beforehand. Therefore, it will be fresh and new to the channel, thus giving the channel far less of a reason to doubt himself or herself.

As always, we would say that if there is any thought which we offer in this channeling circle that troubles any of you, we would ask you to leave it behind without a second thought. For we appreciate your right to complete free will and would not wish to trespass upon that.

We give this instrument the picture of a land of heavenly light. The dark clouds come up and obscure the light. It is as if a great cloud had passed over the sun and for the first time, darkness descended upon this land. The inhabitants of the land, being farmers and humble people, could not comprehend this darkness, as theirs had been a land of perpetual daylight. They wondered to themselves whether this was the end of the world; whether they might now be facing their extinction.

In due time, perhaps not more than an hour or two, the cloud passed. The lightness came back in full splendor. And yet the people were deeply concerned and puzzled. What had happened? What was this thing called darkness? As one, they turned to the wisest among them whom, everyone called Father, and they said, "Father, what is the meaning of darkness?"

We would now transfer this contact to the one known as R. We are those of Laitos.

(R channeling)

We are those of Laitos. The darkness fell on the land …

(Pause)

(Carla channeling)

We are those of Laitos and are again with this instrument. We thank the one known as R for the pleasure of working with his instrument.

We continue with our story. The one known as Father smiled upon his people and said, "I have heard in *The Book of the Ages* of a time when darkness was as normal as light, when they had not simply a resting time, but a night time. Every time there was daylight, then there followed a period of night when there was no light except that which was reflected from what they called their moon."

One of the villagers said, "Then, Father, what is the meaning of the night for us?"

This time we would transfer this contact to the one known as S. We are those of Laitos.

(S channeling)

We are those of Laitos and we are with this instrument.

Father was silent for a moment and then spoke with gravity and said, "Just as the silence has preceded these words I speak to you now, so the darkness precedes the light. It is only when we are in the light that we understand that there is darkness too. The darkness comes to us that we have not had for many, many lifetimes now. And we have grown so exclusively used to the light that we have come to forget even that there is something called the dark.

Yet it is not that the darkness is wrong. It is simply that we have been experiencing a very, very long period of light which we may now call day. It is likely that we will have future experiences again of the dark. It is not for us to be afraid, but to regard this as an opportunity."

We will now pass this …

(L channeling)

We are those of Laitos. Among the people surrounding the Father and asking questions of this phenomenon was a young maiden whose memory became stirred by the discussion of the cycle of light and darkness. She seemed to remember something akin to a dream, but which seemed at the same time to be a distant reality, of floating in what is the form of a nebulous cloud, far removed from her beloved planet and far larger and greater than her present form, where she was pulled and tugged by the descent of darkness into a realm which she did not know.

Yet there was a strong response to this dark calling, which somehow enabled her to travel in consciousness; indeed, more than consciousness, to that place of darkness. Meanwhile she remained in the heavenly realms. The calling and the activity of that place of darkness became a focus of interest in her realm of light. There became a manifestation of a different reality which took on a life of its own, as if it was now living in two places at once.

There was a connection to the light from this dark place of the planet which experienced cycles. All the while there was a connection, a beam of light of consciousness, of spirit of the larger entity to that smaller one.

And as the Father spoke of these cycles of light and dark, and as the memory banks were stirred in the young maiden, she began to become aware of the new matter of this connection and this larger being.

We now pass this contact to the one known as J. We are those of Laitos.

(J channeling)

We are those known to you as those of Laitos. The young maiden, remembering her experiences among the clouds and her feeling of being drawn to this sphere of darkness, remembered her experiences on the plane of darkness. She realized that through her experience of these dark planes, she had something to teach those who were in attendance now. So she gathered the courage to speak of her experiences so that she could calm the fears of those who were fearful amongst the group that was gathered about her.

She recalled that when she was in that place and that time, the darkness had called to her to come into a fuller realization, into a fuller embodiment. She remembered the time that she spent upon this dark planet and the experiences that she had there, when she realized that she was part of the light and that she was on the planet to bring that lightness to the world. So she spoke of her experiences on that world.

We are those of Laitos and we pass this connection on to the one known as M. We are those of Laitos.

(M channeling)

We are those of Laitos. She explained to the crowd in another way the meaning and bent over to a beautiful flower. She picked it as she stood in the crowd. A frightful insect was clicking its grumbling song in the center of this beautiful flower, which was composed of red, yellow and rose, the lower chakra colors.

And everyone was focused on this insect which they had not expected to be in the beautiful flower. And the flower began to engulf the insect. The insect got swallowed up and engulfed in the flower. The flower closed up. Then it was as if a new bud and insect had opened up and spread again in all of its beauty and glory. And the maiden said, "Just as the flower has engulfed the insect that you started to fear, the darkness is part of us, but our light is greater and we can engulf the darkness with our light/love and our love/light and become closer to the Creator.

We pass this contact on …

(Pause)

(Carla channeling)

We are those of Laitos and are with this instrument. We greet each again in love and in light.

So as the maiden shared her flowers, there came to Father's face a smile. "Dear ones," he said, "by your preference and long-standing excellence, you earned for yourselves the right to experience unending light, everlasting sunshine and eternal day. You were offered this because you wished it. Yet, it is so that during this generation's long day, you have not moved forward. You have remained upon a happy plateau. The seeds of darkness slept within your group until the light called to the darkness and the darkness cleaved unto the light.

The energies of creativity and growth seem as though they would grow far better in sunlight than in the nighttime. And yet, it is the darkness of soil that offers fertilizer and deep, sweet food to the seeds that burst forth into the daylight. It is in the darkness of your own hearts, interior, shadowed and private, that you experience the depths of emotion and choose to seek the one infinite Creator. And while the daylight has been a blessing, perhaps, my children, you shall begin to hunger for the darkness as well.

We would transfer this contact to the one known as R. We are those of Laitos.

(R channeling)

We are those of Laitos. We are having difficulty with this instrument.

(Carla channeling)

We are those of Laitos and are again with this instrument. We thank the one known as R for moving ahead with the contact and speaking our identity. We assure the one known as R that with repetition, the sensations which block full awareness of our concepts shall become less and less. We thank the one known as R for offering himself to our service. We would transfer this contact to the one known as S. We are known to you as Laitos.

(S channeling)

We are Laitos and are here with this instrument.

The maiden reflected on these things that she has been told and that more importantly, had began to dawn on her as if they were memories from times of old And as she reflected, a change began to come over her countenance. The innocence of youth seemed to acquire a new aspect and she began to seem older and wiser—in this capacity even as old and as wise as old Father himself. Then she proposed to those who had gathered around that the time had come for a great adventure.

Taking the flower she had in her hand, she strewed the petals, which were caught up by a gust of wind and seemed to multiply and form into an image of a great ship. The lower part of this ship was made of the roots which had belonged to the flower. She invited all of those who would come to enter into the ship, which would carry them into a land where once again light and darkness could be experienced together.

We pass this contact to the one known as L.

(L channeling)

We are those of Laitos. We are now with this instrument.

The ship that was formed was a ship of consciousness. And as the maiden and the others who were ready for the adventure entered the ship, they entered with an awareness and with a new respect for the cycle of light and dark and with the new intention to use and master the darkness and, at the same time, consciously to use and to master the light.

As they moved forward with this intention, they called to themselves a greater awareness of the various powers that they incorporated in order to blend both darkness and light into catalyst for their greater growth and glory and also for their beloved planet.

We now transfer this contact to J. We are those of Laitos.

(J channeling)

We are those known as Laitos. The young maiden, feeling emboldened by her understanding of times past from the deep crevices of her being, began to speak to those who had accompanied her in this great metaphorical ship about a journey into the past or into the alternate realities that had the light and the dark.

She remembered that when she was floating among the clouds that she so loved the light! And yet, the dark was different and so she was curious about it. So she came to understand that which she wished to communicate to those that were with her. And this was that there was nothing to fear. Because there was some fear among the group to begin with. She wished to show them that the light, even though it was most powerful and glorious, had its opposite, which was as glorious and powerful. And there was nothing to fear.

She said, "Just remember that there is new information, new experience, new learning coming in this contrast of light and dark." She saw this new occurrence in the experience of those of her world as an opportunity to appreciate the contrast, to appreciate the light for what it was. They had lost that in that long period of being only in the light, so in this contrast then they could come to appreciate the light more. They could come to appreciate what it was they had in the light alone through the contrast of the darkness that was now upon them.

With the promise that the darkness would return, there was some anticipation of that which they might experience in this darkness. With her experience and her reassurance, then the group began to understand that there were new possibilities awaiting for them in this darkness from whence it would come. And some grew eager at the opportunity to experience the darkness once again.

So it was then with that the maiden became much more deeply grounded in her being and her wisdom began to flow. Her confidence and understanding flowed through her effortlessly, and much joy came to her countenance as she was able to relate and to experience these changes once again.

We now pass this contact on to the one known as M. We are those who answer as Laitos.

(M channeling)

We are those known as Laitos. The community to which the maiden belonged anticipated the fear of the darkness, almost looking forward to it, as if it was another opportunity. The understanding of the young maiden and old Father had helped them. But the anticipation was still tempered with the fear that they would be gripped by the darkness. And they asked the young maiden, "What should we do if the darkness is too great?" Their fear was that the darkness was too much and that the ending would come with the darkness again.

The young maiden said, "There is both the darkness and the light. And what was light becomes darkness, and then light again. You start out with the darkness and the dark clouds, but you can always look above them." And she pointed to the distant horizon.

(Side one of tape ends.)

(M channeling)

And she said, "See. Look at those clouds coming. It is okay. Accept your fear, but love your fear and look above it. Look above it. You can always look above the clouds. You can always look upward towards the light. Look above the clouds."

And everyone did. And above the clouds was a beautiful, tall castle that grew so high up in the sky that they couldn't see the top of it. This uplifted the community. And with that experience they understood that experiencing fear and darkness helps you climb higher, to heights you wouldn't have been able to scale without the dark clouds. You would never have thought to look higher.

We now pass this contact on.

(Carla channeling)

We are those of Laitos and we are again with this instrument.

The maiden gazed with understanding into the eyes of Father. Father nodded an affirmation to her. He held out his hand and she took it. And together they began to ascend the steps of the castle. As she went, she wrapped the petals of her ship about her, gleaming petals of light. As he followed her, hand-in-hand, he wrapped himself in the roots that signified darkness and fertility and growth. And together they danced to the light through the darkness, to the very peak of the castle.

And at the end of their dance, the darkness that lay between the land and the peak of the castle wrapped itself about the light as a lover. And the light in turn wrapped itself about the darkness in response. And in a great swirl of light and dark, those in the heavenly land of light were brought back to where they had begun.

And as the dance of light and dark was done, the maiden and Father said, "Now, would you choose eternal day? Or shall you choose that which seems fearful, but brings growth?" And with boldness, one by one, the farmers of that village chose growth.

Indeed, my friends, there are many times when growth seems to be undesirable. For it moves one from the land of peace, from the garden of Eden, into a dark and troubled time. Yet it is only in the dance of light and dark that the spirit may continue its journey back to the original source of all things. Blessed is each of you who has chosen the way of growth.

We are those of Laitos and are most thankful to have been able to work with each of you this day. We are aware that this is a new experience for some and that the images that we offer sometimes seem illogical or fanciful. We thank each for trusting that which is given and for working with those concepts that are often so difficult to translate into everyday words.

At this time we would leave this instrument and this group, thanking each for the joy of collaboration and for the beauty of your company. We leave you in the love and in the light of the one infinite Creator. We are known to you as Laitos. Adonai. Adonai.

L/L Research

www.llresearch.org

L/L Research is a subsidiary of Rock Creek Research & Development Laboratories, Inc.

P.O. Box 5195
Louisville, KY 40255-0195

Rock Creek is a non-profit corporation dedicated to discovering and sharing information which may aid in the spiritual evolution of humankind.

ABOUT THE CONTENTS OF THIS TRANSCRIPT: This telepathic channeling has been taken from transcriptions of the weekly study and meditation meetings of the Rock Creek Research & Development Laboratories and L/L Research. It is offered in the hope that it may be useful to you. As the Confederation entities always make a point of saying, please use your discrimination and judgment in assessing this material. If something rings true to you, fine. If something does not resonate, please leave it behind, for neither we nor those of the Confederation would wish to be a stumbling block for any.

© 2009 L/L RESEARCH

CHANNELING INTENSIVE 1 - SESSION 15 - SPECIAL MEDITATION
MAY 4, 2008

Group question: Channeling Intensive Meditation[144], May 4, 2008. The question this evening, Q'uo, is we would like to know the nature of the connection between the contact—that would be you—and the channel that channels your words or thoughts, or any Confederation words or thoughts. Could you elaborate on the nature and quality of that connection and how it might be enhanced by the one who is serving as the channel or the instrument?

(Carla channeling)

We are those known to you as the principle of Q'uo. Greetings in the love and in the light of the one infinite Creator in whose service we come to you this day. What a privilege and a pleasure it is, my friends, to be called to your circle of seeking. We thank each soul who has laid aside precious time for seeking the truth. We are most glad to accept the invitation to share our humble thoughts with you on the subject of the nature of the point of contact betwixt source and channel.

As always, however, before we begin, we would ask that each of you employ your powers of discrimination as you hear what we have to say. Use those thoughts of ours that seem helpful to you, by all means, and leave the rest behind without a second thought. This will enable us to speak freely without being concerned that we may be interrupting the process of your evolution or infringing upon your free will. We thank you for this consideration.

The nature of contact betwixt a physical being—that is, a spiritual being which has associated itself with a physical body in your third density—and a non-physical being—that is, a being which does not have a body that would be considered a physical body in third density—begins with a consideration of the nature of the energy body itself. Such a consideration must begin with a look at who you are energetically, and how your energetic system works to create a place for connection. Each of you has studied the material that we of the Confederation have offered you through this instrument over the years about the energy body.

You are aware that, in our opinion, that it is the primary body, even though you are in physical form as far as your physical eyes can see. The creature that you are would be empty and hollow were it not for the interpenetration of your flesh and bones by the energy body which is associated with your infinite and eternal self. The first point of contact to be considered in your question is the contact between you as a physical being and you as an energy being or an essence. Your physical body is a marvel of engineering and design, a self-contained chemical distillery set in delicate parameters for the sole purpose of use by your soul.

---

[144] This Special Meditation was held at the end of the Channeling Intensive 1 make-up session.

Because you have experienced what this instrument calls Derby Weekend, you have been talking about the courage and bravery of the thoroughbreds that run, and especially the incredible courage and self-sacrifice of the filly known as Eight Bells, who gave her life in order to please her master and run the straight race to her very best ability. You may see your physical bodies in the same light. Just as a horse and its rider, your physical body wants to be ridden—waits to be ridden—and loves the rider who rides it. That rider is your energy body, or your soul body, or your spiritual essence.

The connection between the two is delicate, yet very powerful. It was set by intention prior to your joining the physical body with the soul body. Somewhere during the process of your mother's pregnancy, or perhaps just after your mother delivered you into the world—the point of entry of the soul or the energy body into association with the physical body varies greatly—yet eventually you are born and you are inextricably intertwined spirit and flesh, incorporated in one creature of amazing complexity and nuance.

And yet, in the end, moving by very simple principles having to do with attraction, repulsion and the whole principle of choice, this all that you are has brought into your physical manifestation many non-physical items. They include your physical traits such as quickness of mind or quickness of coordination, personality traits such as your preferences for choices of pleasure and choices of work, and your limitations and seeming failings and faults, all of which were carefully placed where they were as they were in order that you in this very short lifetime of yours may have the maximum potential for using what the one known as D called "the day," each brief day of lifetime, to create an ever more just balance within your energy body, within your soul essence between the qualities of love, wisdom, power and peace.

It is the nature of your density that you are not to know the truth of that which we say, nor having any way of proving it. Rather, you take your journey on in a state of unknowing, and as you leap into faith and make your choice for love, you have only the most subjective of feedbacks to reassure you that you are on the right track, on task, and on target.

It is not given you to know if you are drawn to something like channeling simply because you wish to be of service, or if there are other strains of unmanifested, and perhaps undiscovered, reasons for being attracted to the service of offering yourself as channel. It remains for you an act of faith, an act of courage, and an act of absolute dedication to service, so to prepare yourself to be able to receive our thoughts and to transmit them, or translate them as this instrument would say, through your voice, your sensibility and your awareness.

As those who do come to this service seeking to make it better, we are very glad to speak of the second point of connection, which would be the connection betwixt your energy body and our energy body. This instrument has, in teaching during this weekend of study and fellowship, spoken several times about the importance of intent. Within the world of spirit, which is the environment of your energy body, creating an intent is as real as taking a tool would be in the physical world to a board and creating an opening by sawing a hole of a certain shape and size in the material. There is a lot of thought that goes into making a certain opening in a board—perhaps it is supposed to fit onto another board, and is just of this dimension and that thickness—and so the saw must be very clever and the wielder of the saw must be skilled in order that the cut may be smooth, the hole may be appropriately sized, and the fit may be a good one.

When you make your intention, you are creating an opening into your body that is your energy body, that is of a certain nature, of a certain shape shall we say for simplicity's sake. You have crafted that intent by stating precisely what you wish to do, why you wish to achieve contact with the source. You have used the material of your energy body to create this opening. It is not precisely an opening within any of your chakras, but rather it is an opening made by the alignment of your heart chakra, your blue-ray chakra, your indigo-ray chakra, and your violet-ray chakra together with the gateway to intelligent infinity and the octave chakra, or eighth chakra, which rests above your head in time/space.

So it is not only an opening that is not a flat opening, but rather it is a multidimensional opening of a certain shape—that shape being the shape of your desire and your intention—and the clarity and the cut of that shape being made by the degree of clarity which you bring to your service of opening to channel. Thusly, we say to you that the greatest part of cooperating with the process of opening to channel is the degree of clarity, integrity and depth of thoughtfulness with which your intention to offer this service is made.

There is always, in doing this service, the concern on our part that, in your eagerness to be of service, you shall skip the thorough examination of your entire energy body before setting your intention to open to channel. The one known as T was asking earlier if certain blockages that she may have deep within her might keep her from being the best channel that she could be. And we would say to that question that the answer is yes. And not only the blockages that are within her in particular, but in general those blockages which remain within the energy system, and which either acutely or chronically are narrowing the beam of energy which is able to be drawn up through the root chakra, up through the heart, and out through the top of the head.

This is the base node or the foundation energy from which the channeling must proceed. Therefore, we would encourage those who wish to channel to make a daily practice of examining, balancing and freeing the energy body from all distortions that can be found as you examine your thoughts for the day and those things that have occurred to you that would tell you where your energy may be caught within the energy body.

There is no more helpful thing that you can do to prepare for the service of channeling on a regular basis than the daily clearing of your energy body. This entails a great deal, actually, and we would use one word to characterize the nature of work with your energy body. That word is forgiveness. Forgiveness is a very powerful thing. Perhaps you are upset with yourself because you ate that which you shouldn't have eaten, or you spent some time when you should have been doing A, and then instead you preferred to do B. Perhaps you felt that you talk too much, or too little … perhaps many, many things. Whatever those thoughts about yourself, they call for forgiveness from you, not because you are worthy, and not because you are unworthy but are redeemed, but because the nature of you and of everything else in creation is perfection. Shall you hold it against manifestation that it cannot show you that perfection, or shall you by faith alone claim that perfection that exists triumphantly, regardless of appearances? You forgive, because that is the truth of your being. You forgive because in claiming love as your nature, you know that love forgives all.

And when it comes to forgiving others, you go through the same process, although we are aware it is exponentially easier to forgive others than to forgive the self. Therefore, we speak of the self first, and we speak of the self last in asking you always to remember to forgive the self, even if it seems that the self was not involved, and all you have to do is forgive another who has wronged you. Dear ones, this is not the equation as it truly exists. That which is held against another is held against yourself. That which is forgiven another is forgiven yourself, for you and another are one. Therefore, come into a state of forgiveness, sense that all is forgiven, know that love is everything, and in that environment can you set your intention to be of service. The quality and lucidity of your intention create a vector through the gateway to intelligent infinity towards the target that you have selected by the specificity of your intention.

This instrument has talked before about how you are radios and in tuning you are dialing towards the highest and best channel which you can receive on your instrument. Therefore, the tuning process that you have been learning this weekend is very important in terms of the contact that you are able to make, and how securely and soundly that contact is made. Consequently, we are very pleased that each of you has spent much time working with the process of tuning. We encourage you to find your own way. As this instrument has said in her teaching, do not rely upon what she has learned, but only use her suggestions as a starting place and then, by observation and by repetition in your own practice, refine your own way of tuning your mind, body and spirit into alignment with your highest intentions.

It is good that you take time to do this, not only because it is good to tune—that in itself is reason enough to spend the time before making a contact—but there is a further point to be made here, and that is that although it is a tender invasion between an instrument and the source of channeling, it is nevertheless an invasion. We are incorporating our energy into your energy, and that incorporation will last for the duration of the channeling. Consequently, it helps the energy body to have a little time to get ready for this very intimate connection which can be likened to the sexual connection in that it is a connection of power that is made for the purpose of propagating love in a certain vibration.

Our propagation is never intended to take corporeal form. There is no sperm or ovum, there is no child that grows. There is only that most tender and delicate stream of concepts that interpenetrates the sensibility of the channel coming through the gateway of intelligent infinity from that specific point of targeting that has been hit, down through the violet-ray chakra, the indigo-ray chakra, the blue-ray chakra to the heart chakra, and bouncing up again and resting in the blue ray, that throat chakra which we rest in in order to use your vocal apparatus and to offer our concepts to you. It is a penetration in utmost honor and respect in love and in light, and it is blessed and protected by the care and the fastidiousness with which you have prepared yourself for this contact, and by the care with which you have tuned and then challenged the spirit who answers your call.

It is wise indeed when the contact is over and we have withdrawn from your energy body back through the gateway to our resting place in the inner planes of your density for you as an instrument to take that same amount of time to rest and allow the experience to mellow. You may think of it as a time of the gradual return of your full energy to the outside world, or you may think of it as a time of afterglow following the sexual metaphor that we used earlier. For it is a communion of a very high order when an instrument allows the incorporation of the source which is channeled. Your children are your channelings, and you offer them with that same love and devotion that a mother offers to her children.

We thank you for this query, and would request that if there is a follow-up question, that you ask it now. We are those of Q'uo.

S: I have a question. I wonder if you could speak a little bit to the experience of channeling. It often seems to the channel that what we are speaking is actually our own thoughts, and not the thoughts of another. This seems particularly true because the experience requires that we put together sentences the way we would as if we were speaking on our own behalf. Can you give us some guidance about how we might sort out where that which comes from us lies and where that which comes from the source received by the channel lies? Thank you.

We are those of Q'uo, and we believe that we understand your query, my brother. If we understand you correctly, we would say that there should be no thought taken as to whether the thoughts that come to your mind are yours or are ours. The less thought that is taken on a conscious level once the channeling process begins, the cleaner the contact will be, and the more space we shall have in which to work. The reason that it is so difficult to distinguish betwixt one's own thought and the thought of the source that is channeling through your instrument is that there is no difference in the production of a thought by you and the production of a thought by us, as it comes from the world of concepts and ideation into the workaday world of sentences and statements which express the thought or the concept.

Since there is no difference in the feel or texture of thoughts generated from your subconscious processes and the processes of a source channeling through your subconscious into your conscious mind, any thought taken constitutes an element of self-doubt. It invites the consideration of many things by the intellectual or rational mind, and it encourages the distraction of the energies that have been so carefully aligned through the chakras from the heart on upward through the gateway to intelligent infinity. Consequently, once a contact has been accepted, the encouragement of such thoughts is sabotage to your original intent. It is not necessarily a harmful distortion for you to flash upon these thoughts—this is conscious channeling, and the conscious self will be there around the edges, shall we say—but let that conscious self be a spectator, and let the process of allowing the incorporated entity to speak through your instrument to go forward unimpeded by any encouragement whatsoever of that spectator to join into the equation of channeling.

May we answer you further, my brother? We are those of Q'uo.

S: Not on that question. Thank you very much.

We thank you, my brother. May we ask if there is another query at this time? We are those of Q'uo.

G: Q'uo, of the infinite range of reactions that an entity could have upon hearing or reading your words, is there a hoped-for reaction behind your intention when communicating through earthly instruments?

We are those of Q'uo, and are aware of your query, my brother. My brother, it is our hope to share our thoughts. We have no hope that they will be accepted in such and such a way, nor have we any expectation of any particular kind of reaction on the part of those whose questions we answer. Our hope is to express in a voice of love the thoughts that we have to share in the least distorted manner possible. Our hope, in short, is to decrease distortion and enlarge love within the awareness of our self and of those to whom we speak. Our hope is to be part of the light and the love of the one infinite Creator as it's manifested so many ways, seen and unseen, known and unknown. We could never point or predict or narrow the possibilities of reaction that are acceptable to us. It is acceptable to us if entities listen and have no interest in that which we have to say. It is acceptable to us if entities find our work, our thoughts, our opinions of use. It is our pleasure to meet the opportunity that has been given to us in a channeling session to have a conversation with those of you who are yet in third density calling for our help, hoping to hear a voice of love. We hope to be such a voice. Beyond that, we do not have any expectation or desire to see a particular outcome. Were we to do so, we would be less than fully of service to others, and that would never be part of our intention.

May we answer you further, my brother?

G: Not on that question. Thank you, Q'uo.

We thank you, my brother. May we ask then if there is another query at this time? We are those of Q'uo.

S: If no one else has one, I would have one other one. It's a big question, and maybe a brief answer will suffice at this point. Many of us have feelings of having not been treated well. In our response of anger to that, and particularly for those of us who are attempting to develop on the path of service to others, it can be a tendency to hold back on our feelings of anger, and to hold this over long periods of time until it gets to the point where we become sort of numb and unreachable. I wonder if you could speak briefly to the question about how one might clear those frozen energies. Thank you.

We are those of Q'uo, and are aware of your query, my brother. It is indeed so that in most patterns of incarnation within your density, there grow to be in the incarnated mind/body/spirit complex pockets of deeply buried pain. As one can imagine, the effort made to bury the pain is commensurate to the level of the pain—the greater the pain, the more harsh the need will have been to erect defenses around it and enisle[145] it. It is not a desirable situation to have these islands of buried pain.

Although there are methods of systematically going after such buried pain, we would perhaps more happily recommend the natural process of becoming aware of these pockets of pain and suffering through the observation of the self in its reactions to surface catalyst. As events occur on the surface of life in everyday matters, some events trigger reactions that seem out of proportion to the catalyst that provoked them. When an unevenness in the calm of the spirit is detected, that unevenness is worth noting, not in order to judge the self, but in order to play detective in ferreting out the direction of these pockets of deeply held pain.

Naturally, you do not wish to do violence to yourself in the process of digging up this rich ore of experience, and this is why we say that it is better to work with the self in a patient and sustained manner, getting to know the patterns of triggering that you have as an individual, and building your intelligence as to what might be behind these unusually outsized reactions to seemingly mild catalyst. Gradually, you will be begin to be able to close in on the line of thinking or a direction of inference which leads you to a sudden memory of the generation of this old pain. Perhaps you cannot recall the details, but suddenly the pain will present itself to you free from its defenses' guard, so that you are able to realize its strength and see it in its true shape for the first time. When this occurs, embrace this realization and release that deeply held pocket of pain.

A Balm of Gilead for such wounds is forgiveness again, forgiveness of the self, forgiveness of the other, forgiveness of the situation. In many cases, you are forgiving things experienced so early, experienced in your childhood that you shall never have a cognitive awareness of the exact nature of the pain or of the cause of the pain. Yet at the same time that as you are able to lift this ore out of its pocket and set it free, you can sense the lightness of your shoulders that no longer carry this burden, and you can feel the inrush of new energy into your body. And these are the signs that you have successfully released an

---

[145] enisle: to place apart, isolate; to make an island of.

engram of frozen emotion. This is work well done, but we encourage you to do it gently, lovingly and patiently rather than attempting to "clear the decks" and become completely free of all distortion. Such desires are those which create further distortion.

Realize, too, that as you clear out a pocket of pain, you may be dealing with a pocket that is being fed from a still deeper source within your system of energies, so that were you to stop at that point and think to yourself, "Now my work is done," you would be denying yourself the opportunity to move even deeper and to find that original pain that has been feeding the more near-to-the-surface pocket of pain which you have found now. Consequently, do not feel that this is work that can be finished within a lifetime, but rather remain vigilant each day of your life to those things which disturb you and investigate them as you get to know yourself ever better and ever more deeply.

May we answer you further, my brother? We are those of Q'uo.

S: No, thank you very much. That's very helpful.

We thank you, my brother. Is there a final query at this time? We are those of Q'uo.

G: Q'uo, I have one. What categories of questions yield the best results and/or are most suitable for your contact? And if there is time, conversely, what categories of questions are least suitable for your contact?

We are those of Q'uo, and are aware of your query, my brother. We are those who hope to be a source of information helpful to those who are seeking the truth. Consequently, questions which are shaped from spiritual concerns are those that most directly avail themselves to a fruitful discussion by us. We are a voice of love and our energies are nurtured by questions that are couched in loving terms by those seeking in a peaceful way to progress, to know themselves better, and to accelerate the pace of their spiritual evolution. Those questions which baffle our ability to serve are those questions which do not have to do with spiritual concerns in any way that we can find as the question is presented.

And it is to be noted in this regard that this instrument's frequent suggestions to those who would have sessions of channeling with our source to ask for what spiritual principles apply to any given concern are very well founded. The request for spiritual principles opens to us the ability to offer our humble opinions on those subjects. We may not be able to address directly a specific concern, yet if spiritual principles are involved in the query, we may discuss those which we can see may have some use as a resource in considering an issue at hand, whether it be abstractly spiritual or involved in a more specific and earthly concern. Because we are a voice of love, because we come in service to others, those queries asked from a standpoint of fear and service to self are those which most effectively baffle our ability to be of service.

May we answer you further, my brother? We are those of Q'uo.

G: Yes, real quick. Another category of question that may not be suitable which you did not mention is the category of question that may qualify in terms of being about spiritual concerns, but may disqualify itself in that it seeks something that is beyond the instrument's own knowledge base. Is this true?

We are those of Q'uo, and if we understand your query, my brother, it is not so. When a question is beyond an instrument's knowledge base, but yet is that of which we are aware, we are often able to give impressions to an instrument that allow it to create structures of thought that are able to be used by those with the information which the instrument does not have. If the instrument has been able to be lucid and true in the creation of that metaphor which replaces knowledge, then the questioner may then infer from that metaphor of words and sentences the structure of the information that is desired.

May we answer you further, my brother?

G: I'm often in the position of guiding question making by other individuals, and your information was very helpful. No further questions. Thank you.

We thank you, too, my brother, and appreciate your service upon our behalf as you help to prepare those who come to us for a conversation to have the most productive conversation that they may have. We are most grateful for the opportunity to have such conversations. It is our blessing to be called to circles of seeking such as this one, and indeed it is our way of being of service at this point in our own spiritual evolution.

We would at this time thank this group for the beauty of its vibrations, and the blended beauty of its creation of the sacred space of the temple of this session of working. We thank this circle, and we leave this circle in the love and in the light of the one infinite Creator. We are known to you as the principle of Q'uo. Adonai. Adonai, my friends. ✣

L/L Research

L/L Research is a subsidiary of Rock Creek Research & Development Laboratories, Inc.

P.O. Box 5195
Louisville, KY 40255-0195

www.llresearch.org

Rock Creek is a non-profit corporation dedicated to discovering and sharing information which may aid in the spiritual evolution of humankind.

ABOUT THE CONTENTS OF THIS TRANSCRIPT: This telepathic channeling has been taken from transcriptions of the weekly study and meditation meetings of the Rock Creek Research & Development Laboratories and L/L Research. It is offered in the hope that it may be useful to you. As the Confederation entities always make a point of saying, please use your discrimination and judgment in assessing this material. If something rings true to you, fine. If something does not resonate, please leave it behind, for neither we nor those of the Confederation would wish to be a stumbling block for any.

© 2009 L/L Research

Saturday Meditation
May 10, 2008

Group question: The question this evening is about sexual energy exchanges. From the Ra contact we know that two factors which enhance the exchange are extended foreplay, which increases the amount of energy transferred, and both partners dedicating themselves to service to others, which doubles the energy transfer. Also, simultaneous orgasm allows the transfer to be most efficient.

Please speak to the spiritual nature of sexual energy exchanges and how they enhance our magical personalities.

(Carla channeling)

We are those known to you as the principle of Q'uo. We greet you in the love and in the light of the one infinite Creator, in whose service we come to you this evening. We thank you for the privilege of being called to join your circle of seeking this evening. It is a joy to be part of this circle of beautiful, seeking souls. As your auras mingle and create the sacred space of this contact, they show us a beauty that is beyond words.

We thank you so much for this opportunity to share our humble thoughts with you on the subject of sexual energy exchange and the principles involved in maximizing this sacred energy. As always, however, we would preface our discussion by requesting that each maintain the utmost vigilance over his doors of perception. Please use your discrimination. Listen for the voice of your own resonance. If something seems interesting to you, by all means use it, but if something does not, please let it go without a second thought. In this way we can be assured of refraining from infringing in any way upon the process of your spiritual evolution. We thank you for this consideration.

In speaking of sexual energy exchange we need first to move back and prepare the ground, as it were, by offering some thoughts concerning the nature of the energy body and the nature of energy exchanges.

Your energy body is far more full of your essence in the metaphysical sense than is your physical body. It is the body from which your physical body takes its form, but it is non-physical, being electrical in nature. You can think of the universe as a whole as a field of energy, infinite and mysterious. Contained within that vast and unimaginable Creator-field lie the fields of the galaxies, the suns, the planets, and the entities upon those planets, such as yourself.

As you step down orders of magnitude to go from Creator to sub-Logos, to sub-sub-Logos, to sub-sub-sub-Logos, yet still the one infinite Creator is replete in every portion, every energy field, and every iota of the creation. Since all is one, each portion of the One is a hologram of the One. The very cells of your body are full of the information of the Creator and the created.

Your energy body is the governing field of your mind, body and spirit. It joins the physical body at some time around physical birth willingly and consciously interpenetrating the physical body that is the opportunity for a lifetime of experience within the illusion of planet Earth. Throughout your life, then, your energy body and your physical body are indistinguishable in terms of any worldly observation or scientific ability to measure the potential difference betwixt the physical and the metaphysical.

It is the energy body that feeds the perceptions of the physical body. As the physical body, mind and emotions gather catalyst and experience, the harvest of those thoughts and emotions moves into the energy body in an endless loop.

Your energy body is fed by the Logos. In local terms it is fed by the energy of your sun which pours its light, its energy, and power into the Earth. Planet Earth, your mother, receives this energy in infinite amounts and sends it from the very heart and womb of the Earth in a radiating pattern from the very core of the planet, outward in every direction, coming up through the ground so that you may absorb it with your feet as you walk upon the earth. It enters the energy body at the joining of the legs, which is the seat of the red-ray chakra, the first of the seven chakras that together comprise your energy body.

This infinite love/light of the Creator that streams into the red ray will, if not baffled, blocked or narrowed, move freely and powerfully into the heart, letting the heart open and bloom like a flower, thereby setting the stage for the potential for work in consciousness.

Work in consciousness can only take place when the red ray, orange ray, and yellow ray are open and the energy of the Creator is running freely through them, for this is the energy that feeds the heart. When it is limited or constricted, the magical personality shall find itself on very short rations. Once the seeker has set his intention to do work in consciousness, then the higher rays become involved: the blue ray of communication, the indigo ray of faith and being, and of course, the green ray of healing and unconditional love.

It is to be noted that it is not necessary, in order to be of service to others and to graduate from third density, for the higher rays to be used in order to access the gateway to intelligent infinity. Simple, straightforward, unconditional love and the energies of forgiveness and compassion shall carry any seeker through graduation with flying colors. That is far more than enough to use in order to penetrate those energies that move one into higher light.

However, you, as a metaphysical being within incarnation, were indeed given the ability to use the higher chakras and to do work in consciousness. The infinite love/light of the one Creator moves upward, whereas it is the intention set by the magical personality that calls the energy from above down to meet the infinite love/light of the one Creator moving upward. Where those two energies meet is the location where the seeker is able to accomplish work in consciousness whether it be healing, channeling or the radiancy of being.

So, whether we are speaking of healing, the green ray energy, or communication, the blue ray energy, or radiancy of being, the indigo ray, we speak of one process whereby a seeker decides to set his intention to become a priest, a minister of light, and to take upon himself the responsibility of using his power rightly.

Sacred sexuality lies within the precincts of the indigo ray, and indeed, moves into the mystery of the violet ray. It calls down inspiration and information from the Godhead principle Itself, that great Logos that is unconditional love, into the heart of that which joins the physical and the metaphysical being, sexuality.

The potential of sexuality is that it may be sacred. The beginnings of sexuality are simple and primal. Consequently, as the priest and the priestess together set their intention to invite the Creator into the equation of their electrical circuitry, they call down the Logos itself. Yet it begins with the simplest sexual chemistry, that attraction that is purely red ray and that has been so sturdy in its efficiency of propagating the species of humans on planet Earth.

The first point that the one known as Jim made concerning sexuality is that it is helpful to prolong foreplay and we would speak on this to an extent and explore why this is so.

As the two who have set their intent come together, they have simply their intent. They have not developed a structure, metaphysically speaking, in which to express their intent. Whatever two entities do after they have set their intent to share sacred sexuality can be considered foreplay. The ritual of the date is very helpful in this regard.

As each of you has talked around the circle before the meditation this night, each has expressed the feeling of being so terribly busy that he almost cannot catch his breath. The world lies heavy upon the shoulders of those who must earn the living and fulfill the duties of the day. There is a great deal to lay down before one can engage in sacred play. There is much to release of the world and the grime and the weariness of the world.

And so, the two meet, perhaps over a dinner or sharing a glass of wine or coffee, a simple meeting of the eyes and the voices. And each talks, perhaps, about the day, about the concerns, the burdens and the feelings of world-weariness and ennui. And as these are spoken, the energy opens up and the rays begin to clear.

What is not usually understood about red ray is that it is not only the ray of sexuality but also the ray of survival. It is the ray in which you must say either "yes" or "no" to life itself. Many are those whose feelings of depression and unhappiness, for various reasons, has begun to shut down or at least narrow that red ray. Somehow, sharing these woes with another whose ears are open to listen begins to get the red ray open again; begins to make life seem good again. The colors brighten, energies lift, and the conversation goes on.

Much is shared on a personal level, opening up orange ray. And if there is, between the two, the sacrament of marriage, yellow ray is also penetrated. And as the affairs of that particular relationship are discussed, that ray begins to open and relax, as each supports each. Finally each can feel the heart opening because of the gratitude that is felt for the company of the other.

Now, perhaps, there has been a shift in the location and the amount of privacy. Perhaps this is the time when the two lovers become intimate, clothes are shed, the outside world falls away, and the talk deepens. Whatever is said in this opening into blue ray has begun to take on the quality of sacredness, as each listens in complete sympathy and support to what the other has to say. The world seems to brighten more and more, the energy lifts and moves towards the indigo ray, that ray of faith and magic where two beings may become magical together.

When that moment arrives where touch is involved, you can see that there has been a great deal of preparation. Sacred sexuality is not casual in any way. It is as structured as is any magical ritual, yet it is structured within the sensibilities of two priests who are invoking the one infinite Creator as they invoke that connection that is the essence of sexual congress.

We mentioned before that your energy body is an electrical body. As electricity has its path, so your energy body has its points of contact which can form a circuit betwixt two energy bodies, making them one. Those openings are at the lips, the hands, the feet, the groin and the breasts. If two hold hands, they are able to exchange sexual energy. If they touch lips they are able to express sexual energy. If any of those elements touch, sexual energy circuits between the two. When one thinks of sacred sexuality one needs to think in terms of the closing of those circuits.

By the time the first touch occurs, there has been a good deal of power built up by the anticipation of the pleasure of touch. In this regard, the focus of the two entities involved is the key to the ratcheting up of the amperage of the contact betwixt the two. Indeed, this instrument has often found it useful to visualize the circuit that has been closed, seeing how it changes color in intensity, how it is infinite in its play as each touches each and each creates ways to make the other feel good.

It was intended by the Creator that sexuality had the potential of offering to third-density entities an experience of the steady state of the Creator, which would be described by third density entities as orgasm. This is the steady state of the universe. This is the power of unconditional love. This is the engine that drives creation. This is the sunlight that falls upon you. It too, is the fusion of the priest and the priestess expressing unconditional love in a steady state.

As a priest and priestess who are mated become more experienced, each with the other, there begin to be refinements on the art of touching, on the nuances of intimacy, so that each can bring the other very close to the point of orgasm and then remain there, playing with that energy, fueling it, playing again, and fueling again, and not feeling the need to move to orgasm.

We believe this is what the one known as Jim had in mind when he spoke of prolonging foreplay, and this is certainly the major part of being able to move up in orders of magnitude, in terms of the brilliance and the power of the energy exchange involved.

However, it is never to be forgotten that all of the energy centers are involved in sacred sexuality. One cannot play in the fields of the Lord if one does not have the lower chakras running well, glad and free and open and accepting of life and all that it offers.

It is indeed so that when both entities, the priest and the priestess, have consciously dedicated their lives to the service of the one infinite Creator, this doubles the power available to each. This is according to the way of doubling or squares. As in many other kinds of energies, when there are two who together seek, the power of that seeking is doubled.

And we would certainly agree with the one known as Jim that when there is a simultaneous orgasm between the priest and the priestess, the energy exchange is at its most brilliant, focused and collected. It is certainly the most lucid way to experience the fusion of self with self and self with Creator.

Yet, at the same time, we would note that it is possible to have a powerful energy exchange without orgasm, simply because of the intention of the mated pair and their dedication of the time of pleasure and feeling good to the service of the one infinite Creator. There are many among your people who have been well mated and who no longer are able to share the sexuality in the way of their youth. This in no way inhibits their ability to exchange sexual energy, to make each other feel good, and to have sacred play.

Sacred sexuality begins with a person's willingness to become magical. To be able to experience sacred sexuality, a seeker must release those thoughts of himself which limit him. He must find it within himself to accept himself just as he is and to fall in love with himself, casting aside all thought of self-improvement or self judgment. The beginning of the seeker's transition to the magical personality is his total acceptance of himself as he is.

We believe that this is perhaps the critical difficulty with sacred sexuality and is that limiting factor which keeps many from experiencing the full freedom and beauty of sacred sexuality.

Think of yourself not as you see yourself in the mirror but as you feel yourself when you pray for what you most dearly wish. See yourself not as a physical being but as a dreamer, a hoper, a lover of the light, an idealist. See those energies of intention that have nothing to do with the manifestations of the world. This is the beginning of the magical personality: to perceive yourself more truly than you can with the mirrors of the world.

And finally, we would note the impossibility of creating sacred sexuality without context. Such has often been attempted by those who would like to take a shortcut and who perhaps are unable to sustain a committed personal relationship for the length of time that it takes to establish a safe haven where two can trust that they shall not be harmed. Many are those who have attempted to create sacred sexuality by the use of objects, such as prostitutes, where all of the work of the magician is done by one entity in solitude, using the object in order to express the actual sexual energy. This shall never become true sacred sexuality, for there is no energy exchange.

In higher densities this shall be much clearer, for in higher densities entities exchange the dynamic between them upon meeting and so experience a kind of orgasm simply by shaking hands and saying hello, shall we say. There is nothing hidden or shameful. All energies are accepted as clean and beautiful. So entities dwell in an atmosphere of the exchanging of energies at all times.

You who dwell within the veil do not have that luxury. And so, in order to become able to practice as priest and priestess in sacred sexuality, you must create with another that safe place that enables trust and faith to reign supreme. How precious such a relationship is and how much it has to offer!

(Side one of tape ends.)

(Carla channeling)

Before we leave this subject, we would note that including the Creator in all that you do is the way to create your life as magical. The Creator is not "out there," unless you allow the Creator to be far off. The Creator is intimate with you in a very sexual way.

As you move through your everyday chores, invite the Creator to come into your life and power—and mean it—and watch your life transform. You will find yourself exchanging energy in a far more transparent way, and seeing the energy expenditures of others around you. You will feel the energy of the sun and share with that energy, giving your love back to it. And so, an energy exchange is made with the daylight itself. You can do that with each and every thing with which you come in contact.

We wish you the joy of your practice. May we ask if there is a follow-up to this query? We are those of Q'uo.

Jim: We don't have a follow-up to that particular query, but G has given me one that he would like to have asked. It's from J. It reads, "Q'uo, I've been distributing, promoting, and ingesting a substance known as "White Gold" for almost ten years. It's a legal substance. New information from another channel has presented itself to me which suggests that there may be a negative consequence to the DNA of the entity ingesting the substance. I'm deeply concerned that there may be some validity to this statement and am worried that, if it is true, then I may be, in ignorance, distributing a chemical substance which has negative effects on those who ingest it. Is there any information of a spiritual nature that you could offer me involved with the principles of this situation?"

We are those of Q'uo, and are aware of your query, my brother. The spiritual principle which we would mention at this time in connection with your query is the principle of the individuality of response. All is one, yet each entity is as a snowflake, individual and unique. Each unique energy system operates on its own frequency and with its own peculiarities. Therefore, that which may be extremely helpful for one entity may be neutral for another and may be detrimental for another. Only the percentages vary in terms of this being true of virtually any energy or substance that is offered.

Is there another query that we may consider at this time? We are those of Q'uo.

A: Yes, Q'uo. Could you compare and contrast, from the spiritual perspective, the energy exchanges of sacred sex with the energy exchanges in other spiritual dimensions of empathy?

We are those of Q'uo, and believe we understand your query, my brother. When there is an empathic energy exchange, it is an exchange that does not have the element of sexual touch. The nature of the empathic exchange is not necessarily indigo-ray. Empathic exchanges, that is, one entity understanding another to the point where one is able to experience as that entity, are possible in any of the energy centers.

So, my brother, we would say that it is a different animal in terms of its being a more general and more broad category of energy exchange. Yet, certainly, it is, just as is sexual energy exchange, that closing of circuitry of one kind or another where two entities become one.

May we answer you further, my brother?

A: I'm studying a method of providing compassionate empathy in a book called *Nonviolent Communication* by Marshall Rosenberg[146]. I'm not clear what my next question would be about that, but if you see anything spiritual about that, I would be interested.

We are those of Q'uo, and my brother, we encourage you to follow the path of resonance and wish you well with your journey.

Is there a final query at this time? We are those of Q'uo.

R: I have a question about energy exchange. Is there energy exchange between you, as an entity that works with a circle of seeking? I understand there is an energy exchange because you work through the channel and you need to connect with the channel so some energy moves there. But is there a more general energy exchange because this is a circle of seeking and we ask you to join it, so everybody in the circle exchanges energy in some way?

We are those of Q'uo, and grasp your query my brother. The energy exchange betwixt you and us is the energy exchange of Creator and Creator, equal to equal. The precise nature of the exchange again has to do with the individual. Each entity's energy body is unique and each energy body has its ways of receiving and giving energy, not in the specifically sexual sense, but in the sense of having pathways between various of the chakras that are used to working together. This is often a matter that is compounded by the long-held habits of an entity and his tendency to perceive in a certain way.

The energy exchange betwixt spirit in general and yourself in incarnation in general is always deepened and strengthened as the seeker avails himself to the silence and practices meditation and thus becomes able to begin to perceive deeper truths about his own nature. The more deeply that it is possible for you as

---

[146] Marshall Rosenberg, *Nonviolent Communication: A Language of Life*: Encinitas, CA, Puddle Dancer Press, 2003.

an entity to go in opening up and revealing your inner self in terms of opening to contact with us, the more able that we are to become one with you in a very intimate way as we collaborate together to create an instrument whereby perhaps those who seek may find good resources and information for their spiritual journey.

When the dedication is set to serve as a channel and when the self has been opened up fearlessly to that possibility, the stage is set for the most efficient and deep energy exchange betwixt those of us of the time/space realm and you in the space/time realm. It is a beautiful and mysterious collaboration which is hedged in artistry and energy. It is a very creative exchange, as we are sure that you are aware, as you yourself have attempted to open yourself to these energies.

May we answer you further, my brother?

R: No, Q'uo, thank you for your comments and thank you for coming in, being repeatedly willing to answer our numerous questions.

We are those of Q'uo, and are aware of your thanks, my brother. As you know well, our thanks are just as fervent. It is tremendously fulfilling to us to be able to share our thoughts with you and hopefully to be of some small service to those of you who seek so valiantly within the veil on planet Earth.

The instrument becomes weary and we would leave this instrument and this group with thanksgiving and joy, in the love and in the light of the one infinite Creator. We are known to you as the principle of Q'uo. Adonai. Adonai. ✛

L/L Research

L/L Research is a subsidiary of Rock Creek Research & Development Laboratories, Inc.

P.O. Box 5195
Louisville, KY 40255-0195

www.llresearch.org

Rock Creek is a non-profit corporation dedicated to discovering and sharing information which may aid in the spiritual evolution of humankind.

ABOUT THE CONTENTS OF THIS TRANSCRIPT: This telepathic channeling has been taken from transcriptions of the weekly study and meditation meetings of the Rock Creek Research & Development Laboratories and L/L Research. It is offered in the hope that it may be useful to you. As the Confederation entities always make a point of saying, please use your discrimination and judgment in assessing this material. If something rings true to you, fine. If something does not resonate, please leave it behind, for neither we nor those of the Confederation would wish to be a stumbling block for any.

© 2009 L/L Research

Special Meditation
May 13, 2008

Question from Y: I feel as though I have a wall around me that keeps me from communicating with my higher self and my guidance system. If it was set there on purpose before incarnation, please discuss the spiritual principles for making this choice. If it was not set there on purpose, please discuss the spiritual principles involved in taking down this wall.

(Carla channeling)

We are those known to you as the principle of Q'uo. Greetings in the light and in the love of the one infinite Creator, in whose service we come to you this evening. We thank the one known as Y for asking for us to join a circle of seeking in which she may ask some questions. And we thank those who formed [the] circle this evening: one known as R, the one known as G, and the instrument. For each of you to take time out of your busy day to seek the truth and form a sacred circle of working is most impressive to us. We realize how many, many things are upon your minds.

We are honored and privileged to share our humble thoughts with the one known as Y. As always, however, we would ask both Y and all of those who may hear or read these words to use the utmost discrimination, taking what is good from the thoughts that we offer and leaving the rest behind. Follow the path of resonance, my friends, for truly you are the very best judge of that which is important to you and that which will be helpful in your work to accelerate the pace of your spiritual evolution. We thank you for this consideration, for it enables us to speak freely without being concerned that we may infringe upon your free will.

My sister, you asked concerning a wall that seems to have blocked you from being aware of your guidance. And you ask whether it was set by you before incarnation or whether it is something that has occurred during incarnation. We assure you, my sister, that there is no power on Earth or in heaven, shall we say, that could keep you from your guidance. For your guidance is an aspect of yourself. However, there is a tendency in some seekers to create for the self a self-imposed wall, due to the workings of personality and a somewhat low opinion of the self by the self. We might call this factor a low self-worth or the unworthiness factor.

The guidance that you seek so ardently is closer to you than your very breath. And yet when there is within a seeker that [which] is prejudiced against the perfection and the beauty of the self, a glass wall can obstruct the free flow of information betwixt the higher self and the self within incarnation. Let us look at some aspects of this situation, for we feel that there is sure and certain hope that it may be ameliorated, and that you may find yourself being much more able to work with your guidance when some things are taken into consideration of which we would now speak.

The energy body, that time/space body that is pure energy and pure light, is the author of your physical body, holding the template of your physical body during incarnation. It also holds contact with your greater self. You have brought only a part of yourself into incarnation.

It is as though a lifetime were a journey. When your guidance and you decided upon this incarnation and set your intention for it, you packed those things that you would need. You packed your relationships. You packed the gifts you needed in order to perform the services you hoped to offer. And you packed those limitations and challenges that you felt would help you to come into a more balanced configuration of a vibration.

Some entities seek to balance their open and loving hearts with more wisdom. Other wise souls come into incarnation hoping to break open their hearts and link that unconditional love vibration with wisdom in a more balanced and equal fashion. There are also some who seek the right use of power, balancing it either with love or with wisdom or with both. These are the usual areas of which concern the soul going into incarnation.

When the desire is to open the heart on the more stable and continuous basis, that choice has been made by the one who is wise and this is the case with you, my sister. Therefore, you offered to yourself the challenge that wisdom poses for the seeker. The wise seeker knows the self very well. He knows his shortcomings. And the more close to perfection his character may be, the more harsh those shortcomings may seem to him.

In reality, each soul is perfect. We have said before through this instrument that there are no mistakes; there are only surprises. Consequently, know that your guidance is separated from you only by the illusions of thought-forms you have had in place since childhood. They are located within your energy body and they constrict the amount of energy moving into your heart and especially moving from the heart into the blue and indigo chakras.

The way the energy body works, it requires a constant working through all of the chakras, starting with the very basic chakra, the red-ray chakra, and moving up to the orange and yellow rays and then to the green ray. It is a common desire of those who so eagerly seek the presence of the one infinite Creator to spend as much time as possible within the higher chakras, experiencing the infinite light and love of the one Creator. Yet always the entry into the higher chakras must be preceded by work in the lower chakras to clear the way.

Perhaps you know the verse from the *Holy Bible*: "Prepare a road in the desert that makes the crooked places straight"[147]. This is the journey through the lower chakras and it needs to be taken not once but every day; sometimes more than once in a day if there are triggers that you find occurring that pull you away from the open heart.

Let us look a bit more closely at that open heart. As you move into the heart chakra, you move into what could be termed an outer courtyard. You stand before the open heart. And yet there is a gate that you must cross. It is guarded by the lions of discrimination. Those lions guard that gate until such time as you have accepted yourself. It seems a simple thing, and yet for those who are habitually self-critical, it is not so simple at all. How can one forgive oneself for self-perceived faults and errors?

My sister, the way to forgive yourself is to realize that you gaze at the illusion of self, thrown out by your personality shell. You may take it on faith that within that personality shell lies a beautiful, worthy, wonderful, exquisite spirit, unique in all the creation, beloved of the Father beyond all telling. When you see bits of your personality that you would wish to be other than they are, you have allowed yourself to judge yourself. We would ask you then to find it within yourself to refrain from judgment and instead hold out your arms and embrace yourself with your own open heart.

You have come into an illusion upon this planet and your life must be lived within that illusion in order for you to choose, by faith alone, to seek the Creator. And it is in faith that you forgive yourself, accept yourself, and fall in love with yourself.

When you see those faults occurring, do not think judgmental thoughts, but think affectionately, "Ah, there is my personality again," and give yourself a hug. We do not suggest that you cease attempting to become a better person. We encourage that journey

---

[147] *Holy Bible*, Matthew 3: 1-3: "In those days came John the Baptist, preaching in the wilderness of Judaea, and saying, "Repent ye, for he kingdom of heaven is at hand. For this is he that was spoken of by the prophet Esa'aias, saying, "The voice of one crying in the wilderness, prepare ye the way of the Lord. Make his paths straight."

towards the light. However, upon that journey you walk with feet that move through transformation. One of the transformations is to begin to see yourself as a magical, beautiful and entirely worthy being.

We ask you not to see that which is not there. We simply ask you to see that which is not on the surface. We ask you to move deeper and find that portion of yourself that we would call consciousness. You share this consciousness with every third-density entity upon this planet. And, indeed, in the deepest sense you share this consciousness with all there is. For it is the consciousness of the Creator. It is the consciousness of unconditional love. Form a heaven then, when you feel yourself moving into judgment, of choosing to refrain from going further with that thought, and instead taking up that thought of appreciation of the self just as you are.

When you have gathered all of the bits and pieces of self that you might have shrugged aside because they were not your best parts, then and only then can you truly come into the tabernacle of the open heart. It is then that the lions will let you pass.

When you move into the open heart, then remain in silence for awhile. Allow the silence to fill you. For there is information being given to your subconscious mind within that speaking silence. Simply rest, letting the love you have for the Creator flow and radiate until you begin to feel that answering pressure of love from the Creator, that incredibly strong, answering love. Rest there; be fed, and be comforted.

Now we would speak about working with guidance. Working with your guidance is one of the ways in which you use the gateway to intelligent infinity. You open yourself to the metaphysical worlds by the process of tuning yourself up to your highest and best as you move out of the open heart and into the blue-ray chakra, then into the indigo-ray chakra, and from thence into the violet-ray chakra and through the gateway.

Your guidance is a source of inspiration and information and it is most happy to communicate with you. Thusly, after you have spent time resting in the open heart, form your intention to seek your guidance system. You may even say so out loud, or if you are one of those who enjoy working on the computer, type your intention in a new document on your computer: "My intention is to seek the guidance that has been given me in the love and the light of the one infinite Creator."

Then, we would suggest that you simply speak or type or write with the pen and paper the question that you have to ask your guidance. As soon as you have finished writing or typing or asking that question, write or type or say the very next thing that comes into your mind, not checking it, judging it, or evaluating it in any way, but simply letting flow what comes to you.

When that flow has stopped, evaluate it and continue to ask the questions that you wish to ask your guidance and continue, as you finish each question, to let that answer, whatever it may be, flow without judging it in any way. The greatest hindrance besides low self-worth to hearing your guidance is intellectual evaluation.

It is not a logical or rational activity to seek guidance, but it could be classed rather more as one would a musician as he sings or plays, a poet as he writes his poetry, or artist as he manifests on canvas what lies within the precincts of his imagination. It is pure intuition, insight and impulse which is the environment of your guidance's communication with you. Consequently, we suggest that you immediately write or type what comes to you as soon as you have finished your question in order that there is no time or space for your intellect to interrupt this flow.

It is a flow, my sister. It is an energy exchange of a kind. As long as you continue this exercise, you and your guidance are in your own world, a world in which nothing can break in or destroy. For there is nothing of Earth in this vibration between you and guidance. It may seem illogical, my sister, that you and your guidance planned for it to be somewhat difficult for you to contact guidance within incarnation, given that your guidance could help you open your heart and find ways to keep it open in more reliable and steadfast manner.

Yet, it is often the case when planning incarnational lessons that a soul chooses to challenge the self by making it more difficult to reach that which is desired. It increases the factor of suffering within the lifetime while at the same time giving to the seeker the maximum opportunity to exercise the faculty of faith.

Finally, we would note that the habit of meditation on a daily basis creates a very strong background for the seeker who wishes to be more and more in touch with himself and all of his aspects, including his guidance, which is a part of himself. There are many ways to meditate, and we have no opinion as to the best way. For each entity is unique. And for each entity, the best way will be an intimate and deeply personal way.

However you choose to enter the silence, setting your intention shall be your password to that tabernacle that lies within. Your environment may be inside or outside, in the cloister or the forest. We suggest that you seek the silence where you are most comfortable and where you are able to go on a daily basis.

We would ask at this time if there is a follow-up to this query. We are those of Q'uo.

Y: I feel that my heart chakra is open and balanced, at least to the minimum, and that my blue-ray chakra is in the process of opening. Please confirm.

We are those of Q'uo, and we are aware of your query, my sister. We can confirm that which is said, but would enter into some thoughts concerning this judgment. Firstly, as we have said before the heart chakra does not open and then stay open. The energy body as a whole has a basic vibration, which does not change very much at all. But within that range of vibration, there is constant change, just as there is change in your oceans because of the pull of the Moon. You have inner tides, my sister, both daily and at periods longer than a day. Some are cyclical on a regular basis and some are unique to certain phases in your development as a spirit. When you go through dark nights of the soul, the energy in the vibrations changes a bit as you move through challenging times.

And again we would suggest that one key to opening the higher chakras is to be sure that you are getting full power through to the heart from the infinite love and light of the Creator that moves through from the base chakra upwards and out of the top of your head.

If you have issues with sex or love of life; if you find your relationships lacking; if you judge yourself or others; if you find your relationships with your family or your work troubled—all of these things can limit or even stop the flow of energy into the heart. Consequently, always move back with true humility and begin again, each time that you sense that you are being triggered, that you are closing off, shutting down, and limiting the light that can flow into your open heart.

The challenge of the blue-ray chakra is that it takes a well-developed ability to be completely forthright and honest at the level that is not often seen among your peoples and normal conversation. The process of falling in love with yourself is the key in opening the blue-ray chakra.

It is a great challenge to find complete and utter compassion for yourself. It is indeed one of the great challenges which you offer to yourself as you came into the incarnation. The reason that it is the key is that when you have become able to see yourself with eyes of love and love yourself, warts and all, as this instrument would say, you then will find it child's play to have compassion on others. For you are always harder on yourself than on others. That freedom that compassion gives to you is a palpable vibration that can be felt by other selves with whom you're interacting.

When you know that you are perfectly worthy, it is far easier to move through a discussion with someone who may attempt to trigger your feelings of unworthiness, without being swayed from your compassion and your open heart.

This compassion also enables you to listen with enhanced ears, ears enhanced by love. It is not that you become able to rationalize and excuse other entities. Indeed, many is the time that blue-ray communication requires honesty to the point where many would shrink away and not wish to share their shining truth for fear of being rebuffed, rejected or judged. Yet, many times it is just that point of view that you have to offer that is going to be a saving grace for someone else.

Yet in blue ray, with the heart open and fully powering your movement, it is easy to find a compassionate way to share that truth so there is no accusation or judgment, but only the sharing of opinion and emotion. We believe that you will find, my sister, that once you have opened green ray it will springboard you to blue or indigo ray with equal ease.

We wish you the very best of fortune in wending your way through the many mirrors that those about you offer to you. When you are seeking to open your ability to communicate, the one infinite Creator may well see fit to offer you many distorted mirrors upon which to practice your new-found compassion. Gaze steadily into those mirrors. No matter how distorted they may look, they offer you information concerning parts of your shadow side.

It would be helpful for you to store up such conversations with such distorted mirrors of the self and contemplate them at the later time, looking within the self to find the same distortions, no matter how deeply hidden they may be. They too are part of you; they too deserve honor and respect, and the chance to become part of your daylight personality by being asked to help you.

Even the darkest of emotions may become part of your very grit and determination. That energy that was used for anger can become that energy that is unwilling to give up the dream, the hope, the prayer, the intention. Meet yourself in every conversation, not only as you speak, but as others speak to you, and contemplate at your leisure the many facets of yourself.

May we answer any further, my sister, before we go on? We are those of Q'uo.

Y: Please clarify as to whether my heart chakra is open or not.

We are those of Q'uo. We are aware of your query, my sister. You ask concerning whether or not your heart chakra is open. And we would suggest that it is open at a variable degree, depending upon the moment. The original question, we believe, was offering the idea that you felt that your heart chakra was open at least to a minimal degree and with that we certainly agree. However, it is that variability of the moment, that place where you are in the tides of your being and your progress that have caught you sometimes by surprise, so that you didn't even know that your heart had become less powered by unconditional love and was not getting as much energy as the maximum would be.

And again, as we said, the key to this puzzle that you are working is low self-worth. You see, low self-worth occurs both in the orange ray and in the indigo ray, one being on a different level than the other, but both being the same basic structure in terms of vibration. At the orange-ray level, the issue is the relationship of self with self.

Y: Is that why I have lost sexual desire?

We are those of Q'uo, and we believe that we shall do better to take questions in their turn, my sister. Is that satisfactory to you?

Y: Yes, I just thought that sexual desire is related to the orange-ray chakra.

We are those of Q'uo, and would agree that sexual desire is certainly related to all of the chakras. However, the issue of which we are speaking here is that of low self-worth. And we do not believe that that comes from anything but your opinion of yourself.

We were saying that in the orange ray, at that level of the personality, the issue is simply the relationship of self to self, just as if you were either a friend of yourself or were not particularly fond of yourself. And the issue there is simply to become your own friend.

In the indigo ray, the issue becomes steeper and deeper and involves the ability to see yourself at the soul level as an infinitely perfect and beautiful soul, trusting by faith alone that this is true, ignoring at last with great relief the judgment of the earthly personality.

We would ask if there is another query at this time.

Y: I have attributed the recent energy drainages within my chakra body as having to do with a psychic greeting. I was told I have eight entities attached to me. Did I or do I now? What kind of entities are they and what do they want? Can I use the Enochian circle of light to get rid of them? Please, comment on that in any way you think would be helpful without infringing on my free will.

We are those of Q'uo, and we are aware of your query, my sister. Because the question of specific entities attaching themselves to you is part of your active personal seeking at this time, we would step back from the line of infringing upon your free will by saying that all seekers who wish to accelerate the rate of their mental and spiritual evolution will attract those entities who see your light and wish either to gain power over it or to put it out.

Psychic greeting can be something that occurs even within your own personality, as voices from your past spring up from your mind as thought forms, offering you hurtful messages. Whether the psychic resistance comes from within the self or outside of the personality shell, the response that removes psychic greeting is, firstly, to be fearless and secondly, to send love and light to the greeter and to the entire transaction.

A negative entity will be sickened by true love. The challenge here is that it needs to be genuine, heartfelt love, not that which is applied as a Band-Aid from the intellect. This love for the Creator must come from the heart.

Further, we would agree that the Enochian circle of light is one way in which protective forces that are abounding in the unseen realms may be alerted to the need that you may have for strengthening your allegiance to the light and your firm stands within the light. This instrument, being a mystical Christian, leans more towards invoking Jesus the Christ and creating a ring of light in that way across which no mortal error dares to set its foot. However, the way you mentioned is equally efficacious in alerting a large number of those who come in the name of the love and light of the one infinite Creator. The Enochian tradition is millennia long and there are many who dwell in the unseen realms who are allies of all of those who would use those words of beauty and light.

We would suggest that it is inevitable that any seeker who is successful at moving closer to the light within himself will have cyclical periods of seeming psychic resistance. These can be uncomfortable. And yet it is well to look at these times as times to put into practice that which you know to be the truth: that all is one, and that one thing is love.

This instrument has read a book called *Psychic Self Defense* by the one known as Dion[148]. In this book this entity speaks of seeing a ravening wolf during a very difficult time in her life, while she was in her bedroom. She was sitting upon her bed and meditating and suddenly there was a wild wolf at the foot of her bed, crouching, getting ready to jump at her. She knew what she had to do, she said. She opened her arms and embraced the wolf even as it tore and bit into her skin. And as she did so, the wolf melted away and was gone.

Lose all fear, offer the greetings of your best love, and you shall move through these times of resistance with your spirit unquenched and with the constant

---
[148] Dion Fortune, *Psychic Self Defense*: York Beach, Maine, Samuel Weiser, 2001. This book is in print.

growth of maturity as you find yourself able to weather the storms that you have asked to come upon you by your desire to seek the truth.

As one continues to seek, one begins to transform. And in every transformation, various changes occur. Change is by its very definition uncomfortable. One gains comfort by routine. When things fall away from the seeking soul, it feels as though one even may be losing one's self. And so fear may enter in these times of transformation. Rest back into fearlessness and know that all is well, even when the resistance seems the thickest.

Is there a follow-up to this query, my sister? We are those of Q'uo.

Y: I believe I had planned to stay through the difficult times of Earth's shift to fourth density before incarnation. It is my life's goal to ascend while on Earth. It is my desire to stay and serve as teacher/mentor/parent to many children who would lose their earthly parents during that change and to share the best of me with them and teach them the Law of One. I have been calling on the Masters, the Christed Ones, to establish a contact. I feel I could learn many metaphysical teachings from them, which will be helpful and in some cases necessary for physical survival within the small communities which would be left after the shift. Do these Masters hear me? Are they aware of me and my goal, intent and desire?

We are those of Q'uo, and we are aware of your query, my sister. Firstly, we would assure you that your voice has never gone unheard and never will be unheard. For you are precious. And as you seek, so you shall find; as you love, so love is reflected in love. Those with whom you wish to connect are indeed connected with you, and joyfully so.

Secondly, the scenario which is part of your intent is somewhat limiting in that it has a certain view of how the shift shall occur. We might suggest that you release the limited view of what will happen in the future, while maintaining your desire to be of service, to ascend, and to have an ever closer connection with those beings whom you so value.

May we answer you further, my sister, before we leave this instrument? We are those of Q'uo.

Y: There is a young man who has run into me at the book store for the third time now. My first thought was that he is somehow connected with those

Masters, the Christed Ones. He may be some sort of messenger. Can you confirm or tell me anything at all about this?

We are those of Q'uo, and, yes, my sister, we do confirm that.

We are sorry that we must cut this session of working short, but this instrument's energy wanes. May we say again what a delight and a pleasure it has been to communicate with you. Thank you from the bottom of our collective hearts for the beautiful seeking that you share with us and for asking us to share our humble thoughts with you.

We leave this instrument and circle of seeking in the love and in the light of the one infinite Creator. We are known to you as the principle of Q'uo. Adonai. Adonai vasu. ❧

L/L Research

L/L Research is a subsidiary of Rock Creek Research & Development Laboratories, Inc.

P.O. Box 5195
Louisville, KY 40255-0195

www.llresearch.org

Rock Creek is a non-profit corporation dedicated to discovering and sharing information which may aid in the spiritual evolution of humankind.

ABOUT THE CONTENTS OF THIS TRANSCRIPT: This telepathic channeling has been taken from transcriptions of the weekly study and meditation meetings of the Rock Creek Research & Development Laboratories and L/L Research. It is offered in the hope that it may be useful to you. As the Confederation entities always make a point of saying, please use your discrimination and judgment in assessing this material. If something rings true to you, fine. If something does not resonate, please leave it behind, for neither we nor those of the Confederation would wish to be a stumbling block for any.

© 2009 L/L Research

Saturday Meditation
May 24, 2008

Group question: *((Read by G.)* The question as we quote it is, "There is the phrase, 'winning over the self,' which is another way of saying, 'knowing and accepting the self.' Is there a similar process that occurs to that of the calling? Do those portions of the self that desire love gain power so that the more the call is made, the more the desire is made until [the] square of the resistance within the self is overcome?

Carla channeling

We are known to you as the principle of Q'uo. Greetings in the love and in the light of the one infinite Creator, in whose service we come to you this day. Thank you for calling us to your circle of seeking. It is our privilege and our pleasure to respond. We are happy to share our humble thoughts with you. However, as always, we request that you use your discrimination in choosing which thoughts of ours to pick up and which ones to leave behind as you move forward in your own spiritual process. If you will take care to use your discrimination, then we may feel far more free to offer you our thoughts. We thank you for this consideration.

You ask this day concerning the process of knowing yourself and accepting yourself, or, as the one known as G has put it, winning the self over. You wonder if there is a doubling process that takes hold, so that as the process goes on, the energy becomes stronger and the self is gathered into the love and the light of the one infinite Creator ever more quickly.

Certainly, my brother, there is truth in this supposition. Yet, it is not the precise way of the process of gathering the self into the open heart to say that there is a doubling effect as you work more. We shall come back to this idea later because there is, indeed, a doubling effect at work here. It is just somewhat different than your query.

For now, let us look at this process of knowing the self and accepting the self. We would acknowledge that it is impossible to know the self fully. The self is known fully only at the point in the octave of Creation where seventh density is beginning to fade into timelessness and the mind/body/spirit becomes a mind/body/spirit totality. This mind/body/spirit totality offers its mysterious and ever-shifting information to itself in mid-sixth density, allowing that sixth-density version of self to become the higher self, which then, in turn, offers to the third-density incarnate being a source of good information and guidance.

The mind/body/spirit's gift from the higher self, however, is not of the nature of a definite, finite structure or box of contents. It is full of mystery and paradox, as all entities are, because of the fact that they are in the image of the Infinite Creator, whose nature is rich in mystery and paradox. This is why we cannot say that there is precisely a doubling effect as one gets to know oneself better. Because that work is never done.

Indeed, those of us who speak with you this evening feel inadequate to the challenge of expressing in full the nature of ourselves. We have, however, become content to allow the question of self-definition to inhere in our vibrations, or our essence.

What we have to suggest is a discussion of the cycles that are an inevitable portion of the spiritual seeker, and the dynamic between those cycles and that central essence of self which most decidedly does not have all the pieces of self collected, yet is very, very important to the self. That is the part of the self that has focus.

Perhaps you have noticed that there are variations in the amount of focus with which you seek the love and the light of the one Creator. At some points, there is a plain and clear feeling of utter desire and single-minded seeking to know the truth of the creation and to tabernacle in the presence of the one infinite Creator. At other times, it would be possible to say those same words and yet not to be able to feel the intensity of desire because of the fact that you have lost your focus.

The cycles of which we speak are several. The first is the cycle of the beginner on the path and then the more experienced entity on the path. This cycles in an unpredictable and quite slow way, for it is not known when that first rush of excitement shall fade away, once the seeker has awakened and started on the path of his spiritual evolution.

The initial flush of excitement and that wonderful feeling that you have a treasure of great value may last years, or it may last months, or it may last weeks. Inevitably, however, the honeymoon between yourself and the infinite possibilities of seeking the Creator fade and it begins to be possible simply to give lip service to those ideals which have previously moved you almost to tears.

It is as though at times your energy body were [a stream] rushing forward and, at other times, a dry bed. You look at that place where the torrent flew and frothed above all. And, below the place where all that water flowed, it is dry and cracked, and you are in a season of drought within your own spiritual process.

The seeker who wishes to win the self over has one great resource during those dry times within and that is his will. The will of an entity who knows that he is powerful can overcome any resistance within the self, and that faculty of will is fed by memory; the memory of those times when the self was lifted up and things were very clear.

There are times in every seeker's life when the Creator is close and the connection is sweet and pure and strong. In dry times it is extremely helpful for the spiritual seeker to remember those times of torrential inundations of the love and the light of the one infinite Creator.

It is as though your will were a candle that you keep burning day and night. Sometimes it is not needed because the world is full of sunlight. During the dark night of the soul, however, there is only the candle of your will. Feel that steel core within you of will and focus and let it blaze as the candle in good seasons and in poor.

Another cycle about which we will speak is the cycle of physical maturation. A lifetime [encompasses] the rising and the falling. During the times of rising, there is a learning curve going on almost all the time concerning the consensus reality that surrounds the seeker and his skill in being able to function within that consensus reality. At those early times of an incarnation it is often the case that the self cannot be known to the self because there is so much to learn and so much to process that there is no mental or emotional leisure for contemplating the self in a non-attached and witness-like focus.

At the apex of the arch of life, there is a period during which the ability to function within consensus reality has been, if not perfected, brought up to acceptable standards for that which the seeker needs to do in his life, and at that point, he becomes free to choose his thoughts and to follow his thoughts where they might go. It is a blessed time in many ways and yet it carries its own challenges.

When the seeker does focus on knowing himself, he acquires a great deal of information, some of which is trustworthy and some of which is not. This is due to the fact that there are many inner voices which like to share their opinions concerning who you are. Some of those voices are parental. Others are the voices of teachers or other authority figures who instructed you in a certain way that penetrated into your personality shell and became thought forms that took root there. And those voices are still heard.

They are not the voices of yourself. They are voices that are as distorted as any carnival mirror. No parent or authority figure knows you. Indeed, you yourself are struggling to know you. The challenge, as you open up to your own thoughts and the processes of conceptualization as you experience day-by-day, is to find your own voice.

As the sun sets upon an incarnation and the physical body functions less well, it would seem as though one would, once again, have little time for spiritual matters, and, indeed, this is the case with some entities whose older years are confused by failing minds. However, in many cases the summer of the seeker's life may extend right up until the last breath is expelled from the [physical] body that is left at death in order that the spirit may enter again the larger life.

It is well for an entity who is just beginning to be free of the learning process of becoming an adult to realize that there has been a long, slow learning curve that has placed tremendous pressure on the physical organism's mental complex, and especially the emotions. Therefore, as the seeker wakes up and begins to feel free of the learning of consensus reality, it is well for him to begin to gaze within in a way, which again contains that concept of focus and flame.

When the seeker becomes fully aware that every person about him is a mirror for himself, there is in that realization a feeling of "too much information." Shall the seeker take, in complete sincerity, every word that is spoken to him and every interaction with another person as being information about himself? If so, the information stacks up exponentially as the years go by. Yet, it is true that the spiritual seeker is in a hall of mirrors. Each mirror is distorted, yet gives some information.

How does one look at one's self? The eyes look outward. They do not see inward. It is impossible to see yourself as others see you. Consequently, it is very helpful to enter into the game, shall we say, of taking each person as a mirror for yourself, and musing upon what that mirror is telling you.

Some mirrors are difficult to look into. If you are interacting with a murderer, than you must find the murderer within yourself in order for the information that mirror holds to be relevant. Many are the times that you will find yourself avoiding certain situations or certain relationships, and in that avoidance is more information.

This instrument, in describing the green-ray chakra or the heart energy center, wrote that it was like the basilica at St. Peters, that great structure which was the Doge's Chapel and which now is a cathedral.[149] As great and massive as that structure is, it is dwarfed by the size of the plaza which lies in front of the building. In pictures of this Cathedral of St. Mark, that huge forecourt is always mobbed with thousands of tourists, and pigeons walking among the tourists, pecking at whatever the tourists drop to feed them. This is a fairly accurate image for the parts of yourself that are, to some extent, not yet integrated into your essential self.

And here we may use that phrase of "winning over the self," for as you stand in that outer courtyard of the open heart, you can deliberately and consciously move into work within yourself, to take up each wandering [portion] of yourself as you find it, and bring it into your heart.

It is easy to love the parts of yourself that conform to your ideals. Yet the tough truth is that there is much more to the self than those idealistic parts of the self that have been polished and cleaned and are on display, shall we say, in the windows of one's ideas about who one is. All of the rest of the self that lies in the shadows and has not yet been polished, has not yet been picked up, and has certainly not yet been recognized, waits for your attention.

And this is not something that is a linear process. This is something that is like housework. You keep going back to that plaza of the self and recognizing a new portion of yourself from that shadow side. Then it is time to win that heart of the self over, to express your feelings of honor and respect for it, and to ask it to integrate itself into you so that its darkness becomes your strength rather than your weakness. This quest for the self shall never end.

In counterpoint to that truth is the truth that you are already a perfected being. You are already a mind/body/spirit totality. That flame at the very heart of your being is the same flame that burns throughout all densities in the octave of Creation that you now experience. Consequently, in counterpoint to the attempts of the rational mind to

---

[149] This material is in her book, *Living the Law of One – 101: The Choice*: Louisville, Kentucky, L/L Research, [c2008].

know itself, there lies the dynamic of the perfect self, the perfected self, the self that lies within you, undiscovered, for the most part unknown and unexplored.

This is why meditation is so very helpful.

In meditation, you have accepted that intellectually you do not know your essence or your nature.

In meditation, you rest in unknowing.

In meditation, you are not trying to figure anything out.

In meditation, you are no longer talking to yourself, or talking to the Creator, or talking at all.

In this stoppage of the intellectual mind lies a great aid to the seeker who wishes to remain focused. For that flame that burns within you burns within all. There is one flame, one consciousness, one great and utter love. It is a tremendous balm and relief to escape from your personality and all that you think you know, and rest, wrapped in the blanket of warmth that the tabernacle of the open heart offers, cuddled upon the lap of the Almighty with nothing to do except be.

We said earlier that we would move back to the idea of a doubling effect and so we do now. What is doubled has nothing to do with the parts of yourself that you are attempting to know and accept. It has to do with your faith. For that you do not need to reach or strive. You do not need to do anything. For you already are a being created by the infinite One, full of power and beauty.

It is difficult to keep the faith when it is new. It is difficult in the face of one's personal shortcomings, as perceived by the self, to know that all is well. There is so much temptation to reject the self, or parts of the self, in most entities that it is almost irresistible. Yet, having grasped faith, you hold to it and you know that at the depths of your being, you are good in that biblical sense where man was created, and God saw that it was good, and it was very good.[150]

Faith stabilizes you among the chaos of perceptions. Outer perceptions shall always bring conflict. The truth shall always be elusive. Yet as you have faith in yourself and in the innate goodness of your design,

you come through the crisis of not liking aspects of yourself and you find yourself still standing after the storm has passed. The next time there is heavy weather within your heart and mind and soul, you find it easier to maintain faith regardless of the outer picture. And each time thereafter, you find it exponentially easier to remain stable and faithful and serene.

It is a tremendous faculty that is innate within all third-density entities, this faculty of faith. And we encourage contemplation of the word itself, for in it lie untold mysteries and infinite light. It is often a great help when developing the faculty of faith to have something to which to cling, whether it be a person, an ideal, or some image or icon that has special meaning to you.

We would encourage exploring those persons, images, icons and symbols which call you. If you can find one or two that are particularly resonant to you, [then] find ways to have those images in your field of vision as you work and as you play, as you eat and as you sleep. For they shall remind you of who you are and make it ever easier for you to regain that stance of the spiritual seeker which is centered in faith.

We come back to the word "focus," my brother. It is easy to feel the self as a vast collection of somewhat related, but not necessarily coordinated, parts. We ask you to dive deep beneath the surface of that perception into the center of yourself—that center which has never been apart from the one infinite Creator. Dive deep. Dive with love. Dive with absolute surety and faith.

(Side one of tape ends.)

(Carla channeling)

Again and again, may your excursions of faith be filled with light. May you have fair horizons for your travel.

We would at this time ask if there are other queries in this group. We are those of Q'uo.

A: Would you discuss the spiritual principles for converting excess emotion into mental and emotional clarity?

We are Q'uo, and are aware of your query, my brother. The emotions are often given far less respect than they deserve, and this is because they are not seen for the deep, running rivers that they are, but

---

[150] *Holy Bible*, Genesis 1:31: "And God saw every thing that he had made, and, behold, it was very good."

rather are seen as somewhat troublesome hindrances to a calm and orderly life.

We would use the analogy of cooking here and compare the way most entities allow their emotions to run to "fast food." It is easy to get, it is easily eaten, and there is not much nourishment in the food. And so it is with surface emotions. Like rain on hardpan, it is difficult for the emotions to offer any good information or go anywhere. They just hit the consciousness and bounce off and, indeed, do seem quite excessive sometimes.

However, if a chef with great love for the food takes the same ingredients that are in fast food and prepares them carefully and with love, those same ingredients yield much more nourishment. And so it is with emotions. Surface emotions are usually quite impure. However, when one can abide with one's feelings and observe them as though they were guests coming to tea, offering them hospitality and courtesy, sitting with them and listening to them, then the emotions have found respect and honor. And this allows them to go deeper, interconnecting the [surface] self with the deepest part of the roots of consciousness. For this is what emotions eventually become if they are allowed to go through the process of purification.

There is a beauty to each emotion when it has been purified and it is pure feeling with no distortion. Thus, we would say that instead of looking at emotions as something to work around, the one who seeks clarity needs to spend time honoring the emotions that seem so inconvenient and excessive. Physically taking the time to process emotions is very helpful. Emotions call to you and when you can answer by sitting with these guests that are speaking to you in certain colors, then those colors gradually lose the muddy characteristics of surface emotions and become more and more clear.

May we answer you further, my brother? We are those of Q'uo.

A: Yes. Would Q'uo discuss the spiritual principles behind the connection drawn between the theory in non-violent communication that positive emotions indicate that a universal human need has been met and that negative emotions indicate that a universal human need has not been met?

We are those of Q'uo, and we believe we understand your query. We would have no quarrel with the statement that positive emotions indicate that a universal need has been met and negative emotions indicate that a universal need has not been met. We agree completely that the needs and desires of third density entities are universal for, indeed, all is one.

The only reservation that we would have concerning this statement is that there are layers upon layers to emotion and layers upon layers to human need. So, some positive emotions ring false, as do some negative emotions, thereby not offering [truth] to the seeker.

In the sense of attempting to understand one's feelings, it certainly is helpful to compare the concept of emotion with the concept of universal needs, for it seems to give a psychological validation to one's needs so that emotion then is not a thing about which to be embarrassed, but is rather a needed signal for that which is occurring within the personality. Perhaps the spiritual principle that would apply here is that all is one and that just as the baby's cry indicates that it is hungry, that emotion stems from that cry of hunger.

The other spiritual principle that we would invoke is that balancing principle which expresses the infinity and the mystery of human emotion and human nature in general. There are paths that move into mountain upon mountain upon mountain, raising the quality and the purity of human emotion many times for the entity who is willing to penetrate every emotion with his utter attention and respect.

We are those of Q'uo, [and] would ask if there is a final query at this time.

A: Yes, would Q'uo discuss the spiritual principles behind love at first sight, such as in Romeo and Juliet?

We are those of Q'uo, and are aware of your query, my brother. But in this case there does not seem to be a spiritual principle to bring to bear on love at first sight. The classic Romeo and Juliet's love at first sight is a story of entities who were in their early teens. This is a time [of life] when it is unlikely that there is a bleed-through memory of a past life or something of that nature which would create a spiritual nexus within which one might gaze at that attraction.

However, it is so that there is a network which an entity has of souls with whom he has worked in past experiences—past, of course, being a linear term that does not hold in time/space. In that circular time/space where everything is occurring simultaneously, the web of relationships is amazingly extensive. And there are times when one entity meets another and a resonance is set up that is undeniable and is far deeper and more penetrating than the circumstances would normally suggest.

In those cases, it is quite likely that entities who have planned to work together on some service or some incarnational lesson together within an incarnation have found each other. And that is a very hopeful and positive thing for an entity who wishes to do spiritual work. It is greatly helpful to have companions with whom to share one's gifts and with whom to explore one's challenges.

We might note in this regard that there has been a tendency within this group through decades of questions to visit the phenomenon of love at first sight or star-crossed lovers or soul mates. And we would suggest that, in fact, before the Creation has wound to its fullest spiritual gravity and returns to the one infinite Creator, each shall be a soul mate to each.

We would, at this time relinquish this instrument and this contact, for the instrument is growing weary. May we say what a delight and privilege it has been to share this meditation with you and be part of your session of working. We thank you once again for asking for our thoughts. We leave you in the love and the light of the one infinite Creator. We are known to you as the principle of Q'uo. Adonai. Adonai.

L/L Research

L/L Research is a subsidiary of Rock Creek Research & Development Laboratories, Inc.

P.O. Box 5195
Louisville, KY 40255-0195

www.llresearch.org

Rock Creek is a non-profit corporation dedicated to discovering and sharing information which may aid in the spiritual evolution of humankind.

ABOUT THE CONTENTS OF THIS TRANSCRIPT: This telepathic channeling has been taken from transcriptions of the weekly study and meditation meetings of the Rock Creek Research & Development Laboratories and L/L Research. It is offered in the hope that it may be useful to you. As the Confederation entities always make a point of saying, please use your discrimination and judgment in assessing this material. If something rings true to you, fine. If something does not resonate, please leave it behind, for neither we nor those of the Confederation would wish to be a stumbling block for any.

© 2008 L/L RESEARCH

SPECIAL MEDITATION
MAY 27, 2008

Group question: *(Read by Jim.)* Q'uo, the question from D begins with two statements from the L/L Research channeling of March 24, 1991. He says:

"There are two statements that caught my attention. First, Q'uo says, 'Those who are willing to use a crutch in order to vault themselves upward into the light, whether the crutch be drugs or magical rituals or whatever other occult sciences may be used as a gadget, have literally pulled themselves up to a place for which they have not worked and for which they may not be ready.'

"A later quote says, 'Thus it may be seen that those who by any means other than natural move themselves to transformation must needs be responsible for that which has been gained long after the crutch has been thrown away.'

"For several years I have been considering these concepts as it might relate to a particular metaphysical technology. Very recently I have been given the opportunity to enhance this technology. Also, very recently my wife has faced a serious illness, which has forced me to realize at a deeper emotional level how important it is to let everyone find their own path of light. Both situations have brought me to set up this channeling to explore the issues of developing and distributing metaphysical technologies, while respecting the free will of those who might use such technologies.

"The first of three questions I have is, without reference to any particular technology, is it theoretically possible for a metaphysical technology to be self-regulating? That is, could a technology be constructed so that the user would not receive any more metaphysical light than he or she was prepared to integrate? And if this is possible, does Q'uo see that any such self-regulating technologies are currently available on Earth?"

(Carla channeling)

We are known to you as the principle of Q'uo. Greetings in the love and in the light of the one infinite Creator, in whose service we come to you this evening. We wish to thank the one known as D for creating a sacred circle of seeking and we wish to thank those who have joined with the one who is known as D in this circle, the one known as R, the one known as M, the one known as G, the one known as Jim, and the instrument.

We greatly appreciate the privilege of being asked for our opinion, as those who also seek the truth. As always, we would encourage who reads or hears these words to discriminate as you listen to what we have to say, feeling for the path of resonance. If ideas that we offer do not resonate to you, please leave them behind. This strict attention to your own temple gates will enable us to speak freely without being concerned that we may infringe on your free will or disturb the rhythm of your process.

The query concerning the use of metaphysical technology to enhance the natural abilities of seekers is, as the one known as D is well aware, one with many, many layers and levels of consideration. However, the possibility of finding a self-regulatory feature is one which creates the environment for a potential positive gain in the one known as D's being of service to others. There is a delicate situation when we speak concerning an on-going point of spiritual study. Each entity has not only incarnational lessons but permutations of those lessons that are active at any one time, and we must tread carefully to avoid infringing upon the active process that is on-going within the spiritual seeking of the one known as D. So, we may offer some thoughts that may or may not have any interest to you, my brother.

Firstly, the nature of the energy that is used to open the gateway of intelligent infinity consists of three basic components: the will of the seeker; the infinite love/light of the infinite Creator which, moving from the Logos to the heart, is then reflected up through the Earth into the soles of the feet and into the energy body in an infinite supply. And thirdly, there is that vast array of sources of aid and guidance that can be accessed for those who move through the gateway into intelligent infinity.

In the normal course of seeking, the work of the seeker is first to clear his chakras so that the energy from the Earth may flow in infinite supply into the opened heart and then springboard up through the higher chakras through the gateway of intelligent infinity and then, aimed with the clear and lucid intent of the seeker, attract the appropriate source of guidance.

The energy body is crystalline and delicate. Consequently, the energy of the infinite Creator that comes up from the Earth is geared to harmonize with the needs of the energy body. If this love/light encounters a hindrance, it does not push or press but merely awaits the clearing of whatever energy center or centers have been blocked or over-activated. This constitutes a built-in safety mechanism, if you will.

It is in this regard that there is an interesting potential for further consideration by the one known as D. We cannot express through this instrument, who is not in any way an educated scientist, the nature of the contemplation that might prove productive, but can simply say that it is in understanding and being able to measure or identify and otherwise work with this elemental love/light of the one infinite Creator that the possibility barely exists within the technology of which you are aware, of creating your technology in such a way that it rides the love/light energy and is, consequently, created safe because of the natural intelligence or love/light energy, which knows when it may go forward and when it may not.

Were the discovery or integration of the present knowledge base from the study of light and the study of—we give this instrument pictures of a vast array of what look like computer read-outs or languages—to be wedded, then there would be the possibility of offering this regularizing and cohering technology in a way that would not interrupt the natural safeguards of the energy body.

May we ask my brother for the second portion of this query? We are those of Q'uo.

D: Q'uo uses the phrase "by any means other than natural" in the second statement above. Some might say that there is nothing natural about Earth's current environment, given technology such as HAARP, cell phone towers, the web, and alternating-current energies that appear to restrict the natural flow of metaphysical life. I am guessing that some members of the Confederation may see benefits in leveling the playing field on this planet by distributing technologies that counteract these restricting technologies. Is this true? And is it possible that Q'uo's position on such gadgetry might be considered somewhat conservative by other members of the Confederation?

We are those of Q'uo, and are aware of your query, my brother. We are a principle made up of three social memory complexes: a fourth-density social memory complex which is known to you as Hatonn, a fifth-density social member complex which is known to you as Latwii, and a sixth-density social member complex which is known to you as Ra.

Consequently, within our very principle we carry the memory of just such an attempt to aid by technology of a kind, for we offered to those in Egypt, as you all know that area, the technology of the sacred geometry, which is [used in the building of] the pyramid. We were hopeful that with such a device for initiation and healing, the culture of that day might be able to create a new paradigm of unity.

We discovered that, far from creating an effective instrument for healing, we created in the end very shortly after this structure, called the Great Pyramid by this instrument, was completed, that the entities who were supposedly the priests of the Law of One were corrupted by politics and society so that there was no initiation nor was there healing, but that it was to be used only by the elite.

We could offer other examples of the Confederation's experiments in offering technology to, as you say, my brother, level the playing field. Each of them was brought to the environment of your planet in a genuine and utter hope that there could be aid from such devices. We need only mention the [technology used to produce the] atomic bomb to make our point.

Within any Confederation, my brother, there are those who remain hopeful that the next time and the next time, such intervention might be a positive contribution to the spiritual evolution of humankind. And perhaps "conservative" would be an understatement. However, regardless of the opinion of some few who have not learned from experience, we remain serene in our realization that the way to aid humankind is not through outer technology, or any technology, but rather by the continual creation through instruments such as this one of a discussion of the true identity of all humankind.

And in further discussion of how the creation works, we weave a story, my brother, through instruments such as this, a story that offers an explanation on several different levels for the life to which each human being has awakened, and for the larger natural philosophy in which this life has been imbedded, the creation from beginning to end, and each human being's part in that great cycle or octave of creation.

We weave a net of love and it catches people. It helps them to get their feet under them and to realize who they are. The secret to spiritual evolution is that realization that each human being, just as he is, is capable of becoming a person of infinite power and focus.

We hope always in the communications that we offer through instruments such as this one to enlarge that vision of the human being as a living flame, that moment where consciousness and consensus reality meet; two worlds, intersecting at each moment, through the thoughts of the focused human being. Encouraging that focus, encouraging the awareness that each is a portion of the Godhead principle and has not only the honor but the duty to take up the responsibility of Godhead, is one of our most basic hopes from this web of communication which we have been able to offer through instruments such as this one.

We believe our tactics have, though modest and conservative, indeed enlarged the possibility of each individual's acceleration of his mental and spiritual evolution. This instrument saw earlier this evening a *Democracy Now*[151] interview with Utah Phillips. This entity known as Utah spoke of being patient and abiding in the belief system that gave him dignity and integrity. He spoke of finding it difficult to vote when there were no good choices in the elections and, instead, saying, "My ballot is on my back."

As more and more people awaken to who they truly are and become aware of their magical personality and their ability to do work in consciousness, we believe that our discussions of the one great original Thought have a small but contributing part, and we are content, my brother, to share, word by word and concept by concept, this one great original Thought, to the exclusion of more attempts to level the playing field from the outside in.

The magic of all entities in third density lies within them and is awakened by their realization that they are entities of power and that this power is founded in, made up of, and completely melted and dissolved in love. The essence of this love, my brother, can be found in the love/light that, coming from the Logos and bouncing back from the heart of the Earth, constitutes the energy that is fed to the energy body. It is this source of energy that we would encourage you to consider.

We again apologize for being unable to create technical language through this instrument. However, hopefully the rhythms and the emphases of that which we have been able to share through her instrument may be of some help.

Before leaving this question we would wish to express our appreciation of the depth and the intensity of the love and the desire to serve of the one known as D. It is, my brother, a moving thing to see the beauty of your vibrations and, indeed, may we say that this circle of seeking is unusual in its blended auras and its sacred space. There is a great

---

[151] *Democracy Now*, with Amy Goodman, is a news review show on Link TV.

strength in this particular group. It is a pleasure to share this energy with you.

We who are those of Q'uo, ask if we might hear the third part of the main question as this time.

D: Ra has stated that the term "density" refers to the degree that each level of all that is can pack or store metaphysical life. Does the human heart, when its bioelectrical wave forms fall into phase coherence, model how our reality is more able to symmetrically and harmoniously pack metaphysical light as into the third and fourth density? If so, how could a metaphysical technology based on this same principle of phase coherence be most responsibly and effectively used to show individuals that their hearts have the same capacity as the universe at large for this phase shift?

We are those of Q'uo, and are aware of your query, my brother. We must take this query in two parts. Firstly, we would speak of densities and light. The attempt to create fourth-density light, fifth-density light, or sixth-density light out of third-density light is an attempt that is founded in a mistaken assumption and that is that light has a linear progression from density to density. However, it does not.

The photon of third density is not the photon of fourth density. Consequently, no matter how beautifully coherent you create third-density light, you have simply maximized a third-density light. You have not created a fourth-density light. It would be like trying to make an apple into an orange. You can make the best apple, but you cannot make it be an orange.

Fourth-density light has more—we give this instrument a picture of angles of rotation, as if there were a ninety degree shift while in the same plane—which creates an enormously expanded number of surfaces within each portion of light. More surfaces mean more places for information, more choices, more awareness, etc.

Secondly, we believe that there is a very good idea in that of which you speak, in that there is a good deal of power in the purity of colors available when a coherent light is used. There are, we believe, among your peoples, healing modalities that already have begun to investigate the possibilities of using coherent light. They have moved, in terms of their focus, on physical healing rather than moving into the consideration of working with light to create or enhance metaphysical environments.

This work would not be an infringement upon free will, for the optical apparatus of entities is self-limiting as are the physical senses in general, and overload simply removes the possibility of that modality being useful rather than creating difficulties within the energy body which could result in the overloading of one or more of the chakras.

At this time, my brother, we would pause before moving on in order that you may query in any way you wish about these three portions of the main query. Is there a follow-up to this body of discussion at this time? We are those of Q'uo.

D: Yes, the question is, given the self-regulating quality of the technology in question and the instrument's inability to describe technological principles, is there any source of information that the entities using this technology might research or look into in order to enhance this self-regulating quality?

We are those of Q'uo, and are aware of your query, my brother. We may say that the sources are there. However, they are scattered and unrecognized. Consequently, we would suggest to the one known as D that he combine research into light and its nature, especially research done by those who are unrecognized and obscure, with a continuation of his unremitting, unwavering, absolute devotion to the one infinite Creator and to the service of the one infinite Creator, and to maintain that focus while requesting his guidance system to enhance his ability to sense that path of resonance and synchronicity that shall aid him.

May we answer you further, my brother?

D: Yes. Given the ability of education to be helpful to people who are interested in this technology, is there a way to let people who would be interested in this technology know that there is a bio-feedback type of quality within themselves that would allow themselves to use technology in a self-regulating fashion?

We are those of Q'uo, and are aware of your query, my brother. We make this instrument smile with our feelings of *déjà vu*, as this instrument would say, for, indeed, this was precisely what we wished to do with the pyramid in the old times of Egypt. It is possible while a charismatic and persuasive leader is in charge of a place where entities may be aided by such bio-feedback systems for this self-regulatory feature of the individual to be awakened in a safe way.

(Side one of tape ends.)

(Carla channeling)

As soon as the charismatic leader passes from the scene, there are always entities eager to distort and eventually nullify any positive outcome from such attempts to be of service in this wise.

The challenge of those who would attempt to help those of Earth awaken to the sacred nature of every cell in their bodies, their minds, and their spirits is not only in getting their attention, but in keeping it. Those among your peoples have not shown a marked tendency towards persistence in metaphysical seeking. The culture of your civilization has shortened the seeming attention span of most among your people. There needs to be the willingness to become a new person, a different person, a person who creates his own truth and lives according to his own lights. This is entirely possible.

However, it is a challenge to open people up to the concept of starting over and living in an entirely different way, a way which returns the power of life and love to each person and removes that person from the grid, shall we say, of society and culture.

Is there another follow-up, my brother, to this query? We are those of Q'uo.

D: We'd like to ask about another technology, Ark's technology[152], a separate technology, something called Plato's fifteen rings, that has a more rounded type of architecture rather than these sharper types of architecture of the pyramids of the past. Is there a better fit or easier use of this type of technology?

We are those of Q'uo, and are aware of your query, my brother. There is definitely a higher chance that the rounded geometrical shape shall be able to be utilized without the side effects caused by the movement of prana or the love/light of the one infinite Creator through the pointed shape of the pyramid. Instead of the scoop of the pyramid revolving twice before exiting the point of the pyramid, the ring system has the capacity, when developed, to be much more benign.

The challenge in this creation or this technology is the iteration factor that occurs with there being no exit pointed for the light that is generated by the scoop which draws energy into this structure.

We would suggest the contemplation of a system of vents, whether they are of material or intentional, in a spiral fashion that would regularize the passage of the love/light of the infinite Creator through this sacred shape or series of shapes.

We are those of Q'uo, and would ask that if there is a follow-up to this query?

D: Yes. Given that this sacred geometry of the rounded shape is better than the pointed, is there some type of use that this electromagnetic geometry has of making it more effective in the self-regulating feature of the electromagnetic geometry that we were first talking of? Is that anywhere close? Can the self-regulating feature of this rounded geometry be used to enhance the self-regulating feature of the first geometry we were talking about?

We are those of Q'uo, and believe that we are aware of your query, my brother. We can respond in the affirmative with the reservation that the connection and the content of this connection, the nature of it, is both simpler and more unexpected or unimagined than might seem to be so at first glance.

We tread carefully here, my brother, and would suggest that you also tread carefully as you seek in this wise. Cultivate humility, cast aside pride and those previously assumed truths concerning sacred geometry. Look to nature for examples and remain grounded, deeply grounded, into the earth plane as you investigate the possibilities which have opened up to you.

We would at this time ask if there is a follow-up to this query? We are those of Q'uo.

D: I would like to know if there is a better way to state these questions in relation to the people who might use this technology? And if there is a better way to state them, would Q'uo restate them and then answer them?

We are those of Q'uo, and are aware of your query, my brother. We believe that your present queries are perfectly adequate according to your present level of awareness. The clarity of your questions and the depth of spiritual awareness which offers the energy upon which your words come seem to us to be of an

---

[152] Arkadiusz Jadczyk's work may be further examined at www.quantumfuture.net/quantum_future/qf.htm.

entirely adequate order. Were we to rephrase your query, we should be learning for you and this is an infringement upon free will.

May we ask if there is a final query at this time?

D: Considering the quality of phase coherence as it is related to the human heart when it makes certain connections, how can we utilize this principle in generating technologies that are more responsible in relation to the human heart?

We are those of Q'uo and are aware of your query, my brother. We have poked and prodded at this query and cannot find a way into offering information without infringing upon your free will. We are apologetic and yet we come up against the stop of the Law of Confusion.

We may say that the coherence of which you speak is that which the spiritual seeker of third density tends towards or becomes more able to express. Coherence is an excellent word to use when thinking of the human energy body and that consciousness that it contains, eternity and infinity cradled in crystalline structures that seem so fragile and yet are so incredibly powerful.

That is, you see, the challenge of any helping technology: to advance the ability of entities to sense their own coherence and to do so without blowing their circuitry. The quality of faith is the living coherence of the spirit and we encourage you to increase your faith. As you proceed, we wish you light in your research, my brother. You already have the love.

We would at this time thank this instrument and this group and especially the one known as D. It has been a sheer pleasure to converse with this group and we have enjoyed it tremendously. This instrument's energy wanes and we would not harm the instrument. Therefore, we shall at this time take our leave of this instrument and this group. We leave you as we found you, in all that there is—the love and the light of the one infinite Creator. In that coherence, we leave you. We are known to you as the principle of Q'uo. Adonai. Adonai vasu borragus. ✽